# Reading Street

## Grade 4, Unit 4

Puzzles and Mysteries

**PEARSON**
Scott Foresman

scottforesman.com

**Editorial Offices:** Glenview, Illinois • Parsippany, New Jersey • New York, New York
**Sales Offices:** Boston, Massachusetts • Duluth, Georgia • Glenview, Illinois
Coppell, Texas • Sacramento, California • Mesa, Arizona

*We dedicate Reading Street to*
*Peter Jovanovich.*

*His wisdom, courage,*
*and passion for education*
*are an inspiration to us all.*

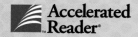
**Accelerated Reader**®

**Cover** Tim Jessell

About the Cover Artist

Tim Jessell draws and paints in Stillwater, Oklahoma. He and his wife are raising three great children, whom he coaches in many sports. When not playing catch or illustrating, Tim trains falcons for the sport of falconry. Occasionally, he can still be found making a racket behind his drum set, with kids dancing around.

ISBN-13: 978-0-328-24382-2

ISBN-10: 0-328-24382-5

Copyright © 2008 Pearson Education, Inc.

All Rights Reserved. Printed in the United States of America. This publication is protected by Copyright, and permission should be obtained from the publisher prior to any prohibited reproduction, storage in a retrieval system, or transmission in any form by any means, electronic, mechanical, photocopying, recording, or likewise. For information regarding permission(s), write to: Permissions Department, Scott Foresman, 1900 East Lake Avenue, Glenview, Illinois 60025.

Many of the designations used by manufacturers and sellers to distinguish their products are claimed as trademarks. Where those designations appear in this book, and Scott Foresman was aware of a trademark claim, the designations have been printed with initial capitals and in cases of multiple usage have also been marked with either ® or ™ where they first appear.

6 7 8 9 10 11 V063 16 15 14 13 12 11 10 09
CC:N1

# Reading

## STREET

Where the
Love of
Reading
Begins

# Reading Street Program Authors

**Peter Afflerbach, Ph.D.**
Professor, Department of
Curriculum and Instruction
University of Maryland at
College Park

**Camille L.Z. Blachowicz, Ph.D.**
Professor of Education
National-Louis University

**Candy Dawson Boyd, Ph.D.**
Professor, School of Education
Saint Mary's College of California

**Wendy Cheyney, Ed.D.**
Professor of Special Education
and Literacy, Florida
International University

**Connie Juel, Ph.D.**
Professor of Education, School of
Education, Stanford University

**Edward J. Kame'enui, Ph.D.**
Professor and Director, Institute for
the Development of Educational
Achievement, University of Oregon

**Donald J. Leu, Ph.D.**
John and Maria Neag Endowed
Chair in Literacy and Technology
University of Connecticut

**Jeanne R. Paratore, Ed.D.**
Associate Professor of Education
Department of Literacy
and Language Development
Boston University

**P. David Pearson, Ph.D.**
Professor and Dean,
Graduate School of Education
University of California, Berkeley

**Sam L. Sebesta, Ed.D.**
Professor Emeritus,
College of Education,
University of Washington, Seattle

**Deborah Simmons, Ph.D.**
Professor, College of Education
and Human Development
Texas A&M University
(Not pictured)

**Sharon Vaughn, Ph.D.**
H.E. Hartfelder/Southland
Corporation Regents Professor
University of Texas

**Susan Watts-Taffe, Ph.D.**
Independent Literacy Researcher
Cincinnati, Ohio

**Karen Kring Wixson, Ph.D.**
Professor of Education
University of Michigan

# Components

## Student Editions (1–6)

## Teacher's Editions (PreK–6)

## Assessment
Assessment Handbook (K–6)

Baseline Group Tests (K–6)

DIBELS™ Assessments (K–6)

ExamView® Test Generator CD-ROM (2–6)

Fresh Reads for Differentiated
Test Practice (1–6)

Online Success Tracker™ (K–6)*

Selection Tests Teacher's Manual (1–6)

Unit and End-of-Year
Benchmark Tests (K–6)

## Leveled Readers
Concept Literacy Leveled Readers (K–1)

Independent Leveled Readers (K)

Kindergarten Student Readers (K)

Leveled Reader Teaching Guides (K–6)

Leveled Readers (1–6)

Listen to Me Readers (K)

Online Leveled Reader Database (K–6)*

Take-Home Leveled Readers (K–6)

## Trade Books and Big Books
Big Books (PreK–2)

Read Aloud Trade Books (PreK–K)

Sing with Me Big Book (1–2)

Trade Book Library (1–6)

## Decodable Readers
Decodable Readers (K–3)

Strategic Intervention
Decodable Readers (1–2)

Take-Home Decodable Readers (K–3)

## Phonics and Word Study
Alphabet Cards in English and Spanish
(PreK–K)

Alphabet Chart in English and Spanish
(PreK–K)

Animal ABCs Activity Guide (K)

Finger Tracing Cards (PreK–K)

Patterns Book (PreK–K)

Phonics Activities CD-ROM (PreK–2)*

Phonics Activities Mats (K)

Phonics and Spelling Practice Book (1–3)

Phonics and Word-Building Board and Letters
(PreK–3)

Phonics Songs and Rhymes Audio CD (K–2)

Phonics Songs and Rhymes Flip Chart (K–2)

Picture Word Cards (PreK–K)

Plastic Letter Tiles (K)

Sound-Spelling Cards and Wall Charts (1–2)

Strategies for Word Analysis (4–6)

Word Study and Spelling Practice Book (4–6)

## Language Arts
Daily Fix-It Transparencies (K–6)

Grammar & Writing Book and
Teacher's Annotated Edition, The (1–6)

Grammar and Writing Practice Book
and Teacher's Manual (1–6)

Grammar Transparencies (1–6)

Six-Trait Writing Posters (1–6)

Writing Kit (1–6)

Writing Rubrics and Anchor Papers (1–6)

Writing Transparencies (1–6)

## Practice and Additional Resources
AlphaBuddy Bear Puppet (K)

Alphasaurus Annie Puppet (PreK)

Amazing Words Posters (K–2)

Centers Survival Kit (PreK–6)

Graphic Organizer Book (2–6)

Graphic Organizer Flip Chart (K–1)

High-Frequency Word Cards (K)

Kindergarten Review (1)

Practice Book and Teacher's Manual (K–6)

Read Aloud Anthology (PreK–2)

Readers' Theater Anthology (K–6)

Research into Practice (K–6)

Retelling Cards (K–6)

Scott Foresman Research Base (K–6)

Skill Transparencies (2–6)

Songs and Rhymes Flip Chart (PreK)

Talk with Me, Sing with Me Chart (PreK–K)

Tested Vocabulary Cards (1–6)

Vocabulary Transparencies (1–2)

Welcome to Reading Street (PreK–1)

## ELL
ELL and Transition Handbook (PreK–6)

ELL Comprehensive Kit (1–6)

ELL Posters (K–6)

ELL Readers (1–6)

ELL Teaching Guides (1–6)

Ten Important Sentences (1–6)

## Digital Components
AudioText CDs (PreK–6)

Background Building Audio CDs (3–6)

ExamView® Test Generator
CD-ROM (2–6)

Online Lesson Planner (K–6)

Online New Literacies Activities (1–6)*

Online Professional Development (1–6)

Online Story Sort (K–6)*

Online Student Editions (1–6)*

Online Success Tracker™ (K–6)*

Online Teacher's Editions (PreK–6)

Phonics Activities CD-ROM (PreK–2)*

Phonics Songs and Rhymes
Audio CD (K–2)

Sing with Me/Background Building
Audio CDs (PreK–2)

Songs and Rhymes Audio CD (PreK)

## My Sidewalks Early Reading Intervention (K)

## My Sidewalks Intensive Reading Intervention (Levels A–E)

## Reading Street for the Guided Reading Teacher (1–6)

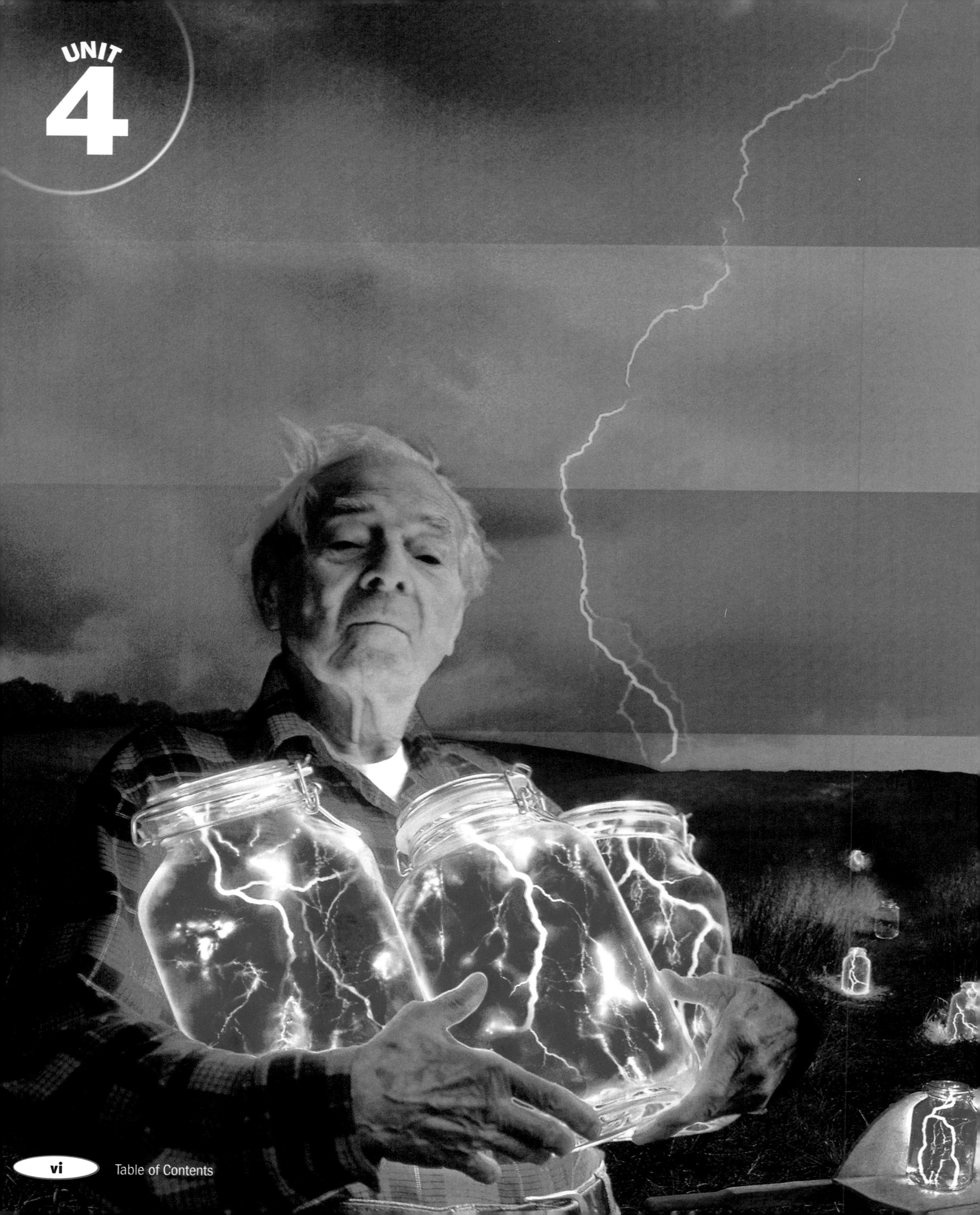
UNIT
4

# PUZZLES AND MYSTERIES

### IS THERE AN EXPLANATION FOR EVERYTHING?

# The Houdini Box

A boy learns the secrets of a famous magician.

**HISTORICAL FICTION**

connect to *SCIENCE*

**Paired Selection**

## So You Want to Be an Illusionist

**EXPOSITORY NONFICTION**

# Encantado: Pink Dolphin of the Amazon

Pink dolphins of the Amazon puzzle scientists.

**EXPOSITORY NONFICTION**

connect to *SCIENCE*

**Paired Selection**

## Mysterious Animals

**EXPOSITORY NONFICTION**

# The King in the Kitchen

A king makes a mysterious mixture.

**PLAY**

connect to *SCIENCE*

**Paired Selection**

## "A Man for All Seasonings," "A Confectioner," and "Expert"

**POETRY**

# Seeker of Knowledge

A Frenchman decodes a mysterious language.

**BIOGRAPHY**

connect to *SOCIAL STUDIES*

**Paired Selection**

## Word Puzzles

**SEARCH ENGINES**

# Encyclopedia Brown and the Case of the Slippery Salamander

A boy detective solves a mystery.

**REALISTIC FICTION**

connect to *SCIENCE*

**Paired Selection**

## Young Detectives of Potterville Middle School

**NEWSPAPER ARTICLE**

# Unit 4
# Skills Overview

| | | **WEEK 1** | **WEEK 2** |
|---|---|---|---|
| | | 396–415 <br> **The Houdini Box/So You Want to Be an Illusionist** <br> *Can you always believe what you see?* <br> HISTORICAL FICTION | 420–439 <br> **Encantado: Pink Dolphin of the Amazon/ Mysterious Animals** <br> *What can explain animal behavior?* <br> EXPOSITORY NONFICTION |
| **Reading** | **Comprehension** | T ◉ **Skill** Compare and Contrast <br> ◉ **Strategy** Predict <br> T REVIEW **Skill** Plot and Character | T ◉ **Skill** Compare and Contrast <br> ◉ **Strategy** Visualize <br> T REVIEW **Skill** Generalize |
| | **Vocabulary** | T ◉ **Strategy** Context Clues | T ◉ **Strategy** Context Clues |
| | **Fluency** | Emotion | Phrasing |
| **Word Work** | **Spelling and Phonics** | Contractions | Final *le, al, en* |
| **Oral Language** | **Speaking/Listening/ Viewing** | Interview <br> Analyze Media | TV Commercial <br> Analyze Commercials |
| **Language Arts** | **Grammar, Usage, and Mechanics** | T Singular and Plural Pronouns | T Subject and Object Pronouns |
| | **Weekly Writing** | Story About a Discovery <br> Writing Trait: Sentences | Travel Brochure <br> Writing Trait: Focus/Ideas |
| | **Unit Process Writing** | Story | Story |
| | **Research and Study Skills** | Instruction Manual | Poster/Announcement |
| | **Integrate Science and Social Studies Standards** | Science Physiology, Physiology/Optics | Science Animal Biology, Ecosystems |

◉ Target Skill    T Tested Skill

| WEEK 3 | WEEK 4 | WEEK 5 |
|---|---|---|
| 444–465<br>**The King in the Kitchen/ A Man for All Seasonings/ A Confectioner/Expert**   **PLAY**<br>*How can a mistake turn into a success?* | 470–487<br>**Seeker of Knowledge/ Word Puzzles**   **BIOGRAPHY**<br>*How can knowing another language create understanding?* | 492–507<br>**Encyclopedia Brown and the Case of the Slippery Salamander/ Young Detectives of Potterville Middle School**   **REALISTIC FICTION**<br>*How can attention to detail help solve a problem?* |
| T ⊙ **Skill** Character and Setting<br>⊙ **Strategy** Monitor and Fix Up<br>T REVIEW **Skill** Graphic Sources | T ⊙ **Skill** Graphic Sources<br>⊙ **Strategy** Ask Questions<br>T REVIEW **Skill** Main Idea | T ⊙ **Skill** Plot<br>⊙ **Strategy** Prior Knowledge<br>T REVIEW **Skill** Compare and Contrast |
| T ⊙ **Strategy** Dictionary/Glossary | T ⊙ **Strategy** Word Structure | T ⊙ **Strategy** Context Clues |
| Stress/Emphasis | Phrasing | Characterization/Dialogue |
| Final *er, ar* | Consonants /j/, /ks/, and /kw/ | Prefixes *un-, dis-, in-* |
| Readers' Theater<br>Analyze Media | Retelling<br>Listen to a Story | Newscast<br>Analyze Media |
| T Pronouns and Antecedents | T Possessive Pronouns | T Contractions and Negatives |
| Business Letter<br>Writing Trait: Voice | Feature Story<br>Writing Trait: Conventions | Plot Summary<br>Writing Trait: Organization/Paragraphs |
| Story | Story | Story |
| Follow and Clarify Directions | Thesaurus | Technology: Card Catalog/Database |
| **Time For Science** Patents, Scientific Invention, Chemistry | **Time For Social Studies** Biography, Egyptology | **Time For Science** Amphibian Biology, Scientific Method |

# Unit 4
# Monitor Progress

| Predictors of Reading Success | | WEEK 1 | WEEK 2 | WEEK 3 | WEEK 4 |
|---|---|---|---|---|---|
| WCPM | **Fluency** | Emotion<br>110–120 WCPM | Phrasing<br>110–120 WCPM | Stress/Emphasis<br>110–120 WCPM | Phrasing<br>110–120 WCPM |
| Vocabulary | **Vocabulary/ Concept Development**<br>(assessed informally) | invisible<br>pretending<br>judge | agility<br>endowed<br>relationship | advertising<br>concentrate<br>secret | converse<br>scholar<br>symbol |
| | **Lesson Vocabulary** | **Strategy**<br>Context Clues<br><br>appeared<br>bustling<br>crumbled<br>escape<br>magician<br>monument<br>vanished | **Strategy**<br>Context Clues<br><br>aquarium<br>dolphins<br>enchanted<br>flexible<br>glimpses<br>pulses<br>surface | **Strategy**<br>Dictionary/ Glossary<br><br>duke<br>dungeon<br>furiously<br>genius<br>majesty<br>noble<br>peasant<br>porridge | **Strategy**<br>Word Structure<br><br>ancient<br>link<br>scholars<br>seeker<br>temple<br>translate<br>triumph<br>uncover |
| Retelling | **Text Comprehension** | **Skill** Compare and Contrast<br><br>**Strategy**<br>Predict | **Skill** Compare and Contrast<br><br>**Strategy**<br>Visualize | **Skill** Character and Setting<br><br>**Strategy**<br>Monitor and Fix Up | **Skill** Graphic Sources<br><br>**Strategy** Ask Questions |

**390e** Puzzles and Mysteries                    Target Skill        SuccessTracker/Unit 4 Benchmark Tested Skills

## ⚙ Make Data–Driven Decisions

**Data Management**
- Assess
- Diagnose
- Prescribe
- Disaggregate

**Classroom Management**
- Monitor Progress
- Group
- Differentiate Instruction
- Inform Parents

# Success ⚙ Tracker™

# ONLINE CLASSROOM

## WEEK 5

Characterization/
Dialogue

**110–120** WCPM

case
court
damage

⚙ ⊙ **Strategy**
Context Clues

amphibians
crime
exhibit
lizards
reference
reptiles
salamanders
stumped

⚙ ⊙ **Skill** Plot

⊙ **Strategy** Prior
Knowledge

## ⚙ Manage Data

- Assign the Unit 4 Benchmark Test for students to take online.

- SuccessTracker records results and generates reports by school, grade, classroom, or student.

- Use reports to disaggregate and aggregate Unit 4 skills and standards data to monitor progress.

- Based on class lists created to support the categories important for AYP (gender, ethnicity, migrant education, English proficiency, disabilities, economic status), reports let you track adequate yearly progress every six weeks.

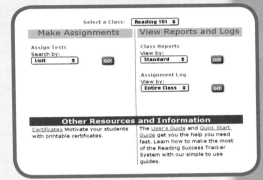

## ⚙ Group

- Use results from Unit 4 Benchmark Tests taken online through SuccessTracker to regroup students.

- Reports in SuccessTracker suggest appropriate groups for students based on test results.

## ⚙ Individualize Instruction

- Tests are correlated to Unit 4 tested skills and standards so that prescriptions for individual teaching and learning plans can be created.

- Individualized prescriptions target instruction and accelerate student progress toward learning outcome goals.

- Prescriptions include resources to reteach Unit 4 skills and standards.

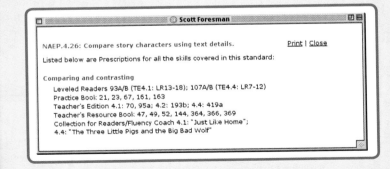

NAEP.4.26: Compare story characters using text details.          Print | Close

Listed below are Prescriptions for all the skills covered in this standard:

Comparing and contrasting
Leveled Readers 93A/B (TE4.1: LR13-18); 107A/B (TE4.4: LR7-12)
Practice Book: 21, 23, 67, 161, 163
Teacher's Edition 4.1: 70, 95a; 4.2: 193b; 4.4: 419a
Teacher's Resource Book: 47, 49, 52, 144, 364, 366, 369
Collection for Readers/Fluency Coach 4.1: "Just Like Home";
4.4: "The Three Little Pigs and the Big Bad Wolf"

# Unit 4
# Grouping for AYP

**STEP 1**

## Diagnose and Differentiate

### Diagnose
To make initial grouping decisions, use the Baseline Group Test or another initial placement test. Depending on children's ability levels, you may have more than one of each group.

### Differentiate

| If... student performance is | Below-Level | then... use the regular instruction and the daily Strategic Intervention lessons, pp. DI·2–DI·50. |
| If... student performance is | On-Level | then... use the regular instruction for On-Level learners throughout each selection. |
| If... student performance is | Advanced | then... use the regular instruction and the daily instruction for notes and activities for Advanced learners, pp. DI·3–DI·51. |

## Group Time

### On-Level
- Explicit instructional routines teach core skills and strategies.
- Independent activities provide practice for core skills and extension and enrichment options.
- Leveled readers (LR1–LR45) provide additional reading and practice with core skills and vocabulary.

### Strategic Intervention
- Daily Strategic Intervention lessons provide more intensive instruction, more scaffolding, more practice with critical skills, and more opportunities to respond.
- Reteach lessons (DI·52–DI·56) provide additional instructional opportunities with target skills.
- Leveled readers (LR1–LR45) build background for the selections and practice target skills and vocabulary.

### Advanced
- Daily Advanced lessons provide compacted instruction for accelerated learning, options for investigative work, and challenging reading content.
- Leveled readers (LR1–LR45) provide additional reading tied to lesson concepts.

Additional opportunities to differentiate instruction:
- Reteach Lessons, pp. DI·52–DI·56
- Leveled Reader Instruction and Leveled Practice, LR1–LR45
- My Sidewalks on Scott Foresman Reading Street Intensive Reading Intervention Program

**MY SiDEWALKS ON**
SCOTT FORESMAN
**READING STREET**
Intensive Reading Intervention

## Monitor Progress

**STEP 2**

- **Guiding comprehension questions** and skill and strategy instruction during reading
- **Monitor Progress boxes** to check comprehension and vocabulary
- **Weekly Assessments** on Day 3 for comprehension, Day 4 for fluency, and Day 5 for vocabulary
- **Practice Book** pages at point of use
- **Weekly Selection Tests** or **Fresh Reads for Differentiated Test Practice**

## Assess and Regroup

**STEP 3**

- **Days 3, 4, and 5 Assessments** Record results of weekly Days 3, 4, and 5 assessments in retelling, fluency, and vocabulary (pp. WA16–WA17) to track student progress.
- **Unit 4 Benchmark Test** Administer this test to check mastery of unit skills.
- Use weekly assessment information, Unit Benchmark Test performance, and the Unit 4 Assess and Regroup (p. WA18) to make regrouping decisions. See the time line below.

*YOU ARE HERE*
*Begin Unit 4*

SCOTT FORESMAN ASSESSMENT

Group Baseline Group Test → Regroup Units 1 and 2 → Regroup Unit 3 → Regroup Unit 4 (p. WA18) → Regroup Unit 5 → END OF YEAR

1      5      10      15      20      25      30

OUTSIDE ASSESSMENT
Initial placement → Outside assessment for regrouping → Outside assessment for regrouping

Outside assessments (e.g., DIBELS) may recommend regrouping at other times during the year.

## Summative Assessment

**STEP 4**

- **Benchmark Assessment** Use to measure a student's mastery of each unit's skills.
- **End-of-Year Benchmark Assessment** Use to measure a student's mastery of program skills covered in all six units.

# Theme Launch

## Discuss the Big Idea

As a class, discuss the Big Idea question, *Is there an explanation for everything?*

Explain that people often search for clues to explain the mysteries around them, such as why animals behave a certain way or how magicians make things disappear.

Ask students to think of events or behaviors they find puzzling or mysterious.

One example of an unsolved mystery is the giant statues located on Easter Island in the Pacific Ocean. Scientists are not certain who carved the volcanic rock, what the statues represent, or why the people who carved the statues disappeared.

## Theme and Concept Connections

Weekly lesson concepts help students connect the reading selections and the unit theme. Theme-related activities throughout the week provide opportunities to explore the relationships among the selections, the lesson concepts, and the unit theme.

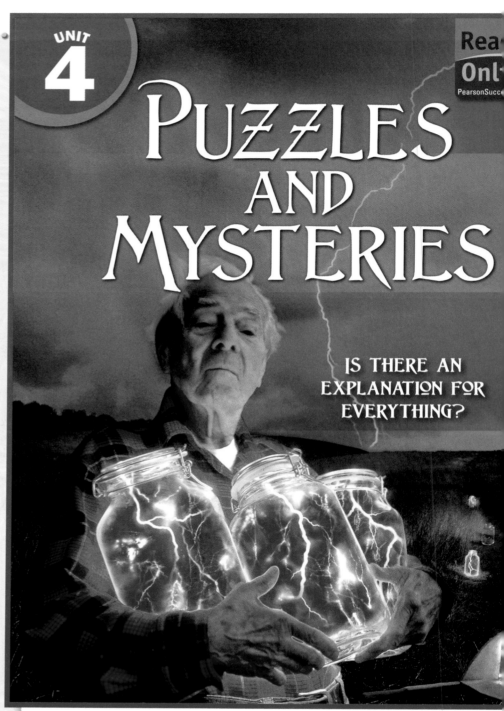

UNIT
4

Rea
Onl

PearsonSucce

# PUZZLES AND MYSTERIES

IS THERE AN EXPLANATION FOR EVERYTHING?

## CONNECTING CULTURES

Use the following selections to help students learn more about mysteries involving nature and ancient civilizations.

**Encantado** Have students discuss unusual attributes of pink dolphins. Students can also speculate on ways to learn more about these mysterious creatures and what it would be like to visit the Amazon.

**Seeker of Knowledge** Have students discuss the importance of Jean-François Champollion's discovery and why scholars want to solve the mysteries of past civilizations. Students can also tell what they enjoy about solving mysteries and puzzles.

**The Houdini Box**

A boy learns the secrets of a famous magician.

HISTORICAL FICTION

**Paired Selection**

**So You Want to Be an Illusionist**

EXPOSITORY NONFICTION

*connect to* SCIENCE

**Encantado: Pink Dolphin of the Amazon**

Pink dolphins of the Amazon puzzle scientists.

EXPOSITORY NONFICTION

**Paired Selection**

**Mysterious Animals**

EXPOSITORY NONFICTION

*connect to* SCIENCE

**The King in the Kitchen**

A king makes a mysterious mixture.

PLAY

**Paired Selection**

**"Who Knows?," "Poetry," "The Seed," and "Carolyn's Cat"**

POETRY

*connect to* SCIENCE

**Seeker of Knowledge**

A Frenchman decodes a mysterious language.

BIOGRAPHY

**Paired Selection**

**Word Puzzles**

SEARCH ENGINES

*connect to* SOCIAL STUDIES

**Encyclopedia Brown and the Case of the Slippery Salamander**

A boy detective solves a mystery.

REALISTIC FICTION

**Paired Selection**

**Young Detectives of Potterville Middle School**

NEWSPAPER ARTICLE

*connect to* SCIENCE

# Unit Inquiry Project

## Unlocking Nature's Mysteries

In the unit inquiry project, students investigate a mystery of nature and uncover the scientific explanation or theories for it. Students may use print or online resources as available.

The project assessment rubric can be found on p. 508a. Discuss the rubric's expectations before students begin the project. **Rubric** `4 3 2 1`

### PROJECT TIMETABLE

| WEEK | ACTIVITY/SKILL CONNECTION |
|------|---------------------------|
| **1** | **IDENTIFY QUESTIONS** Each student chooses a mystery of nature and browses a few Web sites or print reference materials to develop an inquiry question about it. |
| **2** | **NAVIGATE/SEARCH** Students conduct effective information searches and look for text and images that can help them answer their questions. |
| **3** | **ANALYZE** Students explore Web sites or print materials. They analyze the information they have found to determine whether or not it will be useful to them. Students print or take notes on valid information. |
| **4** | **SYNTHESIZE** Students combine relevant information they've collected from different sources to develop answers to their inquiry questions from Week 1. |
| | **ASSESSMENT OPTIONS** |
| **5** | **COMMUNICATE** Each student prepares and presents a short speech describing a mystery of nature and the scientific explanation or theories for it. Students may also write short summaries of their research and compile them into a class book. |

CONCEPT DEVELOPMENT

# Unit 4
# Puzzles and Mysteries

**CONCEPT QUESTION**

Is there an explanation for everything?

---

**Week 1**

**Expand the Concept**

Can you always believe what you see?

**Connect the Concept**

**Literature**

**Develop Language**
*invisible, pretending, judge*

**Teach Content**
Breathing
Illusions
Dai Vernon

**Writing**
Story About a Discovery

**Internet Inquiry**
Perception

---

**Week 2**

**Expand the Concept**

What can explain animal behavior?

**Connect the Concept**

**Literature**

ENCANTADO:

**Develop Language**
*agility, endowed, relationship*

**Teach Content**
Animal Characteristics
Animal Survival
Food Web
Habitat

**Writing**
Travel Brochure

**Internet Inquiry**
Animal Behavior

---

**Week 3**

**Expand the Concept**

How can a mistake turn into a success?

**Connect the Concept**

**Literature**

The King in the Kitchen

**Develop Language**
*advertising, concentrate, secret*

**Teach Content**
Getting a Patent
Inventing Super Glue
Kitchen Chemistry

**Writing**
Business Letter

**Internet Inquiry**
Mistakes and Successes

---

**Week 4**

**Expand the Concept**

How can knowing another language create understanding?

**Connect the Concept**

**Literature**

SEEKER OF KNOWLEDGE

**Develop Language**
*converse, scholar, symbol*

**Teach Content**
Napoleon Bonaparte
The Rosetta Stone

**Writing**
Feature Story

**Internet Inquiry**
Languages

---

**Week 5**

**Expand the Concept**

How can attention to detail help solve a problem?

**Connect the Concept**

**Literature**

The Daily Journal
Young Detectives
of Potterville Middle School

**Develop Language**
*case, damage, court*

**Teach Content**
Salamanders
Experiments

**Writing**
Plot Summary

**Internet Inquiry**
Successful Problem Solving

# Unit 4
# Puzzles and Mysteries

## CONCEPT QUESTION
## Is there an explanation for everything?

## EXPAND THE CONCEPT
## Can you always believe what you see?

TIME FOR **Science**

## CONNECT THE CONCEPT

▶ **Build Background**
*invisible, pretending, judge*

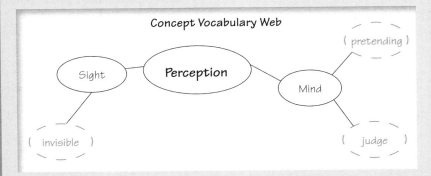

Concept Vocabulary Web

Sight — Perception — Mind

pretending

invisible

judge

▶ **Science Content**
Breathing, Illusions, Dai Vernon

▶ **Writing**
Story About a Discovery

▶ **Internet Inquiry**
Perception

*The Houdini Box*   **392a**

# Preview Your Week

*Can you always believe what you see?*

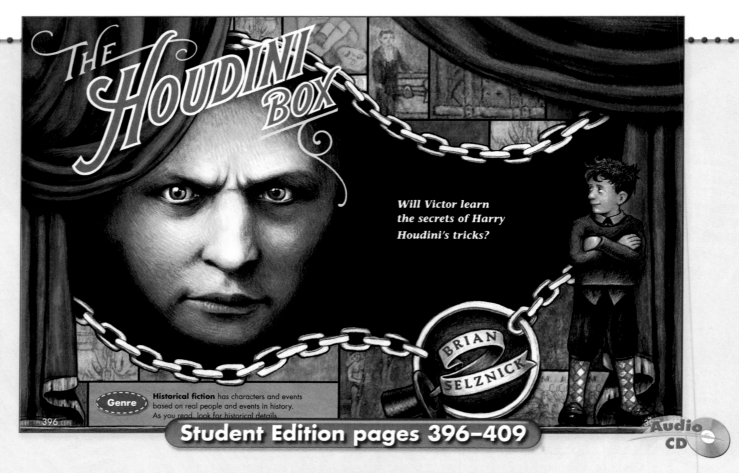

**Will Victor learn the secrets of Harry Houdini's tricks?**

**Genre** Historical fiction has characters and events based on real people and events in history. As you read, look for historical details.

396

**Student Edition pages 396–409**

Audio CD

| | |
|---|---|
| **Genre** | Historical Fiction |
| ⟳ **Vocabulary Strategy** | Context Clues |
| ⟳ **Comprehension Skill** | Compare and Contrast |
| ⟳ **Comprehension Strategy** | Predict |

## Paired Selection

**Reading Across Texts**
Compare Magic Tricks

**Genre**
Expository Nonfiction

**Text Features**
Headings
Captioned Diagrams

### Science in Reading

**Expository Nonfiction**

**Genre**
- Expository nonfiction gives factual information or explanations about a topic.
- Frequently, photos or artwork help explain the information.

**Text Features**
- The author uses headings to organize the text into meaningful parts.
- Captioned diagrams help you "see" and understand information in the text.
- Preview the title, headings, diagrams, and captions. This will prepare you to better understand what you read.

**Link to Science**
Do research in the library or on the Internet to find out more about optical illusions. Re-create one simple optical illusion you find and share it with your class.

412

## So You Want to Be an Illusionist

by Tui T. Sutherland

Most magicians start their careers with illusions. A classic example is pulling a rabbit out of a hat. Harry Houdini wanted to take illusions to a whole new level. And he did.

A lot of magicians make things "disappear"—a rabbit, a coin, even a person. But Harry wanted to perform the biggest disappearing act in the world. That's how he came up with his trick: The Vanishing Elephant.

Harry performed this illusion only in the biggest theaters where there was room on stage for an elephant.

**Predict** What will this article be about?

### Vanishing Elephant

He would start out by introducing his elephant, who was named Jenny. Then Harry's assistants would roll in a very large box on wheels, large enough to hold Jenny. Harry would walk around the box, opening the doors on all sides, so the audience could see that there were no hidden sections at the back. Harry would lead Jenny inside and close all the doors.

A few seconds later, Harry would sweep open the doors again. Jenny was gone. Once again, he'd walk around the box and open all the doors. She had vanished!

Audiences were amazed. How did he do it? The trick was in the construction of the box. But as far as the audience could tell, Harry had made the elephant disappear.

**1** Harry leads Jenny the elephant to a large cabinet on the stage. Jenny enters the cabinet through the curtains and is out of the audience's view.

**2** The cabinet is folded open to reveal that Jenny has vanished.

**3 The Trick** Through spring doors at the rear of the cabinet, Jenny enters a hidden cage on wheels, where she is trained to find her favorite foods.

**4** With the cabinet open, the audience does not see the assistants removing the secret cage.

**Student Edition pages 412–415**

Audio CD

Read It
ONLINE
PearsonSuccessNet.com
• Student Edition
• Leveled Readers

## Leveled Readers

◎ **Skill** Compare and Contrast
◎ **Strategy** Predict
**Lesson Vocabulary**

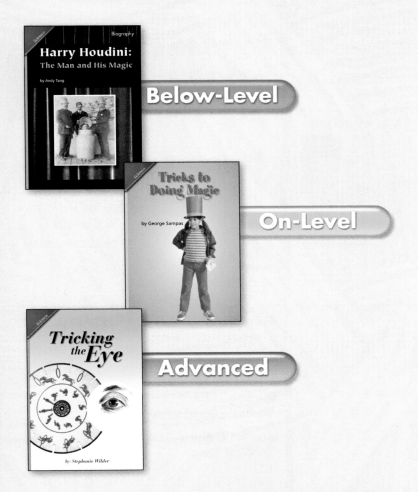

**Below-Level**

**On-Level**

**Advanced**

**ELL Reader**
· Concept Vocabulary
· Text Support
· Language Enrichment

---

## Integrate Science Standards
• Physiology
• Physiology/Optics

✓ **Read**

***The Houdini Box,***
pp. 396–409

**"So You Want to Be an Illusionist,"**
pp. 412–415

### Leveled Readers

**Below-Level** **On-Level** **Advanced**
• Support Concepts • Develop Concepts • Extend Concepts
• Science Extension Activity

### ELL Reader

✓ **Build**
**Concept Vocabulary**
**Perception,** pp. 392l–392m

✓ **Teach**
**Science Concepts**
**Breathing,** p. 399
**Illusions,** p. 405
**Dai Vernon,** p. 413

✓ **Explore**
**Science Center**
**Perform a Trick,** p. 392k

*The Houdini Box* **392c**

# Weekly Plan

## READING

*45–90 minutes*

### TARGET SKILLS OF THE WEEK

- **Comprehension Skill**
  Compare and Contrast

- **Comprehension Strategy**
  Predict

- **Vocabulary Strategy**
  Context Clues

## LANGUAGE ARTS

*30–60 minutes*

### Trait of the Week

**Sentences**

---

## DAY 1  PAGES 392l–394b, 415a, 415e–415k

### Oral Language

**QUESTION OF THE WEEK**  *Can you always believe what you see?*

Read Aloud: "The Emperor's New Clothes" 392m
Build Concepts, 392l

### Comprehension/Vocabulary

Comprehension Skill/Strategy Lesson, 392–393
- Compare and Contrast **T**
- Predict

Build Background, 394a

Introduce Lesson Vocabulary, 394b
*appeared, bustling, crumbled, escape, magician, monument, vanished* **T**

**Read** Leveled Readers

**Grouping Options** 392f–392g

### Fluency

Model Emotion, 392l–392m, 415a

---

**Grammar,** 415e
Introduce Singular and Plural Pronouns **T**

**Writing Workshop,** 415g
Introduce Story About a Discovery
Model the Trait of the Week: Sentences

**Spelling,** 415i
Pretest for Contractions

**Internet Inquiry,** 415k
Identify Questions

---

## DAY 2  PAGES 394–403, 415a, 415e–415k

### Oral Language

**QUESTION OF THE DAY**  *Why is Houdini able to escape, but Victor cannot?*

### Comprehension/Vocabulary

Vocabulary Strategy Lesson, 394–395
- Context Clues **T**

**Read** *The Houdini Box,* 396–403

**Grouping Options** 392f–392g

- Compare and Contrast **T**
- Predict
- Context Clues **T**
- REVIEW Plot and Character **T**

Develop Vocabulary

### Fluency

Echo Reading, 415a

---

**Grammar,** 415e
Develop Singular and Plural Pronouns **T**

**Writing Workshop,** 415g
Improve Writing with Good Beginnings

**Spelling,** 415i
Teach the Generalization

**Internet Inquiry,** 415k
Navigate/Search

---

**DAILY WRITING ACTIVITIES**

**Day 1**  Write to Read, 392

**Day 2**  Words to Write, 395
Strategy Response Log, 396, 403

---

**DAILY SCIENCE CONNECTIONS**

**Day 1**  Perception Concept Web, 392l

**Day 2**  Time for Science: Breathing, 399
Revisit the Perception Concept Web, 403

---

**DAILY SUCCESS PREDICTORS**
for Adequate Yearly Progress

### Monitor Progress and Corrective Feedback

Vocabulary  Check Vocabulary, *392l*

**RESOURCES FOR THE WEEK**

- Practice Book, *pp. 151–160*
- Word Study and Spelling Practice Book, *pp. 61–64*
- Grammar and Writing Practice Book, *pp. 61–64*
- Selection Test, *pp. 61–64*
- Fresh Reads for Differentiated Test Practice, *pp. 91–96*
- The Grammar and Writing Book, *pp. 140–145*

## Grouping Options for Differentiated Instruction

Turn the page for the small group lesson plan.

---

# DAY 3 — PAGES 404–411, 415a, 415e–415k

### Oral Language

**QUESTION OF THE DAY** *Why do people enjoy doing and watching magic tricks so much?*

### Comprehension/Vocabulary

**Read** *The Houdini Box, 404–411*

**Grouping Options** 392f–392g

- Compare/Contrast **T**
- Predict
- Confirm Predictions
- Context Clues **T**
- Develop Vocabulary

Reader Response
Selection Test

### Fluency

Model Emotion, 415a

---

**Grammar,** 415f
Apply Single and Plural Pronouns in Writing **T**

**Writing Workshop,** 411, 415h
Write Now
Prewrite and Draft

**Spelling,** 415j
Connect Spelling to Writing

**Internet Inquiry,** 415k
Analyze Sources

---

**Day 3** Strategy Response Log, 408
Look Back and Write, 410

**Day 3** Time for Science: Illusions, 405
Revisit the *Perception* Concept Web, 409

---

# DAY 4 — PAGES 412–415a, 415e–415k

### Oral Language

**QUESTION OF THE DAY** *What are some things you would and wouldn't like about being an illusionist?*

### Comprehension/Vocabulary

**Read** *"So You Want to Be an Illusionist"* 412–415

**Grouping Options** 392f –392g

Expository Nonfiction
Reading Across Texts
Content-Area Vocabulary

### Fluency

Partner Reading, 415a

---

**Grammar,** 415f
Practice Singular and Plural Pronouns for Standardized Tests **T**

**Writing Workshop,** 415h
Draft, Revise, and Publish

**Spelling,** 415j
Provide a Strategy

**Internet Inquiry,** 415k
Synthesize Information

---

**Day 4** Writing Across Texts, 415

**Day 4** Time for Science: Dai Vernon, 413

---

# DAY 5 — PAGES 415a–415l

### Oral Language

**QUESTION OF THE WEEK** *To wrap up the week, revisit the Day 1 question.*

Build Concept Vocabulary, 415c

### Fluency

**Read** Leveled Readers

**Grouping Options** 392f–392g

Assess Reading Rate, 415a

### Comprehension/Vocabulary

- Reteach Compare and Contrast, 415b **T**
- Steps in a Process, 415b
- Review Context Clues, 415c **T**

---

**Speaking and Viewing,** 415d
Interview
Analyze Media

**Grammar,** 415f
Cumulative Review

**Writing Workshop,** 415h
Connect to Unit Writing

**Spelling,** 415j
Posttest for Contractions

**Internet Inquiry,** 415k
Communicate Results

**Research/Study Skills,** 415l
Instruction Manual

---

**Day 5** Steps in a Process, 415b

**Day 5** Revisit the Perception Concept Web, 415c

---

**KEY** = Target Skill **T** = Tested Skill

Check Retelling, *410*

Check Fluency WCPM, *415a*

Check Vocabulary, *415c*

SUCCESS PREDICTOR

# Small Group Plan for Differentiated Instruction

## Daily Plan AT A GLANCE

### Reading
### Whole Group
- Oral Language
- Comprehension/Vocabulary

### Group Time
#### Differentiated Instruction
Meet with small groups to provide:
- Skill Support
- Reading Support
- Fluency Practice

#### Read

This week's lessons for daily group time can be found behind the Differentiated Instruction (DI) tab on pp. DI·2–DI·11.

### Whole Group
- Fluency

### Language Arts
- Grammar
- Writing
- Spelling
- Research/Inquiry
- Speaking/Listening/Viewing

**Use *My Sidewalks on Reading Street* for Tier III intensive reading intervention.**

---

### DAY 1

| On-Level | Strategic Intervention | Advanced |
|---|---|---|
| **Teacher-Led** *Page DI·3* | **Teacher-Led** *Page DI·2* | **Teacher-Led** *Page DI·3* |
| • Develop Concept Vocabulary | • Reinforce Concepts | • Read Advanced Reader *Tricking the Eye* |
| • Read On-Level Reader *Tricks to Doing Magic* | • Read Below-Level Reader *Harry Houdini: The Man and His Magic* | • Independent Extension Activity |

#### (i) Independent Activities
**While you meet with small groups, have the rest of the class...**

- Visit the Reading/Library Center
- Listen to the Background Building Audio
- Finish Write to Read, p. 392
- Complete Practice Book pp. 153–154
- Visit Cross-Curricular Centers

---

### DAY 2

| On-Level | Strategic Intervention | Advanced |
|---|---|---|
| **Teacher-Led** *Pages Pages 398–403* | **Teacher-Led** *Page DI·4* | **Teacher-Led** *Page DI·5* |
| • Develop Concept Vocabulary | • Practice Lesson Vocabulary | • Extend Vocabulary |
| • Read *The Houdini Box* | • Read Multisyllabic Words | • Read *The Houdini Box* |
| | • Read or Listen to *The Houdini Box* | |

#### (i) Independent Activities
**While you meet with small groups, have the rest of the class...**

- Visit the Reading/Library Center
- Listen to the AudioText for *The Houdini Box*
- Finish Words to Write, p. 395
- Complete Practice Book pp. 155–156
- Write in their Strategy Response Logs, pp. 396, 403
- Visit Cross-Curricular Centers
- Work on inquiry projects

---

### DAY 3

| On-Level | Strategic Intervention | Advanced |
|---|---|---|
| **Teacher-Led** *Pages 404–409* | **Teacher-Led** *Page DI·6* | **Teacher-Led** *Page DI·7* |
| • Read *The Houdini Box* | • Practice Compare and Contrast and Predict | • Extend Compare and Contrast and Predict |
| | • Read or Listen to *The Houdini Box* | • Read *The Houdini Box* |

#### (i) Independent Activities
**While you meet with small groups, have the rest of the class...**

- Visit the Reading/Library Center
- Listen to the AudioText for *The Houdini Box*
- Write in their Strategy Response Logs, p. 408
- Finish Look Back and Write, p. 410
- Complete Practice Book p. 157
- Visit Cross-Curricular Centers
- Work on inquiry projects

① Begin with whole class skill and strategy instruction.

② Meet with small groups to provide differentiated instruction.

③ Gather the whole class back together for fluency and language arts.

## DAY 4

**On-Level**

Teacher-Led
*Pages 412–415*

• **Read** "So You Want to Be an Illusionist"

**Strategic Intervention**

Teacher-Led
*Page DI·8*

• Practice Retelling
• **Read** or Listen to "So You Want to Be an Illusionist"

**Advanced**

Teacher-Led
*Page DI·9*

• **Read** "So You Want to Be an Illusionist"
• Genre Study

### ⓘ Independent Activities

**While you meet with small groups, have the rest of the class...**

• Visit the Reading/Library Center
• Listen to the AudioText for "So You Want to Be an Illusionist"
• Visit the Writing/Vocabulary Center
• Finish Writing Across Texts, p. 415
• Visit Cross-Curricular Centers
• Work on inquiry projects

## DAY 5

**On-Level**

Teacher-Led
*Page DI·11*

• **Reread** Leveled Reader *Tricks to Doing Magic*
• Retell *Tricks to Doing Magic*

**Strategic Intervention**

Teacher-Led
*Page DI·10*

• **Reread** Leveled Reader *Harry Houdini: The Man and His Magic*
• Retell *Harry Houdini: The Man and His Magic*

**Advanced**

Teacher-Led
*Page DI·11*

• **Reread** Leveled Reader *Tricking the Eye*
• Share Extension Activity

### ⓘ Independent Activities

**While you meet with small groups, have the rest of the class...**

• Visit the Reading/Library Center
• Complete Practice Book pp. 158–160
• Visit Cross-Curricular Centers
• Work on inquiry projects

**Grouping** Place English language learners in the groups that correspond to their reading abilities in English.

Use the appropriate Leveled Reader or other text at students' instructional level.

**TiP** Send home the appropriate Multilingual Summary of the main selection on Day 1.

---

**Take It to the NET™ ONLINE**
PearsonSuccessNet.com

**Jeanne Paratore**
For ideas on using repeated readings, see the article "Using Repeated Readings to Promote Reading Success . . ." by J. Turpie and Scott Foresman author J. Paratore.

---

### TEACHER TALK

**Curriculum compacting** is a technique for content acceleration. Students skip work they already have mastered and complete more challenging content.

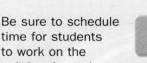

Be sure to schedule time for students to work on the unit inquiry project "Unlocking Nature's Mysteries." This week students develop an inquiry question about a mystery of nature.

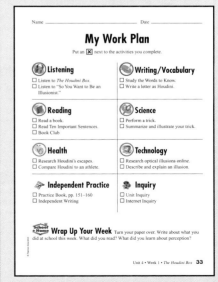

▲ **Group-Time Survival Guide** p. 33, Weekly Contract

*The Houdini Box* **392g**

# ☑ Customize Your Plan *by Strand*

## ORAL LANGUAGE

### Concept Development

Can you always believe what you see?

**CONCEPT VOCABULARY**
*invisible     judge     pretending*

### BUILD

☐ **Question of the Week** Introduce and discuss the question of the week. This week students will read a variety of texts and work on projects related to the concept *perception*. Post the question for students to refer to throughout the week. **DAY 1** *392d*

☐ **Read Aloud** Read aloud "The Emperor's New Clothes." Then begin a web to build concepts and concept vocabulary related to this week's lesson and the unit theme, Puzzles and Mysteries. Introduce the concept words *invisible, judge,* and *pretending* and have students place them on the web. Display the web for use throughout the week. **DAY 1** *392l-392m*

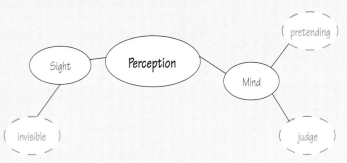

### DEVELOP

☐ **Question of the Day** Use the prompts from the Weekly Plan to engage students in conversations related to this week's reading and the unit theme. **EVERY DAY** *392d-392e*

☐ **Concept Vocabulary Web** Revisit the Perception Concept Web and encourage students to add concept words from their reading and life experiences. **DAY 2** *403*, **DAY 3** *409*

### CONNECT

☐ **Looking Back/Moving Forward** Revisit the Perception Concept Web and discuss how it relates to this week's lesson and the unit theme. Then make connections to next week's lesson. **DAY 5** *415c*

### CHECK

☐ **Concept Vocabulary Web** Use the Perception Concept Web to check students' understanding of the concept vocabulary words *invisible, judge,* and *pretending*. **DAY 1** *392l*, **DAY 5** *415c*

## VOCABULARY

**STRATEGY CONTEXT CLUES** When you are reading, you may come across an unfamiliar word. Sometimes the author has used a synonym or an antonym as a clue to the word's meaning. Synonyms are words that mean almost the same thing. Antonyms are words with opposite meanings.

**LESSON VOCABULARY**
appeared      magician
bustling      monument
crumbled      vanished
escape

### TEACH

☐ **Words to Know** Give students the opportunity to tell what they already know about this week's lesson vocabulary words. Then discuss word meaning. **DAY 1** *394b*

☐ **Vocabulary Strategy Lesson** Use the vocabulary strategy lesson in the Student Edition to introduce and model this week's strategy, *context clues*. **DAY 2** *394-395*

**Vocabulary Strategy Lesson**

### PRACTICE/APPLY

☐ **Leveled Text** Read the lesson vocabulary in the context of leveled text. **DAY 1** *LR1-LR9*

☐ **Words in Context** Read the lesson vocabulary and apply *context clues* in the context of *The Houdini Box.* **DAY 2** *396-403*, **DAY 3** *404-410*

**Leveled Readers**

☐ **Writing/Vocabulary Center** Write a letter as if you were Houdini telling Victor why you gave him the box. **DAY 4** *392k*, **DAY 5** *392k*

**Main Selection—Fiction**

☐ **Homework** Practice Book pp. 154–155. **DAY 1** *394b*, **DAY 2** *395*

☐ **Word Play** Have students brainstorm a list of words (verbs) that show how characters speak. Then have them write lines of dialogue using words from the list and characters from the story. **ANY DAY** *415c*

### ASSESS

☐ **Selection Test** Use the Selection Test to determine students' understanding of the lesson vocabulary words. **DAY 3**

### RETEACH/REVIEW

☐ **Reteach Lesson** If necessary, use this lesson to reteach and review *context clues.* **DAY 5** *415c*

## COMPREHENSION

**👁 SKILL COMPARE AND CONTRAST** To compare is to tell how two ideas or concepts are similar or alike. To contrast is to tell how ideas or concepts are different.

**👁 STRATEGY PREDICT** Active readers predict. They use what they know as well as what the author tells them to form ideas about what might happen next.

### TEACH

❑ **Skill/Strategy Lesson** Use the skill/strategy lesson in the Student Edition to introduce and model *compare and contrast* and *predict*. **DAY 1** *392-393*

**Skill/Strategy Lesson**

❑ **Extend Skills** Teach steps in a process. **ANY DAY** *415b*

### PRACTICE/APPLY

❑ **Leveled Text** Apply *compare and contrast* and *predict* to read leveled text. **DAY 1** *LR1-LR9*

**Leveled Readers**

❑ **Skills and Strategies in Context** Read *The Houdini Box*, using the Guiding Comprehension questions to apply *compare and contrast* and *predict*. **DAY 2** *396-403*, **DAY 3** *404-410*

**Main Selection—Fiction**

❑ **Skills and Strategies in Context** Read "So You Want to Be an Illusionist," guiding students as they apply *compare and contrast* and *predict*. Then have students discuss and write across texts. **DAY 4** *412-415*

**Paired Selection—Nonfiction**

❑ **Homework** Practice Book pp. 153, 157, 158. **DAY 1** *393*, **DAY 3** *409*, **DAY 5** *415b*

❑ **Fresh Reads for Differentiated Test Practice** Have students practice *compare and contrast* with a new passage. **DAY 3**

### ASSESS

❑ **Selection Test** Determine students' understanding of the selection and their use of *compare and contrast*. **DAY 3**

❑ **Retell** Have students retell *The Houdini Box*. **DAY 3** *410-411*

### RETEACH/REVIEW

❑ **Reteach Lesson** If necessary, reteach and review *compare and contrast*. **DAY 5** *415b*

## FLUENCY

**SKILL EMOTION** Reading with emotion is the ability to place emphasis on pause, pitch, and tone of voice to help listeners understand characters and events better.

### TEACH

❑ **Read Aloud** Model fluent reading by rereading "The Emperor's New Clothes." Focus on this week's fluency skill, emotion. **DAY 1** *392l-392m, 415a*

### PRACTICE/APPLY

❑ **Echo Reading** Read aloud selected paragraphs from *The Houdini Box*, placing emphasis on pitch, pause, and tone of voice. Have the class practice, doing three echo readings. **DAY 2** *415a*, **DAY 3** *415a*

❑ **Partner Reading** Have partners practice reading aloud, reading with emotion and offering each other feedback. As students reread, monitor their progress toward their individual fluency goals. **DAY 4** *415a*

❑ **Listening Center** Have students follow along with the AudioText for this week's selections. **ANY DAY** *392j*

❑ **Reading/Library Center** Have students reread a selection of their choice. **ANY DAY** *392j*

❑ **Fluency Coach** Have students use Fluency Coach to listen to fluent readings or practice reading on their own. **ANY DAY**

### ASSESS

❑ **Check Fluency** WCPM Do a one-minute timed reading, paying special attention to this week's skill— emotion. Provide feedback for each student. **DAY 5** *415a*

# ☑ Customize Your Plan *by Strand*

## GRAMMAR

**SKILL SINGULAR AND PLURAL PRONOUNS** Pronouns are words that take the place of nouns. Pronouns that take the place of singular nouns are singular pronouns (*I, me, he, she, him, her,* and *it*). Pronouns that take the place of plural nouns are plural pronouns (*we, us, they,* and *them*).

### TEACH

❏ **Grammar Transparency 16** Use Grammar Transparency 16 to teach singular and plural pronouns. DAY 1 *415e*

**Grammar Transparency 16**

### PRACTICE/APPLY

❏ **Develop the Concept** Review the concept of singular and plural pronouns and provide guided practice. DAY 2 *415e*

❏ **Apply to Writing** Have students review something they have written and tighten it up by using singular and plural pronouns. DAY 3 *415f*

❏ **Test Preparation** Examine common errors in singular and plural pronouns to prepare for standardized tests. DAY 4 *415f*

❏ **Homework** Grammar and Writing Practice Book pp. 61–63. DAY 2 *415e*, DAY 3 *415f*, DAY 4 *415f*

### ASSESS

❏ **Cumulative Review** Use Grammar and Writing Practice Book p. 64. DAY 5 *415f*

### RETEACH/REVIEW

❏ **Daily Fix-It** Have students find and correct errors in grammar, spelling, and punctuation. **EVERY DAY** *415e-415f*

❏ **The Grammar and Writing Book** Use pp. 140–143 of The Grammar and Writing Book to extend instruction for singular and plural pronouns. **ANY DAY**

**The Grammar and Writing Book**

## WRITING

### Trait of the Week

**SENTENCES** Good writers express their thoughts in lively, varied sentences. Sentences that have a natural flow as well as vary in structure and length create a rhythm and style.

### TEACH

❏ **Writing Transparency 16A** Use the model to introduce and discuss the Trait of the Week. DAY 1 *415g*

❏ **Writing Transparency 16B** Use the transparency to show students how good beginnings can improve their writing. DAY 2 *415g*

**Writing Transparency 16A** **Writing Transparency 16B**

### PRACTICE/APPLY

❏ **Write Now** Examine the model on Student Edition p. 411. Then have students write their own stories about a discovery. DAY 3 *411, 415h*, DAY 4 *415h*

> **Prompt** In *The Houdini Box*, a boy discovers the secrets of a great magician. Think about a discovery you have made or would like to make. Now write a story about your discovery.

**Write Now p. 411**

❏ **Writing/Vocabulary Center** Write a letter as if you were Houdini telling Victor why you gave him the box. DAY 4 *392k*, DAY 5 *392k*

### ASSESS

❏ **Writing Trait Rubric** Use the rubric to evaluate students' writing. DAY 4 *415h*

### RETEACH/REVIEW

❏ **The Grammar and Writing Book** Use pp. 140–145 of The Grammar and Writing Book to extend instruction for singular and plural pronouns, good beginnings, and a story about a discovery. **ANY DAY**

**The Grammar and Writing Book**

❶ Use assessment data to determine your instructional focus.

❷ Preview this week's instruction by strand.

❸ Choose instructional activities that meet the needs of your classroom.

## SPELLING

**GENERALIZATION CONTRACTIONS** In contractions, an apostrophe replaces omitted letters: *do not* becomes *don't; there is* becomes *there's*. Because letters are left out in a contraction, the contraction is pronounced differently from the original two words.

### TEACH

❑ **Pretest** Give the pretest for contractions. Guide students in self-correcting their pretests and correcting any misspellings. **DAY 1** *415i*

❑ **Think and Practice** Connect spelling to the phonics generalization for contractions. **DAY 2** *415i*

### PRACTICE/APPLY

❑ **Connect to Writing** Have students use spelling words to write a note inviting a friend to a party. Then review frequently misspelled words: *it's, you're, we're.* **DAY 3** *415j*

❑ **Homework** Word Study and Spelling Practice Book pp. 61–64. **EVERY DAY**

### RETEACH/REVIEW

❑ **Review** Review spelling words to prepare for the posttest. Then provide students with a spelling strategy— problem parts. **DAY 4** *415j*

### ASSESS

❑ **Posttest** Use dictation sentences to give the posttest for words with contractions. **DAY 5** *415j*

## Spelling Words

| | | |
|---|---|---|
| 1. don't | 8. I've | 15. aren't |
| 2. won't* | 9. here's | 16. they're |
| 3. wouldn't | 10. wasn't* | 17. it's |
| 4. there's* | 11. shouldn't | 18. we've |
| 5. we're | 12. couldn't* | 19. when's |
| 6. you're* | 13. where's | 20. haven't |
| 7. doesn't | 14. hadn't | |

## Challenge Words

| | | |
|---|---|---|
| 21. it'll | 23. might've | 25. we'd |
| 22. who'll | 24. mustn't | |

*Word from the selection

## RESEARCH AND INQUIRY

❑ **Internet Inquiry** Have students conduct an Internet inquiry on perception. **EVERY DAY** *415k*

❑ **Instruction Manual** Review what an instruction manual is, its purpose, how it is organized, and discuss how students can use these manuals to learn how to do or build something. **DAY 5** *415l*

❑ **Unit Inquiry** Allow time for students to develop inquiry questions about a mystery of nature. **ANY DAY** *391*

## SPEAKING AND VIEWING

❑ **Interview** Have pairs role-play an interview with a famous magician. **DAY 5** *415d*

❑ **Analyze Media** Have a class discussion on television shows or movies students have seen in which a person or situation is not as it originally appeared to be. **DAY 5** *415d*

# Resources for
# Differentiated Instruction

▶ **Comprehension**

🎯 **Skill** Compare and Contrast

🎯 **Strategy** Predict

▶ **Lesson Vocabulary**

🎯 Context Clues

appeared    bustling    crumbled    escape    monument    vanished    magician

▶ **Science Standards**

• Physiology
• Physiology/Optics

## ONLINE

PearsonSuccessNet.com

Use the Online Database of over 600 books to

• Download and print additional copies of this week's leveled readers.

• Listen to the readers being read online.

• Search for more titles focused on this week's skills, topic, and content.

## On-Level

**On-Level Reader**

*Tricks to Doing Magic* by George Sampas

---

Name _____  **Tricks to Doing Magic**

### Compare and Contrast

• To compare is to describe how two ideas or concepts are similar or alike.
• To contrast is to describe how ideas or concepts are different.

**Directions** Read the paragraphs below. Then answer the questions. *Possible responses given.*

When performing the *Disappearing Person* trick, the magician brings out a tall box. The magician talks and tells jokes or stories to the audience. In the center of the box, is a post that the audience cannot see. There are mirrors from the top to the bottom of the cabinet that swing from the sides to the center post. The magician's assistant steps inside and hides behind the mirrors. Presto! When the magician opens the box, the assistant is gone.

The *Guess Which Hand* trick is also an illusion. The magician keeps the audience's attention by talking and joking with them. First, he shows the audience a quarter. He also has a secret quarter in his belt. He shifts his hands to make it look like he's moving one quarter back and forth. In fact, each hand now has a quarter. When the audience picks which hand has the quarter, the magician shows the other hand. This way, the audience thinks they got it wrong.

1. Compare the magician's interaction with the audience in both tricks.
   The magician talks to the audience to create excitement.
2. Contrast the size of the props in these tricks.
   the first trick uses a large box and another person; the second trick uses only two quarters
3. How are these tricks similar?
   they both involve disappearing props; both rely on the magician's clever talking
4. Compare the set-up or preparation for these tricks.
   for the *Disappearing Person*, the box must be built; for *Which Hand*, the magician needs to collect two quarters
5. Contrast the techniques the magician might use to practice these tricks.
   for the first, the magician creates dramatic presentation with mirrors; for the second, the magician uses his hands to create illusion

🎯 **On-Level Practice** TE p. LR5

---

Name _____  **Tricks to Doing Magic**

### Vocabulary

**Directions** Choose the word from the Word Box that best matches each definition. Write the word on the line.

**Check the Words You Know**

___appeared  ___crumbled  ___magician  ___vanished
___bustling  ___escape  ___monument

1. seemed to be, looked like     appeared
2. disappeared suddenly     vanished
3. made into small pieces     crumbled
4. to get free from     escape
5. one who entertains with magic     magician
6. noisily busy, excited     bustling
7. something set up to honor a person or event     monument

**Directions** Choose the word (or words) from the Word Box that best completes each sentence. Write each word on the line.

8. The crowd outside the magic show was    bustling    with excitement.
9. First the assistant    vanished    from the box, but then she    appeared    again.
10. The magician was so famous that a    monument    was put up to remember him after he died.

🎯 **On-Level Practice** TE p. LR6

## Strategic Intervention

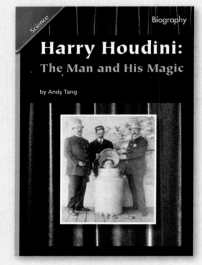

**Harry Houdini:** The Man and His Magic
by Andy Tang

**Below-Level Reader**

---

Name _____  **Harry Houdini**

### Compare and Contrast

• To compare is to tell how two or more things are alike or similar.
• To contrast is to tell how two or more things are different.

**Directions** Read the paragraphs. Then answer the questions below. *Possible responses given.*

For an act called the Metamorphosis, Harry Houdini was handcuffed inside a sack and locked in a trunk. Somehow he would free himself and switch places with his brother, who was standing beside the trunk. In 1899, Houdini developed his handcuff challenge. He said he would pay one hundred dollars to anyone who gave him handcuffs he could not escape from. He never had to pay. In 1913 he introduced his most famous stunt, the Upside-Down Water Torture Cell. In this act, Houdini was locked in a water-filled glass-and-steel cabinet while hanging upside down by his feet.

Houdini explained some of his secrets. Many handcuffs could be opened with properly applied force. Sometimes he carried hidden lock picks or keys. In the Metamorphosis, the trunk had a hidden side panel that allowed Houdini to escape. Houdini also spent hours practicing holding his breath so he could stay submerged in the water trick.

1. Compare the Metamorphosis to the Water Torture Cell by finding one similarity.
   for both, Houdini was trapped inside a device
2. Contrast the Metamorphosis and the Water Torture Cell by finding one difference.
   for both, Houdini was trapped inside a device
3. Compare the Metamorphosis to the handcuff tricks.
   in both, Houdini was stuck because he was locked up
4. Contrast the handcuff tricks with the Water Torture Cell by finding a difference.
   the handcuff tricks did not involve water
5. Find another difference between the Water Torture Cell and the handcuff tricks.
   Houdini did not need to hold his breath

🎯 **Below-Level Practice** TE p. LR2

---

Name _____  **Harry Houdini**

### Vocabulary

**Directions** Choose the word from the Word Box that best matches each definition. Write the word on the line.

**Check the Words You Know**

___appeared  ___crumbled  ___magician  ___vanished
___bustling  ___escape  ___monument

1. The crowds at Houdini's shows were    bustling    with excitement.
2. Many people visit the    monument    that was built to remember the president.
3. In some of Houdini's tricks, the magician or his partner    vanished    from view.
4. After Houdini vanished, he always    appeared    again.
5. The suspense of the crowd    crumbled    as soon as Houdini reappeared.
6. It must have been exciting for the crowd when Houdini pretended to    escape   .
7. To be a good    magician    takes months, sometimes years, of practice.

**Directions** For each vocabulary word, find the root word and write it on the line. Then use the root word or the vocabulary word in a sentence.

8. bustling    bustle
   I went to the mall because I like the bustle of it.
9. crumbled    crumble
   I watched the dirt clod crumble to pieces.
10. vanished    vanish
    I was so embarrassed I wanted to vanish.

🎯 **Below-Level Practice** TE p. LR3

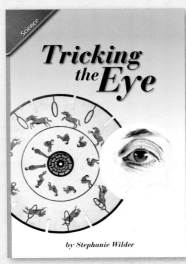

## Advanced Reader

*Tricking the Eye*
by Stephanie Wilder

---

**Name** _____ **Tricking the Eye**

## Compare and Contrast

- To **compare** is to describe how two ideas or concepts are similar or alike.
- To **contrast** is to describe how ideas or concepts are different.
- Clue words like **however, unlike, although,** and **on the other hand** suggest contrasts. Clue words like **also, similarly,** and **like** suggest similarities.

**Directions** Read the paragraphs below. Then answer the questions. *Possible responses given.*

In the early days, the many still pictures that make a cartoon had to be drawn by hand, and this took a lot of work. So animators came up with a few tricks to make their jobs easier. Instead of drawing a whole new picture for every frame, they decided to draw only the parts of the picture that needed to move. Usually this meant making one background drawing. The characters were drawn on clear plastic sheets and laid over the still background. The characters would change and look like they were moving, but only one background drawing was made. This method is called cel animation.

Another old trick is called the slash-and-tear system. Here the moving characters are drawn on regular paper, but then they are cut out. This way the different images of the moving characters can be placed on top of the background drawing. Either way, what you think you see is the characters coming to life.

1. Compare the cel and slash-and-tear systems by finding two things that are similar.
   _both create animated characters; both use a basic background_
2. Contrast the cel and slash-and-tear systems by finding a difference.
   _for the cel system, animators draw the characters on clear plastic; for the_
   _slash-and-tear, animators draw the characters on paper and cut them out_
3. Contrast cel animation with making a cartoon without any tricks.
   _in the first method, the animator draws every single frame from scratch;_
   _with cel animation, the animator only changes the characters_
4. The book *Tricking the Eye* also discusses the use of clay models or puppets in animated films. Contrast this with cel animation.
   _puppets or clay models are three-dimensional; cel animation uses 2-D_
   _techniques_

**Advanced Practice** TE p. LR8

---

**Name** _____ **Tricking the Eye**

## Vocabulary

**Directions** Choose the word from the Word Box that best matches each definition. Write the word on the line.

**Check the Words You Know**
- accommodation
- animate
- cerebral cortex
- computer-assisted animation
- computer-generated animation
- concave
- frames
- illusion
- optical illusion
- perception

1. illusion having to do with sight or seeing _optical illusion_
2. two-dimensional computer animation; a series of still computer images put together to create movement _computer-assisted animation_
3. to make lively _animate_
4. curved inward _concave_
5. the brain's understanding of something _perception_
6. the automatic adjustment of the lens of the eye to see objects at various distances _accommodation_
7. the process by which a computer uses models and formulas to make a still image move in lifelike ways, often in three dimensions _computer-generated animation_
8. part of the brain that receives signals from the senses _cerebral cortex_
9. individual still images that make up a cartoon _frames_
10. something that appears to be different from what it actually is _illusion_

**Advanced Practice** TE p. LR9

---

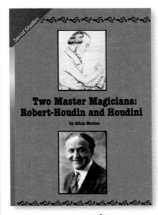

*Two Master Magicians:*
*Robert-Houdin and Houdini*
by Alicia Morton

**ELL Reader**

**ELL Poster 16**

**Teacher's Edition Notes**

ELL notes throughout this lesson support instruction and reference additional resources at point of use.

**Teaching Guide**
**pp. 106–112, 242–243**
- Multilingual summaries of the main selection
- Comprehension lesson
- Vocabulary strategies and word cards
- ELL Reader 4.4.1 lesson

**ELL and Transition Handbook**

**Ten Important Sentences**
- Key ideas from every selection in the Student Edition
- Activities to build sentence power

---

# More Reading

## Readers' Theater Anthology
- Fluency practice
- Five scripts to build fluency
- Poetry for oral interpretation

## Leveled Trade Books

Below-Level

Advanced

On-Level

- Extended reading tied to the unit concept
- Lessons in the Trade Book Library Teaching Guide

---

# School + Home

## Homework
- Family Times Newsletter
- ELL Multilingual Selection Summaries

## Take-Home Books
- Leveled Readers

---

# Cross-Curricular Centers

## Listening

### Listen to the Selections

**MATERIALS** SINGLES
CD player, headphones, AudioText CD, student book

**LISTEN TO LITERATURE** Listen to *The Houdini Box* and "So You Want to Be an Illusionist" as you follow or read along in your book. Listen for comparisons and contrasts in *The Houdini Box*.

If there is anything you don't understand, you can listen again to any section.

## Reading/Library

### Read It Again!

**MATERIALS** SINGLES PAIRS GROUPS
Collection of books for self-selected reading, reading logs, student book

Select a book you have already read. Record the title of the book in your reading log. You may want to read with a partner.

Choose from the following:

- Leveled Readers
- ELL Readers
- Stories Written by Classmates
- Books from the Library
- *The Houdini Box*

**TEN IMPORTANT SENTENCES** Read the Ten Important Sentences for *The Houdini Box.* Then locate the sentences in the student book.

**BOOK CLUB** Read a nonfiction book about Harry Houdini. In a group share some facts you learned about Houdini. Compare *The Houdini Box* with the nonfiction book.

## Health

### Compare Skills

**MATERIALS** SINGLES PAIRS
Student book, resources about Houdini, writing materials

Compare the physical skills Houdini used as an escape artist to an athlete's skills.

1. **Review *The Houdini Box* and search classroom resources about Houdini to find details about the escapes he performed and how he did them.**
2. **Think of the physical skills that Houdini needed to be an escape artist.**
3. **Compare Houdini to a professional athlete. Write a paragraph telling how Houdini and the athlete are alike or different.**

**EARLY FINISHERS** Who do you think has a harder job, Houdini or a professional athlete? Add sentences to your paragraph stating your opinion. Give reasons to support your ideas.

Harry Houdini had to be in good physical shape to perform his escape tricks, just like a professional athlete. To escape from the milk bottle, Houdini had to hold his breath underwater for a long time. He also had to be flexible to squeeze his body into small spaces.

## Scott Foresman Reading Street Centers Survival Kit

Use the *The Houdini Box* materials from the Reading Street Centers Survival Kit to organize this week's centers.

# Writing/ Vocabulary

## Write a *Letter*

**MATERIALS**
Writing materials

`SINGLES`

Write a letter as if you were Houdini telling Victor why you gave him the box.

1. Start your letter with:
   Dear Victor,
   I decided to give you this box because _____.
2. Give reasons why Houdini might have given Victor his box. Use friendly language in your letter.
3. End with a closing and sign the letter.

**EARLY FINISHERS** Write a letter from Victor to Mrs. Houdini telling her how you feel about receiving Houdini's box.

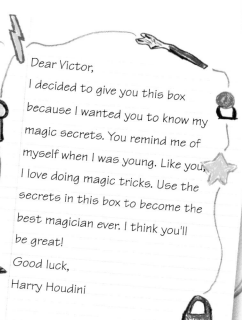

Dear Victor,

I decided to give you this box because I wanted you to know my magic secrets. You remind me of myself when I was young. Like you, I love doing magic tricks. Use the secrets in this box to become the best magician ever. I think you'll be great!

Good luck,

Harry Houdini

# Science

## Perform a *Trick*

**MATERIALS**
Resources of simple science tricks, materials for these tricks, writing materials

`SINGLES`
`PAIRS`

Perform a trick using science.

1. Review the science tricks in classroom resources. Choose a trick to perform.
2. Read the steps of the trick carefully. Gather any materials needed to perform the trick.
3. Follow the steps for the trick.
4. Summarize the trick you performed and the steps you followed. Add pictures to show what you did.

**EARLY FINISHERS** Explain the science that makes the trick work.

### Rising Marble Trick

1. I bent a straw into the shape of an L.
2. I carefully put a marble on top of the short end of the straw.
3. I held the straw near the short end and near my mouth.
4. First, I blew gently and the marble wobbled. Then I blew as hard as I could.

# Technology

## Research Illusions

**MATERIALS**
Internet access, writing materials

`SINGLES`

Search the Internet to find out more about optical illusions.

1. Using a student-friendly search engine and the keywords *optical illusions* find a Web site that shows an optical illusion. Follow classroom rules when searching the Internet.
2. Write an explanation describing the illusion you saw and how it tricks your eyes.

**EARLY FINISHERS** With your teacher's permission, print the optical illusion you found. Add your explanation to the illusion, and display it in the classroom.

### Search Engine

optical illusion

The optical illusion showed horizontal lines against columns of black squares. The lines looked slanted because the black squares weren't in straight columns.

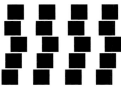

**ALL CENTERS**

- Build vocabulary by finding words related to the lesson concept.
- Listen for comparisons and contrasts.

### Concept Vocabulary

**invisible** not visible; not capable of being seen

**pretending** making believe

**judge** form an opinion or estimate about

### Monitor Progress

**Check Vocabulary**

| **If...** | **then...** review the |
|---|---|
| students are unable to place words on the web, | lesson concept. Place the words on the web and provide additional words for practice, such as *fooled, judge,* and *visible.* |

SUCCESS PREDICTOR

### DAY 1  Grouping Options

**Reading**

**Whole Group**
Introduce and discuss the Question of the Week. Then use pp. 392l–394b.

**Group Time**
**Differentiated Instruction**
**Read** this week's Leveled Readers. See pp. 392f–392g for the small group lesson plan.

**Whole Group**
Use p. 415a.

**Language Arts**
Use pp. 415e–415k.

# Build Concepts

## FLUENCY

**MODEL EMOTION** As you read "The Emperor's New Clothes," use emphasis, pauses, pitch, and tone of voice to convey characters' emotions. For example, read the emperor's statement about not being fit for his job in a worried tone and express the child's surprise at the emperor's lack of clothes.

## LISTENING COMPREHENSION

After reading "The Emperor's New Clothes," use the following questions to assess listening comprehension.

1. **How is the child different from the other characters in the story?** *(Possible response: The child says what he really sees. He isn't worried about looking foolish so he tells the truth.)* **Compare and Contrast**

2. **How is the emperor at the beginning of the story the same and different by the end of the story?** *(Same: Still a good ruler; Different: Now judges people by what they do, not by what they say; doesn't care as much about wearing nice clothes.)* **Compare and Contrast**

## BUILD CONCEPT VOCABULARY

Start a web to build concepts and vocabulary related to this week's lesson and the unit theme.

- Draw the Perception Concept Web.
- Read the sentence with the word *invisible* again. Ask students to pronounce *invisible* and discuss its meaning.
- Place *invisible* in an oval attached to *Sight*. Discuss how *invisible* relates to the concept. Read the sentences in which *judge* and *pretending* appear. Have students pronounce the words, place them on the Web, and explain connections.
- Brainstorm additional words and categories for the Web. Keep the Web on display and add words throughout the week.

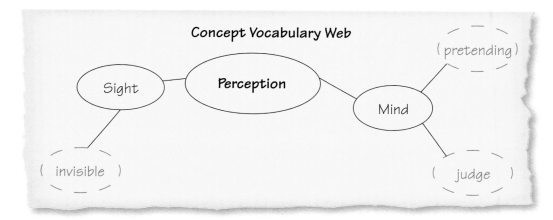

Concept Vocabulary Web

# The Emperor's New Clothes

## by Hans Christian Andersen

Once long ago in a land near the sea ruled an emperor. This emperor was a good ruler, but he was very proud and liked to look his best at all times. This emperor loved beautiful, new clothes.

One day the emperor learned that two weavers had arrived and were looking for work. They said that they could make the best and most beautiful cloth in all the world; however, the cloth was invisible to people who were unfit for their jobs and foolish people could not see the cloth.

The emperor knew he wanted it for two reasons. First, he deserved to have clothes made from the most beautiful cloth. Second, he would be able to tell whether the people who worked for him were fit for their jobs. So he hired the weavers to make the cloth and to sew him clothes made from it.

Every week the emperor sent people to check on the work of the weavers. Every week, the workers watched the weavers pretending to weave cloth. The people could not see the cloth. They thought they could not see the cloth because they were not fit for their jobs. They did not want the emperor to know this, so they told him that the cloth was the most beautiful they had ever seen.

Soon the weavers said the suit was ready. They carried a package to the emperor. They unwrapped the paper and pretended to hold up the suit.

The emperor couldn't see the suit. He thought to himself, "I must not be fit for my job." The emperor would not admit that he could not see the suit. He did not want people to think he was not fit to be emperor or that he was foolish. So he put on a shirt and some tights, and he let the weavers help him put on his new suit. He paid the weavers for their work and thanked them for making him the most beautiful suit he had ever seen.

All the people pretended to see the suit because they did not want to seem foolish. They applauded the emperor as he passed by.

Then a small child saw the emperor and shouted out, "Look, the emperor is only wearing his shirt and tights!" People knew then that they could not see the suit because there was no suit. The emperor and all the people had been fooled by the weavers.

The emperor learned a lesson that day. He learned to judge people by the good work they did, not by how they complimented him. He also learned that it is more important to be known as a good ruler than to be known as a well-dressed ruler. Since that day, the emperor ruled his empire well, and he wore clothes just like everyone else's.

BEFORE READING

SKILLS ⟷ STRATEGIES IN CONTEXT

# Compare/Contrast
# Predict

**Comprehension**

**Skill**
Compare and Contrast

**Strategy**
Predict

 **Compare and Contrast**

- When you compare and contrast, you tell how two or more things are alike and different.

- A chart can help you compare and contrast. You can compare and contrast two things you read about or something you read about with something you already know.

|  | Alike | Different |
|---|---|---|
| Two things in the text |  |  |
| One thing in the text with something I already know |  |  |

 **Strategy: Predict**

Active readers predict. They use what they know as well as what the author tells them to form ideas about what might happen next. When you read, you can also predict how something will be like or unlike something you know about from your own life.

 **Write to Read**

1. Read "How Did He Do That?" Make a chart like the one above to compare and contrast Harry Houdini with the magicians mentioned in the text. If there is a magician you already know about, compare and contrast Houdini with that person.

2. Use your chart to sum up what made Houdini like and unlike other magicians.

392

## OBJECTIVES

- Compare and contrast information.

- Use comparisons and contrasts to make predictions.

### Skills Trace
### Compare and Contrast

| Introduce/Teach | TE: 4.4 392–393, 416–417; 4.5 538–539 |
|---|---|
| Practice | TE: 399, 407, 423, 431, 545, 549<br>PB, 153, 157, 158, 163, 167, 168, 213, 217, 218 |
| Reteach/Review | TE: 4.2 197; 4.3 283; 4.4 415b, 439b, 499, DI·52, DI·53; 4.5 559b, DI·53<br>PB: 76, 106, 196 |
| Test | Selection Test: 61–64, 65–68, 85–88;<br>Benchmark Test: Unit 4 |

## INTRODUCE

Display two objects, such as chalk and a pen, and talk about how they are alike and different. Then write two ideas on the board, such as *freedom* and *good health*. Ask how these ideas are alike and different. *(Possible response: Both are something that most people want. Freedom has to do with what you can and can't do. Good health has to do with your body.)*

Have students read the information on p. 392. Explain the following:

- You can better understand what you read if you compare and contrast it to what you already know.

- Comparing and contrasting can sometimes help you make predictions about what will happen next.

Use Skill Transparency 16 to teach compare and contrast and predict.

**Strategic Intervention**

**Compare and Contrast** Point out Harry Houdini's traits listed in the last paragraph on p. 393 and then ask: *Who else might be described in one or more of these ways?* When students respond, explain that they are comparing and contrasting. Then ask: *In what ways is that person different from Houdini?* When students respond, explain that they are again comparing and contrasting.

**ELL**

**Access Content**

**Beginning/Intermediate** For a Picture It! lesson on compare and contrast, see the ELL Teaching Guide, pp. 106–107.

**Advanced** Have volunteers explain how the word *day* is used in the expressions "greatest magician of his day" (p. 393, paragraph 1) and "In Houdini's day" (p. 393, paragraph 2).

# How Did He Do That?

One day a boy named Erich read a book about a great magician, Robert Houdin. Erich dreamed of becoming a magician himself. He decided to change his name to Harry Houdini. Harry went on to become the greatest magician of his day.

In Houdini's day, magicians sawed ladies in half. They walked through walls. They made people float in the air. In other words, they were masters of illusion. They made things appear to be real that were not.

Yet Houdini did do something real, and he did it better than anyone else could. Houdini ESCAPED! He could get free of ropes and handcuffs and straitjackets and locked boxes—you name it!

Thousands came to see Houdini perform. The suspense would be almost too much to bear. Would Houdini get out alive? He always did. How?

Houdini's secret was this: He exercised to become very strong, he became an expert at locks, and he trained himself to keep calm in dangerous situations. How dangerous? Imagine being chained upside-down in a locked tank filled with water!

**1** **Strategy** Make a prediction. Will this article be about Erich's dream of becoming a magician? What are the clues?

**2** **Skill** This paragraph describes other magicians of Houdini's day. How are they similar to or different from magicians you know of?

**3** **Strategy** Do you predict that Houdini performed the same kind of magic as other magicians? Why or why not?

**4** **Skill** What was different about Houdini's act? Did he do anything like other magicians? Think of magicians you may know about, and complete your graphic organizer.

393

Available as **Skill Transparency** 16

---

**Compare and Contrast**

- To **compare and contrast** means to tell how two or more things are alike and different.
- Clue words such as *like* and *as* can show similarities. Clue words such as *however* and *instead* can show differences.

**Directions** Read the following passage. Then complete the diagram by comparing and contrasting magic tricks with special effects.

Have you seen strange creatures and amazing superheroes in movies? Today's special effects are like the stage magic performed for years and years, but they're even harder to figure out. For years, magicians have used quick hands and distraction to make something seem to appear or disappear. In a similar way, special effects make you think you're

seeing something that doesn't really exist. To create movie magic, special-effects artists use computers to create moving pictures that fool the eye. When you see them unfolding in front of you, both magic tricks and special effects seem real. They both work because of the hard work of people who love to entertain us.

| Special Effects and Magic Tricks | |
|---|---|
| **Alike** | **Different** |
| Both seem real. | 3. how they work to fool the eye: computers vs. quick hands and distraction |
| 1. Both fool the eye. | 4. new practice vs. old |
| 2. Both take hard work. | 5. One is harder to figure out. |

**Practice Book** p. 153

---

## TEACH

**1** **STRATEGY** Use the title, illustrations, and opening sentences to make a prediction.

> **Think Aloud** **MODEL** I think this article will be about Erich's dream of becoming a great magician. The title is "How Did He Do That?," which is what you ask when a magician does a trick. There is an illustration of a chain and a magician's hat, as well as a book about Houdini, who I know was a magician. The first two sentences say that Erich read about a great magician and dreamed of becoming one.

**2** **SKILL** Compare and contrast magicians of Houdini's day with other well-known magicians.

> **Think Aloud** **MODEL** The second paragraph tells how magicians in Houdini's day made things seem real that weren't. Today's magicians are also masters of illusions. I've seen them make people float in the air. I bet today's magicians do some new tricks that magicians long ago didn't do.

## PRACTICE AND ASSESS

**3** **STRATEGY** Possible response: No, Houdini probably performed a different kind of magic. The first sentence talks about what other magicians of Houdini's day did. These magicians may be compared and contrasted with Houdini.

**4** **SKILL** Houdini's act was different because he did something real. He escaped from tough spots. He was like other magicians because he surprised and amazed his audiences.

**WRITE** Have students complete steps 1 and 2 of the Write to Read activity. You might consider using this as a whole-class activity.

| **Monitor Progress** | |
|---|---|
| **Compare and Contrast** | |
| **If…** students are unable to complete **Write to Read** on p. 392, | **then…** use Practice Book p. 153 to provide additional practice. |

## ONLINE

Have students find out more about Harry Houdini by searching the Internet. Have them use a student-friendly search engine and the keywords *Harry Houdini*.

**ELL**

**Build Background** Use ELL Poster 16 to build background and vocabulary for the lesson concept of perception.

▲ **ELL Poster** 16

# Build Background

## ACTIVATE PRIOR KNOWLEDGE

**BEGIN A T-CHART** about magicians.

- Have students write a list of tricks magicians do. Record tricks students know on the left side of a T-chart. Add an idea of your own.
- Have students write any ideas they have about how magicians do their tricks. Record their ideas on the right side of the T-chart.
- Tell students that, as they read, they should look for information about what magicians do and note any new information to add to the chart.

| Magic Tricks | How They're Done |
|---|---|
| 1. Card tricks | 1. Special pack of cards |
| 2. Escape from handcuffs | 2. Hidden tool to pick the lock or a hidden key |
| 3. Draw rabbit from hat | 3. False bottom on hat |

▲ **Graphic Organizer** 25

**BACKGROUND BUILDING AUDIO** This week's audio explores illusions created by a magician. After students listen, discuss what they found out and what surprised them most about a magician's tricks.

**Background Building Audio**

# Introduce Vocabulary

## CONCEPT WEB

Create webs that students can use to make connections among their lesson vocabulary words.

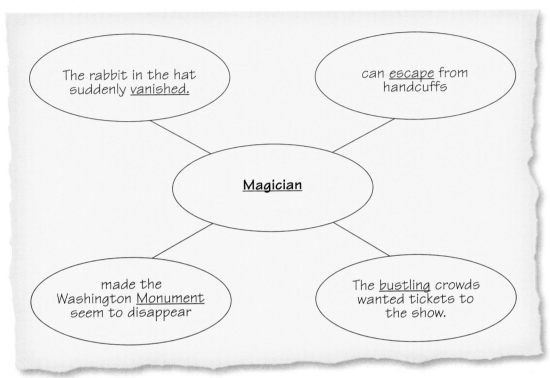

The rabbit in the hat suddenly *vanished.*

can *escape* from handcuffs

Magician

made the Washington *Monument* seem to disappear

The *bustling* crowds wanted tickets to the show.

▲ **Graphic Organizer** 15

Display the lesson vocabulary words, and discuss meanings. Write *magician* in the center of the web. Ask students to suggest possible connections to other lesson vocabulary words. Fill out the web together. Then have students complete other webs with the word *monument* or *bustling* in the center. ***Activate Prior Knowledge***

Point out the suffix *-ian* can mean "someone who is skilled in ___." Ask how knowing the meaning of the suffix helps readers figure out the meaning of *magician. (A magician is someone who is skilled in magic.)* **Suffixes**

Have students use these steps for reading multisyllabic words. (See the Multisyllabic Word Routine on p. DI·1.)

1. **Look for Meaningful Word Parts** (base words, endings, prefixes, suffixes, roots) Think about the meaning of each part. Use the parts to read the word. Model: I see *-ed* at the end of *crumbled. Crumble* means "break into very small pieces," and *-ed* means it happened in the past, so *crumbled* means "broke into very small pieces."

2. **Chunk Words with No Recognizable Parts** Say each chunk slowly. Then say the chunks fast to make a word. Model: *mon, u, ment—monument.*

By the end of the week students should know the lesson vocabulary words. Students can add other selection words to their webs or create new webs.

---

### Lesson Vocabulary

#### WORDS TO KNOW

**T appeared** was seen; came in sight

**T bustling** being noisily busy and in a hurry

**T crumbled** fell to pieces; decayed

**T escape** to get out and away; to get free

**T magician** person who entertains by art or skill of creating illusions, especially a sleight of hand

**T monument** something set up to honor a person or an event. A monument may be a building, pillar, arch, statue, tomb, or stone.

**T vanished** disappeared, especially suddenly

#### MORE WORDS TO KNOW

**engraved** cut deeply in; carved in; carved in an artistic way

**unexplainable** unaccountable; without apparent cause or reason

**T** = Tested Word

---

**Vocabulary**

**Directions** Choose the word from the box that best matches each definition. Write the word on the line.

| monument | 1. something set up to honor a person or an event |
| appeared | 2. was seen |
| vanished | 3. disappeared suddenly |
| bustling | 4. being noisily busy |
| crumbled | 5. fell to pieces |

**Check the Words You Know**
___appeared
___bustling
___crumbled
___escape
___magician
___monument
___vanished

**Directions** To solve this puzzle, write the word that matches each definition. The circled letters will spell a secret word.

6. c r u (m) b l e d
7. v (a) n i s h e d
8. b u s t l i n (g)
9. m a g (i) c i a n
10. e s (c) a p e

6. broke into bits
7. went suddenly from sight
8. loud and in a hurry
9. a performer skilled in illusions
10. to get away or get out

**Write a Note**
Think of something mysterious that happened to you. On a separate sheet of paper, write a note to a friend describing it. Be sure to tell why it puzzled you. Use as many vocabulary words as you can.
**Notes should include specific details that make the mystery vivid.**

**School + Home** Home Activity Your child identified and used vocabulary words from *The Houdini Box.* With your child, take turns telling a story incorporating the vocabulary words. Alternate adding sentences, each sentence containing at least one vocabulary word, until all vocabulary words are included.

▲ **Practice Book** p. 154

# Vocabulary Strategy

## Words to Know

| |
|---|
| magician |
| vanished |
| crumbled |
| bustling |
| escape |
| appeared |
| monument |

**Remember**

Try the strategy. Then, if you need more help, use your glossary or a dictionary.

# Vocabulary Strategy
## for Synonyms and Antonyms

**Context Clues** When you read, you may come across a word you don't know. Sometimes the author will use a synonym or an antonym as a clue to the word's meaning. Synonyms are words that mean almost the same thing. Antonyms are words with opposite meanings.

**1.** Reread the sentence with the unknown word. Look for a synonym or an antonym of the word. If you find one, try it in the sentence. Does the synonym make sense in the sentence? Does the antonym give the sentence an opposite meaning?

**2.** If there is not a synonym or an antonym in the same sentence as the unknown word, check the sentences around it. The author may use a synonym or an antonym there. If you find one, try it in the sentence.

**3.** If you cannot find a synonym or an antonym of the unknown word, think about the context—the meaning of all the sentences together. Decide on a meaning of the word that makes sense in the context.

As you read "A Little Magic," look for synonyms and antonyms to help you understand the meanings of vocabulary words.

394

---

## OBJECTIVE

◎ Use context clues to determine word meaning.

## INTRODUCE

Discuss the strategy for synonyms and antonyms as context clues by using the steps on p. 394.

## TEACH

- Have students think about vocabulary words in context as they read "A Little Magic."
- Model using context clues to determine the meaning of *vanished*.

**Think Aloud**

**MODEL** In paragraph 1, the writer compares a historian to a magician: Just as a magician *brings back* things that have *disappeared*, a historian *calls up* things that have *vanished*. The context shows me that *disappeared* and *vanished* have similar meanings. Both words are opposite to *brings back* and *calls up*. From these clues I can tell that things that have *vanished* are gone.

---

## DAY 2 Grouping Options

**Reading**

**Whole Group** Discuss the Question of the Day. Then use pp. 394–397.

**Group Time** Differentiated Instruction
**Read** *The Houdini Box.* See pp. 392f–392g for the small group lesson plan.

**Whole Group** Use p. 415a.

**Language Arts**
Use pp. 415e–415k.

---

## Strategic Intervention

◎ **Context Clues** Have students reread paragraph 2 of "A Little Magic." Ask them whether *bustling* means "lively" or "quiet" and to explain how the context helped them decide.

**Access Content** Use ELL Poster 16 to preteach vocabulary. Choose from the following to meet language proficiency levels.

**Beginning** Clues in the first paragraph of p. 395 tell that the antonym of *vanished* is *calls up.* Explain that "to call up" means "to bring back."

**Intermediate** After studying the vocabulary words, have students revisit the concept web they began on p. 394b and revise or expand it.

**Advanced** Teach the lesson on pp. 394–395. Have students create a main idea chart to present ways in which a historian is like a magician.

Resources from home-language words may include parents, bilingual staff members, bilingual dictionaries, or online translation sources.

# A Little Magic

A historian is someone who writes about the past. In some ways, he or she is like a **magician.** With a wave of the hand, a magician brings back things that have disappeared. In much the same way, the person who writes history calls up people, places, and events that **vanished** long ago.

A building has **crumbled.** All that is left are a few columns standing on a hill. The writer of history brings it to life. We can see it as a **bustling** center of government in Greece thousands of years ago. It is where men meet to discuss and vote on leaders and wars.

A magician may **escape** from a trunk that has been locked and chained shut. In just a few seconds, he or she is free of the box and has **appeared** on stage. How is this possible?

A historian may draw us to the **monument,** or tombstone, of a great leader. In just a few pages, he or she has brought that person to life with words. We understand what made that person unforgettable.

## Words to Write

Imagine that your school put on a talent show that featured a magic act. Describe the act. Use as many of the Words to Know as you can.

395

## PRACTICE AND ASSESS

- Have students determine the meanings of the remaining words and explain the context clues they used.
- Point out the words *or tombstone* between commas in the last paragraph of p. 395. Explain that when writers give a synonym as a context clue, they often set it off with commas right after the unfamiliar word.
- If students filled out a concept web (p. 394b), they may add connections to one or more vocabulary words. Students could also create a new web listing using the word *historian* in the center, and adding related details that include vocabulary words or other words from the selection.
- Have students complete Practice Book p. 155.

**WRITE** Writing should include several vocabulary words as well as other words that describe a performance of magic.

### Monitor Progress

#### Context Clues

| **If…** students need more practice with the lesson vocabulary, | **then…** use Tested Vocabulary Cards. |

**Vocabulary • Context Clues**

- When you see an unfamiliar word in your reading, use **context clues,** or words around the unfamiliar word. They can help you figure out the word's meaning.
- **Synonyms** are words that mean almost the same things.
- **Antonyms** are words with opposite meanings.

**Directions** Read the following passage about a magician. Then answer the questions below. Look for context clues as you read.

Hundreds of people streamed through the crowded, noisy streets of the bustling market. In the shadow of an old monument, a crowd gathered. All the people were orderly as a man waved his hands over a small boy's head. Then they burst into raucous cheering. The man, a street magician, pulled coins and scarves and white birds from behind the wide-eyed boy's ears. The clever performer took a bow and gave a sly smile to the child's mother. The crowd laughed as a fruit-seller's apples vanished from her basket. They roared when the apples appeared again, one by one, from a policeman's pockets. Even the usually dour blacksmith could not help feeling joyful at the magician's tricks.

Possible answers given.
1. What does *bustling* mean? What clues help you to determine the meaning?
   noisy and busy with activity; crowded and noisy

2. What antonym for *vanished* helps you determine its meaning? What does it mean?
   appeared; went away from view suddenly

3. What antonym for *raucous* helps you find its meaning? What does it mean?
   orderly; harsh, disorderly

4. What does *sly* mean? What words help you determine its meaning?
   sneaky or clever; clever

5. What type of context clue helps you to determine the meaning of *dour?* What does *dour* mean?
   the antonym *joyful;* gloomy or silent

**School Home** **Home Activity** Your child used synonyms and antonyms as clues to understanding new words in a passage. Choose a newspaper or magazine article with your child and take turns naming synonyms and antonyms for words you find in the article.

▲ **Practice Book** p. 155

# Prereading Strategies

## GENRE STUDY

### Historical Fiction

*The Houdini Box* is historical fiction. Explain that historical fiction is realistic fiction that takes place in the past. It mixes facts with imagination. Real people sometimes appear in historical fiction, but dialogue or events involving them are often fictional.

## PREVIEW AND PREDICT

Have students preview the story title and illustrations and discuss who the characters might be and what might happen in the story. Encourage students to use lesson vocabulary words as they talk about what they expect to read.

*Strategy Response Log*

**Predict** Have students write their predictions in their strategy response logs. Students will confirm their predictions in the Strategy Response Log activity on p. 403.

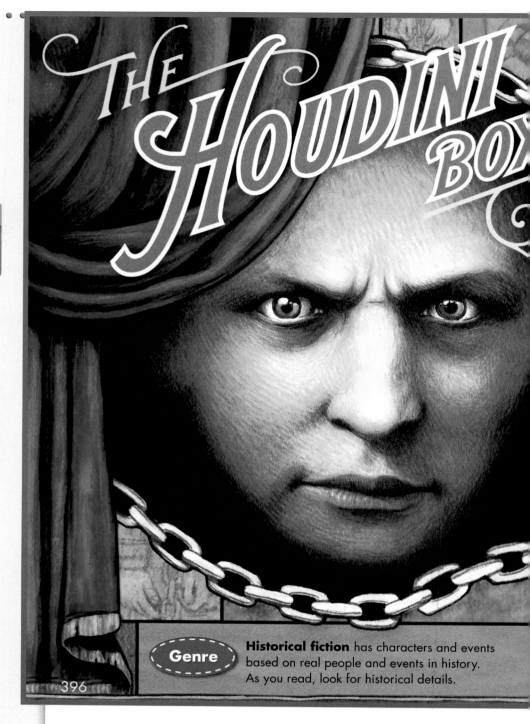

THE HOUDINI BOX

396

**Genre** **Historical fiction** has characters and events based on real people and events in history. As you read, look for historical details.

**ELL**

**Activate Prior Knowledge** Have students share any experiences they've had watching others perform magic tricks or doing magic tricks themselves. Discuss any famous magicians they know about, especially Harry Houdini.

Consider having students read the selection summary in English or in students' home languages. See the Multilingual Summaries in the ELL Teaching Guide, pp. 110–112.

*Will Victor learn the secrets of Harry Houdini's tricks?*

BRIAN SELZNICK

397

## SET PURPOSE

Read p. 399 aloud. Have students recall the discussion about magicians from p. 394a and tell what they want to find out as they read.

Remind students to compare and contrast characters in the story with people they know as they read.

## STRATEGY RECALL

Students have now used these before-reading strategies:

- preview the selection to be aware of its genre, features, and possible content;
- activate prior knowledge about that content and what to expect of that genre;
- make predictions;
- set a purpose for reading.

Remind students to be aware of and flexibly use the during-reading strategies they have learned:

- link prior knowledge to new information;
- summarize text they have read so far;
- ask clarifying questions;
- answer questions they or others pose;
- check their predictions and either refine them or make new predictions;
- recognize the text structure the author is using, and use that knowledge to make predictions and increase comprehension;
- visualize what the author is describing;
- monitor their comprehension and use fix-up strategies.

After reading, students will use these strategies:

- summarize or retell the text;
- answer questions they or others pose;
- reflect to make new information become part of their prior knowledge.

 **AudioText**

*The Houdini Box* **397**

# Guiding Comprehension

**1** 🔄 Compare and Contrast • Inferential

**How is Victor like and unlike Houdini?**

Like Houdini, Victor wants to be a magician. He tries to do an escape trick like Houdini does. Unlike Houdini, Victor isn't successful at escaping.

---

### Monitor Progress

### 🔄 Compare and Contrast

| **If...** students are unable to compare and contrast Victor and Houdini, | **then...** use the skill and strategy instruction on p. 399. |
|---|---|

---

**2** Characters • Inferential

**How would you describe Victor?**

Possible response: He is interested in magic tricks and determined to succeed, even though he keeps failing.

**3** Plot • Inferential

**Remind students that most stories have a problem. What is the problem in this story?**

Victor wants to be a magician like Houdini, but he is unable to perform any of the magic tricks that Houdini can do.

---

**OUDINI** was a magician. He could pull rabbits from hats, make elephants disappear, and do a thousand card tricks. Locks would fall open at his fingertips, and he could escape from ropes and chains and cabinets and coffins. Police from around the world couldn't keep him in their jails, and the oceans couldn't drown him. Bolt Houdini into a metal box and throw him in the water; he will escape. Lock him up in a jail, handcuffed and helpless, in any city in the world—Moscow, New York, Vienna, Paris, or Providence; Houdini will escape.

Everyone was wonderstruck by Houdini, but children were especially delighted. Children want to be able to escape from their rooms when they are sent there for being bad. They want to make their dinners disappear and their parents vanish. They want to pull candy from their pockets without putting any in, turn their sisters into puppies and their brothers into frogs (although some children want to turn their puppies and frogs into sisters and brothers). Children liked Houdini because he could do the unexplainable things that they wanted to do. Houdini was a magician. Magicians can do anything.

398

**Access Content** Explain that an iron milk can (p. 399, paragraph 2) is a large container used on farms to hold milk. It is barely big enough to hold one man, but Houdini was skilled working within small, cramped places. Refer to the picture of a milk can on p. 411.

Victor was ten. He wanted to be a magician too.

When Victor was eight, he read in the newspaper that Houdini had escaped from an iron milk can in under twenty seconds.

Victor found his grandmother's trunk and closed himself inside. The locks snapped shut behind him. He tried and tried, but he could not escape in under twenty seconds. In fact, he could not escape at all. **1**

So Victor cried and yelled until his mother came home and undid the locks. She was very upset that her son had shut himself up in Grandmother's trunk. Victor was very upset that he couldn't get out. **2**

When Victor was nine, he found out that Houdini could hold his breath for over five thousand seconds while escaping from a crate dropped into the ocean. If Houdini could hold his breath for five thousand seconds in his crate in the ocean, then Victor could certainly hold his breath for five thousand seconds in his tub in the bathroom. So during bath time, he put his head underwater and counted as fast as he could. But he never got to five thousand. His mother kept making him get out of the tub and breathe. **3**

399

## Breathing

TIME FOR Science

Houdini was able to hold his breath for a long time. Some of his tricks, such as escaping from a giant milk can full of water, relied on illusion and his ability to stay calm under water. Breathing is an automatic process people usually don't think about. When we inhale, our lungs take in oxygen. Tiny blood vessels in the lungs absorb oxygen into the bloodstream which then delivers it throughout the body. We release carbon dioxide when we exhale.

SKILLS ↔ STRATEGIES IN CONTEXT

# Compare and Contrast

## TEACH

- Remind students that when they compare and contrast they tell how two things are alike and different.
- Model comparing and contrasting Victor and Houdini.

**Think Aloud** **MODEL** I read that Houdini was a magician, and Victor wants to be a magician too. This is a way they are alike. Houdini could do amazing magic tricks, but Victor is unable to do any of them. That is a way they are different. Houdini was a great magician. Victor is just a kid whose mother has to free him from a locked trunk.

## PRACTICE AND ASSESS

Have students compare and contrast the reactions of Victor and his mother when Victor is locked in the trunk. To assess, make sure students can state one way their reactions are alike and different. *(Alike: They are both upset that Victor is locked in the trunk. Different: Victor is upset because he can't get out. His mother is upset because he locked himself in.)*

# Guiding Comprehension

**4** **Compare and Contrast • Critical**

*Text to Self* **Ask students to imagine seeing a famous person in a restaurant or airport. Would you react the same way or a different way as Victor does when he sees Houdini?**

Some students may say they would act like Victor because they would want to talk to someone famous. Others may say they would act differently and not ask so many questions or not bother the celebrity.

**5** **Characters • Inferential**

**What kind of person does Houdini seem to be? How do you know?**

Possible responses: He seems to be kind. He responds to Victor with respect. He smiles at him and offers to write him a letter.

**6** **Plot • Inferential**

**At this point in the story, what can you say about Victor's problem?**

Possible responses: It appears that his problem with escape tricks may be solved, since Houdini says he will write Victor a letter and implies that he will answer Victor's questions.

---

### Monitor Progress

**REVIEW** **Plot and Character**

| **If...** students have difficulty understanding the plot and characters, | **then...** use the skill and strategy instruction on p. 401. |
|---|---|

---

Victor got this idea when he read that Houdini could walk through brick walls. Victor was sure he could do that. First he tried walking slowly into a living-room wall and pushing his way through. Nothing happened. Next he tried backing up across the room and running through the wall. He almost broke the lamp, the table, a few pictures, and his nose—but he didn't make it to the other side. Later that evening, after many unsuccessful hours, Victor finally got through the wall. He used the door.

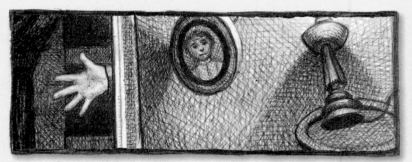

Victor's mother was going crazy unlocking her son from trunks, reminding him to breathe when he took a bath, and telling him not to walk into walls. She decided she would take him to visit Aunt Harriet. Maybe a weekend in the country would calm him down.

It was while they were traveling there that the most incredible thing happened.

Victor was looking around the huge, bustling train station when he saw, way across the crowds, Harry Houdini himself, buying tickets with his wife.

Victor broke free from his mother's hand and ran straight to Houdini. He was filled with questions, millions and billions of questions, but which should he ask first? He took a deep breath, and this is what he said:

400

**Understanding Idioms** Houdini's dialogue on p. 401 includes the idiom *tied you up.* Point out that to "tie someone up" means to delay someone or make someone late. Help students understand the author's use of humor with this idiom by explaining that Houdini was famous for getting tied up—literally—and then escaping.

"How can I escape from my grandmother's trunk in under twenty seconds? How do I hold my breath in the tub without running out of air? 4 Why can't I walk through a wall, like you can? How do you escape from jails and handcuffs and ropes and make elephants disappear? How—"

"Congratulations, my young man," interrupted the smiling magician. "No one has ever asked me so many questions in such a short amount of time. Are you a magician?"

"I want to be one," said Victor.

Houdini remained silent for several moments. After looking at Victor, and then at his wife, he finally said, "Then listen. Give me the tag from your suitcase."

"Why?"

"Your name and address are on it. When I write you a letter, I'll need to know where to send it, won't I?"

Victor immediately undid the little buckle and handed the tag to Houdini.

After reading it, the magician bent down so he was face to face with the boy. He whispered, "You want me to tell you things I can't talk about in the middle of a busy train station, son. And if I'm not mistaken, I see your mother heading this way. If it looks like you're going to get in trouble, you can blame everything on me." Then, grinning ever so slightly, he added, "Tell her Houdini tied you up for a moment. I'll write you a letter. Wait. Just you wait." 5

Houdini slipped the nametag into his pocket and disappeared into the crowd with his wife. 6

401

---

# Plot and Character REVIEW

## TEACH

- Remind students they can learn about characters by noticing what they say and do.

- Explain that the main character's problem often drives the plot. Main events usually focus on the character's efforts to solve the problem.

**Think Aloud** **MODEL** I know that Victor wants to be a magician, but he isn't very successful at escape tricks. Now Houdini says he will write Victor a letter. I think Houdini's promise is a big event in the story's plot because Victor may finally learn how to be a magician.

## PRACTICE AND ASSESS

- Have students read the first paragraph on p. 400 and tell what it shows about Victor's personality. Have them explain how the paragraph helps their understanding of the story's problem. *(It shows how determined Victor is to perform difficult tricks successfully.)*

- To assess, use Practice Book p. 156.

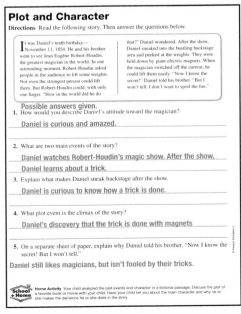

**Plot and Character**

**Directions** Read the following story. Then answer the questions below.

It was Daniel's tenth birthday—November 11, 1854. He and his brother went to see Jean Eugène Robert-Houdin, the greatest magician in the world. In one astounding moment, Robert-Houdin asked people in the audience to lift some weights. Not even the strongest person could lift them. But Robert-Houdin could, with only one finger. "How in the world did he do

that?" Daniel wondered. After the show, Daniel sneaked into the bustling backstage area and peeked at the weights. They were held down by giant electric magnets. When the magician switched off the current, he could lift them easily. "Now I know the secret!" Daniel told his brother. "But I won't tell. I don't want to spoil the fun."

Possible answers given.
1. How would you describe Daniel's attitude toward the magician?
   Daniel is curious and amazed.

2. What are two main events of the story?
   Daniel watches Robert-Houdin's magic show. After the show,
   Daniel learns about a trick.

3. Explain what makes Daniel sneak backstage after the show.
   Daniel is curious to know how a trick is done.

4. What plot event is the climax of the story?
   Daniel's discovery that the trick is done with magnets

5. On a separate sheet of paper, explain why Daniel told his brother, "Now I know the secret! But I won't tell."
   Daniel still likes magicians, but isn't fooled by their tricks.

**School + Home** **Home Activity** Your child analyzed the plot events and character in a fictional passage. Discuss the plot of a favorite book or movie with your child. Have your child tell you about the main character and why he or she makes the decisions he or she does in the story.

▲ **Practice Book** p. 156

# Guiding Comprehension

**7** ⊙ **Predict • Inferential**

**What do you predict will happen when Victor goes to Houdini's house?**

Possible response: Houdini will tell Victor the secrets to his magic tricks.

**8 Author's Craft • Critical**

*Question the Author* **The author writes that the door opens "with a heavy sigh." Why do you think the author uses these words to describe the door?**

Possible response: The words create a tone of mystery and sadness. The woman is sad, but we're not sure why. The author makes us wonder what has happened. (After students read p. 404, point out how this description of the door foreshadows Houdini's death.)

**9 Cause and Effect • Inferential**

**Why does Houdini's wife hand Victor some candy?**

It is Halloween night. She thinks he is out trick-or-treating.

---

The weekend in the country was not as restful as Victor's mother had hoped. Her son was so excited about having seen Houdini that he locked himself in Aunt Harriet's dresser and in the cabinet of her clock. He walked very fast into her walls and almost broke all of her old framed photographs. Aunt Harriet was not sad when they left.

Back at home, Victor locked himself in the closet under the staircase, the cupboard in the kitchen, and his grandmother's trunk. How he hoped Houdini would write him quickly!

Victor thought and dreamt about the magician's letter. When you are a boy expecting the secrets of the world to arrive in the mail, it is almost impossible to be patient. If only Victor were already a magician! A magician could make the letter appear out of thin air. But Victor was still just a boy, and patiently or not, he had to wait. And so he did, until one day when he was locked up tight inside an old suitcase, he finally heard his mother say, "Victor, there's a letter here for you."

She unlocked the suitcase and handed him the letter. The handwriting was thick and round and perfect:

**7** *A thousand secrets await you. Come to my house...*

Then Houdini gave the time and date for the meeting.

But it seemed so far away! Victor knew he couldn't wait so he went to the magician's house that evening.

His hands were shaking as he knocked on the door. With a

**8** heavy sigh it opened, and there before him was Harry Houdini's wife. Victor was suddenly too nervous to speak. He stood silently, staring at the sad woman in the light of the doorway.

402

---

**ⒺⓁⓁ**

**Extend Language** Reread the sentence "Aunt Harriet was not sad when they left." (p. 402, paragraph 1) Have students restate the sentence using synonyms for *not sad*. For example, "Aunt Harriet was *happy* when they left."

She handed him some candy and softly asked, "What are you supposed to be?"

Victor didn't understand what she meant until he saw a ghost, a cowboy, and two little goblins running down the street. In all of his excitement, he had forgotten that tonight was Halloween! **9**

403

## Develop Vocabulary

### PRACTICE LESSON VOCABULARY

Students orally respond *yes* or *no* to each question and provide a reason for each answer. Possible reasons are given.

**1. Is a *magician* likely to sing you a song?** *(No; a magician is someone who performs magic tricks.)*

**2. If prisoners *escape* from jail, would the police want to catch them?** *(Yes; the police would want to put them back in jail.)*

**3. Is a *bustling* park a quiet place?** *(No; it is full of busy, noisy people.)*

### BUILD CONCEPT VOCABULARY

Review previous concept words with students. Ask if students have come across any words today in their reading or elsewhere that they would like to add to the Perception Concept Web, such as *disappear* and *secrets*.

**STRATEGY SELF-CHECK**

# Predict

Ask students to predict what will happen next. Remind them that good predictions are based on what has already happened and what they know. A good prediction may not always come true. Authors often surprise readers.

To help students predict, have them compare and contrast Victor's experiences with their own lives.

## SELF-CHECK

Students can ask themselves questions to assess their ability to use the skill and strategy.

- Did I think about how the story was like or unlike my own life?
- How does comparing and contrasting help me predict?

| **Monitor Progress** | |
|---|---|
| **Compare and Contrast** | |
| **If...** students have difficulty comparing and making predictions, | **then...** revisit the skill lesson on pp. 392–393. Reteach as necessary. |

*Strategy Response Log*

**Confirm Predictions** Have students confirm if previous predictions came true. (See p. 396.) Have them revise their predictions or make new ones about the rest of the story.

# EXTEND SKILLS

## Note

Point out the note on p. 402, and explain that notes are informal writing that often lack many of the features of a formal letter, such as a heading, inside address, and closing. Have students discuss when a note or informal letter is appropriate.

*If you want to teach this story in two sessions, stop here.*

# Guiding Comprehension

*If you are teaching the story in two days, discuss predictions made so far and review the vocabulary.*

**10**  **Vocabulary • Context Clues**

**Have students use a synonym or antonym to determine the meaning of *vanished* on p. 404, paragraph 2. Have them find the context clues and give the meaning.**

Clues: *appeared*, an antonym for *vanished*, is in the next paragraph. Meaning: disappeared.

---

### Monitor Progress

#### Context Clues

| **If...** students have difficulty using context clues, | **then...** use the vocabulary strategy instruction on p. 405. |
|---|---|

---

**11** **Author's Purpose • Critical**

*Question the Author* **Why does the author include this explanation about who Victor's son was named after?**

Possible response: The author wants us to notice that Victor's son has Houdini's first name and maybe question the explanation.

---

## DAY 3 Grouping Options

**Reading**
**Whole Group** Discuss the Question of the Day.

**Group Time** Differentiated Instruction
Read *The Houdini Box.* See pp. 392f–392g for the small group lesson plan.

**Whole Group** Discuss the Reader Response questions on p. 410. Then use p. 415a.

**Language Arts**
Use pp. 415e–415k.

---

And now he knew what he was supposed to be. "I'm a magician!" he said, and handed Mrs. Houdini the letter.

Mrs. Houdini read it and began to cry. She asked him **10** to please wait inside, and vanished up the staircase into the magician's library, a dark place alive with books and dust and magical things. He held his breath, waiting for Houdini to greet him with outstretched arms and lead him back into that mysterious room.

When someone finally appeared in the hallway, though, it was only Mrs. Houdini again, alone. She came to Victor and handed him a small locked box. Then she opened the front door, and as she showed him out, he heard her whisper, "Houdini died today."

The magician's wife closed the door and left Victor alone with the box. "Bye," he said to the door, and went out, into the streets, toward home.

That night, while he was trying to open the lock on the box with pins and pens and all the small keys from the suitcases and clocks around the house, Victor found the owner's initials engraved on the bottom:

# E.W.

This wasn't Houdini's box at all! The owner was E. W. There could be no secrets in here.

404

---

**ELL**

**Understanding Idioms** Point out the expression *cross my heart and hope to die* (p. 405, paragraph 1) is something a child may say to convince someone that they are telling the truth. Students may be amused to know that children believe this oath can be cancelled or made untrue by crossing one's fingers behind the back as it is being said.

Imagine, as you read this, how it would feel if you had one dream, one hope, one mysterious wish, and then saw it disappear into thin air. That's how Victor felt, and that's why he did what he did next. He took the box that belonged to E. W. and buried it forever at the bottom of his closet. As he closed the door, he made this promise: "Houdini is gone. I will never think about him again or try to do any of his tricks. Cross my heart and hope to die."

So Victor grew up and got married. He and his wife had a child, and they named him Harry (in honor of Aunt Harriet, who had passed away one October long ago; he was not named in honor of a certain magician, because Victor said he never, not even once, thought about Houdini).

One chilly day, several years later, Victor and Harry were playing ball in a large field near a graveyard behind their house. Victor was pitching and Harry was swinging his bat, but he could never quite hit the ball. It was nearing dark, and there was time for just one more try. Victor gave Harry a few last-minute batting tips, and then, with all the gentle power that he had, threw the day's final pitch to his son.

405

## Illusions

Magicians' tricks are often based on illusions. The magician uses props, unseen hand movements, or distractions to make the audience believe they are seeing the impossible happen, such as a person floating in air or a person being sawed in half. An optical illusion happens when the eyes see something different from what it really is. For example, a dark house looks smaller than a white house of the same size because of the way our eyes and brain process color and surrounding backgrounds. A person wearing vertical stripes may look taller or thinner than when the same person wears horizontal stripes because our eyes don't move up and down as easily as they move from side to side.

## VOCABULARY STRATEGY
# Context Clues

## TEACH

- Remind students that synonyms are words that mean almost the same thing. Antonyms are words with opposite meanings.
- Read p. 404, paragraphs 2 and 3. Model using an antonym to determine the meaning of *vanished*.

**Think Aloud** **MODEL** I'll check the sentences around *vanished* for clues. The third paragraph says Mrs. Houdini "finally appeared." I think *vanished* and *appeared* are opposites. I can check by using *appeared* in the sentence to see if it means the opposite. "She asked him to please wait inside, and *appeared*." This is the opposite of what happened, so *vanished* means the opposite of *appeared*. It means *disappeared*.

## PRACTICE AND ASSESS

Have students reread p. 399, paragraphs 3 and 4, and use context clues to determine the meaning of *escape*. *(Clue:* he couldn't get out. *Meaning: get out, get free.)*

## EXTEND SKILLS

### Hyperbole

Explain that *hyperbole* is exaggeration. The author overstates something to make a point or be humorous. The author uses hyperbole when he writes that Victor took the box and "buried it forever" in his closet. Forever is a long time. The author uses exaggeration to show the humorous side of this serious young boy. Have students find other examples of hyperbole in the story (e.g., *millions and billions of questions*, p. 400) and use one or two in sentences of their own.

# Guiding Comprehension

 **Details • Literal**

**What is the monument that Victor and his son find in the graveyard?**

It is Houdini's gravestone.

**13 Draw Conclusions • Inferential**

**Why are the initials *E. W.* important to Victor?**

Those are the initials on the box that Mrs. Houdini gives him. Now Victor knows the box really did belong to Houdini.

**14**  **Predict • Critical**

**What do you think Victor will do next?**

Possible response: He will go home and look for the box since he now knows it really belonged to Houdini.

| Monitor Progress | |
|---|---|
| **Predict** | |
| **If...** students are unable to make a reasonable prediction, | **then...** use the skill and strategy instruction on p. 407. |

Harry closed his eyes, and at exactly the right moment, he swung his bat. He heard a loud crash, opened his eyes, and was amazed to see the ball fly through the sky and land somewhere in the middle of the graveyard.

406

**ELL**

**Fluency** Students may be confused by sentences that contain pronouns such as *it* that don't have antecedents, prior noun references. On p. 407, paragraph 2, the sentence that begins "It wasn't until he traced the first letters with his fingers..." may be clearer as two sentences: "He traced the first letters with his fingers. Then he understood what he was reading."

Victor congratulated his son, and together they climbed over the iron fence to look for the winning baseball. At last they found it, lying in the corner of a dark monument. Whether it had landed there by chance, or by some strange, powerful magic, no one will ever know. But the ball that Victor's son had hit so perfectly had come to rest right on the grave of Houdini! **12**

Victor read the monument. Two smaller words appeared directly below "Houdini," and Victor said them over and over again because they seemed so familiar. It wasn't until he traced the first letters with his fingers that he understood what he was reading. This was Houdini's real name.

Before he became Houdini, the magician had been a boy named Ehrich Weiss. E. W.! **13**

**14**

407

---

# Compare/Contrast Predict

## TEACH

Have students compare the monument in the graveyard with the box Victor received years ago. How are they alike? *(They both have the letters E and W on them.)* How are Victor's feelings different now than when he first received the box? *(Then: He felt disappointed and hopeless. Now: He is excited and hopeful.)* Then model how to make a prediction based on these comparisons and contrasts.

 **Think Aloud**

**MODEL** Now that I have compared the letters on the monument to the initials on the box, I can predict what Victor will do. He was sad and hopeless when he thought the box did not belong to Houdini. Now that he knows it did belong to Houdini, he is excited about what might be inside the box. I think Victor will try to find the box and open it to see what is inside. I wonder what he'll find.

## PRACTICE AND ASSESS

- Have students make predictions about what Victor might find in the box.

- To assess, make sure that predictions are reasonable based on story details about Houdini.

# Guiding Comprehension

**15** 🔄 **Confirm Predictions • Critical**

**Did your prediction match what happens in the story? If not, why do you think it didn't match?**

Possible response: I predicted Victor would open the box, and he did. But I thought we would find out what is in the box, and we don't know for sure. I guess the author wants to keep some things secret.

**16** **Plot • Inferential**

**Reread p. 399, paragraph 3, at the beginning of the story. Compare it to the last sentence of the story. Do you think this a satisfying ending to the story? Tell why or why not.**

Possible response: Yes, it is a satisfying ending because Victor has finally accomplished what he tried over and over again to do as a boy. He has solved the "problem" of the story.

**17** 🔄 **Compare and Contrast • Critical**

*Text to World* **What did you learn about magicians from this story that you didn't know before? What more would you like to learn?**

Possible response: I learned about some of the tricks that magicians do, like walking through walls and escaping from locked trunks. But the story doesn't tell how these tricks are done. I'd like to learn the secrets to magicians' tricks.

## Strategy Response Log

**Summarize** When students finish reading the selection, provide this prompt: Imagine you are asked to write a summary for the book cover of *The Houdini Box*. Describe the story's main characters and plot in four or five sentences.

Victor's head spun, and he laughed out loud. Carrying his son, he ran out of the graveyard, through the baseball field, and into his house.

He was out of breath and crazy with excitement, but he couldn't tell his wife or son what was going on. He waited until they were fast asleep, and then he snuck upstairs into the attic.

Victor found the forgotten box in a moonlit corner under a steady leak in the roof. He carefully picked it up and dried it off. His hand brushed across the lock, and it suddenly crumbled. The water had rusted through the tiny thing completely. How easy it would be to open the box now!

408

**ELL**

**Understanding Idioms** The idiomatic phrase *Victor's head spun* (p. 408, paragraph 1) can be restated as "Victor felt dizzy and confused." Encourage students to record English idioms and their meanings in language journals, word lists, or computer files of English vocabulary.

And that night, while his wife and son slept downstairs and the attic shadows vanished in the pale, blue fall of moonlight, Victor locked himself inside his *grandmother's* trunk and escaped in under twenty seconds.  **15** **16**

**17**

↻ STRATEGY SELF-CHECK

# Confirm Predictions

Students can confirm their predictions by comparing and contrasting what actually happened in the story to their predictions. Have them identify story clues they used to make predictions and tell whether the ending surprised them. Use Practice Book p. 157.

## SELF-CHECK

Students can ask themselves these questions to assess understanding of the story.

- Did I use clues in the story to make predictions?
- Did I compare and contrast my predictions to what actually happened in the story?

### Monitor Progress

↻ **Compare and Contrast**

| **If...** students are having difficulty using comparisons and contrasts to confirm their predictions, | **then...** use the Reteach lesson on p. 415b. |
| --- | --- |

---

**Compare and Contrast**

- To **compare and contrast** means to tell how two or more things are alike and different.
- Clue words such as *like* and *as* can show similarities. Clue words such as *however* and *instead* can show differences.

**Directions** Read the following passage. Then answer the questions below.

Is the hand quicker than the eye? Sometimes. A magician may use quick, careful hand movements to make you think you have seen or heard something you haven't. Magicians also use optical illusions, images that fool the eye. These illusions often use mirrors, painted backdrops, or special lighting.

Optical illusions make you think you see something on the stage that is not there. Magicians also use illusions of sound to confuse an audience. You may hear someone's voice sounding like it comes from a box that is actually empty. You may hear the sound of a coin hitting the floor even if no coin has been dropped. Illusions like these make magic seem real.

1. How are the hand movements and optical illusions used by magicians similar?
   Both are intended to fool the eye.

2. How are these two kinds of visual tricks used by magicians different?
   Hand movements use the body, but optical illusions can use mirrors.

3. How does the sound of a voice contrast with the use of hand movements?
   A voice is something you hear, not something you see.

4. Name one other comparison or contrast you could make using this passage.
   Mirrors and backdrops are different kinds of optical illusions.

5. On a separate sheet of paper, predict how a magician might be able to fool one of our other senses, such as the sense of touch or smell.
   Possible answer: They might make a cool thing look hot.

**Home Activity** Your child compared and contrasted ideas in a passage and also used these ideas to make a prediction. Have your child compare and contrast two performers or entertainers. Then ask your child to predict other ways two entertainers could be alike and different.

▲ **Practice Book** p. 157

---

## Develop Vocabulary

### PRACTICE LESSON VOCABULARY

Students respond orally to each question and provide a reason for their response. Possible reasons are given.

**1. Would you be more likely to see a *monument* in a park or at a carnival?** *(A park; a monument honors a person and is usually in a respectful, quiet place.)*

**2. Which is more likely to have *crumbled* when stepped on, a cookie or an apple?** *(A cookie; it is soft and easily falls into pieces.)*

**3. If you ate the last muffin on the plate, would you say the muffin had *appeared* or *vanished*?** *(Vanished; it was gone.)*

---

### BUILD CONCEPT VOCABULARY

Review previous concept words. Ask if students have come across any word that they would like to add to the Perception Concept Web, such as *magical* and *mysterious*.

*The Houdini Box* 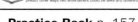 **409**

# Reader Response

## Open for Discussion Personal Response

**Think Aloud** **MODEL** I wonder how Houdini learned those amazing tricks. Did someone teach him, or did he figure out how to do those tricks by himself?

## Comprehension Check Critical Response

**1.** Possible response: It shows Victor's feelings of surprise and hope when he finds out Houdini will write him a letter. **Author's Purpose**

**2.** Before: He is excited and hopeful. After: He is disappointed and gives up his dreams. His feelings change because he thinks the box doesn't belong to Houdini. **Compare and Contrast**

**3.** Possible response: Yes, because now he can learn Houdini's secrets. **Predict**

**4.** Responses should show an understanding of words related to Houdini, such as *magician* and *vanished*. **Vocabulary**

**Think and Explain** For test practice, assign a 10–15 minute time limit. For assessment, see the Scoring Rubric at the right.

## Retell

Have students retell *The Houdini Box*.

| **Monitor Progress** |
| --- |
| **Check Retelling** Rubric [4] [3] [2] [1] |
| **If...** students have difficulty retelling the story, | **then...** use the Retelling Cards and the Scoring Rubric for Retelling on p. 411 to assist fluent retelling. |
| | SUCCESS PREDICTOR |

**Check Retelling** Have students use the story's illustrations to guide their retellings. Model retelling by talking about the first illustration. For more ideas on assessing students' retellings, see the ELL and Transition Handbook.

**410**

---

# Reader Response

**Open for Discussion** Houdini was a great magician who performed amazing tricks. What did you wonder about Houdini as you read *The Houdini Box*?

**1.** Brian Selznick, the author of *The Houdini Box*, drew his own pictures for the story to help communicate certain feelings. What do you think the picture of Victor on page 401 communicates to the reader? **Think Like an Author**

**2.** How does Victor feel before and after he visits Houdini's house? Why do you think his feelings change? **Compare and Contrast**

**3.** Do you think Victor's life will change now that he has opened Houdini's box? Why or why not? **Predict**

**4.** Write a poster advertising a new movie about Houdini. Use words from the Words to Know list and the story. **Vocabulary**

**Look Back and Write** Did Victor learn the secrets of Houdini's tricks? Why do you think as you do? Support your answer with details from the story.

Meet author **and illustrator Brian Selznick on page 775.**

410

---

## Scoring Rubric | Look Back and Write

**Top-Score Response** A top-score response uses details from the selection to support an opinion that Victor did or did not learn Houdini's secrets.

**Example of a Top-Score Response** Victor did find Houdini's secrets in the box marked E.W. (Houdini's real initials). At the beginning of the story, Victor keeps getting locked in his grandmother's trunk. But after opening the mystery box, he is able to escape from his grandmother's trunk in less than twenty seconds. This could only be magic.

**For additional rubrics, see p. WA10.**

# Write Now

## Story About a Discovery

**Prompt**

In *The Houdini Box*, a boy discovers the secrets of a great magician. Think about a discovery you have made or would like to make. Now write a story about your discovery.

**Student Model**

**Writer sets the scene of the story.**

Last weekend, my grandmother asked me to help her with some spring cleaning. We started with her closet. As I picked up a scarf that had fallen, something caught my eye. What was this shimmering fabric? I carefully pulled down the hanger. It was a gown fit for a movie star!

"What's this, Gran?" I asked.

"Oh, that old thing," she said. Then she smiled.

**Interrogative and exclamatory sentences catch the reader's interest.**

Next, I went to dust the top shelf. My hand hit something. It rolled. I fished for it and pulled out a microphone! Was there something about my granny that I didn't know?

**Writer adds variety by using dialogue.**

"What about this?" I asked.

"Oh, that's for when I do concerts," she stated.

"Concerts?" I cried.

"Oh, yes," she smiled. "You don't know everything about your granny."

**Use the model to help you write your own discovery story.**

411

# Write Now

**Look at the Prompt** Each sentence in the prompt has a purpose.

- Sentence 1 presents a topic.
- Sentence 2 suggests students think about the topic.
- Sentence 3 tells what to write—a story.

## Strategies to Develop Sentences

Have students

- write a strong opening sentence.
- practice rewriting declarative sentences as interrogative or exclamatory sentences.
- look for opportunities to tell the story using dialogue.

NO: My sister had a secret. She wouldn't tell me anything.

YES: "What's that?" I asked my sister. "Nothing," she said, with an odd grin.

For additional suggestions and rubric, see pp. 415g–415h.

## Writer's Checklist

☑ **Focus** Do sentences stick to a discovery?

☑ **Organization** Do transitons connect ideas?

☑ **Support** Do details tell about the discovery?

☑ **Conventions** Are singular and plural pronouns used correctly? Is dialogue punctuated correctly?

---

## Scoring Rubric | Narrative Retelling

| Rubric 4 3 2 1 | 4 | 3 | 2 | 1 |
|---|---|---|---|---|
| **Connections** | Makes connections and generalizes beyond the text | Makes connections to other events, stories, or experiences | Makes a limited connection to another event, story, or experience | Makes no connection to another event, story, or experience |
| **Author's Purpose** | Elaborates on author's purpose | Tells author's purpose with some clarity | Makes some connection to author's purpose | Makes no connection to author's purpose |
| **Characters** | Describes the main character(s) and any character development | Identifies the main character(s) and gives some information about them | Inaccurately identifies some characters or gives little information about them | Inaccurately identifies the characters or gives no information about them |
| **Setting** | Describes the time and location | Identifies the time and location | Omits details of time or location | Is unable to identify time or location |
| **Plot** | Describes the problem, goal, events, and ending using rich detail | Tells the problem, goal, events, and ending with some errors that do not affect meaning | Tells parts of the problem, goal, events, and ending with gaps that affect meaning | Retelling has no sense of story |

## Retelling Plan

☑ **This week assess Strategic Intervention students.**

☐ **Week 2** Assess Advanced students.

☐ **Week 3** Assess Strategic Intervention students.

☐ **Week 4** Assess On-Level students.

☐ **Week 5** Assess any students you have not yet checked during this unit.

Use the Retelling Chart on p. TR16 to record retelling.

**Selection Test** To assess with *The Houdini Box,* use Selection Tests, pp. 61–64.

**Fresh Reads for Differentiated Test Practice** For weekly leveled practice, use pp. 91–96.

SUCCESS PREDICTOR

# Science in Reading

## PREVIEW/USE TEXT FEATURES

Encourage students to look at text features as they preview. After they preview, ask:

- **What do the headings tell readers?** *(the names of the illusions the author tells about)*
- **How do the diagrams help readers?** *(They show how the illusions are done.)*

### Link to Science

Help students brainstorm keywords such as *magic tricks, card tricks,* and *optical illusions.*

---

## DAY 4 Grouping Options

**Reading**

**Whole Group** Discuss the Question of the Day.

**Group Time** Differentiated Instruction
**Read** "So You Want to Be an Illusionist." See pp. 392f–392g for the small group lesson plan.

**Whole Group** Use p. 415a.

**Language Arts**
Use pp. 415e–415k.

---

## Science in Reading

# So You Want to Be an Illusionist

### Expository Nonfiction

**Genre**

- Expository nonfiction gives factual information or explanations about a topic.
- Frequently, photos or artwork help explain the information.

**Text Features**

- The author uses headings to organize the text into meaningful parts.
- Captioned diagrams help you "see" and understand information in the text.

**Link to Science**

Magicians' tricks are not the only illusions. Optical illusions are tricks some images play on your eyes. Do research in the library or on the Internet to learn more about optical illusions. Share examples with the class.

by Tui T. Sutherland

**M**ost magicians start their careers with illusions. A classic example is pulling a rabbit out of a hat. Harry Houdini wanted to take illusions to a whole new level. And he did.

A lot of magicians make things "disappear"—a rabbit, a coin, even a person. But Harry wanted to perform the biggest disappearing act in the world. That's how he came up with his trick: The Vanishing Elephant.

Harry performed this illusion only in the biggest theaters where there was room on stage for an elephant.

**Predict** What will this article be about?

412

---

| Content-Area Vocabulary | Science |
|---|---|
| **illusion** | something that appears to be different from what it actually is |
| **illusionist** | a person who performs illusions, or magic tricks |

**Access Content** Spanish-speaking students may mistake the word *illusions* with the Spanish word *ilusión,* which means "hope" or "wish" (although many magicians do start their careers with *ilusión).* In this context, an *illusion* is something that appears to be different from what it actually is.

# Vanishing Elephant

He would start out by introducing his elephant, who was named Jenny. Then Harry's assistants would roll in a very large box on wheels, large enough to hold Jenny. Harry would walk around the box, opening the doors on all sides, so the audience could see that there were no hidden sections at the back. Harry would lead Jenny inside and close all the doors.

A few seconds later, Harry would sweep open the doors again. Jenny was gone. Once again, he'd walk around the box and open all the doors. She had vanished!

Audiences were amazed. How did he do it? The trick was in the construction of the box. But as far as the audience could tell, Harry had made the elephant disappear.

Harry leads Jenny the elephant to a large cabinet on the stage. Jenny enters the cabinet through the curtains and is out of the audience's view.

The cabinet is folded open to reveal that Jenny has vanished.

## The Trick

Through spring doors at the rear of the cabinet, Jenny enters a hidden cage on wheels, where Jenny is trained to find her favorite foods.

With the cabinet open, the audience does not see the assistants removing the secret cage.

413

# Dai Vernon

TIME FOR Science

Dai Vernon was born in Ottawa, Canada, in 1894. He grew up to become a skilled magician, serving as teacher and mentor to many young illusionists. He is best remembered as "the man who fooled Houdini." Harry Houdini once said he could figure out any trick if he saw it performed three times. Vernon thought he could outwit Houdini with his card trick called the Ambitious Card. In this trick, one particular card seems to move independently all over the deck. Vernon performed the trick for Houdini repeatedly, not just three times, but eight times! Still, Houdini was unable to figure out how the trick was done. From then on, whenever Vernon performed, he was billed as "the man who fooled Houdini."

## EXPOSITORY NONFICTION

Use the sidebar on p. 412 to guide discussion.

- Remind students expository nonfiction provides facts and explanations.
- Explain that authors of expository nonfiction often use headings, diagrams, and captions to assist readers.
- Discuss the organization of this article. (*opening paragraphs*, *heading*, *text*, *diagram*, *captions*)

Audio CD  AudioText

### Predict

Possible response: This article might tell me how to do some of the tricks Harry Houdini did.

## Strategies for Nonfiction

**USE DIAGRAMS** Explain that some authors include diagrams to help readers understand the text. Diagrams can be used to find answers to test questions. Provide the following strategy.

### Use the Strategy

1. Read the test question and identify the information you need to find.
2. Study the diagrams in the article to see if any of them relate to the information you need to answer the test question.
3. If you find a match, look over the diagram and study its captions to find an answer to the test question.

**GUIDED PRACTICE** Have students discuss how they would use the strategy to answer the following question.

How did Houdini know Jenny the elephant would go through the spring doors into the hidden cage?

**INDEPENDENT PRACTICE** After students answer the following test question, discuss the process they used to find information.

How did assistants help Houdini perform the Brick Wall trick? Use two details from the article to support your answer.

# Brick Wall Trick

Another one of his illusions used screens and an actual brick wall. Harry would have a team of bricklayers build a wall down the center of the stage, right in front of the audience. The stage floor was covered with a large sheet, pinned underneath the wall, and Harry would ask volunteers to come up and stand around the edges of the sheet. Then he would stand on one side of the wall, and his assistants would put a screen around him. They would put another screen on the other side of the wall. Then everyone would stand back and wait.

Harry, waving his hand over the top of the screen, would call, "You see, I am over here!" Then the hand would disappear, his assistants would take away the screen, and—no Harry. A moment later, Harry would walk out from behind the screen—on the other side of the wall.

How did he do it? The people onstage would see that he didn't walk around the back. The audience had seen the wall being built, so they knew there wasn't a secret door or way through it. And surely the sheet on the stage floor guaranteed that he hadn't somehow gone under the wall.

Well, not exactly. In actual fact, that's just what he did. There was a trapdoor in the stage just under the wall. Once everything was in place, one of his assistants would hide under the stage and open the trapdoor. There was just enough room for Harry to squeeze between the bottom of the wall and the sheet. Everyone standing on the sheet kept it from moving while Harry squeezed through. They thought they were preventing Houdini from tricking them. Instead, they were actually helping him.

414

**Independent Practice** Write the Independent Practice test question on the board. Define *assistants* as "people who help you." Have students look at the diagram on p. 415, and note the people helping Houdini in each illustration. Let pairs generate sentences telling how each person is providing assistance. (e.g., *He is building a wall.*)

**1** A sheet is laid on the stage floor and a brick wall is built on a wheeled frame.

**2** Audience volunteers inspect the wall as assistants place screens on both sides of the wall.

**3** Houdini moves behind the screen on one side of the wall and then emerges from the other side.

**4** The Trick

stage

trapdoor

An assistant releases a trapdoor below the stage, allowing the sheet to sag just enough for Houdini to crawl beneath the wall.

## Reading Across Texts

You read about magic tricks in both *The Houdini Box* and "So You Want to Be an Illusionist." Which trick impressed you the most?

**Writing Across Texts** Write about why you chose the trick you did.

🎯 **Compare & Contrast** | How useful is the art compared to the text?

415

---

## CONNECT TEXT TO TEXT

### Reading Across Texts

Review both selections and help students make a list of the illusions mentioned or discussed. Give groups an opportunity to talk about each illusion, sharing why they were or were not impressed as they read about it. Each student can then identify the one illusion that impresses him or her the most.

**Writing Across Texts** Have students write a paragraph that includes the name of the illusion and some details to describe it. Have them include an explanation of why they chose the illusion.

🎯 **Compare & Contrast**

Responses will vary depending on students' learning styles. Visual learners might say the art is more useful than the text since it explains and "demonstrates" the illusion.

## Fluency Assessment Plan

☑ **This week assess Advanced students.**

☐ **Week 2** Assess Strategic Intervention students.

☐ **Week 3** Assess On-Level students.

☐ **Week 4** Assess Strategic Intervention students.

☐ **Week 5** Assess any students you have not yet checked during this unit.

Set individual goals for students to enable them to reach the year-end goal.

• Current Goal: 110–120 WCPM

• Year-End Goal: 130 WCPM

For English Language learners, reading aloud song lyrics, favorite poems, and very short, engaging stories provides good opportunities to increase oral reading fluency.

To develop fluent readers, use Fluency Coach.

### DAY 5    Grouping Options

**Reading**
**Whole Group**
Revisit the Question of the Week.

**Group Time**
**Differentiated Instruction**
*Reread* this week's Leveled Readers. See pp. 392f–392g for the small group lesson plan.

**Whole Group**
Use p. 415b–415c.

**Language Arts**
Use pp. 415d–415l.

---

### EMOTION

# Fluency

#### DAY 1

**Model** Reread aloud "The Emperor's New Clothes" on p. 392m. Explain that you will read with emotion to help listeners understand characters and events better and to make the story more enjoyable. Model for students as you read.

#### DAY 2

**Echo Reading** Read aloud p. 402, paragraphs 2–3, expressing Victor's excitement and impatience. Practice as a class by doing three echo readings.

#### DAY 3

**Model** Read aloud p. 405, paragraph 1. Have students notice how your voice drops with disappointment at the end of the first sentence and the strong emotion in your voice as you read Victor's vow. Practice as a class by doing three echo readings of this paragraph.

#### DAY 4

**Partner Reading** Have partners practice reading aloud p. 405, paragraph 1, three times. Students should read with emotion and offer each other feedback.

### Monitor Progress    Check Fluency WCPM

As students reread, monitor their progress toward their individual fluency goals. Current Goal: 110–120 words correct per minute. End-of-Year Goal: 130 words correct per minute.

**If...** students cannot read fluently at a rate of 110–120 words correct per minute,
**then...** make sure students practice with text at their independent level. Provide additional fluency practice, pairing nonfluent readers with fluent readers.

**If...** students already read at 130 words correct per minute,
**then...** they do not need to reread three to four times.

**SUCCESS PREDICTOR**

#### DAY 5

**Assessment**
**Individual Reading Rate** Use the Fluency Assessment Plan and do a one-minute timed reading of either selection from this week to assess students in Week 1. Pay special attention to this week's skill, emotion. Provide corrective feedback for each student.

# RETEACH

# ⟳ Compare and Contrast

## TEACH

Review the definition of *compare and contrast* on p. 392. Students can complete Practice Book p. 158 on their own or as a class. As they read the Practice Book passage, have them think about how Kim's performance is the same and different in the two shows. They could also circle sentences that tell how the second show was different to help them complete the chart.

## ASSESS

Have students use pp. 400 and 402 to compare and contrast Victor's behavior before and after he meets Houdini. *(Victor is still locking himself in things and walking into walls, but he is doing everything a lot faster because he is excited about Houdini writing to him.)*

For additional instruction on compare and contrast, see DI·52.

# EXTEND SKILLS

# Steps in a Process

## TEACH

Steps in a process are the steps involved in making or doing something. When following the steps to make a craft project, cook a dish, or do a magic trick, it helps to use these strategies:

- Read all the steps to make sure you understand the process.
- Think about the final result.
- Look at any illustrations and match them to the written steps.

Ask students to read the steps for making an elephant disappear on p. 413. Then have them explain the steps in their own words.

## ASSESS

Have students write and illustrate the steps for doing a magic trick or making a favorite recipe. To assess, check that students have included all the steps, listed them in the right order, and illustrated them in a helpful way.

---

## OBJECTIVES

- ⟳ Compare and contrast events and characters in a story.
- ● Understand steps in a process.

### Skills Trace
#### ⟳ Compare and Contrast

| | |
|---|---|
| Introduce/Teach | TE: 4.4 392–393, 416–417; 4.5 538–539 |
| Practice | TE: 399, 407, 423, 431, 545, 549 PB: 153, 157, 158, 163, 167, 168, 213, 217, 218 |
| Reteach/Review | **TE: 4.2 197; 4.3 283; 4.4 415b, 439b, 499, DI•52, DI•53; 4.5 559b, DI•53 PB: 76, 106, 196** |
| Test | Selection Test: 61–64, 65–68, 85–88; Benchmark Test: Unit 4 |

**Access Content** Reteach the skill by reviewing the Picture It! lesson on compare and contrast in the ELL Teaching Guide, pp. 106–107.

---

**Compare and Contrast**

- To **compare and contrast** means to tell how two or more things are alike and different.
- Clue words such as *like* and *as* can show similarities. Clue words such as *however* and *instead* can show differences.

**Directions** Read the following passage. Then complete the diagram by comparing and contrasting.

Yesterday, when Kim performed her magic act for her family, she was calm and skillful. But today Kim was nervous. She was doing the same magic tricks for all her friends. Everything started well, as her vanishing coin trick worked perfectly. But with her second trick, things started to go wrong. Kim was trying to guess the card a friend had picked. Kim lost count of the cards in her hand and didn't get it right. Then her deck of cards showered to the floor. Maybe, Kim thought, she should stick to family shows!

**First Show and Second Show**

| Alike | Different |
|---|---|
| 1. Kim performed the same tricks each time. | 3. Kim felt calm the first time, but nervous the second time. |
| 2. The coin trick worked in both shows. | 4. During the second show, the second trick failed. |
| | 5. The deck of cards fell on the floor in the second show. |

**Home Activity** Your child compared and contrasted events described in a written passage. Work with your child to compare and contrast two dinners he or she had this week. Then see if your child can predict how the next dinner will be alike and different from those.

▲ **Practice Book** p. 158

# Vocabulary and Word Study

## VOCABULARY STRATEGY

### Context Clues

**SYNONYMS AND ANTONYMS** Remind students that a synonym or antonym may be a context clue they can use to figure out a word's meaning. Point out that when a sentence includes an antonym, it may also contain a word that shows contrast, such as *not* or *but*. Display or read aloud sentences in which an antonym or synonym is a clue to an unfamiliar word, such as those listed below. Have students tell what the unfamiliar word means and how they know.

### Sentences with Synonyms or Antonyms

*Victor was diligent and not at all lazy about learning how to escape.*

*Victor breathed in, but he had to exhale long before he counted to five thousand.*

*Houdini, the world's most famous magician, could not remain anonymous in the crowd.*

*The congested train station was as crowded as he'd ever seen it.*

## Speaking Words

Point out the author of *The Houdini Box* uses verbs such as *said, added, asked,* and *interrupted* to indicate how characters say dialogue in the story. Challenge students to brainstorm as many words as they can to show how characters speak. Then have pairs write lines of dialogue using some of the listed words and characters from the story. Partners can read aloud their dialogue with expression for the class.

| | | | |
|---|---|---|---|
| yelled | whispered | mumbled | gasped |
| stated | repeated | replied | hissed |

## BUILD CONCEPT VOCABULARY
### Perception

**LOOKING BACK** Remind students of the question of the week: *Can you always believe what you see?* Discuss how this week's Concept Web of vocabulary words relates to the theme of perception. Ask students if they have any words or categories to add. Discuss whether words and categories are appropriately related to the concept.

**MOVING FORWARD** Preview the title of the next selection, *Encantado: Pink Dolphin of the Amazon.* Ask students which Concept Web words might apply to the new selection based on the title alone.

Put a star next to these words on the Web.

Display the Concept Web and revisit the vocabulary words as you read the next selection to check predictions.

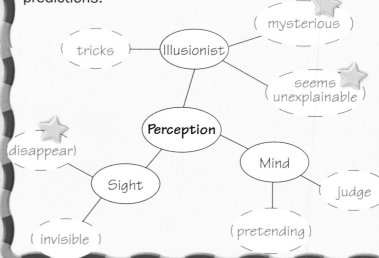

### Monitor Progress
#### Check Vocabulary

| If... students suggest words or categories that are not related to the concept, | then... review the words and categories on the Concept Web and discuss how they relate to the lesson concept. |
|---|---|

SUCCESS PREDICTOR

# Speaking and Viewing

## SPEAKING

## Interview

**SET-UP** Have pairs find out about a famous magician and then role-play an interview with that person. One student will be the interviewer and the other will play the role of the magician.

**TOPICS** Have students conduct a quick Internet search using a student-friendly search engine to find the names of famous magicians or choose one of the following: David Copperfield, Harry Blackstone, Harry Houdini, William Ellsworth Robinson.

**ORGANIZATION** Have each pair find biographical information about their magician and organize it into categories, such as the magician's early life, how the person became a magician, and the magician's most famous tricks. They can brainstorm possible questions and answers but shouldn't write a script. Point out that open-ended questions elicit more details than *yes-no* questions.

### Rehearsal Tips

- Know the topics to discuss so you can focus on listening to responses instead of the next question.
- If someone doesn't answer a question fully, ask a follow-up question.
- Look at the person answering the question, not at your notes.

## VIEWING

## Analyze Media

Discuss television shows or movies students have seen in which a person or situation is not as it originally appeared to be. For example, *The Wizard of Oz* is a movie in which the main character's adventure is actually a dream. Group students who have seen the same show together to discuss the following questions.

1. **What surprised you in this show?**

2. **How were you fooled into thinking things were different than they really were, and how did you recognize the mistaken conclusions you had drawn?**

3. **How did you feel when you realized the situation was not as you thought?**

Responses will vary but students should be able to support their ideas with specific examples from the TV show or movie they watched.

## ELL

**Support Vocabulary** Use the following to review and extend vocabulary and to explore lesson concepts further:
- ELL Poster 16, Days 3–5 instruction
- Vocabulary Activities and Word Cards in ELL Teaching Guide, pp. 108–109

**Assessment** For information on assessing students' speaking, listening, and viewing, see the ELL and Transition Handbook.

# Grammar  Singular and Plural Pronouns

## OBJECTIVES

- Define and identify singular and plural pronouns.
- Use singular and plural pronouns correctly in writing.
- Become familiar with pronoun assessment on high-stakes tests.

### Monitor Progress

**Grammar**

| If... students have difficulty understanding singular and plural pronouns, | then... provide additional instruction and practice in The Grammar and Writing Book pp. 140–143. |
|---|---|

## DAILY FIX-IT

This week use Daily Fix-It Transparency 16.

**Spiral REVIEW**

## ELL

**Grammar Support** See the Grammar Transition lessons in the ELL and Transition Handbook.

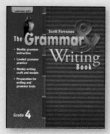

▲ **The Grammar and Writing Book** For more instruction and practice, use pp. 140–143.

---

## DAY 1   Teach and Model

### DAILY FIX-IT

1. Whens the magic show! *(When's; show?)*

2. Bill think its' at seven o'clock. *(thinks it's)*

### READING-GRAMMAR CONNECTION

Write the following sentences on the board:

> *Victor and his mother met Harry Houdini.*

> *They met him.*

Explain that the underlined words in sentence 2 are **pronouns.** They replace the underlined noun phrase and proper noun in sentence 1. Point out that *him* is a **singular pronoun** and *they* is a **plural pronoun.**

Display Grammar Transparency 16. Read aloud the definitions and sample sentences. Work through the items.

---

### Singular and Plural Pronouns

**Pronouns** are words that take the place of nouns. Pronouns that take the place of singular nouns are **singular pronouns.** *I, me, he, she, him, her,* and *it* are singular pronouns. Pronouns that take the place of plural nouns are **plural pronouns.** *We, us, they,* and *them* are plural pronouns.

The man met the magicians at the train station.

He met them at the train station.

Always capitalize the singular pronoun *I*. When you talk about yourself and another person, name yourself last. The pronoun *you* can be singular or plural.

**Directions** Write the pronoun in each sentence.

1. I want to learn more about Harry Houdini.
2. He was a famous magician.
3. Tell us about Houdini's tricks.
4. Houdini got into a crate and had it lowered into the ocean.
5. People were amazed when they saw Houdini escape.
6. You would enjoy reading about Houdini.

I
He
us
it
they
You

**Directions** Choose a pronoun in ( ) to replace each underlined noun or noun phrase. Write the pronoun on the line.

7. Mother did not know what to do with Victor. (She, We)
8. Victor was always getting into trouble. (They, He)
9. She even had to remind Victor to breathe in the bath. (him, us)
10. Mother and Victor went to see Victor's Aunt Harriet. (They, He)
11. Victor made Aunt Harriet very upset. (her, you)
12. Later, Victor visited the Houdinis at home. (they, them)

She
He
him
They
her
them

Unit 4 The Houdini Box                    Grammar **16**

▲ **Grammar Transparency** 16

---

## DAY 2   Develop the Concept

### DAILY FIX-IT

3. He pulled a rabbit out of a hat and then putted them back again. *(put it)*

4. Harry Houdini performed on stage, she also performed in movies. *(stage. He)*

### GUIDED PRACTICE

Review the concept of singular and plural pronouns.

- **Pronouns** are words that take the place of nouns.
- Pronouns that take the place of singular nouns are called **singular pronouns.** *I, me, he, she, him, her,* and *it* are singular pronouns.
- Pronouns that take the place of plural nouns are **plural pronouns.** *We, us, they,* and *them* are plural pronouns. *You* can be used as both a singular and a plural pronoun.

**HOMEWORK** Grammar and Writing Practice Book p. 61.

---

### Singular and Plural Pronouns

**Pronouns** are words that take the place of nouns. Pronouns that take the place of singular nouns are **singular pronouns.** *I, me, he, she, him, her,* and *it* are singular pronouns. Pronouns that take the place of plural nouns are **plural pronouns.** *We, us, they,* and *them* are plural pronouns.

Sam and I enjoy reading about Harry Houdini.

We enjoy reading about him.

Always capitalize the singular pronoun *I*. When you talk about yourself and another person, name yourself last. The pronoun *you* can be singular or plural.

**Directions** Circle the pronoun in each sentence.

1. I am reading about Harry Houdini in school.
2. He was born in Hungary but raised in the United States.
3. Harry married Wilhelmina Rahner, and together they performed magic tricks.
4. Houdini's escapes still amaze us today.
5. If you want to learn more, read books about Houdini.

**Directions** Choose a pronoun in ( ) to replace each underlined noun or noun phrase. Write the pronoun on the line.

6. The class enjoyed reading about Houdini's tricks. (She, We)

_____We_____

7. Houdini often had the police lock Houdini in a prison cell. (it, him)

_____him_____

8. He always escaped from the cell. (it, us)

_____it_____

**Home Activity** Your child learned about singular and plural pronouns. Have your child tell you what he or she did today. Ask your child to identify any singular or plural pronouns he or she uses.

▲ **Grammar and Writing Practice Book** p. 61

---

# DAY 3 — Apply to Writing

## DAILY FIX-IT

5. People were amazed by houdini's incredible escape's. *(Houdini's; escapes)*

6. A century ago he will perform magic on stage. With his wife. *(he performed; stage with)*

## USE PRONOUNS IN WRITING

Point out that using pronouns can make sentences smoother and less wordy.

*Wordy:* Dave will show you Dave's card trick when Dave has learned the card trick.

*Not Wordy:* Dave will show you his card trick when he has learned it.

• Have students review something they have written to see if they can tighten it by replacing any nouns or noun phrases with pronouns.

**HOMEWORK** Grammar and Writing Practice Book p. 62.

---

### Singular and Plural Pronouns

**Directions** On the lines below, write pronouns to replace the underlined nouns or noun phrases in the sentences.

**1.** Magicians rarely tell people how magicians do their tricks. **2.** For example, Harry Houdini did not reveal to the public how Harry Houdini got out of handcuffs or locked chests. **3.** He left spectators puzzled because he wanted spectators to return to see another show. **4.** If he told how a trick was done, no one would want to see the trick again. **5.** I wish he could tell the person writing this a few of his secrets!

1. ___they___
2. ___he___
3. ___them___
4. ___it___
5. ___me___

**Directions** Write a paragraph about a magic trick you have seen or a trick you know how to do. Underline any singular or plural pronouns that you use.

**Possible answer:**

I once saw a magician pull a rabbit out of a hat. First, he showed us that the hat was empty. Then he covered it with a cloth. Next, he said, "Make me a rabbit," and he pulled a rabbit out by the ears.

**Home Activity** Your child learned how to use singular and plural pronouns in writing. Have your child write an e-mail to a friend or relative. Ask your child to print it and show you the singular and plural pronouns.

▲ **Grammar and Writing Practice Book** p. 62

---

# DAY 4 — Test Preparation

## DAILY FIX-IT

7. Pick a card and tell me what they is? *(it is.)*

8. I thinks you chosed the ace of spades. *(think you chose)*

## STANDARDIZED TEST PREP

### Test Tip

If you are writing about yourself and another person and are uncertain about whether to use the pronoun *I* or *me*, say the sentence without the other person's name. The correct form of the pronoun generally becomes clear.

*Example:* He gave the rabbit to John and ___.

He gave the rabbit to *I*. (That doesn't sound right.)

He gave the rabbit to *me*. (That sounds right.)

He gave the rabbit to *John and me*.

**HOMEWORK** Grammar and Writing Practice Book p. 63.

---

### Singular and Plural Pronouns

**Directions** Write the letter of the word that completes each sentence in the paragraph.

1. Next month ___ am going to perform magic tricks for the class. 2. I will ask a student to pick a card, and I will guess what ___ is. 3. Then I will pull white mice out of my pockets and let ___ loose in the classroom. 4. I think that Ms. Lopez might not want ___ to do this trick. 5. ___ is afraid of mice! 6. I will also ask students if ___ want me to cut them in half. 7. Maybe ___ can get Ms. Lopez to volunteer! 8. Reader, do ___ think she will?

1. A me
   B us
   **C I**
   D we

2. A they
   **B it**
   C him
   D I

3. **A it**
   B they
   C he
   **D them**

4. A she
   B we
   C I
   **D me**

5. **A She**
   B Her
   C They
   D I

6. A them
   **B they**
   C us
   D she

7. **A we**
   B us
   C them
   D me

8. A she
   B it
   **C you**
   D them

**Home Activity** Your child prepared for taking tests on singular and plural pronouns. Have your child write a list of the pronouns he or she has learned. Ask your child to tell you a story, using as many of the pronouns as possible.

▲ **Grammar and Writing Practice Book** p. 63

---

# DAY 5 — Cumulative Review

## DAILY FIX-IT

9. I seen a circus performer hang from her teeths. *(saw [or have seen]; teeth))*

10. Has you ever tryed a magic trick? *(Have; tried)*

## ADDITIONAL PRACTICE

Assign pp. 140–143 in The Grammar and Writing Book.

**EXTRA PRACTICE** Grammar and Writing Practice Book p. 137.

**TEST PREPARATION** Grammar and Writing Practice Book pp. 155–156.

## ASSESSMENT

**CUMULATIVE REVIEW** Grammar and Writing Practice Book p. 64.

---

### Singular and Plural Pronouns

**Directions** Underline the pronoun in the sentence if it is a singular pronoun. Circle the pronoun if it is a plural pronoun.

1. Wilhelmina Rahner was 18 when she married Harry Houdini.
2. Together they traveled around the country performing magic.
3. A wealthy man named Martin Beck saw them perform.
4. Beck hired the Houdinis to perform for him.
5. The Houdini's act was amazing, and crowds flocked to see it.

**Directions** Replace each underlined noun or noun phrase with a pronoun from the box. Write the new sentence and underline the pronoun you chose.

| her | you | we | them | us |

6. Sarah and I are pretending that Sarah and I are Houdini and his wife.
   Sarah and I are pretending that **we** are Houdini and his wife.

7. We are learning tricks and will perform the tricks for the class.
   We are learning tricks and will perform **them** for the class.

8. We are hoping our audience will find Sarah and me amazing.
   We are hoping our audience will find **us** amazing.

**Home Activity** Your child reviewed singular and plural pronouns. Read an article in a magazine or newspaper with your child. Ask him or her to identify examples of singular and plural pronouns in the article.

▲ **Grammar and Writing Practice Book** p. 64

# Writing Workshop
## Story About a Discovery

## OBJECTIVES

- Identify qualities of a story about a discovery.
- Write a story about a discovery with a good beginning.
- Focus on sentences.
- Use a rubric.

**Genre** Story About a Discovery
**Writer's Craft** Good Beginnings
**Writing Trait** Sentences

**Sentences** Read imperative, exclamatory, and interrogative sentences aloud to English learners, using tone to show how these sentences add excitement to writing. Let your voice also reflect the punctuation at the end of these sentences.

## Writing Traits

**FOCUS/IDEAS** Strong supporting details make the topic clear and interesting.

**ORGANIZATION/PARAGRAPHS** The story has a beginning, middle, and end. It leads up to the author's discovery that his brother was not telling the truth.

**VOICE** The writer's voice is direct and friendly. He lets the reader know how he felt (*scared and curious*).

**WORD CHOICE** The writer uses exact nouns (*flashlight, baseball bat*), strong verbs (*clumped*), and vivid images.

**SENTENCES** Sentences are varied in kind and length. The writer uses dialogue, questions, and exclamations.

**CONVENTIONS** There is excellent control and accuracy.

---

## DAY 1 — Model the Trait

### READING-WRITING CONNECTION

- The variety of sentences in *The Houdini Box* hooks the reader and keeps the story interesting.
- Students will write a **story about a discovery** using a variety of sentence types to create excitement and a good beginning.

**MODEL SENTENCES** Discuss Writing Transparency 16A. Then discuss the model and the writing trait of sentences.

**Think Aloud** I see that throughout the model the writer uses different types of sentences. I see an exclamation: "Don't go down there alone!" and a question: "What if they clumped upstairs?" These different types of sentences make the writing interesting. The writer also starts with a good beginning that makes me want to keep reading.

### Story About a Discovery

A good story keeps the reader interested from beginning to end. The opening sentence should catch the reader's interest. In a **story about a discovery**, like the one below, it is a good idea not to reveal the actual discovery until the very end.

#### The Bear Facts

A good beginning catches the reader's interest.
> When I was four years old, I went bear hunting with my dad in the basement. My brother had told me about the bears. "Don't go down there alone!" he warned me.

The writer explains his feelings.
> I was very scared and very curious. Why hadn't I ever heard the bears clumping around? What if they clumped upstairs?

> It was my dad who suggested the hunt. I took a flashlight, and my dad carried a baseball bat. We hunted and hunted, but there were no bears.

Dialogue makes the story realistic.
> "I guess they've moved out," my dad said. "I'll lock up just in case."

A discovery rounds off the story.
> That's when I discovered that my brother didn't always tell the truth.

Unit 4 The Houdini Box — Writing Model **16A**

▲ **Writing Transparency** 16A

---

## DAY 2 — Improve Writing

### WRITER'S CRAFT
### Good Beginnings

Display Writing Transparency 16B. Read the directions and work together to discuss good beginnings.

**Think Aloud** **CREATE A GOOD BEGINNING** Tomorrow we will be writing a story about a discovery. Before I write, I will ask myself, *What is an interesting or exciting discovery that I have made? or Is there a discovery that someone else has made that I would like to write about?* My story should have a strong and exciting beginning. I could begin with a question or an exclamation to get the reader's attention.

**GUIDED WRITING** Some students may need help identifying good beginnings. Have students look at stories and articles in their reading texts and discuss what makes each a good beginning.

### Good Beginnings

What happens when you start reading something that seems dull? You probably stop reading! If you want people to read your writing, you need a **good beginning**. Start with a question, an interesting fact, a funny remark, or an exclamation. Look at the examples below.

- Snow is made up of tiny ice crystals that form in the clouds.
- Much of the Northern Hemisphere experiences snow during the winter months.
- My friends and I like to play in the snow.
- Snowflakes are like the cookies my sister and I make.

Which beginning do you think is most interesting?

**Directions** A and B are the titles of two articles. The numbered sentences are possible beginnings for these articles. Choose the sentence that you think is the best beginning for each article. Write the number next to the article title.

_5_ **A** "Harry Houdini: Escape Artist"
_7_ **B** "Life in Antarctica"

1. Harry Houdini was born in 1874.
2. Penguins, seals, whales, and many other creatures live in Antarctica.
3. Antarctica is a cold place where few people live.
4. One of the people I am most interested in is Harry Houdini.
5. Imagine yourself locked in a crate and lying on the ocean floor.
6. Antarctica is a large, cold continent at the extreme south of the world.
7. How can living creatures survive in a world of eternal ice and snow?
8. I think one of the greatest magicians who ever lived was Harry Houdini.

**Directions** The sentences below need a good beginning to make them into an effective paragraph. Write two or three sentences that get the paragraph off to a good start.

You can go for walks with a dog, but you can't with a cat. Dogs can retrieve balls, play hide and seek, and shake hands. They know when you are sad or sick. Cats can't do any of these things. That's why dogs are better than cats.

Possible answer: Which do you like better, dogs or cats? There's no question in my mind. Dogs are better.

Unit 4 The Houdini Box — Writer's Craft **16B**

▲ **Writing Transparency** 16B

## DAY 3 Prewrite and Draft

### READ THE WRITING PROMPT
on page 411 in the Student Edition.

*In The Houdini Box, a boy discovers the secrets of a great magician.*

*Think about a discovery you have made or would like to make.*

*Now write a story about your discovery.*

#### Writing Test Tips
- Tell your story as it happened. Make sure the time order is clear.
- Keep the reader interested by including a little suspense.
- Use dialogue to make your story realistic.

**GETTING STARTED** Students can do any of the following:

- Create a graphic organizer or story map to plot out the events in their story.
- Write several opening sentences, including a question, exclamation, and quotation. Then read them aloud to a partner to see which is most effective.
- Make a list of details that will make their story more exciting. They can refer to this list as they write.

## DAY 4 Draft and Revise

### EDITING/REVISING CHECKLIST
☑ Have I written a good beginning?
☑ Is the story well organized and the discovery clear?
☑ Are singular and plural pronouns used effectively?
☑ Are contractions spelled correctly?

See the *Grammar and Writing Book*, pp. 140–145.

#### Revising Tips

#### Sentences
- Support sentence variety by using sentences of different lengths.
- Look for places to use interrogative, exclamatory, or imperative sentences.
- Check to make sure sentences do not all begin with the same word.

**PUBLISHING** Assemble students' stories in a binder with an alphabetical index of things discovered. Some students may wish to revise their work later.

**ASSESSMENT** Use the scoring rubric to evaluate students' work.

## DAY 5 Connect to Unit Writing

| | Story |
|---|---|
| Week 1 | Story About a Discovery 415g–415h |
| Week 2 | Travel Brochure 439g–439h |
| Week 3 | Business Letter 465g–465h |
| Week 4 | Feature Story 487g–487h |
| Week 5 | Plot Summary 507g–507h |

### PREVIEW THE UNIT PROMPT
*Write a story about something that happens on a real or an imaginary trip. Try to include suspense or humor and dialogue.*

#### APPLY
- A story has a beginning, middle, and end and focuses on one incident or event.
- A good beginning will grab the reader's attention.

## Writing Trait Rubric

| | 4 | 3 | 2 | 1 |
|---|---|---|---|---|
| **Sentences** | Good variety of sentence lengths and structures; includes dialogue | Some variety of sentence lengths and structures; some dialogue | Sentences mostly lacking in fluency and variety; no dialogue | Sentences choppy and dull |
| | Interesting and exciting story | Some excitement to story | Story lacking in excitement | Boring or confusing story |

# Spelling & Phonics Contractions

## OBJECTIVE

● Spell words with contractions.

### Generalization

**Connect to Phonics** In contractions, an apostrophe replaces omitted letters: *do not* becomes *don't; there is* becomes *there's*. Because letters are left out in a contraction, the contraction is pronounced differently from the original two words.

### Spelling Words

| | |
|---|---|
| 1. don't | 11. shouldn't |
| 2. won't* | 12. couldn't* |
| 3. wouldn't | 13. where's |
| 4. there's* | 14. hadn't |
| 5. we're | 15. aren't |
| 6. you're* | 16. they're |
| 7. doesn't | 17. it's |
| 8. I've | 18. we've |
| 9. here's | 19. when's |
| 10. wasn't* | 20. haven't |

### Challenge Words

| | |
|---|---|
| 21. it'll | 24. mustn't |
| 22. who'll | 25. we'd |
| 23. might've | |

*Word from the selection

**Spelling/Phonics Support** See the ELL and Transition Handbook for spelling support.

## DAY 1 Pretest and Sort

### PRETEST

Use the Dictation Sentences from Day 5 to administer the pretest. Read the word, read the sentence, and then read the word again. Guide students in self-correcting their pretests and correcting any misspellings.

#### Monitor Progress

**Spelling**

| If... students misspell more than 5 pretest words, | then... use words 1–10 for Strategic Intervention. |
|---|---|
| If... students misspell 1–5 pretest words, | then... use words 1–20 for On-Level practice. |
| If... students correctly spell all pretest words, | then... use words 1–25 for Advanced Learners. |

**HOMEWORK** Spelling Practice Book, p. 61.

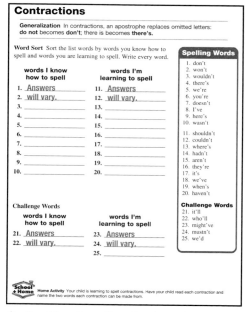

▲ **Spelling Practice Book** p. 61

## DAY 2 Think and Practice

### TEACH

In contractions, apostrophes replace omitted letters. Write *do not* and *don't* on the board. Point out that in the contraction, *don't,* the words are combined and the letter *o* in *not* is replaced by an apostrophe. Guide students in finding the pattern in *wouldn't* and *doesn't*.

contraction
don't

**FIND THE PATTERN** Ask students to identify the contraction in each of the spelling words. Have them separate the contracted words, and identify the letter that has been replaced by an apostrophe. Point out that *won't* is irregular—*will not*.

**HOMEWORK** Spelling Practice Book, p. 62.

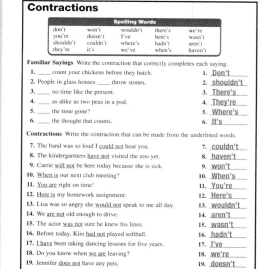

▲ **Spelling Practice Book** p. 62

# DAY 3 | Connect to Writing

## WRITE A NOTE

Ask students to write a note inviting a friend to a party. The note should use at least four of the spelling words.

### Frequently Misspelled Words

*it's*    *you're*

*we're*

These words may seem easy to spell, but they often are misspelled by fourth-graders. Alert students to these frequently misspelled words.

**HOMEWORK** Spelling Practice Book, p. 63.

### Contractions

**Proofread Riddles** Circle six spelling errors in Vicki's list of riddles. Write the words correctly on the lines. Rewrite the sentence that ends with the wrong punctuation mark.

Why don't rivers go out of style?
Because (theyr'e) always current!

(When'is) fishing not a good way to relax?
When you're a worm!

(Whats) better than a talking dog?
A spelling bee!

What driver (does't) need a license.
A screwdriver!

Why should you wear a watch in the desert?
Because there's a spring inside.

Why (woudn't) the letter E spend any money?
Because (its) always in debt.

| | | | |
|---|---|---|---|
| 1. | they're | 2. | When's |
| 3. | What's | 4. | doesn't |
| 5. | wouldn't | 6. | it's |
| 7. | What driver doesn't need a license? | | |

**Missing Words** Circle the contraction that is spelled correctly. Write it.

8. (We've) We'ev  chosen you for our team.    8. We've
9. There  ar'nt  (aren't)  any more books on the shelf.    9. aren't
10. The puppy  (wouldn't)  woudn't  come when I called.    10. wouldn't
11. Hear's  (Here's)  my missing shoe!    11. Here's
12. Nick  (doesn't)  dosen't  like ice cream.    12. doesn't

**Spelling Words**
don't
won't
wouldn't
there's
we're
you're
doesn't
I've
here's
wasn't
shouldn't
couldn't
where's
hadn't
aren't
they're
it's
we've
when's
haven't

**Frequently Misspelled Words**
it's
we're
you're

**Home Activity** Your child identified misspelled contractions. Write each contraction, omitting the apostrophes. Have your child add the missing apostrophe to each word.

▲ **Spelling Practice Book** p. 63

# DAY 4 | Review

## REVIEW CONTRACTIONS

There is one spelling word on the list in which the spelling of the base word changes to form a contraction. Have students find it and name the base word. *(Will not changes to won't.)*

### Spelling Strategy
### Problem Parts

An apostrophe in a word can supply a clue that the word is a contraction. Remind students to think about what letter or letters the apostrophe is replacing to help with word meaning.

**HOMEWORK** Spelling Practice Book, p. 64.

### Contractions

**Spelling Words**

| don't | won't | wouldn't | there's | we're |
|---|---|---|---|---|
| you're | doesn't | I've | here's | wasn't |
| shouldn't | couldn't | where's | hadn't | aren't |
| they're | it's | we've | when's | haven't |

**Writing Contractions** Words from the first and second columns can be combined to form a contraction. Write the contraction.

| | First Word | Second Word | | Contraction |
|---|---|---|---|---|
| 1. | do | not | 1. | don't |
| 2. | will | not | 2. | won't |
| 3. | there | has | 3. | there's |
| 4. | we | have | 4. | we've |
| 5. | you | are | 5. | you're |
| 6. | here | is | 6. | here's |
| 7. | have | not | 7. | haven't |
| 8. | it | has | 8. | it's |
| 9. | are | not | 9. | aren't |
| 10. | they | are | 10. | they're |
| 11. | where | is | 11. | where's |
| 12. | should | not | 12. | shouldn't |
| 13. | does | not | 13. | doesn't |
| 14. | could | not | 14. | couldn't |
| 15. | when | is | 15. | when's |
| 16. | was | not | 16. | wasn't |
| 17. | would | not | 17. | wouldn't |
| 18. | I | have | 18. | I've |
| 19. | we | are | 19. | we're |
| 20. | had | not | 20. | hadn't |

**Home Activity** Your child has learned to read, write, and spell contractions. Say the two words from the first and second columns of the chart. Have your child say and spell the contraction.

▲ **Spelling Practice Book** p. 64

# DAY 5 | Posttest

## DICTATION SENTENCES

1. Don't be late for dinner.

2. I won't forget my homework.

3. I wouldn't do that if I were you.

4. There's plenty here for everyone.

5. We're going to have a big party.

6. You're invited to our party.

7. The project doesn't have a deadline.

8. I've done some amazing things.

9. Here's the book you've been looking for.

10. He wasn't late.

11. You shouldn't do that.

12. I couldn't do that if I tried.

13. Where's my favorite shirt?

14. If I hadn't been late, I would have seen the whole movie.

15. Aren't we there yet?

16. They're the nicest people I know.

17. It's been a long time since I last saw you.

18. We've been waiting all day.

19. When's dinner?

20. I haven't been here since last year.

## CHALLENGE

21. It'll be a long time before that happens.

22. Who'll be going to the party?

23. If I had known, I might've done things differently.

24. We mustn't be late for school.

25. We'd better be going now.

| New Literacies | |
|---|---|
| Day 1 | **Identify Questions** |
| Day 2 | **Navigate/Search** |
| Day 3 | **Analyze** |
| Day 4 | **Synthesize** |
| Day 5 | **Communicate** |

## NEW LITERACIES

# Internet Inquiry Activity

## EXPLORE PERCEPTION

Use the following 5-day plan to help students conduct this week's Internet inquiry activity on perception. Remind students to follow classroom rules when using the Internet.

### DAY 1

**Identify Questions** Discuss the lesson focus question: *Can you always believe what you see?* Help students identify ideas for specific inquiry questions about perception. For example, students may want to learn about a magic trick, optical illusion, or other aspects of visual perception. Have students work individually, in pairs, or in small groups to write inquiry questions.

### DAY 2

**Navigate/Search** Have students use student-friendly search engines to perform Internet searches. Then they can identify sites they want to use for their research. If allowed, instruct students on how to bookmark promising sites. Explain that a site may not have exactly the information they expect, so effective researchers identify a few likely sites to explore in more depth.

### DAY 3

**Analyze** Have students analyze the Web sites they identified on Day 2 and gather information that answers their inquiry questions. Remind them it is sometimes appropriate to revise their inquiry question during this stage. For example, they might discover there is not enough information available about a particular magic trick they're exploring. In that case, it would be appropriate to choose a different trick to research.

### DAY 4

**Synthesize** Have students synthesize the information they identified as relevant on Day 3. They may want to create diagrams or numbered, illustrated lists that explain how a specific trick or illusion is done or how the eye perceives something a certain way.

### DAY 5

**Communicate** Have students share their inquiry results. Each student can display a poster explaining the topic for the class and, if appropriate, provide a demonstration.

## RESEARCH/STUDY SKILLS
# Instruction Manual

## OBJECTIVES

- Review terms related to procedures, instructions, and manuals.
- Use a manual to learn how to do something.

## TEACH

Explain that **procedures** and **instructions** are directions for using or doing something. A **manual** is a written set of instructions, usually published in booklet or book form. Display the instruction manual for a common product, such as a camera, and review the following features:

- An **index** or **table of contents** helps readers find specific information.
- **Step-by-step directions** listed in order make it easy for readers to see what to do. Steps are often numbered.
- **Photos, illustrations,** and **diagrams** make directions clearer and easier to follow.
- **Labels** show the working parts readers need to identify.
- **Warnings** tell about special hazards.

Distribute manuals to small groups. Have each group examine its manual. Then ask them to answer questions such as these:

1. **What is the purpose of the manual?**
2. **How is information in the manual organized?**
3. **What kind of graphics does the manual include?**
4. **Are the manual's instructions easy to follow? Why or why not?**

### Numbered Steps

#### Section I: Getting Started

1. To **turn on** the camera, press the power button in the upper left hand corner. The viewfinder light will begin blinking, and the lens cover will open once the power is turned on.

2. To **turn off** the camera, press the power button in the upper left hand corner.

**IMPORTANT:** When not in use, the camera should be turned off. Leaving the power on will cause batteries to run down, and the lens will NOT be covered.

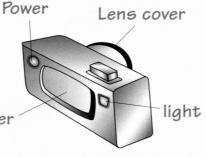

Power    Lens cover

View finder    light

Warning

## ASSESS

As students work with manuals, check that they can identify and explain the purpose of the table of contents, index, steps, labels, warnings, and illustrations. Have them explain or demonstrate a set of instructions.

For more practice or to assess students, use Practice Book pp. 159–160.

---

**Procedures and Instructions/Manual**

- **Procedures and instructions** are directions for using or doing something. Instructions are given in order and often include numbered steps. Read through all the instructions before you begin. Then do what is directed, one step at a time.
- A **manual** usually takes the form of a booklet or handbook. It contains a written set of instructions that help the reader understand, use, or build something. Take note of illustrations, diagrams, headings, labels, and sections (including index and table of contents). Also watch for warnings about special hazards.

**Directions** Read the following instructions. Then answer the questions below.

> **The Great Houdini Ring Escape**
> 1. Tie a ring with a "fake knot." Poke a loop of string through a finger ring. Bring the loop all the way back and over the ring. Then pull the ends of the string to make a "knot." Show your audience, but not too closely.
> 2. Ask someone to hold the two ends of the string. Make sure the string sags.
> 3. Put a scarf over the ring.
> 4. Reach under the scarf. Remove the ring by pushing the loop up and back over the ring.
> 5. Show the ring you're holding to the audience and remove the scarf to reveal the empty string.

1. What is the purpose of these instructions?
   The instructions explain how to perform a magic trick.
2. What does the audience see at the end of the first step? The last step?
   The audience sees a ring that seems to be tied on a string; The audience sees the ring separated from the string.
3. Which step in this procedure involves an audience member?
   Step 2 of the procedure involves an audience member.
4. Why is it important that the instructions are followed in order?
   Possible answer: The success of the trick depends on following the steps in order.
5. What skills are required to perform this procedure successfully?
   use quick, smooth hand movements; tie a 'fake' knot

**School + Home** Home Activity Your child analyzed a set of instructions. Find or create a set of simple instructions that tell how to do a household chore. Read over the instructions together, noting the steps to do the procedure.

▲ **Practice Book** p. 159

---

**Directions** Read over this table of contents for a manual of magic tricks. Then answer the questions below.

**WARNING** Magic tricks require much practice. These tricks must be practiced until you can do them without even thinking.

6. What is the purpose of this manual?
   The manual provides instructions for doing magic tricks.
7. According to the table of contents, how many sections does this manual contain? Which section might explain the kinds of tricks performed by Houdini?
   thirteen sections; The section "Escape Tricks" might explain tricks like those performed by Houdini.
8. In which section would you find magic tricks from Japan? Math tricks?
   "Magic Around the World"; "Number Magic"
9. What page would you turn to for instructions on making a nickel disappear? For definitions of magic terms?
   page 24; page 138
10. What message does the warning contain? How do warnings help readers?
    The warning reminds readers that tricks require much practice. Warnings alert readers to important information.

**School + Home** Home Activity Your child analyzed the table of contents of a manual. Together, look through a manual, such as one for a camera or telephone. Invite your child to explain various features of the manual.

▲ **Practice Book** p. 160

# Assessment Checkpoints *for the Week*

## Selection Assessment

Use pp. 61–64 of Selection Tests to check:

 **Selection Understanding**

 **Comprehension Skill**
*Compare and Contrast*

 **Selection Vocabulary**

| | |
|---|---|
| *appeared* | *magician* |
| *bustling* | *monument* |
| *crumbled* | *vanished* |
| *escape* | |

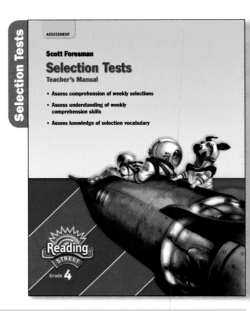

ASSESSMENT

**Scott Foresman**
**Selection Tests**
Teacher's Manual

- Assess comprehension of weekly selections
- Assess understanding of weekly comprehension skills
- Assess knowledge of selection vocabulary

Reading STREET Grade 4

## Leveled Assessment

On-Level
Strategic Intervention
Advanced

Use pp. 91–96 of Fresh Reads for Differentiated Test Practice to check:

 **Comprehension Skill**
*Compare and Contrast*

 **REVIEW Comprehension Skill**
*Plot and Character*

 **Fluency** *Words Correct Per Minute*

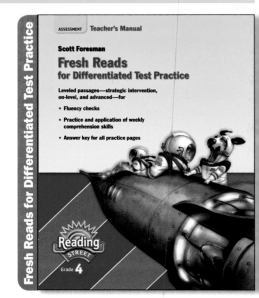

ASSESSMENT   Teacher's Manual

**Scott Foresman**
**Fresh Reads**
**for Differentiated Test Practice**

Leveled passages—strategic intervention, on-level, and advanced—for

- Fluency checks
- Practice and application of weekly comprehension skills
- Answer key for all practice pages

Reading STREET Grade 4

## Managing Assessment

Use Assessment Handbook for:

 **Observation Checklists**

 **Record-Keeping Forms**

 **Portfolio Assessment**

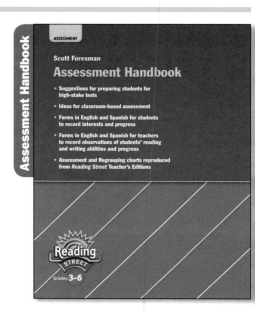

ASSESSMENT

**Scott Foresman**
**Assessment Handbook**

- Suggestions for preparing students for high-stake tests
- Ideas for classroom-based assessment
- Forms in English and Spanish for students to record interests and progress
- Forms in English and Spanish for teachers to record observations of students' reading and writing abilities and progress
- Assessment and Regrouping charts reproduced from *Reading Street* Teacher's Editions

Reading STREET Grades 3–6

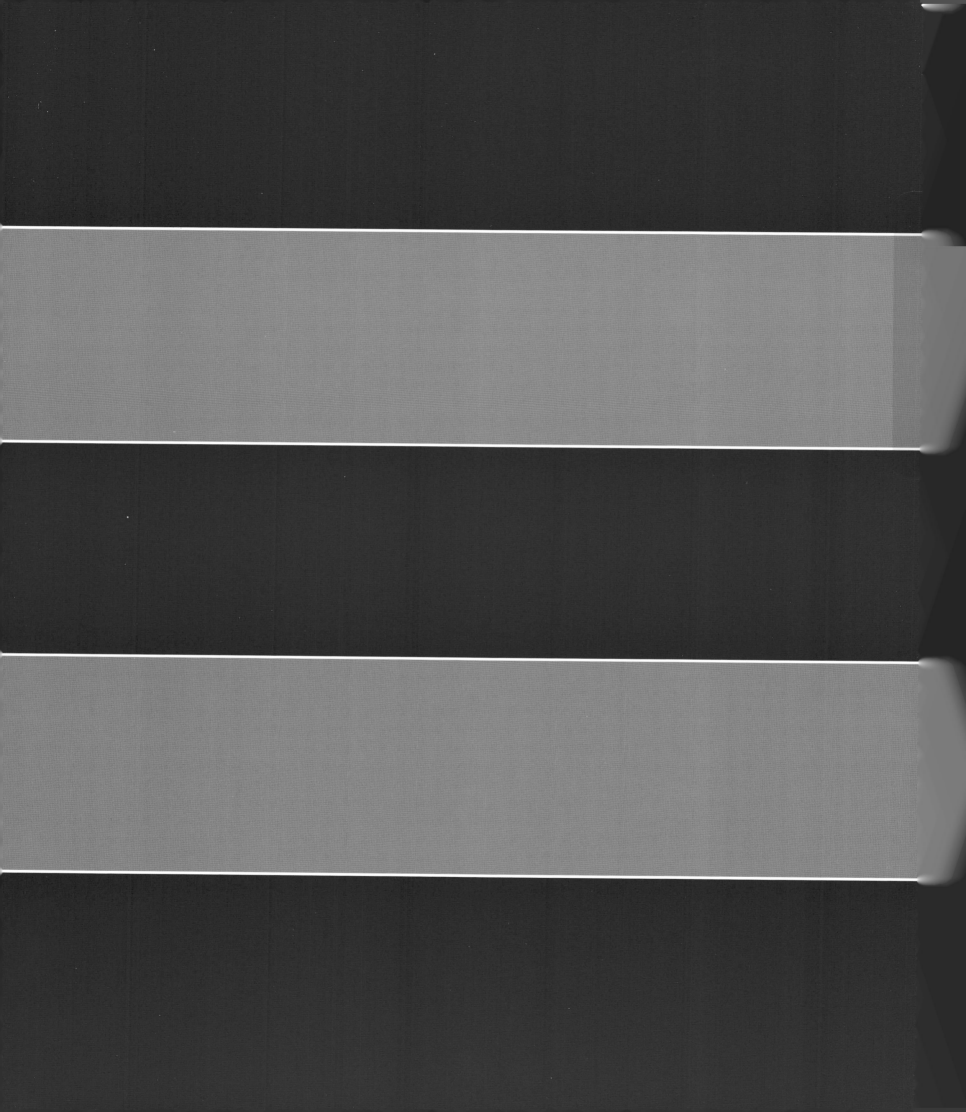

# Unit 4
# Puzzles and Mysteries

## CONCEPT QUESTION
### Is there an explanation for everything?

## EXPAND THE CONCEPT
## What can explain animal behavior?

TIME FOR Science

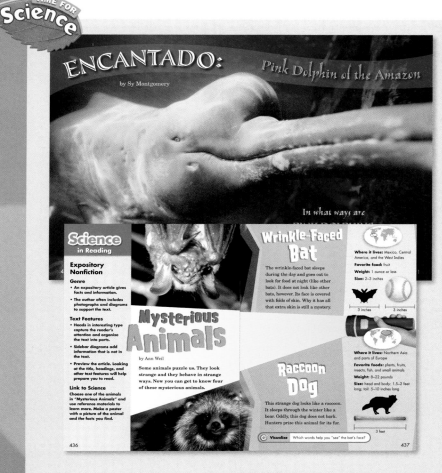

## CONNECT THE CONCEPT

▶ **Build Background**
*agility, endowed, relationship*

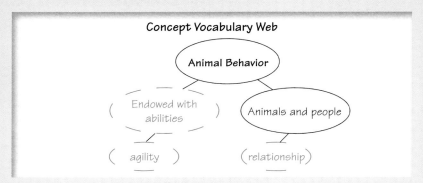

Concept Vocabulary Web

- Animal Behavior
  - Endowed with abilities
  - Animals and people
  - agility
  - relationship

▶ **Science Content**
Animal Characteristics, Animal Survival, Food Web, Habitat

▶ **Writing**
Travel Brochure

▶ **Internet Inquiry**
Animal Behavior

# Preview Your Week

*What can explain animal behavior?*

## ENCANTADO: Pink Dolphin of the Amazon
by Sy Montgomery

In what ways are PINK DOLPHINS mysterious?

**Genre** Expository nonfiction provides factual information about a topic. As you read, look for facts about pink dolphins to add to your knowledge of animals.

**Student Edition pages 420–433**

**Genre** Expository Nonfiction

**Vocabulary Strategy** Context Clues

**Comprehension Skill** Compare and Contrast

**Comprehension Strategy** Visualize

## Paired Selection

**Reading Across Texts**

Identify Animals from South America

**Genre**

Expository Nonfiction

**Text Features**

Headings with Interesting Typeface

Sidebar Diagrams

### Science in Reading

**Expository Nonfiction**

**Genre**
- An expository article gives facts and information.
- The author often includes photographs and diagrams to support the text.

**Text Features**
- Headings in an interesting typeface capture the reader's attention and organize the text into parts.
- Sidebar diagrams add information that is not in the text.
- Preview the article. Looking at the title, headings, and other text features will help prepare you to read.

**Link to Science**
Choose one of the animals in "Mysterious Animals" and use reference materials to learn more about it. Make a poster with a picture of the animal and the facts you find.

## Mysterious Animals
by Ann Weil

Some animals puzzle us. They look strange and they behave in strange ways. Now you can get to know four of these mysterious animals.

### Wrinkle-Faced Bat

The wrinkle-faced bat sleeps during the day and goes out to look for food at night (like other bats). It does not look like other bats, however. Its face is covered with folds of skin. Why it has all that extra skin is still a mystery.

**Where it lives:** Mexico, Central America, and the West Indies
**Favorite food:** fruit
**Weight:** 1 ounce or less
**Size:** 2–3 inches

3 inches    3 inches

### Raccoon Dog

This strange dog looks like a raccoon. It sleeps through the winter like a bear. Oddly, this dog does not bark. Hunters prize this animal for its fur.

**Where it lives:** Northern Asia and parts of Europe
**Favorite foods:** plants, fruits, insects, fish, and small animals
**Weight:** 8–22 pounds
**Size:** head and body: 1.5–2 feet long; tail: 5–10 inches long

3 feet

**Visualize** Which words help you "see" the bat's face?

436

**Student Edition pages 436–439**

**Read It**
**ONLINE**
PearsonSuccessNet.com
• Student Edition
• Leveled Readers

## Leveled Readers

◉ **Skill** Compare and Contrast
◉ **Strategy** Visualize
**Lesson Vocabulary**

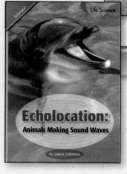
**Dolphins** by Morgan Lloyd
**Below-Level**

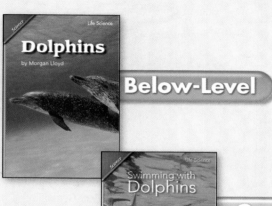
**Swimming with Dolphins** by Stephanie Wilder
**On-Level**

**Echolocation: Animals Making Sound Waves**
**Advanced**

**ELL Reader**
• Concept Vocabulary
• Text Support
• Language Enrichment

Life in the Amazon Rain Forest by Ronald Scheibel

---

**TIME FOR Science**

## Integrate Science Standards
• Animal Biology
• Ecosystems

✓ **Read**

***Encantado: Pink Dolphin of the Amazon,***
pp. 420–433

**"Mysterious Animals,"**
pp. 436–439

### Leveled Readers

**Below-Level** • Support Concepts
**On-Level** • Develop Concepts
**Advanced** • Extend Concepts • Science Extension Activity

### ELL Reader

✓ **Build**
## Concept Vocabulary
**Animal Behavior,** pp. 416l–416m

✓ **Teach**
## Science Concepts
**Animal Characteristics,** p. 425
**Animal Survival,** p. 431
**Food Web,** p. 437
**Habitat,** p. 439

✓ **Explore**
## Science Center
**Find Dolphin Facts,** p. 416k

*Encantado* **416c**

# Weekly Plan

## READING

*45–90 minutes*

### TARGET SKILLS OF THE WEEK

**Comprehension Skill**
Compare and Contrast

**Comprehension Strategy**
Visualize

**Vocabulary Strategy**
Context Clues

## LANGUAGE ARTS

*30–60 minutes*

### Trait of the Week

**Focus/Ideas**

---

## DAY 1
PAGES 416l–418b, 439a, 439e–439k

### Oral Language

**QUESTION OF THE WEEK** *What can explain animal behavior?*

Read Aloud: "Sugar: Cross Country Traveler" 416m
Build Concepts, 416l

### Comprehension/Vocabulary

Comprehension Skill/Strategy Lesson, 416–417

Compare and Contrast **T**

Visualize

Build Background, 418a

Introduce Lesson Vocabulary, 418b
*aquarium, dolphins, enchanted, flexible, glimpses, pulses, surface* **T**

**Read** Leveled Readers

**Grouping Options** 416f–416g

### Fluency

Model Juncture, 416l–416m, 439a

---

**Grammar,** 439e
Introduce Subject and Object Pronouns **T**

**Writing Workshop,** 439g
Introduce Travel Brochure
Model the Trait of the Week: Focus/Ideas

**Spelling,** 439i
Pretest for Final *le, al, en*

**Internet Inquiry,** 439k
Identify Questions

---

**Day 1** Write to Read, 416

---

**Day 1** Animal Behavior Concept Web, 416l

---

## DAY 2
PAGES 418–429, 439a, 439e–439k

### Oral Language

**QUESTION OF THE DAY** *Why do you think a pink dolphin is called* encantado *or "enchanted"?*

### Comprehension/Vocabulary

Vocabulary Strategy Lesson, 418–419

Context Clues **T**

**Read** *Encantado,* 420–429

**Grouping Options**
416f–416g

Compare and Contrast **T**

Visualize

Context Clues **T**

**REVIEW** Generalize **T**

Develop Vocabulary

### Fluency

Echo Reading, 439a

---

**Grammar,** 439e
Develop Subject and Object Pronouns **T**

**Writing Workshop,** 439g
Improve Writing with Sensory Details

**Spelling,** 439i
Teach the Generalization

**Internet Inquiry,** 439k
Navigate/Search

---

**Day 2** Words to Write, 419
Strategy Response Log, 420, 429

---

**Day 2** Time for Science: Animal Characteristics, 425
Revisit the Animal Behavior Concept Web, 429

---

## DAILY WRITING ACTIVITIES

## DAILY SCIENCE CONNECTIONS

## DAILY SUCCESS PREDICTORS
for Adequate Yearly Progress

### Monitor Progress and Corrective Feedback

**Vocabulary**      Check Vocabulary, *416l*

## RESOURCES FOR THE WEEK

- Practice Book, *pp. 161–170*
- Word Study and Spelling Practice Book, *pp. 65–68*
- Grammar and Writing Practice Book, *pp. 65–68*

- Selection Test, *pp. 65–68*
- Fresh Reads for Differentiated Test Practice, *pp. 97–102*
- The Grammar and Writing Book, *pp. 146–151*

### Grouping Options for Differentiated Instruction
Turn the page for the small group lesson plan.

# DAY 3   PAGES 430–435, 439a, 439e–439k

## Oral Language

**QUESTION OF THE DAY** *Why do you think the pink dolphins' behavior remains a mystery today?*

## Comprehension/Vocabulary

**Read** *Encantado,* 430–435

**Grouping Options** 416f–416g

- Compare and Contrast **T**
- Visualize
- Develop Vocabulary

Reader Response
Selection Test

## Fluency

Model Phrasing, 439a

---

**Grammar,** 439f
Apply Subject and Object Pronouns in Writing **T**

**Writing Workshop,** 435, 439h
Write Now
Prewrite and Draft

**Spelling,** 439j
Connect Spelling to Writing

**Internet Inquiry,** 439k
Analyze Sources

---

**Day 3**   Strategy Response Log, 432
Look Back and Write, 434

---

**Day 3**   Revisit the Animal Behavior Concept Web, 433

# DAY 4   PAGES 436–439, 439a, 439e–439k

## Oral Language

**QUESTION OF THE DAY** *Why is it important to find out more about the behavior of dolphins and other "Mysterious Animals"?*

## Comprehension/Vocabulary

**Read** "Mysterious Animals," 436–439

**Grouping Options** 416f–416g

Expository Nonfiction
Reading Across Texts
Content-Area Vocabulary

## Fluency

Partner Reading, 439a

---

**Grammar,** 439f
Practice Subjective and Objective Pronouns for Standardized Tests **T**

**Writing Workshop,** 439h
Draft, Revise, and Publish

**Spelling,** 439j
Provide a Strategy

**Internet Inquiry,** 439k
Synthesize Information

---

**Day 4**   Writing Across Texts, 439

---

**Day 4**   Time for Science: Food Web, 437; Habitat, 439

# DAY 5   PAGES 439a–439l

## Oral Language

**QUESTION OF THE WEEK** *To wrap up the week, revisit the Day 1 question.*

   Build Concept Vocabulary, 439c

## Fluency

**Read** Leveled Readers

**Grouping Options** 416f–416g

Assess Reading Rate, 439a

## Comprehension/Vocabulary

- Reteach Compare and Contrast, 439b **T**
- Persuasive Devices, 439b
- Context Clues, 439c **T**

---

**Speaking and Listening,** 439d
TV Commercial
Analyze Commercials

**Grammar,** 439f
Cumulative Review

**Writing Workshop,** 439h
Connect to Unit Writing

**Spelling,** 439j
Posttest for Final *le, al, en*

**Internet Inquiry,** 439k
Communicate Results

**Research/Study Skills,** 439l
Poster/Announcement

---

**Day 5**   Persuasive Devices, 439b

---

**Day 5**   Revisit the Animal Behavior Concept Web, 439c

---

**KEY** ⦿ = Target Skill   **T** = Tested Skill

Comprehension    Check Retelling, *434*

Fluency    Check Fluency WCPM, *439a*

Vocabulary    Check Vocabulary, *439c*

**SUCCESS PREDICTOR**

# Small Group Plan for Differentiated Instruction

## Daily Plan AT A GLANCE

### Reading
**Whole Group**
- Oral Language
- Comprehension/Vocabulary

### Group Time
**Differentiated Instruction**

Meet with small groups to provide:
- Skill Support
- Reading Support
- Fluency Practice

**Read**

This week's lessons for daily group time can be found behind the Differentiated Instruction (DI) tab on pp. DI·12–DI·21.

**Whole Group**
- Fluency

### Language Arts
- Grammar
- Writing
- Spelling
- Research/Inquiry
- Speaking/Listening/Viewing

**Use *My Sidewalks on Reading Street* for Tier III intensive reading intervention.**

---

### DAY 1

**On-Level**
**Teacher-Led**
*Page DI·13*
- Develop Concept Vocabulary
- **Read** On-Level Reader *Swimming with Dolphins*

**Strategic Intervention**
**Teacher-Led**
*Page DI·12*
- Reinforce Concepts
- **Read** Below-Level Reader *Dolphins*

**Advanced**
**Teacher-Led**
*Page DI·13*
- **Read** Advanced Reader *Echolocation*
- Independent Extension Activity

#### (i) Independent Activities
**While you meet with small groups, have the rest of the class...**

- Visit the Reading/Library Center
- Listen to the Background Building Audio
- Finish Write to Read, p. 416
- Complete Practice Book pp. 163–164
- Visit Cross-Curricular Centers

---

### DAY 2

**On-Level**
**Teacher-Led**
*Pages 422–429*
- Develop Concept Vocabulary
- **Read** *Encantado: Pink Dolphin of the Amazon*

**Strategic Intervention**
**Teacher-Led**
*Page DI·14*
- Practice Lesson Vocabulary
- Read Multisyllabic Words
- **Read** or Listen to *Encantado: Pink Dolphin of the Amazon*

**Advanced**
**Teacher-Led**
*Page DI·15*
- Extend Vocabulary
- **Read** *Encantado: Pink Dolphin of the Amazon*

#### (i) Independent Activities
**While you meet with small groups, have the rest of the class...**

- Visit the Reading/Library Center
- Listen to the AudioText for *Encantado: Pink Dolphin of the Amazon*
- Finish Words to Write, p. 419
- Complete Practice Book pp. 165–166
- Write in their Strategy Response Logs, pp. 420, 429
- Visit Cross-Curricular Centers
- Work on inquiry projects

---

### DAY 3

**On-Level**
**Teacher-Led**
*Pages 430–433*
- **Read** *Encantado: Pink Dolphin of the Amazon*

**Strategic Intervention**
**Teacher-Led**
*Page DI·16*
- Practice Compare and Contrast and Visualize
- **Read** or Listen to *Encantado: Pink Dolphin of the Amazon*

**Advanced**
**Teacher-Led**
*Page DI·17*
- Extend Compare and Contrast and Visualize
- **Read** *Encantado: Pink Dolphin of the Amazon*

#### (i) Independent Activities
**While you meet with small groups, have the rest of the class...**

- Visit the Reading/Library Center
- Listen to the AudioText for *Encantado: Pink Dolphin of the Amazon*
- Write in their Strategy Response Logs, p. 432
- Finish Look Back and Write, p. 434
- Complete Practice Book p. 167
- Visit Cross-Curricular Centers
- Work on inquiry projects

① Begin with whole class skill and strategy instruction.

② Meet with small groups to provide differentiated instruction.

③ Gather the whole class back together for fluency and language arts.

**DAY 4**

### On-Level
**Teacher-Led**
*Pages 436–439*
- **Read** "Mysterious Animals"

### Strategic Intervention
**Teacher-Led**
*Page DI · 18*
- Practice Retelling
- **Read** or Listen to "Mysterious Animals"

### Advanced
**Teacher-Led**
*Page DI · 19*
- **Read** "Mysterious Animals"
- Genre Study

## ⓘ Independent Activities

**While you meet with small groups, have the rest of the class…**

- Visit the Reading/Library Center
- Listen to the AudioText for "Mysterious Animals"
- Visit the Writing/Vocabulary Center
- Finish Writing Across Texts, p. 439
- Visit Cross-Curricular Centers
- Work on inquiry projects

**DAY 5**

### On-Level
**Teacher-Led**
*Page DI · 21*
- **Reread** Leveled Reader *Swimming with Dolphins*
- Retell *Swimming with Dolphins*

### Strategic Intervention
**Teacher-Led**
*Page DI · 20*
- **Reread** Leveled Reader *Dolphins*
- Retell *Dolphins*

### Advanced
**Teacher-Led**
*Page DI · 21*
- **Reread** Leveled Reader *Echolocation*
- Share Extension Activity

## ⓘ Independent Activities

**While you meet with small groups, have the rest of the class…**

- Visit the Reading/Library Center
- Complete Practice Book pp. 168–170
- Visit Cross-Curricular Centers
- Work on inquiry projects

**Grouping** Place English language learners in the groups that correspond to their reading abilities in English.

Use the appropriate Leveled Reader or other text at students' instructional level.

**TIP** Send home the appropriate Multilingual Summary of the main selection on Day 1.

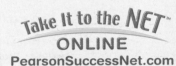

## Take It to the NET ONLINE
**PearsonSuccessNet.com**

**Sharon Vaughn**
For research on intervention, see the article "Group Size and Time Allotted to Intervention" by S. Linan-Thompson and Scott Foresman author S. Vaughn.

### TEACHER TALK

Text written at a student's **instructional reading level** is text in which no more than about one in ten words is difficult for the student to read.

Be sure to schedule time for students to work on the unit inquiry project "Unlocking Nature's Mysteries." This week students conduct information searches for text and images to help them answer their questions.

**Looking Ahead**

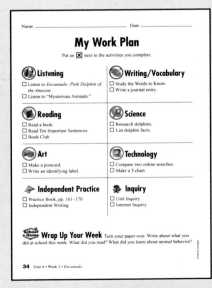

▲ **Group-Time Survival Guide** p. 34, Weekly Contract

*Encantado* **416g**

# Customize Your Plan *by Stran...*

## ORAL LANGUAGE

### Concept Development

**What can explain animal behavior?**

**CONCEPT VOCABULARY**

agility     endowed     relationship

### BUILD

☐ **Question of the Week** Introduce and discuss the question of the week. This week students will read a variety of texts and work on projects related to the concept *animal behavior.* Post the question for students to refer to throughout the week. **DAY 1** *416d*

☐ **Read Aloud** Read aloud "Sugar Cross-Country Traveler." Then begin a web to build concepts and concept vocabulary related to this week's lesson and the unit theme, Puzzles and Mysteries. Introduce the concept words *agility, endowed,* and *relationship* and have students place them on the web. Display the web for use throughout the week. **DAY 1** *416l–416m*

Animal Behavior

Endowed with abilities

Animals and people

agility

relationship

### DEVELOP

☐ **Question of the Day** Use the prompts from the Weekly Plan to engage students in conversations related to this week's reading and the unit theme. **EVERY DAY** *416d–416e*

☐ **Concept Vocabulary Web** Revisit the Animal Behavior Concept Web and encourage students to add concept words from their reading and life experiences. **DAY 2** *429,* **DAY 3** *433*

### CONNECT

☐ **Looking Back/Moving Forward** Revisit the Animal Behavior Concept Web and discuss how it relates to this week's lesson and the unit theme. Then make connections to next week's lesson. **DAY 5** *439c*

### CHECK

☐ **Concept Vocabulary Web** Use the Animal Behavior Concept Web to check students' understanding of the concept vocabulary words *agility, endowed,* and *relationship.* **DAY 1** *416l,* **DAY 5** *439c*

## VOCABULARY

**STRATEGY CONTEXT CLUES** When you read, you may find that the meaning of a word you know does not make sense in a sentence. This may be because the word is a multiple-meaning word, or a word with more than one meaning.

**LESSON VOCABULARY**

aquarium     glimpses
dolphins     pulses
enchanted    surface
flexible

### TEACH

☐ **Words to Know** Give students the opportunity to tell what they already know about this week's lesson vocabulary words. Then discuss word meaning. **DAY 1** *418b*

☐ **Vocabulary Strategy Lesson** Use the vocabulary strategy lesson in the Student Edition to introduce and model this week's strategy, *context clues.* **DAY 2** *418–419*

**Vocabulary Strategy Lesson**

### PRACTICE/APPLY

☐ **Leveled Text** Read the lesson vocabulary in the context of leveled text. **DAY 1** *LR10–LR18*

☐ **Words in Context** Read the lesson vocabulary and apply *context clues* in the context of *Encantado: Pink Dolphin of the Amazon.* **DAY 2** *420–429,* **DAY 3** *430–434*

**Leveled Readers**

☐ **Writing/Vocabulary Center** Write a journal entry about your day after your imaginary trip with Moises. **DAY 4** *416k,* **DAY 5** *416k*

**Main Selection—Nonfiction**

☐ **Homework** Practice Book pp. 164–165. **DAY 1** *418b,* **DAY 2** *419*

☐ **Word Play** Have pairs select several words from *Encantado* and write clues for each word. Then have pairs use those clues to create a word puzzle. **ANY DAY** *439c*

### ASSESS

☐ **Selection Test** Use the Selection Test to determine students' understanding of the lesson vocabulary words. **DAY 3**

### RETEACH/REVIEW

☐ **Reteach Lesson** If necessary, use this lesson to reteach and review *context clues.* **DAY 5** *439c*

① Use assessment data to determine your instructional focus.

② Preview this week's instruction by strand.

③ Choose instructional activities that meet the needs of your classroom.

## COMPREHENSION

**SKILL COMPARE AND CONTRAST**  To compare is to tell how two ideas or concepts are similar or alike. To contrast is to tell how ideas or concepts are different.

**STRATEGY VISUALIZE**  Visualizing is the ability to create pictures in your mind while reading. Visualizing can help you "see" how things are alike and different.

### TEACH

❏ **Skill/Strategy Lesson** Use the skill/strategy lesson in the Student Edition to introduce and model *compare and contrast* and *visualize*. **DAY 1** *416-417*

Skill/Strategy Lesson

❏ **Extend Skills** Teach persuasive devices. **ANY DAY** *439b*

### PRACTICE/APPLY

❏ **Leveled Text** Apply *compare and contrast* and *visualize* to read leveled text. **DAY 1** *LR10-LR18*

❏ **Skills and Strategies in Context** Read *Encantado: Pink Dolphin of the Amazon,* using the Guiding Comprehension questions to apply *compare and contrast* and *visualize.* **DAY 2** *420-429,* **DAY 3** *430-434*

Leveled Readers

❏ **Skills and Strategies in Context** Read "Mysterious Animals," guiding students as they apply *compare and contrast* and *visualize.* Then have students discuss and write across texts. **DAY 4** *436-439*

Main Selection—Nonfiction

❏ **Homework** Practice Book pp. 163, 167, 168. **DAY 1** *417,* **DAY 3** *433,* **DAY 5** *439b*

Paired Selection— Nonfiction

❏ **Fresh Reads for Differentiated Test Practice** Have students practice *compare and contrast* with a new passage. **DAY 3**

### ASSESS

❏ **Selection Test** Determine students' understanding of the selection and their use of *compare and contrast*. **DAY 3**

❏ **Retell** Have students retell *Encantado: Pink Dolphin of the Amazon.* **DAY 3** *434-435*

### RETEACH/REVIEW

❏ **Reteach Lesson** If necessary, reteach and review *compare and contrast*. **DAY 5** *439b*

## FLUENCY

**SKILL PHRASING**  Phrasing is grouping related words in a meaningful way. Phrasing allows the reader and listener to better understand the text.

### TEACH

❏ **Read Aloud** Model fluent reading by rereading "Sugar Cross-Country Traveler." Focus on this week's fluency skill, phrasing. **DAY 1** *416l-416m, 439a*

### PRACTICE/APPLY

❏ **Echo Reading** Read aloud selected paragraphs from *Encantado,* placing emphasis on the use of punctuation to group phrases. Then practice as a class, doing three echo readings. **DAY 2** *439a ,* **DAY 3** *439a*

❏ **Partner Reading** Have partners practice reading aloud, reading with careful phrasing, and pausing briefly after clauses and punctuation marks. Have partners offer each other feedback. As students reread, monitor their progress toward their individual fluency goals. **DAY 4** *439a*

❏ **Listening Center** Have students follow along with the AudioText for this week's selections. **ANY DAY** *416j*

❏ **Reading/Library Center** Have students reread a selection of their choice. **ANY DAY** *416j*

❏ **Fluency Coach** Have students use Fluency Coach to listen to fluent readings or practice reading on their own. **ANY DAY**

### ASSESS

❏ **Check Fluency** WCPM Do a one-minute timed reading, paying special attention to this week's skill—phrasing. Provide feedback for each student. **DAY 5** *439a*

# ☑ Customize Your Plan *by Strand*

## GRAMMAR

**SKILL SUBJECT AND OBJECT PRONOUNS** A subject pronoun is used in the subject of a sentence. Examples of singular subject pronouns are *you, he, she, it,* and *I*. An object pronoun is used in the predicate of a sentence after an action verb or with a preposition, such as *for, at, into, with,* or *to*. Examples of singular object pronouns are *you, he, she, it,* and *I*. Plural object pronouns are *you, them,* and *us*.

### TEACH

☐ **Grammar Transparency 17** Use Grammar Transparency 17 to teach subject and object pronouns. DAY 1 *439e*

**Grammar Transparency 17**

### PRACTICE/APPLY

☐ **Develop the Concept** Review the concept of subject and object pronouns and provide guided practice. DAY 2 *439e*

☐ **Apply to Writing** Have students review something they have written and check use of subject and object pronouns. **DAY 3** *439f*

☐ **Test Preparation** Examine common errors in subject and object pronouns to prepare for standardized tests. DAY 4 *439f*

☐ **Homework** Grammar and Writing Practice Book pp. 65–67. DAY 2 *439e*, DAY 3 *439f*, DAY 4 *439f*

### ASSESS

☐ **Cumulative Review** Use Grammar and Writing Practice Book p. 68. DAY 5 *439f*

### RETEACH/REVIEW

☐ **Daily Fix-It** Have students find and correct errors in grammar, spelling, and punctuation. **EVERY DAY** *439e–439f*

☐ **The Grammar and Writing Book** Use pp. 146–149 of The Grammar and Writing Book to extend instruction for subject and object pronouns. **ANY DAY**

**The Grammar and Writing Book**

## WRITING

### Trait of the Week

**FOCUS/IDEAS** Good writers focus on a main idea and develop this idea with strong supporting details. Having a purpose for writing, such as to inform, to persuade, or to entertain, helps keep focus on the main idea.

### TEACH

☐ **Writing Transparency 17A** Use the model to introduce and discuss the Trait of the Week. DAY 1 *439g*

☐ **Writing Transparency 17B** Use the transparency to show students how sensory details can improve their writing. DAY 2 *439g*

**Writing Transparency 17A** **Writing Transparency 17B**

### PRACTICE/APPLY

☐ **Write Now** Examine the model on Student Edition p. 435. Then have students write their own travel brochures. DAY 3 *435, 439h*, DAY 4 *439h*

> **Prompt** *Encantado: Pink Dolphin of the Amazon* describes the Amazon rainforest. Think about a place you know and like. Now write a travel brochure describing that place.

**Write Now p. 435**

☐ **Writing/Vocabulary Center** Write a journal entry about your day after your imaginary trip with Moises. DAY 4 *416k*, DAY 5 *416k*

### ASSESS

☐ **Writing Trait Rubric** Use the rubric to evaluate students' writing. DAY 4 *439h*

### RETEACH/REVIEW

☐ **The Grammar and Writing Book** Use pp. 146–151 of The Grammar and Writing Book to extend instruction for subject and object pronouns, sensory details, and travel brochures. **ANY DAY**

**The Grammar and Writing Book**

## SPELLING

GENERALIZATION **FINAL *LE, AL, EN*** The schwa sound in final syllables is often spelled differently: *jungle, animal.*

### TEACH

❑ **Pretest** Give the pretest for words with final *le, al, en*. Guide students in self-correcting their pretests and correcting any misspellings. **DAY 1** *439i*

❑ **Think and Practice** Connect spelling to the phonics generalization for final *le, al, en*. **DAY 2** *439i*

### PRACTICE/APPLY

❑ **Connect to Writing** Have students use spelling words to write an advertisement for a one-day tour. Then review frequently misspelled words: *people, hospital*. **DAY 3** *439j*

❑ **Homework** Word Study and Spelling Practice Book pp. 65–68. **EVERY DAY**

### RETEACH/REVIEW

❑ **Review** Review spelling words to prepare for the posttest. Then provide students with a spelling strategy—problem parts. **DAY 4** *439j*

### ASSESS

❑ **Posttest** Use dictation sentences to give the posttest for words with final *le, al, en*. **DAY 5** *439j*

### Spelling Words

| | | |
|---|---|---|
| 1. chicken | 8. needle* | 15. spiral |
| 2. eleven | 9. single | 16. marble |
| 3. given | 10. citizen | 17. oval* |
| 4. jungle* | 11. threaten* | 18. mumble |
| 5. national | 12. diagonal | 19. tangle |
| 6. several* | 13. paddle* | 20. frighten |
| 7. natural* | 14. animal* | |

### Challenge Words

| | | |
|---|---|---|
| 21. strengthen | 23. individual | 25. three-dimensional |
| 22. knuckle | 24. cubicle | |

*Word from the selection

## RESEARCH AND INQUIRY

❑ **Internet Inquiry** Have students conduct an Internet inquiry on animal behavior. **EVERY DAY** *439k*

❑ **Poster/Announcement** Review the elements of announcements and posters and have students analyze a poster or announcement looking for answers to the questions *Who? What? When? Where? Why?* and *How?* **DAY 5** *439l*

❑ **Unit Inquiry** Allow time for students to conduct information searches for text and images to help them answer their questions. **ANY DAY** *391*

## SPEAKING AND VIEWING

❑ **TV Commercial** Have students work in groups to create a TV commercial advertising tours to vacation destinations. **DAY 5** *439d*

❑ **Analyze Commercials** Have students listen to a recording of an actual radio or TV commercial and answer questions. **DAY 5** *439d*

# Resources for Differentiated Instruction

## LEVELED READERS

▶ **Comprehension**
- ◎ **Skill** Compare and Contrast
- ◎ **Strategy** Visualize

▶ **Lesson Vocabulary**
- ◎ Context Clues

aquarium  dolphins  flexible  enchanted  glimpses  surface  pulses

▶ **Science Standards**
- • Animal Biology
- • Ecosystems

## Leveled Reader Database

### ONLINE
### PearsonSuccessNet.com

Use the Online Database of over 600 books to
- • Download and print additional copies of this week's leveled readers.
- • Listen to the readers being read online.
- • Search for more titles focused on this week's skills, topic, and content.

---

## On-Level

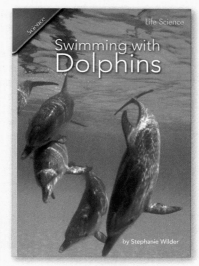

Life Science
**Swimming with Dolphins**
by Stephanie Wilder

**On-Level Reader**

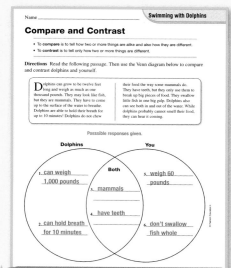

**On-Level Practice** TE p. LR14

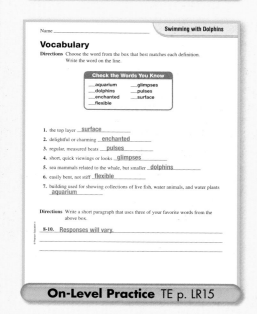

**On-Level Practice** TE p. LR15

---

## Strategic Intervention

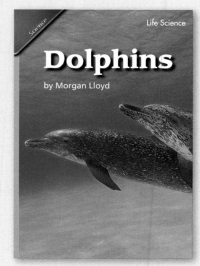

Life Science
**Dolphins**
by Morgan Lloyd

**Below-Level Reader**

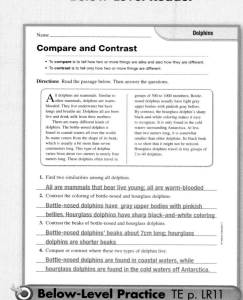

**Below-Level Practice** TE p. LR11

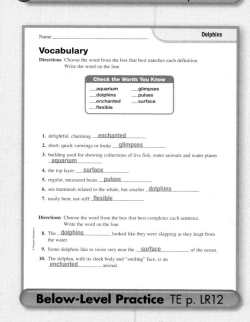

**Below-Level Practice** TE p. LR12

## Advanced

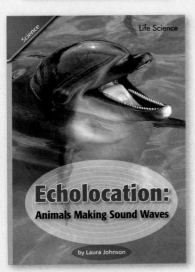

**Advanced Reader**

---

Name _____ Echolocation

**Compare and Contrast**

- To **compare** is to tell how two or more things are alike and also how they are different.
- To **contrast** is to tell only how two or more things are different.

**Directions** Read the following passage and answer the questions below.

Both bats and dolphins use echolocation, an ability to "see" using sound. Dolphins use their jaws, not their ears, to feel vibrations. Dolphins produce sounds called echolocation clicks. These clicks are short sound waves that bounce off objects in the water, then bounce back to the dolphin's jaw and then to the brain. Dolphins then create a mental picture of what is in the water around them. Echolocation clicks also can help a dolphin tell the direction an object is traveling, its speed, size and shape. Dolphins' tiny ear holes are only for hearing sounds above the surface of the water.

Bats produce their sound pulses differently than dolphins do. Dolphins produce sound in their nasal passages. Bats have a larynx or voice box that produces sound. Some bats send their sounds out of their mouths. Others snort the sound out of their noses. Bats' large ears can catch sound waves. When they catch sound waves, bats direct them to sound-sensitive cells inside their ears. These cells pass along signals to the brain.

1. What is one similarity between how bats and dolphins hear?
   They both use echolocation.
2. Contrast how dolphins and bats produce sounds.
   Dolphins produce sound in their nasal passages; bats have a larynx.
3. Contrast the way dolphins and bats receive echolocation sounds.
   Bats receive sounds in their ears; dolphins receive sounds to their jaws.
4-5. Compare and contrast dolphins' and bats' ears.
   Bat ears are usually large; dolphins' ears are small. Bat ears are key to their use of echolocation; dolphin ears are useful only for hearing sounds above water.

**Advanced Practice** TE p. LR17

---

Name _____ Echolocation

**Vocabulary**

**Directions** Choose the word from the box that best matches each definition. Write the word on the line.

**Check the Words You Know**
- anvil
- cochlea
- echolocation
- hammer
- larynx
- lymph
- melon
- nose leaves
- pinna
- stirrup

1. the skin-covered outer part of an ear  pinna
2. the outermost bone of three tiny bones in the middle ear  hammer
3. the fluid in the cochlea  lymph
4. a method of finding objects by using sound waves or vibrations  echolocation
5. the flaps of skin on a bat's nose that direct sound forward  nose leaves
6. the fat-filled area in the front of a dolphin's head that focuses the echolocation clicks as they leave the dolphin's head  melon
7. voice box  larynx
8. a spiral-shaped tube in the inner ear  cochlea
9. the innermost of three tiny bones in the middle ear  stirrup
10. the central bone of three tiny bones in the middle ear  anvil

**Advanced Practice** TE p. LR18

---

**ELL Reader**

**ELL Poster 17**

**Teacher's Edition Notes**

ELL notes throughout this lesson support instruction and reference additional resources at point of use.

**Teaching Guide pp. 113–119, 244–245**
- Multilingual summaries of the main selection
- Comprehension lesson
- Vocabulary strategies and word cards
- ELL Reader 4.4.2 lesson

**ELL and Transition Handbook**

**Ten Important Sentences**
- Key ideas from every selection in the Student Edition
- Activities to build sentence power

---

## More Reading

**Readers' Theater Anthology**
- Fluency practice
- Five scripts to build fluency
- Poetry for oral interpretation

**Leveled Trade Books**

Below-Level

On-Level

Advanced

- Extended reading tied to the unit concept
- Lessons in the Trade Book Library Teaching Guide

---

## School + Home

**Homework**
- Family Times Newsletter
- ELL Multilingual Selection Summaries

**Take-Home Books**
- Leveled Readers

# Cross-Curricular Centers

## Listening

### Listen to the Selections

**MATERIALS** SINGLES
CD player, headphones, AudioText CD, student book

**LISTEN TO LITERATURE** Listen to *Encantado* and "Mysterious Animals" as you follow or read along in your book. Listen for comparisons and contrasts in *Encantado.*

If there is anything you don't understand, you can listen again to any section.

## Reading/Library

### Read It AGAIN!

**MATERIALS** SINGLES PAIRS GROUPS
Collection of books for self-selected reading, reading logs, student book

Select a book you have already read. Record the title of the book in your reading log. You may want to read with a partner.

Choose from the following:

- Leveled Readers
- ELL Readers
- Stories Written by Classmates
- Books from the Library
- *Encantado*

**TEN IMPORTANT SENTENCES** Read the Ten Important Sentences for *Encantado.* Then locate the sentences in the student book.

**BOOK CLUB** Get together with a group and discuss the writing style in *Encantado.* Talk about how the author could have written it differently and if you would have enjoyed reading it more or less that way.

## Art

### Make a Postcard

**MATERIALS** SINGLES
Postcard-sized paper or note cards, art and writing materials, student book

Make a postcard about the Amazon.

1. Choose something interesting about the Amazon, such as a plant, animal, building, or person, to show on a postcard.
2. Use the photographs and details from *Encantado* to help you draw a picture on the front of your postcard.
3. Add a label on the back of your postcard identifying what you drew.

**EARLY FINISHERS** Add a message on the back of your postcard telling something you learned about the Amazon.

## Scott Foresman Reading Street Centers Survival Kit
Use the *Encantado* materials from the Reading Street
Centers Survival Kit to organize this week's centers.

# Writing/Vocabulary

## Write a Journal Entry

**MATERIALS**
Student book, writing
materials

`SINGLES`
`PAIRS`

Imagine you're at the jungle lodge
after your trip with Moises. Write a
journal entry telling about your day.

1. Look back at *Encantado* to find
   details about the canoe trip.
2. Scan *Letters Home from Yosemite*
   on pp. 116–127 to get ideas for your
   journal entry.
3. Write a journal entry as if you were
   in the canoe. Describe a few things
   you saw and heard on the trip.
4. Tell whether you liked or didn't like
   the trip. Explain why.

**EARLY FINISHERS** Act out a canoe
trip through the Amazon. One
person can play a tour guide and
the other can be a tourist. Use
selection details and Words to
Know in your performance.

Dear Diary,
Today I took a cool canoe
trip in the Amazon. It was
scary at first. I almost
hit my head on a wasp's
nest and came close
to a tree full of biting
ants. But seeing the pink
dolphins was great! They
kept popping up near our
canoe and made funny
blowing sounds. It was a
great day.

# Science

## Find Dolphin Facts

**MATERIALS**
Resources on dolphins,
Internet access, writing and
art materials

`SINGLES`

Learn more about dolphins.

1. Use classroom resources or search
   the Internet to learn more about dolphins. Follow classroom rules when
   searching the Internet. Use the keyword *dolphins* and a student-friendly
   search engine.
2. List five facts you learned about
   dolphins.

**EARLY FINISHERS** Draw a picture of
a dolphin and label its important
parts.

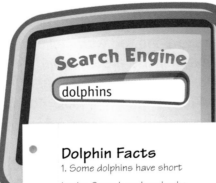

### Search Engine
`dolphins`

### Dolphin Facts
1. Some dolphins have short
beaks. Some have long beaks.
2. They can weigh up to 300
pounds and grow over 8 feet
long.
3. They eat squid or small fish.

**ALL CENTERS**

# Technology

## Compare Sources

**MATERIALS**
Online encyclopedia, Internet
access, writing materials,
T-chart

`PAIRS`
`GROUPS`

Compare searching an online
encyclopedia to an Internet
search.

1. Think of an Amazon animal that you'd
   like to know more about.
2. Work with a partner or group. Search
   an online encyclopedia for information about the animal. Use a student-
   friendly search engine for information
   about the same animal. Follow classroom rules when searching the
   Internet.
3. Compare your two searches. Write
   notes in a T-chart telling what animal
   you researched and what you liked or
   didn't like about each search.

**EARLY FINISHERS** Discuss with a
partner or group whether computer
searches about animals are better
than using books or magazines.
Give reasons for your opinion.

| Online Encyclopedia Search | Internet Search |
|---|---|
| Did a search on centipedes | Did a search on centipedes |
| Found a whole article on centipedes | Lots of Web sites but some didn't have facts that I wanted |
| Only had 1 picture | Found pictures of centipedes but they take a long time to download |

*Encantado* **416k**

- Build vocabulary by finding words related to the lesson concept.
- Listen for comparisons.

## Concept Vocabulary

**agility** the ability to move quickly and easily; nimbleness

**endowed** born with; provided with some ability, quality, or talent

**relationship** condition that exists between people or groups that deal with each other

### Monitor Progress

#### Check Vocabulary

| If... | then... review the lesson concept. Place the words on the web and provide additional words for practice, such as *leaped* and *affection*. |
|---|---|
| students are unable to place words on the web, | |

SUCCESS PREDICTOR

### DAY 1   Grouping Options

**Reading**

**Whole Group**
Introduce and discuss the Question of the Week. Then use pp. 416l–418b.

**Group Time**
*Differentiated Instruction*
**Read** this week's Leveled Readers. See pp. 416f–416g for the small group lesson plan.

**Whole Group**
Use p. 439a.

**Language Arts**
Use pp. 439e–439k.

# Build Concepts

## FLUENCY

**MODEL JUNCTURE** As you read "Sugar," emphasize examples of juncture—phrasing or chunking groups of words together in a way that reflects understanding of the text and engages readers. Pay special attention to prepositional phrases, setting them off with pauses.

## LISTENING COMPREHENSION

After reading "Sugar," use the following questions to assess listening comprehension.

1. **How is Sugar like other cats?** *(Possible responses: She purrs and plays in the sun. She hunts mice and crickets. She has fur and is agile.)* **Compare and Contrast**

2. **How is Sugar different from other cats?** *(Possible response: She has a mysterious sense of geography and a hip deformity. She has a strong bond with people, not just with the house she lived in.)* **Compare and Contrast**

## BUILD CONCEPT VOCABULARY

Start a web to build concepts and vocabulary related to this week's lesson and the unit theme.

- Draw the Animal Behavior Web.

- Read the sentence with the word *endowed* again. Ask students to pronounce *endowed* and discuss its meaning.

- Place *Endowed with abilities* in an oval attached to *Animal Behavior.* Explain that animals are *endowed,* or born, with some behaviors and abilities. Read the sentences in which *agility* and *relationship* appear. Have students pronounce the words, place them on the Web, and provide reasons.

- Brainstorm additional words and categories for the Web. Keep the Web on display and add words throughout the week.

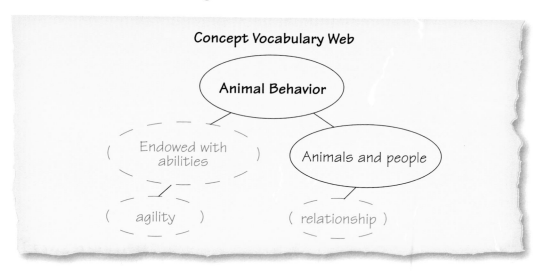

Concept Vocabulary Web

# SUGAR
## Cross-Country Traveler

### by Jean Craighead George

*Sugar appeared to be like any normal house cat that purred and played in the sun, but the Woods family soon learned that she was endowed with a mysterious sense of geography that has yet to be explained.*

When she was several years old, Sugar walked into the Woods' farmhouse in California. Her long, creamy hair and copper eyes provoked admiration, and she soon had bowls of cream and bits of fish set before her. She also demanded affection, and when Mrs. Woods picked her up to stroke her beautiful fur and say nice things to her, her fingers found a deformity in Sugar's left hip. It did not seem to interfere with the cat's stride or agility, but it was there.

Gradually she bonded not with the house, as do most cats, but with Mr. and Mrs. Woods. The relationship between them deepened over the years. The only problem Sugar presented her owners was that she would not ride in cars. They could not take her on vacations; they could not take her on visits to family and friends. Sugar seemed to be saying to them that her deformed hip was due to an automobile accident. But they could not know. Sugar brought them mice and crickets, told them with a "meow" that she was hungry. Or with a "merow" that she wanted the door opened, but where she came from and what had happened to her remained her secret.

Then came the crisis. The Woodses had the opportunity to move to a farm in Oklahoma, and they did not turn it down. Feeling that it would be cruel to force Sugar to ride fifteen hundred miles in a car, they did what they thought best. They gave Sugar to a neighbor who was eager to have her. Although they would miss her, they knew she had a good home, and they drove away satisfied that Sugar would be happy.

Two weeks after the Woodses left California, Sugar disappeared.

Fourteen months later, Mrs. Woods was in her barn working when a part-Persian cat leaped through the window and landed softly on her shoulder.

Mrs. Woods took her in her arms. She saw the cream-colored fur and the copper eyes. Then she ran her fingers over the hip.

"Sugar," she said. "It's you!"

Mrs. Woods called her friend in California. "Yes," she said, "Sugar did run away."

No one had given her a ride; no one had reported seeing her. Sugar had crossed fifteen hundred miles of deserts and mountains. She had passed through or around towns. She had eaten well, avoided cars, and had somehow found the Woodses on their new farm in Oklahoma.

Even now, scientists wonder what signals from the earth Sugar listened to on her long journey across the southwestern United States.

**BEFORE READING**

## Activate Prior Knowledge

Before students listen to the Read Aloud, have them share their experiences of pets that have done interesting and amazing things.

## Set Purpose

Read aloud the title and ask students to predict what the selection will be about.

Read the introduction aloud. Have students listen for ways a special cat named Sugar is similar to and different from other cats.

## Creative Response

If Sugar could speak, what would she say about her trip? Have pairs improvise a dialogue between Mrs. Woods and Sugar. Encourage students playing Sugar to act and sound cat-like. **Drama**

**Build Background** Before students listen to the Read Aloud, explain that the phrase *endowed with a mysterious sense of geography* in the introduction means the cat could find her way around and no one could explain how.

**Homework** Send home this week's Family Times newsletter.

**SUCCESS PREDICTOR**

**Vocabulary**

SKILLS ⟷ STRATEGIES IN CONTEXT

# Compare/Contrast
# Visualize

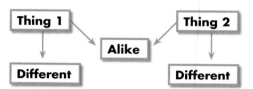

## OBJECTIVES

◎ Compare and contrast to improve comprehension.

◎ Visualize to compare and contrast.

| Skills Trace |  |
| --- | --- |
| **◎ Compare and Contrast** |  |
| Introduce/Teach | TE: 4.4 392–393, 416–417; 4.5 538–539 |
| Practice | TE: 399, 407, 423, 431, 545, 549<br>PB: 153, 157, 158, 163, 167, 168, 213, 217, 218 |
| Reteach/Review | TE: 4.2 197; 4.3 283; 4.4 415b, 439b, 499, DI-52, DI-53; 4.5 559b, DI-53<br>PB: 76, 106, 196 |
| Test | Selection Test: 61–64, 65–68, 85–88;<br>Benchmark Test: Unit 4 |

## INTRODUCE

Show photos of two animals that live in the rain forest, such as a pink dolphin and a caiman (pictured on p. 423). Have students use the photos and prior knowledge to tell how the animals are alike and different. (*Possible response: Alike: Both live in the rain forest. Both swim. Different: Caimans have legs; dolphins have flippers. Caimans are reptiles; dolphins are mammals.*)

Have students read the information on p. 416. Explain the following:

• You compare and contrast things by telling how they are alike and different.

• Visualizing, or picturing in your mind, the things being described can help you compare and contrast them.

Use Skill Transparency 17 to teach compare and contrast and visualize.

---

**Comprehension**

**Skill**
Compare and Contrast

**Strategy**
Visualize

##  Compare and Contrast

• To compare and contrast is to tell how two or more things are alike and different.

• Clue words such as *like* and *as* show similarities. Clue words such as *but, instead,* and *unlike* show differences.
Often, however, there are no clue words.

| Thing 1 | | Thing 2 |
| --- | --- | --- |
| ↓ | Alike | ↓ |
| Different | | Different |

## Strategy: Visualize

Good readers visualize as they read. This means they create pictures in their minds. Sensory words such as *sticky* and *crackle* can help you experience what you are reading. You can use visualizing to help you compare and contrast as you read. It will help you "see" how things are alike and different.

## Write to Read

1. Read "It's a Jungle Out There!" Make a graphic organizer like the one above to compare and contrast the rain forest and jungle.

2. Suppose you take a trip through the rain forest and then the jungle. Write a letter home about what you see and do in each.

416

---

**Strategic Intervention**

◎ **Compare and Contrast** If students have difficulty using the graphic organizer on p. 416, help them use a different compare-and-contrast chart, such as a T-chart or a Venn diagram, to compare and contrast the jungle and rain forest.

**ELL**

**Access Content**

**Beginning/Intermediate** For a Picture It! lesson on compare and contrast, see the ELL Teaching Guide, pp. 113–114.

**Advanced** Before reading "It's a Jungle Out There!" have volunteers explain the figurative meaning of the title.

# 'S A JUNGLE OUT THERE!

Well, actually, it's a tropical rain forest out there. t's easy to confuse the terms *rain forest* and *jungle*, ut they don't mean exactly the same thing. A jungle s a particular part of the rain forest.

In the rain forest, thousands and thousands of uge trees grow so close together that their tops verlap to form a kind of roof high above the forest oor. This leafy roof is called the canopy.

You can walk around fairly well on the forest floor under the canopy. That's because the tops of the tall trees grow so thickly together that they shut out most of the sunlight. Plants need sunlight to grow, but there's not enough light for them to grow under the canopy.

The jungle is another matter. In the rain forest here are clearings (for example, on the banks of ivers) where there are not as many gigantic trees. Iere the sunlight can reach the ground, so smaller rees and plants can grow. And do they ever! This vild, thick tangle of plants is the jungle. You would eed a big, sharp knife called a machete to hack our way through it. Good luck!

> **1 Strategy** Visualize a rain forest tree. See its height, its colors, its trunk, and its leaves. Now picture thousands of such trees together.

> **2 Skill** The topic is shifting to the jungle. Pay attention to how it is both like and unlike the rain forest.

> **3 Skill** Ask yourself how this is different from the rain forest.

> **4 Strategy** Picture yourself trying to go through the jungle.

417

Available as **Skill Transparency** 17

---

## TEACH

**1 STRATEGY** Model visualizing trees in the rain forest.

> **Think Aloud** **MODEL** I'm thinking about the description of the rain forest and try- ing to picture it in my mind. First, I picture a single tree with a tall trunk and large green leaves at the very top. Now I'll visualize thousands of trees together, forming a leafy rooftop canopy.

**2 SKILL** Model identifying comparisons and contrasts.

> **Think Aloud** **MODEL** So far, the article has described the rain forest. The sen- tence *The jungle is another matter* tells me the next part will describe how the jungle is different from the rain forest. When I read this section, I will pay atten- tion to how the jungle is like and unlike the rain forest.

## PRACTICE AND ASSESS

**3 SKILL** The rain forest canopy blocks sun- light, so small trees and plants cannot grow there, unlike the thick growth on the floor of the jungle.

**4 STRATEGY** Responses should mention struggling to walk through thick plants and using a machete to cut a path.

**WRITE** Have students complete steps 1 and 2 of the Write to Read activity. You might con- sider using this as a whole-class activity.

| Monitor Progress |
|:---:|
| **Compare and Contrast** |

| If... students are unable to complete **Write to Read** on p. 416, | then... use Practice Book p. 163 to provide additional practice. |
|---|---|

---

## Compare and Contrast

- To **compare and contrast** means to tell how two or more things are alike and different.
- Clue words such as *like* and *as* can show similarities. Clue words such as *however* and *instead* can show differences.

**Directions** Read the following passage and complete the diagram below.

All rain forests have four levels of growth that animals live in, from the forest floor to the emergent trees peaking out above the canopy. Although each rain forest is home to many animals, the animals differ from rain forest to rain forest. In Australia, a bird of paradise soars among the trees, but in South American rain forests, you may spot a scarlet macaw.

You'll notice a colorful cockatoo perching on a branch in Australia. In South America, however, howler monkeys hang out on the limbs. You might be frightened by the frilled lizard lurking in the Australian rain forest. But in South America, you'll have to watch for large animals, such as jaguars, stalking their prey.

**Australian Rain Forest**

**South American Rain Forest**

**Alike**
many animals live here
1. **four layers of growth**

**Different**
birds of paradise
2. **cockatoo**
3. **frilled lizards**

**Different**
scarlet macaw
4. **howler monkey**
5. **jaguars**

**School + Home** Home Activity Your child compared and contrasted details of a nonfiction passage. Read a book or article about animals and work with your child to find similarities and differences between two animals.

**Practice Book** p. 163

Have students find out more about pink dolphins using a student-friendly search engine on the Internet. Have them use the keywords *Amazon River* and *dolphins* for their search.

**Build Background** Use ELL Poster 17 to build background and vocabulary for the lesson concept of animal behavior.

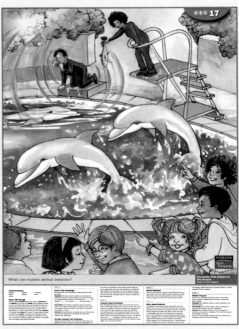

▲ **ELL Poster** 17

# Build Background

## ACTIVATE PRIOR KNOWLEDGE

**BEGIN A KWL CHART** about pink dolphins.

- Have students write as many facts as they can about dolphins. Record what students know on a KWL chart.

- Have students write three questions they would like to find out about pink dolphins of the Amazon. Record questions on the KWL chart. Add a question of your own.

- Tell students that, as they read, they should look for answers to their questions and note any new information to add to the chart.

**Topic** Dolphins

| K | W | L |
|---|---|---|
| Dolphins live in water and are usually found in the ocean.<br><br>Dolphins are usually grey in color. | How does a dolphin survive in the Amazon river?<br><br>Why are some dolphins pink? | |

▲ **Graphic Organizer** 4

**BACKGROUND BUILDING AUDIO** This week's audio explores endangered animals in the Amazon. After students listen, discuss what they found out and what surprised them about animals in the Amazon.

**Background Building Audio**

# Introduce Vocabulary

## WORD RATING CHART

Create a word rating chart in which students tell how well they know the vocabulary words.

**Word Rating Chart**

| Word | Know | Have Seen | Don't Know |
|------|------|-----------|------------|
| aquarium | | ✓ | |
| dolphins | ✓ | | |
| enchanted | | ✓ | |
| flexible | | | ✓ |
| glimpses | | | ✓ |
| pulses | | ✓ | |
| surface | ✓ | | |

▲ **Graphic Organizer** 5

Display the lesson vocabulary words and a word rating chart. Talk about each word. Have students create their own word rating charts, placing a checkmark in the column that describes what they know about each word. Allow students to use their glossaries to learn more about words they have only seen or don't know at all. **Activate Prior Knowledge**

Point out the prefix *aqua-* in *aquarium*. Tell students that it comes from a Latin word meaning "water." Have students name or look up other words that begin with *aqua* or *aque*, such as *aquaplane, aquamarine, aquacade, aquatic,* and *aqueduct*. Discuss meanings and their connections to water. **Latin Roots**

By the end of the week, students should be able to demonstrate their knowledge of lesson vocabulary words. Have them revise their word rating charts and use these words in sentences.

Use the Multisyllabic Word Routine on p. DI·1 to help students read multisyllabic words.

## Lesson Vocabulary

### WORDS TO KNOW

**T aquarium** building used for showing collections of live fish, water animals, and water plants

**T dolphins** any of numerous sea mammals related to the whale, but smaller. Dolphins have beaklike snouts and remarkable intelligence.

**T enchanted** delighted greatly; charmed

**T flexible** easily bent; not stiff; bending without breaking

**T glimpses** short, quick views or looks

**T pulses** regular, measured beats

**T surface** the top of the ground or soil, or of a body of water or other liquid

### MORE WORDS TO KNOW

**destination** place to which someone or something is going or is being sent

**submerged** put under water; covered with water

**teem** to be full of; abound; swarm

**T** = Tested Word

---

**Vocabulary**

**Directions** Choose the word from the box that best matches each definition. Write the word on the line.

pulses _____ 1. regular, measured beats

flexible _____ 2. easily bent

enchanted _____ 3. greatly delighted, charmed

glimpses _____ 4. short, quick views or looks

surface _____ 5. the top of the ground or soil, or of a body of water

**Check the Words You Know**
__aquarium
__dolphins
__enchanted
__flexible
__glimpses
__pulses
__surface

**Directions** Choose the word from the box that best completes each sentence. Write the word on the line shown to the left.

aquarium _____ 6. The show at the ____ features dolphins and sharks.

Dolphins _____ 7. ____ are mammals that live in the sea.

surface _____ 8. In one trick, a baby dolphin jumps above the ____ of the water.

enchanted _____ 9. The crowd is ____ by the magic of the dolphins' tricks.

glimpses _____ 10. Through portholes, visitors can catch ____ of the creatures underwater.

**Write an Advertisement**

Imagine that you run an aquarium and want people to attend your dolphin show. On a separate sheet of paper, write an advertisement that will persuade people to come. Use colorful words to make the show sound like fun. Use as many vocabulary words as you can.

Advertisements should included vivid words that appeal to emotions as well as vocabulary words. They should feature enjoyable aspects of the show.

**Home Activity** Your child identified and used vocabulary words from *Encantado: Pink Dolphin of the Amazon*. Together, write your own short story that takes place at the ocean, a lake, or a river. Try to use all of the vocabulary words in the story.

▲ **Practice Book** p. 164

# Vocabulary Strategy

## OBJECTIVE

 Use context clues to determine word meaning.

## INTRODUCE

Discuss the strategy for context clues with multiple-meaning words by using the steps on p. 418.

## TEACH

- Have students read "Dolphins," paying attention to how vocabulary is used.

- Model using context clues to determine another meaning of *pulses.*

**Think Aloud**

**MODEL** In paragraph 3, I read that dolphins send out *pulses* of sound. I know I can feel the *pulse* of blood in my wrist, but what are *pulses* of sound? My pulse makes a regular beat, so maybe a pulse of sound is a beat of sound. That meaning for *pulses,* "regular beats," makes sense in the context.

## DAY 2 Grouping Options

**Reading**

**Whole Group** Discuss the Question of the Day. Then use pp. 418–421.

**Group Time** Differentiated Instruction
**Read** *Encantado.* See pp. 416f–416g for the small group lesson plan.

**Whole Group** Use p. 439a.

**Language Arts**
Use pp. 439e–439k.

---

**Words to Know**

| dolphins |
| surface |
| pulses |
| aquarium |
| flexible |
| enchanted |
| glimpses |

**Remember**

Try the strategy. Then, if you need more help, use your glossary or a dictionary.

# Vocabulary Strategy
## for Multiple-Meaning Words

**Context Clues** When you read, you may find that the meaning of a word you know does not make sense in a sentence. This may be because the word is a multiple-meaning word, or a word with more than one meaning. For example, *story* can mean "an account of what happened." It can also mean "a lie, or falsehood."

**1.** Try the meaning you know. Does it make sense in the sentence?

**2.** If it does not make sense, think of another meaning for the word. Try that meaning in the sentence. Does it make sense?

**3.** If necessary, consider other meanings for the word. Decide on the best meaning and read on.

As you read "Dolphins," look for words that can have more than one meaning. Try each meaning to see which one makes sense in the sentence.

418

---

**Strategic Intervention**

 **Context Clues** Display a familiar word used in a new way; for example: *Our school won the swimming <u>meet</u>.* Have students tell why the more familiar meaning does not fit and offer a likely alternative meaning.

**E L L**

**Access Content** Use ELL Poster 17 to preteach vocabulary. Choose from the following to meet language proficiency levels.

**Beginning** Have students continue their Word Rating Chart (p. 418b) by predicting meanings for words rated *Have Seen.*

**Intermediate** Pairs can create vocabulary frames (Graphic Organizer 6) for words they find challenging.

**Advanced** Teach the lesson on pp. 418–419. Have students speak any word cognates from their home language to identify similarities.

Resources from home-language words may include parents, bilingual staff members, bilingual dictionaries, or online translation sources.

# Dolphins

Dolphins are animals that live in the sea. Unlike many sea animals, they are mammals, not fish.

Dolphins have long, smooth bodies, and flippers, not fins. When they swim, they move their tails up and down, not side to side like fish do. Dolphins have to go to the surface of the water to breathe. They breathe through a hole on top of their head.

Dolphins use sounds to find things. They send out pulses of sound. The sounds bounce off an object and back to the dolphins. They use the sounds to tell where the object is.

If you take an expedition to an aquarium or a zoo, you will most likely see bottle-nosed dolphins. They are the ones that look like they are smiling. They are also friendly and smart. They can be trained to jump through hoops, throw balls through nets, and "walk" backwards on the water using their flexible tails.

People have long been enchanted by dolphins. The ancient Greeks drew pictures of them on pottery and walls. For centuries sailors have believed that catching glimpses of dolphins following their ships would bring them good luck.

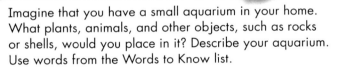

## Words to Write

Imagine that you have a small aquarium in your home. What plants, animals, and other objects, such as rocks or shells, would you place in it? Describe your aquarium. Use words from the Words to Know list.

419

## Connect to Phonics

**Word Study/Decoding** Explain that students can break words into syllables, or sound chunks, and read each part separately before putting them together to form the word. Model identifying syllabication by using *enchanted* from p. 419, paragraph 5. Have students suggest other multisyllabic words they know. Have them break each word into sound chunks, read each separately, and then put them back together. Check dictionaries or glossaries for correct syllabication.

## PRACTICE AND ASSESS

- Have students determine the meanings of the remaining words and explain the context clues they used.
- Point out that the way a word is used in a sentence—its part of speech—is a context clue. Have students reread the sentence with the noun *surface* on p. 419, paragraph 2. Then display this sentence, and have students tell what *surface* means in this context: *Dolphins must surface to breathe.* (verb; "to rise to the top layer of water")
- If students filled out a vocabulary frame (p. 418), they may fill out another frame with a different vocabulary word or a challenging word related to dolphins.
- Have students complete Practice Book p. 165.

**WRITE** Writing should include several vocabulary words as well as words about plants, animals, and other objects in a home aquarium.

### Monitor Progress

#### Context Clues

| **If...** students need more practice with the lesson vocabulary, | **then...** use Tested Vocabulary Cards. |
| --- | --- |

### Vocabulary · Context Clues

- Some words have more than one meaning.
- **Context clues,** the words around these multiple-meaning words, can help you decide the correct meaning of the word. If it doesn't make sense in the sentence, try another meaning.

**Directions** Read the following passage. Then answer the questions below.

> Kerry was enchanted by his visit to this delightful place, the rain forest. Just beneath the surface of the water, he saw fish unlike any of those in his aquarium at home. The trees grew so large that their branches reached out into the water, like flexible arms bending out into his boat. He was surprised when he caught glimpses of dolphins making their way down the long river. Kerry knew he would not have enough time to absorb everything that he saw. He knew he would return to learn more about this amazing world so different from where he lives.

Possible answers given.

1. Which context clues tell you that *enchanted* means "greatly delighted, charmed"?

   this delightful place

2. *Glimpses* can mean "sees" or "short views." How is it used in the passage? How can you tell?

   Glimpses means "short views"; "When he caught" is a clue.

3. *Surface* can mean "the outside or top of anything" or "to rise up." How is it used in the passage? How can you tell?

   the outside or top of anything; just beneath, the water

4. Which context clues tell you that *flexible* means "easily bent"?

   arms bending

5. *Absorb* can mean "to soak up" or "to learn." How is it used in the passage? How can you tell?

   to learn; "He knew he would return to learn more" is a clue.

**Home Activity** Your child identified and used context clues to understand words that have multiple meanings. Read a story or nonfiction article with your child. Find words that have more than one meaning and figure out which meaning goes with each word.

▲ **Practice Book** p. 165

# Prereading Strategies

## GENRE STUDY

### Expository Nonfiction

*Encantado* is expository nonfiction. Tell students that expository nonfiction explains a topic or idea and gives information about the real world.

## PREVIEW AND PREDICT

Have students preview the selection title and photographs and discuss the topics or ideas they think this selection will cover. Point out the word *Encantado* in the title and have students discuss possible meanings.

## Strategy Response Log

**Activate Prior Knowledge** Have students write what they know about the Amazon River environment in their strategy response logs. Students will monitor their comprehension in the Strategy Response Log activity on p. 429 by revising their ideas based on what they have read.

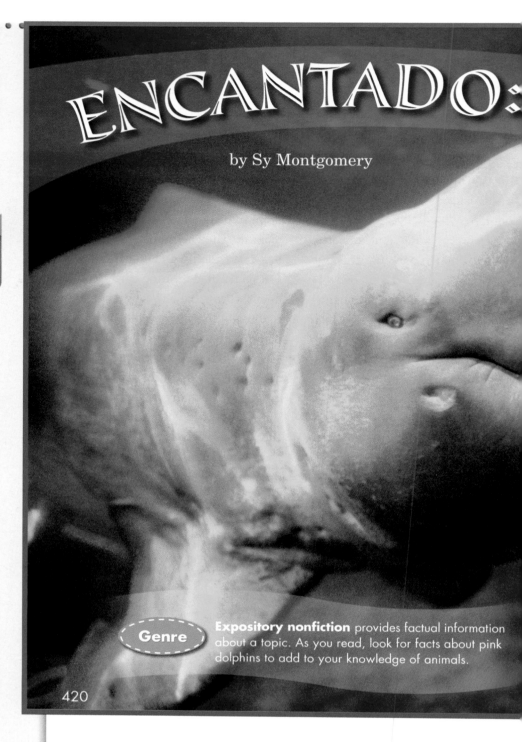

ENCANTADO:

by Sy Montgomery

**Genre**

**Expository nonfiction** provides factual information about a topic. As you read, look for facts about pink dolphins to add to your knowledge of animals.

420

**ELL**

**Access Content** Lead a picture walk to establish the setting. Scan the captions to preview the content.

Consider having students read the selection summary in English or in students' home languages. See the Multilingual Summaries in the ELL Teaching Guide, pp. 117–119.

# Pink Dolphin of the Amazon

In what ways are
PINK DOLPHINS
mysterious?

421

## SET PURPOSE

Ask students to tell how they think the selection relates to the theme of Unit 4, "Puzzles and Mysteries." Have them read on to confirm whether or not their ideas are accurate.

Remind students to visualize as they read to help them compare and contrast.

## STRATEGY RECALL

Students have now used these before-reading strategies:

- preview the selection to be aware of its genre, features, and possible content;
- activate prior knowledge about that content and what to expect of that genre;
- make predictions;
- set a purpose for reading.

Remind students that, as they read, they should monitor their own comprehension. If they realize something does not make sense, they can regain their comprehension by using fix-up strategies they have learned, such as:

- use phonics and word structure to decode new words;
- use context clues or a dictionary to figure out meanings of new words;
- adjust their reading rate—slow down for difficult text, speed up for easy or familiar text, or skim and scan just for specific information;
- reread parts of the text;
- read on (continue to read for clarification);
- use text features such as headings, subheadings, charts, illustrations, and so on as visual aids to comprehension;
- make a graphic organizer or a semantic organizer to aid comprehension;
- use reference sources, such as an encyclopedia, dictionary, thesaurus, or synonym finder;
- use another person, such as a teacher, a peer, a librarian, or an outside expert, as a resource.

After reading, students will use these strategies:

- summarize or retell the text;
- answer questions they or others pose;
- reflect to make new information become part of their prior knowledge.

AudioText

# Guiding Comprehension

**1**  **Compare and Contrast • Critical**
*Text to Self* **How is the weather in the Amazon like the weather where you live? How is it different?**

Responses will vary, but should describe at least one way local weather and Amazon weather are alike and one way local weather is different from Amazon weather.

| Monitor Progress |
|---|
|  **Compare and Contrast** |
| **If...** students are unable to compare and contrast the weather, **then...** use the skill and strategy instruction on p. 423. |

**2** **Predict • Inferential**
**What animal do you think an *encantado* may be?**

Possible response: An *encantado* may be a pink dolphin.

**Tech Files**
ONLINE

Students can search an online encyclopedia or the Internet to find out more about the Amazon River environment. Have them use the keywords *Amazon River* for their search.

## ENCOUNTERS *with* ENCANTADOS

You're traveling to a world that is full of water.

In the Amazon, the wet season lasts half the year. During the rainiest part of the wet season, from March through May, it rains every day. Not all day but every day. Sometimes the rain lasts less than an hour, and then the bright, hot sun comes out to burn your skin. But every day there is some **1** kind of downpour.

The wet season is the best time of year to explore the Amazon. You'll soon see why. So bring a poncho. On your expedition, you will watch the rain remake this jungle world. Swollen with rainwater, the Amazon River and its many branches—smaller rivers called tributaries—overflow their dry-season banks. The rivers flood people's gardens. Water

422

**ELL**

**Context Clues** Help students use context to figure out the meaning of *downpour* (p. 422, paragraph 2). Point out that the previous sentences all refer to rain and the wet season. Then act out the two parts that form *downpour: down* (point from the sky downward) and *pour* (pantomime pouring from a pitcher).

covers the village soccer fields. The school playgrounds are underwater. Instead of taking a school bus to class, the kids take a canoe.

The village school is like a treehouse, perched high on stilts. Many of the village houses are built on stilts, too. Others float on the river, like rafts. People have to tie their floating houses to big trees so they don't drift away.

On your expedition, you'll sleep in a jungle lodge on stilts. You'll visit Amazon villages where the little girls play with real baby caimans (a kind of crocodile) the way girls at home play with dolls—and where the people will tell you stories about amazing creatures they call "encantados."

*Encantado* means the same thing in Portuguese (the language most people speak in Brazil) and in Spanish (which people speak in Peru and many other South American countries). It means "enchanted." And once you meet an encantado on the river, you'll know why.

Some village houses float on the river.

**SKILLS ◆▶ STRATEGIES IN CONTEXT**

# Compare and Contrast

## TEACH

- Remind students that when we compare and contrast two or more things, we tell how they are alike and different.

- Model how to compare and contrast the weather in the Amazon with the weather where you live as you read p. 422, paragraph 2.

**Think Aloud** **MODEL** As I read this paragraph I think about how the weather is the same and different from my home town. The text says that during the wet season it rains every day from March to May. I know we don't have a wet season like that here. It says sometimes it only rains for an hour and then the sun comes out. I can picture that. It sometimes rains hard like that here, and then the sun comes out. I know what that's like.

## PRACTICE AND ASSESS

- Ask students what the author compares baby caimans to on p. 423, paragraph 2. *(dolls)*

- To assess, have students compare and contrast the houses in Amazon villages with houses where they live. *(Possible response: People live in houses in the Amazon just like they do here. The houses here are not built on stilts and do not float like some houses in the Amazon.)*

# Guiding Comprehension

**③ Generalize • Inferential**

**Reread p. 424, paragraph 1. Identify a generalization in the text.**

Everything about them sounds impossible: pink dolphins!

| Monitor Progress |
| --- |
| **REVIEW Generalize** |

| **If...** students have difficulty identifying a generalization, | **then...** use the skill and strategy instruction on p. 425. |
| --- | --- |

**④ ⊚ Compare and Contrast • Inferential**

**How are pink dolphins different from ocean dolphins?**

Possible responses: Pink dolphins don't have fins on their backs like ocean dolphins do. Pink dolphins are flexible while ocean dolphins are not. Pink dolphins do not leap out of the water like ocean dolphins.

**⑤ Alliteration • Critical**

**What is it called when a pink dolphin touches its tail to its nose? Tell why this name is an alliteration.**

Dolphin doughnut. It's an alliteration because the *d* sound is repeated at the beginning of each word.

## WHALES of the AMAZON

Everything about them sounds impossible: pink dolphins! Dolphins who live in rivers, not in the ocean. And not just any rivers: these are rain-forest dolphins, who swim in a ③ submerged jungle.

And look how they do it. Unlike the athletic dolphins who jump through hoops for aquarium shows, pink dolphins don't leap out of the water. Watch: they swim slowly, low in the water. They don't look like "regular" dolphins, either: Unlike the ones who swim in the sea, the pink dolphin doesn't have a tall, pointed fin on the back, sticking out of the water like a shark's. Pink dolphins just have a low ridge, which makes ④ them difficult to spot.

Besides making sounds from their mouths, dolphins (as well as many whales) can also send out pulses of sound, like an invisible beam of light, from inside their foreheads. The sound beams are too high-pitched for our ears. Listening with the help of special underwater microphones and recording devices, scientists have learned that these sounds are a series of pulsed clicks. The clicks travel through the water. When they hit an object—a tree branch, a tasty fish, or even a swimming person—the sounds come bouncing back to the dolphin. That's right—it's an echo. Dolphins can locate objects by their echoes. That's why this sense is called echolocation. It's also sometimes called sonar, which ships and submarines use to probe the water, too.

In fact, the echoes form a three-dimensional image in the dolphin's brain, allowing the animal to "see" not only the object's shape and size but also its insides.

424

**Extend Language** Help students use a T-chart to jot down details to differentiate pink dolphins from ocean dolphins. Sample entries may be "lives in rivers/lives in oceans; doesn't jump/jumps; doesn't have a pointed fin/has a pointed fin; can bend/can't bend."

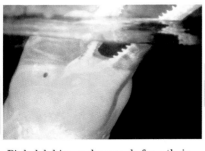

Pink dolphins make sounds from their mouths. They also send out pulses of sound from inside their foreheads.

Dolphin doughnut: a pink dolphin touches its tail to its nose.

In addition to this super-sonar, pink dolphins have another special talent. Ocean dolphins' bodies don't bend very well. They'd never be able to get around all the branches in the Amazon. Pink dolphins can bend their bodies to twist gracefully through the underwater treetops. They are so flexible they can even touch their tail to their nose—like a dolphin doughnut.

Because of their unique flexibility, pink dolphins can also swim in shallow waters that ocean dolphins can't manage. Sometimes they get stuck—but not for long. You probably have already noticed that pink dolphins have really big front flippers—almost like wings. At moments like these, those flippers come in handy. Pink dolphins can use their front flippers not just to swim but also to crawl—both out of and back into the water!

Sometimes pink dolphins' behavior seems downright weird. Here's another example: sometimes they sleep upside down. Imagine finding a 300-pound dolphin floating upside down like a dead goldfish! Why do they do this? Why don't other dolphins?

No one knows. And that's just one of the mysteries about them.

425

### Animal Characteristics

**TIME FOR Science**

In addition to the differences in color, movement, and flexibility mentioned on these pages, pink dolphins and other river dolphins differ from ocean dolphins in other ways. River dolphins have long, slender beaks and rounded, melon-shaped foreheads. Most ocean dolphins have shorter, distinct beaks. River dolphins do not dive like ocean dolphins. They spend most of their time on the bottom of the river, looking for food.

# Generalize REVIEW

## TEACH

- Remind students that a generalization is a type of conclusion in which a broad statement is made based on several examples.

- Model how to identify the generalization on p. 424, paragraph 1.

**Think Aloud** **MODEL** As I read, I look for statements that sound like rules. I also look for clue words that may indicate generalizations. In the first sentence, the author states that *everything* about pink dolphins sounds impossible. The word *everything* tells me that the author is generalizing.

## PRACTICE AND ASSESS

- Ask students to identify the generalization on p. 425, paragraph 3, and explain why it is a generalization. *(Generalization: Sometimes pink dolphins' behavior seems downright weird. Explanation: The word* sometimes *indicates a generalization, and the statement applies to many examples.)*

- To assess, use Practice Book p. 166.

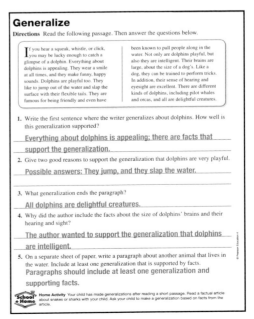

**Generalize**

**Directions** Read the following passage. Then answer the questions below.

If you hear a squeak, whistle, or click, you may be lucky enough to catch a glimpse of a dolphin. Everything about dolphins is appealing. They wear a smile at all times, and they make funny, happy sounds. Dolphins are playful. They like to jump out of the water and slap the surface with their flexible tails. They are famous for being friendly and even have

been known to pull people along in the water. Not only are dolphins playful, but also they are intelligent. Their brains are large, about the size of a dog's. Like a dog, they can be trained to perform tricks. In addition, their sense of hearing and eyesight are excellent. There are different kinds of dolphins, including pilot whales and orcas, and all are delightful creatures.

1. Write the first sentence where the writer generalizes about dolphins. How well is this generalization supported?
   Everything about dolphins is appealing; there are facts that support the generalization.

2. Give two good reasons to support the generalization that dolphins are very playful.
   Possible answers: They jump, and they slap the water.

3. What generalization ends the paragraph?
   All dolphins are delightful creatures.

4. Why did the author include the facts about the size of dolphins' brains and their hearing and sight?
   The author wanted to support the generalization that dolphins are intelligent.

5. On a separate sheet of paper, write a paragraph about another animal that lives in the water. Include at least one generalization that is supported by facts.
   Paragraphs should include at least one generalization and supporting facts.

**School + Home** **Home Activity** Your child has made generalizations after reading a short passage. Read a factual article about snakes or sharks with your child. Ask your child to make a generalization based on facts from the article.

▲ **Practice Book** p. 166

# Guiding Comprehension

**6** Vocabulary • Context Clues

**Based on the context of p. 427, paragraph 2, what is the meaning of *thread*?**

*Thread* means to carefully find a pathway through the river for the canoe.

---

### Monitor Progress

#### Context Clues

| **If...** students have difficulty using context to determine the meaning of *thread*, | **then...** use the vocabulary strategy instruction on p. 427. |

---

**7** Classify • Critical

**How does Moises classify the trees along the river?**

He classifies the trees by the dangerous sap and spines of two trees, and the beneficial flowers of another.

Moises Chavez at the helm of the canoe.

## NIGHTMARE DREAM WORLD

Canoeing through the flooded forest feels like a dream. Strange lives cling to every tree. Fist-sized, hairy megalomorph spiders, who look like tarantulas, hunt for bugs in tree holes. The purselike nests of little birds called oropendulas hang from the tips of branches. Centipedes curl in the cracks of bark. Snails cling to the undersides of leaves.

"Duck!" Moises Chavez (MOY-sess SHAH-vez), your Peruvian guide, calls out from the front of the boat.

A duck? Where? But no—he motions you to get your head down, fast. You don't want to smack your head on a low branch as the canoe glides beneath it. Particularly this branch—because hanging down from it is a wasp nest the size of a pumpkin.

426

**Extend Language** Point out that the word *like* is sometimes added to a noun and used as an adjective. Have students tell what they think *purselike* means on p. 426, paragraph 2, and how this adjective helps them visualize what the nests look like.

Fortunately, Moises knows these waterways well. He can warn you of the dangers. He grew up in the Amazon rain forest. His father was a teacher working in Amazonian Indian villages. Moises speaks some of the Indian languages, as well as Spanish and English. He has learned many of the jungle's secrets, including where to find the pink dolphins.

Today he's taking you to his favorite lake, where he knows you'll see pink dolphins. But to get there, you have to thread **6** through twisting waterways, the heart of the Amazon rain forest.

Trees poke out of the water on all sides. Moises explains that it's important to keep your hands away from the sides of the boat. It's easy to see why. Some of the trees have spines growing out of their trunks. "They're sharp as needles," he says. "Don't touch the trees! See this guy"—he points to a tree with smooth bark—"this guy has sap that can burn your skin. And this guy," he says, pointing to a short tree with yellow flowers, "from its leaves you can make a tea to cure yellow fever. And this guy—" **7**

Electric eels live in the Amazon River.

A centipede.

Hairy megalomorph spiders defend themselves with the hairs on their legs.

427

↻ **VOCABULARY STRATEGY**

# Context Clues

## TEACH

- Tell students that they can use context clues to help them figure out the correct meaning of a word with more than one meaning.
- Read p. 427, paragraphs 2 and 3. Model using context clues to determine the meaning of the word *thread.*

**Think Aloud** **MODEL** Moises Chavez is trying to guide the canoe on the river in the heart of the rain forest, but it is difficult. The author says Moises has to thread the canoe through the twisting waterways. Thread is used in sewing but that doesn't make sense here. I know another meaning of thread is to carefully make your way through something. I'll try using that meaning instead. "To get there, you have to carefully make your way through the twisting waterways." That makes sense.

## PRACTICE AND ASSESS

Have students use context clues to determine the meaning of *heart* on p. 427, paragraph 2. *(the innermost part; middle; center)*

# Guiding Comprehension

**8** **Cause and Effect • Literal**

**What would happen if your canoe bumped the tangarana tree?**

Thousands of tangarana ants would think I was attacking their home and would jump off the tree and into the canoe and sting me.

**9** **Author's Craft • Critical**

*Question the Author* **Why does the author compare Moises's pushing aside some tree branches to pushing aside a curtain on a stage? How does this comparison make the reader feel about Moises's action?**

Possible response: When Moises pushes aside the tree branches, the dolphin's lake is revealed like the set of a play is revealed when the curtain on a stage is opened. This comparison makes the reader feel that Moises's action is exciting and dramatic.

**10** **Visualize • Inferential**

**What words in the selection help you visualize how the lake looks in the dry season and the wet season?**

Dry: "a puddle." Wet: "full of rainwater," "larger than a thousand football fields," "a figure eight."

---

BANG!

Your canoe has come to an abrupt halt. The bottom is hung up on an underwater tree limb.

Your canoe is stuck in the treetops!

But Moises quickly gets the situation under control by pushing against a tree to free the canoe.

You're over the log, but you're not out of trouble.

"Watch out!" calls Moises. "Tangarana tree!"

Moises recognizes the tree's long, oval leaves right away. And he also knows that its hollow stems teem with thousands of stinging black tangarana ants. Each ant is more than an inch long. When something bumps against the tree, the ants think it's an attack on their home. Bravely, they'll rush to defend it. They'll even jump off branches into your

**8** canoe to sting you if they think their tree is threatened.

At the last minute, with some skilled paddling, Moises veers the canoe away from its dangerous path. You miss the ant tree by inches.

And then, pushing aside some branches like a curtain

**9** on a stage, Moises reveals your destination: the dolphin lake. You've made it.

During the dry season, the lake is little more than a puddle. But now, full of rainwater, it covers an area larger than a thousand football fields. It's shaped like a figure eight, with the

**10** crown of a mimosa tree poking up the middle.

Across the lake you can hear a dolphin blowing: "CHHHAAA!"

Some trees protect themselves with sharp spines.

428

**ELL**

**Understanding Idioms** Explain that the idiom *You've made it* (p. 428, paragraph 8) means "You have arrived at your destination."

Encourage students to record English idioms and their meanings in language journals, word lists, or computer files of English vocabulary.

The tangarana tree is home to thousands of stinging black tangarana ants.

429

 STRATEGY SELF-CHECK

# Visualize

Explain to students that they can visualize, or create pictures in their minds, to help them compare and contrast as they read.

Ask students to compare and contrast the dolphin lake during the dry season and the wet season. Have them reread p. 428, paragraph 9, and visualize the lake in each season to help them compare and contrast. *(Possible response: The lake is really small during the dry season. During the wet season, it is huge and shaped like a figure eight with the top of a tree in the middle.)*

## SELF-CHECK

Students can ask themselves these questions to assess their ability to use the skill and strategy.

- Was I able to visualize the lake to help me compare and contrast?
- Which words and phrases from the selection helped me to visualize?
- Did I compare and contrast the dolphin lake during the dry season and the wet season?

| Monitor Progress |
| --- |
| **Compare and Contrast** |

| If... students have difficulty visualizing to compare and contrast, | then... revisit the skill lesson on pp. 416–417. Reteach as necessary. |
| --- | --- |

*Strategy Response Log*

**Monitor Comprehension** Have students look at what they previously wrote about the Amazon River environment. (See p. 420.) Ask them to think about what they have read so far and revise their ideas based on the selection.

## Develop Vocabulary

### PRACTICE LESSON VOCABULARY

Students orally respond *true* or *false* to each statement and provide a reason for each answer. Possible reasons are given.

**1. *Dolphins* are a kind of fish.** *(False; dolphins are mammals.)*

**2. An *aquarium* is a building used for showing water animals.** *(True; dolphins sometimes live in aquariums.)*

**3. An *enchanted* evening may be described as being delightful.** *(True; something that is enchanted is delightful.)*

### BUILD CONCEPT VOCABULARY

Review previous concept words with students. Ask if students have met any words today in their reading or elsewhere that they would like to add to the Animal Behavior Concept Web, such as *echolocation*, *attack*, and *defend*.

*If you want to teach this selection in two sessions, stop here.*

*Encantado* **429**

# Guiding Comprehension

*If you are teaching the selection in two days, discuss comparisons and contrasts read so far and review the vocabulary.*

**11** 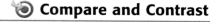 **Compare and Contrast • Inferential**

**Compare and contrast an aquarium tank with the dolphin lake.**

Possible response: An aquarium tank and the dolphin lake both contain water, but the water in the lake is dark, while the water in an aquarium tank is clear. You can see dolphins underwater in a tank. It is difficult to see dolphins underwater in the lake.

| **Monitor Progress** | |
|---|---|
| <img_2> **Compare and Contrast** | |
| **If...** students are unable to compare and contrast an aquarium tank and the dolphin lake, | **then...** use the skill and strategy instruction on p. 431. |

**12 Simile • Literal**

**To what does the author compare the pink dolphin's whirling movements?**

A Ferris wheel

## DAY 3  Grouping Options

**Reading**
**Whole Group** Discuss the Question of the Day.

**Group Time** Differentiated Instruction
Read *Encantado.* See pages 416f–416g for the small group lesson plan.

**Whole Group** Discuss the Reader Response questions on p. 434. Then use p. 439a.

**Language Arts**
Use pp. 439e–439k.

## REFLECTIONS *on the* WATER

You're surrounded.

At first, it seemed that you would see the dolphins only far away—just a pink shimmer on the water's surface. At first glance, you weren't sure whether you really saw one or just imagined it.

But Moises had a great idea. "Let's call them," he suggested. He leaned over the side of the canoe and, reaching underwater, banged on the side of the boat with his knuckles. The dolphins responded. And now they are all around you.

Right behind your canoe, you hear one blow. You twirl around, but all you see is the dolphin's wake, the wave it made when it dived just a split second ago. Then—"CHAAHHH!" A dolphin surfaces in front. "Look!" cries Moises—but you see only a trail of bubbles.

*A diving dolphin leaves a wake and a trail of bubbles.*

430

**Context Clues** Help students understand the meaning of *wake* in this context: ". . . all you see is the dolphin's wake" (p. 430, paragraph 4). The following phrase explains that it is "the wave it made when it dived." Explain that boats also leave wakes. That is, they leave a track in the water as they move through it.

This pink dolphin looks almost like a reflection on the water.

SPLASH! Off to your left, a big pink form has surfaced. But by the time you turn, you see only a tail.

If the water were clear, as in an aquarium tank, you could see them swimming beneath the surface. But the water in the lake is as dark as night. It's not polluted; it's stained with natural chemicals from decaying rain-forest leaves.

Because of the dark water, it's impossible to count the dolphins. It certainly seems there are several. After all, one **11** surfaced in back of the boat, then one in front of the boat. Another rose to the side. Does that mean there were three dolphins?

Maybe not. Remember that pink dolphins, with their bendy bodies, don't have to swim in a straight line. You can't predict where they might surface next. They can turn and twist beneath the water, even whirl around like a Ferris wheel. Maybe **12** the three glimpses you had were all of the same dolphin.

How would you tell? Most animals, including dolphins, look as different from one another as people do. You just have to learn to see the differences. Some are bigger than the others, some are darker. One might have a notch or a scar on the back or head. One might have a bent snout.

431

## Animal Survival

All dolphins, including pink dolhins, have a layer of blubber. Blubber is fat that lies underneath the skin of a dolphin, making up eighteen to twenty percent of a dolphin's body weight. The dolphin's species, habitat, and size will determine its body weight. Blubber insulates the dolphin and also acts as an energy reserve. The thickness of the layer of blubber can change with the seasons. Dolphins use their fins, flippers, and flukes to conserve or dispel heat.

# Compare/Contrast Visualize

## TEACH

Read the first three paragraphs of p. 431 aloud to students. Use this text to model how to visualize to help compare and contrast an aquarium tank with the dolphin lake.

**Think Aloud** **MODEL** As I read this text, I can picture an aquarium tank in my mind. The water is clear and I can see many dolphins swimming around. Then I can visualize the dolphin lake. The water is dark and I can't see the dolphins below the surface.

## PRACTICE AND ASSESS

Have students reread p. 431, paragraph 5. Ask them to choose the statement that best describes dolphins and people. *(Choice a)*

a) Like people, dolphins look different from one another.

b) Unlike people, dolphins look alike.

c) Like people, dolphins do not have differences.

# Guiding Comprehension

**13** **Cause and Effect • Inferential**

**Why is it difficult for scientists to study pink dolphins?**

Possible response: They are hard to see in the Amazon River. They don't leap out of the water, and the river water is dark.

**14** **Summarize • Critical**

*Text to World* **How can what we've learned about pink dolphins help us answer our questions on the KWL chart? Use this information to summarize what we've learned.**

Summaries should include information about the color and flexibility of pink dolphins.

## Strategy Response Log

**Summarize** When students finish reading the selection, provide this prompt: Imagine a friend has asked you what *Encantado* is about. In four or five sentences, explain the important points in the selection.

---

But here's the problem: because pink dolphins don't leap out of the water, and because the lake water is so dark, you never see much of any individual dolphin at one time. You get

**13** only little glimpses: the glistening pink top of a head here, a tail there, a quick look at the low fin on the back here. And you can't identify them by color, because these dolphins grow pinker with exercise, just as people do.

For half an hour, the dolphins, whether one or several, continue to visit near your canoe. Could they be as curious about you as you are about them?

As you and Moises paddle back to the lodge for dinner, you're full of questions about the dolphins. How many of them visit the lake? Do they stay there all year, or do they move to other lakes and rivers? Are there mothers with babies among them? What kinds of fish do they like to eat?

Moises knows a lot about the wildlife in the Amazon. But even he doesn't know the answers to your questions. "The

**14** bufeo*, they are very mysterious," he says.

*****Bufeo colorado** (Boo-FEY-oh co-low-RAH-doe) is another name for the pink dolphin. *Bufeo* is the local word for *dolphin*. *Colorado* is a Spanish word that means "ruddy or reddish."

Because they are difficult to study in the wild, pink dolphins remain a mystery to scientists.

432

---

**ELL**

**Extend Language** Encourage students to restate the phrase "You get only little glimpses" (p. 432, paragraph 1) using a synonym for *little glimpses.* For example, "You get only a quick peek."

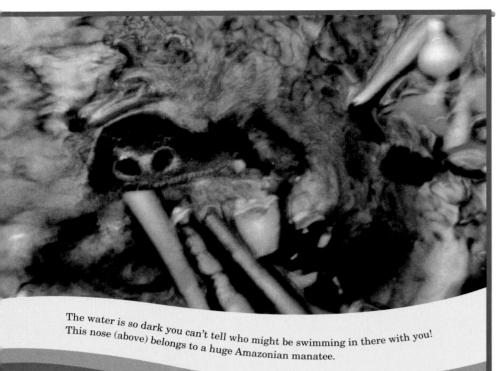

The water is so dark you can't tell who might be swimming in there with you! This nose (above) belongs to a huge Amazonian manatee.

433

## Develop Vocabulary

### PRACTICE LESSON VOCABULARY

Students respond orally to each question.

**1. Are *pulses* regular beats or soft noises?** *(Regular beats)*

**2. Is the *surface* of the lake the top or the bottom of the lake?** *(The top)*

**3. If you caught *glimpses* of a pink dolphin, did you see it for a long time or a short time?** *(For a short time)*

### BUILD CONCEPT VOCABULARY

Review previous concept words with students. Ask if students have met any words today in their reading or elsewhere that they would like to add to the Animal Behavior Concept Web, such as *surfaced* and *exercise*.

 **STRATEGY SELF-CHECK**

# Visualize

Ask students to name two ways that people and dolphins are alike. Encourage them to create pictures in their minds to help. *(Possible response: People and dolphins are curious about visitors to the places where they live. Individual people and individual dolphins do not look alike.)* Use Practice Book p. 167.

## SELF-CHECK

Students can ask themselves these questions to assess understanding of the selection.

- Was I able to picture and name two ways that people and dolphins are alike?
- Did I use words from the selection to help me visualize the similarities?

| **Monitor Progress** | |
|---|---|
| **Compare and Contrast** | |
| **If...** students are having difficulty visualizing to compare and contrast, | **then...** use the Reteach lesson on p. 439b. |

### Compare and Contrast

- To **compare and contrast** means to tell how two or more things are alike and different.
- Clue words such as *like* and *as* can show similarities. Clue words such as *however* and *instead* can show differences.

**Directions** Read the following passage. Then answer the questions below.

When Sir Henry Johnston went to the Congo rain forest in 1899, he found a mysterious animal. Its legs and back end were black-and-white striped, like a zebra's. Its body looked something like a donkey's, but with dark brown fur that felt like velvet. And its neck was long, like a giraffe's. What could this be? This unusual animal is the okapi. Unlike most other mammals, it has only one home, the rain forest of the Congo. At first, explorers thought the okapi was related to the horse. However, they were surprised to find out that instead it is a member of the giraffe family. If you see this strange animal at a zoo, you may be surprised too.

1. What is the author trying to compare and contrast? Which words show comparison and contrast?

   okapis with zebras, donkeys, giraffes, and horses; like, unlike, however, and instead

2. How is the okapi similar to other animals?

   It has a zebra's stripes, a donkey's body, and a giraffe's neck.

3. How is it different from other animals?

   The okapi is different because it has all these characteristics.

4. How is the okapi different from what explorers expected?

   The okapi is a member of the giraffe family, not the horse family.

5. Which three phrases in the passage help you to visualize this animal?

   Possible answer: black-and-white striped, dark brown fur that felt like velvet, and long neck.

**Home Activity** Your child compared and contrasted details of a nonfiction passage. Read a newspaper article with your child about a strange or unusual event. Ask your child to compare and contrast the unusual event with more ordinary events. Have your child pick out details that help him or her visualize the event.

▲ **Practice Book** p. 167

# Reader Response

## Open for Discussion  Personal Response

**Think Aloud** **MODEL** The sight of houses on stilts along the river impressed me. Seeing the pink dolphins alongside the canoe was also impressive.

## Comprehension Check  Critical Response

**1.** Possible response: The author makes it seem as if the reader is on the journey. Sample sentence: *You're traveling to a world that is full of water.* **Author's Purpose**

**2.** Possible response: The pink dolphin has a flexible body that can bend and twist. This helps it swim in the shallow, crowded river. **Compare and Contrast**

**3.** Responses will vary but the comparison should include details about daily life in the Amazon during the rainy season and the student's daily life. **Visualize**

**4.** Responses should include lesson vocabulary and describe a trip to a dolphin show. **Vocabulary**

**Look Back and Write** For test practice, assign a 10–15 minute time limit. For assessment, see the Scoring Rubric at the right.

## Retell

Have students retell *Encantado: Pink Dolphin of the Amazon.*

### Monitor Progress

**Check Retelling**  Rubric 4 3 2 1

| If... students have difficulty retelling the selection, | then... use the Retelling Cards and the Scoring Rubric for Retelling on p. 435 to assist fluent retelling. |
|---|---|

SUCCESS PREDICTOR

**Check Retelling** Have students use the selection's illustrations, captions, and other text features to guide their retellings. For more ideas on assessing students' retellings, see the ELL and Transition Handbook.

# Reader Response

**Open for Discussion** A person who reads about travel is an armchair traveler. So you are an armchair traveler. Which sights and sounds impressed you as you traveled in the Amazon rain forest?

**1.** How does the author involve you in her journey to the Amazon? Find sample sentences that show how she brings the reader along to the rain forest. **Think Like an Author**

**2.** Reread pages 424–425. Describe the special body structure of the pink dolphin. What is it able to do because of this body structure? **Compare and Contrast**

**3.** Use details from the selection to create a mental image of daily life in the Amazon during the rainy season. What is it like? How does it compare to your own daily life? **Visualize**

**4.** Write an article for the school newspaper about a class trip to a dolphin show. Make it exciting for your classmates. Use words from the Words to Know list and the selection. **Vocabulary**

**Look Back and Write** Why are pink dolphins called *encantado,* or "enchanted"? Support your answer with details from the selection.

Meet author **Sy Montgomery on page 772.**

---

**Scoring Rubric** | **Look Back and Write**

**Top-Score Response** A top-score response will use details from the selection to explain why pink dolphins are called "enchanted."

**Example of a Top-Score Response** There are many reasons why the pink dolphins of the Amazon are called *encantado* or "enchanted." So many things make them unique and mysterious. First of all, they are pink! They also live in jungle rivers, not in the ocean. Their flexible bodies curve and twist around the jungle's trees and plants. However, the dolphins are not easy to see, which makes them even more mysterious and magical.

**For additional rubrics, see p. WA10.**

# Write Now

## Travel Brochure

### Prompt

*Encantado: Pink Dolphin of the Amazon* describes the Amazon rain forest.

Think about a place you know and like.

Now write a travel brochure describing that place.

**Writing Trait**

Your travel brochure should **focus** on one place. Use strong, supporting details to express your **ideas.**

**Student Model**

*Introductory paragraph engages the reader and focuses on the topic.*

Are you looking for a quiet getaway? Are you looking for an exciting adventure? Whatever the answer, the White Mountains are for you. With mountains, lakes, forests, and beautiful towns, this is the ideal place for your next vacation.

*Supporting details describe the place.*

Come in the summer to hike, swim, or just sit on the porch. There are quaint hotels and log cabins in every kind of setting. State parks and beaches are excellent places to walk and relax. There are hundreds of species of trees, flowers, and birds to be seen. Don't forget your binoculars!

Come in the winter to ski, snowboard, and ice-skate. Test your skill on ski trails—Great Gulf and The Big Drop. Or why not try something new? How about ice fishing or snow sculpture?

*Final sentence summarizes the brochure.*

Whatever the season, whatever the reason, the White Mountains have it all!

**Use the model to help you write your own travel brochure.**

435

# Write Now

**Look at the Prompt** Have students identify and discuss key words and phrases in the prompt. *(travel brochure, describing)*

**Strategies to Develop Focus/Ideas**

Have students

- take out details that don't focus on the main idea.
- provide strong, supporting details to describe the place.
- anticipate and answer questions the reader might have about the place.

NO: Madison is great.

YES: A world-class city with a university at its center and a lake on either side—Madison is the place for you!

For additional suggestions and rubric, see pp. 439g–439h.

## Hints for Better Writing

- Carefully read the prompt.
- Use a graphic organizer to plan your writing.
- Support your ideas with information and details.
- Use words that help readers understand.
- Proofread and edit your work.

## Scoring Rubric | Expository Retelling

| Rubric 4 3 2 1 | 4 | 3 | 2 | 1 |
|---|---|---|---|---|
| Connections | Makes connections and generalizes beyond the text | Makes connections to other events, texts, or experiences | Makes a limited connection to another event, text, or experience | Makes no connection to another event, text, or experience |
| Author's Purpose | Elaborates on author's purpose | Tells author's purpose with some clarity | Makes some connection to author's purpose | Makes no connection to author's purpose |
| Topic | Describes the main topic | Identifies the main topic with some details early in retelling | Identifies the main topic | Retelling has no sense of topic |
| Important Ideas | Gives accurate information about events, steps, and ideas using details and key vocabulary | Gives accurate information about events, steps, and ideas with some detail and key vocabulary | Gives limited or inaccurate information about events, steps, and ideas | Gives no information about events, steps, and ideas |
| Conclusions | Draws conclusions and makes inferences to generalize beyond the text | Draws conclusions about the text | Is able to tell some learnings about the text | Is unable to draw conclusions or make inferences about the text |

## Retelling Plan

☑ **Week 1** Assess Strategic Intervention students.

☑ **This week assess Advanced students.**

☐ **Week 3** Assess Strategic Intervention students.

☐ **Week 4** Assess On-Level students.

☐ **Week 5** Assess any students you have not yet checked during this unit.

**Use the Retelling Chart on p. TR17 to record retelling.**

**Selection Test** To assess with *Encantado,* use Selection Tests, pp. 65–68.

**Fresh Reads for Differentiated Test Practice** For weekly leveled practice, use pp. 97–102.

SUCCESS PREDICTOR

Retelling

# Science in Reading

## OBJECTIVES

- Examine features of expository nonfiction.
- Practice a test-taking strategy.
- Compare and contrast across texts.

## PREVIEW/USE TEXT FEATURES

As students preview "Mysterious Animals," have them look at the headings and sidebars on pp. 437–439. After they preview, ask:

- **How do the headings help organize the text?** *(They organize the text into sections describing different animals.)*

- **Why do you think the sidebar information on the animals was presented in this format?** *(Possible response: It's a quick way to list important facts about each animal.)*

**Link to Science**

Have students choose an animal and make a list of questions they would like to answer.

## DAY 4 Grouping Options

**Reading**

**Whole Group** Discuss the Question of the Day.

**Group Time** Differentiated Instruction
**Read** "Mysterious Animals." See pp. 416f–416g for the small group lesson plan.

**Whole Group** Use p. 439a.

**Language Arts**
Use pp. 439e–439k.

---

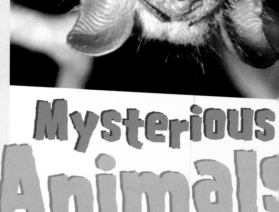

## Science in Reading

### Expository Nonfiction

**Genre**

- An expository article gives facts and information.

- The author often includes photographs and diagrams to support the text.

**Text Features**

- Heads in interesting type capture the reader's attention and organize the text into parts.

- Sidebar diagrams add information that is not in the text.

- Preview the article. Looking at the title, headings, and other text features will help prepare you to read.

**Link to Science**

Choose one of the animals in "Mysterious Animals" and use reference materials to learn more. Make a poster with a picture of the animal and the facts you find.

# Mysterious Animals

by Ann Weil

Some animals puzzle us. They look strange and they behave in strange ways. Now you can get to know four of these mysterious animals.

436

---

| Content-Area Vocabulary | Science |
|---|---|
| **rodent** | type of mammal with large front teeth used for gnawing. Rats, mice, squirrels, and beavers are rodents. |
| **webbed** | having the toes joined by a web such as ducks or other waterfowl. |

**Build Background** Preview the headings with students and link them to the photographs. Be sure students understand which animals are being discussed in each section.

# Wrinkle-Faced Bat

The wrinkle-faced bat sleeps during the day and goes out to look for food at night (like other bats). It does not look like other bats, however. Its face is covered with folds of skin. Why it has all that extra skin is still a mystery.

**Where it lives:** Mexico, Central America, and the West Indies

**Favorite food:** fruit

**Weight:** 1 ounce or less

**Size:** 2–3 inches

3 inches        3 inches

**Where it lives:** Northern Asia and parts of Europe

**Favorite foods:** plants, fruits, insects, fish, and small animals

**Weight:** 8–22 pounds

**Size:** head and body: 1.5–2 feet long; tail: 5–10 inches long

3 feet

# Raccoon Dog

This strange dog looks like a raccoon. It sleeps through the winter like a bear. Oddly, this dog does not bark. Hunters prize this animal for its fur.

**Visualize** Which words help you "see" the bat's face?

437

## EXPOSITORY NONFICTION

Use the sidebar on p. 436 to guide discussion.

- Explain that expository nonfiction provides information about the real world.
- Tell students sometimes expository nonfiction includes diagrams and photographs to illustrate the information.
- Discuss the specific information provided by the photographs and diagrams in this article.

 **AudioText**

**Visualize**

Words: *wrinkle-faced, folds of skin, extra skin*

## Food Web

**TIME FOR Science**

A food web is a connection between several living things that are linked because each uses another as food. All food webs begin with the sun. Plants take energy from the sun and change it to food. Rodents eat plants and sometimes insects. The bush dog is a carnivore (meat-eater) that eats mainly rodents. Thus, the bush dog belongs to a predator food web in which a larger animal eats a smaller animal that eats plants that get their food from the sun.

## Strategies for Nonfiction

**USE SIDEBARS** Explain that sidebars often highlight facts not stated in the text. When expository nonfiction contains sidebar information, such as the lists of facts and diagrams in "Mysterious Animals," we can use it to answer test questions. Provide the following strategy.

### Use the Strategy

1. Read the test question and identify key words and phrases.
2. Scan the bold text and diagrams in the sidebars, looking for matches to your key words or phrases.
3. Decide if you can answer the question by looking at one sidebar's information and diagram or if you need to compare and contrast information from all the sidebars.

**GUIDED PRACTICE** Have students discuss how they would use the strategy to answer the following question.

Of all the animals described in "Mysterious Animals," which one weighs the least? How do you know? Use details from the selection to support your answer.

**INDEPENDENT PRACTICE** After students answer the following test question, discuss the process they used to find information.

About how long is a bush dog from head to tail? Name an object that is about this long. Use details from the selection to support your answer.

# Grasshopper Mouse

This small mouse is not timid or quiet. It has sharp teeth and big jaw muscles for killing and eating its prey. Unlike some other mice, it does not squeak softly. Instead, it stands on its back legs and roars! Its cry can be heard more than 100 yards away.

**Where it lives:** North Ameri

**Favorite foods:** insects and small animals

**Weight:** 1–2 ounces

**Size:** 2 inches tall with a hea body length of 3–5 inches

3 inches

**Compare & Contrast** Think beyond the obvious when you compare.

438

**Guided Practice** Help students locate the weight of each animal in the sidebars. Ask: *Which weighs less, an object that weighs one pound or one ounce?* If necessary, let students hold objects that weigh about an ounce (a paper clip) and about a pound (a textbook). Then have students work in pairs to decide which animal weighs the least.

# Bush Dog

These dogs are equally at home on land and in the water. With their webbed feet, they can swim and dive underwater. Though they may swim like fish, these strange dogs sound like birds. Their "bark" resembles a whistle or chirp.

## Reading Across Texts

*Encantado* takes place in Brazil, a country in South America. Which of the animals in "Mysterious Animals" also makes its home in South America?

**Writing Across Texts** Tell two ways in which pink dolphins and one of these animals are alike and two ways in which they are different.

**Where it lives:** parts of Central and South America

**Favorite foods:** birds and rodents

**Weight:** 11–15 pounds

**Size:** head and body: 1.75–2.5 feet; tail: 4–6 inches

3 feet

439

## CONNECT TEXT TO TEXT

### Reading Across Texts

Have students scan the sidebar maps in this selection to locate the animal found in South America. *(the bush dog)*

**Writing Across Texts** Have students use a graphic organizer to compare and contrast two ways pink dolphins are like one of the mysterious animals and two ways they are different.

**◎ Compare & Contrast**

Encourage students to think about characteristics beyond size and shape when comparing animals, such as how the animals move or communicate.

## Habitat

A habitat is a place where a living thing lives or grows. The grasshopper mouse's habitat is the desert and dry grasslands of the western United States and northern Mexico. Grasshopper mice often live in burrows dug by other animals, such as a gopher. They eat insects such as beetles, grasshoppers, and scorpions. They also hunt and kill other small rodents, such as prairie voles, kangaroo rats, and white-footed mice.

TIME FOR Science

## Fluency Assessment Plan

☑ **Week 1** Assess Advanced students.
☑ **This week assess Strategic Intervention students.**
☐ **Week 3** Assess On-Level students.
☐ **Week 4** Assess Strategic Intervention students.
☐ **Week 5** Assess any students you have not yet checked during this unit.

Set individual goals for students to enable them to reach the year-end goal.
- Current Goal: 110–120 WCPM
- Year-End Goal: 130 WCPM

For English language learners, emphasize repeated readings to build fluency with enjoyable passages in English, with as much teacher guidance as feasible.

To develop fluent readers, use Fluency Coach.

### DAY 5 — Grouping Options

**Reading**
**Whole Group**
Revisit the Question of the Week.

**Group Time**
**Differentiated Instruction**
**Reread** this week's Leveled Readers. See pp. 416f–416g for the small group lesson plan.

**Whole Group**
Use p. 439b–439c.

**Language Arts**
Use pp. 439d–439l.

## PHRASING
# Fluency

### DAY 1

**Model** Reread aloud "Sugar" on p. 416m. Explain you will group words that go together, pausing after phrases and sentences. This makes reading sound smooth and helps convey meaning. Model for students as you read.

### DAY 2

**Echo Reading** Read aloud the last four paragraphs on p. 428. Have students note how you use punctuation to group phrases. Have students practice as a class, doing three echo readings of the last four paragraphs, p. 428

### DAY 3

**Model** Read aloud the last paragraph on p. 422. Point out how readers can use commas, dashes, and periods to group text and determine the length of pauses. Practice as a class by doing three echo readings.

### DAY 4

**Partner Reading** Have partners practice reading aloud the last paragraph on p. 422 three times. Students should group words such as prepositional phrases and offer one another feedback.

### Monitor Progress | Check Fluency WCPM

As students reread, monitor their progress toward their individual fluency goals. Current Goal: 110–120 words correct per minute. End-of-Year Goal: 130 words correct per minute.

**If...** students cannot read fluently at a rate of 110–120 words correct per minute,
**then...** make sure students practice with text at their independent level. Provide additional fluency practice, pairing nonfluent readers with fluent readers.

**If...** students already read at 130 words correct per minute,
**then...** they do not need to reread three to four times.

**SUCCESS PREDICTOR**

### DAY 5

**Assessment**
**Individual Reading Rate** Use the Fluency Assessment Plan and do a one-minute timed reading of either selection from this week to assess students in Week 2. Pay special attention to this week's skill, juncture. Provide corrective feedback for each student.

## RETEACH

# ◎ Compare and Contrast

## TEACH

Review the definition of *compare and contrast* on p. 416. Students can complete Practice Book p. 168 on their own or as a class. Tell students to use information from the passage to complete the phrases describing how bats and butterflies are alike and different. Point out clue words that indicate a comparison or contrast, such as *both, too,* and *on the other hand.*

## ASSESS

Ask students to read about raccoon dogs and bush dogs on pp. 437 and 439 and compare and contrast the animals. *(Both are dogs and both have fur. A bush dog's bark sounds like a whistle or chirp, but raccoon dogs do not bark.)*

For additional instruction on compare and contrast, see DI·53.

## EXTEND SKILLS

# Persuasive Devices

## TEACH

Writers sometimes use persuasive devices in an attempt to convince or persuade the reader to agree with their point of view.

- Writers may try to influence readers by using strong words, making vague statements, or including expert statements.
- Look for persuasive devices in writing to help you determine whether or not to believe a writer's claims.

Have students read the first sentence on p. 426 and discuss how the phrase *feels like a dream* is used as a persuasive device.

## ASSESS

Have small groups find examples of persuasive devices on p. 430 and write an explanation of how the author uses these devices to influence the reader.

## OBJECTIVES

- ◎ Compare and contrast two or more things.
- ● Identify persuasive devices in writing.

### Skills Trace
#### ◎ Compare and Contrast

| | |
|---|---|
| Introduce/Teach | TE: 4.4 392–393, 416–417; 4.5 538–539 |
| Practice | TE: 399, 407, 423, 431, 545, 549 PB: 153, 157, 158, 163, 167, 168, 213, 217, 218 |
| ▶ Reteach/Review | **TE: 4.2 197; 4.3 283; 4.4 415b, 439b, 499, DI•52, DI•53; 4.5 559b, DI•53 PB: 76, 106, 196** |
| Test | Selection Test: 61–64, 65–68, 85–88; Benchmark Test: Unit 4 |

## ELL

**Access Content** Reteach the skill by reviewing the Picture It! lesson on compare and contrast in the ELL Teaching Guide, pp. 113–114.

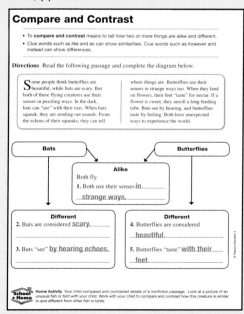

▲ **Practice Book** p. 168

# Vocabulary and Word Study

## VOCABULARY STRATEGY

### Context Clues

**MULTIPLE-MEANING WORDS** Remind students that if they come upon a familiar word that does not seem to make sense in a sentence, it may be a multiple-meaning word. They should reread the sentence and look for clues around it to other possible meanings. Have students review *Encantado* to find multiple-meaning words, such as those in the left column of the chart. Have them write what the word means in the context of this selection and what other meaning it has.

| Word | Meaning in Selection | Alternate Meaning |
|---|---|---|
| branches (p. 422) | smaller rivers | tree parts |
| stilts (p. 423) | | |
| pitched (p. 424) | | |
| thread (p. 427) | | |
| spines (p. 427) | | |
| figure (p. 428) | | |
| wake (p. 430) | | |

### Mystery Word Puzzles

Pairs can create word puzzles by writing clues for several words from *Encantado*, and drawing a series of blank boxes for the letters. Puzzle-makers may want to circle one blank in each answer so that the circled letters spell another mystery word.

1. | e | n | c | a | n | t | a | d | o |

2. | e | c | h | o |

1. "Enchanted" in Spanish
2. Pulse of sound that bounces back

## BUILD CONCEPT VOCABULARY

### Animal Behavior

**LOOKING BACK** Remind students of the question of the week: *What can explain animal behavior?* Discuss how this week's Concept Web of vocabulary words relates to the theme of animal behavior. Ask students if they have any words or categories to add. Discuss if words and categories are appropriately related to the concept.

**MOVING FORWARD** Preview the title of the next selection, *The King in the Kitchen*. Ask students which Concept Web words might apply to the new selection based on the title alone.

Put a star next to these words on the web.

Display the Concept Web and revisit the vocabulary words as you read the next selection to check predictions.

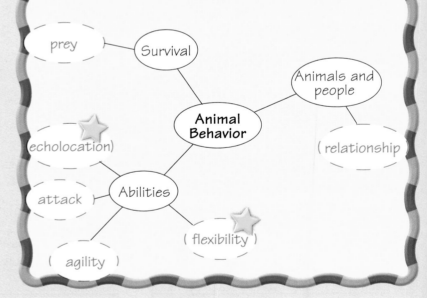

### Monitor Progress

#### Check Vocabulary

| If... students suggest words or categories that are not related to the concept, | then... review the words and categories on the Concept Web and discuss how they relate to the lesson concept. |
|---|---|

SUCCESS PREDICTOR

# Speaking and Listening

## SPEAKING

## TV Commercial

**SET-UP** Have students use the travel brochures they wrote in this week's Writing Workshop as the basis for one-minute TV commercials advertising tours to destinations from their brochures.

**PLANNING** Have groups meet and discuss the purpose of the TV commercial and choose the information they want to emphasize for the audience. Have them assign jobs to produce the commercial.

**MULTIMEDIA PRESENTATION** Remind students that TV commercials use words, sights, and sounds to sell products or services. Suggest students use background music or visual aids in their presentations. If recording equipment is available, students could videotape their commercials and then play them for the class.

### Rehearsal Tips
- Don't stop if you fumble a line. Just keep going.
- After the first rehearsal, jot down notes about things you like and things you may want to change.
- Discuss possible changes as a group and incorporate them into the next rehearsal.
- Decide on a final version before performing your commercial.

## LISTENING

## Analyze Commercials

**MEDIA TECHNIQUES** Have students listen to the TV commercials produced by their classmates or play a recording of an actual radio or TV commercial. Ask them to pay particular attention to the way sound is used in the commercial, including music and the use of actors' voices. After listening to the commercial, have individuals or small groups answer these questions orally or in writing:

1. **What is the purpose of the commercial?**
   *(Students should identify the commercial's specific persuasive purpose to get them to buy or do something. They may also point out that it provides information about a specific product or service.)*

2. **What kinds of sounds did the commercial use? Why do you think those sounds were chosen?**
   *(Students should note any spoken dialogue, singing, music, or specific sound effects and describe their impact on listeners.)*

3. **Think about the ways the actors said their lines. Did their acting affect your feelings about the commercial's message? How?**
   *(Students should cite details about the actors' performances and their effects.)*

### ELL

**Support Vocabulary** Use the following to review and extend vocabulary and to explore lesson concepts further:
- ELL Poster 17, Days 3–5 instruction
- Vocabulary Activities and Word Cards in ELL Teaching Guide, pp. 115–116

**Assessment** For information on assessing students' speaking and listening, see the ELL and Transition Handbook.

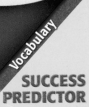

Vocabulary

**SUCCESS PREDICTOR**

# Grammar Subject and Object Pronouns

### Monitor Progress

**Grammar**

| If... students have difficulty understanding subject and object pronouns, | then... provide additional instruction and practice in The Grammar and Writing Book pp. 146–149. |
|---|---|

### DAILY FIX-IT

This week use Daily Fix-It Transparency 17.

**Spiral REVIEW**

### ELL

**Grammar Support** See the Grammar Transition lessons in the ELL and Transition Handbook.

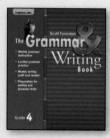

▲ **The Grammar and Writing Book** For more instruction and practice, use pp. 146–149.

---

## DAY 1  Teach and Model

### DAILY FIX-IT

1. Bob paddled threw the jungel in search of the pink dolphin. *(through; jungle)*

2. He gone on the trip last year with Carlos and I. *(went; me)*

- - - - - - - - - - - - - - - - - - - - -

### READING-GRAMMAR CONNECTION

Write this sentence about *Encantado* on the board:

> *She saw the pink dolphins, and they amazed her.*

Explain that *she* is the subject of the sentence and is a **subject pronoun.** The pronoun *her* follows the action verb *amazed* and is an **object pronoun.**

Display Grammar Transparency 17. Read aloud the definitions and sample sentences. Work through the items.

**Subject and Object Pronouns**

A **subject pronoun** is used in the subject of a sentence. Singular subject pronouns are *I, you, he, she,* and *it.* Plural subject pronouns are *we, you,* and *they.* When you use a person's name and a pronoun in a compound subject, be sure to use a subject pronoun.

| **Singular Subject Pronouns** | <u>She</u> went to Brazil. Luisa and <u>I</u> stayed home. |
|---|---|
| **Plural Subject Pronouns** | <u>We</u> looked for dolphins. <u>They</u> were hard to see. |

An **object pronoun** is used in the predicate of a sentence after an action verb or with a preposition, such as *for, at, into, with,* or *to.* Singular object pronouns are *me, you, him, her,* and *it.* Plural object pronouns are *us, you,* and *them.* When you use a person's name and a pronoun in a compound object, be sure to use an object pronoun.

| **Singular Object Pronouns** | The dolphin saw <u>her</u>. It looked at Luisa and <u>me</u>. |
|---|---|
| **Plural Object Pronouns** | We photographed <u>them</u>. They swam with <u>us</u>. |

**Directions** Write *SP* if the underlined pronoun is a subject pronoun. Write *OP* if it is an object pronoun.

1. <u>He</u> knows where to find the dolphins.  **SP**
2. Who saw <u>them</u> first?  **OP**
3. That dolphin is playing with <u>us</u>.  **OP**
4. <u>It</u> is swimming under the canoe.  **SP**
5. <u>I</u> could stay here forever.  **SP**
6. Please help <u>me</u> paddle this canoe.  **OP**
7. After a day or two, <u>we</u> will visit the dolphins again.  **SP**
8. Let's photograph Carlos and <u>her</u> in the canoe.  **OP**
9. I'll see the dolphins with <u>you</u>.  **OP**
10. <u>They</u> will swim up to us if we are quiet.  **SP**

Unit 4 Encantado  **Grammar 17**

▲ **Grammar Transparency** 17

---

## DAY 2  Develop the Concept

### DAILY FIX-IT

3. What an amazing color. That dolphin is. *(color that dolphin is!)*

4. It has long flippers and it's body is very flexible. *(flippers, and its)*

- - - - - - - - - - - - - - - - - - - - -

### GUIDED PRACTICE

Review the concept of subject and object pronouns.

- When a pronoun is used as the subject of a sentence, it is called a **subject pronoun.** *I, you, he, she, it, we,* and *they* are subject pronouns.

- Pronouns that are used after action verbs or as objects of prepositions are called **object pronouns.** *Me, you, him, her, it, us* and *them* are object pronouns.

**HOMEWORK** Grammar and Writing Practice Book p. 65. Work through the first two items with the class.

**Subject and Object Pronouns**

A **subject pronoun** is used in the subject of a sentence. Singular subject pronouns are *I, you, he, she,* and *it.* Plural subject pronouns are *we, you,* and *they.* When you use a person's name and a pronoun in a compound subject, be sure to use a subject pronoun.

| **Singular Subject Pronoun** | <u>He</u> saw the dolphin. Jo and <u>I</u> took photographs. |
|---|---|
| **Plural Subject Pronoun** | <u>We</u> swam with the dolphins. <u>They</u> are very fast. |

An **object pronoun** is used in the predicate of a sentence after an action verb or with a preposition, such as *for, at, into, with,* or *to.* Singular object pronouns are *me, you, him, her,* and *it.* Plural object pronouns are *us, you,* and *them.* When you use a person's name and a pronoun in a compound object, be sure to use an object pronoun.

| **Singular Object Pronoun** | The rain soaked <u>her</u>. Give the camera to Jo and <u>me</u>. |
|---|---|
| **Plural Object Pronoun** | We watched <u>them</u>. They played with Bill and <u>us</u>. |

**Directions** Write each subject pronoun.

1. We are studying the rain forests in class. **We**
2. I would love to learn more about them. **I**
3. Sarah, Maria, and she are showing us a forest model. **she**
4. It looks really interesting to me. **It**
5. Next week you and Jaime will tell us about the dolphins. **you**

**Directions** Write each object pronoun.

6. She explained why the forests are important to us. **us**
7. Please tell me how to save the forests. **me**
8. They are doing more research with Karl and her. **her**
9. Next week I will help them write a report. **them**
10. If we do a good job, Ms. Lopez will give us extra credit. **us**

**Home Activity** Your child learned about subject and object pronouns. Have your child explain the difference between subject pronouns and object pronouns by using the words *I, me, she,* and *her* in oral sentences.

▲ **Grammar and Writing Practice Book** p. 65

---

# DAY 3 — Apply to Writing

5. If you see a pink dolphin in its naturel habitat take a photograph. *(natural habitat, take)*

6. My friends and I am really excited, we expect to learn a lot. *(are; excited. We)*

## USE SUBJECT/OBJECT PRONOUNS

Explain that using both subject and object pronouns makes writing less wordy by avoiding repeated nouns.

*Too Wordy:* Todd and I said Todd and I wanted to see the dolphins. When Todd and I did, Todd and I were thrilled.

*Less Wordy:* Todd and I said we wanted to see the dolphins. When we did, we were thrilled.

**HOMEWORK** Grammar and Writing Practice Book p. 66.

### Subject and Object Pronouns

**Directions** Complete the numbered sentences with pronouns from the box. Use each pronoun once.

| you | us | it | I | she | me | they | him |
|-----|-----|-----|-----|-----|-----|-----|-----|

1. Bill, Valya, and ___ want to visit Brazil in the rainy season. 2. We will take waterproof clothing with ___. We want to see the pink dolphins. 3. ___ live in shallow river waters. The trip was Bill's idea. 4. It came to ___ when he read *Encantado*. 5. He persuaded Valya and ___ to go. 6. Unfortunately, we have no money for the flight, but we hope to earn ___ by selling cookies. Valya is a good cook. 7. ___ has some great recipes. 8. Do ___ think we will raise enough money?

1. ___I___      5. ___me___
2. ___us___     6. ___it___
3. ___They___   7. ___She___
4. ___him___    8. ___you___

**Directions** Imagine your class took a trip to the rain forest. Write a paragraph describing what it was like. Underline subject pronouns and circle object pronouns.
Possible answer:

We went to the rain forest along the Amazon. It is a very big river. Ms. Lopez gave us all umbrellas. One of the monkeys threw a banana peel at her. I didn't see any dolphins. However, we could hear them.

*School-Home Connection* **Home Activity** Your child learned how to use subject and object pronouns in writing. Have your child write a postcard from a rain forest. Ask him or her to identify subject pronouns and object pronouns in the message.

▲ **Grammar and Writing Practice Book** p. 66

---

# DAY 4 — Test Preparation

7. Are there any mooses in the amazon rain forest? *(moose; Amazon)*

8. You and me should eat before we gone to school. *(I; go)*

## STANDARDIZED TEST PREP

### Test Tip

You may be asked to identify the correct pronoun in a phrase such as *Alex and I* or *Emily and him*. Decide whether the subject pronoun or object pronoun is correct by saying the sentence with just the pronoun and not the rest of the phrase.

*Example:* I saw the dolphins.
<u>Alex and I</u> saw the dolphins.
I showed *him* the dolphins.
I showed *Emily and him* the dolphins.

**HOMEWORK** Grammar and Writing Practice Book p. 67.

### Subject and Object Pronouns

**Directions** Write the letter of the word that completes each numbered sentence.

1. "Look at the size of that spider!" Jesse said to ___. 2. ___ was enormous. 3. The spider looked at ___ and waved a hairy leg. 4. Jesse and ___ didn't wait to see what it would do. 5. ___ ran as fast as we could to our camp.
6. "What's going on?" Jaime asked Jesse and ___.
7. "A spider out there scared ___," said Jesse.
8. Jaime gave ___ a funny look. 9. "Spiders see me and ___ run away," he laughed.
Jaime went out to look for the spider. 10. I wonder what happened to ___.

1. A I
   B we
   C they
   **D me**

2. A You
   B They
   **C It**
   D Him

3. **A us**
   B she
   C we
   D I

4. **A I**
   B me
   C him
   D her

5. A Us
   **B We**
   C Them
   D Me

6. A I
   B we
   **C me**
   D he

7. **A us**
   B yous
   C I
   D we

8. A he
   **B him**
   C I
   D we

9. **A they**
   B he
   C it
   D me

10. A he
    **B him**
    C she
    D her

*School-Home Connection* **Home Activity** Your child prepared for taking tests on subject and object pronouns. Have your child write lists of the subject pronouns and object pronouns. Ask him or her to use the pronouns in sentences as you say them.

▲ **Grammar and Writing Practice Book** p. 67

---

# DAY 5 — Cumulative Review

9. Millions of ants live in this tree, it is the thier home. *(tree. It; their)*

10. Ouch? Now they has a painful sting. *(Ouch!; have)*

## ADDITIONAL PRACTICE

Assign pp. 146–149 in The Grammar and Writing Book.

**EXTRA PRACTICE** Grammar and Writing Practice Book p. 138.

**TEST PREPARATION** Grammar and Writing Practice Book pp. 155–156.

## ASSESSMENT

**CUMULATIVE REVIEW** Grammar and Writing Practice Book p. 68.

### Subject and Object Pronouns

**Directions** Write *SP* if the underlined pronoun is a subject pronoun. Write *OP* if it is an object pronoun.

1. <u>We</u> are rapidly destroying the rain forests. ___SP___
2. People cut down trees and use <u>them</u> for fuel or buildings. ___OP___
3. Then <u>they</u> farm the land. ___SP___
4. Saving the forests is a job for you and <u>me</u>. ___OP___

**Directions** Write each subject pronoun.

5. In a few minutes I will give you a report. ___I___
6. It describes how people can save the forests. ___It___
7. Later, we can discuss conservation. ___we___
8. Ms. Lopez and you can look at my photographs. ___you___

**Directions** Write each object pronoun.

9. We could not see them in the black water. ___them___
10. One swam right under us. ___us___
11. You could almost reach over the side and touch it. ___it___
12. It thrills me to watch the dolphins. ___me___

**Directions** Choose the correct subject or object pronoun in () to complete each sentence. Write the pronoun on the line.

13. Jonas and (I, me) present information about recycling. ___I___
14. Jonas tells Claire and (I, me) to help set up a video. ___me___
15. The video shows (they, them) how discarded plastic harms wildlife. ___them___
16. Students ask (he, him) questions about recycling. ___him___
17. Jonas tells the students and (we, us) how to conserve natural resources. ___us___
18. He and (they, them) will work together. ___They___

*School-Home Connection* **Home Activity** Your child reviewed subject and object pronouns. Listen with your child to the radio or TV for a minute. Ask him or her to identify some subject and object pronouns in the broadcast.

▲ **Grammar and Writing Practice Book** p. 68

# Writing Workshop  Travel Brochure

## OBJECTIVES

- Identify the characteristics of a travel brochure.
- Write part of a travel brochure using sensory details.
- Focus on focus/ideas.
- Use a rubric.

**Genre** Travel Brochure
**Writer's Craft** Sensory Details
**Writing Trait** Focus/Ideas

**Focus/Ideas** Talk with English learners about what they plan to write. Record ideas and help them generate language for support. Help them tighten their focus by eliminating unrelated details. See more writing support in the ELL and Transition Handbook.

## Writing Traits

**FOCUS/IDEAS** Strong supporting details make the topic clear and interesting.

**ORGANIZATION/PARAGRAPHS** Paragraphs are organized in the order of the seasons.

**VOICE** The writer speaks directly to the reader with enthusiasm and passion.

**WORD CHOICE** The writer uses exact nouns (*bluebells*), strong verbs (*capture, wander*), and vivid images (*crystal dance floor*).

**SENTENCES** Sentences are varied in kind and length. The writer effectively uses imperative sentences.

**CONVENTIONS** There is excellent control and accuracy.

---

## DAY 1  Model the Trait

### READING-WRITING CONNECTION

- *Encantado* focuses on the pink dolphins of the Amazon and the rain forest that surrounds them.
- Sensory details help focus the reader on the topic.
- Students will write a **travel brochure,** using sensory details to draw the reader into the destination.

**MODEL FOCUS/IDEAS** Discuss Writing Transparency 17A. Then discuss the model and the writing trait of focus/ideas.

 In the first paragraph the writer identifies the place to focus the reader on the topic. I know this brochure is about Lake Marisa. I also see that the supporting details give more information about this place. I don't see any unrelated or unnecessary information. Each paragraph gives details about a different season.

### Travel Brochure

A **travel brochure** tries to persuade readers to visit the place it describes. The writer of a travel brochure uses vivid, lively images to bring the place to life.

#### A Lake for All Seasons

**Opening sentence makes the topic clear.** At any time of year, Lake Marisa is the ideal place for a quiet getaway. Its peaceful waters capture the deep blue of a summer sky.

**Vivid images appeal to the senses.** In the fall, Lake Marisa glitters with red and orange. Admire the golden forest and feel the sharp touch of the new season.

Winter brings its own special beauty. The trees are clothed in white, and the lake is a crystal dance floor.

**The writer addresses the reader directly.** And don't forget the spring. Take time in May to wander on a carpet of bluebells and to smell the fragrance of new life.

**The ending neatly rephrases the opening.** Summer, fall, winter, or spring, Lake Marisa is the perfect break.

Unit 4 Encantado  Writing Model **17A**

▲ **Writing Transparency** 17A

---

## DAY 2  Improve Writing

### WRITER'S CRAFT
### Sensory Details

Display Writing Transparency 17B. Read the directions and work together to identify sensory details.

#### SENSORY DETAILS

*Think Aloud* Tomorrow we will be writing a travel brochure about a place we know and like. I know that sensory details will help the reader focus on that place. I'm going to think about my five senses, what I see, hear, smell, taste, and touch in this place. For example, if I think about the ocean, I could describe the salty taste of the water or the rushing sound of the surf.

**GUIDED WRITING** Some students may need more help with sensory details. Work with them to find sensory details in *Encantado* or another reading selection. Discuss to which sense each detail appeals.

### Sensory Details

To bring a description to life, writers use **sensory details**. Sensory details tell how something looks, sounds, smells, tastes, or feels. These kinds of details make writing vivid and real and help readers experience what the writer is describing.

| | |
|---|---|
| **Sight** | the glistening, black surface of the water |
| **Sound** | a slow, deep gurgling |
| **Touch** | the damp, slippery skin of a frog |
| **Smell** | a stench of rotting plants |
| **Taste** | soft and sweet, like an overripe banana |

**Directions** Decide which sense the writer is appealing to in each sentence in the paragraph. Write *sight, sound, touch, smell,* or *taste* on the numbered lines below.

(1) Thousands of trees rose around me like the walls of an enormous green prison. (2) The heat made my skin prickle and burn. (3) Golden sunlight filtered through the leaves. (4) The air was thick with the odor of mud and flowers. (5) My boots sank into the soft and spongy earth. (6) I licked the salty sweat from my lips. (7) A howler monkey shrieked like a mad woman in the branches above. (8) Then the terrible silence returned.

1. sight
2. touch
3. sight
4. smell
5. touch
6. taste
7. sound
8. sound

**Directions** Write a paragraph about a summer day. Use sentences that appeal to at least four of the five senses. **Possible answer:**
I love hot summer days. The sun sparkles on the fountain in the park and burns the back of your neck. Kids laugh and shout in the playground. The smell of popcorn drifts through the air. And I can almost taste the ice cream!

Unit 4 Encantado  Writer's Craft **17B**

▲ **Writing Transparency** 17B

# DAY 3 Prewrite and Draft

**READ THE WRITING PROMPT**

on page 435 in the Student Edition.

*Encantado: Pink Dolphin of the Amazon describes the Amazon rain forest.*

*Think about a place you know and like.*

*Now write a travel brochure describing that place.*

### Writing Test Tips

- Keep in mind that your purpose is to persuade people to visit a place.
- Use details that help readers get the "feel" of the place.
- Use dialogue to make your story realistic.

**GETTING STARTED** Students can do any of the following:

- Make a chart with the headings *Sight, Sound, Smell, Taste,* and *Touch.* They can then complete the chart with sensory details about their place.
- Shut their eyes and imagine the place they are describing. Ask themselves, "What do I see and hear?"
- Make a list of the top ten reasons to visit their place.

# DAY 4 Draft and Revise

**EDITING/REVISING CHECKLIST**

☑ Have I included sensory details?

☑ Is the main idea clear?

☑ Are subject and object pronouns used correctly?

☑ Are words ending in *-le, -al,* and *-en* spelled correctly?

See *The Grammar and Writing Book,* pp. 146–151.

### Revising Tips

## Focus/Ideas

- Make sure the place you are describing is central to your writing.
- Eliminate unnecessary details.
- Stick to your purpose, which is to inform and persuade your readers.

**PUBLISHING** Have students create folding brochures with text and photographs or illustrations. Some students may wish to revise their work later.

**ASSESSMENT** Use the scoring rubric to evaluate students' work.

# DAY 5 Connect to Unit Writing

| Story | |
|---|---|
| Week 1 | Story About a Discovery 415g–415h |
| Week 2 | Travel Brochure 439g–439h |
| Week 3 | Business Letter 465g–465h |
| Week 4 | Feature Story 487g–487h |
| Week 5 | Plot Summary 507g–507h |

**PREVIEW THE UNIT PROMPT**

*Write a story about something that happens on a real or an imaginary trip. Try to include suspense or humor and dialogue.*

**APPLY**

- A story has a beginning, middle, and end and focuses on one incident or event.
- Sensory details help readers "see" the characters and setting.

## Writing Trait Rubric

| | 4 | 3 | 2 | 1 |
|---|---|---|---|---|
| **Focus/Ideas** | Ideas focused and clearly described; many vivid sensory details | Ideas focused; some sensory details | Focus inconsistent; few sensory details | Description unfocused; no sensory details |
| | Travel brochure that vividly informs reader about the place | Travel brochure that adequately informs reader about the place | Travel brochure generally informative, but focus confusing or vague at times | Travel brochure unsuccessful in informing reader about a place |

# Spelling & Phonics  Final *le, al, en*

## OBJECTIVE

● Spell words with final *le, al, en*.

### Generalization

**Connect to Phonics** The schwa sound in final syllables is often spelled differently: *jungle, animal.*

## Spelling Words

1. chicken
2. eleven
3. given
4. jungle*
5. national
6. several*
7. natural*
8. needle*
9. single
10. citizen
11. threaten*
12. diagonal
13. paddle*
14. animal*
15. spiral
16. marble
17. oval*
18. mumble
19. tangle
20. frighten

### Challenge Words

21. strengthen
22. knuckle
23. individual
24. cubicle
25. three-dimensional

*Word from the selection

## ELL

**Spelling/Phonics Support** See the ELL and Transition Handbook for spelling support.

---

## DAY 1  Pretest and Sort

### PRETEST

Use the Dictation Sentences from Day 5 to administer the pretest. Read the word, read the sentence, and then read the word again. Guide students in self-correcting their pretests and correcting any misspellings.

#### Monitor Progress

**Spelling**

|  |  |
|---|---|
| **If...** students misspell more than 5 pretest words, | **then...** use words 1–10 for Strategic Intervention. |
| **If...** students misspell 1–5 pretest words, | **then...** use words 1–20 for On-Level practice. |
| **If...** students correctly spell all pretest words, | **then...** use words 1–25 for Advanced Learners. |

**HOMEWORK** Spelling Practice Book, p. 65.

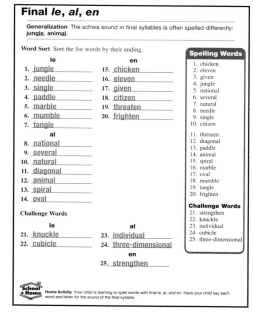

▲ **Spelling Practice Book** p. 65

---

## DAY 2  Think and Practice

### TEACH

The schwa sound in final syllables is often spelled differently. Write *chicken* and *national* on the board. Point out that the final vowel sound in *chicken* sounds the same as the final vowel sound in *national*, and that they are both the schwa sound. Guide students in finding the schwa sound in other list words.

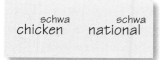

**FORM WORD GROUPS** Ask students to identify the schwa sound in each of the spelling words. Have them group words by how the schwa sound is spelled.

**HOMEWORK** Spelling Practice Book, p. 66.

▲ **Spelling Practice Book** p. 66

---

## DAY 3 — Connect to Writing

### WRITE AN ADVERTISEMENT

Ask students to write an advertisement for a one-day tour using as many of the spelling words as possible.

#### Frequently Misspelled Words

people    hospital

These words may seem easy to spell, but they are often misspelled by fourth-graders. Alert students to these frequently misspelled words.

**HOMEWORK** Spelling Practice Book, p. 67.

---

**Final le, al, en**

**Proofread a Story** Melissa is writing a story. Proofread her first paragraph. Circle six spelling errors. Write the words correctly. Find a run-on sentence and write it correctly.

| Spelling Words |
|---|
| chicken |
| eleven |
| given |
| jungle |
| national |
| several |
| natural |
| needle |
| single |
| citizen |
| threaten |
| diagonal |
| paddle |
| animal |
| spiral |
| marble |
| oval |
| mumble |
| tangle |
| frighten |

The Mysterious Path

All elevin students zigzagged in a diagone path across the wet field. Then they entered a forest that was as dark as a jungal the students had to walk through the tangle of bushes in a single line. Every thorn scratched like a needel Even though the students tried to hold their voices to a soft mumble, they couldn't help but frightan some of the animals. An animal ran across their path and snarled, trying to threaten these strange peeple

1. eleven          2. diagonal
3. jungle          4. needle
5. frighten        6. people
7. Then they entered a forest that was dark as a jungle. The students had to walk through the tangle of bushes in a single line.

**Frequently Misspelled Words**

people
hospital

**Proofread Words** Fill in the circle beside the word that is spelled correctly. Write the word.

8. ○ ovel   ● oval   ○ ovle          8. oval
9. ○ nationel  ○ nationle  ● national   9. national
10. ● citizen  ○ citisan  ○ citizin   10. citizen
11. ○ marbl  ○ marbel  ● marble   11. marble
12. ● spiral  ○ spirle  ○ spirel   12. spiral

**School + Home** **Home Activity** Your child identified misspelled words that end with le, al, and en. Say list words that end with the schwa-l sound and have your child tell whether the final syllable is spelled with an le or al.

▲ **Spelling Practice Book** p. 67

---

## DAY 4 — Review

### REVIEW FINAL le, al, en

Have each student create a fill-in-the-blanks puzzle, by writing ten list words with letters missing. They can exchange puzzles with a partner and complete the puzzles.

#### Spelling Strategy
#### Problem Parts

Correct pronunciation can help with correct spelling. Have students say each word correctly, listening to the sound of each letter. Then have students say the word again as they write it.

**HOMEWORK** Spelling Practice Book, p. 68.

---

**Final le, al, en**

| Spelling Words | | | | |
|---|---|---|---|---|
| chicken | eleven | given | jungle | national |
| several | natural | needle | single | citizen |
| threaten | diagonal | paddle | animal | spiral |
| marble | oval | mumble | tangle | frighten |

**Word Match** Add le, al, or en to complete each word. Write it.

1. anim___          1. animal
2. citiz___         2. citizen
3. padd___          3. paddle
4. threat___        4. threaten
5. diagon___        5. diagonal
6. elev___          6. eleven
7. giv___           7. given
8. marb___          8. marble
9. spir___          9. spiral
10. fright___       10. frighten

**Word Scramble** Rewrite the list words.

11. aglent          11. tangle
12. glujen          12. jungle
13. aovl            13. oval
14. lenede          14. needle
15. legins          15. single
16. bummel          16. mumble
17. alveres         17. several
18. intanola        18. national
19. unatral         19. natural
20. kecchin         20. chicken

**School + Home** **Home Activity** Your child has learned to read, write, and spell words with el, al, and en endings. Have your child pick the ten hardest words in the list. Write them as your child dictates them. Make mistakes and have your child correct your spelling.

▲ **Spelling Practice Book** p. 68

---

## DAY 5 — Posttest

### DICTATION SENTENCES

1. That was the best chicken soup I've ever had.
2. The number that follows ten is eleven.
3. I would have given it to you if you had asked.
4. Many plants grow in a jungle.
5. We went to a national park.
6. There are several kinds of roses in my garden.
7. It is important to preserve natural resources.
8. I need to thread this needle.
9. I followed every single rule.
10. Almost every citizen of the town saw the parade.
11. You should not threaten people.
12. Draw a diagonal line.
13. I left the paddle in the canoe.
14. I saw that animal at the zoo.
15. The room had a spiral staircase.
16. The bowl is made of marble.
17. An egg is shaped like an oval.
18. When I feel shy I tend to mumble.
19. Try not to tangle the cord.
20. Thunder does not frighten me.

### CHALLENGE

21. Exercise will strengthen your muscles.
22. I bruised my knuckle with the hammer.
23. Every individual person is different.
24. My father works in a cubicle.
25. A cube is a three-dimensional figure.

**OBJECTIVES**

- Formulate an inquiry question that is connected to this week's lesson focus.

- Effectively and efficiently find, evaluate, and communicate information related to an inquiry question using electronic sources.

| New Literacies | |
|---|---|
| Day 1 | Identify Questions |
| Day 2 | Navigate/Search |
| Day 3 | Analyze |
| Day 4 | Synthesize |
| Day 5 | Communicate |

## NEW LITERACIES

# Internet Inquiry Activity

## EXPLORE ANIMAL BEHAVIOR

Use the following 5-day plan to help students conduct this week's Internet inquiry activity on animal behavior. Remind students to follow classroom rules when using the Internet.

### DAY 1

**Identify Questions** Discuss the focus question: *What can explain animal behavior?* Have students brainstorm different kinds of animal behaviors they find odd or interesting. Have students work individually, in pairs, or in small groups to write an inquiry question about an animal behavior they want to understand.

### DAY 2

**Navigate/Search** Instruct students to begin a simple Internet search using a student-friendly search engine and keywords related to their question. They should identify a few sites to explore further and record their URLs or bookmark them, if allowed.

### DAY 3

**Analyze** Have students explore the Web sites they identified on Day 2. Point out that many Web sites contain links to other Web sites and discuss how these can help them find additional information to answer their inquiry question. Links are often underlined or highlighted in different colored text. While these links may take students to Web sites that provide valuable information on a subject not listed in the original search engine results, caution students to manage their time wisely. They should allow a specific amount of time to gather information and sufficient time to read and analyze it.

### DAY 4

**Synthesize** Have students synthesize relevant information from Day 3. It may be helpful for students to use a concept web to organize their information. For example, students may write an animal behavior in the center circle and use the other circles to list details, such as descriptions of the behavior, reasons for it, and how scientists discovered the reasons.

### DAY 5

**Communicate** Students can use a word processing program to write a paragraph or short report about their inquiry results. Have them share their work in small groups.

## RESEARCH/STUDY SKILLS
# Poster/Announcement

### TEACH

Have students describe the kinds of posters or announcements they see around school. Then ask: *Where else might you find announcements?* Students may mention the library or bus stop. Explain elements of announcements and posters.

- An **announcement** tells about an upcoming event. It usually answers the questions *Who? What? When? Where? Why?* and *How?*

- A **poster** is a type of announcement that is large. It often uses color and large type to emphasize information and to grab readers' attention.

Display a poster or distribute copies of an announcement for an upcoming school event. Have students look for information in the poster or announcement that answers the questions *Who? What? When? Where? Why?* and *How?* Then discuss these questions:

1. **What is the purpose of this announcement?**
2. **What does the announcement emphasize? How?**

### ASSESS

Have pairs make an announcement or poster for a community event that answers the questions *Who? What? When? Where? Why?* and *How?*

For more practice or to assess students, use Practice Book pp. 169–170.

## OBJECTIVES

- Review the elements of a poster and an announcement.
- Identify information in a poster or an announcement.

---

### Poster/Announcement

- A **poster** is an **announcement** for an event. Posters are large in size. Usually they use color and large type to attract attention.
- Posters answer these questions about an event: Who? What? When? Where? How? Why?

**Directions** Read this poster. Then complete the chart by telling how the poster answers the questions.

> See the Top Trainers in America!
> *All-New Dolphin Show*
> Springfield City Aquarium
> **Saturday, March 8**
> 11:00 A.M.
> Only $1 per person
> Proceeds Benefit the Red Cross

| Who? | top trainers in America |
| --- | --- |
| What? | 1. all-new dolphin show |
| When? | 2. Saturday, March 8, at 11:00 A.M. |
| Where? | 3. Springfield City Aquarium |
| Why? | 4. to benefit the Red Cross |

5. On a large sheet of paper, make a colorful poster for a school event. Choose the most important information. Make sure your poster tells who, what, when, why, how, and where.

   Check that students' posters are colorful and use big letters. They should tell who, what, when, why, how, and where.

▲ **Practice Book** p. 169

---

**Directions** Read over this announcement. Then answer the questions below.

> **HELP SAVE THE RAIN FOREST!**
> Come hear
> **Manuel Ortega,**
> Costa Rican Biologist
> *"What Kids Can Do to Save the Rain Forest"*
> Don't miss this multimedia presentation for children ages 8–11. Enjoy activities, animals, and rain forest snacks. Bring your questions.
> **January 12, 5 P.M.**
> Santa Fe Public Library
> 2100 S. Rio Grande Way

6. What is the purpose of this announcement?
   It announces a "save the rain forest" event.

7. What is the event? Who is featured?
   It's a multimedia presentation about how children can help save the rain forest; Biologist Manuel Ortega is featured.

8. When and where is the event taking place?
   The event is at 5 P.M. January 12 at the Santa Fe Public Library.

9. Why do you think the event is taking place?
   to educate children about saving the rain forest

10. What does this announcement emphasize? How?
    the title of the presentation and the appeal of saving the rain forest; It uses bolder typefaces for these elements.

**Home Activity** Your child learned about announcements. With your child, think of a school or community activity that is coming up. Work with your child to write an announcement to post. Make sure your child includes answers to these questions: who, what, when, why, how, and where?

▲ **Practice Book** p. 170

# Assessment Checkpoints *for the Week*

## Selection Assessment

**Use pp. 65–68 of** Selection Tests **to check:**

 **Selection Understanding**

 **Comprehension Skill**
*Compare and Contrast*

 **Selection Vocabulary**

| | |
|---|---|
| aquarium | glimpses |
| dolphins | pulses |
| enchanted | surface |
| flexible | |

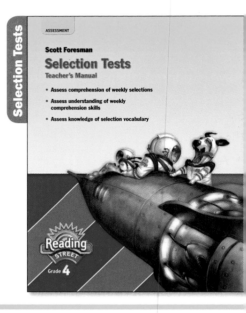

ASSESSMENT

Scott Foresman
**Selection Tests**
Teacher's Manual

- Assess comprehension of weekly selections
- Assess understanding of weekly comprehension skills
- Assess knowledge of selection vocabulary

Reading STREET
Grade 4

---

## Leveled Assessment

 On-Level
Strategic Intervention
Advanced

**Use pp. 97–102 of** Fresh Reads for Differentiated Test Practice **to check:**

 **Comprehension Skill**
*Compare and Contrast*

 **REVIEW** **Comprehension Skill** *Generalize*

 **Fluency** *Words Correct Per Minute*

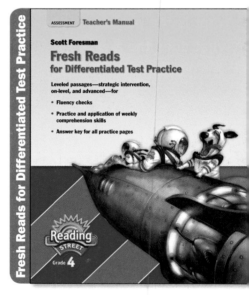

ASSESSMENT   Teacher's Manual

Scott Foresman
**Fresh Reads**
**for Differentiated Test Practice**

Leveled passages—strategic intervention, on-level, and advanced—for

- Fluency checks
- Practice and application of weekly comprehension skills
- Answer key for all practice pages

Reading STREET
Grade 4

---

## Managing Assessment

**Use** Assessment Handbook **for:**

 **Observation Checklists**

 **Record-Keeping Forms**

 **Portfolio Assessment**

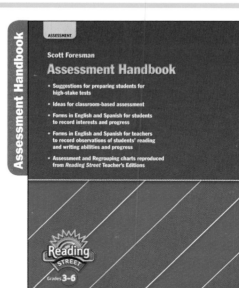

ASSESSMENT

Scott Foresman
**Assessment Handbook**

- Suggestions for preparing students for high-stake tests
- Ideas for classroom-based assessment
- Forms in English and Spanish for students to record interests and progress
- Forms in English and Spanish for teachers to record observations of students' reading and writing abilities and progress
- Assessment and Regrouping charts reproduced from *Reading Street* Teacher's Editions

Reading STREET
Grades 3–6

# Unit 4
# Puzzles and Mysteries

**CONCEPT QUESTION**

Is there an explanation for everything?

## Week 3

**EXPAND THE CONCEPT**

## How can a mistake turn into a success?

## CONNECT THE CONCEPT

▶ **Build Background**
*advertising, concentrate, secret*

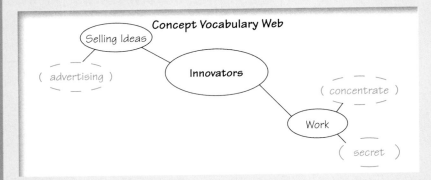

Concept Vocabulary Web

▶ **Science Content**
Getting a Patent, Inventing Super Glue, Kitchen Chemistry

▶ **Writing**
Business Letter

▶ **Internet Inquiry**
Mistakes and Successes

# Preview Your Week

*How can a mistake turn into a success?*

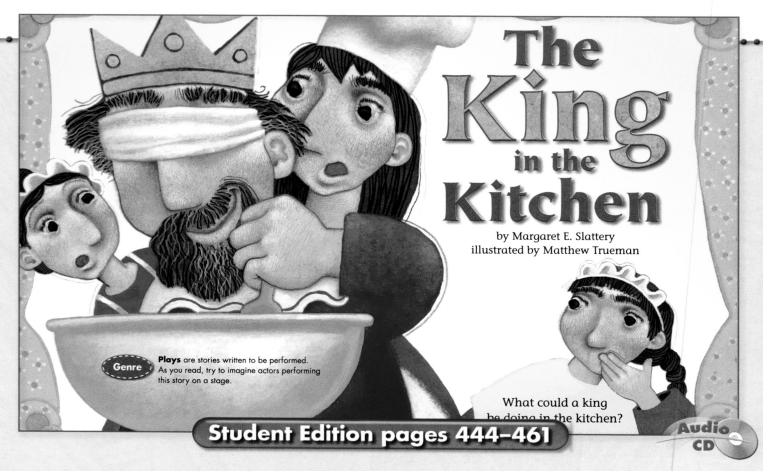

**The King in the Kitchen**
by Margaret E. Slattery
illustrated by Matthew Trueman

**Genre** Plays are stories written to be performed. As you read, try to imagine actors performing this story on a stage.

What could a king be doing in the kitchen?

Audio CD

**Student Edition pages 444–461**

**Genre** Play
**Vocabulary Strategy** Dictionary/Glossary
**Comprehension Skill** Character and Setting
**Comprehension Strategy** Monitor and Fix Up

## Paired Selection

**Reading Across Texts**
Link Words from Poems to Play

**Genre**
Poetry

**Text Features**
Lines End with Rhyming Words
Rhythm

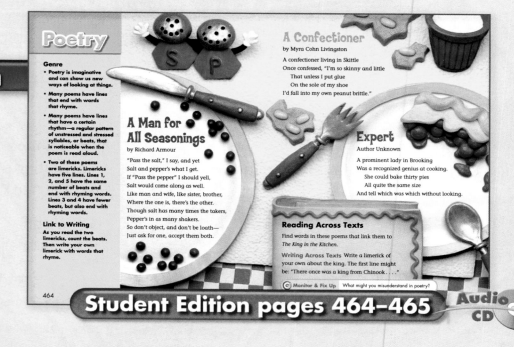

### Poetry

**Genre**
- Poetry is imaginative and can show us new ways of looking at things.
- Many poems have lines that end with words that rhyme.
- Many poems have lines that have a certain rhythm—a regular pattern of unstressed and stressed syllables, or beats, that is noticeable when the poem is read aloud.
- Two of these poems are limericks. Limericks have five lines. Lines 1, 2, and 5 have the same number of beats and end with rhyming words. Lines 3 and 4 have fewer beats, but also end with rhyming words.

**Link to Writing**
As you read the two limericks, count the beats. Then write your own limerick with words that rhyme.

**A Confectioner**
by Myra Cohn Livingston

A confectioner living in Skittle
Once confessed, "I'm so skinny and little
    That unless I put glue
    On the sole of my shoe
I'd fall into my own peanut brittle."

**A Man for All Seasonings**
by Richard Armour

"Pass the salt," I say, and yet
Salt and pepper's what I get.
If "Pass the pepper" I should yell,
Salt would come along as well.
Like man and wife, like sister, brother,
Where the one is, there's the other.
Though salt has many times the takers,
Pepper's in as many shakers.
So don't object, and don't be loath—
Just ask for one, accept them both.

**Expert**
Author Unknown

A prominent lady in Brooking
Was a recognized genius at cooking.
    She could bake thirty pies
    All quite the same size
And tell which was which without looking.

**Reading Across Texts**
Find words in these poems that link them to *The King in the Kitchen*.

**Writing Across Texts** Write a limerick of your own about the king. The first line might be: "There once was a king from Chinook. . . ."

Monitor & Fix Up What might you misunderstand in poetry?

Audio CD

**Student Edition pages 464–465**

**Read It**
**ONLINE**
PearsonSuccessNet.com
- Student Edition
- Leveled Readers

## Leveled Readers

◎ **Skill** Character and Setting

◎ **Strategy** Monitor and Fix Up

**Lesson Vocabulary**

**Below-Level**

**On-Level**

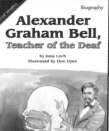

**Advanced**

**ELL Reader**
- Concept Vocabulary
- Text Support
- Language Enrichment

---

TIME FOR **Science**

## Integrate Science Standards
- Patents
- Scientific Invention
- Chemistry

✓ **Read**

**The King in the Kitchen,** pp. 444–461

**"A Man for All Seasonings," "A Confectioner," and "Expert,"** pp. 464–465

### Leveled Readers

**Below-Level**    **On-Level**    **Advanced**

- Support Concepts   • Develop Concepts   • Extend Concepts

### ELL Reader

✓ **Build**
**Concept Vocabulary**
   **Innovators,** pp. 440l–440m

✓ **Teach**
**Science Concepts**
   **Getting a Patent,** p. 457
   **Inventing Super Glue,** p. 459
   **Kitchen Chemistry,** p. 465

✓ **Explore**
**Science Center**
   **Find a New Use,** p. 440k

*The King in the Kitchen*   **440c**

# Weekly Plan

## READING

*45–90 minutes*

### TARGET SKILLS OF THE WEEK

- **Comprehension Skill**
  Character and Setting
- **Comprehension Strategy**
  Monitor and Fix Up
- **Vocabulary Strategy**
  Dictionary/Glossary

## LANGUAGE ARTS

*30–60 minutes*

### Trait of the Week

**Voice**

---

### DAY 1
PAGES 440l–442b, 465a, 465e–465k

**Oral Language**

**QUESTION OF THE WEEK** *How can a mistake turn into a success?*

Read Aloud: "Corn Flake Kings" 440m
Build Concepts, 440l

**Comprehension/Vocabulary**

Comprehension Skill/Strategy Lesson, 440–441
- Character and Setting **T**
- Monitor and Fix Up
Build Background, 442a

Introduce Lesson Vocabulary, 442b
*duke, dungeon, furiously, genius, majesty, noble, peasant, porridge* **T**

**Read** Leveled Readers

**Grouping Options** 440f–440g

**Fluency**

Model Stress/Emphasis, 440l–440m, 465a

---

**Grammar,** 465e
Introduce Pronouns and Antecedents **T**

**Writing Workshop,** 465g
Introduce Business Letter
Model the Trait of the Week: Voice

**Spelling,** 465i
Pretest for Final *er, ar*

**Internet Inquiry,** 465k
Identify Questions

---

### DAY 2
PAGES 442–451, 465a, 465e–465k

**Oral Language**

**QUESTION OF THE DAY** *How would you feel if you were the Cook, and the King visited your kitchen?*

**Comprehension/Vocabulary**

Vocabulary Strategy Lesson, 442–443
- Dictionary/Glossary **T**

**Read** *The King in the Kitchen,* 444–451

**Grouping Options** 440f–440g

- Character and Setting **T**
- Monitor and Fix Up
- **REVIEW** Graphic Sources **T**
Develop Vocabulary

**Fluency**

Choral Reading, 465a

---

**Grammar,** 465e
Develop Pronouns and Antecedents **T**

**Writing Workshop,** 465g
Improve Writing with Elaborate

**Spelling,** 465i
Teach the Generalization

**Internet Inquiry,** 465k
Navigate/Search

---

| DAILY WRITING ACTIVITIES | **Day 1** Write to Read, 440 | **Day 2** Words to Write, 443 / Strategy Response Log, 444, 451 |
|---|---|---|
| DAILY SCIENCE CONNECTIONS | **Day 1** Innovators Concept Web, 440l | **Day 2** Revisit the Innovators Concept Web, 451 |

---

**DAILY SUCCESS PREDICTORS**
for Adequate Yearly Progress

**Monitor Progress and Corrective Feedback**

Vocabulary    Check Vocabulary, *440l*

**Grouping Options for Differentiated Instruction**

Turn the page for the small group lesson plan.

## DAY 3 PAGES 452–463, 465a, 465e–465k

### Oral Language

**QUESTION OF THE DAY** *Do you think the King, the Princess, and the Peasant will live happily ever after? Why or why not?*

### Comprehension/Vocabulary

**Read** *The King in the Kitchen, 452–461*

**Grouping Options** 440f–440g

- Character **T**
- Monitor and Fix Up
- Dictionary/ Glossary **T**
- Develop Vocabulary

Reader Response
Selection Test

### Fluency

Model Stress/Emphasis, 465a

---

**Grammar,** 465f
Apply Pronouns and Antecedents in Writing **T**

**Writing Workshop,** 463, 465h
Write Now
Prewrite and Draft

**Spelling,** 465j
Connect Spelling to Writing

**Internet Inquiry,** 465k
Analyze Sources

---

**Day 3** Strategy Response Log, 460
Look Back and Write, 462

---

**Day 3** Time for Science: Getting a Patent, 457;
Inventing Super Glue, 459
Revisit the Innovators Concept Web, 461

## DAY 4 PAGES 464–465a, 465e–465k

### Oral Language

**QUESTION OF THE DAY** *What kind of person would be a genius in a kitchen?*

### Comprehension/Vocabulary

**Read** "A Man for All Seasonings," "A Confectioner," and "Expert," 464–465

**Grouping Options** 440f–440g

Poetry
Reading Across Texts
Content-Area Vocabulary

### Fluency

Partner Reading, 465a

---

**Grammar,** 465f
Practice Pronouns and Antecedents for Standardized Tests **T**

**Writing Workshop,** 465h
Draft, Revise, and Publish

**Spelling,** 465j
Provide a Strategy

**Internet Inquiry,** 465k
Synthesize Information

---

**Day 4** Writing Across Texts, 465

---

**Day 4** Time for Science: Kitchen Chemistry, 465

## DAY 5 PAGES 465a–465l

### Oral Language

**QUESTION OF THE WEEK** *To wrap up the week, revisit the Day 1 question.*

Build Concept Vocabulary, 465c

### Fluency

**Read** Leveled Readers

**Grouping Options** 440f–440g

Assess Reading Rate, 465a

### Comprehension/Vocabulary

- Reteach Character and Setting, 465b **T**
- Rhyme, 465b
- Review Dictionary/Glossary, 465c **T**

---

**Speaking and Viewing,** 465d
Readers' Theater
Analyze Media

**Grammar,** 465f
Cumulative Review

**Writing Workshop,** 465h
Connect to Unit Writing

**Spelling,** 465j
Posttest for Final *er, ar*

**Internet Inquiry,** 465k
Communicate Results

**Research/Study Skills,** 465l
Follow and Clarify Directions

---

**Day 5** Rhyme, 465b

---

**Day 5** Revisit the Innovators Concept Web, 465c

---

**KEY** ◉ = Target Skill **T** = Tested Skill

---

**Comprehension** Check Retelling, *462*

**Fluency** Check Fluency WCPM, *465a*

**Vocabulary** Check Vocabulary, *465c*

**SUCCESS PREDICTOR**

# Small Group Plan for Differentiated Instruction

## Daily Plan AT A GLANCE

### Reading
**Whole Group**
- Oral Language
- Comprehension/Vocabulary

### Group Time
**Differentiated Instruction**

Meet with small groups to provide:
- Skill Support
- Reading Support
- Fluency Practice

**Read**

This week's lessons for daily group time can be found behind the Differentiated Instruction (DI) tab on pp. DI·22–DI·31.

### Whole Group
- Fluency

### Language Arts
- Grammar
- Writing
- Spelling
- Research/Inquiry
- Speaking/Listening/Viewing

**Use My Sidewalks on Reading Street for Tier III intensive reading intervention.**

---

## DAY 1

| On-Level | Strategic Intervention | Advanced |
|---|---|---|
| **Teacher-Led** Page DI·23 | **Teacher-Led** Page DI·22 | **Teacher-Led** Page DI·23 |
| • Develop Concept Vocabulary<br>• **Read** On-Level Reader *The Amazing, Incredible Idea Kit* | • Reinforce Concepts<br>• **Read** Below-Level Reader *Inventing Oatmeal* | • **Read** Advanced Reader *Alexander Graham Bell*<br>• Independent Extension Activity |

### *(i)* Independent Activities
While you meet with small groups, have the rest of the class...

- Visit the Reading/Library Center
- Listen to the Background Building Audio
- Finish Write to Read, p. 440
- Complete Practice Book pp. 173–174
- Visit Cross-Curricular Centers

---

## DAY 2

| On-Level | Strategic Intervention | Advanced |
|---|---|---|
| **Teacher-Led** Pages 446–451 | **Teacher-Led** Page DI·24 | **Teacher-Led** Page DI·25 |
| • **Read** *The King in the Kitchen* | • Practice Lesson Vocabulary<br>• Read Multisyllabic Words<br>• **Read** or Listen to *The King in the Kitchen* | • Extend Vocabulary<br>• **Read** *The King in the Kitchen* |

### *(i)* Independent Activities
While you meet with small groups, have the rest of the class...

- Visit the Reading/Library Center
- Listen to the AudioText for *The King in the Kitchen*
- Finish Words to Write, p. 443
- Complete Practice Book pp. 175–176
- Write in their Strategy Response Logs, pp. 444, 451
- Visit Cross-Curricular Centers
- Work on inquiry projects

---

## DAY 3

| On-Level | Strategic Intervention | Advanced |
|---|---|---|
| **Teacher-Led** Pages 452–461 | **Teacher-Led** Page DI·26 | **Teacher-Led** Page DI·27 |
| • **Read** *The King in the Kitchen* | • Practice Character and Setting and Monitor and Fix Up<br>• **Read** or Listen to *The King in the Kitchen* | • Extend Character and Setting and Monitor and Fix Up<br>• **Read** *The King in the Kitchen* |

### *(i)* Independent Activities
While you meet with small groups, have the rest of the class...

- Visit the Reading/Library Center
- Listen to the AudioText for *The King in the Kitchen*
- Write in their Strategy Response Logs, p. 460
- Finish Look Back and Write, p. 462
- Complete Practice Book p. 177
- Visit Cross-Curricular Centers
- Work on inquiry projects

① Begin with whole class skill and strategy instruction.

② Meet with small groups to provide differentiated instruction.

③ Gather the whole class back together for fluency and language arts.

## DAY 4

### On-Level
**Teacher-Led**
*Pages 464–465*

- **Read** "A Man for All Seasonings," "A Confectioner," and "Expert"

### Strategic Intervention
**Teacher-Led**
*Page DI · 28*

- Practice Retelling
- **Read** or Listen to "A Man for All Seasonings," "A Confectioner," and "Expert"

### Advanced
**Teacher-Led**
*Page DI · 29*

- **Read** "A Man for All Seasonings," "A Confectioner," and "Expert"
- Genre Study

### ⓘ Independent Activities

**While you meet with small groups, have the rest of the class...**

- Visit the Reading/Library Center
- Listen to the AudioText for "A Man for All Seasonings," "A Confectioner," and "Expert"

- Visit the Writing/Vocabulary Center
- Finish Writing Across Texts, p. 465
- Visit Cross-Curricular Centers
- Work on inquiry projects

## DAY 5

### On-Level
**Teacher-Led**
*Page DI · 31*

- **Reread** Leveled Reader *The Amazing, Incredible Idea Kit*

  Retell *The Amazing, Incredible Idea Kit*

### Strategic Intervention
**Teacher-Led**
*Page DI · 30*

- **Reread** Leveled Reader *Inventing Oatmeal*
- Retell *Inventing Oatmeal*

### Advanced
**Teacher-Led**
*Page DI · 31*

- **Reread** Leveled Reader *Alexander Graham Bell*
- Share Extension Activity

### ⓘ Independent Activities

**While you meet with small groups, have the rest of the class...**

- Visit the Reading/Library Center
- Complete Practice Book pp. 178–180

- Visit Cross-Curricular Centers
- Work on inquiry projects

**Grouping** Place English language learners in the groups that correspond to their reading abilities in English.

Use the appropriate Leveled Reader or other text at students' instructional level.

**TIP** Send home the appropriate Multilingual Summary of the main selection on Day 1.

**ONLINE**
**PearsonSuccessNet.com**

**P. David Pearson**
For ideas on teaching comprehension, see the article "Developing Expertise in Reading Comprehension" by Scott Foresman author P. D. Pearson and others.

### TEACHER TALK

**Fix-up strategies** are strategies readers use when they realize they do not understand something. Adjusting reading rate, rereading, and using a reference source are a few fix-up strategies.

Be sure to schedule time for students to work on the unit inquiry project "Unlocking Nature's Mysteries." This week students analyze the information they have found from Web sites or print materials.

*Looking Ahead*

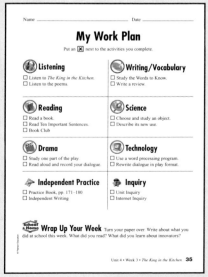

▲ **Group-Time Survival Guide**
p. 35, Weekly Contract

*The King in the Kitchen* **440g**

# ☑ Customize Your Plan *by Strand*

## ORAL LANGUAGE

### Concept Development

How can a mistake turn into a success?

**CONCEPT VOCABULARY**

advertising    concentrate    secret

### BUILD

❑ **Question of the Week** Introduce and discuss the question of the week. This week students will read a variety of texts and work on projects related to the concept *innovators*. Post the question for students to refer to throughout the week. **DAY 1** *440d*

❑ **Read Aloud** Read aloud "Corn Flake Kings." Then begin a web to build concepts and concept vocabulary related to this week's lesson and the unit theme, Puzzles and Mysteries. Introduce the concept words *advertising, concentrate,* and *secret* and have students place them on the web. Display the web for use throughout the week. **DAY 1** *440l–440m*

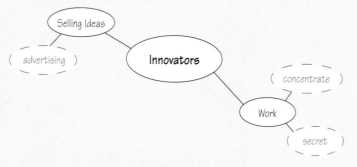

### DEVELOP

❑ **Question of the Day** Use the prompts from the Weekly Plan to engage students in conversations related to this week's reading and the unit theme. **EVERY DAY** *440d–440e*

❑ **Concept Vocabulary Web** Revisit the Innovators Concept Web and encourage students to add concept words from their reading and life experiences. **DAY 2** *451,* **DAY 3** *461*

### CONNECT

❑ **Looking Back/Moving Forward** Revisit the Innovators Concept Web and discuss how it relates to this week's lesson and the unit theme. Then make connections to next week's lesson. **DAY 5** *465c*

### CHECK

❑ **Concept Vocabulary Web** Use the Innovators Concept Web to check students' understanding of the concept vocabulary words *advertising, concentrate,* and *secret.* **DAY 1** *440l,* **DAY 5** *465c*

## VOCABULARY

❑ **STRATEGY DICTIONARY/ GLOSSARY** Dictionaries and glossaries provide alphabetical lists of words and their meanings. A dictionary is its own book, but a glossary is part of a book.

**LESSON VOCABULARY**

| | |
|---|---|
| duke | majesty |
| dungeon | noble |
| furiously | peasant |
| genius | porridge |

### TEACH

❑ **Words to Know** Give students the opportunity to tell what they already know about this week's lesson vocabulary words. Then discuss word meaning. **DAY 1** *442b*

❑ **Vocabulary Strategy Lesson** Use the vocabulary strategy lesson in the Student Edition to introduce and model this week's strategy, *dictionary/ glossary.* **DAY 2** *442–443*

**Vocabulary Strategy Lesson**

### PRACTICE/APPLY

❑ **Leveled Text** Read the lesson vocabulary in the context of leveled text. **DAY 1** *LR19–LR27*

**Leveled Readers**

❑ **Words in Context** Read the lesson vocabulary and apply *dictionary/ glossary* in the context of *The King in the Kitchen.* **DAY 2** *444–451,* **DAY 3** *452–462*

❑ **Writing/Vocabulary Center** Write a review of *The King in the Kitchen.* **DAY 4** *440k,* **DAY 5** *440k*

**Main Selection—Drama**

❑ **Homework** Practice Book pp. 174–175. **DAY 1** *442b,* **DAY 2** *443*

❑ **Word Play** Have students find words related to cooking in *The King in the Kitchen.* Then have students sort the words into categories such as tools, cookbook words, and actions. **ANY DAY** *465c*

### ASSESS

❑ **Selection Test** Use the Selection Test to determine students' understanding of the lesson vocabulary words. **DAY 3**

### RETEACH/REVIEW

❑ **Reteach Lesson** If necessary, use this lesson to reteach and review *dictionary/glossary.* **DAY 5** *465c*

## COMPREHENSION

**◉ SKILL CHARACTER AND SETTING** A character in a story is a person or animal that takes part in the events of the story. The setting is the time and place in which the story events happen.

**◉ STRATEGY MONITOR AND FIX UP** At times when reading, you may realize that you did not understand what you just read. Good readers make sure they understand what they read. If they don't, they use text features to fix up the problem.

### TEACH

☐ **Skill/Strategy Lesson** Use the skill/strategy lesson in the Student Edition to introduce and model *character and setting* and *monitor and fix up.* **DAY 1** 440-441

☐ **Extend Skills** Teach rhyme. **ANY DAY** 465b

**Skill/Strategy Lesson**

### PRACTICE/APPLY

☐ **Leveled Text** Apply *character and setting* and *monitor and fix up* to read leveled text. **DAY 1** LR19–LR27

☐ **Skills and Strategies in Context** Read *The King in the Kitchen,* using the Guiding Comprehension questions to apply *character and setting* and *monitor and fix up.* **DAY 2** 444–451, **DAY 3** 452–462

**Leveled Readers**

☐ **Skills and Strategies in Context** Read the poems, guiding students as they apply *character and setting* and *monitor and fix up.* Then have students discuss and write across texts. **DAY 4** 464–465

**Main Selection—Drama**

☐ **Homework** Practice Book pp. 173, 177, 178. **DAY 1** 441, **DAY 3** 461, **DAY 5** 465b

**Paired Selection—Poetry**

☐ **Fresh Reads for Differentiated Test Practice** Have students practice *character and setting* with a new passage. **DAY 3**

### ASSESS

☐ **Selection Test** Determine students' understanding of the selection and their use of *character and setting.* **DAY 3**

☐ **Retell** Have students retell *The King in the Kitchen.* **DAY 3** 462–463

### RETEACH/REVIEW

☐ **Reteach Lesson** If necessary, reteach and review *character and setting.* **DAY 5** 465b

## FLUENCY

**SKILL STRESS/EMPHASIS** When reading, it is vital to stress important words for emphasis. A good reader will emphasize words by saying them with more stress, using a stronger voice, or higher pitch.

### TEACH

☐ **Read Aloud** Model fluent reading by rereading "Corn Flake Kings." Focus on this week's fluency skill, stress/emphasis. **DAY 1** 440l–440m, 465a

### PRACTICE/APPLY

☐ **Choral Reading** Read aloud selected paragraphs from *The King in the Kitchen,* stressing important words for emphasis. Then practice as a class, doing three choral readings. **DAY 2** 465a, **DAY 3** 465a

☐ **Partner Reading** Have partners practice reading aloud dramatically, stressing important words and offering each other feedback. As students reread, monitor their progress toward their individual fluency goals. **DAY 4** 465a

☐ **Listening Center** Have students follow along with the AudioText for this week's selections. **ANY DAY** 440j

☐ **Reading/Library Center** Have students reread a selection of their choice. **ANY DAY** 440j

☐ **Fluency Coach** Have students use Fluency Coach to listen to fluent readings or practice reading on their own. **ANY DAY**

### ASSESS

☐ **Check Fluency WCPM** Do a one-minute timed reading, paying special attention to this week's skill—stress/emphasis. Provide feedback for each student. **DAY 5** 465a

# ☑ Customize Your Plan *by Strand*

## GRAMMAR

**SKILL PRONOUNS AND ANTECEDENTS**    A pronoun takes the place of a noun. An antecedent, or referent, is the noun to which the pronoun refers. A pronoun and its antecedent must agree in number and gender.

### TEACH

- ❑ **Grammar Transparency 18** Use Grammar Transparency 18 to teach pronouns and antecedents. DAY 1 *465e*

**Grammar Transparency 18**

### PRACTICE/APPLY

- ❑ **Develop the Concept** Review the concept of pronouns and antecedents and provide guided practice. DAY 2 *465e*

- ❑ **Apply to Writing** Have students review something they have written and check their use of pronouns and antecedents. DAY 3 *465f*

- ❑ **Test Preparation** Examine common errors in pronouns and antecedents to prepare for standardized tests. DAY 4 *465f*

- ❑ **Homework** Grammar and Writing Practice Book pp. 69–71. DAY 2 *465e*, DAY 3 *465f*, DAY 4 *465f*

### ASSESS

- ❑ **Cumulative Review** Use Grammar and Writing Practice Book p. 72. DAY 5 *465f*

### RETEACH/REVIEW

- ❑ **Daily Fix-It** Have students find and correct errors in grammar, spelling, and punctuation. **EVERY DAY** *465e-465f*

- ❑ **The Grammar and Writing Book** Use pp. 152–155 of The Grammar and Writing Book to extend instruction for pronouns and antecedents. **ANY DAY**

**The Grammar and Writing Book**

## WRITING

### Trait of the Week

**VOICE**    Good writers have a strong voice—a personality that comes through in the tone and style of their writing. Voice shows that a writer knows and cares about a topic. A strong voice speaks directly to readers and keeps their attention.

### TEACH

- ❑ **Writing Transparency 18A** Use the model to introduce and discuss the Trait of the Week. DAY 1 *465g*

- ❑ **Writing Transparency 18B** Use the transparency to show students how elaboration can improve their writing. DAY 2 *465g*

**Writing Transparency 18A**     **Writing Transparency 18B**

### PRACTICE/APPLY

- ❑ **Write Now** Examine the model on Student Edition p. 463. Then have students write their own business letters. DAY 3 *463, 465h*, DAY 4 *465h*

  **Prompt** In *The King in the Kitchen*, the king starts a glue business. Think about a new product that you might like to invent. Now write a business letter asking a company to help you sell your product.

**Write Now p. 463**

- ❑ **Writing/Vocabulary Center** Write a review of *The King in the Kitchen*. DAY 4 *440k*, DAY 5 *440k*

### ASSESS

- ❑ **Writing Trait Rubric** Use the rubric to evaluate students' writing. DAY 4 *465h*

### RETEACH/REVIEW

- ❑ **The Grammar and Writing Book** Use pp. 152–157 of The Grammar and Writing Book to extend instruction for pronouns and antecedents, elaboration, and business letters. **ANY DAY**

**The Grammar and Writing Book**

## SPELLING

**GENERALIZATION WORDS WITH FINAL *ER, AR*** Final syllables with *er* and *ar* often sound alike, but are spelled differently: *calendar, summer.*

### TEACH

❑ **Pretest** Give the pretest for words with final *er, ar*. Guide students in self-correcting their pretests and correcting any misspellings. **DAY 1** *465i*

❑ **Think and Practice** Connect spelling to the phonics generalization for final *er, ar*. **DAY 2** *465i*

### PRACTICE/APPLY

❑ **Connect to Writing** Have students use spelling words to write a letter to a friend, a relative or the editor of a newspaper. Then review frequently misspelled words: *another, let's, that's*. **DAY 3** *465j*

❑ **Homework** Word Study and Spelling Practice Book pp. 69–72. **EVERY DAY**

### RETEACH/REVIEW

❑ **Review** Review spelling words to prepare for the posttest. Then provide students with a spelling strategy—problem parts. **DAY 4** *465j*

### ASSESS

❑ **Posttest** Use dictation sentences to give the posttest for words with final *er, ar*. **DAY 5** *465j*

### Spelling Words

| | | |
|---|---|---|
| 1. brother | 8. regular | 15. never* |
| 2. together* | 9. summer | 16. shelter |
| 3. dinner* | 10. clever* | 17. cellar |
| 4. popular | 11. supper | 18. caterpillar |
| 5. center* | 12. pitcher | 19. theater |
| 6. calendar | 13. filter | 20. deliver* |
| 7. similar | 14. hangar | |

### Challenge Words

| | | |
|---|---|---|
| 21. character | 23. receiver | 25. binocular |
| 22. singular | 24. spectacular | |

*Word from the selection

## RESEARCH AND INQUIRY

❑ **Internet Inquiry** Have students conduct an Internet inquiry on how mistakes can lead to successes. **EVERY DAY** *465k*

❑ **Follow and Clarify Directions** Review the strategies for following and clarifying directions and discuss how students can use these strategies to help them complete a task. **DAY 5** *465l*

❑ **Unit Inquiry** Allow time for students to analyze the information they have researched from web sites and print materials. **ANY DAY** *391*

## SPEAKING AND VIEWING

❑ **Readers' Theater** Have students work in groups to perform a dramatic reading from *The King in the Kitchen*. **DAY 5** *465d*

❑ **Analyze Media** Have students view a scene from a television play or a movie to analyze and answer questions on how the actors delivered their lines. **DAY 5** *465d*

# Resources for
# Differentiated Instruction

## LEVELED READERS

▶ **Comprehension**
- 🎯 **Skill** Character and Setting
- 🎯 **Strategy** Monitor and Fix Up

▶ **Lesson Vocabulary**
- 🎯 Dictionary/Glossary

duke · dungeon · furiously · genius · majesty · peasant · noble · porridge

▶ **Science Standards**
- Patents
- Scientific Invention
- Chemistry

## Leveled Reader Database

### ONLINE

PearsonSuccessNet.com

Use the Online Database of over 600 books to

- Download and print additional copies of this week's leveled readers.
- Listen to the readers being read online.
- Search for more titles focused on this week's skills, topic, and content.

---

### On-Level

Social Studies
**The Amazing, Incredible Idea Kit**
by Vana Dougias
illustrated by Burgundy Beam

**On-Level Reader**

Name _____ Incredible Idea Kit

**Character and Setting**
- A **character** in a story is a person or animal that takes part in the events in a story.
- The **setting** is the time and place in which the events happen in a story.

**Directions** Complete the following chart about the main characters in *The Amazing, Incredible Idea Kit*. Make sure to give evidence from the story to support your ideas.
Possible responses given.

**Characters: Paul and Beatrice**

| Say/Think | Does | Others Say/Think |
|---|---|---|
| 1. Granny Mae is interesting and wise, p. 5; like to hear about Granny Mae's life, p. 9 | 2. help each other; created the idea kit, pp. 5, 22; listen to their parents, p. 20; work hard, p. 21 | 3. Granny Mae thinks Paul and Beatrice are smart and excellent students, p. 10; Mr. O'Hara thinks they made the best science fair exhibit, p. 23 |

**Directions** Describe the setting during the time when Granny Mae was a governess for James and Anastasia.

4–5. The setting was England when Granny Mae was a college student. The house of the Goslings might have been in the country, because it had a garden for parties.

🎯 **On-Level Practice** TE p. LR23

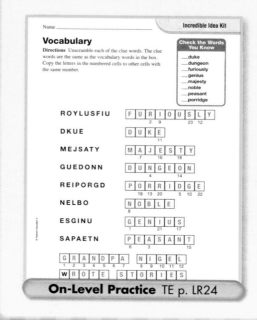

Name _____ Incredible Idea Kit

**Vocabulary**

**Check the Words You Know**
___ duke
___ dungeon
___ furiously
___ genius
___ majesty
___ noble
___ peasant
___ porridge

**Directions** Unscramble each of the clue words. The clue words are the same as the vocabulary words in the box. Copy the letters in the numbered cells to other cells with the same number.

ROYLUSFIU — F U R I O U S L Y
DKUE — D U K E
MEJSATY — M A J E S T Y
GUEDONN — D U N G E O N
REIPORGD — P O R R I D G E
NELBO — N O B L E
ESGINU — G E N I U S
SAPAETN — P E A S A N T

G R A N D P A N I G E L
W R O T E S T O R I E S

🎯 **On-Level Practice** TE p. LR24

---

### Strategic Intervention

Social Studies
**Inventing Oatmeal**
by Christian Downey

**Below-Level Reader**

Name _____ Inventing Oatmeal

**Character and Setting**
- A **character** in a story is a person or animal that takes part in the events in a story.
- The **setting** is the time and place in which the events happen in a story.

**Directions** Complete the following table using evidence from the story *Inventing Oatmeal*. Remember, there is more than one setting and more than one important character in the story.
Possible responses given.

| Setting | Setting |
|---|---|
| The first part of the story takes place in the present, in the garage of Grace and Ben | The second part of the story takes place during the Middle Ages in an imaginary castle in England |
| Evidence pictures on p. 3–8 show Grace and Ben in modern clothes | Evidence p. 8, "'Picture us in a castle,'" he said, "we will be in England during the Middle Ages!'" |
| **Character** An important character in the story is Grace | **Character** An important character in the story is Ben |
| Some of the traits of this character are that she likes science projects, being clean, she is interested in other times and places | Some of the traits of this character are that he likes science projects, he has a good imagination |
| evidence p. 3, she and Ben like to work on science projects; she wishes she could travel back to the Middle Ages | evidence p. 3, both like to work on science projects; Grace how to imagine that they are in the Middle Ages |

🎯 **Below-Level Practice** TE p. LR20

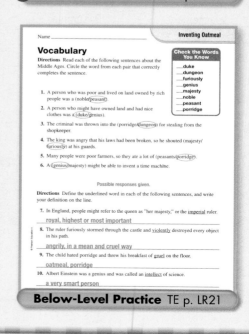

Name _____ Inventing Oatmeal

**Vocabulary**

**Check the Words You Know**
___ duke
___ dungeon
___ furiously
___ genius
___ majesty
___ noble
___ peasant
___ porridge

**Directions** Read each of the following sentences about the Middle Ages. Circle the word from each pair that correctly completes the sentence.

1. A person who was poor and lived on land owned by rich people was a (noble/peasant).
2. A person who might have owned land and had nice clothes was a (duke/genius).
3. The criminal was thrown into the (porridge/dungeon) for stealing from the shopkeeper.
4. The king was angry that his laws had been broken, so he shouted (majesty/furiously) at his guards.
5. Many people were poor farmers, so they ate a lot of (peasants/porridge).
6. A (genius/majesty) might be able to invent a time machine.

Possible responses given.

**Directions** Define the underlined word in each of the following sentences, and write your definition on the line.

7. In England, people might refer to the queen as "her majesty," or the *imperial* ruler.
   royal, highest or most important

8. The ruler furiously stormed through the castle and *violently* destroyed every object in his path.
   angrily, in a mean and cruel way

9. The child hated porridge and threw his breakfast of *gruel* on the floor.
   oatmeal, porridge

10. Albert Einstein was a genius and was called an *intellect* of science.
    a very smart person

🎯 **Below-Level Practice** TE p. LR21

## Advanced

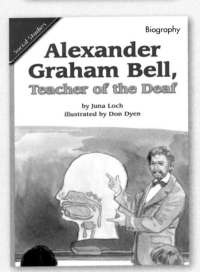

Biography

Social Studies

# Alexander Graham Bell,
## Teacher of the Deaf

by Juna Loch
illustrated by Don Dyen

**Advanced Reader**

---

Name _____

Alexander Graham Bell

### Character and Setting

• A **character** in a story is a person or animal that takes part in the events in a story.
• The **setting** is the time and place in which the events happen in a story.

**Directions** Answer the following questions using details from *Alexander Graham Bell, Teacher of the Deaf.*

Possible responses given.

1. Describe the character of the narrator. Tell the pages in the book where you find your evidence.

   He is a talking dog who thinks he is handsome, and never lies, p.4. He also loves his master, Alexander Graham Bell, pp.15, 18.

2. How do you learn about the narrator's character traits—through what the narrator says or thinks, what he does, or what others say or think about him?

   Through what he thinks and what he does with his master.

3. Describe Alexander Graham Bell. Tell the pages in the book where you find your evidence.

   He was always interested in how things work, p.4. He wanted to help deaf people talk and he worked hard, p. 10.

4. How does the reader learn about Alexander Graham Bell's character traits?

   Through what the narrator says and through what Bell does.

5. How does the setting of the story influence what Alexander Graham Bell does in his life?

   The story is set before the telephone was invented. People far away from each other had to use a telegraph. Bell wanted to invent something to allow people to speak to each other from great distances.

**Advanced Practice** TE p. LR26

---

Name _____

Alexander Graham Bell

### Vocabulary

**Directions** Use each of the following words in an original sentence about Alexander Graham Bell.

**Check the Words You Know**
____communicate
____dedicated
____frequency
____harmonic
____membrane
____patent
____vibrations
____visible

Possible responses given.

1. frequency

   Bell thought that frequency was the key to creating a telephone.

2. harmonic

   Bell and Watson worked together on the Harmonic Telegraph.

3. vibrations

   Bell knew that different objects make different vibrations.

4. communicate

   Bell wanted to help the deaf communicate with others.

5. membrane

   Bell's telephone had a membrane that vibrated and made sound.

6. visible

   The sound waves in Bell's telephone were not visible.

7. dedicated

   Bell was dedicated to helping deaf people.

8. patent

   Bell was the first to get a patent for the telephone.

**Advanced Practice** TE p. LR27

---

# ELL

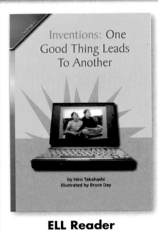

Inventions: One Good Thing Leads To Another

by Hiro Takahashi
illustrated by Bruce Day

**ELL Reader**

**ELL Poster 18**

### Teacher's Edition Notes

ELL notes throughout this lesson support instruction and reference additional resources at point of use.

**Teaching Guide
pp. 120–126, 246–247**

• Multilingual summaries of the main selection
• Comprehension lesson
• Vocabulary strategies and word cards
• ELL Reader 4.4.3 lesson

**ELL and Transition Handbook**

**Ten Important Sentences**

• Key ideas from every selection in the Student Edition
• Activities to build sentence power

---

## More Reading

### Readers' Theater Anthology

• Fluency practice
• Five scripts to build fluency
• Poetry for oral interpretation

### Leveled Trade Books

Below-Level

On-Level

Advanced

• Extended reading tied to the unit concept
• Lessons in the Trade Book Library Teaching Guide

---

# School + Home

### Homework

• Family Times Newsletter
• ELL Multilingual Selection Summaries

### Take-Home Books

• Leveled Readers

---

*The King in the Kitchen*

**440i**

# Cross-Curricular Centers

 **Listening**

## Listen to the Selections

**MATERIALS** `SINGLES`
CD player, headphones, AudioText CD, student book

**LISTEN TO LITERATURE** Listen to *The King in the Kitchen,* "A Man for All Seasonings," "A Confectioner," and "Expert" as you follow or read along in your book. Listen for details about characters and setting in *The King in the Kitchen.*

If there is anything you don't understand, you can listen again to any section.

---

 **Reading/Library**

## Read It Again!

**MATERIALS** `SINGLES` `PAIRS` `GROUPS`
Collection of books for self-selected reading, reading logs, student book

Select a book you have already read. Record the title of the book in your reading log. You may want to read with a partner.

Choose from the following:

- Leveled Readers
- ELL Readers
- Stories Written by Classmates
- Books from the Library
- *The King in the Kitchen*

**TEN IMPORTANT SENTENCES** Read the Ten Important Sentences for *The King in the Kitchen.* Then locate the sentences in the student book.

**BOOK CLUB** Get together with a group and discuss how reading a play is like and unlike reading other kinds of stories. Tell what you like or don't like about reading plays.

---

 **Drama**

## Read Aloud Dialogue

**MATERIALS** `PAIRS` `GROUPS`
Student book, writing materials, audiotape recorder

Read dialogue with expression.

1. **Work with a partner or group to choose part of the play to read aloud.**
2. **Review your character's dialogue. Identify the emotions of your character and how the lines should be read.**
3. **Take notes about stage directions or punctuation clues that help you figure out how to say your lines.**
4. **Read aloud with your partner or group. Record your performance.**

**EARLY FINISHERS** Read your lines again. Add facial expressions and body movement as you read aloud. *Drama*

**Scene:** King coming into the kitchen

**My Character:** Cook
**Stage directions:** tearfully, flustered
Go up on question mark.
She's worried that she's in trouble.

**Cook:** (stammers) I-I did.

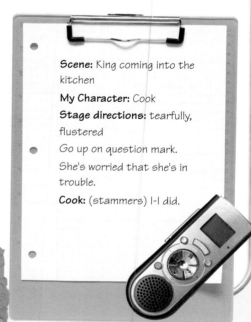

## Scott Foresman Reading Street Centers Survival Kit

Use *The King in the Kitchen* materials from the Reading Street Centers Survival Kit to organize this week's centers.

 **Writing/ Vocabulary**

# Write a Review

**MATERIALS** **SINGLES**
Writing materials, student book

Write a review of *The King in the Kitchen*.

1. Imagine you are a theater critic. Look back over the play to recall main events.
2. Begin your review with a short summary of the play.
3. Tell what you liked or didn't like about the play. Give reasons to support your opinions. Tell if you think others should see the play.

**EARLY FINISHERS** Compare *The King in the Kitchen* with your favorite book, TV show, or movie. Tell which one you like better and why.

> *The King in the Kitchen* is a funny play about a king with a crazy idea. He hates the soup his cook makes and thinks he can do better with his eyes covered. But the king doesn't know how to cook. I won't give away the ending. It's a fun surprise! Go see this play because it will make you laugh.

 **Science**

# Find a New Use

**MATERIALS** **PAIRS**
Everyday objects, writing and art materials

Work with a partner to brainstorm a new use for a familiar object.

1. Choose an object and study it carefully. What kind of parts does it have? How does it work?
2. Think of a new way that someone could use the object.
3. Write a few sentences describing the object's new use. Draw a picture to show how to use it.

**EARLY FINISHERS** Make an advertisement selling the object's new use. Include persuasive words in your advertisement.

### A Paper Clip Key Holder

You can use a paper clip to hold your house key. Just unbend one end and slide your key over it. Then bend the end back into place. Carry the clip in your pocket or hang it on a hook.

 **Technology**

# Write a Play

**MATERIALS** **PAIRS**
Word processing program, student book, printer

Adapt dialogue from a story and make it look like a play.

1. Scan your student book to find a few lines of dialogue between two characters in a story that isn't a play.
2. Use a word processing program to make the dialogue look like a play. Use *The King in the Kitchen* as a model. For example, use bold, capital letters for a character's name before a line of dialogue.
3. Follow classroom rules for printing your scene.

**EARLY FINISHERS** Add your own dialogue to your new play.

> MRS. HOUDINI (Hands VICTOR candy and asks softly): What are you supposed to be?
>
> VICTOR (Excited): I'm a magician! (Hands MRS. HOUDINI the letter.)

**ALL CENTERS** 🕐

*The King in the Kitchen* (440k)

## OBJECTIVES

- Build vocabulary by finding words related to the lesson concept.
- Listen to determine setting and draw conclusions about characters.

### Concept Vocabulary

**advertising** the act of bringing to public notice by radio or TV announcements, published notices, posters, or other means

**concentrate** pay close attention; focus the mind

**secret** something kept from the knowledge of others

### Monitor Progress

#### Check Vocabulary

| If... | then... review the |
|---|---|
| students are unable to place words on the web, | lesson concept. Place the words on the web and provide additional words for practice, such as *experimenting* and *manufacturers*. |

**SUCCESS PREDICTOR**

## DAY 1 Grouping Options

**Reading**
**Whole Group**
Introduce and discuss the Question of the Week. Then use pp. 440l–442b.

**Group Time**
**Differentiated Instruction**
**Read** this week's Leveled Readers. See pp. 440f–440g for the small group lesson plan.

**Whole Group**
Use p. 465a.

**Language Arts**
Use pp. 465e–465k.

# Build Concepts

## FLUENCY

**MODEL STRESS/EMPHASIS** As you read "Corn Flake Kings," model how to stress important words for emphasis. Preview the selection to identify key terms and main ideas to emphasize. You may want to read a few sentences with inappropriate stresses and discuss the impact on meaning.

## LISTENING COMPREHENSION

After reading "Corn Flake Kings," use the following questions to assess listening comprehension.

1. **When and where was the first dry breakfast cereal made?** *(in 1894 in the town of Battle Creek [Michigan])* **Setting**

2. **Based on details from the selection, what words would you use to describe the Kellogg brothers?** *(Possible responses: persistent, innovative, hard working, determined, creative, successful)* **Characters**

## BUILD CONCEPT VOCABULARY

Start a web to build concepts and vocabulary related to this week's lesson and the unit theme.

- Draw the Innovators Concept Web and define the word for students.
- Read the sentence with the word *secret* again. Ask students to pronounce *secret* and discuss its meaning.
- Place *secret* in an oval attached to *Work* and discuss how these concepts are related. Read the sentences in which *advertising* and *concentrate* appear. Have students pronounce the words, place them on the Web, and provide reasons.
- Brainstorm additional words and categories for the Web. Keep the Web on display and add words throughout the week.

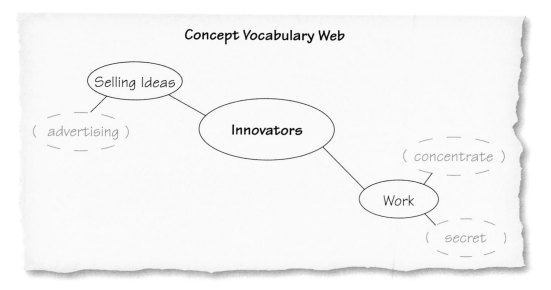

Concept Vocabulary Web

# Corn Flake Kings

### by Meredith Hooper

*Two brothers, Dr. John Kellogg and Will Keith Kellogg, invented breakfast cereal by accident as they prepared food for patients at the Sanitarium in Battle Creek, Michigan, where John worked. Soon competitors–a man named Post and others–were selling the brothers' inventions.*

Dr. John and Will Keith Kellogg made the first pre-cooked flaked cereal in 1894. Dr. John was experimenting with wheat, which he boiled for varying lengths of time, and then pushed through rollers. Will scraped the sticky dough off the rollers with a knife. Nothing useful could be done with this mess. One batch of boiled wheat got left for several days; no one had time to do anything with it. In the end the brothers decided to put it through the rollers, although it was very moldy, to see what would happen. Out came large thin flakes, each grain of wheat forming one flake. The flakes were baked in the oven and emerged crisp and tasty. After more experimenting, the Kelloggs found out how to leave the boiled wheat long enough to produce flakes, without the wheat becoming moldy.

Even though they were tough and rather tasteless, the wheat flakes were instantly popular with the Sanitarium patients. The secret of how to make them leaked out; soon there were dozens of manufacturers copying the recipe.

Battle Creek suffered a breakfast-food rush. Post's success and the various Kellogg inventions brought hundreds of hopeful money-makers into the town to try their luck at making a breakfast food in a box.

Will Keith could see all the Sanitarium food inventions being taken over and developed by other people. He was determined not to let this happen to the best invention of them all, corn flakes. Will Keith Kellogg set up in Battle Creek the Toasted Corn Flake Company.

The packets of corn flakes rolled out of Will Keith's factory in Battle Creek in ever increasing numbers. The taste of corn flakes had been improved by adding malt, sugar, and salt for flavor. Like Post, with Postum, he spent huge amounts on advertising, using especially the new invention, radio. Free samples of Toasted Corn Flakes were given away to millions of housewives. Breakfast-food manufacturers were some of the first to concentrate on *children*: If children wanted Kellogg's Corn Flakes, then their mothers would probably buy them. Give-away presents were included in each packet: cut-outs, sets of cards, models. William Keith Kellogg became known as the "Corn Flake King," and his products were made and sold around the world. Fifty years after the company began, the factories at Battle Creek alone produced six million packets of cereals a day, and a million of these were corn flakes.

SKILLS ←→ STRATEGIES IN CONTEXT

# Character/Setting
# Monitor/Fix Up

## OBJECTIVES

- Identify characters and setting in a story.
- Use monitoring and fix-up strategies to clarify understanding of text.

### Skills Trace

**Literary Elements: Character and Setting**

| Introduce/Teach | TE: 4.4 440–441, 488–489; 4.6 686–687 |
| --- | --- |
| Practice | TE: 171, 449, 455, 459, 497, 693, 699, 703<br>PB: 173, 177, 178, 193, 197, 198, 277, 278 |
| Reteach/Review | TE: 4.2 171; 4.4 401, 465b, 507b,<br>DI·54; 4.5 621; 4.6 711b, DI·54<br>PB: 66, 156, 246 |
| Test | Selection Test: 69–72, 77–80,<br>109–112; Benchmark Test: Unit 4 |

## INTRODUCE

Discuss a character from a recently read story. Ask volunteers to describe him or her, giving examples of what the character says and does. Ask what the character is like. *(Responses should include character traits.)*

Have students read the information on p. 440. Explain the following:

- We learn a lot about characters by what they say, what they do, and what other characters say about them.
- The setting is when and where a story takes place.
- Looking back over the text is a good way to get a better idea of what a character is like.

Use Skill Transparency 18 to teach character, setting, and fix-up strategies.

**Comprehension**

**Skill**
Character and Setting

**Strategy**
Monitor and Fix Up

## Character and Setting

- Characters are the people in a story. You can learn about characters by noticing what they say and do and by noticing how they interact with other characters.
- The setting is the time and place of a story.

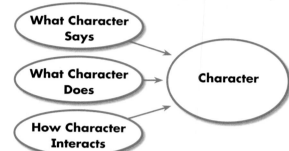

What Character Says → Character
What Character Does →
How Character Interacts →

### Strategy: Monitor and Fix Up

Good readers make sure they understand what they read. If they don't, they may use text features to fix up the problem. A play's text features can help you. For example, directions in parentheses tell you how a character should speak and act.

## Write to Read

1. Read "Frog Prince: The Sequel." Make a graphic organizer like the one above for the character of the Bad Fairy.

2. Use your graphic organizer to write a paragraph describing the Bad Fairy.

440

**Strategic Intervention**

**Character and Setting** You may wish to tell the classic story of "The Frog Prince" to students to give them prior knowledge of what happens when a princess kisses a frog. To help students get a better idea of character, read aloud p. 441 with expression before applying the skills and strategies. Have students find the words in the Princess's dialogue that tell where the call takes place.

## ELL

**Access Content**

**Beginning/Intermediate** For a Picture It! lesson on character and setting, see the ELL Teaching Guide, pp. 120–121.

**Advanced** Before reading "Frog Prince: The Sequel," discuss what a *sequel* is. Then have students use the title to predict when the events in the sequel take place.

# Frog Prince: The Sequel

**CHARACTERS:** BAD FAIRY, PRINCESS

*A telephone conversation in fairy tale land.*

**BAD FAIRY:** Nasty Spells Complaint Department. What do you want? •

**PRINCESS:** Hello, this is the princess up at the castle.

**BAD FAIRY:** Just a minute, Sweetie. Let me pull up your file. Oh, right, right. You kissed the frog and turned him back into a prince. How's that working out?

**PRINCESS:** It's totally not!

**BAD FAIRY:** What's the problem? He's not *handsome* enough for you? •

**PRINCESS:** No, no, it's not that. I mean, he's a really cute guy and everything, but . . .

**BAD FAIRY:** But what?

**PRINCESS:** He jumps out at people. And he makes these disgusting rib-bet noises. And—and he eats flies!

**BAD FAIRY:** Boys will be boys. (*She chuckles.*)

**PRINCESS:** But he's not acting like a boy. He's acting like a *frog!*

**BAD FAIRY:** (*in a no-nonsense way*) • Sorry, Sweetie. We have a strict no-returns policy on frogs turned human.

**PRINCESS:** Then what am I going to do?

**BAD FAIRY:** Live hoppily ever after? •

**1** **Skill** Where does the Bad Fairy work? What does she say? What do these things tell you about her?

**2** **Strategy** The word *handsome* is in italics. That's a signal that the Bad Fairy should emphasize it. How should she say this line?
(a) in a sweet way
(b) in a mocking way
(c) in a sad way

**3** **Strategy** If you are not sure about how the Bad Fairy should say these lines, reread the stage direction.

**4** **Skill** How would you describe the Bad Fairy after reading this line?

441

Available as **Skill Transparency** 18

---

## Character and Setting

- **Characters** are people in a story. You can learn what characters are like by noticing what they say and do and how they interact with other characters.
- **Setting** is the time and place in which the story occurs.

**Directions** Read the following passage and complete the diagram below.

Long ago and in a faraway place, a royal family lived in a castle. Princess Lil was a lovely girl, but she was clumsy. The king and queen called a duchess to the castle. "How do you do?" said Princess Lil, knocking over a spinning wheel. The duchess gave the princess twenty lessons in grace and balance. "I think I am getting better," Princess Lil said as she tripped over her royal throne.

The duchess came to love Lil for her kind sweetness. Lil never blamed anyone else for her clumsiness, and she always tried to help pick up what she knocked over. These were very rare things for a princess to do. Princess Lil offered other people so much more than grace and balance. Did Princess Lil learn to be graceful? No, but the duchess learned a lesson in kindness.

Possible answers given.

**What Princess Lil Says:**
1. "How do you do?"

**What Princess Lil Does:**
2. knocks things over and tries to pick things up

**How the Duchess Reacts to Princess Lil:**
3. The duchess learned to be kind from Lil.

**Princess Lil's Character Traits**
4. lovely, sweet, kind, helpful, honest

5. Write a sentence to describe the setting of this story.
The setting is a castle at some time in the past.

*School + Home* **Home Activity** Your child read a short story and analyzed one of the characters and the setting. Read a fairy tale with your child. Work with your child to identify the setting and the traits of the main character.

**Practice Book** p. 173

---

## TEACH

**1** **SKILL** Use dialogue to model identifying characters and setting.

*Think Aloud* **MODEL** The Bad Fairy works at the Nasty Spells Complaint Department. I can also tell that she's not going to be a nice fairy because her name is "Bad Fairy." Also she says "What do you want?" That is not very polite.

**2** **STRATEGY** Use text features to model how to monitor and fix up problems with comprehension.

*Think Aloud* **MODEL** I wasn't sure at first how the Bad Fairy would say that sentence, but I noticed that *handsome* is in italics. I stopped and thought about it. I already know that the Bad Fairy doesn't seem to be sympathetic to the Princess. Besides, she's a bad fairy. So I think the Bad Fairy is saying *handsome* in a mocking way. *(b)*

## PRACTICE AND ASSESS

**3** **STRATEGY** She says these lines in a no-nonsense way, so she is not sympathetic.

**4** **SKILL** The Bad Fairy is making fun of the Princess, so she is not very nice to her.

**WRITE** Have students complete steps 1 and 2 of the Write to Read activity with a partner or as a whole-class activity.

---

### Monitor Progress

#### Character and Setting

| **If...** students are unable to complete **Write to Read** on p. 440, | **then...** use Practice Book p. 173 to provide additional practice. |
| --- | --- |

## Tech Files
### ONLINE

Students can search the Internet to find out about inventions and inventors. Have them use a student-friendly search engine and the keywords *inventions, inventors,* or the name of an inventor.

**Build Background** Use ELL Poster 18 to build background and vocabulary for the lesson concept of inventions.

▲ **ELL Poster** 18

# Build Background

## ACTIVATE PRIOR KNOWLEDGE

**BEGIN A STORY PREDICTIONS CHART** about the play.

- Have students preview the selection title and illustrations. Encourage students to predict what might happen in the story. Remind them they have probably read other stories about kings. What kinds of things usually happen in these stories?

- Record what students predict in the first column on a story predictions chart.

- Help students think about what clues they use in making their predictions. Record clues in the second column.

- After students have read the story, they will write in the third column what actually happened in the story and compare what happened with what they predicted might happen.

Title  The King in the Kitchen

| What might happen? | What clues do I have? | What did happen? |
|---|---|---|
| A king might decide he wants to trade places with the cook. | The title

Pictures of a king cooking, with the cook looking on | |

▲ **Graphic Organizer** 7

**BACKGROUND BUILDING AUDIO** This week's audio explores putting on a play. After students listen, discuss what they found out and what surprised them most about the tasks involved in putting on a play.

**Background Building Audio**

# Introduce Vocabulary

## WORD-DEFINITION MATCH

Guide students in a matching activity with prepared cards of lesson vocabulary words and definitions.

| | |
|---|---|
| Duke | Nobleman of the highest title, ranking just below a prince |

Read aloud lesson vocabulary words, and have students tell what they know about them. Write lesson vocabulary words and definitions on separate cards to distribute to students. One student holds up his or her card and reads the definition. The student with the lesson vocabulary word that matches the definition holds up the card and says the word. Have the class decide whether the match is correct. **Activate Prior Knowledge**

Explain that feelings suggested by a word are called its *connotations*. Ask students which of the lesson vocabulary words seem to have a favorable, or positive, connotation, and which have a negative connotation. **Connotation**

By the end of the week, students should know the lesson vocabulary words. They can reuse the cards to make word-definition matches again. This time, the student holding the lesson vocabulary word uses it in an oral sentence.

Use the Multisyllabic Word Routine on p. DI·1 to help students read multisyllabic words.

---

### Lesson Vocabulary

#### WORDS TO KNOW

**T duke** nobleman of the highest title, ranking just below a prince

**T dungeon** a dark underground room or cell to hold prisoners

**T furiously** with unrestrained energy, speed, etc.

**T genius** person having very great natural power of mind

**T majesty** title used in speaking to or of a king, queen, emperor, empress, etc.

**T noble** high or great by birth, rank, or title

**T peasant** farmer of the working class in Europe, Asia, and Latin America

**T porridge** food made of oatmeal or other grain boiled in water or milk until it thickens

---

#### MORE WORDS TO KNOW

**exiled** forced to leave your country or home, often by law as a punishment; banished

**inferior** not very good; below most others; low in quality

**treasury** money owned; funds

**T** = Tested Word

---

**Vocabulary**

**Directions** Choose the word from the box that best matches each definition. Write the word on the line.

| | | |
|---|---|---|
| furiously | 1. with unrestrained energy | **Check the Words You Know** |
| noble | 2. high and great by birth, rank, or title | duke |
| | | dungeon |
| majesty | 3. title used in speaking to or of a king, queen, emperor, etc. | furiously |
| | | genius |
| genius | 4. one who has great natural power of mind | majesty |
| | | noble |
| | | peasant |
| peasant | 5. a farmer of the working class | porridge |

**Directions** Choose the word from the box that fits best in each sentence. Write the word on the line shown to the left.

porridge — 6. On cold mornings, I like to eat ____ made from oats.

majesty — 7. Her ____ walks with dignity and grace.

genius — 8. Only a ____ could have understood the difficult code.

dungeon — 9. The prisoner in the ____ never saw the sun.

duke — 10. Among royalty, a ____ is the husband of a duchess.

**Write a Diary**

Imagine that you were living a long time ago and you played games with knights, princes, and princesses. On a separate sheet of paper, write an entry in your diary about the games you played. Use as many vocabulary words as you can.

Diary entries should include vocabulary words and specific details.

**School + Home Home Activity** Your child identified and used vocabulary words from *The King in the Kitchen*. Play a vocabulary game with your child where you give clues to the vocabulary words and your child tries to guess the word.

▲ **Practice Book** p. 174

# Vocabulary Strategy

## OBJECTIVE

⊙ Use a dictionary or glossary to determine word meaning.

## INTRODUCE

Discuss the strategy for finding words in a dictionary or glossary by using the steps on p. 442.

## TEACH

- Have students read "Keeping a Secret," paying attention to how vocabulary is used.

- Model using a dictionary to determine the meaning of *peasant*.

**Think Aloud** **MODEL** I'm not sure what *peasant* means so I'll look in a dictionary. First I'll find the words beginning with *p*. Then I'll find *peasant* and read the entry. It means "a farmer of the working class." That meaning makes sense in the sentence.

- You may also wish to model using the glossary to determine the meaning of *peasant* or another vocabulary word.

**Words to Know**

majesty

genius

peasant

noble

duke

furiously

dungeon

porridge

# Vocabulary Strategy
## for Unfamiliar Words

**Dictionary/Glossary** You can use a glossary or a dictionary to find out the meaning of an unfamiliar word. A glossary is part of a book. It lists important words and their meanings. A dictionary is its own book. It gives the meanings of most of the words in a language. The words in a glossary or dictionary are listed in alphabetical order.

**1.** Look at the first letter in the unfamiliar word.

**2.** Open the glossary or dictionary to the section for that letter.

**3.** Find the word.

**4.** Read the entry for the word. If the word has more than one meaning, decide which meaning fits in the sentence.

**5.** Try that meaning in the sentence to see if it makes sense.

As you read "Keeping a Secret," use a glossary or dictionary to find the meanings of unfamiliar vocabulary words.

442

## DAY 2 Grouping Options

**Reading**
**Whole Group** Discuss the Question of the Day. Then use pp. 442–445.

**Group Time** Differentiated Instruction
**Read** *The King in the Kitchen.* See pp. 440f–440g for the small group lesson plan.

**Whole Group** Use p. 465a.

**Language Arts**
Use pp. 465e–465k.

### Strategic Intervention

⊙ **Dictionary/Glossary** Show students how to use guide words at the top of a glossary or dictionary page. If the word has more than one meaning, have them discuss which meaning makes sense in the sentence.

**Access Content** Use ELL Poster 18 to preteach vocabulary. Choose from the following to meet language proficiency levels.

**Beginning** Have students use vocabulary frames to record definitions.

**Intermediate** Use the title "Keeping a Secret" and vocabulary words to complete the Story Prediction from Vocabulary A graphic organizer.

**Advanced** Teach the lesson on pp. 442–443. Have pairs quiz each other by making flash cards of the vocabulary words.

Resources for home-language words may include parents, bilingual staff members, bilingual dictionaries, or online translation sources.

# Keeping a Secret

Once upon a time, there was a king who had really big ears. The only person who knew this was the king's barber. The king told the barber, "Never tell anyone what you have seen." The barber nodded vigorously and replied, "Oh, yes, of course, your Majesty."

The barber was a genius at snipping hair but not at keeping secrets. He went into a field and dug a hole. He whispered into the hole, "The king has really big ears." Then he filled the hole and went home.

Oats grew in the field and when the wind blew, the oats whispered, "The king has really big ears." A peasant heard the oats. He told his wife, who told the neighbors, who told the noble lord, who told the duke, who told everyone else.

The king soon realized that everyone knew his secret. He confronted the barber and shouted furiously, "Guards, take this man to the dungeon!"

Alone in the dark dungeon, the poor barber puzzled over how the secret had gotten out. A guard brought him a bowl of porridge (which is made from oats). As the barber lifted the bowl, he heard a faint whisper, "The king has really big ears."

## Words to Write

Why do you think the barber couldn't keep a secret? What would you have told him to do? Write your advice to the barber. Use words from the Words to Know list.

443

## PRACTICE AND ASSESS

- Explain that not every unfamiliar word needs to be looked up in a dictionary or glossary. Readers can read on to determine if the word's meaning is essential to understanding.

- Have students determine the meanings of the remaining words and tell if they used context clues, word structure, or a glossary or dictionary to find the meanings.

- If you played a word-definition match game (p. 442b), have students reuse the cards to make matches again. Students can also take turns selecting a vocabulary word card and using the word in a sentence.

- Have students complete Practice Book p. 175.

**WRITE** Writing should include vocabulary words and some advice to the barber.

### Monitor Progress

#### Dictionary/Glossary

| **If...** students need more practice with the lesson vocabulary, | **then...** use Tested Vocabulary Cards. |
|---|---|

---

#### Vocabulary • Dictionary/Glossary

- **Dictionaries** and **glossaries** provide alphabetical lists of words and their meanings. A dictionary is its own book, but a glossary is part of a book.
- Sometimes using context clues won't help you figure out the meaning of an unfamiliar word. When this happens, you can use a dictionary or glossary to find the word's meaning.

**Directions** Read the following passage. Look for context clues as you read to help you define each word in the table. Use a dictionary or glossary if necessary.

One cold night, the royal cook was furiously fixing porridge for the servants. He threw some oats into a pot. Then he tossed in some dried-up apples and crumbly pieces of nuts. He flung in the last of the honey from the honey jar. He splashed in water and let the ingredients boil. To his surprise, the king entered the kitchen and wanted to eat what he was cooking. "Your Majesty, it's for the servants. I'll make you a noble feast instead," he said. The king replied, "That's not necessary. Besides, I'm famished."

After he tasted the porridge, he began to gulp more and more. "You're a genius, Cook!" he said. "And it's good for a chilly morning. It's perfect for our royal breakfast."

| Word | Definition |
|---|---|
| furiously | 1. with unrestrained energy |
| Majesty | 2. title used for a king or queen |
| porridge | 3. food made from boiled oatmeal or other grain |
| genius | 4. a person with a powerful mind |

5. Use a dictionary or glossary to find the definition for *famished*.

very hungry

**Home Activity** Your child learned to understand unfamiliar words after looking them up in a dictionary or glossary. Work with your child to identify unfamiliar words in a story. Have him or her look them up in a dictionary and see which meaning fits best in the sentence.

▲ **Practice Book** p. 175

# Prereading Strategies

## OBJECTIVES

- Understand characters and setting to improve comprehension.
- Monitor comprehension and use fix-up strategies to understand characters and setting.

## GENRE STUDY

### Play

*The King in the Kitchen* is a play. Explain that a play is written for the stage where the play will be performed. It has stage directions written in parentheses to help readers imagine the action and setting as the playwright intended.

## PREVIEW AND PREDICT

Have students preview the title and illustrations. Discuss what they think the problem will be in the play. Encourage students to use lesson vocabulary words as they talk about their predictions.

### Strategy Response Log

**Predict** Have students write their predictions in their strategy response logs. Students will confirm their predictions in the Strategy Response Log activity on p. 451.

**Genre** **Plays** are stories written to be performed. As you read, try to imagine actors performing this story on a stage.

444

### ELL

**Access Content** Preview the format of the play; point out that each name in boldface represents a character that is speaking.

Consider having students read the selection summary in English or in students' home languages. See the Multilingual Summaries in the ELL Teaching Guide, pp. 124–126.

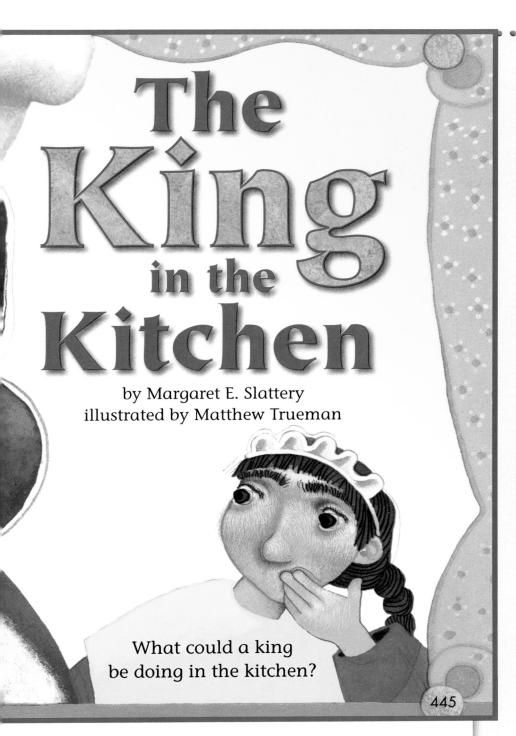

# The King in the Kitchen

by Margaret E. Slattery
illustrated by Matthew Trueman

What could a king
be doing in the kitchen?

445

## SET PURPOSE

Read the cast of characters and the description of the setting aloud to students. Have them consider their preview discussion and state why they want to read the play.

Remind students to use the stage directions to help them if they have trouble understanding the characters and setting as they read.

## STRATEGY RECALL

Students have now used these before-reading strategies:

- preview the selection to be aware of its genre, features, and possible content;
- activate prior knowledge about that content and what to expect of that genre;
- make predictions;
- set a purpose for reading.

Remind students to be aware of and flexibly use the during-reading strategies they have learned:

- link prior knowledge to new information;
- summarize text they have read so far;
- ask clarifying questions;
- answer questions they or others pose;
- check their predictions and either refine them or make new predictions;
- recognize the text structure the author is using, and use that knowledge to make predictions and increase comprehension;
- visualize what the author is describing;
- monitor their comprehension and use fix-up strategies.

After reading, students will use these strategies:

- summarize or retell the text;
- answer questions they or others pose;
- reflect to make new information become part of their prior knowledge.

Audio CD   AudioText

# Guiding Comprehension

**1** **Graphic Sources • Critical**

**Look at the pictures of the characters. What do they tell you about the play and what it will be like?**

Possible response: The pictures show all the characters who have parts in the play. The style of the illustrations tells me that this play will probably be funny. There are a king and a princess, so I think this will be set in the past and it might be a fairy tale.

---

### Monitor Progress

**REVIEW** Graphic Sources

| If... students are unable to use graphic sources to help them understand the play, | then... use the skill and strategy instruction on p. 447. |
| --- | --- |

---

**2** **Cause and Effect • Inferential**

**Why does the King send the Peasant to the dungeon?**

The Peasant asks to marry the Princess. The King wants her to marry the Duke.

**3**  **Character • Inferential**

**What do you know about the King?**

He loses his temper and his treasury is almost empty.

**Characters**

COOK

1ST KITCHEN MAID

2ND KITCHEN MAID

PEASANT

KING

PRINCESS

GUARD

DUKE

**SETTING:** *The palace kitchen. Large table with pots and pans is upstage center. Several stools are placed around stage.*

**AT RISE:** COOK *is standing behind table, fussing with the pots and pans.* 1ST KITCHEN MAID *sits on a stool, peeling potatoes.* GUARD *enters, leading* PEASANT *by the arm. They start to walk across the stage.*

**COOK** *(Looking up):* Ho, there! You! Guard!

**GUARD** *(Stopping):* What is it, Cook?

**COOK:** Where are you taking that man?

**GUARD:** To the dungeon.

**1ST KITCHEN MAID:** Oh, my!

446

---

**E L L**

**Context Clues** Help students use context to figure out what a *dungeon* is (p. 446, line 10). Cook's question on p. 447, "Why, what's he done, poor fellow?" indicates that the dungeon must be a place where people are punished, like a jail. A dungeon is a dark, underground jail.

**COOK:** To the dungeon! Why, what's he done, poor fellow?

**PEASANT:** It was nothing, really. All I did was to ask the King for the Princess's hand in marriage.

**GUARD:** And him a peasant!

**COOK:** A peasant! Why, a peasant can't marry the Princess.

**PEASANT:** I don't see why not. I'm handsome and clever, and I'm awfully fond of the Princess. She's awfully fond of me too.

**1ST KITCHEN MAID** *(Staring):* She is?

**PEASANT:** Oh, my, yes. I come to the palace every day to deliver vegetables. The Princess thinks I'm wonderful, and I think she's wonderful.

**COOK:** The Princess can't marry a peasant, I tell you. She has to marry someone rich and famous and noble and—

**1ST KITCHEN MAID:** Like the Duke.

**PEASANT:** The Duke is fifty years old, and dull too. The Princess will never marry him.

**COOK:** The Princess will marry whomever her father tells her to marry. I'm sure he'll want a wealthy son–in–law because they say the Royal Treasury is almost empty.

**GUARD:** Besides, I told you not to ask the King today. If you'd asked him some other time, he might only have exiled you. But he's awfully upset today.

**COOK:** Why?

**GUARD:** It was the soup you sent up. He said it was horrible and threw it on the floor.

**1ST KITCHEN MAID:** Oh, my!

447

---

# Graphic Sources REVIEW

## TEACH

- Remind students that illustrations with captions often give information that is not in the text.
- Model using the illustrations on the top of p. 446.

**Think Aloud** **MODEL** The pictures on this page show me the characters in the play. Knowing the characters involved will help me keep track of what happens. These pictures are drawn like cartoons, so that makes me think this play will be funny.

## PRACTICE AND ASSESS

- Have students find other pictures that suggest the play is a humorous one. *(Possible response: The picture of the King, the Cook, and Kitchen Maids on p. 449 is funny.)*
- To assess, use Practice Book p. 176.

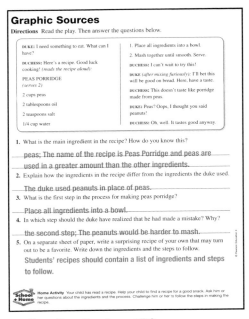

▲ **Practice Book** p. 176

*The King in the Kitchen* **447**

# Guiding Comprehension

**④ Author's Purpose • Critical**

*Question the Author* **Why do you think the author has the Peasant singing as he goes to the dungeon?**

Possible response: The author wants to show that the Peasant doesn't take being sent to the dungeon seriously. The author also wants us to laugh and know this is a funny play.

**⑤  Setting • Inferential**

**How does the setting add to the silliness of the story?**

We don't expect to see a king in the palace kitchen.

**⑥ Character • Inferential**

**So far, what kind of character do you think the King is? Explain your answer.**

Possible response: He is silly and demanding. He has never been in a kitchen, but he thinks he can make better soup than the Cook.

---

### Monitor Progress

#### Character and Setting

| **If**... students are unable to analyze the King's character and the setting, | **then**... use the skill and strategy instruction on p. 449. |
|---|---|

---

**GUARD:** Well, come on, peasant. *(Takes PEASANT's arm and starts toward door.)*

**④ PEASANT** *(Sings to tune of "London Bridge")*: To the dungeon we must go, we must go, we must go. To the dungeon— *(Exits with GUARD)*

**COOK** *(Tearfully)*: Oh, dear, the King didn't like the soup and I took such trouble with it.

**2ND KITCHEN MAID** *(Rushing in breathlessly)*: Cook, Cook! Something terrible!

**COOK:** What's the matter?

**2ND KITCHEN MAID:** It's the King. He's coming here!

**COOK** *(Flustered)*: What?

**1ST KITCHEN MAID:** The King! But he's never been in the kitchen before.

**⑤ COOK:** This is terrible. Here now, both of you start working. We'll have to straighten this kitchen up. *(ALL rush around, trying to straighten up, bumping into each other and dropping pots and pans.)*

**⑥ KING** *(Striding in)*: Well, so this is the kitchen. *(Looks around.)* Hmm. At least you're working. Now, who made that awful soup?

**COOK** *(Curtsies)*: I—I did, your Majesty.

**KING:** It was horrible! Horrible, do you hear me?

**COOK:** But, your Majesty, it's really not my fault. The ingredients we've been getting lately have been very inferior.

**KING:** Stuff and nonsense! I could make a better soup than that with my eyes shut. In fact, I'll do it!

448

---

**ELL**

**Understanding Idioms** The statement "We'll have to straighten this kitchen up" (p. 448, line 16) contains the idiom *straighten up*. This sentence can be restated as "We'll have to clean this kitchen."

# Character and Setting

## TEACH

Read the dialogue between the King and the Cook on p. 448. Remind students that what a character says and does can tell us a lot about what the character is like. Then model how to interpret the character's actions.

**Think Aloud** **MODEL** First the King sends the Peasant to the dungeon because the Peasant wants to marry the Princess. Then the King goes to the kitchen for the first time and proclaims that he can make better soup with his eyes shut. His words and actions tell me that he is used to getting his own way and also that he is one silly king.

## PRACTICE AND ASSESS

- Have students work in pairs to describe what they think the Peasant is like. Have them begin a list of traits by considering what the Peasant has said about himself (*I'm handsome and clever*) and what he has done (*asked to marry a princess*).
- To assess, make sure students' lists show at least two traits.

## EXTEND SKILLS

### Dialogue

As students read the dialogue in the play, explain that actors playing the parts would not read the stage directions aloud. Encourage students to imagine they are the actual characters so they can put expression in the characters' voices to show the audience the characters' traits. Since this play is a comedy, they can exaggerate these traits for a more comedic effect.

# Guiding Comprehension

**7** ◎ **Character • Inferential**

**Does the King know a lot about cooking? How can you tell?**

No, he doesn't seem to know a lot about cooking. He doesn't know what anything is in the kitchen.

**8** ◎ **Monitor and Fix Up • Critical**

**If you have trouble following the action on this page, what text feature would help you?**

The stage directions, which are in parentheses and italics, would help because they tell what the characters are doing.

**9** **Compare and Contrast • Critical**

*Text to Text* **How is this play like and unlike other stories about kings and princesses that you have read?**

Possible response: Like other stories, the Princess wants to marry someone her father doesn't approve of. Unlike other stories, this king is rather silly.

---

**2ND KITCHEN MAID** (*Shocked*)*:* Your Majesty!

**KING:** Yes, that's exactly what I'll do. And with my eyes shut. Now, out of my way, everybody. (*Marches behind table, looking at things on it. Picks up mixing spoon.*) What's this?

**COOK:** A mixing spoon, your Majesty.

**KING:** Well, I guess I'll need it. Now let me see, what do I want?

**2ND KITCHEN MAID:** Maybe a bowl, your Majesty? (*Hands him a bowl.*)

**KING:** Of course. The very thing. You're a smart girl. (*Puts bowl on table.*) All right, I'm ready. Now, Cook, give me your apron.

**COOK:** But your Majesty—

**KING:** Hurry up! (*Takes apron from* COOK *and puts it on.*) Now, I'll show you I can do this with my eyes shut. Tie something around my eyes, Cook.

**COOK:** Your Majesty, I don't really think—

**KING:** Be quick about it. (COOK *ties dish towel around* KING*'s eyes.*) There! I'm ready to begin.

**1ST KITCHEN MAID:** What will you do first, your Majesty?

**KING:** Ah, let me see. Have we any water?

**COOK:** Oh, a nice kettle full, your Majesty.

**KING:** Well, pour some in the bowl. (COOK *pours some in.*) Now, I think I'd like a little flour. (COOK *dumps some in a bowl.* KING *feels about table and picks up a bottle.*) What's this?

**COOK:** That's sauce, your Majesty. You don't want that for soup.

**KING:** Silence! That's exactly what I do want.

450

---

Ⓔ Ⓛ Ⓛ

**Assess Content** Explain that the long dashes at the end of some of Cook's statements ("But your Majesty—") indicate that Cook was interrupted. Ask students to think of how these statements might have ended had they not been interrupted.

**COOK:** But, your Majesty—

**KING:** Who's making this, you or I?

**COOK:** You are, your Majesty.

**KING:** Very well then. *(Pours some sauce in bowl.)* Now, what next?

**1ST KITCHEN MAID:** Maybe a little salt.

**KING:** That's just what I was about to say myself. Put some in. *(KITCHEN MAID pours a little salt in a teaspoon and dumps it in.)* How much did you put in?

**1ST KITCHEN MAID:** Oh, just a dash, as the good cookbooks say.

**KING** *(Screaming):* Cookbooks! Cookbooks! What do I care about cookbooks? You, Cook! Do you use cookbooks?

**COOK:** Oh, yes, your Majesty.

**KING:** Then that's what's the matter with your cooking. No imagination. Who ever heard of a dash of salt? We want this to have flavor, don't we? Here, where's that salt shaker? *(Pulls towel off eyes and grabs up shaker.)* This is the way to do it. *(Holds salt shaker in both hands upside-down over bowl. Shakes it furiously.)* There, that's better. *(Stirs it vigorously with mixing spoon. Enter PRINCESS.)*

**PRINCESS:** Oh, here you are, Father. I've been looking everywhere for you.

**KING:** Now, now, my dear, don't bother me. I'm very busy.

**PRINCESS:** Father, I must talk to you. Have you seen my peasant anywhere? He's usually here by eleven o'clock with the vegetables.

**KING:** Oh, him. Yes, I saw him and threw him in the dungeon.

**PRINCESS** *(Shrieking):* What! **9**

451

---

## Develop Vocabulary

### PRACTICE LESSON VOCABULARY

Students respond orally to each question.

**1. If you run *furiously*, do you run slowly or fast?** *(Fast)*

**2. Does a king or a *duke* have more power in a kingdom?** *(A king has more power.)*

**3. Does a *noble* person have a high or low rank in society?** *(High rank)*

**4. Would a *peasant* more likely live in a hut or a castle?** *(A peasant would more likely live in a hut.)*

### BUILD CONCEPT VOCABULARY

Review previous concept words with students. Ask if students have come across any words today in their reading that they would like to add to the Innovators Concept Web, such as *ingredients* and *clever*.

---

STRATEGY SELF-CHECK

# Monitor and Fix Up

Ask students to summarize what happens when the King makes the soup. If students have trouble, remind them to use the stage directions in parentheses to help them follow the action. *(Possible response: The King puts a bowl on the table. Cook ties a towel around his eyes. Cook pours water and flour in the bowl, and the King pours sauce in. The Kitchen Maid puts in a little salt, but then the King pulls off his blindfold and shakes a lot of salt into the bowl and mixes it all up.)*

Students can use a story sequence chart to summarize the characters, setting, and events in the play so far. Have them write one or two adjectives on the chart to describe each main character.

## SELF-CHECK

Students can ask themselves questions to assess their ability to use the skill and strategy.

- Did I understand what the characters did and how they spoke as I read the play?

- Did I use the stage directions to help me understand the characters and setting?

### Character and Setting

| If... students have difficulty describing the characters and setting, | then... revisit the skill lesson on pp. 440–441. Reteach as necessary. |
|---|---|

**Confirm Predictions** Provide the following prompt: Was your prediction accurate? (See p. 444.) Revisit your prediction or make a new prediction about the rest of the play.

*If you want to teach this play in two sessions, stop here.*

# Guiding Comprehension

*If you are teaching the play in two days, discuss characters and setting and review the vocabulary.*

**10 Plot • Literal**

**Why can't the Princess marry the Peasant?**

The King needs money, so he wants the Princess to marry someone with lots of money.

**11 Vocabulary • Dictionary/Glossary**

**You can use a glossary to determine the meaning of an unfamiliar word. Use your glossary to find the meaning of *porridge* on the last line of p. 452.**

It means "a food made of oatmeal or other grain boiled in water or milk until it thickens."

---

### Monitor Progress

#### Dictionary/Glossary

| **If...** students have difficulty using a glossary to find the meaning of *porridge*, | **then...** use the vocabulary strategy instruction on p. 453. |
|---|---|

---

## DAY 3 Grouping Options

**Reading**

**Whole Group** Discuss the Question of the Day.

**Group Time** Differentiated Instruction
**Read** *The King in the Kitchen.* See pp. 440f–440g for the small group lesson plan.

**Whole Group** Discuss the Reader Response questions on p. 462. Then use p. 465a.

**Language Arts**
Use pp. 465e–465k.

---

**KING** *(Looking around at things on table and stroking chin):* Now let me see, what next?

**PRINCESS:** But, Father, why?

**KING:** Are you still here? Go away.

**PRINCESS:** Father, why did you throw him in the dungeon?

**KING:** Who?

**PRINCESS** *(Stamping foot):* Father, stop it. You know who I mean.

**KING:** Oh, that peasant. Yes, I had to throw him in the dungeon. He had the colossal nerve to ask for your hand in marriage.

**PRINCESS** *(Clapping hands):* He did? You have to let him out of the dungeon. I want to marry him.

**10 KING:** Nonsense, you can't marry a peasant and you know it. What this family needs is a relative with some money. Now find someone with royal blood and lots of money and you can marry him.

**PRINCESS** *(Sitting down on chair and crying):* I want to marry my peasant.

**KING:** There, don't cry. Look at this nice thing Daddy made for you here. See? *(Holds bowl out to her.)*

**PRINCESS** *(Sniffing):* What is it?

**KING:** I don't know. Why don't you taste it?

**PRINCESS** *(Peering at it):* It looks awful. What do you suppose it is, Cook?

**COOK** *(Coming over and taking bowl):* I'm sure I don't know, your **11** Highness. *(Stirs it around a little.)* It's not porridge.

452

---

### ELL

**Fluency** The last line on p. 453 contains an unwieldy sentence with two negative contractions. It can be restated as "Maybe he is not so dull. Maybe he can tell what this is."

**KING:** Of course it's not porridge. It's—it's—well, don't all of you stand there. What is it?

**1ST KITCHEN MAID:** I really don't think it's soup.

**2ND KITCHEN MAID:** Nor stew.

**KING** (Stroking chin): Hmm. This is a problem. (Paces floor.) I have it! One of my wonderful ideas!

**COOK:** Oh, dear! (KITCHEN MAIDS groan.)

**PRINCESS:** Oh, Father, what is it this time?

**KING:** We'll have a contest. Whoever can guess what this is, wins a reward.

**COOK:** And what will the reward be, your Majesty?

**KING:** Why, the hand of the Princess in marriage, of course.

**PRINCESS** (Jumping up): Father!

**KING:** Certainly. You want to have a lovely wedding and get lots of presents, don't you?

**PRINCESS:** Yes, but—

**KING:** Now, let me see. Whom shall we have enter the contest?

**1ST KITCHEN MAID:** What about the Duke, your Majesty?

**KING:** Of course. Now, Kitchen Maid, run quickly and tell the Guard to tell the Footman to send the Duke here immediately. (Exit 1ST KITCHEN MAID.)

**PRINCESS:** But I don't want to marry the Duke. He's the dullest man in the palace.

**KING:** Well he can't be so dull he won't be able to tell what this is.

453

---

**VOCABULARY STRATEGY**

# Dictionary/ Glossary

## TEACH

- Ask students how a glossary is useful. Remind them that the glossary lists words in alphabetical order, and the guide words can help them locate a word more quickly.

- Read the last line on p. 452. Model using a glossary to find the meaning of *porridge*.

**Think Aloud** **MODEL** A glossary is good to use because it is smaller than a dictionary. Like a dictionary, a glossary has guide words at the top of the pages to help me find the word *porridge*. When I find the guide words that come before and after *porridge*, I look for the word on that page. There it is. *Porridge* is a noun and is a "food made of oatmeal or other grain boiled in water or milk until it thickens." Does this meaning fit in the sentence? Yes, it does. The King made something that might be mistaken for cooked oatmeal.

## PRACTICE AND ASSESS

- Have students use the glossary to determine the meaning of *furiously* on p. 451, line 18. (with unrestrained energy, speed, etc.)

- To assess, have students act out the meaning of this word or use it in a sentence.

## EXTEND SKILLS

### Alphabetical Order

As students review use of dictionaries and glossaries, explain that sometimes words are spelled the same until the fourth or fifth letter. Write on the board the words *beads*, *beach*, and *beacon*. Ask students which would appear first in a dictionary and why. Students may write words that fit this pattern on individual cards and use them to test classmates.

*The King in the Kitchen*    **453**

# Guiding Comprehension

**12**  **Character • Critical**

*Question the Author* **Why do you think the author chose to have the Duke compliment the King when he enters?**

Possible response: The author wants us to know that the Duke is a flatterer.

---

**Monitor Progress**

 **Character and Setting**

| **If**... students have difficulty understanding how the author establishes the Duke's character, | **then**... use the skill and strategy instruction on p. 455. |
|---|---|

---

**13 Dialogue • Inferential**

**To whom is the Duke speaking when he says "And, your Highness" in his second speech on p. 454? How do you know?**

He is speaking to the Princess. The stage directions say "Bows to PRINCESS."

**14 Predict • Inferential**

**What do you think has happened to the Duke? Why isn't he speaking?**

Possible responses: Either the mixture he ate tastes so awful that he can't speak, or he can't open his mouth.

---

**PRINCESS:** How will you know if he's right anyway? You don't know what it is yourself.

**KING:** Nonsense! Why, it's—it's—*(Noise outside.)* Ah, here comes the Duke now. *(Enter* GUARD *and* DUKE.*)*

**DUKE:** Ah, your Majesty, good afternoon. Making a little tour of the kitchens, I see? We in this country are so fortunate to have a king who takes an interest in these simple matters. I have always said—

**KING:** Save that for an after-dinner speech.

**DUKE:** Ahem, yes. And, your Highness. *(Bows to* PRINCESS.*)* How beautiful you look today!

**KING:** All right, all right, let's get on with it. Now, Duke, can you tell me what I've made here in this bowl? *(Points to bowl* COOK *is holding.)*

**DUKE:** Er—what *you've* made, your Majesty?

**KING:** Yes, of course I made it. And if you can tell me what it is, you win the hand of the Princess in marriage.

**DUKE:** Well, that would indeed be an honor. *(Takes bowl.)* Now let me see. *(Stirs it around.)* Ah–er—could it be—pudding?

**KING:** Pudding! Of course not, you nincompoop! Why would I make a pudding? You must really be dull.

**DUKE:** Oh, no I'm not—not at all, your Majesty. Maybe if I could just taste it—*(Takes some up on mixing spoon.)* I'm sure it will be delicious. *(Puts spoon to mouth.)*

**KING:** Well?

**DUKE** *(Choking and coughing):* Ah—ugh—er *(Claps hand over mouth.)*

454

---

**ELL**

**Extend Language** Sometimes people talk with disfluencies, or filler words, when they can't think of what to say next. In Spanish, people say *pues* or *eh*. In French, people say *eu* and *em*. Have students study the disfluencies the Duke uses *(ah, er, ugh)*, and compare them to those they use in their home languages.

**KING:** What? Speak up, man!

**DUKE** *(Muttering through hand over mouth):* Ug—mmph—mm—er—

**KING:** What is he trying to say?

455

SKILLS ↔ STRATEGIES IN CONTEXT

# Character Monitor and Fix Up

## TEACH

Model monitoring comprehension and using text features to help draw conclusions about the Duke's character on p. 454.

**Think Aloud** **MODEL** First the Duke compliments the King for being in the kitchen. He sounds like he's trying to flatter the King. When I read his next speech I got a little confused, because he says "And, your Highness." I thought he was talking to the King, but he wouldn't tell the King he was beautiful. The stage directions in parentheses say "Bows to Princess." That helps me figure out that he is talking to the Princess now, and he is flattering her too.

## PRACTICE AND ASSESS

- Have students read the rest of p. 454 and find two words the King uses to describe the Duke. Do they think the King is correct? *(The King calls the Duke a "nincompoop" and "dull." Most students should agree with the King.)*

- To assess, make sure students can describe the Duke's character in their own words.

# Guiding Comprehension

**15** **Author's Craft • Critical**

*Question the Author* **On the bottom of p. 456, the Princess and the Peasant use almost the same language in addressing one another. Why did the author write the lines this way?**

Possible response: The repeated phrases are humorous. By repeating the same words, it exaggerates the humor.

**16**  **Vocabulary • Dictionary/Glossary**

**Have students use a dictionary to determine the meaning of *blood* on p. 457, line 8.**

It means "relationship by descent from a common ancestor; family; parentage."

| Monitor Progress | |
|---|---|
| **Dictionary/Glossary** | |
| **If...** students have difficulty using a dictionary to determine the meaning of *blood*, | **then...** use the vocabulary strategy instruction on p. 457. |

**17** **Character • Inferential**

**The Peasant says that of course he will win the contest. What does this tell you about his character?**

Possible response: He is a confident person and believes in his abilities.

---

**PRINCESS:** I don't know. I told you he was dull.

**DUKE** *(Sitting down on stool in corner):* Mmph—er—*(Covers face with hands.)*

**PRINCESS:** Well, there you are, Father. He doesn't know what you've made so I don't have to marry him.

**COOK:** Congratulations, your Highness.

**KING:** Well, just because he's dull doesn't mean everyone is. Let's see, whom shall we ask next? *(Looks about room.)* Ah, what about you, Guard?

**PRINCESS:** Father!

**GUARD:** Oh, I'm afraid it wouldn't be fair for me to enter the contest, your Majesty. I'm already married.

**KING:** Well, don't stand there gaping. Go and find someone. *(Exit GUARD.)*

**PRINCESS:** Father, this is so silly.

**KING:** Not at all. By now I'm curious myself to find out what I've made. It's too thick for soup.

**COOK:** And too thin for porridge. *(Enter GUARD.)*

**GUARD:** Your Majesty, I have someone for the contest.

**KING:** Well, send him in, send him in.

**GUARD** *(Calling offstage):* All right, you. Come on in. *(Enter PEASANT.)*

**15** **PRINCESS:** My peasant! My very own dear peasant!

**PEASANT** *(Going down on one knee before PRINCESS):* My Princess! My very own dear Princess!

**KING:** What is all this?

456

---

**ELL**

**Understanding Idioms** Emphasize the importance of word stress within a sentence. In the statement "Well, <u>there</u> you are, Father," if the underlined word is stressed, it implies that the Princess has found her Father. What she means to say is "Well, there you <u>are</u>," which is an idiom meaning "See, I told you." Have students practice stressing different words in the sentence, and discuss the change in meaning.

**PEASANT** *(Rising):* Your Majesty, this is an unexpected pleasure. But you really didn't have to come all the way down to the kitchen to see me. I would have been glad to come upstairs to the throne room.

**KING:** Who let you out of the dungeon?

**GUARD:** I did, your Majesty. You said you wanted someone to enter the contest.

**KING:** Guard! I didn't tell you to empty out the dungeon. Can't you find anyone in this palace with royal blood?

**PRINCESS:** Oh, this is wonderful! Father, please let him try. He's so clever! You will win the contest so you can marry me, won't you, dear peasant?

**PEASANT:** Of course. What is the contest? **17**

**KING:** I've made a perfectly wonderful dish of something or other, and whoever can tell me what it is, receives the hand of the Princess in marriage.

**PRINCESS:** Go ahead, dear. Guess what Father's made.

**PEASANT** *(Goes over to bowl. Sniffs. Stirs it a little. Sniffs again):* Ah!

**KING:** Delicious, isn't it?

**PEASANT:** Indeed, yes. *(Peers at it.)* Let me see. Ah, of course! I have it. *(Sits down on chair.)*

**PRINCESS** *(Excitedly):* What is it? What is it?

**PEASANT:** Now just a minute—*(Takes off shoe, picks up a little of the liquid on a spoon and drops it on edge of sole. Makes motions of pressing sole tight against shoe.)* There!

**KING:** What are you doing?

457

⟳ VOCABULARY STRATEGY

# Dictionary/ Glossary

## TEACH

- Remind students that sometimes a word has more than one meaning in a dictionary entry. All the meanings must be read to determine the correct meaning in the play's context.

- Read lines 7–8 on p. 457. Model using the dictionary to determine the correct meaning of *blood*.

**Think Aloud**  **MODEL** When I'm not sure about a word's meaning, I look for the meaning in the dictionary. When I look up *blood*, I see that it has more than one meaning. I read each meaning and decide that the meaning of *blood* in this context is "family relationship" or "parentage." That makes sense. The King wants his daughter to marry someone who is part of a royal family.

## PRACTICE AND ASSESS

Have students use the dictionary to determine the meaning of the word *hand* in the phrase *hand of the Princess* on p. 457, line 14. *(a pledge or permission to marry)*

## Getting a Patent

**TIME FOR Science**

If a person invents something new, he or she can obtain a patent. A patent protects the inventor from others claiming to have invented it first. It also means that any money made from the invention goes to the inventor. The United States Patent and Trademark Office issues patents for such things as machines, manufactured articles, new and useful processes, designs, or new varieties of plants. Anyone inventing something must first find out if the idea is original by researching the patents already filed. Plans, details, and a complete description must accompany the patent application. If the idea is judged new, the United States Patent and Trademark Office issues a patent that is good for twenty years.

# Guiding Comprehension

**18** **Main Idea • Literal**

**What did the King make?**

A strong glue

**19** ⟳ **Character • Critical**

**The Princess calls the Peasant "clever" and the Peasant calls the King a "genius." Who do you think is the smartest character? Why?**

Possible response: The Peasant is the smartest because he figured out a use for the mixture.

| Monitor Progress |
| --- |
| ⟳ **Character** |

| If... students have difficulty judging the characters, | then... use the skill and strategy instruction on p. 459. |
| --- | --- |

**20** **Draw Conclusions • Critical**

**Would you want this king to rule your country? Explain.**

Possible response: No, because he doesn't act like he is very smart.

458

**ELL**

**Context Clues** Help students use context clues to figure out the meaning of *It serves him right* (p. 459, next-to-last line). The following sentence says that "the fellow ought to have known better," so it probably means that he deserved what he got.

**PEASANT** *(Putting shoe back on):* Now we'll see. *(Gets up and walks around a little. Then bends down and looks at shoe.)* Ah–ha, just as I thought! Congratulations, your Majesty.

**KING:** What for?

**PEASANT:** You have just made a bowl of the most wonderful glue I've ever seen. **18**

**KING** *(Bellowing):* What!

**PRINCESS:** Glue!

**COOK:** Glue!

**KITCHEN MAIDS** *(Together):* Glue!

**PEASANT:** You are a genius! An absolute genius. Why, this glue is strong as iron. See? *(Lifts up foot.)* The sole of my shoe was almost falling off. Now it's on tight as new.

**KING:** So you think I'm a genius, do you?

**PEASANT:** Certainly. You'll be famous. Rich, too. We'll put this in bottles and sell it everywhere. Let's see. We could call it King's Glue. *(Sings)*

> Go out today and buy King's Glue.
> Through thick and thin, it sticks with you.

**PRINCESS:** I knew you were clever. We gave some to the Duke **19** and he didn't know what it was.

**PEASANT:** The Duke ate some? *(Rushes over to* DUKE. *Peers at him.)* Just as I thought. His teeth are stuck together.

**KITCHEN MAIDS** *(Together):* Oh my! *(Hurry over and look at* DUKE.)

**KING:** It serves him right. The fellow ought to have known better than to eat glue. Here, Guard, take him off to the Royal Dentist.

**20**

459

## SKILLS ⟷ STRATEGIES IN CONTEXT

# Character

## TEACH

- Authors don't always tell us everything about a character. We must draw conclusions based on what characters say or do.

- Model drawing conclusions about the Peasant.

 **MODEL** The Peasant has an original idea for the stuff the King made. I would never have thought to try it out as a glue. But mixing flour and water is a way to make glue or paste. Not only does he come up with a good idea, but he even thinks of a name for the glue and a song to help sell it. The Peasant really does seem to be very smart.

## PRACTICE AND ASSESS

- Have students review what the Princess has said and done in the play. How would they describe her character?

- To assess, be sure students have examples to support their ideas.

## Inventing Super Glue

**TIME FOR Science**

Super glue can be found in almost any household. It is used to repair everything from cracked teacups to broken chairs. This miraculous glue was discovered quite by accident. Dr. Harry Coover, an inventor and chemist, was working with plastics to develop gunsights for soldiers in World War II. He found that cyanoacrylate monomers were sticky and had unusual adhesive properties. They immediately bonded with anything they touched. Years later, Coover recognized the potential for such a glue and applied for a patent. By 1958, super glue was flying off the store shelves. Dr. Coover became a TV celebrity for his invention and appeared on the TV show *"I've Got a Secret."* When Coover retired, he had more than 460 patents.

# Guiding Comprehension

**21** **Character • Inferential**

**What clues in the play show how the King feels about making new batches of his glue by himself?**

He sends everyone away, so he shows that he thinks that he is better off doing it without help from Cook and the Kitchen Maids. He sings as he works, which shows that he is happy about it.

**22** **Summarize • Critical**

**Have students complete the predictions chart they started on p. 442a by summarizing what happened in the play. Were your predictions accurate?**

Possible response: The King decides to cook soup in the kitchen. He says whoever can guess what he made can marry the Princess. The Peasant guesses the King made glue. He marries the Princess and the King starts selling his glue.

**23** **Compare and Contrast • Critical**

*Text to Self* **Which character in the play reminds you of someone you know?**

Possible response: The Princess reminds me of my sister. She is always arguing with my dad.

*Strategy Response Log*

**Summarize** When students finish reading the selection, provide this prompt: Imagine a producer wants to stage *The King in the Kitchen* and asks you what it is about. In four or five sentences, summarize what happens in the play.

**DUKE** (*Getting up*): Mmph! (GUARD *takes him by arm and leads him off.*)

**KING** (*Stirring spoon in bowl*): It does look a little like glue. How clever I am.

**PRINCESS** (*To* PEASANT): You've won the contest! Now we can be married.

**KING:** This is terrible. What will my Prime Minister say when he hears I am to have a peasant for a son–in–law?

**PEASANT:** Never you mind. When we tell him how much money will go into the Royal Treasury from your glue, he won't care about anything. Of course, it will mean you will have to spend most of your time in the kitchen.

**KING:** It's not so bad down here. And I'll always have something to eat. As for you, Cook—

**COOK:** Y–y–yes, your Majesty?

**KING:** Off to cooking school you go, and don't come back till you have a diploma. Take the Kitchen Maids with you. (*Exit* COOK *and* KITCHEN MAIDS.)

**21** **KING:** Now you two run along. I want to start working.

**PEASANT:** All right, your Majesty. See you at the wedding. (*Exit* PRINCESS *and* PEASANT.)

**22** **KING** (*Fussing about with pots and pans*): Now let me see. What did I do first? (*Places pan in front of him and pours some water in.*) Did I put one cup of flour in? Or was it two? And how much salt? (*Picks up shaker and shakes some in.*) Oh, well—(*Stirs it up singing.*)

Go out today and buy King's Glue.
**23** Through thick and thin, it—sticks—with—you!

460

**ELL**

**Understanding Idioms** The King's jingle contains two idioms: *through thick and thin* and *it sticks with you*. Both are also plays on words. *Through thick and thin* means "through good times and bad times," but it also describes the consistency of glue. *It sticks with you* means "it will always be with you, like a friend," but it also makes reference to the stickiness of glue.

The End

461

# Monitor and Fix Up

Have students retell the play, focusing on the characters and setting. Ask them to identify places in the play where they didn't understand what was happening. What fix-up strategies did they use to help them understand? Use Practice Book p. 177.

## SELF-CHECK

Students can ask themselves these questions to assess understanding of the play.

- Did I interpret the actions and dialogue of the characters to learn what they were like?
- Did I use the play's stage directions to help me understand the characters and setting?

| Monitor Progress |
| --- |
| 🎯 **Character and Setting** |

| If... students are having difficulty describing characters and setting and using text features to help, | then... use the Reteach lesson on p. 465b |
| --- | --- |

---

## Develop Vocabulary

### PRACTICE LESSON VOCABULARY

As a class, complete the following sentences orally. Possible responses are given.

**1.** You might find a *dungeon* in (*the basement of a castle*).

**2.** If you call someone Your *Majesty*, then you are speaking to (*royalty; a king or queen*).

**3.** A *genius* who takes a test is likely to (*do very well on it*).

---

### BUILD CONCEPT VOCABULARY

Review previous concept words with students. Ask if students have come across any words today in their reading that they would like to add to the Innovators Concept Web, such as *curious* and *genius*.

---

**Character and Setting**

- **Characters** are people in a story. You can learn what characters are like by noticing what they say and do and how they interact with other characters.
- **Setting** is the time and place in which the story occurs.

**Directions** Read the following passage. Then answer the questions below.

> One snowy morning, Jorie was doing something she wasn't supposed to do. She went out of her backyard and climbed boldly onto the top of a big hill covered with ice and snow. From there she could see the hills of Utah all around, white and rolling. "I dare you to come up here too!" she called to her brother below. "You're going to get in trouble again!" he replied.
>
> As Jorie stood and waved at him, she lost her balance. Plop! She landed on a patch of ice and began to slip down the hill. "Whoop! Out of the way!" she howled with glee as she whizzed past. "That was so much fun!" she told her brother with a big smile. "Jou try it!" Jorie and her brother spent the whole day sliding down the snowy hill.

Possible answers given.

1. When Jorie climbs onto the icy hill, what do her actions tell you about her?

   She is bold and daring.

2. "I dare you to come up here," Jorie says. What tone of voice do you think she was using? What do these words show about her?

   teasing; Jorie is playful and fearless.

3. What does Jorie's brother's reaction to Jorie's dare tell you about her?

   Jorie can be mischievous and disobedient.

4. What is the setting of the story? How is the setting important?

   a snowy morning in the hills of Utah; Without the snowy hill,
   Jorie wouldn't have dared her brother to climb it.

5. Look back in the story and find words that show Jorie's expressions and feelings. Write these down. What do these words tell you about Jorie?

   howled with glee, big smile; Jorie is joyful and fun-loving.

**Home Activity** Your child described the character and setting of a story. Read a seasonal story with your child. Work together to identify the setting and the traits of the main character.

▲ **Practice Book** p. 177

# Reader Response

## Open for Discussion **Personal Response**

**MODEL** I think I'd like to play the Peasant. He gets to sing and realizes the King's "invention" is glue. Three adjectives to describe him are *silly, funny,* and *clever.*

## Comprehension Check **Critical Response**

1. Responses will vary, but could explain that accidental inventions could be humorous or entertaining. **Author's Purpose**

2. Setting: The setting is the kitchen of a palace. The stage directions identify the setting. 🎯 **Setting**

3. Possible response: The Peasant helped the King realize he invented something wonderful. 🎯 **Character**

4. Royals: The King, the Princess, the Duke; Servants: The Peasant, the Cook, the Kitchen Maids, the Guard. Students may include other words from the play sorted by rank. 🎯 **Vocabulary**

**Look Back and Write** For test practice, assign a 10–15 minute time limit. For assessment, see the Scoring Rubric at the right.

## Retell

Have students retell *The King in the Kitchen.*

| Monitor Progress | |
|---|---|
| **Check Retelling** Rubric 4 3 2 1 | |
| If... students have difficulty retelling the play, | then... use the Retelling Cards and the Scoring Rubric for Retelling on p. 463 to assist fluent retelling. **SUCCESS PREDICTOR** |

**Check Retelling** Encourage students to use the illustrations, names of speakers, stage directions, and other text features of a play to guide their retellings. For more ideas on assessing students' retellings, see the ELL and Transition Handbook.

# Reader Response

**Open for Discussion** Suppose your class is putting on a performance of *The King in the Kitchen.* Which character would you like to play? Why? What are three adjectives that describe that character?

1. Suppose someone says, "This play isn't real. It could never happen!" What do you think the author would say? **Think Like an Author**

2. The setting is the time and place in which a story occurs. What is the setting of *The King in the Kitchen?* What details in the text and the illustrations help you determine this? **Character and Setting**

3. The Princess loves the Peasant because he's clever. Think about what you know about being clever. How was the Peasant clever in his encounter with the King? **Monitor and Fix Up**

4. Some of the characters in the play are royals. Some are servants. Make a chart. List the characters in each category. Add other words you know that fit into each category. **Vocabulary**

**Look Back and Write** The King went to the kitchen to find out who made his soup. What else did he accomplish while he was there? Support your answer with details from the play.

Meet illustrator **Matthew Trueman on page 783.**

462

---

**Scoring Rubric** | **Look Back and Write**

**Top-Score Response** A top-score response uses details from the selection to explain that the King created an amazing new glue in the kitchen.

**Example of a Top-Score Response** The King went to the kitchen to discover who made his soup. He said that he could make a better soup with his eyes closed. He added a little bit of this and that. When he was finished, it didn't look like soup, porridge, or stew. The peasant figured out it was an amazing glue!

**For additional rubrics, see p. WA10.**

# Write Now

## Business Letter

### Prompt

In *The King in the Kitchen*, the king starts a glue business.

Think about a new product that you might like to invent.

Now write a business letter asking a company to help you sell your product.

### Writing Trait

Writers use a strong **voice** to speak directly to readers. The voice in your business letter should be persuasive, enthusiastic, and direct.

### Student Model

**Writer engages the reader with the opening question.**

Dear Sir or Madam:

Are you looking for the next breakthrough in pet care? If so, my new invention is for you. The Cat's Pajamas are the latest and greatest thing for cats.

**Voice is enthusiastic and persuasive.**

Like you, I love my cat. But sleeping with a cat on your bed can be a furry mess. Cat hair is everywhere! Not anymore! The Cat's Pajamas are a safe and comfortable set of pajamas for your cat. You wear pajamas, why not FiFi?

I have dozens of styles and sizes ready for production. All I need is a partner to help me get the pajamas into pet stores. I believe your company is the perfect partner. I love your other products, such as Puppy Paw Mittens and Hamster Hats.

**Closing gives contact information.**

Please contact me at 806-222-3456.

Sincerely,

Greta Stone

**Use the model to help you write your own business letter.**

463

# Write Now

**Look at the Prompt** Each sentence in the prompt has a purpose.

- Sentence 1 presents a topic.
- Sentence 2 suggests students think about the topic.
- Sentence 3 tells what to write—a business letter.

## Strategies to Develop Voice

Have students

- imagine they are receiving the letter. Are they convinced about the product?
- read their letters aloud. Does the voice sound enthusiastic and persuasive?

NO: I made a new juice. It tastes good.

YES: Like most kids, I'm tired of apple juice. That's why I invented *Bubble Apple*—a fantastic, fizzy new taste!

For additional suggestions and rubric, see pp. 465g–465h.

## Writer's Checklist

- ☑ **Focus** Are sentences about the new product?
- ☑ **Organization** Are ideas in an order that makes sense?
- ☑ **Support** Do details support the persuasive voice?
- ☐ **Conventions** Does writer use the correct format for a business letter?

## Scoring Rubric — Narrative Retelling

| Rubric 4 3 2 1 | 4 | 3 | 2 | 1 |
|---|---|---|---|---|
| Connections | Makes connections and generalizes beyond the text | Makes connections to other events, stories, or experiences | Makes a limited connection to another event, story, or experience | Makes no connection to another event, story, or experience |
| Author's Purpose | Elaborates on author's purpose | Tells author's purpose with some clarity | Makes some connection to author's purpose | Makes no connection to author's purpose |
| Characters | Describes the main character(s) and any character development | Identifies the main character(s) and gives some information about them | Inaccurately identifies some characters or gives little information about them | Inaccurately identifies the characters or gives no information about them |
| Setting | Describes the time and location | Identifies the time and location | Omits details of time or location | Is unable to identify time or location |
| Plot | Describes the problem, goal, events, and ending using rich detail | Tells the problem, goal, events, and ending with some errors that do not affect meaning | Tells parts of the problem, goal, events, and ending with gaps that affect meaning | Retelling has no sense of story |

## Retelling Plan

- ☑ **Week 1** Assess Strategic Intervention students.
- ☑ **Week 2** Assess Advanced students.
- ☑ **This week assess Strategic Intervention students.**
- ☐ **Week 4** Assess On-Level students.
- ☐ **Week 5** Assess any students you have not yet checked during this unit.

Use the Retelling Chart on p. TR16 to record retelling.

**Selection Test** To assess with *The King in the Kitchen*, use Selection Tests, pp. 69–72.

**Fresh Reads for Differentiated Test Practice** For weekly leveled practice, use pp. 103–108.

SUCCESS PREDICTOR

# Poetry

- Examine features of poetry.
- Practice a test-taking strategy.
- Compare and contrast across texts.

## PREVIEW

Have students preview the poems and describe ways they are alike and different. Prompt them to think about the number of lines, rhythms, and topics. Read aloud the information under Genre, and then ask:

- **Which two poems are limericks?**
  ("A Confectioner" and "Expert")

## Link to Writing

Suggest students brainstorm rhyming words about cooking, such as *book/cook, pot/hot, foil/boil.*

**DAY 4** Grouping Options

**Reading**
**Whole Group** Discuss the Question of the Day.

**Small Group** Differentiated Instruction
Read poetry. See pp. 440f–440g for the small group lesson plan.

**Whole Group** Use p. 465a.

**Language Arts**
Use pp. 465e–465k.

---

# Poetry

## Genre

- **Poetry is imaginative and can show us new ways of looking at things.**

- **Many poems have lines that end with words that rhyme.**

- **Many poems have lines that have a certain rhythm—a regular pattern of unstressed and stressed syllables, or beats, that is noticeable when the poem is read aloud.**

- **Two of these poems are limericks. Limericks have five lines. Lines 1, 2, and 5 have the same number of beats and end with rhyming words. Lines 3 and 4 have fewer beats, but also end with rhyming words.**

## Link to Writing

As you read the two limericks, count the beats. Then write your own limerick with words that rhyme.

# A Man for All Seasonings

by Richard Armour

"Pass the salt," I say, and yet
Salt and pepper's what I get.
If "Pass the pepper" I should yell,
Salt would come along as well.
Like man and wife, like sister, brother,
Where the one is, there's the other.
Though salt has many times the takers,
Pepper's in as many shakers.
So don't object, and don't be loath—
Just ask for one, accept them both.

464

### Content-Area Vocabulary    Science

| | |
|---|---|
| confectioner | a person who makes or sells candies, ice creams, or cakes |
| genius | a person who has a great natural ability |
| seasonings | things that give a better flavor. Salt, pepper, and herbs are seasonings. |

# A Confectioner
by Myra Cohn Livingston

A confectioner living in Skittle
Once confessed, "I'm so skinny and little
      That unless I put glue
      On the sole of my shoe
I'd fall into my own peanut brittle."

## Expert
Author Unknown

A prominent lady in Brooking
Was a recognized genius at cooking.
      She could bake thirty pies
      All quite the same size
And tell which was which without looking.

**Reading Across Texts**
Find words in these poems that link them to *The King in the Kitchen*.

**Writing Across Texts** Write a limerick of your own about the king. The first line might be: "There once was a king from Chinook. . . ."

**Monitor & Fix Up** | What might you misunderstand in poetry?

465

## Kitchen Chemistry

People use chemistry in cooking every day. Heat is usually the energy that changes mixtures into something new and good to eat. For example, when dough is baked in an oven, the sticky mixture turns into bread. In peanut brittle, sugar and butter are heated until they form a sticky liquid. Peanuts are added and when the mixture cools, it hardens and becomes crunchy peanut brittle.

TIME FOR Science

## POETRY
Use the sidebar on p. 464 to guide discussion.
- Explain poetry can express different moods. Some poems, such as limericks, are humorous and meant to entertain.
- Poetry differs from fiction by using fewer words to express the writer's thoughts.
- Discuss how the poets use rhyme and rhythm in these poems about cooking.

Audio CD   **AudioText**

**Monitor and Fix Up**

Possible response: You might misunderstand where a thought begins and ends.

## CONNECT TEXT TO TEXT

### Reading Across Texts
Have students work in small groups to find the related words and compile a list.

**Writing Across Texts** Students can use their lists as a source to rhyme in their limericks.

## EXTEND SKILLS

### Rhyme in Poetry

Explain that rhyming patterns identify which lines of a poem end in rhyming words. Tell students that the rhyming pattern for a couplet is *aabbccdd*. Write these letters on the board. Then have students follow in their books as you read aloud "A Man for All Seasonings." Call on volunteers to identify the rhyming words. As they do, underline the letter pairs that represent them.

Write *aabba* on the board. Explain that limericks are always five lines and that the *aabba* rhyming pattern shows that lines 1, 2, and 5 end with rhyming words and that lines 3 and 4 also end in rhyming words. Then follow the procedure used with the couplet.

## Fluency Assessment Plan

☑ **Week 1** Assess Advanced students.
☑ **Week 2** Assess Strategic Intervention students.
☑ **This week assess On-Level students.**
☐ **Week 4** Assess Strategic Intervention students.
☐ **Week 5** Assess any students you have not yet checked during this unit.

Set individual goals for students to enable them to reach the year-end goal.
• Current Goal: 110–120 wcpm
• Year-End Goal: 130 wcpm

Provide opportunities for students to read one-on-one with an aide or parent volunteer, if possible. The adult models by reading first, and the child reads and rereads the same text, with adult guidance. Allow extra repetitions for English language learners, to improve their fluency.

 To develop fluent readers, use Fluency Coach.

### DAY 5   Grouping Options

**Reading**
**Whole Group**
Revisit the Question of the Week.

**Small Group**
**Differentiated Instruction**
Reread this week's Leveled Readers. See pp. 440f–440g for the small group lesson plan.

**Whole Group**
Use p. 465b–465c.

**Language Arts**
Use pp. 465d–465l.

## STRESS/EMPHASIS
# Fluency

### DAY 1

**Model** Reread "Corn Flake Kings" on p. 440m. Explain that you will emphasize important words by saying them with more expression, using a stronger voice or higher pitch. Model as you read.

### DAY 2

**Choral Reading** Read aloud the last six speeches on p. 451. Have students notice how you emphasize *that's* in the first sentence, *here* in the Princess's first speech, and *very* in the King's reply. Practice with three choral readings.

### DAY 3

**Model** Read aloud the last seven speeches on p. 452. Discuss which words to stress, such as *nonsense, can't, needs, money, awful,* and *not.* Practice as a class by doing three choral readings.

### DAY 4

**Partner Reading** Partners practice reading aloud the last seven speeches on p. 452, three times. Students should read dramatically, stressing important words, and then offer each other feedback.

---

### Monitor Progress   Check Fluency wcpm

As students reread, monitor their progress toward their individual fluency goals. Current Goal: 110–120 words correct per minute. End-of-Year Goal: 130 words correct per minute.

**If...** students cannot read fluently at a rate of 110–120 words correct per minute,
**then...** make sure students practice with text at their independent level. Provide additional fluency practice, pairing nonfluent readers with fluent readers.

**If...** students already read at 130 words correct per minute,
**then...** they do not need to reread three to four times.

SUCCESS PREDICTOR

---

### DAY 5

**Assessment**
**Individual Reading Rate** Use the Fluency Assessment Plan and do a one-minute timed reading of either selection from this week to assess students in Week 3. Pay special attention to this week's skill, stress/emphasis. Provide corrective feedback for each student.

# RETEACH

## ⊙ Character/Setting

### TEACH

Review the definitions of *character* and *setting* on p. 440. Students can complete Practice Book p. 178 on their own or as a class. As they work on number 4, remind them to list one trait for each example listed in the smaller ovals that tells what Jake says and does and how he affects his father.

### ASSESS

Have students discuss the King's personality in *The King in the Kitchen*. Then have students write what the King would likely say or do after his daughter's wedding. *(Dialogue should reflect the King making some silly comment about the wedding.)*

For additional instruction on character, see DI·54.

## EXTEND SKILLS

# Rhyme

### TEACH

Rhyme is two or more words that have the same ending sound. The words *yet* and *get* are an example from "A Man for All Seasonings" on p. 464.

- Rhyming words do not necessarily end with the same letters. The words *loan* and *bone* rhyme, even though the endings are spelled differently.
- Two-syllable words can rhyme just in the last syllable *(obey, today)* or in the first syllable with the same last syllable *(topping, shopping)*.

Work with students to identify more rhyming words in "A Man for All Seasonings." *(yell/well, brother/other, takers/shakers)*

### ASSESS

Have students list rhyming words in "Expert" on p. 465. *(Brooking, cooking, looking; pies, size)* Have them identify the two words that are spelled differently but still rhyme. *(pies, size)*

---

## OBJECTIVES

- ⊙ Identify character traits and setting.
- ● Identify rhyme in poetry.

### Skills Trace

#### ⊙ Character and Setting

| Introduce/Teach | TE: 4.4 440–441, 488–489; 4.6 686–687 |
| --- | --- |
| Practice | TE: 171, 449, 455, 459, 497, 693, 699, 703<br>PB: 173, 177, 178, 193, 197, 198, 273, 277, 278 |
| **Reteach/Review** | **TE: 4.2 171; 4.4 401, 465b, 507b, DI•54, DI•56; 4.5 621; 4.6 711b, DI•54**<br>**PB: 66, 156, 246** |
| Test | Selection Test: 69–72, 77–80, 109–112; Benchmark Test: Unit 4 |

**Access Content** Reteach the skill by reviewing the Picture It! lesson on character and setting in the ELL Teaching Guide, pp. 120–121.

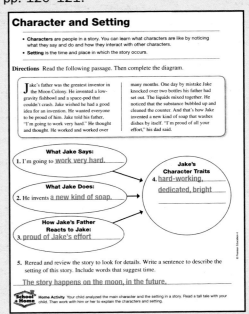

▲ **Practice Book** p. 178

*Words Correct Per Minute*
**SUCCESS PREDICTOR**

# Vocabulary and Word Study

## ◎ Dictionary/ Glossary

**UNFAMILIAR WORDS** Remind students that they can use a dictionary or glossary to look up the meanings of unfamiliar words. Have students select unfamiliar words from the stage directions of *The King in the Kitchen* and demonstrate the steps they use to find the appropriate meaning in a dictionary. Then have them take notes about their dictionary search as shown below.

Unfamiliar Word: curtsies

Guide Words on Page: curly/cuspidor

Entry Word: curtsy (also spelled "curtsey")

Part of Speech: verb

Meaning in Play: to make a bow of respect—The cook bows to
show respect for the King.

## Cooking Terms

Have small groups review *The King in the Kitchen* to find words related to cooking. Tell them to brainstorm more cooking words and sort them into categories. They may use some of the words in a creative recipe for a new dish.

| Actions | Tools | Cookbook Words |
|---|---|---|
| peel | teaspoon | recipe |
| stir | mixing bowl | ingredients |
| shake | colander | dash |
| pour | spatula | |
| dice | | |
| crumble | | |
| sprinkle | | |
| broil | | |
| sauté | | |

## Innovators

**LOOKING BACK** Review the question of the week with students: *How can a mistake turn into a success?* Discuss how this week's Concept Web of vocabulary words relates to the theme of innovators. Ask students if they have any words or categories to add. Discuss if words and categories are appropriately related to the concept.

**MOVING FORWARD** Preview the title of the next selection, *Seeker of Knowledge.* Ask students which Concept Web words might apply to the new selection based on the title alone. Put a star next to these words on the web.

Display the Concept Web and revisit the vocabulary words as you read the next selection to check predictions.

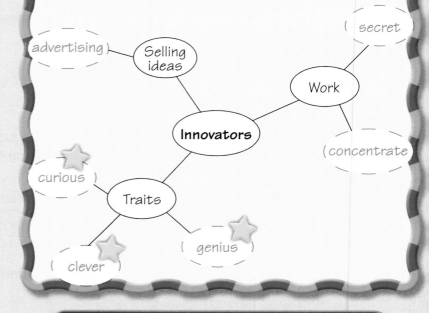

### Monitor Progress

#### Check Vocabulary

| **If...** students suggest words or categories that are not related to the concept, | **then...** review the words and categories on the Concept Web and discuss how they relate to the lesson concept. |
|---|---|

SUCCESS PREDICTOR

# Speaking and Viewing

## Readers' Theater

**SET-UP** Have groups of students choose a short scene from *The King in the Kitchen* for a dramatic reading. Explain the scene should have a beginning and ending, such as when the Duke enters and leaves the kitchen.

**PLANNING** Have group leaders assign parts for members of each group. Suggest they prepare by discussing character traits and how each character might sound as he or she speaks.

**REHEARSAL** Tell actors to practice saying their lines, using different vocal inflections and stresses. Remind them to follow any stage directions in parentheses about how to express themselves. Have them practice quietly alone first and then as a group. Set aside time for each group to perform for the class.

### Delivery Tips
- Use a voice that's appropriate for your character.
- Vary your tone of voice to express the character's emotions and to keep the audience interested.
- Wait for cues from other actors before you speak, unless you are supposed to interrupt someone.

## Analyze Media

Have students view a scene of a television play or a movie. Tell them to pay attention to the ways the actors deliver their lines. After viewing, ask partners to answer the following questions, orally or in writing:

1. **How do the characters reveal their personalities by the way they speak and move?**

2. **Is the conflict of the play or movie expressed through the characters' dialogue or their actions?**

3. **Did this scene make you want to see the rest of the play or movie? Why or why not?**

You may want to show the scene again and discuss it with the class as it's playing. Have students imagine they are directing the scene and tell other ways it could have been staged and recorded.

**Support Vocabulary** Use the following to review and extend vocabulary and to explore lesson concepts further:
- ELL Poster 18, Days 3–5 instruction
- Vocabulary Activities and Word Cards in ELL Teaching Guide, pp. 122–123

**Assessment** For information on assessing students' speaking, listening, and viewing, see the ELL and Transition Handbook.

# Grammar  Pronouns and Antecedents

## OBJECTIVES

- Define and identify pronouns and antecedents.
- Use pronouns that agree with their antecedents.
- Use pronouns and antecedents correctly in writing.
- Become familiar with pronoun assessment on high-stakes tests.

### Monitor Progress

**Grammar**

| If... students have difficulty identifying pronouns and antecedents, | then... provide additional instruction and practice in The Grammar and Writing Book pp. 152–155. |
|---|---|

## DAILY FIX-IT

This week use Daily Fix-It Transparency 18.

Spiral REVIEW

## ELL

**Grammar Support** See the Grammar Transition lessons in the ELL and Transition Handbook.

▲ **The Grammar and Writing Book**
For more instruction and practice, use pp. 152–155.

---

## DAY 1  Teach and Model

### DAILY FIX-IT

1. You and me can cook dinner togethar if we agree on a menu. *(I; together)*

2. We can invite José and she to help? *(her to help.)*

### READING-GRAMMAR CONNECTION

Write this sentence about *The King in the Kitchen* on the board:

*The King took the <u>soup</u> and threw <u>it</u> on the floor.*

Explain that the **pronoun** *it* refers to *soup. Soup* is the **antecedent** of *it.*

Display Grammar Transparency 18. Read aloud the definitions and sample sentences. Work through the items.

---

### Pronouns and Antecedents

A **pronoun** takes the place of a noun or nouns. An **antecedent,** or referent, is the noun or nouns to which the pronoun refers. A pronoun and its antecedent must agree in number and gender.

Before you use a pronoun, ask yourself whether the antecedent is singular or plural. If the antecedent is singular, decide whether it is masculine, feminine, or neuter. Then choose a pronoun that agrees. In the following sentences, the antecedents are underlined once; the pronouns are underlined twice.

The <u>maid</u> was sitting at a table, where <u>she</u> was peeling potatoes.
The <u>cook</u> and the <u>maid</u> were amazed when <u>they</u> saw the King in the kitchen.

**Directions** Match the pronoun with the noun or noun phrase that could be its antecedent. Write the letter of the correct antecedent next to the pronoun.

| | | | |
|---|---|---|---|
| B | 1. it | A | two kitchen maids |
| D | 2. we | B | dungeon |
| E | 3. he | C | the Princess |
| A | 4. they | D | the peasant and I |
| C | 5. she | E | the King |

**Directions** Write the correct pronoun in ( ) to complete each sentence. The antecedents of the pronouns have been underlined to help you.

6. <u>Cook</u> spoke to the <u>guard</u> when (he, it) walked through her kitchen. **he**
7. The <u>King</u> made Cook blindfold (her, him). **him**
8. He had tried Cook's <u>soup</u> and said (he, it) was awful. **it**
9. <u>Cook</u> told him that (she, them) had worked hard to make the soup. **she**
10. The <u>Princess and the peasant</u> said that (she, they) were in love. **they**
11. The King called for <u>Cook</u> and sent (it, her) to cooking school. **her**
12. When <u>you</u> and I read this play, (we, they) acted it out. **we**

Unit 4 The King in the Kitchen                Grammar **18**

▲ **Grammar Transparency** 18

---

## DAY 2  Develop the Concept

### DAILY FIX-IT

3. The egg cracked. When we put her in the boiling water. *(cracked when; it)*

4. What a mess you has made in the kitchen. *(have; kitchen!)*

### GUIDED PRACTICE

Review the concept of pronouns and their antecedents.

- A **pronoun** is a word that takes the place of a noun or nouns.
- The word that a pronoun replaces is called its **antecedent.**
- A pronoun should agree with its antecedent in number and gender.

**HOMEWORK** Grammar and Writing Practice Book p. 69. Work through the first two items with the class.

---

### Pronouns and Antecedents

A **pronoun** takes the place of a noun or nouns. An **antecedent,** or referent, is the noun or nouns to which the pronoun refers. A pronoun and its antecedent must agree in number and gender.

Before you use a pronoun, ask yourself whether the antecedent is singular or plural. If the antecedent is singular, decide whether it is masculine, feminine, or neuter. Then choose a pronoun that agrees. In the following sentences, the antecedents are underlined once; the pronouns are underlined twice.

The <u>King</u> didn't like the soup, so <u>he</u> decided to cook for himself.
The <u>Princess and the peasant</u> told the King that <u>they</u> wanted to get married.

**Directions** Write the letter of the pronoun next to the noun or noun phrase that could be its antecedent.

| | | | |
|---|---|---|---|
| D | 1. soup | A | he |
| E | 2. the kitchen maid | B | us |
| C | 3. the guard and the peasant | C | them |
| B | 4. the Princess and me | D | it |
| A | 5. the Duke | E | she |

**Directions** Write the correct pronoun in ( ) to complete each sentence. The antecedents of the pronouns have been underlined to help you.

6. The <u>Princess and the peasant</u> talked each day when (they, she) met. **they**
7. The <u>Princess</u> knew what (her, she) wanted. **she**
8. Did the <u>King</u> think that Cook was trying to poison (him, it)? **him**
9. The <u>Duke</u> couldn't talk after (him, he) ate the King's awful food. **he**
10. The <u>maids</u> were glad that the King was nice to (her, them). **them**

**Home Activity** Your child learned about pronouns and antecedents. Ask your child to explain to you how a pronoun can change with a different antecedent.

▲ **Grammar and Writing Practice Book** p. 69

---

# DAY 3 — Apply to Writing

## D A I L Y   F I X - I T

5. We will make soup for suppar if you give him a good recipe. *(supper; us)*

6. Cooking is hard work, its also a lot of fun. *(work. It's)*

## WRITE CLEAR ANTECEDENTS

Explain that if a pronoun's antecedent is confusing, the sentence should be rewritten.

*Unclear:* Joe and my brother have dinner when he comes to town.

*Clear:* Joe and my brother have dinner when Joe comes to town.

Have students review something they have written to see if they can improve it by clarifying pronoun references.

**HOMEWORK** Grammar and Writing Practice Book p. 70.

### Pronouns and Antecedents

**Directions** Write a pronoun to complete each sentence.

1. Bill and his little sister Janice decided to make "no bake" cookies when ____ were alone in the house one afternoon. 2. Bill wanted to make a recipe that ____ had seen in a magazine. 3. Janice said that ____ would help. 4. Bill gave Janice a plastic bottle of chocolate syrup and told ____ to squeeze it into a bowl. 5. Janice took the cap off the syrup and squirted ____ into a bowl. 6. A few minutes later chocolate syrup was all over the floor. Bill and Janice were trying to clean ____ up when their mother came home.
7. "What are you doing?" ____ asked Bill.
8. "Janice made a mess," ____ replied.
9. Their mother was cross with Bill and told ____ not to blame his sister. 10. She made Bill and Janice finish washing the floor and told ____ not to cook alone in the future.

1. ____they____   6. ____it____
2. __he _or_ they__   7. ____she____
3. ____she____   8. ____he____
4. ____her____   9. ____him____
5. ____it____   10. ____them____

**Directions** Write a paragraph about a time you helped in the kitchen. Use pronouns to make your writing smooth. Underline the pronouns.
**Possible answer:**

I helped Grandma frost a birthday cake. We put sugar and butter in a bowl. I stirred them and added some color. Grandma spread the frosting on the cake. Then she gave me sprinkles, and I put them on the top.

**Home Activity** Your child learned how to use pronouns and antecedents in writing. Have your child write two or three sentences about someone in the family, using pronouns and antecedents. Ask him or her to point out the pronouns and their antecedents.

▲ **Grammar and Writing Practice Book** p. 70

---

# DAY 4 — Test Preparation

## D A I L Y   F I X - I T

7. Pams dessert look more like a pancake than a birthday cake. *(Pam's; looks)*

8. If you've got any left please give some more to Julia and I. *(left, please; me)*

### STANDARDIZED TEST PREP

#### Test Tip

Watch out for sentences with *everyone, someone,* or *everybody* as the subject. If these words are pronoun antecedents, they require a singular pronoun, such as *he, she, him,* or *her.*

*No:* Everyone bowed their head.

*Yes:* Everyone bowed his head.

*Yes:* Everyone bowed her head.

**HOMEWORK** Grammar and Writing Practice Book p. 71.

### Pronouns and Antecedents

**Directions** Read the following story. Mark the letter of the pronoun that correctly completes each sentence. The antecedents of the pronouns have been underlined.

1. One day the King announced that ___ would give a diamond ring to the person who made the best bowl of soup. 2. Cooks came from all over the kingdom, bringing their soup recipes with ___. 3. The King tried all the soups, but ___ did not please him. 4. "___ want a simple soup that won't make me fat," the King said. 5. A little kitchen maid heard the King say this and knew what ___ would do. 6. She boiled some water and poured ___ into a bowl. 7. Then she brought the "soup" to the King and put it before ___. 8. "Try this soup," she said. "___ is simple and won't make you fat." 9. The King tried a spoonful of the hot water. "This is delicious," ___ announced. 10. He gave the girl the diamond ring and made ___ head cook.

1. A she
   B it
   C him
   **D** he
2. A they
   B her
   C she
   **D** them
3. **A** they
   B them
   C she
   D we
4. A Me
   **B** I
   C Us
   D Him
5. A her
   B he
   **C** she
   D it

6. A us
   B her
   **C** it
   D them
7. A he
   **B** him
   C it
   D you
8. **A** It
   B She
   C We
   D I
9. A we
   **B** they
   C us
   **D** me
10. A she
    B it
    **C** her
    D me

**Home Activity** Your child prepared for taking tests on pronouns and antecedents. Say the names of people your child knows. Have him or her talk about these people, replacing their names with pronouns.

▲ **Grammar and Writing Practice Book** p. 71

---

# DAY 5 — Cumulative Review

## D A I L Y   F I X - I T

9. The cooks in this restaurant work very hard but she don't get paid very much. *(hard, but they)*

10. It's one of the best places to eat in New York, we must go there. *(York. We)*

### ADDITIONAL PRACTICE

Assign pp. 152–155 in The Grammar and Writing Book.

**EXTRA PRACTICE** Grammar and Writing Practice Book p. 139.

**TEST PREPARATION** Grammar and Writing Practice Book pp. 155–156.

### ASSESSMENT

**CUMULATIVE REVIEW** Grammar and Writing Practice Book p. 72.

### Pronouns and Antecedents

**Directions** Match the pronoun with the noun or noun phrase that could be its antecedent. Write the letter of the correct antecedent next to the pronoun.

__C__ 1. it   A mixing bowls
__D__ 2. we   B the King's son
__B__ 3. he   C soup dish
__A__ 4. they   D Cook and I
__E__ 5. she   E the Queen

**Directions** Write a pronoun to replace each underlined noun or noun phrase.

6. The King said that the King didn't like Cook's soup. ____he____
7. He said the soup was horrible and threw the soup on the floor. ____it____
8. Cook said that Cook had worked hard to make it. ____she____
9. The maids were frightened when the maids heard about the King. ____they____
10. When the King entered the kitchen, Cook curtsied to the King. ____him____
11. The King gave Cook a towel and made Cook blindfold him. ____her____
12. The Princess and the peasant said that the Princess and the peasant were getting married. ____they____

**Directions** Circle the pronoun in ( ) to complete each sentence. The antecedents of the pronouns are underlined.

13. The King was concerned that (it, **he**) would get fat.
14. The young maid was clever, and (her, **she**) had a good idea.
15. The maid created "soup" from water, and she fooled the King with (them, **it**).
16. The King liked the young maid's "soup" and gave (she, **her**) a job in his kitchen.

**Home Activity** Your child reviewed pronouns and antecedents. Ask your child to find examples of pronouns and antecedents in reading matter around the house.

▲ **Grammar and Writing Practice Book** p. 72

# Writing Workshop  Business Letter

## OBJECTIVES

- Identify the characteristics of a business letter.
- Write a business letter, elaborating on the ideas expressed.
- Focus on voice.
- Use a rubric.

**Genre** Business Letter
**Writer's Craft** Elaborate
**Writing Trait** Voice

**Voice** Show pictures that convey people's feelings, such as being proud or frightened. Model discussion of these feelings: "The girl is proud of her drawing." Explain that *proud* tells a feeling. Remind language learners to show their feelings when they write.

## Writing Traits

**FOCUS/IDEAS** The writer clearly describes his new product. He directly states his purpose—to find a sales partner.

**ORGANIZATION/PARAGRAPHS** The letter is organized to describe the product, make a request, and give contact information. Greeting, body, and closing are included.

**VOICE** The writer's voice is businesslike, persuasive, enthusiastic, and direct.

**WORD CHOICE** The writer uses persuasive language *(simple and safe)* and telling details *(it costs just pennies).*

**SENTENCES** Sentences are varied in kind and length. The writer effectively uses an interrogative sentence.

**CONVENTIONS** There is excellent control and accuracy.

### READING-WRITING CONNECTION

- In *The King in the Kitchen,* we hear the unique voice of each character.
- Writers use a strong voice and elaboration to explain their point of view clearly.
- Students will write a **business letter** using a unique voice to make their request strong and clear.

**MODEL VOICE** Discuss Writing Transparency 18A. Then discuss the model and the writing trait of voice.

 **Think Aloud** I see that the writer creates a strong voice by speaking directly to the reader. This letter begins with a clear statement about the purpose of the letter. The writer also uses positive words, such as *simple, safe,* and *strong,* to describe the product. The writer's enthusiasm for the product really shines through.

---

### Business Letter

A **business letter** is written to an organization or a company. The writer might be buying or selling something, asking for information, or looking for a job. A business letter should be informative, precise, and clear.

#### A Very Sticky Business

Dear Sir or Madam:

*Opening sentence makes the purpose of the letter clear.*
    I am writing about a new product that I believe could change the world. King's Glue is simple and safe to use, yet strong enough for any job. It can fix anything in an instant, and it costs just pennies to make.

*Details elaborate on the opening sentence.*
    I am producing large quantities of King's Glue in the Royal Kitchens. Several vats of it are ready for use. All I need is a partner to help sell it. Will you be that partner?

*Request is clearly made.*
*Ending sums up proposal and gives contact information.*
    With my glue and your sales force, we could alter forever the way people stick things together. Please contact me at the Palace if you are interested in this project.

Yours truly,
The King

Unit 4 The King in the Kitchen        Writing Model **18A**

▲ **Writing Transparency** 18A

### WRITER'S CRAFT
### Elaborate

Display Writing Transparency 18B. Read the directions and work together to discuss examples of elaboration.

 **Think Aloud** **ELABORATE** Tomorrow we will be writing a business letter describing a new product. We will need to elaborate on our product idea and the reasons someone should buy it. I'm going to write the name of my product in the center of a web, and then list as many details as I can about the product and its uses. I'm going to explain each idea as fully and clearly as I can.

**GUIDED WRITING** Some students may need more help with elaborating. Give them practice by working with them as they rewrite sentences replacing words such as *stuff, things, lots,* and *nice* with more exact, exciting details.

---

### Elaborate

Writing can be undeveloped or unclear if the writer does not **elaborate** his or her ideas. Exact nouns, strong verbs, and vivid sensory details can make writing fresh and clear.

**Before elaboration**   Cook made something.
**After elaboration**    Cook prepared a soup that tasted like ditch water.
**Before elaboration**   The Princess was happy.
**After elaboration**    The Princess shouted for joy and hugged her father.

**Directions** Replace the underlined word or phrase with interesting, exact details. Write the new sentence. **Possible answers:**

1. I like cooking stuff.
   I like cooking hamburgers over a charcoal grill.

2. She baked a nice dessert.
   She baked an angel food cake that was as light as air.

3. The kitchen was full of things.
   The kitchen was full of greasy plates and burned pans.

4. He ate a lot.
   He ate until his buttons popped off.

5. The kitchen was big.
   The kitchen was the size of a football stadium.

**Directions** Make the paragraph below more interesting by elaborating the ideas.

The King did not like his dinner. He was very angry. He went to the kitchen. We were frightened. **Possible answer:**
The King took his dinner tray and hurled it off the balcony. He became red in the face and bellowed at his servants. Then he stormed down to the kitchen, slamming the door after him. We shook with fear and hid in the broom closet.

Unit 4 The King in the Kitchen        Writer's Craft **18B**

▲ **Writing Transparency** 18B

# DAY 3 Prewrite and Draft

## READ THE WRITING PROMPT

on page 463 in the Student Edition.

*In* The King in the Kitchen, *the king starts a glue business.*

*Think about a new product that you might like to invent.*

*Now write a business letter asking a company to help you sell your product.*

### Writing Test Tips

- Remember that your purpose is to interest the reader in your product.
- Include specific details that show how your product is special.
- Speak directly and enthusiastically to the person reading the letter.

**GETTING STARTED** Students can do any of the following:

- Create a concept web with the name of their product in the center.
- Brainstorm with a group to come up with the idea for a new product. Have each member of the group take turns providing details about the product.
- Complete the following sentences in as many ways as possible: "You need to buy this product because...."

# DAY 4 Draft and Revise

## EDITING/REVISING CHECKLIST

☑ Have I elaborated effectively on my product?

☑ Is my purpose clear?

☑ Are pronouns and their antecedents used correctly?

☑ Are words ending in *-er* and *-ar* spelled correctly?

See *The Grammar and Writing Book,* pp. 152–157.

### Revising Tips

#### Voice

- Support a strong and enthusiastic voice by speaking directly to your reader.
- Make sure your word choice is precise and objective.
- Sound businesslike, but friendly.

**PUBLISHING** Have students type their letters on word processors, formatting them correctly with invented addresses. Some students may wish to revise their work later.

**ASSESSMENT** Use the scoring rubric to evaluate students' work.

# DAY 5 Connect to Unit Writing

| | Story |
|---|---|
| Week 1 | Story About a Discovery 415g–415h |
| Week 2 | Travel Brochure 439g–439h |
| Week 3 | Business Letter 465g–465h |
| Week 4 | Feature Story 487g–487h |
| Week 5 | Plot Summary 507g–507h |

## PREVIEW THE UNIT PROMPT

*Write a story about something that happens on a real or an imaginary trip. Try to include suspense or humor and dialogue.*

**APPLY**

- A story has a beginning, middle, and end and focuses on one incident or event.
- Writers of fiction elaborate on ideas in order to bring their stories to life.

## Writing Trait Rubric

| | 4 | 3 | 2 | 1 |
|---|---|---|---|---|
| **Voice** | Direct, enthusiastic, and persuasive voice | Voice generally enthusiastic and persuasive | Voice with isolated examples of enthusiasm and persuasiveness, but generally flat | Writing flat and uninteresting |
| | Business letter with effective and convincing voice | Business letter generally effective with convincing voice | Business letter minimally effective; misses opportunities to create a unique voice | Business letter unconvincing with weak voice |

# Spelling & Phonics Words with final *er, ar*

## Spelling Words

1. brother
2. together*
3. dinner*
4. popular
5. center*
6. calendar
7. similar
8. regular
9. summer
10. clever*
11. supper
12. pitcher
13. filter
14. hangar
15. never*
16. shelter
17. cellar
18. caterpillar
19. theater
20. deliver*

### Challenge Words

21. character
22. singular
23. receiver
24. spectacular
25. binocular

*Word from the selection

**Spelling/Phonics Support** See the ELL and Transition Handbook for spelling support.

## DAY 1 Pretest and Sort

### PRETEST

Use the Dictation Sentences from Day 5 to administer the pretest. Read the word, read the sentence, and then read the word again. Guide students in self-correcting their pretests and correcting any misspellings.

| Monitor Progress | |
|---|---|
| **Spelling** | |
| **If...** students misspell more than 5 pre-test words, | **then...** use words 1–10 for Strategic Intervention. |
| **If...** students misspell 1–5 pretest words, | **then...** use words 1–20 for On-Level practice. |
| **If...** students correctly spell all pretest words, | **then...** use words 1–25 for Advanced Learners. |

**HOMEWORK** Spelling Practice Book, p. 69.

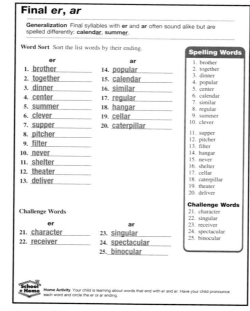

▲ **Spelling Practice Book** p. 69

## DAY 2 Think and Practice

### TEACH

Final syllables with *er* and *ar* often sound alike but are spelled differently. Write *shelter* and *cellar* on the board. Point out that although they sound the same, their endings are spelled differently. Guide students in noting the different endings.

shelt**er**    cell**ar**

**FILL IN BLANKS** Ask students to work in pairs to write spelling words on slips of paper with the final *e* or *a* missing. Then have students exchange slips of paper and fill in the missing letter.

**HOMEWORK** Spelling Practice Book, p. 70.

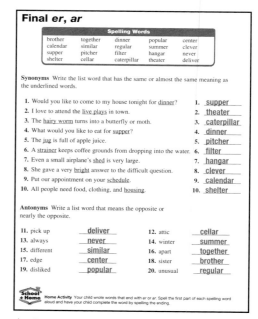

▲ **Spelling Practice Book** p. 70

# DAY 3 Connect to Writing

## WRITE A LETTER

Ask students to write a letter using at least four of the spelling words. The letter can be to a friend, a relative, or the editor of a newspaper.

### Frequently Misspelled Words

another   let's
that's

These words may seem easy to spell, but they are often misspelled by fourth-graders. Alert students to these frequently misspelled words.

**HOMEWORK** Spelling Practice Book, p. 71.

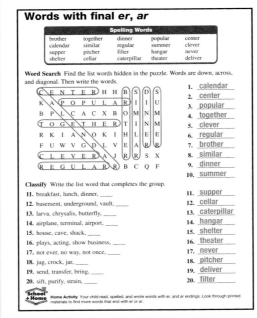

▲ **Spelling Practice Book** p. 71

# DAY 4 Review

## REVIEW FINAL er, ar

Have each student create a hidden word puzzle. They can exchange puzzles with a partner to review the spelling words.

### Spelling Strategy
### Problem Parts

Since the ending sounds er and ar provide little clue as to the spelling of a word, have students try visualization instead. Have them look at the word, say it, and listen to the sounds. Then spell the word aloud and think about its spelling. Is there anything special to remember? Have students picture the word with their eyes shut, then look at the word and write it. Finally, cover the word, picture it, and write it again. Check the spelling.

**HOMEWORK** Spelling Practice Book, p. 72.

▲ **Spelling Practice Book** p. 72

# DAY 5 Posttest

## DICTATION SENTENCES

1. My brother and I went swimming.
2. We rode on the same sled together.
3. Later, we had dinner.
4. Blue is a popular color.
5. We went to the recreation center.
6. We marked the date on the calendar.
7. We have similar glasses.
8. I am a regular visitor to the zoo.
9. In the summer we go swimming.
10. My sister can do many clever dives.
11. Don't be late for supper.
12. There's nothing better than a pitcher of cold water.
13. It's time to change the air filter.
14. The airplane is in the hangar.
15. I am never late for a meal.
16. Seek shelter if it starts to rain.
17. I keep my tools in the cellar.
18. I saw a caterpillar in the grass.
19. On rainy days we go to the theater to see a movie.
20. We would like you to deliver the pizza.

## CHALLENGE

21. My uncle is an interesting character.
22. Write the singular and plural forms.
23. He holds the telephone receiver upside down.
24. The fireworks show is always spectacular.
25. Most animals have binocular vision.

*The King in the Kitchen*    **465j**

## OBJECTIVES

- Formulate an inquiry question that is connected to this week's lesson focus.
- Effectively and efficiently find, evaluate, and communicate information related to an inquiry question using electronic sources.

### New Literacies

| Day 1 | Identify Questions |
| --- | --- |
| Day 2 | Navigate/Search |
| Day 3 | Analyze |
| Day 4 | Synthesize |
| Day 5 | Communicate |

## NEW LITERACIES

# Internet Inquiry Activity

## EXPLORE MISTAKES AND SUCCESSES

Use the following 5-day plan to help students conduct this week's Internet inquiry activity on how mistakes can lead to successes. Remind students to follow classroom rules when using the Internet.

### DAY 1

**Identify Questions** Discuss the lesson focus question: *How can a mistake turn into a success?* List examples students already know and add some of your own, such as penicillin and bubble gum. Have students work individually, in pairs, or in small groups to write an inquiry question they want to answer.

### DAY 2

**Navigate/Search** Students already focused on a specific mistake can use related keywords to identify helpful Web sites to explore on Day 3. Students who wish to find out about other accidental inventions or discoveries may need guidance since student-friendly search engines may produce limited results for this broad subject. Demonstrate a search on a major search engine using the keywords *accidental inventions* or *science mistakes* and suggest grade-appropriate sites students can explore further.

### DAY 3

**Analyze** Have students explore the Web sites identified on Day 2. Point out that efficient researchers first scan a site to find important information and then read relevant sections more closely. Students can use text features such as subheads and graphics to help them scan efficiently. Online encyclopedias often highlight the appearance of search words in the text. You can also demonstrate how to use a computer's "find" feature (usually in the Edit menu) that searches the site for a specific word or phrase and highlights it.

### DAY 4

**Synthesize** Have students synthesize relevant information from Day 3. One way students can organize information is to prepare index cards sorted by topic and subtopic. Students can lay out their index cards in a logical arrangement to create an organization for their Day 5 reports.

### DAY 5

**Communicate** Have students share their inquiry results by writing a report. Encourage them to use subheads identifying topics of individual sections.

# Follow and Clarify Directions

## TEACH

Ask students why it's important to follow directions when cooking or constructing something. Review these strategies for following directions.

● Before you begin, read all of the **directions**. This will help you understand how complicated the task is and how long it will take.

● Look for **numbered steps**. Directions are usually numbered. The numbers tell the sequence in which the steps should be done.

● After reading the first step, do what it says before going on to the next step.

● Visualize the **end result**. This will help you understand how the steps are connected and what you are working toward.

● Study any **illustrations** or **diagrams**. They can help **clarify** written steps.

Give pairs of students a set of written directions, such as a recipe or science experiment. Have them use the directions to complete the task. Then ask:

**1. What is the first thing you should do?** *(Read all the directions.)*

**2. What would happen if you didn't follow the directions in order?** *(Possible response: The end product may not be correct.)*

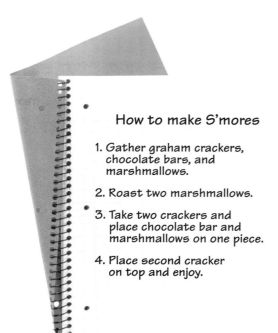

**How to make S'mores**

1. Gather graham crackers, chocolate bars, and marshmallows.

2. Roast two marshmallows.

3. Take two crackers and place chocolate bar and marshmallows on one piece.

4. Place second cracker on top and enjoy.

## ASSESS

As students work with the directions, check that they follow the steps in order and pay attention to numbers and diagrams.

For more practice or to assess students, use Practice Book pp. 179–180.

### Practice Book p. 179

**Follow and Clarify Directions**

- Follow directions, or instructions, in order. Directions are usually numbered.
- Read through all the directions before you begin. Then do what is instructed, one step at a time.
- Try to visualize the end result of the directions to see where you are headed.

**Directions** Read the directions in this recipe. Then answer the questions below.

> **Ants on a Log**
> (two servings)
> This is a healthy snack for camping.
> **INGREDIENTS**
> 2 large celery stalks
> 1/3 cup peanut butter
> 1/4 cup raisins
>
> **PREPARATION**
> 1. Wash and dry two celery stalks.
> 2. Cut off the leafy tops with a kitchen knife. Cut each celery stalk into four parts.
> 3. Spread peanut butter into the groove on the celery pieces. Now they look like logs.
> 4. Press raisins onto the "logs" for "ants."
> 5. Enjoy!

Possible answers given.

1. What is the end result of this recipe?
   a snack called "Ants on a Log"

2. What is the first step in the directions?
   Wash and dry two celery sticks.

3. Which other steps are completed before spreading the peanut butter?
   cutting off the leafy tops and cutting the celery into pieces

4. Why can't step 4 be done before step 3?
   The raisins wouldn't stick without the peanut butter.

5. Why do you think this snack is called "Ants on a Log"? Explain what helps you to visualize it.
   It ends up looking like ants on a log. Students might point out specific descriptions that help in visualizing the recipe.

### Practice Book p. 180

**Directions** Read over these directions. Then answer the questions below.

> You may have seen sand castles on the beach or watched the results of a sand castle building contest live or on television. Here's the best way to build your own sand castle.
> 1. Choose sand that is moist enough to stick together. Fine, flat-grained sand is best. This sand is often found near the high-water line.
> 2. Start by making a pile of sand about 1 foot to 1 1/2 feet high. Its height and width will depend on what you want your castle to look like. Work from the top down to the base for the best results.
> 3. Pack the sand-pile down and make a smooth, flat top.
> 4. Use a shovel edge or ruler to carve the castle's tower and walls. You can also use pails, shovels, cans, spoons, melon-ballers, and so on.
> 5. Move down the pile in a stairstep fashion. Be creative, creating towers and walls.
> 6. Remember that sand castles have a very short life. Don't spend a long time trying to make a single perfect window on one tower. Instead, have fun and remember what you might try differently on your next attempt.

6. What is the purpose of these directions?
   The directions tell how to build a sand castle.

7. How high should your pile of sand be?
   1 foot to 1 1/2 feet tall

8. Should you work from the bottom up or from the top down?
   You should build from the top down.

9. Name some items you might use in building your sand castle.
   Possible answers: pail, can, melon-baller

10. Why shouldn't you worry much about your first attempt at building a sand castle?
    Possible answer: Sand castles don't last long, so there's no point in worrying about making it perfect. You can always make another.

**School + Home** **Home Activity** Your child learned about following directions. With your child, read the directions for a card or board game. Try to follow them, step by step. Help your child to clarify each step in the directions.

# Assessment Checkpoints *for the Week*

## Selection Assessment

**Use pp. 69–72 of** Selection Tests **to check:**

 **Selection Understanding**

 **Comprehension Skill**
*Character and Setting*

 **Selection Vocabulary**

| | |
|---|---|
| duke | majesty |
| dungeon | noble |
| furiously | peasant |
| genius | porridge |

Selection Tests

ASSESSMENT

**Scott Foresman**
**Selection Tests**
Teacher's Manual

* Assess comprehension of weekly selections
* Assess understanding of weekly comprehension skills
* Assess knowledge of selection vocabulary

Reading STREET
Grade 4

## Leveled Assessment

On-Level
Strategic Intervention
Advanced

**Use pp. 103–108 of** Fresh Reads for Differentiated Test Practice **to check:**

 **Comprehension Skill**
*Character and Setting*

 REVIEW **Comprehension Skill**
*Graphic Sources*

 **Fluency** *Words Correct Per Minute*

Fresh Reads for Differentiated Test Practice

ASSESSMENT    Teacher's Manual

**Scott Foresman**
**Fresh Reads**
**for Differentiated Test Practice**

Leveled passages—strategic intervention, on-level, and advanced—for

* Fluency checks
* Practice and application of weekly comprehension skills
* Answer key for all practice pages

Reading STREET
Grade 4

## Managing Assessment

**Use** Assessment Handbook **for:**

 **Observation Checklists**

 **Record-Keeping Forms**

 **Portfolio Assessment**

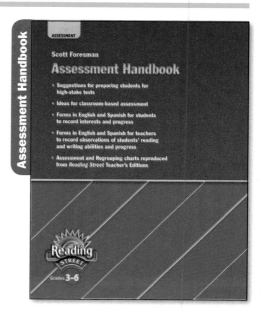

Assessment Handbook

ASSESSMENT

**Scott Foresman**
**Assessment Handbook**

* Suggestions for preparing students for high-stake tests
* Ideas for classroom-based assessment
* Forms in English and Spanish for students to record interests and progress
* Forms in English and Spanish for teachers to record observations of students' reading and writing abilities and progress
* Assessment and Regrouping charts reproduced from *Reading Street Teacher's Editions*

Reading STREET
Grades 3–6

# Unit 4
# Puzzles and Mysteries

## CONCEPT QUESTION
## Is there an explanation for everything?

**Week 1**

Can you always believe what you see?

**Week 2**

What can explain animal behavior?

**Week 3**

How can a mistake turn into a success?

**Week 4**

How can knowing another language create understanding?

**Week 5**

How can attention to detail help solve a problem?

## EXPAND THE CONCEPT
## How can knowing another language create understanding?

## CONNECT THE CONCEPT

▶ **Build Background**
*converse, scholar, symbol*

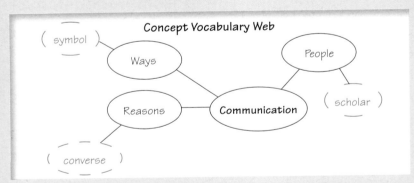

Concept Vocabulary Web

▶ **Social Studies Content**
Napoleon Bonaparte, The Rosetta Stone

▶ **Writing**
Feature Story

▶ **Internet Inquiry**
Languages

# Preview Your Week

*How can knowing another language create understanding?*

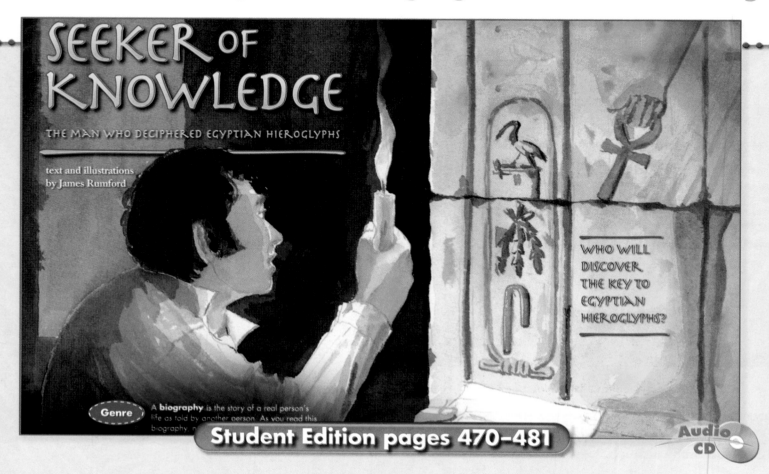

SEEKER OF KNOWLEDGE

THE MAN WHO DECIPHERED EGYPTIAN HIEROGLYPHS

text and illustrations by James Rumford

WHO WILL DISCOVER THE KEY TO EGYPTIAN HIEROGLYPHS?

**Genre** A **biography** is the story of a real person's life as told by another person. As you read this biography, n

**Student Edition pages 470–481**

Audio CD

| | |
|---|---|
| **Genre** | Biography |
| **Vocabulary Strategy** | Word Structure |
| **Comprehension Skill** | Graphic Sources |
| **Comprehension Strategy** | Ask Questions |

## Paired Selection

**Reading Across Texts**

Compare and Contrast Symbols

**Genre**

Search Engines

**Text Features**

Search Window

Search Button

Result List

Reading Online

SOCIAL STUDIES

**Search Engines**

**Genre**
- A tool called a search engine can help you find Web sites on the Internet.
- You can focus your search by brainstorming a list of important words, or keywords.

**Text Features**
- Every search engine has a window in which you type keywords.
- Clicking on the SEARCH button starts the search.
- Search results are displayed in a list below the search window. Each item is a link to a Web site that contains the keywords.

**Link to Social Studies**
How do hearing-impaired people communicate? Search the Internet for information on ASL, American Sign Language.

**Word Puzzles**

To Jean-François Champollion, the Rosetta Stone was a giant word puzzle. If you wanted to know more about word puzzles, you could type "word puzzles" into a search engine window and click the SEARCH button.

The search engine might come up with a long list of Web sites about word puzzles. You might find results such as these:

1. **Word Puzzles** Word Puzzles: Your guide to the best Web sites for **word puzzles**—including acrostics, cryptograms, riddles, and word searches. The best Web sites for acrostics, cryptograms, riddles, word searches, and other **word puzzles**.

2. **Rebus Stories.** Rebus Stories lets you make Web pages of stories you write where some of the words are replaced with pictures (called **rebuses**). Create your own **word puzzles.**

The Rebus Stories link reminds you of the Rosetta Stone because Egyptian writing told stories in pictures. You click on that link.

**Ask Questions** What questions do you have about search engines?

**Student Edition pages 484–487**

Audio CD

**Read It**
ONLINE
PearsonSuccessNet.com
- **Student Edition**
- **Leveled Readers**

## Leveled Readers

◎ **Skill** Graphic Sources

◎ **Strategy** Ask Questions

**Lesson Vocabulary**

**Below-Level**

**On-Level**

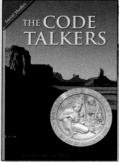

**Advanced**

**ELL Reader**
- Concept Vocabulary
- Text Support
- Language Enrichment

---

Time for
**SOCIAL STUDIES**

## Integrate Social Studies Standards
- **Biography**
- **Egyptology**

✓ **Read**

***Seeker of Knowledge,***
pp. 470–481

**"Word Puzzles,"**
pp. 484–487

### Leveled Readers

| Below-Level | On-Level | Advanced |
|---|---|---|
| • Support Concepts | • Develop Concepts | • Extend Concepts<br>• Social Studies Extension Activity |

### ELL Reader

✓ **Build**
**Concept Vocabulary**
**Communication,**
pp. 466l–466m

✓ **Teach**
**Social Studies Concepts**
**Napoleon Bonaparte,** p. 475
**The Rosetta Stone,** p. 479

✓ **Explore**
**Social Studies Center**
**Create a Code,** p. 466k

# Weekly Plan

## READING

*45–90 minutes*

### TARGET SKILLS OF THE WEEK

**Comprehension Skill**
Graphic Sources

**Comprehension Strategy**
Ask Questions

**Vocabulary Strategy**
Word Structure

---

## DAY 1
**PAGES 466l–468b, 487a, 487e–487k**

### Oral Language

**QUESTION OF THE WEEK** *How can knowing another language create understanding?*

Read Aloud: "Silent Debate," 466m
Build Concepts, 466l

### Comprehension/Vocabulary

Comprehension Skill/Strategy Lesson, 466–467
 Graphic Sources **T**
 Ask Questions
Build Background, 468a
Introduce Lesson Vocabulary, 468b
*ancient, link, scholars, seeker, temple, translate, triumph, uncover* **T**

Read Leveled Readers

Grouping Options 466f–466g

### Fluency

Model Phrasing, 466l–466m, 487a

---

## DAY 2
**PAGES 468–477, 487a, 487e–487k**

### Oral Language

**QUESTION OF THE DAY** *Why does Jean Francois care so much about learning a lost language?*

### Comprehension/Vocabulary

Vocabulary Strategy Lesson, 468–469
 Word Structure **T**

Read *Seeker of Knowledge,* 470–477

Grouping Options
466f–466g

 Graphic Sources **T**
 Ask Questions
 Word Structure **T**
**REVIEW** Main Idea **T**
Develop Vocabulary

### Fluency

Echo Reading, 487a

---

## LANGUAGE ARTS

*30–60 minutes*

### Trait of the Week

**Conventions**

---

**Grammar,** 487e
Introduce Possessive Pronouns **T**

**Writing Workshop,** 487g
Introduce Feature Story

**Spelling,** 487i
Pretest for Consonants /j/, /ks/, and /kw/

**Internet Inquiry,** 487k
Identify Questions

---

**Grammar,** 487e
Develop Possessive Pronouns **T**

**Writing Workshop,** 487g
Improve Writing with Show, Don't Tell

**Spelling,** 487i
Teach the Generalization

**Internet Inquiry,** 487k
Navigate/Search

---

### DAILY WRITING ACTIVITIES

**Day 1** Write to Read, 466

**Day 2** Words to Write, 469
Strategy Response Log, 470, 477

---

### DAILY SOCIAL STUDIES CONNECTIONS

**Day 1** Communication Concept Web, 466l

**Day 2** Time for Social Studies: Napoleon Bonaparte, 475
Revisit the Communication Concept Web, 477

---

### DAILY SUCCESS PREDICTORS
for Adequate Yearly Progress

### Monitor Progress and Corrective Feedback

**Vocabulary**  Check Vocabulary, *466l*

**RESOURCES FOR THE WEEK**

- Practice Book, *pp. 181–190*
- Word Study and Spelling Practice Book, *pp. 73–76*
- Grammar and Writing Practice Book, *pp. 73–76*
- Selection Test, *pp. 73–76*
- Fresh Reads for Differentiated Test Practice, *pp. 109–114*
- The Grammar and Writing Book, *pp. 158–163*

**Grouping Options for Differentiated Instruction**

Turn the page for the small group lesson plan.

## DAY 3   PAGES 478–483, 487a, 487e–487k

### Oral Language

**QUESTION OF THE DAY** *Why was Jean-Francois's discovery important?*

### Comprehension/Vocabulary

**Read** *Seeker of Knowledge, 478–483*

**Grouping Options**
466f–466g

- 🔊 Ask Questions
- 🔊 Word Structure **T**
- Develop Vocabulary

Reader Response

Selection Test

### Fluency

Model Phrasing, 487a

**Grammar,** 487f
Apply Possessive Pronouns in Writing **T**

**Writing Workshop,** 483, 487h
Write Now
Prewrite and Draft

**Spelling,** 487j
Connect Spelling to Writing

**Internet Inquiry,** 487k
Analyze Sources

**Day 3**   Strategy Response Log, 480
      Look Back and Write, 482

**Day 3**   Time for Social Studies: The Rosetta
      Stone, 479
      Revisit the Communication Concept Web, 481

## DAY 4   PAGES 484–487a, 487e–487k

### Oral Language

**QUESTION OF THE DAY** *What can you learn from graphic symbols that you see today, such as computer icons?*

### Comprehension/Vocabulary

**Read** "Word Puzzles," 484–487

**Grouping Options**
466f–466g

Search Engines
Reading Across Texts

### Fluency

Partner Reading, 487a

**Grammar,** 487f
Practice Possessive Pronouns for
    Standardized Tests **T**

**Writing Workshop,** 487h
Draft, Revise, and Publish

**Spelling,** 487j
Provide a Strategy

**Internet Inquiry,** 487k
Synthesize Information

**Day 4**   Writing Across Texts, 487

**Day 4**   Social Studies Center: Create a Code, 466k

## DAY 5   PAGES 487a–487l

### Oral Language

**QUESTION OF THE WEEK** *To wrap up the week, revisit the Day 1 question.*
Build Concept Vocabulary, 487c

### Fluency

**Read** Leveled Readers

**Grouping Options** 466f–466g

Assess Reading Rate, 487a

### Comprehension/Vocabulary

- 🔊 Reteach Graphic Sources, 487b **T**
- How Art Complements Text, 487b
- 🔊 Review Word Structure, 487c **T**

**Speaking and Listening,** 487d
Retelling
Listen to a Story
**Grammar,** 487f
Cumulative Review
**Writing Workshop,** 487h
Connect to Unit Writing
**Spelling,** 487j
Posttest for Consonants /j/, /ks/, and /kw/
**Internet Inquiry,** 487k
Communicate Results
**Research/Study Skills,** 487l
Thesaurus
**Extend Skills,** 487b
How Art Complements Text

**Day 5**   How Art Complements Text, 487b

**Day 5**   Revisit the Communication Concept
      Web, 487c

**KEY** 🔊 = Target Skill   **T** = Tested Skill

**Comprehension**   Check Retelling, *482*

**Fluency**   Check Fluency WCPM, *487a*

**Vocabulary**   Check Vocabulary, *487c*

**SUCCESS PREDICTOR**

# Small Group Plan *for Differentiated Instruction*

## Daily Plan AT A GLANCE

### Reading
**Whole Group**
- Oral Language
- Comprehension/Vocabulary

### Group Time
**Differentiated Instruction**

Meet with small groups to provide:
- Skill Support
- Reading Support
- Fluency Practice

*Read*

This week's lessons for daily group time can be found behind the Differentiated Instruction (DI) tab on pp. DI·32–DI·41.

### Whole Group
- Fluency

### Language Arts
- Grammar
- Writing
- Spelling
- Research/Inquiry
- Speaking/Listening/Viewing

**Use *My Sidewalks on Reading Street* for Tier III intensive reading intervention.**

---

## DAY 1

| On-Level | Strategic Intervention | Advanced |
|---|---|---|
| **Teacher-Led**<br>*Page DI · 33* | **Teacher-Led**<br>*Page DI · 32* | **Teacher-Led**<br>*Page DI · 33* |
| • Develop Concept Vocabulary<br>• Read On-Level Reader *Cracking the German Code* | • Reinforce Concepts<br>• Read Below-Level Reader *The Rosetta Stone and the Secret of Hieroglyphics* | • Read Advanced Reader *The Code Talkers*<br>• Independent Extension Activity |

 **Independent Activities**

While you meet with small groups, have the rest of the class...

- Visit the Reading/Library Center
- Listen to the Background Building Audio
- Finish Write to Read, p. 466
- Complete Practice Book pp. 183–184
- Visit Cross-Curricular Centers

---

## DAY 2

| On-Level | Strategic Intervention | Advanced |
|---|---|---|
| **Teacher-Led**<br>*Pages 472–477* | **Teacher-Led**<br>*Page DI · 34* | **Teacher-Led**<br>*Page DI · 35* |
| • Read *Seeker of Knowledge* | • Practice Lesson Vocabulary<br>• Read Multisyllabic Words<br>• Read or Listen to *Seeker of Knowledge* | • Extend Vocabulary<br>• Read *Seeker of Knowledge* |

 **Independent Activities**

While you meet with small groups, have the rest of the class...

- Visit the Reading/Library Center
- Listen to the AudioText for *Seeker of Knowledge*
- Finish Words to Write, p. 469
- Complete Practice Book pp. 185–186
- Write in their Strategy Response Logs, pp. 470, 477
- Visit Cross-Curricular Centers
- Work on inquiry projects

---

## DAY 3

| On-Level | Strategic Intervention | Advanced |
|---|---|---|
| **Teacher-Led**<br>*Pages 478–481* | **Teacher-Led**<br>*Page DI · 36* | **Teacher-Led**<br>*Page DI · 37* |
| • Read *Seeker of Knowledge* | • Practice Graphic Sources and Ask Questions<br>• Read or Listen to *Seeker of Knowledge* | • Extend Graphic Sources and Ask Questions<br>• Read *Seeker of Knowledge* |

 **Independent Activities**

While you meet with small groups, have the rest of the class...

- Visit the Reading/Library Center
- Listen to the AudioText for *Seeker of Knowledge*
- Write in their Strategy Response Logs, p. 480
- Finish Look Back and Write, p. 482
- Complete Practice Book p. 187
- Visit Cross-Curricular Centers
- Work on inquiry projects

# ☑ Customize Your Plan by Strand

## ORAL LANGUAGE

**SOCIAL STUDIES**

### Concept Development

How can knowing another language create understanding?

**CONCEPT VOCABULARY**
converse    scholar    symbol

### BUILD

☐ **Question of the Week** Introduce and discuss the question of the week. This week students will read a variety of texts and work on projects related to the concept *communication*. Post the question for students to refer to throughout the week. **DAY 1** 466d

☐ **Read Aloud** Read aloud "Silent Debate." Then begin a web to build concepts and concept vocabulary related to this week's lesson and the unit theme, Puzzles and Mysteries. Introduce the concept words *converse, scholar,* and *symbol* and have students place them on the web. Display the web for use throughout the week. **DAY 1** 466l-466m

### DEVELOP

☐ **Question of the Day** Use the prompts from the weekly Plan to engage students in conversations related to this week's reading and the unit theme. **EVERY DAY** 466d-466e

☐ **Concept Vocabulary Web** Revisit the Communication Concept Web and encourage students to add concept words from their reading and life experiences. **DAY 2** 477, **DAY 3** 481

### CONNECT

☐ **Looking Back/Moving Forward** Revisit the Communication Concept Web and discuss how it relates to this week's lesson and the unit theme. Then make connections to next week's lesson. **DAY 5** 487c

### CHECK

☐ **Concept Vocabulary Web** Use the Communication Concept Web to check students' understanding of the concept vocabulary words *converse, scholar,* and *symbol*. **DAY 1** 466l, **DAY 5** 487c

## VOCABULARY

**STRATEGY WORD STRUCTURE**
When you are reading and see an unfamiliar word, use what you know about Greek or Latin roots to try to figure out the meaning.

**LESSON VOCABULARY**

| | |
|---|---|
| ancient | temple |
| link | translate |
| scholars | triumph |
| seeker | uncover |

### TEACH

☐ **Words to Know** Give students the opportunity to tell what they already know about this week's lesson vocabulary words. Then discuss word meaning. **DAY 1** 468b

☐ **Vocabulary Strategy Lesson** Use the vocabulary strategy lesson in the Student Edition to introduce and model this week's strategy, word structure. **DAY 2** 468-469

*Vocabulary Strategy Lesson*

### PRACTICE/APPLY

☐ **Leveled Text** Read the lesson vocabulary in the context of leveled text. **DAY 1** LR28-LR36

☐ **Words in Context** Read the lesson vocabulary and apply word structure in the context of *Seeker of Knowledge*. **DAY 2** 470-477, **DAY 3** 478-482

*Leveled Readers*

☐ **Writing/Vocabulary Center** Make a picture glossary of the Words to Know. **ANY DAY** 466k

*Main Selection—Nonfiction*

☐ **Homework** Practice Book pp. 184-185. **DAY 1** 468b, **DAY 2** 469

☐ **Word Play** Have students identify compound words from *Seeker of Knowledge* and then draw symbols to represent several of the compound words on their list. **ANY DAY** 487c

### ASSESS

☐ **Selection Test** Use the Selection Test to determine students' understanding of the lesson vocabulary words. **DAY 3**

### RETEACH/REVIEW

☐ **Reteach Lesson** If necessary, use this lesson to reteach and review word structure. **DAY 5** 487c

① Begin with whole class skill and strategy instruction.

② Meet with small groups to provide differentiated instruction.

③ Gather the whole class back together for fluency and language arts.

**DAY 4**

### On-Level
**Teacher-Led**
*Pages 484–487*
- **Read** "Word Puzzles"

### Strategic Intervention
**Teacher-Led**
*Page DI · 38*
- Practice Retelling
- **Read** or Listen to "Word Puzzles"

### Advanced
**Teacher-Led**
*Page DI · 39*
- **Read** "Word Puzzles"
- Genre Study

## ⓘ Independent Activities

**While you meet with small groups, have the rest of the class...**

- Visit the Reading/Library Center
- Listen to the AudioText for "Word Puzzles"
- Visit the Writing/Vocabulary Center

- Finish Writing Across Texts, p. 487
- Visit Cross-Curricular Centers
- Work on inquiry projects

**DAY 5**

### On-Level
**Teacher-Led**
*Page DI · 41*
- **Reread** Leveled Reader *Cracking the German Code*
- Retell *Cracking the German Code*

### Strategic Intervention
**Teacher-Led**
*Page DI · 40*
- **Reread** Leveled Reader *The Rosetta Stone and the Secret of Hieroglyphics*
- Retell *The Rosetta Stone and the Secret of Hieroglyphics*

### Advanced
**Teacher-Led**
*Page DI · 41*
- **Reread** Leveled Reader *The Code Talkers*
- Share Extension Activity

## ⓘ Independent Activities

**While you meet with small groups, have the rest of the class...**

- Visit the Reading/Library Center
- Complete Practice Book pp. 188–190

- Visit Cross-Curricular Centers
- Work on inquiry projects

**ELL**

**Grouping** Place English language learners in the groups that correspond to their reading abilities in English.

Use the appropriate Leveled Reader or other text at students' instructional level.

**TIP** Send home the appropriate Multilingual Summary of the main selection on Day 1.

---

**Take It to the NET™**
**ONLINE**
PearsonSuccessNet.com

**Peter Afflerbach**
For ideas on assessing engagement, see the article "Engaged Assessment of Engaged Readers" by Scott Foresman author Peter Afflerbach.

---

**TEACHER TALK**

A **Latin or Greek root** is a meaningful word part that cannot stand alone (such as *aud, cred, auto, bio*) but appears in combination with affixes or other roots.

---

**Looking Ahead**

Be sure to schedule time for students to work on the unit inquiry project "Unlocking Nature's Mysteries." This week students combine the information they have collected to answer their inquiry questions.

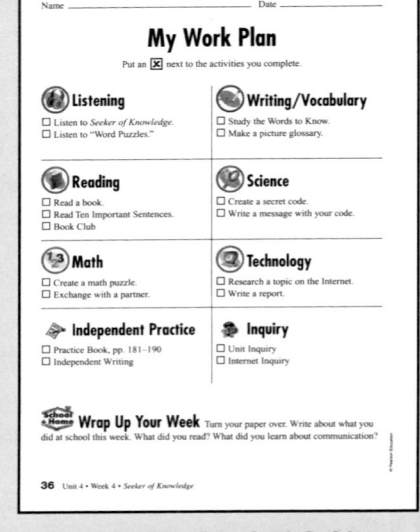

| Name | Date |

## My Work Plan
Put an ☒ next to the activities you complete.

**Listening**
☐ Listen to *Seeker of Knowledge.*
☐ Listen to "Word Puzzles."

**Writing/Vocabulary**
☐ Study the Words to Know.
☐ Make a picture glossary.

**Reading**
☐ Read a book.
☐ Read Ten Important Sentences.
☐ Book Club

**Science**
☐ Create a secret code.
☐ Write a message with your code.

**Math**
☐ Create a math puzzle.
☐ Exchange with a partner.

**Technology**
☐ Research a topic on the Internet.
☐ Write a report.

**Independent Practice**
☐ Practice Book, pp. 181–190
☐ Independent Writing

**Inquiry**
☐ Unit Inquiry
☐ Internet Inquiry

**Wrap Up Your Week** Turn your paper over. Write about what you did at school this week. What did you read? What did you learn about communication?

36  Unit 4 • Week 4 • *Seeker of Knowledge*

▲ **Group-Time Survival Guide**
p. 36, Weekly Contract

*Seeker of Knowledge*   **466g**

**①** Use assessment data to determine your instructional focus.

**②** Preview this week's instruction by strand.

**③** Choose instructional activities that meet the needs of your classroom.

466g-2

# COMPREHENSION

**SKILL GRAPHIC SOURCES** Graphic sources show information visually. They include maps, photographs and captions, time lines, and diagrams. Graphic sources can help you understand the information in the text.

**STRATEGY ASK QUESTIONS** Asking questions before, during and after reading helps focus the reading because you are looking for specific answers. Preview the text and look at the graphic sources in the text to help better understand what you will be reading.

## TEACH

☐ **Skill/Strategy Lesson** Use the skill/strategy lesson in the Student Edition to introduce and model *graphic sources* and *ask questions*. DAY 1 466-467

☐ **Extend Skills** Teach how art complements text. **ANY DAY** 487b

**Skill/Strategy Lesson**

## PRACTICE/APPLY

☐ **Leveled Text** Apply *graphic sources* and *ask questions* to read leveled text. DAY 1 LR28-LR36

**Leveled Readers**

☐ **Skills and Strategies in Context** Read *Seeker of Knowledge*, using the Guiding Comprehension questions to apply *graphic sources* and *ask questions*. DAY 2 470-477, DAY 3 478-482

**Main Selection—Nonfiction**

☐ **Skills and Strategies in Context** Read "Word Puzzles," guiding students as they apply *graphic sources* and *ask questions*. Then have students discuss and write across texts. DAY 4 484-487

☐ **Homework** Practice Book pp. 183, 187, 188. DAY 1 467, DAY 3 481, DAY 5 487b

**Paired Selection—Nonfiction**

☐ **Fresh Reads for Differentiated Test Practice** Have students practice *graphic sources* with a new passage. DAY 3

## ASSESS

☐ **Selection Test** Determine students' understanding of the selection and their use of *graphic sources*. DAY 3

☐ **Retell** Have students retell *Seeker of Knowledge*. DAY 3 482-483

## RETEACH/REVIEW

☐ **Reteach Lesson** If necessary, reteach and review *graphic sources*. DAY 5 487b

# FLUENCY

**SKILL PHRASING** Phrasing is grouping related words in a meaningful way to help listeners understand the story.

## TEACH

☐ **Read Aloud** Model fluent reading by rereading "Silent Debate." Focus on this week's fluency skill, phrasing. DAY 1 466l-466m, 487a

## PRACTICE/APPLY

☐ **Echo Reading** Read aloud selected paragraphs from *Seeker of Knowledge*, modeling how you use commas and dashes as phrasing cues and how you carefully pronounce foreign names. Then practice as a class, doing three echo readings. DAY 2 487a, DAY 3 487a

☐ **Partner Reading** Have partners practice reading aloud, reading with careful logical phrasing and offering each other feedback. As students reread, monitor their progress toward their individual fluency goals. DAY 4 487a

☐ **Listening Center** Have students follow along with the AudioText for this week's selections. **ANY DAY** 466j

☐ **Reading/Library Center** Have students reread a selection of their choice. **ANY DAY** 466j

☐ **Fluency Coach** Have students use Fluency Coach to listen to fluent readings or practice reading on their own. **ANY DAY**

## ASSESS

☐ **Check Fluency** WCPM Do a one-minute timed reading, paying special attention to this week's skill—phrasing. Provide feedback for each student. DAY 5 487a

# Customize Your Plan *by Strand*

## GRAMMAR

**POSSESSIVE PRONOUNS** Possessive pronouns show who or what owns, or possesses, something.

### TEACH

☐ **Grammar Transparency 19** Use Grammar Transparency 19 to teach possessive pronouns. DAY 1 *487e*

**Grammar Transparency 19**

### PRACTICE/APPLY

☐ **Develop the Concept** Review the concept of possessive pronouns and provide guided practice. DAY 2 *487e*

☐ **Apply to Writing** Have students review something they have written and check it for use of possessive pronouns. DAY 3 *487f*

☐ **Test Preparation** Examine common errors in possessive pronouns to prepare for standardized tests. DAY 4 *487f*

☐ **Homework** Grammar and Writing Practice Book pp. 73–75. DAY 2 *487e*, DAY 3 *487f*, DAY 4 *487f*

### ASSESS

☐ **Cumulative Review** Use Grammar and Writing Practice Book p. 76. DAY 5 *487f*

### RETEACH/REVIEW

☐ **Daily Fix-It** Have students find and correct errors in grammar, spelling, and punctuation. **EVERY DAY** *487e–487f*

☐ **The Grammar and Writing Book** Use pp. 158–161 of The Grammar and Writing Book to extend instruction for possessive pronouns. **ANY DAY**

**The Grammar and Writing Book**

## WRITING

### Trait of the Week

**CONVENTIONS** Conventions are special rules for written language. Conventions are signals that writers use to make their meaning clear to readers.

### TEACH

☐ **Writing Transparency 19A** Use the model to introduce and discuss the Trait of the Week. DAY 1 *487g*

☐ **Writing Transparency 19B** Use the transparency to show students how "show, don't tell" can improve their writing. DAY 2 *487g*

**Writing Transparency 19A**  **Writing Transparency 19B**

### PRACTICE/APPLY

☐ **Write Now** Examine the model on Student Edition p. 483. Then have students write their own feature stories. DAY 3 *483, 487h*, DAY 4 *487h*

**Prompt** *Seeker of Knowledge* describes how Jean-François Champollion learned the secrets of Egyptian hieroglyphics. Think about an interesting person, place, or event. Now write a feature story about that person, place, or event.

**Write Now p. 483**

☐ **Writing/Vocabulary Center** Make a picture glossary of the Words to Know. **ANY DAY** *466k*

### ASSESS

☐ **Writing Trait Rubric** Use the rubric to evaluate students' writing. DAY 4 *487h*

### RETEACH/REVIEW

☐ **The Grammar and Writing Book** Use pp. 158–163 of The Grammar and Writing Book to extend instruction for possessive pronouns, show, don't tell, and feature stories. **ANY DAY**

**The Grammar and Writing Book**

## SPELLING

**GENERALIZATION CONSONANTS /J/, /KS/, AND /KW/** The sound /j/ can be spelled *ge* and *dge*: char*ge*, bri*dge*. The sounds /ks/ and /kw/ can be spelled *xc*, *x*, and *qu*: e*xc*ept, e*x*pect, e*qu*al.

### TEACH

❑ **Pretest** Give the pretest for words with consonants /j/, /ks/, and /kw/. Guide students in self-correcting their pretests and correcting any misspellings. DAY 1 *487i*

❑ **Think and Practice** Connect spelling to the phonics generalization for consonants /j/, /ks/, and /kw/. DAY 2 *487i*

### PRACTICE/APPLY

❑ **Connect to Writing** Have students use spelling words to write a poster promoting some fictional event. Then review frequently misspelled words: *except, off, something.* DAY 3 *487j*

❑ **Homework** Word Study and Spelling Practice Book pp. 73-76. **EVERY DAY**

### RETEACH/REVIEW

❑ **Review** Review spelling words to prepare for the posttest. Then provide students with a spelling strategy—problem parts. DAY 4 *487j*

### ASSESS

❑ **Posttest** Use dictation sentences to give the posttest for words with consonants /j/, /ks/, and /kw/. DAY 5 *487j*

## Spelling Words

| | | |
|---|---|---|
| 1. village | 8. question | 15. excellent |
| 2. except* | 9. equal | 16. exercise |
| 3. explain | 10. queen | 17. quart |
| 4. quick | 11. excited | 18. liquid |
| 5. charge | 12. expect | 19. quilt |
| 6. bridge | 13. Texas | 20. expert |
| 7. knowledge* | 14. fudge | |

### Challenge Words

| | | |
|---|---|---|
| 21. expedition | 23. inquire | 25. advantage |
| 22. aquarium | 24. frequent | |

*Word from the selection

## RESEARCH AND INQUIRY

❑ **Internet Inquiry** Have students conduct an Internet inquiry on communication and languages. **EVERY DAY** *487k*

❑ **Thesaurus** Review the features of a thesaurus and discuss how students can use a thesaurus to enhance their writing. DAY 5 *487l*

❑ **Unit Inquiry** Allow time for students to combine the information they have collected to answer their inquiry questions. **ANY DAY** *391*

## SPEAKING AND LISTENING

❑ **Retelling** Have students retell *Seeker of Knowledge* or another favorite story they have read. DAY 5 *487d*

❑ **Listen to a Story** Have students either listen to a recorded reading of a story or invite a professional storyteller to class. Then have students answer questions. DAY 5 *487d*

# Resources for
# Differentiated Instruction

## LEVELED READERS

▶ **Comprehension**
  ◎ **Skill** Graphic Sources
  ◎ **Strategy** Ask Questions
▶ **Lesson Vocabulary**
  ◎ Word Structure

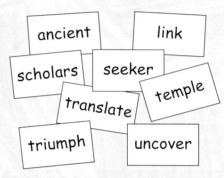

ancient · link · scholars · seeker · translate · temple · triumph · uncover

▶ **Social Studies Standards**
  • **Biography**
  • **Egyptology**

## Leveled Reader Database

### ONLINE
PearsonSuccessNet.com

Use the Online Database of over 600 books to
• Download and print additional copies of this week's leveled readers.
• Listen to the readers being read online.
• Search for more titles focused on this week's skills, topic, and content.

---

## On-Level

Cracking the German Code
by Rena Korb

**On-Level Reader**

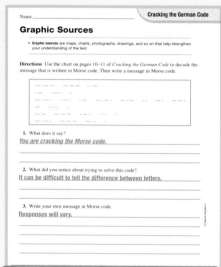

Name _____ Cracking the German Code

**Graphic Sources**

• **Graphic sources** are maps, charts, photographs, drawings, and so on that help strengthen your understanding of the text.

**Directions** Use the chart on pages 10–11 of *Cracking the German Code* to decode the message that is written in Morse code. Then write a message in Morse code.

**1.** What does it say?
You are cracking the Morse code.

**2.** What did you notice about trying to solve this code?
It can be difficult to tell the difference between letters.

**3.** Write your own message in Morse code.
Responses will vary.

◎ **On-Level Practice** TE p. LR32

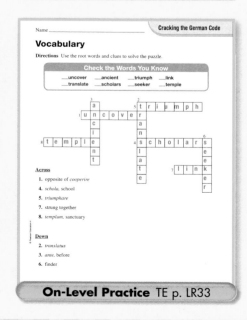

Name _____ Cracking the German Code

**Vocabulary**

**Directions** Use the root words and clues to solve the puzzle.

**Check the Words You Know**
__uncover __ancient __triumph __link
__translate __scholars __seeker __temple

**Across**
1. opposite of *cooperire*
4. *schola*, school
5. *triumphare*
7. strung together
8. *templum*, sanctuary

**Down**
2. *translatus*
3. *ante*, before
6. finder

◎ **On-Level Practice** TE p. LR33

---

## Strategic Intervention

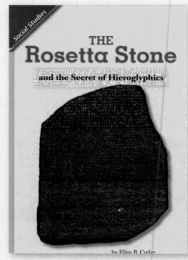

THE Rosetta Stone
and the Secret of Hieroglyphics
by Ellen B. Cutler

**Below-Level Reader**

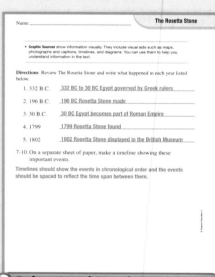

Name _____ The Rosetta Stone

• **Graphic Sources** show information visually. They include visual aids such as maps, photographs and captions, timelines, and diagrams. You can use them to help you understand information in the text.

**Directions** Review The Rosetta Stone and write what happened in each year listed below.
1. 332 B.C. _332 BC to 30 BC Egypt governed by Greek rulers_
2. 196 B.C. _196 BC Rosetta Stone made_
3. 30 B.C. _30 BC Egypt becomes part of Roman Empire_
4. 1799 _1799 Rosetta Stone found_
5. 1802 _1802 Rosetta Stone displayed in the British Museum_

7-10. On a separate sheet of paper, make a timeline showing these important events.

Timelines should show the events in chronological order and the events should be spaced to reflect the time span between them.

◎ **Below-Level Practice** TE p. LR29

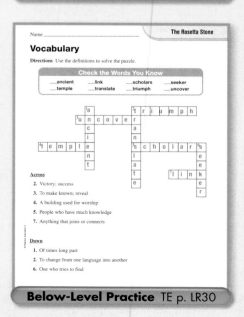

Name _____ The Rosetta Stone

**Vocabulary**

**Directions** Use the definitions to solve the puzzle.

**Check the Words You Know**
__ancient __link __scholars __seeker
__temple __translate __triumph __uncover

**Across**
2. Victory; success
3. To make known; reveal
4. A building used for worship
5. People who have much knowledge
7. Anything that joins or connects

**Down**
1. Of times long past
2. To change from one language into another
6. One who tries to find

◎ **Below-Level Practice** TE p. LR30

# Advanced

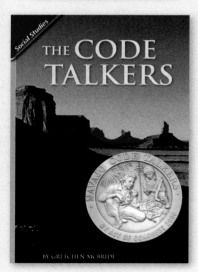

**Advanced Reader**

---

**Advanced Practice** TE p. LR35

---

**Advanced Practice** TE p. LR36

---

# ELL

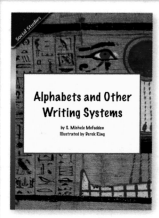

**ELL Reader**

**ELL Poster 19**

**Teacher's Edition Notes**

ELL notes throughout this lesson support instruction and reference additional resources at point of use.

**Teaching Guide
pp. 127–133, 248–249**

• Multilingual summaries of the main selection

• Comprehension lesson

• Vocabulary strategies and word cards

• ELL Reader 4.4.4 lesson

**ELL and Transition Handbook**

**Ten Important Sentences**

• Key ideas from every selection in the Student Edition

• Activities to build sentence power

---

# More Reading

**Readers' Theater Anthology**

• Fluency practice

• Five scripts to build fluency

• Poetry for oral interpretation

**Leveled Trade Books**

• Extended reading tied to the unit concept

• Lessons in the Trade Book Library Teaching Guide

---

**Homework**

• Family Times Newsletter

• ELL Multilingual Selection Summaries

**Take-Home Books**

• Leveled Readers

# Cross-Curricular Centers

## Listening

### Listen to the Selections

**MATERIALS** `SINGLES`
CD player, headphones, AudioText CD, student book

**LISTEN TO LITERATURE** Listen to *Seeker of Knowledge* and "Word Puzzles" as you follow or read along in your book. Look at pictures of the selection's events and ancient Egyptian letters as you listen to *Seeker of Knowledge*.

If there is anything you don't understand, you can listen again to any section.

## Reading/Library

### Read It Again!

**MATERIALS** `SINGLES` `PAIRS` `GROUPS`
Collection of books for self-selected reading, reading logs, student book

Select a book you have already read. Record the title of the book in your reading log. You may want to read with a partner.

Choose from the following:

- **Leveled Readers**
- **ELL Readers**
- **Stories Written by Classmates**
- **Books from the Library**
- *Seeker of Knowledge*

**TEN IMPORTANT SENTENCES** Read the Ten Important Sentences for *Seeker of Knowledge*. Then locate the sentences in the student book.

**BOOK CLUB** Discuss with a group the writing style of *Seeker of Knowledge*. Tell another way the author could have written this biography and if you would have enjoyed that way more.

Classroom Library

## Math

### Create a Math Puzzle

**MATERIALS** `PAIRS`
Writing materials

Create a number pattern puzzle for a partner to solve.

1. **Think of a number pattern. Start by thinking of a rule for your pattern, such as "add 5." The "key" to solving number pattern puzzles is to figure out the rule for the pattern.**
2. **Write a set of four or five numbers that follow your rule, such as "3, 8, 13, 18. . . . "**
3. **Exchange patterns with a partner, figure out the rule for your partner's pattern, and write the next three numbers for it.**

**EARLY FINISHERS** Write a pattern that uses a two-step rule, such as "add 5, subtract 1." List four or five numbers that follow the rule. Exchange patterns with a partner and solve.

*3, 8, 13, 18, 23, 28, 33*

*Rule: Add 5.*

## Scott Foresman Reading Street Centers Survival Kit

Use the *Seeker of Knowledge* materials from the Reading Street Centers Survival Kit to organize this week's centers.

## Writing/Vocabulary

# Make a *Glossary*

**MATERIALS** `GROUPS`
Writing and art materials, slips of paper, stapler, student book

Make a picture glossary of the Words to Know from the selection.

1. Have each member of the group choose a Word to Know from p. 468. Write each word at the top of a slip of paper.

2. Draw a picture under each word to show what it means. Look at the glossary at the back of your student book for ideas.

3. Put your words in alphabetical order, and staple the left side of the slips of paper to make a glossary booklet.

**EARLY FINISHERS** Under each picture, write an example sentence using the word.

## Social Studies

# Create a **Code**

**MATERIALS** `SINGLES` `PAIRS`
Writing materials, student book

Create your own secret code and write a message.

1. Write the alphabet in order and draw a symbol to represent each letter. Look at the symbols on p. 477 of the student book for ideas.

2. On a separate sheet of paper, write a short message using the symbols from your code instead of letters. If a letter appears more than once, be sure to use the same symbol.

**EARLY FINISHERS** Exchange messages with a partner and figure out one another's code. Then exchange alphabet keys to write the messages. Discuss how the key "unlocks" the secrets of a code.

## Technology

# Write a *Report*

**MATERIALS** `SINGLES`
Internet access or encyclopedia on CD, word processing program

Research and write a report.

1. **Choose a topic from the selection to research, such as the Rosetta Stone.**

2. **Search the Internet or an electronic encyclopedia for facts. Follow classroom rules for searching the Internet.**

3. **Use specific keywords to narrow your search, such as the keywords *ancient Egypt* instead of just *Egypt*.**

4. **Write a report telling what you learned. Identify the sources you used. Remember to restate facts in your own words.**

**EARLY FINISHERS** Discuss your research with others. Tell which keywords did or didn't work. Talk about why you should use your own words to restate facts.

**Search Engine**

Rosetta Stone

The Rosetta Stone helped scholars figure out how to read ancient Egyptian hieroglyphics. It was found in 1799 by French soldiers in Egypt. It's made of black basalt.

- Build vocabulary by finding words related to the lesson concept.
- Listen for causes and effects.

## Concept Vocabulary

**converse** to talk together in an informal way

**scholar** a learned person; person having much knowledge

**symbol** something that stands for or represents something else

## Monitor Progress

### Check Vocabulary

| If... | then... review the |
|---|---|
| students are unable to place words on the web, | lesson concept. Place the words on the web and provide additional words for practice, such as *sign language* and *understand*. |

**SUCCESS PREDICTOR**

## DAY 1 Grouping Options

**Reading**
**Whole Group**
Introduce and discuss the Question of the Week. Then use pp. 466l–468b.

**Small Group**
**Differentiated Instruction**
**Read** this week's Leveled Readers. See pp. 466f–466g for the small group lesson plan.

**Whole Group**
Use p. 487a.

**Language Arts**
Use pp. 487e–487k.

# Build Concepts

## FLUENCY

**MODEL PHRASING** As you read "Silent Debate," model how to group words into meaningful phrases to help listeners understand the story. You may want to model using a bad break in middle of a phrase and then rereading the phrase correctly to show the impact of phrasing on meaning.

## LISTENING COMPREHENSION

After reading "Silent Debate," use the following questions to assess listening comprehension.

1. **What causes the misunderstandings between the scholar and the boatman?** (Possible response: Each one thinks the symbols mean something different.) **Cause and Effect**

2. **Why does the scholar have the boatman turn the boat around?** (He figures if a Korean boatman is this smart, the Korean scholars must be brilliant, and he doesn't need to test their wits.) **Cause and Effect**

## BUILD CONCEPT VOCABULARY

Start a web to build concepts and vocabulary related to this week's lesson and the unit theme.

- Draw the Communication Concept Web.

- Read the sentence with the word *converse* again. Ask students to pronounce *converse* and discuss its meaning.

- Place *converse* in an oval attached to *Reasons*. Discuss how these concepts are related to communication. Read the sentences in which *scholar* and *symbol* appear. Have students pronounce the words, place them on the Web, and provide reasons.

- Brainstorm additional words and categories for the Web. Keep the Web on display and add words throughout the week.

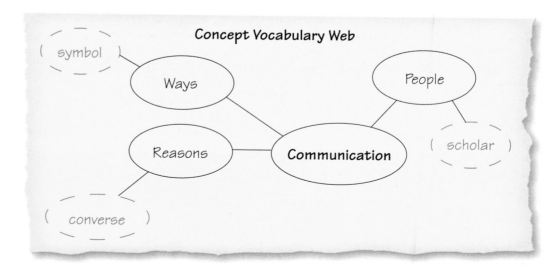

Concept Vocabulary Web

# Silent Debate

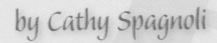

## by Cathy Spagnoli

Once a Chinese scholar heard of Korea's learned people and went to test the wits of the great thinkers there. After a long, weary trip, he found himself in a boat being ferried toward a large and important Korean city.

As he watched the strong boatman row, he had an idea.

"It is always interesting to find out how clever the working people are in a land," thought the scholar. "Let me test this boatman and see if he has a spark of intelligence." Since the Chinese scholar spoke little Korean, and the Korean boatman knew no Chinese, the scholar decided to converse in a kind of sign language.

Carefully he placed his fingers in the shape of a circle, the symbol of the universe. By this, he wanted to inquire if the boatman knew any of heaven's secrets. Now this boatman spared not a thought about the universe, but instead spent all of his time thinking about the rice cakes which he loved to eat. So when he saw the circle sign, he thought the scholar was asking, "Do you like round rice cakes?"

Well, there was no doubt about that: he liked *all* rice cakes. But he was especially fond of the square kind of rice cake. So to answer, he held up his fingers in the shape of a square, as if to say, "Of course I like round rice cakes, but I prefer the square variety."

The scholar gasped in amazement. For he saw the square as the sign of the earth, and imagined the boatman had replied, "Yes, I know all about the heavens. And I know as well about the earth and its secrets."

Wondering if he had misunderstood, the scholar decided to try one more question. He held up three fingers, as if to say, "Do you know even three of the five important Confucian relationships?"

The boatman, still dreaming of his rice cakes, saw the three fingers and thought, "Ah, he's asking me if I eat three rice cakes at a time." Now this was a silly question, for if you adore rice cakes you never stop with just three. So the boatman quickly held up five fingers, meaning, "Only three? Never. I *always* eat five rice cakes at a time."

The scholar almost fell into the water. For he understood the answer to be, "I know not just three; I understand all five of those important relationships."

"Incredible," whispered the scholar. "This boatman knows so much. If a mere boatman has such learning, then the scholars will be impossible to debate with. They must be truly brilliant. What a land of learning."

Then the Chinese scholar had the boatman turn the boat round and he quickly returned to his own home. He told everyone there about the wondrous learning to be found in Korea. And never again did he try to visit that land of intellectual giants, Korea.

SKILLS ⬌ STRATEGIES IN CONTEXT

# Graphic Sources
# Ask Questions

## OBJECTIVES

- Interpret graphic sources.
- Ask questions to enhance understanding of graphic sources.

### Skills Trace
#### Graphic Sources

| | |
|---|---|
| Introduce/Teach | TE: 4.3 338–339; 4.4 466–467; 4.6 738–739 |
| Practice | TE: 345, 351, 473, 477, 745, 753<br>PB: 133, 137, 138, 183, 187, 188, 293, 297, 298 |
| Reteach/Review | TE: 4.3 359b, DI·55; 4.4 447, 487b, DI·55; 4.6 677, 723, 761b, DI·56<br>PB: 176, 266, 286 |
| Test | Selection Test: 53–56, 73–76, 117–120; Benchmark Test: Unit 6 |

## INTRODUCE

Display a book with graphic sources, such as a social studies textbook. Point out a map, diagram, chart, or bar graph. Ask why authors use these graphics in their books. *(Authors use them to explain an idea or show information in a visual way.)*

Have students read the information on p. 466. Explain the following:

- Graphic sources show information in a visual way. Sometimes they can show things you can't learn from text alone.
- Ask yourself questions about graphic sources that accompany the material you read. This will help you to understand them better.

Use Skill Transparency 19 to teach graphic sources and asking questions.

**Comprehension**

**Skill**
Graphic Sources

**Strategy**
Ask Questions

## Graphic Sources

- A graphic source, such as a picture, a map, or a chart, organizes information and makes it easy to see.
- You can use a graphic source to help you understand what you read.

### Strategy: Ask Questions

Active readers ask themselves questions before they read, while they read, and after they read. Look at a graphic source before you read. Ask yourself, "What does this show? What do I think the article will be about?" As you read, ask, "How does this graphic source compare with the text?" After you read, ask, "Do I understand this graphic source now? Do I have any questions about it?"

1. Read "Picture This." Draw a shape like an Egyptian cartouche (see below). Write your name in the cartouche in hieroglyphics.

2. Write a sentence using hieroglyphics. Exchange your sentence with a partner. Write each other's sentences in English.

466

### Strategic Intervention

**Graphic Sources** Have small groups discuss the chart on p. 467 in detail. Ask questions such as: *How would you write the sound /b/ in hieroglyphics? What does the almost oval shape in the fifth column stand for? Why do you think the author included this chart with the article?* Then let students brainstorm questions to ask each other.

**Access Content**

**Beginning/Intermediate** For a Picture It! lesson on graphic sources, see the ELL Teaching Guide, pp. 127–128.

**Advanced** Before reading "Picture This," have students explain the play on words used in the title.

# Picture This.

In ancient Egypt, people used a form of picture writing known as **hieroglyphics.** This word means "sacred writing." Hieroglyphics were carved on the walls of temples and tombs, but they were used on other things as well. For example, a cartouche was an oval figure that contained the name of a ruler in hieroglyphics.

English writing is made up of letters. The letters represent the sounds of the language. Hieroglyphics were just pictures–no letters at all! Sometimes a picture stood for the thing it showed. For example, sometimes ∿∿∿ meant "water." Other times ∿∿∿ stood for the sound /nnn/ from the Egyptian word for *water*. This chart shows hieroglyphics that can be used for English letters.

**1 Strategy** Look at the chart below. Ask, "What does this chart show? What will this article be about?"

**2 Skill** Look below to see how this information relates to the chart.

**Skill** Which hieroglyphic can be used for *d*? Which letters have the same hieroglyphic?

**3**

| D | H | L | O/U/W | S/Z | U/W/O |
|---|---|---|---|---|---|
| (1) Hand (5) | House (9) | Lion (13) | Lasso (18) | Cloth (22) | Chick (26) |
| **E/I/Y** | **H** | **M** | **P** | **SH/CH** | **X** |
| (2) Two Strokes (6) | Flax (10) | Owl (14) | Door (19) | Pool (23) | Basketcloth (27) |
| **F/V** | **I/Y/E** | **M** Bar (15) | **Q** | **T** | **Y/E/I** |
| (3) Viper (7) | Reed (11) | Slope (20) | Loaf (24) | Double Reed (28) | |
| **G** | **J** | **N** Water (16) | **R** | **TH** | **Z/S** |
| (4) Jar (8) | Cobra (12) | **N** Crown (17) | Mouth (21) | Rope (25) | Bolt (29) |

**4 Strategy** What questions do you have about this chart?

467

Available as **Skill Transparency** 19

---

**Practice Book** p. 183

---

## TEACH

**1 STRATEGY** Model asking questions before reading.

**Think Aloud** **MODEL** Before I even start reading, I want to know about the chart. I first ask myself what it shows. It looks like a bunch of pictures with words below them. I then ask myself what I think the article will be about. I'm sure it will have something to do with these pictures and how they represent words.

**2 SKILL** Model using a graphic source to better understand the text.

**Think Aloud** **MODEL** When I look at the chart, I see the water symbol is next to the letter *N* and next to the word *water*. That's what the text says too. The symbol can represent a sound or a word. If I look at the rest of the chart, I can tell that this is also true of other symbols.

## PRACTICE AND ASSESS

**3 SKILL** The picture of the hand can be used for *d*. Many letters have the same hieroglyphic (e.g., O/U/W, C/K, E/I/Y).

**4 STRATEGY** Responses will vary, but questions should relate to specific symbols or the overall purpose of the chart.

**WRITE** Have students complete steps 1 and 2 of the Write to Read activity. You might consider modeling this by writing your own name first, before students work in pairs.

| **Monitor Progress** | |
|---|---|
| **◎ Graphic Sources** | |
| **If…** students are unable to complete **Write to Read** on p. 466, | **then…** use Practice Book p. 183 to provide additional practice. |

## Tech Files ONLINE

Students may want to learn more about Egyptian hieroglyphics. Suggest using a student-friendly search engine and the key-words *Egypt* and *hieroglyphics* to find Web sites with information about this ancient language.

## ELL

**Build Background** Use ELL Poster 19 to build background and vocabulary for the lesson concept of communication.

▲ **ELL Poster** 19

# Build Background

## ACTIVATE PRIOR KNOWLEDGE

**BEGIN A KWL CHART** about ancient Egyptian writing.

- Identify Egypt on a world map. Talk about the people of ancient Egypt.
- Ask students what they know about ancient Egyptian writing. Write their ideas in the first column of a KWL chart.
- Have students tell what they would like to learn about ancient Egyptian writing. Write their questions in the second column of the chart. Add a question of your own.
- Tell students that as they read *Seeker of Knowledge* they will learn many things about ancient Egyptian writing. They can write what they learn in the last column of the chart.

Topic <u>Ancient Egyptian Writing</u>

| K | W | L |
|---|---|---|
| It used lots of pictures.<br><br>Scientists have found it on cave walls. | How many different pictures were there?<br><br>How did ancient Egyptians know what the pictures meant?<br><br>Were there letters too? | |

▲ **Graphic Organizer** 4

**BACKGROUND BUILDING AUDIO** This week's audio explores Egyptian hieroglyphics and how symbols become words. After students listen, invite them to tell what they learned and what surprised them most about Egyptian hieroglyphics.

**Background Building Audio**

# Introduce Vocabulary

## WORD RATING CHART

List lesson vocabulary words in a word rating chart for students to assess their level of understanding of the words.

### Word Rating Chart

| Word | Know | Have Seen | Don't Know |
|------|------|-----------|------------|
| ancient | ✓ | | |
| link | | ✓ | |
| scholars | | | ✓ |
| seeker | | | ✓ |
| temple | | ✓ | |
| translate | ✓ | | |
| triumph | | ✓ | |
| uncover | ✓ | | |

▲ Graphic Organizer 5

Discuss what it means to "know" a word: to recognize it in print, to understand how it is used, and to use it in speech and writing. Explain that before reaching that level of understanding, readers may be familiar with the word because they have seen or heard it. Other words may be completely unknown. Read aloud the lesson vocabulary words. Each student decides which column to check to rate his or her own level of understanding. **Activate Prior Knowledge**

Have students with check marks in the "Know" column tell what the words mean. Students then use their glossary to find or verify the meanings of all the listed words. **Unfamiliar Words**

By the end of the week, students should know all lesson vocabulary words. Have them revise their charts and demonstrate their understanding by using lesson vocabulary words in oral sentences.

Use the Multisyllabic Word Routine on p. DI·1 to help students read multisyllabic words.

## Lesson Vocabulary

### WORDS TO KNOW

**T ancient** of times long past

**T link** anything that joins or connects, as a loop of a chain does

**T scholars** learned people; people having much knowledge

**T seeker** one who tries to find; one who searches

**T temple** building used for the service or worship of God or gods

**T translate** to change from one language into another

**T triumph** victory; success

**T uncover** to make known; reveal; expose

### MORE WORDS TO KNOW

**decipher** to change something in cipher or code to ordinary language; decode

**hieroglyphs** pictures, characters, or symbols standing for words, ideas, or sounds. The ancient Egyptians used hieroglyphs instead of an alphabet like ours.

**spellbound** too interested to move; fascinated

**T** = Tested Word

### Vocabulary

**Directions** Choose the word from the box that best matches each definition. Write the word on the line.

link _____ 1. anything that joins or connects

triumph _____ 2. victory; success

uncover _____ 3. to make known; to reveal

ancient _____ 4. of times long past

scholars _____ 5. people who have much knowledge

**Check the Words You Know**
___ ancient
___ link
___ scholars
___ seeker
___ temple
___ translate
___ triumph
___ uncover

**Directions** Choose the word from the box that best fits in each sentence. Write the word on the line.

Always on a quest, the knight was a 6. seeker _____ of a holy vessel. After many years, he found the object of his search in a sacred 7. temple _____. After his discovery, his next task was to 8. translate _____ the writing inscribed on it. The writing was in an 9. ancient _____ language used thousands of years earlier. The knight's discovery was hailed throughout the kingdom as a 10. triumph _____.

**Write a News Report**
On a separate sheet of paper, write a news report announcing the discovery of a new language. You will need research to help you tell how, when, where, and by whom the discovery was made. Use as many vocabulary words as possible.
News reports should include vocabulary words and details about the language's discovery.

**School + Home** **Home Activity** Your child identified and used vocabulary words from *Seeker of Knowledge*. Have your child create a story about finding a secret treasure. Ask your child to use the vocabulary from the lesson in the story.

▲ **Practice Book** p. 184

# Vocabulary Strategy

## INTRODUCE

Discuss the strategy for word structure by using the steps on p. 468.

## TEACH

- Have students read "The Rosetta Stone," taking note of prefixes, suffixes, base words, and Greek and Latin roots as they read.

- Model using knowledge of *trans-* to determine the meaning of *translate.*

**Think Aloud** **MODEL** The context tells me that Greek writing was used to *translate* the Egyptian writing. I know other words that begin with *trans-*: *transfer, transact, transform.* These words have to do with changing from one to another. The word *translate* probably means "to change from one language to another."

**Words to Know**

ancient

temple

scholars

seeker

translate

link

triumph

uncover

**Remember**

Try the strategy. Then, if you need more help, use your glossary or a dictionary.

# Vocabulary Strategy
## for Greek and Latin Roots

**Word Structure** Many words in English come from the Greek and Latin languages. You may be able to use what you already know about Greek and Latin words to help you figure out the meaning of an unknown word.

**1.** Check the word for any Greek or Latin word parts whose meanings you already know. For example, you might know that the *trans-* in *translate* means "across, through, or beyond."

**2.** Use the meaning of the word part to help you figure out the meaning of the unknown word.

**3.** Check the word to see if it looks like another word you know. For example, the *schol-* in *scholars* may remind you of the word *school.*

**4.** Use the meaning of the similar word to help you figure out the meaning of the unknown word.

As you read "The Rosetta Stone," use what you know about Greek and Latin words to help you figure out the meanings of unknown vocabulary words.

468

---

**DAY 2**   **Grouping Options**

**Reading**
**Whole Group** Discuss the Question of the Day. Then use pp. 468–471.

**Small Group** **Differentiated Instruction**
*Read* *Seeker of Knowledge.* See pp. 466f–466g for the small group lesson plan.

**Whole Group** Use p. 487a.

**Language Arts**
Use pp. 487e–487k.

**Strategic Intervention**

⊙ **Word Structure** Offer a list of words to sort by prefix and number: *unicycle, United States; bicycle, biweekly; tricycle, tricolor flag.*

**ELL**

**Access Content** Use ELL Poster 19 to preteach vocabulary. Choose from the following to meet language proficiency levels.

**Beginning** Use the Multilingual Lesson Vocabulary list that begins on p. 272 of the ELL Teaching Guide, and other resources, to provide translations of the tested words.

**Intermediate** Have students identify English words with Latin roots that may have cognates in other languages.

**Advanced** Teach the lesson on pp. 468–469. Have students discuss words rated as *Don't Know* in their word rating charts (p. 468b).

Resources for home-language words may include parents, bilingual staff members, bilingual dictionaries, or online translation sources.

# The Rosetta Stone

In 1799, a French army officer found a stone slab near the city of Rosetta in Egypt. On the stone was the same announcement in three different languages. At the top was hieroglyphics, a writing that uses pictures or symbols to stand for ideas and sounds. This writing was used in ancient Egypt. In the middle was an Egyptian language called demotic. At the bottom was the Greek language.

For more than 3,000 years, the ancient Egyptians used hieroglyphics on their temple walls and monuments. But over time the language was forgotten.

For hundreds of years, scholars were unable to figure out how to read hieroglyphics.

Jean-François Champollion was a French scholar who wanted to be the first to read hieroglyphics. He studied the language his whole life. He was a true seeker of knowledge. He used the Greek part of the Rosetta Stone to translate the Egyptian part. The Rosetta Stone gave him a link between the known and the unknown.

Champollion's work was a triumph. It allowed other scholars to uncover the history of ancient Egypt.

## Words to Write

Imagine that you have made an important discovery. Write about your discovery. Use words from the Words to Know list.

469

---

## PRACTICE AND ASSESS

- Have students determine the meanings of the remaining words and explain the strategies they used.
- Display the word *hieroglyphics.* Students can use a dictionary to find the word and information about its Greek roots. (*hiero* means "sacred"; *glyphic* means "carving")
- If you began a Word Rating Chart (p. 468b), have students reassess their ratings.
- Have students complete Practice Book p. 185.

**WRITE** Writing should include vocabulary words as well as other words that name and describe an imaginary discovery.

### Monitor Progress

#### Word Structure

| If... students need more practice with the lesson vocabulary, | then... use Tested Vocabulary Cards. |

---

### Vocabulary • Word Structure

- When you see an unknown word, you can use what you know about **Greek and Latin roots** to help you figure out the word's meaning.
- The Latin word *ante* means "before," as in the word *antechamber.* The word *scholarly* comes from the Latin word *scholaris,* meaning "of a school." The word *celebrity* comes from the Latin word *celebrare,* which means "to honor."

**Directions** Read the following passage. Look for Latin roots as you read. Then answer the questions below.

Since ancient times, breaking an enemy's code has been very important. During World War II, Allied code-breakers worked hard to uncover the secrets found in German codes. From 1939 to 1945, these scholars used their knowledge of math and technology to crack the codes of German communications. If code breakers could translate a message, spies might be caught and lives could be saved. Breaking a code was a triumph to celebrate!

Possible answers given.

1. How is the meaning of *ancient* similar to the meaning of the Latin word *ante*?
   *Ante* means before, and ancient times came before today.

2. How is the meaning of *scholars* related to the meaning of the Latin word *scholaris*?
   Scholars study at a school to learn something.

3. *Translate* comes from the Latin word *translatus,* meaning "carried across or transferred." How is the meaning of *translate* similar to the meaning of *translatus*?
   When you translate something, you carry its meaning across into a different language.

4. Which word above comes from the Latin word *triumphus,* meaning "victory"?
   triumph

5. How does knowing the meaning of the Latin word *celebrare* help you understand the meaning of *celebrate*?
   To celebrate something is to honor an event or an achievement.

**School + Home** Home Activity Your child identified and used Latin roots to understand unfamiliar words. Work with your child to identify words with Latin or Greek roots in an article. Use a dictionary to confirm meanings.

▲ **Practice Book** p. 185

# Prereading Strategies

- Use graphic sources to better understand text.
- Ask questions to improve comprehension of graphic sources.

## GENRE STUDY

### Biography

*Seeker of Knowledge* is a biography. Remind students that a biography tells about all or part of the life of a real person. This biography tells about the life of Jean-François Champollion.

## PREVIEW AND PREDICT

Have students preview the title, illustrations, and graphic sources that accompany this selection. Discuss what students think *Seeker of Knowledge* will be about. Encourage them to use lesson vocabulary words as they talk about their predictions.

*Strategy Response Log*

**Graphic Organizer** Have students draw a web with the name *Jean-François Champollion* in the middle. They can add details to this web as they read and will update it for the Strategy Response Log activity on p. 477.

# SEEKER OF KNOWLEDGE

### THE MAN WHO DECIPHERED EGYPTIAN HIEROGLYPHS

text and illustrations
by James Rumford

**Genre** A **biography** is the story of a real person's life as told by another person. As you read this biography, notice how the author uses words and images to tell his story.

470

---

**ELL**

**Access Content** The question on p. 471 uses a less common meaning of *key*. Restate as "Who will discover what Egyptian hieroglyphs mean?"

Consider having students read the selection summary in English or in students' home languages. See the Multilingual Summaries in the ELL Teaching Guide, pp. 131–133.

WHO WILL DISCOVER THE KEY TO EGYPTIAN HIEROGLYPHS?

471

## SET PURPOSE

Direct student attention to the pictures and captions in the margins on pp. 472–473. Ask them what they hope to find out about these pictures as they read *Seeker of Knowledge*.

Remind students that the graphic sources that accompany this text will help them understand what they read.

## STRATEGY RECALL

Students have now used these before-reading strategies:

- preview the selection to be aware of its genre, features, and possible content;
- activate prior knowledge about that content and what to expect of that genre;
- make predictions;
- set a purpose for reading.

Remind students that, as they read, they should monitor their own comprehension. If they realize something does not make sense, they can regain their comprehension by using fix-up strategies they have learned, such as:

- use phonics and word structure to decode new words;
- use context clues or a dictionary to figure out meanings of new words;
- adjust their reading rate—slow down for difficult text, speed up for easy or familiar text, or skim and scan just for specific information;
- reread parts of the text;
- read on (continue to read for clarification);
- use text features such as headings, subheadings, charts, illustrations, and so on as visual aids to comprehension;
- make a graphic organizer or a semantic organizer to aid comprehension;
- use reference sources, such as an encyclopedia, dictionary, thesaurus, or synonym finder;
- use another person, such as a teacher, a peer, a librarian, or an outside expert, as a resource.

After reading, students will use these strategies:

- summarize or retell the text;
- answer questions they or others pose;
- reflect to make new information become part of their prior knowledge.

 **AudioText**

# Guiding Comprehension

**1** 🎯 **Graphic Sources • Inferential**

**What picture do you see after the word *discoveries* on p. 472, paragraph 3? What does it mean?**

There is a picture of a bird. The "key" in the margin explains that this bird is part of the word *discover* in ancient Egyptian writing.

---

### Monitor Progress

🎯 **Graphic Sources**

| If... students are unable to explain what the picture after the word *discoveries* means, | then... use the skill and strategy instruction on p. 473. |
|---|---|

---

**2** **Cause and Effect • Inferential**

**Why did Jean-François study books about Egypt?**

Possible response: He wanted to learn as much as he could so he could figure out the key to Egyptian hieroglyphs.

**3** **Compare and Contrast • Critical**

*Text to Self* **Think about what you have read so far about Jean-François Champollion. In what ways is he like you? In what ways is he different?**

Responses will vary, but students should compare and contrast some aspects of Jean-François's personality and characteristics with their own.

There is a jumping, free-spirited kid goat in the Egyptian word "imagine."

There is a sharp-eyed ibis bird in the word "discover."

There is a long-necked, far-seeing giraffe in "predict."

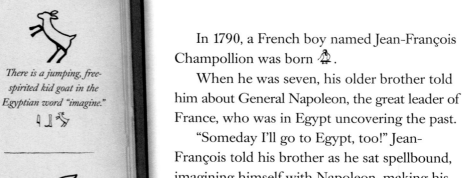

In 1790, a French boy named Jean-François Champollion was born 🐦.

When he was seven, his older brother told him about General Napoleon, the great leader of France, who was in Egypt uncovering the past.

"Someday I'll go to Egypt, too!" Jean-François told his brother as he sat spellbound, imagining himself with Napoleon, making his own discoveries 🐦.

When Jean-François was eleven, he went to school in the city of Grenoble. There, his brother took him to meet 👥 a famous scientist who had been in Egypt with Napoleon.

The scientist's house was filled with Egyptian treasures. Each one captured the boy's imagination.

472

**ELL**

**Access Content** Have students look at the surrounding text to understand the sentence "Then I will one day" (p. 473, paragraph 3). Ask: *What will Jean-François do one day?* Refer them to paragraph 1, in which Jean-François asks: "Can anyone read their writing?" The scientist replies that no one ever has, to which Jean-François answers: "Then I will one day (read their writing)."

"Can anyone read their writing?" asked Jean-François.

"No. No one," the scientist replied.

"Then I will one day," said Jean-François, and he left the house full of enthusiasm, sure that he would be the first to discover the key to Egyptian hieroglyphs.

Back home, his brother helped him get **2** down all the books they had on Egypt. On moonlit nights, Jean-François stayed up reading long after he should have been asleep.

His brother nicknamed him "the Egyptian" and bought him notebooks. Jean-François filled them with hieroglyphs. There were prowling lions, angry monkeys, trumpeting elephants, and sharp-eyed ibis birds with their long, curved bills. He could not read the Egyptian words, but he dreamed that one day he would, as he sailed up  the Nile. **3**

*Jean-François had a favorite animal. It was the lion because there was one in his name:* JEAN-FRANÇOIS CHAMPOL**LION.**

*There are strongly woven sandals firmly planted on the ground in "never give up."*

473

## SKILLS ⟷ STRATEGIES IN CONTEXT

# Graphic Sources

## TEACH

- Remind students that graphic sources, such as charts, graphs, drawings, maps, and diagrams, are included to help readers better understand the text.

- Model using the graphic sources on p. 472.

**Think Aloud** **MODEL** I see a little picture next to the word *discoveries*. It looks like a bird. I think the picture must have something to do with the word *discoveries*, but I'm not sure how it's related. I look at the drawings in the margin to see if I can figure out the connection. The second drawing looks just like the picture next to the word *discoveries*. Under the drawing, the caption says, "There is a sharp-eyed ibis bird in the word *discover*." It makes sense that a sharp-eyed bird can help discover things. This bird must be a part of the Egyptian symbol that stands for *discoveries*. Now I know why the author put this symbol next to the word.

## PRACTICE AND ASSESS

- For practice, have pairs discuss the other symbols and explanations in the margins of pp. 472–473.

- To assess students' understanding of how graphic sources assist readers, have them explain the purpose of the graphics on this page. *(Possible response: The selection is about ancient hieroglyphs. The drawings within the text and in the margins help readers visualize what of these symbols looked like.)*

# Guiding Comprehension

**4** Draw Conclusions • Critical

**Were the scholars wise to turn Jean-François away when he came to see the Rosetta Stone? Why or why not?**

Possible response: No. Jean-François was young, but he was brilliant and determined. He could have helped the scholars.

**5** Sequence • Literal

**Why did Jean-François leave Paris?**

He returned to Grenoble to teach school.

**6** Main Idea/Details • Inferential

**What is the main idea on these two pages? What details support that idea?**

Main idea: Jean-François is determined to decipher ancient Egyptian writing. Supporting details: He has a fire burning bright in his eyes. He has already learned all the known ancient languages. He is a seeker of knowledge. He will not rest until he has the answer. He dreams of discovery.

| Monitor Progress |
| --- |
| **REVIEW Main Idea** |

| **If...** students have difficulty identifying the main idea and supporting details on these pages, | **then...** use the skill and strategy instruction on p. 475. |
| --- | --- |

When Jean-François finished school at sixteen, his brother took him to Paris to meet  the scholars who were studying a black stone from Rosetta, Egypt. The stone was covered with Egyptian and Greek words and told of a king of Egypt named Ptolemy. By reading the Greek, the scholars hoped to decipher the Egyptian. But the work was difficult—certainly too difficult for a boy—

**4** and the scholars turned Jean-François away.

They did not see the fire burning bright in his eyes. They did not recognize the genius who

474

**ELL**

**Build Background** Explain that a *pharaoh* (p. 475, paragraph 1) was a ruler of ancient Egypt.

had already learned all the known ancient languages. They did not know that he was a seeker of knowledge, one who would not rest until he had found the answer.

Jean-François gathered his notebooks and ⑤ returned to Grenoble. There he taught school. His students often came to hear him talk about Egypt—her pharaohs and gods and the mysterious writing.

Once, even Napoleon came to Grenoble and sat up all night, listening spellbound as Jean-François told the great man of his dreams.

Napoleon promised to send Jean-François to Egypt when he conquered the world. Napoleon dreamed of glory. Jean-François dreamed of discovery 🖐. ⑥

There are two regal, heads-up-high leopards in the word "glory."

Thoth, one of the ancient gods

475

## Napoleon Bonaparte

### Time for SOCIAL STUDIES

Napoleon Bonaparte became the Emperor of France in 1804. Sometimes called "the Little Corporal" because of his small stature, Napoleon was not content to just govern France. He was determined to increase France's territory. By 1807, Napoleon ruled much of continental Europe, but he was never able to conquer England. Many called the French leader a power-hungry conqueror, but Napoleon insisted that he himself brought order out of chaos. In 1815, Napoleon was finally overthrown at the historic Battle of Waterloo in Belgium.

# Main Idea REVIEW

## TEACH

Remind students that a main idea is the most important point about a topic. Supporting details tell more about a main idea.

**Think Aloud** **MODEL** In the first paragraph, Jean-François goes to Paris to learn about the Rosetta Stone. In the next paragraph, the author tells me that he has a "fire burning in his eyes." In the last paragraphs, I read that even Napoleon is spellbound when Jean-François tells about his dreams. All of these details tell how determined Jean-François is to decipher the ancient Egyptian hieroglyphs. That must be the main idea.

## PRACTICE AND ASSESS

- Have students revisit p. 473 and determine the main idea of the last paragraph. (*Jean-François studied Egyptian hieroglyphs.*)
- To assess, use Practice Book p. 186.

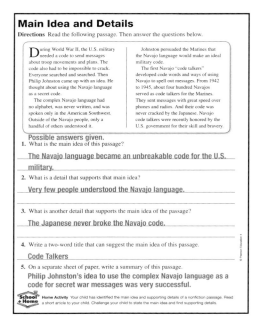

**Main Idea and Details**

**Directions** Read the following passage. Then answer the questions below.

During World War II, the U.S. military needed a code to send messages about troop movements and plans. The code also had to be impossible to crack. Everyone searched and searched. Then Philip Johnston came up with an idea. He thought about using the Navajo language as a secret code.

The complex Navajo language had no alphabet, was never written, and was spoken only in the American Southwest. Outside of the Navajo people, only a handful of others understood it.

Johnston persuaded the Marines that the Navajo language would make an ideal military code.

The first Navajo "code talkers" developed code words and ways of using Navajo to spell out messages. From 1942 to 1945, about four hundred Navajos served as code talkers for the Marines. They sent messages with great speed over phones and radios. And their code was never cracked by the Japanese. Navajo code talkers were recently honored by the U.S. government for their skill and bravery.

Possible answers given.
1. What is the main idea of this passage?
   The Navajo language became an unbreakable code for the U.S. military.
2. What is a detail that supports that main idea?
   Very few people understood the Navajo language.
3. What is another detail that supports the main idea of the passage?
   The Japanese never broke the Navajo code.
4. Write a two-word title that can suggest the main idea of this passage.
   Code Talkers
5. On a separate sheet of paper, write a summary of this passage.
   Philip Johnston's idea to use the complex Navajo language as a code for secret war messages was very successful.

**School Home** **Home Activity** Your child has identified the main idea and supporting details of a nonfiction passage. Read a short article to your child. Challenge your child to state the main idea and find supporting details.

▲ **Practice Book** p. 186

# Guiding Comprehension

**7** Cause and Effect • Inferential

**Why did Jean-François hide in the woods?**

People were mad at him because he had been a friend of Napoleon's. He was afraid they might hurt him.

**8** Details • Literal

**What did an Englishman finally discover about the hieroglyphs on the Rosetta Stone?**

Some hieroglyphs represented letters.

**9** Graphic Sources • Critical

**How do the drawings in this selection help you better understand the text?**

Possible response: The text tells about hieroglyphs and the work people are doing to try to understand them. The drawings show some actual hieroglyphs so that readers can better visualize and relate to what people are so curious about.

---

### Monitor Progress

#### Graphic Sources

| If... students have difficulty understanding how the drawings support the text, | then... use the skill and strategy instruction on p. 477. |
| --- | --- |

---

**Tech Files ONLINE**

Students can search an online encyclopedia or the Internet to find out more about the Battle of Waterloo. Suggest that they use the keywords *Napoleon* and *Battle of Waterloo* for their search.

---

*There is a roaming, black-as-night jackal in the word "mystery."*

---

*There is an unblinking crocodile lurking in the word "trouble."*

476

But a few months later, Napoleon was defeated at the Battle of Waterloo. France was now defenseless. Her enemies poured in. They surrounded Grenoble and in the early morning bombarded the city. Jean-François ran to save his notebooks from the flames.

**7** The people were angry with Napoleon and anyone who knew him. They pointed fingers at Jean-François and called him a traitor. He fled into the woods, leaving his notebooks behind. There he lived like a hunted dog. It was weeks before it was safe to come out and months before he saw his notebooks again.

---

**Extend Language** In English, names of ships, countries, and oceans are sometimes referred to using a feminine pronoun, as in *Her enemies poured in* (p. 476, paragraph 1). The use of gender-specific pronouns in these cases should not be confused with the grammatical gender used in Spanish or French (such as *"el país"* or *"la batalla"*).

During these troubled times, scholars everywhere were racing to solve the mystery of Egyptian writing. Unbelievable things were said. Ridiculous books were written. No one had the answer. Then an Englishman discovered that a few of the hieroglyphs on the Rosetta Stone were letters, and he **8** deciphered King Ptolemy's name. Everyone said that the Englishman would be the first to unlock the door to Egypt's past—everyone except Jean-François 👣.

When Jean-François was thirty, he gathered up his notebooks and left Grenoble. He made his way back to Paris—to his brother.

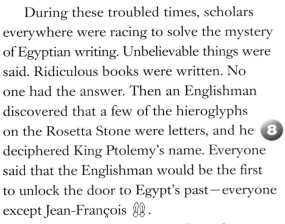

The letter **P** in Ptolemy's name

The letter **T** in Ptolemy's name

To Jean-François, this was the letter **A**.

**9**

The letter **W**

477

## Develop Vocabulary

### PRACTICE LESSON VOCABULARY

Students can answer the following questions orally.

1. **If something is *ancient*, is it very old or new?** *(Very old)*

2. **Do *scholars* have great wealth or great knowledge?** *(Knowledge)*

3. **Is a *seeker* a person who is looking or a person who is eating?** *(A person who is looking)*

4. **If you *uncover* a secret, do you find it out or hide it?** *(Find it out)*

### BUILD CONCEPT VOCABULARY

Review previous concept words with students. Ask if students have come across any words today in their reading or elsewhere that they would like to add to the Communication Concept Web, such as *notebooks*.

**SKILLS ↔ STRATEGIES IN CONTEXT**

# Graphic Sources Ask Questions

## TEACH

- Remind students that authors use graphic sources to support or organize information in text. When readers encounter graphic sources, they need to ask themselves questions such as: *How does this relate to the text? What information is it giving?*

- Model asking questions about the graphic sources on pp. 476–477.

**Think Aloud** **MODEL** In the first paragraph, there is a picture next to the word *ran*. I should ask: *Why is this picture included? What does it mean?* In the margin, there are pictures with short explanations. I should ask: *What do these pictures show? What do the explanations tell me?*

## PRACTICE AND ASSESS

Have students ask and answer questions about specific graphics in this selection. (Example: *What do the sandals on p. 477, paragraph 1, show? Why are they included? The sandals are part of the hieroglyph for "never give up" [see p. 473]. Jean-François refused to give up.*)

*Strategy Response Log*

**Update Graphic Organizer** Have students update their webs on Jean-François Champollion. (See p. 470.) Have them review what they have read about Jean-François so far and record or revise details in their webs.

*If you want to teach this selection in two sessions, stop here.*

# Guiding Comprehension

*If you are teaching the selection in two days, discuss graphic sources used in the selection so far and review the vocabulary.*

**10** 🔊 **Vocabulary • Word Structure**

**The Latin root *script* means "write." Have students use it to determine the meaning of the word *inscriptions* on p. 478.**

Possible response: Inscriptions are writings written or carved into a surface.

### Monitor Progress

#### 🔊 Word Structure

| **If...** students are unable to use the root to determine the meaning of *inscriptions,* | **then...** use the vocabulary strategy instruction on p. 479. |
|---|---|

**11** **Author's Craft • Inferential**

*Question the Author* **Why do you think the author wrote the last three lines on p. 479 instead of just writing, "and there was an echo in the room"?**

Possible response: The author wanted to give a more vivid and dramatic picture of the thrill Jean-François felt.

## DAY 3 Grouping Options

**Reading**
**Whole Group** Discuss the Question of the Day.

**Small Group** Differentiated Instruction
**Read** *Seeker of Knowledge.* See pp. 466f–466g for the small group lesson plan.

**Whole Group** Discuss the Reader Response questions on p. 482. Then use p. 487a.

**Language Arts**
Use pp. 487e–487k.

**10** In Paris, Jean-François studied the Rosetta Stone and other inscriptions. He compared the Greek letters with the Egyptian hieroglyphs and herded together his own alphabet of eagles 𓅂 and lions 𓃭 and dark-eyed chicks 𓅭. But this wonderful list of letters was no help in reading the language. There were too many pictures he did not understand. What to make of a fish with legs 𓆟, a jackal with wings 𓃥, or an ibis god with a long, curved bill 𓅞? There had to be a link between the pictures and the Egyptian letters. But what was it? Jean-François slept little. He ate almost nothing.

Then, on a September morning in 1822, Jean-François found 𓅓 a small package on his doorstep—from a friend in Egypt! In it were the names of pharaohs copied

478

## VOCABULARY STRATEGY
# Word Structure

### TEACH

- Remind students that many English words have Greek and Latin origins.
- Review the meaning of some Greek and Latin word parts such as these: *tri-* means "three," *-ology* means "the study of," and *photo* means "light."
- Model using a Greek or Latin root to determine the meaning of the word *inscriptions* on p. 478.

**Think Aloud** **MODEL** The first sentence says that Jean-François studied the Rosetta Stone and other *inscriptions*. I know that the Latin root *script* means "write." I also know that there was writing carved on the Rosetta Stone. If Jean-François studied this stone and other *inscriptions*, that must mean he studied this stone and other "writings."

### PRACTICE AND ASSESS

Have students explain how they can use the Latin root *cent* ("one hundred") to help determine the meaning of the word *centuries* on p. 479, last line. (Centuries *means "hundreds of years."*)

from a temple wall. Each name was a jigsaw puzzle of letters and pictures. Jean-François studied the names and saw the link! The pictures were sounds, too. Not single letters, but syllables, even whole words!

One of the names drew him. It began with the hieroglyph of an old, silent friend perched on a sacred staff . This was a picture of the god of writing, Thoth, followed by the letters *m* 𓏠 and *s* 𓊃.

"Thothmes!" Jean-François suddenly exclaimed, and the rushing sound of the pharaoh's name, as if carried on wings across the centuries, filled the room. **11**

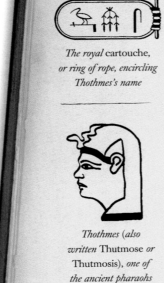

*The royal* cartouche, *or ring of rope, encircling Thothmes's name*

*Thothmes (also written* Thutmose *or* Thutmosis), *one of the ancient pharaohs*

479

## The Rosetta Stone

**Time for SOCIAL STUDIES**

The Rosetta Stone was discovered near the Egyptian city of Rosetta. Made of black basalt and weighing just under a ton, the stone is 3'8" tall, 2'4" across, and 11" thick. It is missing its upper left corner and a small part of its lower right corner. The inscription on the stone is an announcement, or decree, from King Ptolemy V, a 13-year-old Egyptian king. Written on the first anniversary of his coronation, the decree lists the good deeds of the young king. Since shortly after its discovery, the Rosetta Stone has been on exhibit in the British Museum in London since 1802. It was moved only once; in 1917 during World War I, museum caretakers were concerned about heavy bombing and moved the stone to a safe place fifty feet below ground. After two years, it was returned to the museum, where it is still housed today.

# Guiding Comprehension

**12**  **Ask Questions • Critical**

**What questions should you ask yourself about the pictures in the margin on p. 480?**

Possible responses: Do I understand these pictures? Why are they here?

**13 Character • Inferential**

**How do you think Jean-François felt when he was sent on the expedition to Egypt? Explain your answer.**

Possible response: He was very excited. He had dreamed about studying in Egypt since he was a child.

**14 Compare and Contrast • Critical**

*Text to World* **Compare Jean-François Champollion's accomplishment to the accomplishment of another historical figure, such as Christopher Columbus or Benjamin Franklin. Whose accomplishment was more important? Why?**

Responses will vary, but students should compare Jean-François's accomplishment to the accomplishment(s) of some other historical figure. They should make judgments regarding whose work was more important and give valid support for their opinions.

*Strategy Response Log*

**Summarize** Imagine a teacher has asked you to report on the life of Jean-François Champollion. In a few sentences, summarize the highlights of his life.

---

**12**

*There is a blue lotus, its center as bright as the yellow sun, in the word "joy."*

*There are rippling river waves in the word "Nile."*

Jean-François raced down the street to his brother's office. He burst through the door, exclaiming, "I have the key!"

Then he collapsed. He had not eaten. He had not slept. For five days, he lay near death.

On the fifth day, he awoke. "Pen and paper," he whispered, and he wrote of his discovery to the world.

People all over France celebrated his triumph as Jean-François became the first to translate the ancient writing and open the door to Egypt's past.

480

**ELL**

**Access Content** Guide students in asking themselves which meaning of the word *key* applies to the sentence, "I have the key!" (p. 480, paragraph 1). Explain one meaning of *key* is "a list or table of abbreviations or symbols," and another is "the answer to a puzzle or problem."

A few years later, the people of France sent Jean-François to Egypt on an expedition to uncover  more secrets. He knew Egypt so well in his mind that he felt he was going home. As Jean-François had imagined a thousand times in his dreams, he sailed up the Nile. **13**

Once ashore, he entered the ruins of a temple. A magnificent flock of ibis suddenly rose up from the reeds and took flight.

Below, the ibis saw the seeker of knowledge touch the stone walls.

His fingers dipped into the carved pictures. He pressed his ear to the stone and listened to the ancient voices. **14**

481

## Develop Vocabulary

### PRACTICE LESSON VOCABULARY

Have students complete the following sentences. Possible responses are given.

1. When there is a *link* between two things, there is a (*connection*).
2. A *temple* is a place of (*worship*).
3. When you *translate* something, you (*change it from one language to another language*).
4. A *triumph* is a (*victory*).

### BUILD CONCEPT VOCABULARY

Review previous concept words with students. Ask if students have come across any words today in their reading or elsewhere that they would like to add to the Communication Concept Web, such as *inscriptions* and *key*.

**STRATEGY SELF-CHECK**

# Ask Questions

Remind students that good readers ask themselves questions about the graphic sources they encounter in their reading. Guide them as they brainstorm and then answer questions about the pictures that accompany this selection. Use Practice Book p. 187.

## SELF-CHECK

Students can ask themselves these questions to assess understanding of the selection.

- Was I able to ask myself questions to help me better understand the graphic sources?
- Was I able to use the graphic sources to understand the selection better?

### Monitor Progress

#### Graphic Sources

| **If...** students have difficulty asking questions about graphic sources, | **then...** use the Reteach lesson on p. 487b. |
|---|---|

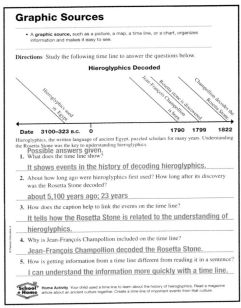

▲ **Practice Book** p. 187

# Reader Response

## Open for Discussion **Personal Response**

**MODEL** I think Jean-François Champollion would talk about how fascinated he was by ancient Egyptian writing. It was a puzzle he had to solve.

## Comprehension Check **Critical Response**

1. Responses should include the idea that the author wants to help us understand and appreciate hieroglyphs. ***Author's Purpose***

2. Yes, it helps. The graphics help show how hieroglyphs tell about ancient Egyptian beliefs. ⊙ ***Graphic Sources***

3. Possible question: How did Jean-François learn so much about hieroglyphs? Answer: He studied hard and worked with lots of smart people. ⊙ ***Ask Questions***

4. Responses will vary, but students should create pictures to represent words and/or sounds in words. ⊙ ***Vocabulary***

**Look Back and Write** For test practice, assign a 10–15 minute time limit. For assessment, see the Scoring Rubric at the right.

## Retell

Have students retell *Seeker of Knowledge.*

### Monitor Progress
#### Check Retelling [4][3][2][1] Rubric

| If... students have difficulty retelling the selection, | then... use the Retelling Cards and the Scoring Rubric for Retelling on p. 483 to assist fluent retelling. |
|---|---|

SUCCESS PREDICTOR

**Check Retelling** Have students use the selection illustrations to guide their retellings. Let students listen to other retellings before attempting their own. For more ideas on assessing students' retellings, see the ELL and Transition Handbook.

---

# Reader Response

**Open for Discussion** Imagine that you are Jean-François Champollion. How would you answer these questions: What made you so determined to decipher hieroglyphs? Why was it so important?

1. The author of this biography placed small pictures among his sentences. Choose one and explain why you think the author included it. **Think Like an Author**

2. On many pages of the selection, part of a notebook appears next to the text. What is the purpose of this graphic element? Does it help you better understand the reading? How so? **Graphic Sources**

3. What questions did you have about Jean-François as you read about him? How were your questions answered? **Ask Questions**

4. Create a hieroglyph for some of the words on the Words to Know list or in the selection. **Vocabulary**

**Look Back and Write** Jean-François was the first to uncover the secrets of Egyptian hieroglyphs, but he had help along the way. Who were the people who helped him? Use details from the biography to support your answer.

**Meet author and illustrator James Rumford on page 777.**

482

---

**Scoring Rubric** **Look Back and Write**

**Top-Score Response** A top-score response will use details from the biography to identify the people who helped Jean-François Champollion.

**Example of a Top-Score Response** Jean-François' brother was a huge help. He found Jean-François books about Egypt. When Jean-François was a teenager, his brother took him to Paris to meet scholars. Jean-François was also greatly helped by his Egyptian friend who sent him the names of the pharaohs that proved to be the key to the puzzle.

**For additional rubrics, see p. WA10.**

# Write Now

## Feature Story

### Prompt

*Seeker of Knowledge* describes how Jean-François Champollion learned the secrets of Egyptian hieroglyphics.

Think about an interesting person, place, or event.

Now write a feature story about that person, place, or event.

**Writing Trait**

**Conventions** are the rules about grammar, spelling, punctuation, and capitalization. Correct use of conventions makes writing clear.

**Student Model**

**Opening clearly introduces topic.**

Mama Gina's is not an ordinary restaurant. It is the place everyone goes for good food and fun. But have you met the woman behind the pasta?

**Conventions include correct uses of possessive pronouns and quotations.**

Mama Gina came from Italy twenty years ago with her husband and four children. "I always loved cooking," she told me. "So I decided to make it my business."

Ten years later, Mama Gina's is a family favorite. The twenty tables are covered with white tablecloths. Hanging plants decorate the dining room. There is a vase of fresh flowers on each table.

**Writer uses details to describe the place.**

"I wanted my restaurant to feel like home," she explained. As soon as the food arrives, you're glad you're home.

**Use the model to help you write your own feature story.**

483

---

# Write Now

**Look at the Prompt** Have students identify and discuss key words and phrases in the prompt. *(interesting person, place, or event; feature story)*

## Strategies to Develop Conventions

Have students

- trade stories with a partner to peer-edit.
- use a dictionary to confirm spelling of unfamiliar words.
- read their feature stories aloud. Do possessive pronouns agree with their antecedents?

NO: One of the authors signed their latest bestseller.

YES: One of the authors signed her latest bestseller.

For additional suggestions and rubric, see pp. 487g–487h.

### Hints for Better Writing

- Carefully read the prompt.
- Use a graphic organizer to plan your writing.
- Support your ideas with information and details.
- Use words that help readers understand.
- Proofread and edit your work.

---

## Scoring Rubric | Expository Retelling

| Rubric 4 3 2 1 | 4 | 3 | 2 | 1 |
|---|---|---|---|---|
| **Connections** | Makes connections and generalizes beyond the text | Makes connections to other events, texts, or experiences | Makes a limited connection to another event, text, or experience | Makes no connection to another event, text, or experience |
| **Author's Purpose** | Elaborates on author's purpose | Tells author's purpose with some clarity | Makes some connection to author's purpose | Makes no connection to author's purpose |
| **Topic** | Describes the main topic | Identifies the main topic with some details early in retelling | Identifies the main topic | Retelling has no sense of topic |
| **Important Ideas** | Gives accurate information about events, steps, and ideas using details and key vocabulary | Gives accurate information about events, steps, and ideas with some detail and key vocabulary | Gives limited or inaccurate information about events, steps, and ideas | Gives no information about events, steps, and ideas |
| **Conclusions** | Draws conclusions and makes inferences to generalize beyond the text | Draws conclusions about the text | Is able to draw few conclusions about the text | Is unable to draw conclusions or make inferences about the text |

### Retelling Plan

☑ **Week 1** Assess Strategic Intervention students.

☑ **Week 2** Assess Advanced students.

☑ **Week 3** Assess Strategic Intervention students.

☑ **This week assess On-Level students.**

☐ **Week 5** Assess any students you have not yet checked during this unit.

**Use the Retelling Chart on p. TR17 to record retelling.**

**Selection Test** To assess with *Seeker of Knowledge*, use Selection Tests, pp. 73–76.

**Fresh Reads for Differentiated Test Practice** For weekly leveled practice, use pp. 109–114.

**SUCCESS PREDICTOR**

# Reading Online

- Examine the features of search engines.
- Compare and contrast across texts.

## PREVIEW/USE TEXT FEATURES

Have students preview "Word Puzzles." Ask:

- **What information goes in a search window?** (Keywords related to the topic you want to know more about)

- **What is the next step after you get the results of your search?** (Look at the list of Web sites and click on a link to go to a Web site you want to explore.)

If students have difficulty explaining these steps, use the Technology Tools Box below.

## Link to Social Studies

Help students identify effective keywords to use in their searches. Discuss the possible results that different keywords might produce. Point out the problems of using keywords that are too broad or too specific.

### DAY 4 Grouping Options

**Reading**
**Whole Group** Discuss the Question of the Day.

**Small Group** Differentiated Instruction
Read "Word Puzzles." See pp. 466f–466g for the small group lesson plan.

**Whole Group** Use p. 487a.

**Language Arts**
Use pp. 487e–487k.

## Reading Online
New Literacies: **PearsonSuccessNet.com**

### Search Engines

**Genre**
- A tool called a search engine can help you find Web sites on the Internet.
- You can focus your search by brainstorming a list of important words, or keywords.

**Text Features**
- Every search engine has a window in which you type keywords.
- Clicking on the SEARCH button starts the search.
- Search results are displayed in a list below the search window. Each item is a link to a Web site that contains the keywords.

**Link to Social Studies**
How do hearing-impaired people communicate? Search the Internet for information on ASL, American Sign Language.

# Word Puzzles

To Jean-François Champollion, the Rosetta Stone was a giant word puzzle. If you wanted to know more about word puzzles, you could type "word puzzles" into a search engine window and click the SEARCH button.

For more practice
**Take It to the Net**
PearsonSuccessNet.com

484

## TECHNOLOGY TOOLS

### Search Engines

**Search Window** Type keywords you want to research here. Remember to click on the window before typing. For some search engines, you click on a Go button instead of a Search button to start the search. You can also press the Enter or Return key on your keyboard.

**Results** The results of a search are listed below the Search window. They are sites that include the keywords. Be sure to read the description of each site to see if it will be helpful for your research. Click on highlighted or underlined links to explore helpful Web sites.

 **Back** After you visit a site, you may want to return to the search results page and choose a different Web site to explore. If so, click on the Back button. You may need to click it more than once to return to the search results page.

See the Technology Tools Box on p. 84 for information on using the Forward, Stop, Refresh, and Home buttons.

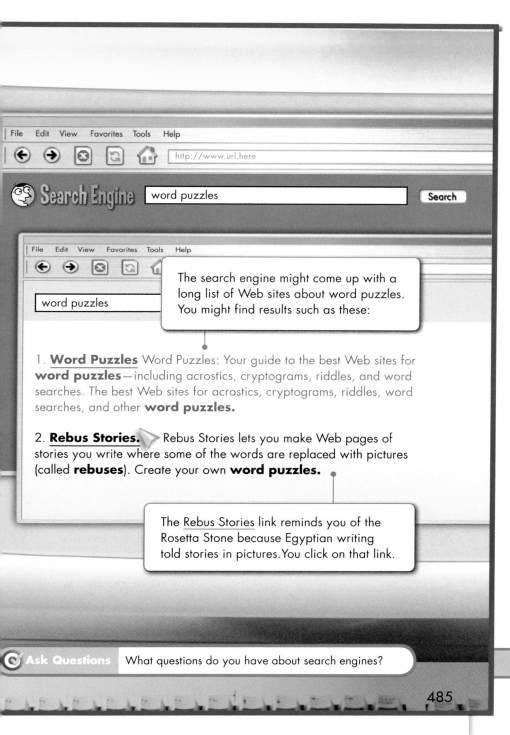

File   Edit   View   Favorites   Tools   Help

http://www.url.here

Search Engine | word puzzles | **Search**

The search engine might come up with a long list of Web sites about word puzzles. You might find results such as these:

1. **Word Puzzles** Word Puzzles: Your guide to the best Web sites for **word puzzles**—including acrostics, cryptograms, riddles, and word searches. The best Web sites for acrostics, cryptograms, riddles, word searches, and other **word puzzles.**

2. **Rebus Stories.** Rebus Stories lets you make Web pages of stories you write where some of the words are replaced with pictures (called **rebuses**). Create your own **word puzzles.**

The Rebus Stories link reminds you of the Rosetta Stone because Egyptian writing told stories in pictures. You click on that link.

**Ask Questions** What questions do you have about search engines?

485

# NEW LITERACIES: Search Engines

Use the sidebar on p. 484 to guide discussion.

- Tell students that search engines may look different, but they all work basically the same way. Like a car engine makes a car go quickly, a search engine does a fast search, scanning sites on the Internet quickly using the key-words typed into the search windows.

- Emphasize the importance of using informa-tion in search engine results to make good choices about which sites to explore further. For example, if a student was interested in riddles, the first site on p. 485 would be more helpful than the second site.

- Discuss what students would do if a search yielded a hundred results.

Audio CD **AudioText**

**Ask Questions**

Possible response: How do I pick the best key-words? How do search engines work? Why do I sometimes get results that don't seem related to my search?

# WEB-IQUETTE

## Search Engines

Tell students that while search engines are a quick and efficient way to find information, there are rules of etiquette they should follow:

- Follow classroom rules for using the Internet, bookmarking Web sites, and printing.

- Do research on a student-friendly search engine approved for use in your classroom or at home. If you are not using a student-friendly engine, avoid inappropriate sites with adult content. Close all "pop-up" advertis-ing windows immediately.

- Read results information carefully and explore only the Web sites that will likely give you helpful, credible information.

- Use your search time wisely. Brainstorm your keywords on paper before you log on. If sharing the computer with others, log off promptly when your time is up.

**ELL**

**Access Content** Preview the selection with students. Provide context by displaying examples of word puzzles such as acrostics, word searches, and rebus stories. To solve the rebus sentences on p. 487, suggest students write the word for each picture in order and then read the sentence.

## Strategies for Navigation

**USE TITLES** Point out that some searches may provide many results, more than a student has time to read. To be efficient, good researchers use Web site titles listed in search results to make decisions about which sites to visit. Like book titles, a Web site title gives clues to the main idea or focus of the site.

### Use the Strategy

1. The next time you use a search engine and get many results, scan Web site titles before you click on any links.

2. Look for titles that match or are closely related to keywords used for your search. Then ask yourself: *What does the title tell me about the Web site? Is this Web site likely to have the helpful, credible information I need?*

3. Click on links to a few sites that you predict will be most helpful.

**PRACTICE** Think about the ways you use Web site titles when searching online at home and at school.

• Think about the topic you want to research and make a list of the kinds of information you want to find. Underline keywords to use for your search and to match to Web site titles.

• The next time you use a search engine, type your keywords in the search window. Compare Web site titles in the results to your keywords and predict which sites will be most helpful. Check a few sites to see if your predictions were accurate. Take notes about successful and unsuccessful searches.

The link takes you to the Rebus Stories Web site. This is what you see:

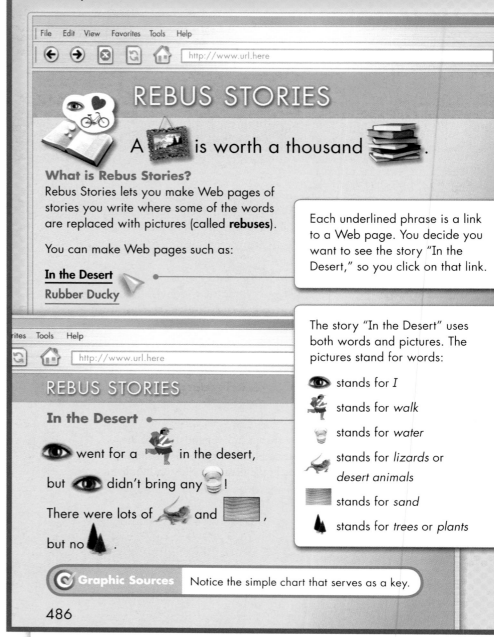

**ELL**

**Guided Practice** If time allows, have students log onto the Internet. Model how to use titles to evaluate search engine results. Help them make connections between the steps they are doing and related vocabulary terms.

REBUS STORIES

**Other Rebuses**
Can you figure out what each of these rebus sentences says?

👁 ❤ **2** ride my 🚲 **2** 🏫 every day.

Did **U C** that 🏀 dunk that 🏀 ?

👵 went **2** her 📖 **2** get her poor 🐕
a 🦴 .

### Reading Across Texts

Both selections tell about how using symbols can be a way to communicate. How are Egyptian hieroglyphics and rebuses alike and different?

**Writing Across Texts** Write a rebus story that tells something about Jean-François Champollion.

487

## CONNECT TEXT-TO-TEXT

### Reading Across Texts
Suggest students use a Venn diagram or T-chart to compare and contrast characteristics of hieroglyphs and rebuses.

**Writing Across Texts** Have students review the characteristics of rebuses they listed before creating their stories. You might have students write the story in words first and then look for words they can easily replace with rebuses.

 **Graphic Sources**

Discuss the purpose of a key. Ask students where else they have seen keys used to explain symbols. *(maps, pictographs)*

## Fluency Assessment Plan

- ☑ **Week 1** Assess Advanced students.
- ☑ **Week 2** Assess Strategic Intervention students.
- ☑ **Week 3** Assess On-Level students.
- ☑ **This week assess Strategic Intervention students.**
- ☐ **Week 5** Assess any students you have not yet checked during this unit.

Set individual goals for students to enable them to reach the year-end goal.
- Current Goal: 110–120 WCPM
- Year-End Goal: 130 WCPM

Bulid students' fluency by encouraging them to repeatedly read aloud passages from familiar and favorite selections, including books that reflect their cultures.

To develop fluent readers, use Fluency Coach.

### DAY 5 Grouping Options

**Reading**
**Whole Group**
Revisit the Question of the Week.

**Small Group**
**Differentiated Instruction**
**Reread** this week's Leveled Readers. See pp. 466f–466g for the small group lesson plan.

**Whole Group**
Use p. 487b–487c.

**Language Arts**
Use pp. 487d–487l.

---

PHRASING
# Fluency

### DAY 1

**Model** Reread "Silent Debate" on p. 466m aloud. Explain that you will help listeners make sense of the story by grouping related words together. Point out how inappropriate phrasing can confuse listeners. Model as you read.

### DAY 2

**Echo Reading** Read aloud p. 474, paragraph 1. Have students notice how you use commas and dashes as phrasing cues and how you pronounce foreign names carefully. Practice as a class by doing three echo readings.

### DAY 3

**Model** Read aloud p. 477, paragraph 1. Have students notice how you pause at logical breaks in the text to give listeners a chance to think about meaning. Practice as a class by doing three echo readings of this paragraph.

### DAY 4

**Partner Reading** Have partners practice reading aloud p. 477, paragraph 1, three times, using logical phrasing. Remind them to self-correct if they make mistakes and to offer each other feedback.

### Monitor Progress | Check Fluency WCPM

As students reread, monitor their progress toward their individual fluency goals. Current Goal: 110–120 words correct per minute. End-of-Year Goal: 130 words correct per minute.

**If...** students cannot read fluently at a rate of 110–120 words correct per minute,
**then...** make sure students practice with text at their independent level. Provide additional fluency practice, pairing nonfluent readers with fluent readers.

**If...** students already read at 130 words correct per minute,
**then...** they do not need to reread three to four times.

**SUCCESS PREDICTOR**

### DAY 5

**Assessment**
**Individual Reading Rate** Use the Fluency Assessment Plan and do a one-minute timed reading of either selection from this week to assess students in Week 4. Pay special attention to this week's skill, phrasing. Provide corrective feedback for each student.

## RETEACH

# Graphic Sources

## TEACH

Review the description of *graphic sources* on p. 466. Students can complete Practice Book p. 188 on their own or as a class. Point out some of the places and geographic features shown on the map in the Practice Book. Remind students to read the caption before and after looking at the map.

## ASSESS

Have students look at the hieroglyphs in the margin on p. 476. Ask them what the hieroglyph for *trouble* looks like. *(It looks like a crocodile about to eat a bird.)* How does the caption help us understand the hieroglyph? *(It points out the crocodile in the hieroglyph.)*

For additional instruction on graphic sources, see DI·55.

## EXTEND SKILLS

# How Art Complements Text

## TEACH

Art enhances and complements text to make reading more enjoyable and understandable. Art can present some information more easily than words.

• Art can call attention to the text that is most important.

• In nonfiction, illustrations often provide additional important information.

Point out the two kinds of art on pp. 476–477, illustrations and hieroglyphs. Ask why both types of art were included. Have students' consider what the art provides that the text does not. *(The illustrations show more of the setting and people's emotions. The hieroglyphs show what ancient Egyptian writing looks like.)*

## ASSESS

Have students write a paragraph telling how the illustration on p. 478 helps readers understand Jean-François's feelings at this time in his life.

---

## OBJECTIVES

◎ Use graphic sources to understand information.

● Analyze how art complements text.

### Skills Trace

◎ **Graphic Sources**

| Introduce/Teach | TE: 4.3 338–339; 4.4 466–467; 4.6 738–739 |
| Practice | TE: 345, 351, 473, 477, 745, 753 PB: 133, 137, 138, 183, 187, 188, 293, 297, 298 |
| Reteach/Review | TE: 4.3 359b, DI•55; 4.4 447, 487b, DI•55; 4.6 677, 723, 761b, DI•56 PB: 176, 266, 286 |
| Test | Selection Test: 53–56, 73–76, 117–120; Benchmark Test: Unit 6 |

## ELL

**Access Content** Reteach the skill by reviewing the Picture It! lesson on graphic sources in the ELL Teaching Guide, pp. 127–128.

---

**Graphic Sources**

• A **graphic source,** such as a picture, a map, a time line, or a chart, organizes information and makes it easy to see.

**Directions** Study the map below, which shows locations in *Seeker of Knowledge.* Answer the questions that follow.

3. At the mouth of what river does Rosetta lie? In which part of Egypt is Rosetta located?

   the Nile River; Rosetta is in the northern part of Egypt.

4. What does the caption tell you about the importance of the places on the map?

   The caption explains that both locations are related to the history of the Rosetta Stone.

Jean-François Champollion of Grenoble, France, decoded the Rosetta Stone, which was found in Rosetta, Egypt.

1. Paris is where scholars studied the Rosetta Stone. In which direction did the Rosetta Stone travel to reach Paris?

   The Rosetta Stone traveled northwest.

2. What separates France from Rosetta, Egypt, where the Rosetta Stone was found?

   the Mediterranean Sea

5. On a separate sheet of paper, write what you learned from the map. What does the map show you?
   Possible answer: I learned how far from home the Rosetta Stone traveled.

**School + Home** **Home Activity** Your child answered questions about locations on a map. Ask your child to draw a map from your home to a familiar location. Be sure to include specific landmarks on the map.

▲ **Practice Book** p. 188

# Vocabulary and Word Study

## VOCABULARY STRATEGY
### Word Structure

**GREEK AND LATIN ROOTS** Remind students that they can use Greek and Latin roots to help figure out the meanings of some words. Explain that the Latin root *scrib* or *scrip* means "to write." Discuss the meaning of *inscriptions*. Display other words with the root *scrib* or *scrip* such as those shown below, and have students explain how each word relates to writing. Provide example phrases or sentences as needed.

| Words with scrib(e) | Words with script |
|---|---|
| describe | description |
| scribble | manuscript |
| scribe | script |
| inscribe | prescription |
| subscribe | subscription |
| transcribe | transcription |

### Compound Hieroglyphs

Write *spellbound* on the board and point out that it is a compound word. Remind students that compound words are two smaller words joined together to make a new word with a new meaning. Have pairs identify other compound words in *Seeker of Knowledge*, such as *nickname, moonlit, notebooks, everywhere,* and so on. Then challenge them to draw symbols to represent a few of the compound words they found. Pairs can exchange drawings and try to decipher one another's compound hieroglyphs.

## BUILD CONCEPT VOCABULARY
### Communication

**LOOKING BACK** Review the question of the week with students: *How can knowing another language create understanding?* Discuss how this week's Concept Web of vocabulary words relates to the theme of communication. Ask students if they have any words or categories to add. Discuss whether words and categories are appropriately related to the concept.

**MOVING FORWARD** Preview the title of the next selection, *Encyclopedia Brown and the Case of the Slippery Salamander.* Ask students which Concept Web words might apply to the new selection based on the title alone. Put a star next to these words on the web.

Display the Concept Web and revisit the vocabulary words as you read the next selection to check predictions.

### Monitor Progress

#### Check Vocabulary

| **If...** students suggest words or categories that are not related to the concept, | **then...** review the words and categories on the Concept Web and discuss how they relate to the lesson concept. |
|---|---|

SUCCESS PREDICTOR

# Speaking and Listening

## SPEAKING

## Retelling

**SET-UP** Have students retell *Seeker of Knowledge* or another story they read this week to share with the class.

**PLANNING** Explain that retelling a story means telling what happened using your own words. Have students review the story they wish to retell and make a list of the sequence of events. Students can refer to this list as they retell the story. Remind students a retelling should include the story's most important events.

**REHEARSAL** Give students an opportunity to rehearse their retellings in front of small groups. Encourage students to offer each other feedback on how they can improve their retellings.

### Delivery Tips

- Tell the story events in order.
- Scan your audience as you talk, making eye contact with different students.
- Use an expressive voice as you retell the story. If appropriate, raise your voice in some parts; whisper in others.
- Use gestures to communicate ideas and grab the audience's attention. For example, you might spread your arms wide to indicate a huge size or crouch to show fear.

## LISTENING

## Listen to a Story

Have students listen to a short story. Invite a professional storyteller to the class or have students listen to a recorded reading of a story using an AudioText CD or a library resource. Before students listen, ask them to think about the following questions. After listening, discuss their answers to the questions.

1. **How does the storyteller's tone of voice make the story meaningful and enjoyable?**
2. **Does the storyteller read at the same speed throughout the story or does the speed vary?**
3. **What else does the storyteller do that makes it easier for a listener to follow and enjoy this story?**

**Support Vocabulary** Use the following to review and extend vocabulary and to explore lesson concepts further:
- ELL Poster 19, Days 3–5 instruction
- Vocabulary Activities and Word Cards in ELL Teaching Guide, pp. 129–130

**Assessment** For information on assessing students' speaking and listening, see the ELL and Transition Handbook.

# Grammar Possessive Pronouns

### OBJECTIVES

- Define and identify possessive pronouns.
- Learn which possessive pronouns are used before nouns and which are used alone.
- Use possessive pronouns correctly in writing.
- Become familiar with possessive pronoun assessment on high-stakes tests.

### Monitor Progress

**Grammar**

| If... students have difficulty identifying possessive pronouns, | then... provide additional instruction and practice in The Grammar and Writing Book pp. 158–161. |
|---|---|

## DAILY FIX-IT

This week use Daily Fix-It Transparency 19.

*Spiral REVIEW*

**Grammar Support** See the Grammar Transition lessons in the ELL and Transition Handbook.

▲ **The Grammar and Writing Book** For more instruction and practice, use pp. 158–161.

## DAILY FIX-IT

1. We were excited to see the mummie's on are museum trip. *(mummies; our)*

2. One mummy was partly unwrapped so that we seen it's face. *(saw its)*

### READING-GRAMMAR CONNECTION

Write this sentence about *Seeker of Knowledge* on the board:

> Jean-François studied hieroglyphs and learned <u>their</u> secrets.

Explain that the word *their* is a **possessive pronoun**. It is used in place of the possessive noun *hieroglyphs'*.

Display Grammar Transparency 19. Read aloud the definitions and sample sentences. Work through the items.

**Possessive Pronouns**

**Possessive pronouns** show who or what owns, or possesses, something. *My, mine, your, her, hers, his, its, our, ours, their,* and *theirs* are possessive pronouns.
- Use *my, your, her, our,* and *their* before nouns.
  I study at <u>my</u> desk. Claire read <u>her</u> book. Experts shared <u>their</u> discoveries.
- Use *mine, yours, hers, ours,* and *theirs* alone.
  The desk is <u>mine</u>. The book was <u>hers</u>. The discoveries were <u>theirs</u>.
- *His* and *its* can be used both before nouns and alone.
  Jean-François did <u>his</u> work. The work was <u>his</u>.
  The Egyptian alphabet revealed <u>its</u> secrets. The secrets were <u>its</u>.
- Do not use an apostrophe with a possessive pronoun.

**Directions** Write the possessive pronoun in each sentence.
1. Ancient Egyptians left many samples of their writing. **their**
2. The Egyptian alphabet was very different from ours. **ours**
3. Some of its letters were pictures of animals. **its**
4. Jean-François concentrated on his work for years. **his**
5. I have written about him in my research paper. **my**

**Directions** Write the possessive pronoun in ( ) that correctly completes each sentence.
6. (Our, Ours) class is studying ancient Egypt. **Our**
7. Maria told us about hieroglyphs in (her, hers) oral report. **her**
8. Julio and Pam made a model of the Rosetta Stone for (their, theirs) presentation. **their**
9. I wrote about Jean-François Champollion for (my, mine). **mine**
10. What will you do for (your, yours)? **yours**

Unit 4 Seeker of Knowledge                Grammar **19**

▲ **Grammar Transparency** 19

## DAILY FIX-IT

3. What a lot of hieroglyphs there were, how did people learn to read them. *(were! How; them?)*

4. I'm glad we read *Seeker of Knowledje* before we gone to the museum. *(Knowledge; went)*

### GUIDED PRACTICE

Review the concept of possessive pronouns.

- **Possessive pronouns** show who or what possesses something.
- The possessive pronouns *my, your, her, our,* and *their* are used before nouns.
- The possessive pronouns *mine, yours, hers, ours,* and *theirs* are used alone.
- Possessive pronouns *his* and *its* are used before nouns and alone.

**HOMEWORK** Grammar and Writing Practice Book p. 73.

**Possessive Pronouns**

**Possessive pronouns** show who or what owns, or possesses, something. *My, mine, your, yours, her, hers, his, its, our, ours, their,* and *theirs* are possessive pronouns.
- Use *my, your, her, our,* and *their* before nouns.
  I study <u>my</u> notes. Marie looked at <u>her</u> drawing. Let us show you <u>our</u> alphabet.
- Use *mine, yours, hers, ours,* and *theirs* alone.
  These notes are <u>mine</u>. The drawing was <u>hers</u>. This alphabet is <u>ours</u>.
- *His* and *its* can be used both before nouns and alone.
  Jean-François followed <u>his</u> plan. The plan was <u>his</u>.
  The tomb guarded <u>its</u> secrets. The secrets were <u>its</u>.
- Do not use an apostrophe with a possessive pronoun.

**Directions** Circle the possessive pronoun in each sentence.
1. Justine and I are preparing (our) report on hieroglyphs.
2. We are learning how Jean-François Champollion made (his) discoveries.
3. You can see examples in (your) book of how the Egyptians wrote.
4. Modern writing is very different from (theirs).
5. Justine will focus on (their) use of pictures.

**Directions** Write the possessive pronoun in ( ) that correctly completes each sentence.
6. The Raymonds went to Egypt, but their trip was different from (our, ours). **ours**
7. She has shown us (hers, her) photographs and videos. **her**
8. You should show the class (your, yours) drawings of Egypt. **your**
9. Ms. Raymond's pictures were better than (my, mine)! **mine**
10. Can you help me make my pictures as good as (yours, your)? **yours**

School-Home CONNECTION **Home Activity** Your child learned about possessive pronouns. Ask your child to use possessive pronouns in sentences about friends or family members and their belongings.

▲ **Grammar and Writing Practice Book** p. 73

# DAY 3 — Apply to Writing

## DAILY FIX-IT

5. If you show me your poster I will show you mines. *(poster,; mine)*

6. Your's is bigger but I like mine better. *(Yours; bigger, but)*

## USE POSSESSIVE PRONOUNS

Explain to students that using too many possessive nouns can make writing awkward. Use possessive pronouns whenever possible to make writing smoother.

*Awkward:* John gave me John's book.

*Smooth:* John gave me his book.

- Have students review something they have written to see if they can improve it by using possessive pronouns in place of possessive nouns.

**HOMEWORK** Grammar and Writing Practice Book p. 74.

### Possessive Pronouns

**Directions** Write a possessive pronoun to replace the underlined words or phrases.

1. Jen and I are studying how the ancient Egyptians built <u>the ancient Egyptians'</u> pyramids. 2. Jen has borrowed a book from <u>Jen's</u> uncle. 3. It says that <u>the Pharaoh Khufu</u> built <u>the Pharaoh Khufu's</u> pyramid out of huge stone blocks. 4. Long ramps were used to put each stone in <u>each stone's</u> place. 5. Jen and I are each planning to build a model pyramid for <u>Jen and my</u> report. 6. Jen is making <u>Jen's</u> pyramid out of clay.

1. ____their____
2. ____her____
3. ____his____
4. ____its____
5. ____our____
6. ____hers____

**Directions** Write a paragraph about something that you have enjoyed making for homework or as a class project. Underline any possessive pronouns you use.

Possible answer:

Last year <u>our</u> class made pictures of the *Mayflower*. I drew <u>my</u> picture in crayon. Carolyn painted <u>hers</u>. Ms. Raymond hung up all <u>our</u> pictures. Later <u>my</u> dad and I used <u>his</u> saw to make a model of the *Mayflower*.

**Home Activity** Your child learned how to use possessive pronouns in writing. Ask your child to write a journal entry titled *My Day*. Have him or her identify possessive pronouns in the entry.

▲ **Grammar and Writing Practice Book** p. 74

# DAY 4 — Test Preparation

## DAILY FIX-IT

7. The jackals in the hieroglyphs looks a little like our wolfs. *(look; wolves)*

8. Jen and me made a copy of one line of hieroglyphs, it took a long time. *(I; hieroglyphs. It)*

## STANDARDIZED TEST PREP

### Test Tip

It is easy to confuse the possessive pronoun *its* with the contraction *it's*, which means *it is*. Keep in mind that possessive pronouns never use apostrophes.

*Possessive Pronoun:* The bird is in <u>its</u> nest.

*Contraction:* <u>It's</u> sitting very still.

Both: <u>It's</u> hatching <u>its</u> eggs.

**HOMEWORK** Grammar and Writing Practice Book p. 75.

### Possessive Pronouns

**Directions** Mark the letter of the possessive pronoun that correctly completes each sentence.

1. ___ class went to the museum and learned about ancient Egypt.
   A We
   B Ours
   C Us
   **D Our**

2. The Egyptians preserved the bodies of ___ dead.
   **A their**
   B its
   C his
   D they

3. When a king died, ___ body was placed in a great tomb.
   A its
   B their
   **C his**
   D him

4. Papyrus was a common plant, and ___ stems were used to make paper.
   A their
   **B its**
   C it
   D they

5. Queen Cleopatra lost ___ war against the Romans.
   A its
   B she
   C hers
   **D her**

6. When we do our Egypt reports, ___ will be about hieroglyphs.
   A I
   **B mine**
   C me
   D my

7. I will draw hieroglyphs on ___ poster.
   A me
   **B my**
   C mine
   D ours

8. Will you do ___ on mummies?
   A ours
   B their
   **C yours**
   D you

**Home Activity** Your child prepared for taking tests on possessive pronouns. Give your child a newspaper or magazine article to read. Ask him or her to highlight the possessive pronouns.

▲ **Grammar and Writing Practice Book** p. 75

# DAY 5 — Cumulative Review

## DAILY FIX-IT

9. Life in ancient egypt must of been very hard. *(Egypt, must have)*

10. Egyptians used flour with sand in it, this damaged there teeth. *(it. This; their)*

## ADDITIONAL PRACTICE

Assign pp. 158–161 in The Grammar and Writing Book.

**EXTRA PRACTICE** Grammar and Writing Practice Book p. 140.

**TEST PREPARATION** Grammar and Writing Practice Book pp. 155–156.

## ASSESSMENT

**CUMULATIVE REVIEW** Grammar and Writing Practice Book p. 76.

### Possessive Pronouns

**Directions** Write the possessive pronoun in ( ) that correctly completes each sentence.

1. The students in (our, ours) class have each chosen a hieroglyph to study.
   ____our____

2. Every hieroglyph has (theirs, its) own meaning.
   ____its____

3. Marie has found a hieroglyph that looks like (her, hers) dog!
   ____her____

4. (My, Mine) is a bird with a long beak.
   ____Mine____

5. I am getting good at drawing (my, mine) hieroglyph.
   ____my____

6. Some students are making models of (theirs, their) hieroglyphs.
   ____their____

**Directions** Write a possessive pronoun to replace the underlined words or phrases.

7. Ancient Egyptians ate bread as part of <u>ancient Egyptians'</u> daily diet.
   ____their____

8. A family sometimes kept a goat and made cheese from a <u>goat's</u> milk.
   ____its____

**Home Activity** Your child reviewed possessive pronouns. With your child, look through the headlines or titles in newspapers or magazines. Challenge your child to find ten examples of possessive pronouns.

▲ **Grammar and Writing Practice Book** p. 76

# Writing Workshop *Feature Story*

## OBJECTIVES

- Identify the characteristics of a feature story.
- Write a feature story with emphasis on showing, not telling.
- Focus on conventions.
- Use a rubric.

**Genre** Feature Story
**Writer's Craft** Show, Don't Tell
**Writing Trait** Conventions

**Conventions** In assessing the writing of language learners, remember that a consistent grammatical error may reflect the writing conventions of the home language. Address the skill by using the appropriate Grammar Transition lessons in the ELL and Transition Handbook.

## Writing Traits

**FOCUS/IDEAS** The writer clearly introduces Ms. Kim. Her purpose is to interest readers of the school paper.

**ORGANIZATION/PARAGRAPHS** The writer tells a step-by-step story about Ms. Kim. There is a brief introduction and conclusion.

**VOICE** The tone is friendly and informative. The use of everyday language is appropriate.

**WORD CHOICE** The writer includes specific information (*Room 3; second-grade*). Details show, rather than tell, the reader about Ms. Kim.

**SENTENCES** Sentences are varied in kind and length. Quotations add interest.

**CONVENTIONS** There is excellent control and accuracy, including correct use of possessive pronouns.

---

## DAY 1 — Model the Trait

### READING-WRITING CONNECTION

- The author of *Seeker of Knowledge* uses writing conventions to clearly communicate the story.
- Conventions help communicate ideas clearly.
- Students will write a **feature story** in which they show, rather than tell, and use writing conventions accurately.

**MODEL CONVENTIONS** Discuss Writing Transparency 19A. Then discuss the model and the writing trait of conventions.

**Think Aloud** This feature story is easy to read because conventions are used correctly. I see where sentences begin and end. The quotations are set off by commas and quotation marks. Other commas also make the story easy to read. They tell me where to pause, such as in the second sentence of the first paragraph.

---

### Feature Story

A **feature story** tells about something that is current and interesting to your readers. The topic may be an event in your town or school or a person that you think your readers would like to know more about. A feature story is factual, but the writing is friendly—and never boring!

**Meet Ms. Kim**

*Opening clearly introduces topic.*
Have you noticed the woman who is always smiling outside Room 3? That's Ms. Kim, our school's new second-grade teacher.

*Writer gives necessary background information.*
Ms. Kim came from Korea to live in this country seventeen years ago.

"I couldn't speak a word of English, and I was afraid of everything," Ms. Kim told me.

*Details help show, not tell, how Ms. Kim felt.*
"On the first day of school, I just stood in a corner and clutched my lunch box tightly."

*Quotations make writing interesting.*
"My teacher's name was Ms. Gleason. She took my hand and showed me my seat. And she was smiling all the time. That's when I knew I had to become a teacher."

So when you see Ms. Kim, say hello to her. And don't forget to smile!

Unit 4 *Seeker of Knowledge*          Writing Model **19A**

▲ **Writing Transparency** 19A

---

## DAY 2 — Improve Writing

### WRITER'S CRAFT
### Show, Don't Tell

Display Writing Transparency 19B. Read the directions and work together to locate examples of "show, don't tell."

**Think Aloud** **SHOW, DON'T TELL** Tomorrow we will be writing a feature story about a person we find interesting. We need to show, rather than tell, details about that person. For example, if I write about my favorite basketball star, I might say: "The top of his head brushes the door frame," rather than "he is very tall."

**GUIDED WRITING** Some students may need more help with showing rather than telling. Write *I was scared* on the board. Under *scared* list other familiar adjectives—*sick, sad, tired, angry*, etc. Discuss with students ways of showing these feelings in their writing.

---

### Show, Don't Tell

When you describe something, **show, don't tell**, your readers what you mean. You might be describing an old house, a new puppy, or stage fright. In each case, showing is more effective than telling.

**Tell**   That house is old.
**Show**  The paint is peeling, and tiles have fallen off the roof.
**Tell**   My puppy is cute.
**Show**  My puppy wriggles and wags her tail when she sees me.
**Tell**   I was scared.
**Show**  My tongue dried up, and my knees began to shake.

**Directions** Rewrite the numbered sentences so that they show rather than tell what the writer means.

The big report was due tomorrow, and I couldn't settle down to work. (1) My little brother was noisy. (2) The room was messy. (3) I was tired. Suddenly, my mom knocked on the door. "Look outside," she said. (4) It was snowing. "There's no school tomorrow," she said. (5) I was happy. Possible answers:

1. My little brother was screaming in his bedroom.
2. The floor was covered with books and papers.
3. My eyelids were drooping, and I just wanted to sleep.
4. The street was covered with snow, and more was drifting down.
5. I smiled for the first time all day.

**Directions** Imagine that you are in a strange place, such as a desert, a jungle, or a pharaoh's tomb. Describe what you see, feel, hear, touch, and smell.
Possible answer: The air is thick and stale. Black shadows fill the corners of the chamber. The beam from my flashlight glints off the pharaoh's treasure. I plunge my hand into the jewels. Crash! The heavy stone door slams shut behind me.

Unit 4 *Seeker of Knowledge*          Writer's Craft **19B**

▲ **Writing Transparency** 19B

# DAY 3 Prewrite and Draft

## READ THE WRITING PROMPT

on page 483 in the Student Edition.

Seeker of Knowledge *describes how Jean-François Champollion learned the secrets of Egyptian hieroglyphics.*

*Think about an interesting person, place, or event.*

*Now write a feature story about that person, place, or event.*

### Writing Test Tips

- Remember that your readers are your classmates. Write with them in mind.
- Use people's actual words when possible.
- Create a smooth style by varying your sentences in kind and length.

**GETTING STARTED** Students can do any of the following:

- Create a Questions and Answers chart for their topic, with questions on the left side and answers on the right.
- Work in small groups to brainstorm possible topics. What kind of feature stories would their friends like to read?
- Make a list of sources, such as an interview, magazine article, or website.

# DAY 4 Draft and Revise

## EDITING/REVISING CHECKLIST

☑ Does my writing help the reader "see" what is happening?

☑ Have I kept my audience in mind?

☑ Are possessive pronouns used correctly?

☑ Are words with the consonant sounds /j/, /ks/, and /kw/ spelled correctly?

See *The Grammar and Writing Book,* pp. 158–163.

### Revising Tips

#### Conventions

- Check to see that all sentences are complete and have correct capitalization and punctuation.
- Make all subjects and verbs agree.
- Check the punctuation of any direct speech.

**PUBLISHING** Students can illustrate their stories and print them in columns, as in a newspaper or magazine. Some students may wish to revise their work later.

**ASSESSMENT** Use the scoring rubric to evaluate students' work.

# DAY 5 Connect to Unit Writing

| Story | |
|---|---|
| Week 1 | Story About a Discovery 415g–415h |
| Week 2 | Travel Brochure 439g–439h |
| Week 3 | Business Letter 465g–465h |
| Week 4 | Feature Story 487g–487h |
| Week 5 | Plot Summary 507g–507h |

## PREVIEW THE UNIT PROMPT

*Write a story about something that happens on a real or an imaginary trip. Try to include suspense or humor and dialogue.*

### APPLY

- A story has a beginning, middle, and end and focuses on one incident or event.
- Stories are most effective when the writer shows readers exactly what people, places, and things look, sound, smell, taste, and feel like.

## Writing Trait Rubric

| | 4 | 3 | 2 | 1 |
|---|---|---|---|---|
| **Conventions** | Excellent control and accuracy; very few or no errors in punctuation, capitalization, and grammar | Good control and accuracy; few errors | Weak control and accuracy; errors that may make writing hard to read | Serious errors that prevent understanding |
| | Feature story extremely clear and easy to read | Feature story clear; a few errors that do not interfere with meaning | Feature story weakened by frequent errors | Feature story confusing because of serious errors |

# Spelling & Phonics  Consonants /j/, /ks/, and /kw/

## OBJECTIVE

● Spell words with consonant sounds /j/, /ks/, and /kw/.

### Generalization

**Connect to Phonics** The sound /j/ can be spelled *ge* and *dge: charge*, *bridge*. The sounds /ks/ and /kw/ can be spelled *xc, x,* and *qu: except, expect, equal.*

### Spelling Words

| | |
|---|---|
| 1. village | 11. excited |
| 2. except* | 12. expect |
| 3. explain | 13. Texas |
| 4. quick | 14. fudge |
| 5. charge | 15. excellent |
| 6. bridge | 16. exercise |
| 7. knowledge* | 17. quart |
| 8. question | 18. liquid |
| 9. equal | 19. quilt |
| 10. queen | 20. expert |

### Challenge Words

| | |
|---|---|
| 21. expedition | 24. frequent |
| 22. aquarium | 25. advantage |
| 23. inquire | |

*Word from the selection

**Spelling/Phonics Support** See the ELL and Transition Handbook for spelling support.

---

## PRETEST

Use the Dictation Sentences from Day 5 to administer the pretest. Read the word, read the sentence, and then read the word again. Guide students in self-correcting their pretests and correcting any misspellings.

### Monitor Progress

#### Spelling

| If... students misspell more than 5 pretest words, | then... use words 1–10 for Strategic Intervention. |
|---|---|
| If... students misspell 1–5 pretest words, | then... use words 1–20 for On-Level practice. |
| If... students correctly spell all pretest words, | then... use words 1–25 for Advanced Learners. |

**HOMEWORK** Spelling Practice Book, p. 73.

### Consonants /j/, /ks/, and /kw/

**Generalization** The sound /j/ can be spelled **ge** and **dge**: **charge**, **bridge**. The sounds /ks/ and /kw/ can be spelled **xc, x,** and **qu**: **except, expect, equal.**

**Word Sort** Sort the words by their spelling of /j/, /kw/, and /ks/.

**ge**
1. village
2. charge

**dge**
3. bridge
4. knowledge
5. fudge

**xc**
6. except
7. excited
8. excellent

**x**
9. explain
10. expect
11. Texas
12. exercise
13. expert

**qu**
14. quick
15. question
16. equal
17. queen
18. quart
19. liquid
20. quilt

**Challenge Words**

**ge**
21. advantage

**x**
22. expedition

**qu**
23. aquarium
24. inquire
25. frequent

**Spelling Words**
1. village
2. except
3. explain
4. quick
5. charge
6. bridge
7. knowledge
8. question
9. equal
10. queen
11. excited
12. expect
13. Texas
14. fudge
15. excellent
16. exercise
17. quart
18. liquid
19. quilt
20. expert

**Challenge Words**
21. expedition
22. aquarium
23. inquire
24. frequent
25. advantage

**Home Activity** Your child is learning to spell words with ge, dge, xc, x, and qu. Have your child circle d in the dge words and c in the xc words.

▲ **Spelling Practice Book** p. 73

---

## TEACH

The sound /j/ can be spelled *ge* and *dge.* The sounds /ks/ and /kw/ can be spelled *xc, x,* and *qu.* Write *village* and *bridge* on the board. Point out the different spellings. Then write *except* and *explain*, again pointing out the different spellings. Finally write *quilt*, and point out how *q* and *u* go together. Guide students in finding these letter patterns in other spelling words.

village   bridge

**FIND THE PATTERN** Ask students to identify the /j/, /ks/, and /kw/ sounds in each of the spelling words. Have them group the words according to the way each of these consonant sounds is spelled.

**HOMEWORK** Spelling Practice Book, p. 74.

### Consonants /j/, /ks/, and /kw/

**Spelling Words**

| village | except | explain | quick | charge |
|---|---|---|---|---|
| bridge | knowledge | question | equal | queen |
| excited | expect | Texas | fudge | excellent |
| exercise | quart | liquid | quilt | expert |

**Missing Words** Write the list word that completes the sentence.

1. The capital of ____ is Austin.    — 1. Texas
2. Some books are full of information, learning, and ____.    — 2. knowledge
3. Stores and places of business are found in the ____.    — 3. village
4. The royal subjects bowed before the ____.    — 4. queen
5. A good rainy day activity is making chocolate ____.    — 5. fudge
6. Two pints are equal to one ____.    — 6. quart
7. A lot of work goes into making a handmade ____.    — 7. quilt
8. Water is a colorless, odorless, tasteless ____.    — 8. liquid
9. A healthy diet and ____ is the path to good health.    — 9. exercise
10. Four quarts are ____ to one gallon.    — 10. equal
11. The ____ was built over the sparkling river.    — 11. bridge
12. We were ____ to go to the amusement park.    — 12. excited

**Categorizing** Write the list word that completes each word group.

13. outstanding, superb, ____    — 13. excellent
14. but, excluding, ____    — 14. except
15. ask, query, ____    — 15. question
16. cost, fee, ____    — 16. charge
17. describe, clarify, ____    — 17. explain
18. fast, speedy, ____    — 18. quick
19. specialist, authority, ____    — 19. expert
20. demand, await, ____    — 20. expect

**Home Activity** Your child wrote words spelled with with ge, dge, xc, x, and qu. Say the dge and g words, and ask your child to spell them.

▲ **Spelling Practice Book** p. 74

# DAY 3 Connect to Writing

## WRITE A POSTER

Ask students to write a poster promoting some fictional event using at least five of the spelling words. The event might be a school play, a carnival, or a charitable event.

### Frequently Misspelled Words

except    off
something

These words may seem easy to spell, but they are frequently misspelled by fourth-graders. Alert students to these frequently misspelled words.

**HOMEWORK** Spelling Practice Book, p. 75.

### Consonants /j/, /ks/, and /kw/

**Proofread an Ad** Ed wants the newspaper ad about his gas station to be perfect. Circle the six misspelled words and write them correctly. Circle the word with a capitalization error and write it correctly.

Drive into Ed's Gas Station!
We have the lowest gas prices in the village.
Try us for a (qwick) oil change or tire repair.
We offer (eggscellent) repair and (exspert) service.
Ask us any question about your car.
We have knowledge about every make and model car.
We (explane) the problem to you before we fix it.
Your car will be fit for a king or (qween).
Open everyday (exsept sunday)

**Spelling Words**
village
except
explain
quick
charge
bridge
knowledge
question
equal
queen

excited
expect
Texas
fudge
excellent
exercise
quart
liquid
quilt
expert

1. quick _____  2. excellent _____  3. expert _____
4. explain _____  5. queen _____  6. except _____
7. Sunday _____

**Proofread Words** Circle the misspelled list word. Write it correctly.

8. Everyone was (ekscited) when the circus came to town.   8. excited _____
9. The class will expand their (knowlei) about other countries.   9. knowledge _____
10. The (brige) was closed for construction.   10. bridge _____
11. There was no admission (chardge) for students.   11. charge _____
12. All team members get (equel) playing time.   12. equal _____

**Frequently Misspelled Words**
except
off
something

School+Home **Home Activity** Your child identified misspelled words with ge, dge, xc, x, and qu. Misspell the list words your child did not use on this page, and have your child correct them.

▲ **Spelling Practice Book** p. 75

# DAY 4 Review

## REVIEW CONSONANT SOUNDS /j/, /ks/, AND /kw/

Have each student write a list of spelling words that includes intentionally misspelled words. Then have students exchange lists with a partner to find and correct mistakes.

### Spelling Strategy
### Problem Parts

Sounds with multiple spellings require special strategies to master. Tell students to underline the letter combinations that are the subject of this lesson, and then to think of words they already know with those same letter combinations. Have them use the known words and the spelling words together in sentences.

**HOMEWORK** Spelling Practice Book, p. 76.

### Consonants /j/, /ks/, and /kw/

**Spelling Words**
| village | except | explain | quick | charge |
| bridge | knowledge | question | equal | queen |
| excited | expect | Texas | fudge | excellent |
| exercise | quart | liquid | quilt | expert |

**Crossword Puzzle** Write list words to fill in the puzzle.

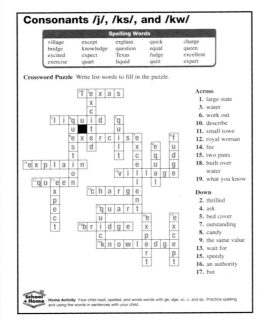

**Across**
1. large state
3. water
6. work out
10. describe
11. small town
12. royal woman
14. fee
15. two pints
18. built over water
19. what you know

**Down**
2. thrilled
4. ask
5. bed cover
7. outstanding
8. candy
9. the same value
13. wait for
15. speedy
16. an authority
17. but

School+Home **Home Activity** Your child read, spelled, and wrote words with ge, dge, xc, x, and qu. Practice spelling and using the words in sentences with your child.

▲ **Spelling Practice Book** p. 76

# DAY 5 Posttest

## DICTATION SENTENCES

1. They lived in a little <u>village</u>.
2. I did all my chores <u>except</u> for one.
3. Can you <u>explain</u> why you did that?
4. Try to be <u>quick</u> in getting here.
5. How much do they <u>charge</u> to get in?
6. We drove over the <u>bridge</u>.
7. The more you learn, the more <u>knowledge</u> you gain.
8. If you don't know something, ask a <u>question</u>.
9. If we both get <u>equal</u> amounts, it will be fair.
10. The <u>queen</u> sat next to the king.
11. I am <u>excited</u> about going to the fair.
12. You should <u>expect</u> me to be there around noon.
13. Her nephew lives in <u>Texas</u>.
14. My favorite candy is <u>fudge</u>.
15. You did an <u>excellent</u> job on the test.
16. Regular <u>exercise</u> will help you stay fit.
17. I will buy a <u>quart</u> of milk.
18. Water is a <u>liquid</u>.
19. I like my <u>quilt</u> on cold nights.
20. My mom is an <u>expert</u> at chess.

## CHALLENGE

21. The explorers went on an <u>expedition</u> to the North Pole.
22. I have some beautiful tropical fish in my <u>aquarium</u>.
23. I would like to <u>inquire</u> about the cost of this toy.
24. I make <u>frequent</u> trips to the park.
25. Being taller may give you an <u>advantage</u>.

- Formulate an inquiry question that is connected to this week's lesson focus.
- Effectively and efficiently find, evaluate, and communicate information related to an inquiry question using electronic sources.

| New Literacies | |
| --- | --- |
| Day 1 | Identify Questions |
| Day 2 | Navigate/Search |
| Day 3 | Analyze |
| Day 4 | Synthesize |
| Day 5 | Communicate |

## NEW LITERACIES

# Internet Inquiry Activity

## EXPLORE LANGUAGES

Use the following 5-day plan to help students conduct this week's Internet inquiry activity on communication and languages. Remind students to follow classroom rules for using the Internet.

### DAY 1

**Identify Questions** Discuss the lesson focus question: *How can knowing another language create understanding?* Identify ideas for language inquiry questions. For example, students might want to learn about an alternative form of communication, such as American Sign Language or Braille, or they may want to learn about particular alphabets or forms of writing. Have students work individually, in pairs, or in groups to write an inquiry question.

### DAY 2

**Navigate/Search** Discuss how to narrow or expand a search if keywords do not yield good results. Have students researching similar topics work together so they can problem-solve as a group. Review the meanings of URL extensions (.com, .org, .net, .edu) and discuss how to use extensions to identify a few helpful, credible sites to explore further.

### DAY 3

**Analyze** Have students visit the Web sites identified on Day 2. Suggest they scan each site for relevant information and use a graphic organizer, such as a multi-column chart, to keep track of the information they gather. If some students struggle with answering their inquiry questions, remind them it is sometimes necessary to revise a question to fit information gathered thus far.

### DAY 4

**Synthesize** Have students synthesize information from Day 3. Remind them *synthesizing* means combining information from a variety of sources in a logical manner. Suggest they look for related pieces of information they can group into categories. Be sure they know how to document each of the sources they choose to use.

### DAY 5

**Communicate** Have students create fact sheets on their topics to share with their classmates. Ask students who explored a specific language to teach the class a few words or phrases in that language.

## RESEARCH/STUDY SKILLS
# Thesaurus

**OBJECTIVES**

- Review terms related to a thesaurus.
- Use a thesaurus to locate synonyms and antonyms.

## TEACH

Write this sentence on the board: *The hieroglyphs were written on a big rock that sat near a noisy river.* Ask students where they could look to find a new, interesting word to replace *big* in the sentence. *(in a thesaurus)* Explain that a **thesaurus** is a special dictionary that lists synonyms, antonyms, and other related words in alphabetical order. Point out that some word processing programs include a thesaurus. Discuss these terms:

- **Synonyms** are words with similar meanings.
- **Antonyms** are words with opposite meanings.
- The **part of speech** tells how the word is used, such as a noun or verb.
- If an **entry word** has **multiple meanings**, synonyms are given for each meaning.

Distribute thesauruses to pairs of students to examine. Then ask pairs to use their thesaurus to answer questions like these:

1. **What are some synonyms for the word *big*?** *(Possible responses: huge, enormous, monstrous)*
2. **What are some antonyms for the word *big*?** *(Possible responses: little, tiny, miniature)*
3. **Which base word would you look for to find synonyms for *written*?** *(write)*
4. **Under what part of speech would you look to find synonyms for *rock* in the sentence on the board?** *(noun)*

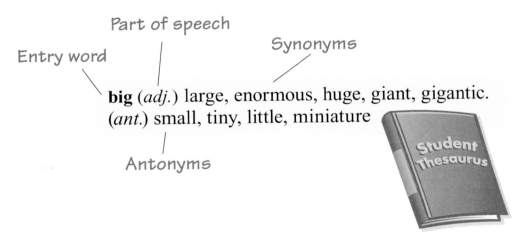

Part of speech

Entry word

Synonyms

**big** *(adj.)* large, enormous, huge, giant, gigantic.
*(ant.)* small, tiny, little, miniature

Antonyms

Student Thesaurus

## ASSESS

As students work with the thesauruses, check whether they can find specific entries and identify synonyms, antonyms, related words, and parts of speech within each entry. Then have them rewrite the sentence on the board, using the thesaurus for ideas.

For more practice or to assess students, use Practice Book pp. 189–190.

---

**Thesaurus**

- A thesaurus is a kind of dictionary that lists **synonyms** (words with the same or similar meanings), **antonyms** (words with opposite meanings), and other related words. Parts of speech are listed to show how a word is used. If a word has multiple meanings, synonyms for each meaning are given.
- You can use a thesaurus to help you find new and interesting words so you don't repeat the same words too often in your writing.

**Directions** If you opened a page in a student thesaurus, you might find these listings. Use them to answer the questions below.

> **soundless** (adj.) still, mute, quiet. See SILENT.
>
> **spark** (n.) **1. flash:** flicker, flare, sparkle, glow, glint, glimmer; **2. stimulus:** goad, spur, motivation, inspiration.
>
> **spark** (v.) **1. flash:** flicker, flare, sparkle, glint; **2. stimulate:** goad, spur, motivate, inspire, ignite, start, activate. (ant) extinguish, douse.
>
> **sparkle** (v.) **1. with light:** glitter, shine, flicker, glint, glimmer, glow, dazzle, shimmer: *The silver ornaments sparkle in the firelight.* **2. with intelligence:** be lively, be vivacious, be the life of the party, shine, dazzle: *Her stories sparkle with clever humor.*
>
> **sparse** (adj.) scanty, meager, slight, scarce, thin, poor, spare, skimpy, few and far between. (ant) thick, abundant, plentiful.

1. How many synonyms are there for *sparse* on this thesaurus page? What part of speech are they?

   nine; They are adjectives.

2. Which numbered list of synonyms would you use for *sparkle* as it is used in this sentence: "The crystal candlesticks sparkle brightly on the mantle." Why?

   list 1; The sentence refers to glowing "with light."

3. Look at this sentence: "A spark of understanding appeared in Jeff's eyes as he read the explanation." Would you look at the entries for the noun or the verb *spark* to replace *spark* with a synonym?

   Spark is used as a noun in the sentence, so you should look at the listing for noun (n).

▲ **Practice Book** p. 189

---

Possible answers given.

4. Rewrite the following sentence using a synonym for the verb *spark.* "The teacher's goal was to *spark* the students' interest in chemistry."

   The teacher's goal was to stimulate the students' interest in chemistry.

5. Give an antonym for *sparse.*

   thick, abundant, plentiful

6. Use an antonym for the verb *spark* in this sentence: "A thick, dull-looking textbook will probably _____ a student's interest in any subject."

   extinguish, douse

7. Give three synonyms for *soundless.* Do they have exactly the same meaning?

   still, mute, quiet; No, there are small differences in their meanings.

8. Where does the entry for *soundless* indicate you might find more synonyms for the word?

   It indicates that you should look under *silent.*

9. How are the two meanings for the verb *spark* like the two meanings for the noun *spark*? How do they differ?

   The meanings of the verbs and nouns are related, and some meanings use the same words; the two meanings of each noun and verb are different from one another.

10. Why would you use a thesaurus when you write? Explain your answer.

   A thesaurus would help me keep from using the same words over and over again, and would make my writing more interesting.

**School + Home** Home Activity Your child learned about using a thesaurus as a resource. Ask your child to use a thesaurus to find synonyms for a word picked at random from a newspaper article.

▲ **Practice Book** p. 190

# Assessment Checkpoints *for the Week*

## Selection Assessment

**Use pp. 73–76 of** Selection Tests **to check:**

 **Selection Understanding**

 **Comprehension Skill** *Graphic Sources*

 **Selection Vocabulary**

| | |
|---|---|
| ancient | temple |
| link | translate |
| scholars | triumph |
| seeker | uncover |

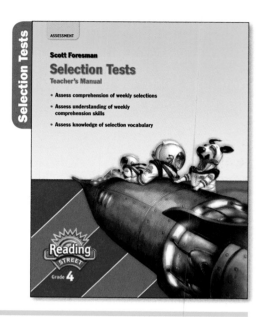

ASSESSMENT

**Scott Foresman**
**Selection Tests**
Teacher's Manual

- Assess comprehension of weekly selections
- Assess understanding of weekly comprehension skills
- Assess knowledge of selection vocabulary

Reading STREET
Grade 4

Selection Tests

## Leveled Assessment

On-Level

Strategic Intervention

Advanced

**Use pp. 109–114 of** Fresh Reads for Differentiated Test Practice **to check:**

 **Comprehension Skill** *Graphic Sources*

 REVIEW **Comprehension Skill** *Main Idea*

 **Fluency** *Words Correct Per Minute*

ASSESSMENT Teacher's Manual

**Scott Foresman**
**Fresh Reads**
**for Differentiated Test Practice**

Leveled passages—strategic intervention, on-level, and advanced—for

- Fluency checks
- Practice and application of weekly comprehension skills
- Answer key for all practice pages

Reading STREET
Grade 4

Fresh Reads for Differentiated Test Practice

## Managing Assessment

**Use** Assessment Handbook **for:**

 **Observation Checklists**

 **Record-Keeping Forms**

 **Portfolio Assessment**

ASSESSMENT

**Scott Foresman**
**Assessment Handbook**

- Suggestions for preparing students for high-stake tests
- Ideas for classroom-based assessment
- Forms in English and Spanish for students to record interests and progress
- Forms in English and Spanish for teachers to record observations of students' reading and writing abilities and progress
- Assessment and Regrouping charts reproduced from *Reading Street Teacher's Editions*

Reading STREET
Grades 3–6

Assessment Handbook

# Unit 4
# Puzzles and Mysteries

## CONCEPT QUESTION
## Is there an explanation for everything?

## EXPAND THE CONCEPT
## How can attention to detail help solve a problem?

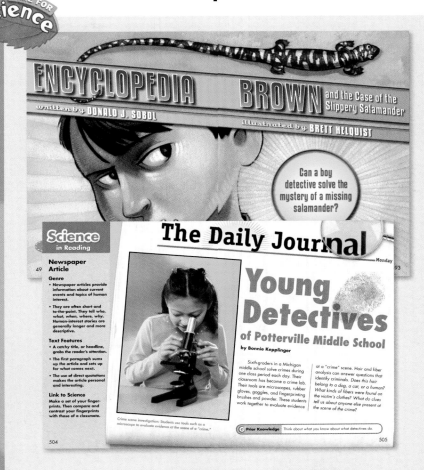

## CONNECT THE CONCEPT

▶ **Build Background**
*case, damage, court*

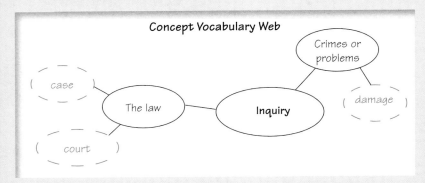

Concept Vocabulary Web

▶ **Science Content**
Salamanders, Experiments

▶ **Writing**
Plot Summary

▶ **Internet Inquiry**
Successful Problem Solving

*Encyclopedia Brown and the Case of the Slippery Salamander*   **488a**

# Preview Your Week

*How can attention to detail help solve a problem?*

ENCYCLOPEDIA BROWN and the Case of the Slippery Salamander

written by DONALD J. SOBOL

illustrated by BRETT HELQUIST

Can a boy detective solve the mystery of a missing salamander?

**Genre** Realistic fiction tells about events that could really happen. As you read, think about how the events in this story are similar to events in real life.

**Student Edition pages 492–500**

Audio CD

**Genre** Realistic Fiction
**Vocabulary Strategy** Context Clues
**Comprehension Skill** Plot
**Comprehension Strategy** Prior Knowledge

## Paired Selection

**Reading Across Texts**
Connect Encyclopedia Brown to Real-life Forensics

**Genre**
Newspaper Article

**Text Features**
Catchy Title or Headline
First Paragraph Summary
Direct Quotations

### Science in Reading

**Newspaper Article**

**Genre**
• Newspaper articles provide information about current events and topics of human interest.
• News stories are usually short and to-the-point. They tell who, what, when, where, and why. Human-interest stories are generally longer and more descriptive.

**Text Features**
• A catchy title, or headline, grabs the reader's attention.
• The first paragraph summarizes the article and prepares readers for what comes next.
• The use of direct quotations makes the article personal and interesting.

**Link to Science**
Make a set of fingerprints. Then compare and contrast your fingerprints with those of a classmate.

Crime scene investigation: Students use tools such as a microscope to evaluate evidence at the scene of a "crime."

504

## The Daily Journal
*Monday*

# Young Detectives
### of Potterville Middle School
by Bonnie Kepplinger

Sixth-graders in a Michigan middle school solve crimes during one class period each day. Their classroom has become a crime lab. Their tools are microscopes, rubber gloves, goggles, and fingerprinting brushes and powder. These students work together to evaluate evidence at a "crime" scene. Hair and fiber analysis can answer questions that identify criminals. Does this hair belong to a dog, a cat, or a human? What kinds of fibers were found on the victim's clothes? What do clues tell us about anyone else present at the scene of the crime?

**Prior Knowledge** Think about what you know about what detectives do.

**Student Edition pages 504–507**

Audio CD

## Leveled Readers

◉ **Skill** Plot
◉ **Strategy** Prior Knowledge
**Lesson Vocabulary**

**Below-Level**

**On-Level**

**Advanced**

**ELL Reader**

· Concept Vocabulary
· Text Support
· Language Enrichment

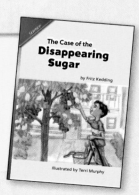

The Case of the
**Disappearing Sugar**
by Fritz Kedding

Illustrated by Terri Murphy

---

TIME FOR **Science**

## Integrate Science Standards

• Amphibian Biology
• Scientific Method

✓ **Read**

***Encyclopedia Brown and the Case of the Slippery Salamander,***
pp. 492–500

**"Young Detectives of Potterville Middle School,"**
pp. 504–507

### Leveled Readers

**Below-Level**     **On-Level**     **Advanced**

• Support Concepts  • Develop Concepts  • Extend Concepts

### ELL Reader

✓ **Build**
**Concept Vocabulary**
Inquiry,
pp. 488l–488m

✓ **Teach**
**Science Concepts**
Salamanders, p. 495
Experiments, p. 505

✓ **Explore**
**Science Center**
Research Reptiles &
Amphibians, p. 488k

*Encyclopedia Brown and the Case of the Slippery Salamander*   **488c**

# Weekly Plan

## READING

*45-90 minutes*

### TARGET SKILLS OF THE WEEK

- **Comprehension Skill**
  Plot
- **Comprehension Strategy**
  Prior Knowledge
- **Vocabulary Strategy**
  Context Clues

## LANGUAGE ARTS

*30-60 minutes*

### Trait of the Week

**Organization/Paragraphs**

---

### DAY 1 — PAGES 488l–490b, 507a, 507e–507k

#### Oral Language

**QUESTION OF THE WEEK** *How can attention to detail help solve a problem?*

Read Aloud: "Something Fishy," 488m
Build Concepts, 488l

#### Comprehension/Vocabulary

Comprehension Skill/Strategy Lesson, 488–489
- Plot **T**
- Prior Knowledge

Build Background, 490a

Introduce Lesson Vocabulary, 490b
*amphibians, crime, exhibit, lizards, reference, reptiles, salamanders, stumped* **T**

**Read** Leveled Readers

**Grouping Options** 488f–488g

#### Fluency

Model Characterization/Dialogue
488l–488m, 507a

---

**Grammar,** 507e
Introduce Contractions and Negatives **T**

**Writing Workshop,** 507g
Introduce Plot Summary

**Spelling,** 507i
Pretest for Prefixes: *un-, dis-,* and *in-*

**Internet Inquiry,** 507k
Identify Questions

---

### DAY 2 — PAGES 490–497, 507a, 507e–507k

#### Oral Language

**QUESTION OF THE DAY** *What talents and strategies does Encyclopedia use to solve cases?*

#### Comprehension/Vocabulary

Vocabulary Strategy Lesson, 490–491
- Context Clues **T**

**Read** *Encyclopedia Brown and the Case of the Slippery Salamander,* 492–497

**Grouping Options** 488f–488g

- Plot **T**
- Context Clues **T**
Develop Vocabulary

#### Fluency

Echo Reading, 507a

---

**Grammar,** 507e
Develop Contractions and Negatives **T**

**Writing Workshop,** 507g
Improve Writing with Eliminate Wordiness

**Spelling,** 507i
Teach the Generalization

**Internet Inquiry,** 507k
Navigate/Search

---

| DAILY WRITING ACTIVITIES | **Day 1** Write to Read, 488 | **Day 2** Words to Write, 491<br>Strategy Response Log, 492, 497 |
|---|---|---|
| DAILY SCIENCE CONNECTIONS | **Day 1** Inquiry Concept Web, 488l | **Day 2** Time for Science: Salamanders, 495<br>Revisit the Inquiry Concept Web, 497 |

---

### DAILY SUCCESS PREDICTORS
for Adequate Yearly Progress

#### Monitor Progress and Corrective Feedback

| Vocabulary | Check Vocabulary, *488l* | |
|---|---|---|

**RESOURCES FOR THE WEEK**

- Practice Book, *pp. 191–200*
- Word Study and Spelling Practice Book, *pp. 77–80*
- Grammar and Writing Practice Book, *pp. 77–80*

- Selection Test, *pp. 77–80*
- Fresh Reads for Differentiated Test Practice, *pp. 115–120*
- The Grammar and Writing Book, *pp. 164–169*

## Grouping Options for Differentiated Instruction
Turn the page for the small group lesson plan.

# DAY 3
**PAGES 498–503, 507a, 507e–507k**

## Oral Language

**QUESTION OF THE DAY**  *How is the Encyclopedia Brown story like and unlike a puzzle?*

## Comprehension/Vocabulary

**Read** *Encyclopedia Brown and the Case of the Slippery Salamander, 498-503*

**Grouping Options**
488f–488g

⊙ Prior Knowledge

**REVIEW** Compare and Contrast **T**

Develop Vocabulary

Reader Response

Selection Test

## Fluency

Model Characterization/Dialogue, 507a

---

**Grammar,** 507f
Apply Contractions and Negatives in Writing **T**

**Writing Workshop,** 502, 507h
Write Now
Prewrite and Draft

**Spelling,** 507j
Connect Spelling to Writing

**Internet Inquiry,** 507k
Analyze Sources

---

**Day 3**  Strategy Response Log, 502
Look Back and Write, 501

**Day 3**  Revisit the Inquiry Concept Web, 499

# DAY 4
**PAGES 504–507a, 507e–507k**

## Oral Language

**QUESTION OF THE DAY**  *Would you like a crime lab class in your school? What skills would you like to learn in such a class?*

## Comprehension/Vocabulary

**Read** *"Young Detectives of Potterville Middle School," 504–507*

**Grouping Options**
488f–488g

Newspaper Article

Reading Across Texts

Content-Area Vocabulary

## Fluency

Partner Reading,  507a

---

**Grammar,** 507f
Practice Contractions and Negatives for Standardized Tests **T**

**Writing Workshop,** 507h
Draft, Revise, and Publish

**Spelling,** 507j
Provide a Strategy

**Internet Inquiry,** 507k
Synthesize Information

---

**Day 4**  Writing Across Texts, 507

**Day 4**  Time for Science: Experiments, 505

# DAY 5
**PAGES 507a–507l**

## Oral Language

**QUESTION OF THE WEEK**  *To wrap up the week, revisit the Day 1 question.*
Build Concept Vocabulary,  507c

## Fluency

**Read** Leveled Readers

**Grouping Options** 488f–488g

Assess Reading Rate,  507a

## Comprehension/Vocabulary

⊙ Reteach Plot, 507b **T**

Idioms, 507b

⊙ Review Context Clues, 507c **T**

---

**Speaking and Viewing,** 507d
Newscast
Analyze Media

**Grammar,** 507f
Cumulative Review

**Writing Workshop,** 507h
Connect to Unit Writing

**Spelling,** 507j
Posttest for Prefixes *un-*, *dis-*, and *in-*

**Internet Inquiry,** 507k
Communicate Results

**Research/Study Skills,** 507l
Card Catalog/Database

---

**Day 5**  Idioms, 507b

**Day 5**  Revisit the Inquiry Concept Web, 507c

---

**KEY** ⊙ = Target Skill  **T** = Tested Skill

Check Retelling, *501*

Check Fluency WCPM, *507a*

Check Vocabulary, *507c*

**SUCCESS PREDICTOR**

# Small Group Plan *for Differentiated Instruction*

### Reading
**Whole Group**
- Oral Language
- Comprehension/Vocabulary

### Group Time
**Differentiated Instruction**

Meet with small groups to provide:
- Skill Support
- Reading Support
- Fluency Practice

### Read

This week's lessons for daily group time can be found behind the Differentiated Instruction (DI) tab on pp. DI·42–DI·51.

### Whole Group
- Fluency

### Language Arts
- Grammar
- Writing
- Spelling
- Research/Inquiry
- Speaking/Listening/Viewing

**Use *My Sidewalks on Reading Street* for Tier III intensive reading intervention.**

---

## DAY 1

| On-Level | Strategic Intervention | Advanced |
|---|---|---|
| **Teacher-Led** *Page DI·43* | **Teacher-Led** *Page DI·42* | **Teacher-Led** *Page DI·43* |
| • Develop Concept Vocabulary<br>• Read *The Case of the Missing Iguana* | • Reinforce Concepts<br>• Read Below-Level Reader *Top Hat, the Detective* | • Read Advanced Reader *Professor Science and the Salamander Stumper*<br>• Independent Extension Activity |

### ⓘ Independent Activities
**While you meet with small groups, have the rest of the class...**

- Visit the Reading/Library Center
- Listen to the Background Building Audio
- Finish Write to Read, p. 488
- Complete Practice Book, pp. 193–194
- Visit Cross-Curricular Centers

---

## DAY 2

| On-Level | Strategic Intervention | Advanced |
|---|---|---|
| **Teacher-Led** *Pages 492–497* | **Teacher-Led** *Page DI·44* | **Teacher-Led** *Page DI·45* |
| • Read *Encyclopedia Brown* | • Practice Lesson Vocabulary<br>• Read Multisyllabic Words<br>• Read or Listen to *Encyclopedia Brown* | • Extend Vocabulary<br>• Read *Encyclopedia Brown* |

### ⓘ Independent Activities
**While you meet with small groups, have the rest of the class...**

- Visit the Reading/Library Center
- Listen to the AudioText for *Encyclopedia Brown*
- Finish Words to Write, p. 488
- Complete Practice Book, pp. 195–196
- Write in their Strategy Response Logs, pp. 492, 497
- Visit Cross-Curricular Centers
- Work on inquiry projects

---

## DAY 3

| On-Level | Strategic Intervention | Advanced |
|---|---|---|
| **Teacher-Led** *Pages 498–500* | **Teacher-Led** *Page DI·46* | **Teacher-Led** *Page DI·47* |
| • Read *Encyclopedia Brown* | • Practice Plot and Prior Knowledge<br>• Read or Listen to *Encyclopedia Brown* | • Extend Plot and Prior Knowledge<br>• Read *Encyclopedia Brown* |

### ⓘ Independent Activities
**While you meet with small groups, have the rest of the class...**

- Visit the Reading/Library Center
- Listen to the AudioText for *Encyclopedia Brown*
- Write in their Strategy Response Logs, p. 502
- Finish Look Back and Write, p. 501
- Complete Practice Book, p. 197
- Visit Cross-Curricular Centers
- Work on inquiry projects

① Begin with whole class skill and strategy instruction.

② Meet with small groups to provide differentiated instruction.

③ Gather the whole class back together for fluency and language arts.

**On-Level**

Teacher-Led
Pages 504–507

- **Read** "Young Detectives of Potterville Middle School"

**Strategic Intervention**

Teacher-Led
Page DI · 48

- Practice Retelling
- **Read** or Listen to "Young Detectives of Potterville Middle School"

**Advanced**

Teacher-Led
Page DI · 49

- **Read** "Young Detectives of Potterville Middle School"
- Genre Study

DAY 4

## ⓘ Independent Activities

**While you meet with small groups, have the rest of the class...**

- Visit the Reading/Library Center
- Listen to the AudioText for "Young Detectives of Potterville Middle School"
- Visit the Writing/Vocabulary Center
- Finish Writing Across Texts, p. 507
- Visit Cross-Curricular Centers
- Work on inquiry projects

---

**On-Level**

Teacher-Led
Page DI · 51

- **Reread** Leveled Reader *The Case of the Missing Iguana*
- Retell *The Case of the Missing Iguana*

**Strategic Intervention**

Teacher-Led
Page DI · 50

- **Reread** Leveled Reader *Top Hat, the Detective*
- Retell *Top Hat, the Detective*

**Advanced**

Teacher-Led
Page DI · 51

- **Reread** Leveled Reader *Professor Science and the Salamander Stumper*
- Share Extension Activity

DAY 5

## ⓘ Independent Activities

**While you meet with small groups, have the rest of the class...**

- Visit the Reading/Library Center
- Complete Practice Book pp. 198–200
- Visit Cross-Curricular Centers
- Work on inquiry projects

---

 ELL

**Grouping** Place English language learners in the groups that correspond to their reading abilities in English.

Use the appropriate Leveled Reader or other text at students' instructional level.

**TiP** Send home the appropriate Multilingual Summary of the main selection on Day 1.

---

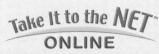

Take It to the NET™
**ONLINE**
PearsonSuccessNet.com

**Sharon Vaughn**
For ideas on professional development, see the article "The Role of Mentoring . . ." by M. Coleman and Scott Foresman author S. Vaughn.

---

### TEACHER TALK

An **idiom** is a phrase that cannot be understood from the ordinary meaning of the words that form it, such as "hold your tongue." Idioms are especially difficult for English language learners.

Be sure to schedule time for students to work on the unit inquiry project "Unlocking Nature's Mysteries." This week students prepare short speeches explaining their mystery of nature. They may also compile a class book.

Looking Ahead

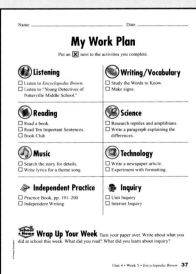

▲ **Group-Time Survival Guide**
p. 37, Weekly Contract

# ☑ Customize Your Plan *by Strand*

## ORAL LANGUAGE

 *Science*

### Concept Development

How can attention to detail help solve a problem?

**CONCEPT VOCABULARY**

case    court    damage

### BUILD

☐ **Question of the Week** Introduce and discuss the question of the week. This week students will read a variety of texts and work on projects related to the concept *inquiry*. Post the question for students to refer to throughout the week. **DAY 1**

☐ **Read Aloud** Read aloud "Something Fishy." Then begin a web to build concepts and concept vocabulary related to this week's lesson and the unit theme, Puzzles and Mysteries. Introduce the concept words *case, court,* and *damage* and have students place them on the web. Display the web for use throughout the week. **DAY 1** *488l–488m*

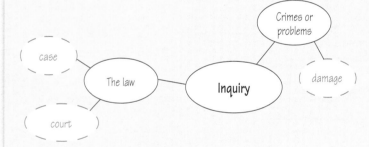

Crimes or problems

case

The law    Inquiry    damage

court

### DEVELOP

☐ **Question of the Day** Use the prompts from the Weekly Plan to engage students in conversations related to this week's reading and the unit theme. **EVERY DAY** *488d–488e*

☐ **Concept Vocabulary Web** Revisit the Inquiry Concept Web and encourage students to add concept words from their reading and life experiences. **DAY 2** *497,* **DAY 3** *499*

### CONNECT

☐ **Looking Back** Revisit the Inquiry Concept Web and discuss how it relates to this week's lesson and the unit theme. **DAY 5** *507c*

### CHECK

☐ **Concept Vocabulary Web** Use the Inquiry Concept Web to check students' understanding of the concept vocabulary words *case, court,* and *damage.* **DAY 1** *488l,* **DAY 5** *507c*

## VOCABULARY

⟳ **STRATEGY CONTEXT CLUES** When you are reading, you may come across an unfamiliar word. Sometimes the author has used a synonym or an antonym as a clue to the word's meaning. Synonyms are words that mean almost the same thing. Antonyms are words with opposite meanings.

**LESSON VOCABULARY**

| | |
|---|---|
| amphibians | reference |
| crime | reptiles |
| exhibit | salamanders |
| lizards | stumped |

### TEACH

☐ **Words to Know** Give students the opportunity to tell what they already know about this week's lesson vocabulary words. Then discuss word meaning. **DAY 1** *490b*

☐ **Vocabulary Strategy Lesson** Use the vocabulary strategy lesson in the Student Edition to introduce and model this week's strategy, *context clues.* **DAY 2** *490–491*

**Vocabulary Strategy Lesson**

### PRACTICE/APPLY

☐ **Leveled Text** Read the lesson vocabulary in the context of leveled text. **DAY 1** *LR37–LR45*

☐ **Words in Context** Read the lesson vocabulary and apply *context clues* in the context of *Encyclopedia Brown and the Case of the Slippery Salamander.* **DAY 2** *492–497,* **DAY 3** *498–501*

**Leveled Readers**

☐ **Writing/Vocabulary Center** Make aquarium signs using Words to Know. **ANY DAY** *488k*

**Main Selection—Fiction**

☐ **Homework** Practice Book pp. 194–195. **DAY 1** *490b,* **DAY 2** *491*

☐ **Word Play** Compile and illustrate a class chart on animal classifications including groupings such as reptiles, amphibians, and mammals. **ANY DAY** *507c*

### ASSESS

☐ **Selection Test** Use the Selection Test to determine students' understanding of the lesson vocabulary words. **DAY 3**

### RETEACH/REVIEW

☐ **Reteach Lesson** If necessary, use this lesson to reteach and review *context clues.* **DAY 5** *507c*

**①** Use assessment data to determine your instructional focus.

**②** Preview this week's instruction by strand.

**③** Choose instructional activities that meet the needs of your classroom.

## COMPREHENSION

**⊙ SKILL PLOT** A story's plot is the important parts of a story. The parts of a plot include the conflict, rising action, climax, and resolution.

**⊙ STRATEGY PRIOR KNOWLEDGE** Prior knowledge is what the reader already knows about a subject. Good readers use their prior knowledge to help them understand what they read.

### TEACH

☐ **Skill/Strategy Lesson** Use the skill/ strategy lesson in the Student Edition to introduce and model *plot* and *prior knowledge*. DAY 1 *488-489*

*Skill/Strategy Lesson*

☐ **Extend Skills** Teach idioms. **ANY DAY** *507b*

### PRACTICE/APPLY

☐ **Leveled Text** Apply *plot* and *prior knowledge* to read leveled text. DAY 1 *LR37-LR45*

*Leveled Readers*

☐ **Skills and Strategies in Context** Read *Encyclopedia Brown and the Case of the Slippery Salamander*, using the Guiding Comprehension questions to apply *plot* and *prior knowledge*. DAY 2 *492-497*, DAY 3 *498-501*

*Main Selection—Fiction*

☐ **Skills and Strategies in Context** Read "The Daily Journal," guiding students as they apply *plot* and *prior knowledge*. Then have students discuss and write across texts. DAY 4 *504-507*

*Paired Selection—Nonfiction*

☐ **Homework** Practice Book pp. 193, 197, 198. DAY 1 *489*, DAY 3 *500*, DAY 5 *507b*

☐ **Fresh Reads for Differentiated Test Practice** Have students practice *plot* with a new passage. DAY 3

### ASSESS

☐ **Selection Test** Determine students' understanding of the selection and their use of *plot*. DAY 3

☐ **Retell** Have students retell *Encyclopedia Brown and the Case of the Slippery Salamander*. DAY 3 *501-502*

### RETEACH/REVIEW

☐ **Reteach Lesson** If necessary, reteach and review *plot*. DAY 5 *507b*

## FLUENCY

**SKILL CHARACTERIZATION/DIALOGUE** Using tone of voice, volume and pitch will convey each character's personality and emotions as well as make the dialogue sound like a real-life conversation.

### TEACH

☐ **Read Aloud** Model fluent reading by rereading "Something Fishy." Focus on this week's fluency skill, characterization/dialogue. DAY 1 *488l-488m, 507a*

### PRACTICE/APPLY

☐ **Echo Reading** Read aloud selected paragraphs from *Encyclopedia Brown*, emphasizing the expression and emotion in the dialogue. Then practice as a class, doing three echo readings. DAY 2 *507a*, DAY 3 *507a*

☐ **Partner Reading** Have partners practice reading in which their voices reflect expression and offer each other feedback. As students reread, monitor their progress toward their individual fluency goals. DAY 4 *507a*

☐ **Listening Center** Have students follow along with the AudioText for this week's selections. **ANY DAY** *488j*

☐ **Reading/Library Center** Have students reread a selection of their choice. **ANY DAY** *488j*

☐ **Fluency Coach** Have students use Fluency Coach to listen to fluent readings or practice reading on their own. **ANY DAY**

### ASSESS

☐ **Check Fluency** WCPM Do a one-minute timed reading, paying special attention to this week's skill— characterization/dialogue. Provide feedback for each student. DAY 5 *507a*

# ☑ Customize Your Plan *by Strand*

## GRAMMAR

**SKILL CONTRACTIONS AND NEGATIVES** A contraction is a shortened form of two words. An apostrophe takes the place of one or more letters. Some contractions are formed from a pronoun and a verb: *she is = she's*. Other contractions combine a verb and the word *not*: *would not = wouldn't*.

### TEACH

❑ **Grammar Transparency 20** Use Grammar Transparency 20 to teach contractions and negatives. **DAY 1** *507e*

**Grammar Transparency 20**

### PRACTICE/APPLY

❑ **Develop the Concept** Review the concept of contractions and negatives and provide guided practice. **DAY 2** *507e*

❑ **Apply to Writing** Have students review something they have written and apply contractions and negatives. **DAY 3** *507f*

❑ **Test Preparation** Examine common errors in contractions and negatives to prepare for standardized tests. **DAY 4** *507f*

❑ **Homework** Grammar and Writing Practice Book pp. 77–79. **DAY 2** *507e*, **DAY 3** *507f*, **DAY 4** *507f*

### ASSESS

❑ **Cumulative Review** Use Grammar and Writing Practice Book p. 80. **DAY 5** *507f*

### RETEACH/REVIEW

❑ **Daily Fix-It** Have students find and correct errors in grammar, spelling, and punctuation. **EVERY DAY** *507e–507f*

❑ **The Grammar and Writing Book** Use pp. 164–167 of The Grammar and Writing Book to extend instruction for contractions and negatives. **ANY DAY**

**The Grammar and Writing Book**

## WRITING

### Trait of the Week

**ORGANIZATION AND PARAGRAPHS** Good writers organize their writing. They write in an order that will help readers understand what they have to say and show connections among their ideas.

### TEACH

❑ **Writing Transparency 20A** Use the model to introduce and discuss the Trait of the Week. **DAY 1** *507g*

❑ **Writing Transparency 20B** Use the transparency to show students how eliminating wordiness can improve their writing. **DAY 2** *507g*

**Writing Transparency 20A**   **Writing Transparency 20B**

### PRACTICE/APPLY

❑ **Write Now** Examine the model on Student Edition p. 503. Then have students write their own plot summaries. **DAY 3** *503, 507h*, **DAY 4** *507h*

> **Prompt** The plot of *Encyclopedia Brown and the Case of the Slippery Salamander* includes a problem, rising action, a climax, and resolution. Think about the plot of a favorite book or movie. Now write a plot summary explaining to a friend what happened in that book or movie.

**Write Now p. 503**

❑ **Writing/Vocabulary Center** Make aquarium signs using Words to Know. **ANY DAY** *488k*

### ASSESS

❑ **Writing Trait Rubric** Use the rubric to evaluate students' writing. **DAY 4** *507h*

### RETEACH/REVIEW

❑ **The Grammar and Writing Book** Use pp. 164–169 of The Grammar and Writing Book to extend instruction for contractions and negatives, eliminating wordiness, and plot summary. **ANY DAY**

**The Grammar and Writing Book**

① Use assessment data to determine your instructional focus.

② Preview this week's instruction by strand.

③ Choose instructional activities that meet the needs of your classroom.

## SPELLING

**GENERALIZATION PREFIXES *UN-*, *DIS-*, AND *IN-*** When adding prefixes *un-*, *dis-*, and *in-*, make no change in the base word: <u>dis</u>count, <u>un</u>certain, <u>in</u>complete. Adding these prefixes does not change the sound of the base word.

### TEACH

❏ **Pretest** Give the pretest for words with prefixes *un-*, *dis-*, and *in-*. Guide students in self-correcting their pretests and correcting any misspellings. **DAY 1** *507i*

❏ **Think and Practice** Connect spelling to the phonics generalization for prefixes *un-*, *dis-*, and *in-*. **DAY 2** *507i*

### PRACTICE/APPLY

❏ **Connect to Writing** Have students use spelling words to write an invitation to some fictional event. Then review frequently misspelled words: *until, into.* **DAY 3** *507j*

❏ **Homework** Phonics and Spelling Practice Book pp. 77–80. **EVERY DAY**

### RETEACH/REVIEW

❏ **Review** Review spelling words to prepare for the posttest. Then provide students with a spelling strategy— problem parts. **DAY 4** *507j*

### ASSESS

❏ **Posttest** Use dictation sentences to give the posttest for words with prefixes *un-*, *dis-*, and *in-*. **DAY 5** *507j*

### Spelling Words

| | | |
|---|---|---|
| 1. distrust | 8. disorder | 15. disrepair |
| 2. uncertain | 9. discount | 16. inability |
| 3. incomplete | 10. indirect | 17. disapprove |
| 4. unlikely* | 11. unopened | 18. unsolved |
| 5. unfair | 12. disrespect | 19. disobey |
| 6. discontinue | 13. unimportant | 20. unsuspecting |
| 7. unaware | 14. unlisted | |

### Challenge Words

| | | |
|---|---|---|
| 21. disintegrate | 23. unconscious | 25. intolerant |
| 22. disillusioned | 24. unappetizing | |

*Word from the selection

## RESEARCH AND INQUIRY

❏ **Internet Inquiry** Have students conduct an Internet inquiry on problem solving. **EVERY DAY** *507k*

❏ **Card Catalog/Database** Review terms associated with a card catalog and library database and discuss how students can use these resources to find information. **DAY 5** *507l*

❏ **Unit Inquiry** Allow time for students to prepare short speeches explaining a mystery of nature and to compile a class book. **ANY DAY** *391*

## SPEAKING AND VIEWING

❏ **Newscast** Have students create and present a newscast with the feature being an investigative report on a problem at school. **DAY 5** *507d*

❏ **Analyze Media** Have students work in small discussion groups to talk about an episode of a TV series or a movie they have watched recently and answer questions. **DAY 5** *507d*

# Resources for
# Differentiated Instruction

## LEVELED READERS

▶ **Comprehension**
- 🎯 **Skill** Plot
- 🎯 **Strategy** Prior Knowledge

▶ **Lesson Vocabulary**
- 🎯 **Context Clues**

amphibians · stumped · crime · exhibit · lizards · reference · reptiles · salamanders

▶ **Science Standards**
- **Amphibian Biology**
- **Scientific Method**

### Leveled Reader Database ONLINE
PearsonSuccessNet.com

Use the Online Database of over 600 books to

- Download and print additional copies of this week's leveled readers.
- Listen to the readers being read online.
- Search for more titles focused on this week's skills, topic, and content.

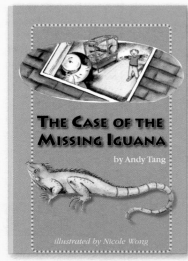

**On-Level Reader**

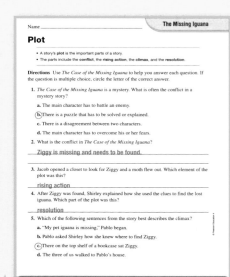

🎯 **On-Level Practice** TE p. LR41

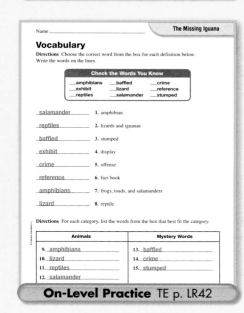

**On-Level Practice** TE p. LR42

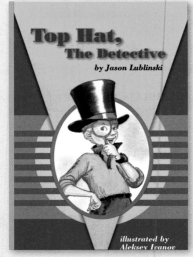

**Below-Level Reader**

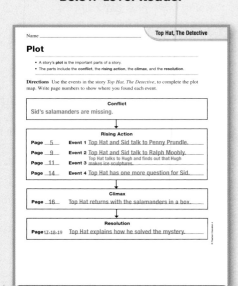

🎯 **Below-Level Practice** TE p. LR38

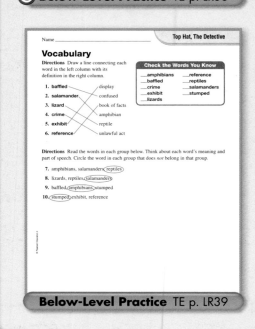

**Below-Level Practice** TE p. LR39

## Advanced

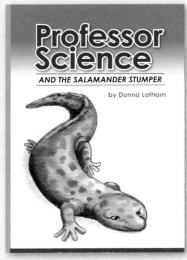

**Advanced Reader**

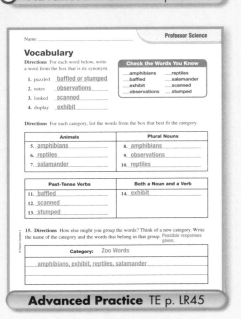

**Advanced Practice** TE p. LR44

**Advanced Practice** TE p. LR45

---

The Case of the
**Disappearing
Sugar**

by Fritz Kedding

Illustrated by Terri Murphy

**ELL Reader**

**ELL Poster 20**

### Teacher's Edition Notes

ELL notes throughout this lesson support instruction and reference additional resources at point of use.

**Teaching Guide
pp. 134–140, 250–251**
- Multilingual summaries of the main selection
- Comprehension lesson
- Vocabulary strategies and word cards
- ELL Reader 4.4.5 lesson

**ELL and Transition Handbook**

**Ten Important Sentences**
- Key ideas from every selection in the Student Edition
- Activities to build sentence power

---

## More Reading

### Readers' Theater Anthology
- Fluency practice
- Five scripts to build fluency
- Poetry for oral interpretation

### Leveled Trade Books

- Extended reading tied to the unit concept
- Lessons in the Trade Book Library Teaching Guide

---

### Homework
- Family Times Newsletter
- ELL Multilingual Selection Summaries

### Take-Home Books
- Leveled Readers

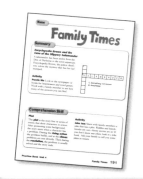

# Cross-Curricular Centers

## Listening

### Listen to the *Selections*

**MATERIALS** `SINGLES`
CD player, headphones, AudioText CD, student book

**LISTEN TO LITERATURE** Listen to *Encyclopedia Brown and the Case of the Slippery Salamander* and "Young Detectives of Potterville Middle School" as you follow or read along in your book. Listen for the story's problem and climax in *Encyclopedia Brown*.

If there is anything you don't understand, you can listen again to any section.

## Reading/ Library

### Read It *Again!*

**MATERIALS** `SINGLES` `PAIRS` `GROUPS`
Collection of books for self-selected reading, reading logs, student book

Select a book you have already read. Record the title of the book in your reading log. You may want to read with a partner.

Choose from the following:

- Leveled Readers
- ELL Readers
- Stories Written by Classmates
- Books from the Library
- *Encyclopedia Brown and the Case of the Slippery Salamander*

**TEN IMPORTANT SENTENCES** Read the Ten Important Sentences for *Encyclopedia Brown and the Case of the Slippery Salamander.* Then locate the sentences in the student book.

**BOOK CLUB** Have each person in a group read another *Encyclopedia Brown* mystery. Take turns telling about the story you read and what you like or don't like about these mysteries.

## Music

### Write a *Theme Song*

**MATERIALS** `PAIRS` `GROUPS`
Student book, writing and art materials, audiotape player

Write a theme song for a TV series starring Encyclopedia Brown.

1. **Look back at the story to find details about Encyclopedia Brown, his family, and how he solves crimes.**
2. **Write lyrics for a theme song about Encyclopedia Brown. It should help viewers understand what the TV series is about and make them want to watch it.**
3. **Sing the song and record it.**

**EARLY FINISHERS** Sketch pictures for the opening credits of the TV series. Use ideas from your song. *Drama*

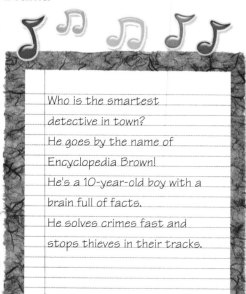

Who is the smartest detective in town?
He goes by the name of Encyclopedia Brown!
He's a 10-year-old boy with a brain full of facts.
He solves crimes fast and stops thieves in their tracks.

## Scott Foresman Reading Street Centers Survival Kit

Use the *Encyclopedia Brown* materials from the Reading Street Centers Survival Kit to organize this week's centers.

## Writing/ Vocabulary

# Make Signs

**MATERIALS**
Art and writing materials, student book

`SINGLES` `PAIRS`

Make aquarium signs using Words to Know.

1. Look at the list of Words to Know on p. 490 in the student book and find story details about the aquarium.
2. Make signs for the aquarium. For example, tell people about an exhibit or things to do while visiting the aquarium.
3. Include Words to Know in your signs. Use clear, simple language. Add pictures or symbols.
4. Display your signs in the classroom.

**EARLY FINISHERS** Imagine you are a tour guide at the aquarium. Create a speech welcoming visitors. Use ideas from your signs. *Drama*

# Welcome to the Den of Darkness Exhibit

Find Fred, the tiger salamander, in the Amphibians section.

Look for the lizards in the Reptiles section.

## Science

# Research Reptiles & Amphibians

**MATERIALS**
Resources about reptiles and amphibians, writing materials

`SINGLES`

Find differences between reptiles and amphibians.

1. Use classroom resources to gather information about reptiles and amphibians.
2. Look for facts that describe differences between these animals, such as their skin, the way they reproduce, or what their babies look like.
3. Write a short paragraph describing these differences.

**EARLY FINISHERS** Create a chart showing the information in your paragraph.

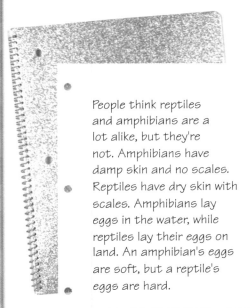

People think reptiles and amphibians are a lot alike, but they're not. Amphibians have damp skin and no scales. Reptiles have dry skin with scales. Amphibians lay eggs in the water, while reptiles lay their eggs on land. An amphibian's eggs are soft, but a reptile's eggs are hard.

## Technology

# Write an Article

**MATERIALS**
Word processing program, clip art, printer

`SINGLES`

Write a newspaper article about the aquarium theft.

1. Review the story to recall details about the theft at the aquarium and how the thief was caught.
2. Using a word processing program, write a newspaper article to tell what happened. Your article should answer *who*, *what*, *where*, *when*, and *how* questions.
3. Use a bigger, dark font size for the title. Use narrow margins for the text. Use a format tool to show the text in columns.
4. Follow classroom rules for printing.

**EARLY FINISHERS** Insert clip art into your article, or print out your story and draw a picture for it.

### Crook Caught with Stolen Salamander

Chief Brown arrested the thief who stole Fred, the tiger salamander, from the aquarium yesterday. Sam Maine, a caretaker at the aquarium, admitted to stealing the rare amphibian. The case was solved because Maine called salamanders, lizards.

**ALL CENTERS**

## OBJECTIVES

- Build vocabulary by finding words related to the lesson concept.
- Listen to identify parts of a story's plot.

### Concept Vocabulary

**case** matter for a court of law to decide

**damage** harm or injury that lessens the value or usefulness

**court** an assembly of persons (judges) who are chosen to administer justice

### Monitor Progress

**Check Vocabulary**

| If... | then... review the |
| --- | --- |
| students are unable to place words on the web, | lesson concept. Place the words on the web and provide additional words for practice, such as *disputes* and *righteous*. |

**SUCCESS PREDICTOR**

## DAY 1    Grouping Options

**Reading**

**Whole Group**
Introduce and discuss the Question of the Week. Then use pp. 488l–490b.

**Small Group**
**Differentiated Instruction**
**Read** this week's Leveled Readers. See pp. 488f–488g for the small group lesson plan.

**Whole Group**
Use p. 507a.

**Language Arts**
Use pp. 507e–507k.

# Build Concepts

## FLUENCY

**MODEL CHARACTERIZATION/DIALOGUE** As you read dialogue in "Something Fishy," model how to use tone of voice, volume, pitch, and emphasis to convey each character's personality and emotions and to make dialogue sound realistic. Point out clues you use to develop a distinct voice for each character's dialogue.

## LISTENING COMPREHENSION

After reading "Something Fishy," use the following questions to assess listening comprehension.

1. **What is the story's main problem?** *(A poor traveler stops and smells the fish, reminding him of his childhood. The fish seller wants to charge the traveler for sampling the smells of his fish.)* **Plot**

2. **How does the magistrate solve the problem?** *(Possible response: He makes the traveler pay the fish seller with the shadow of a silver coin.)* **Plot**

## BUILD CONCEPT VOCABULARY

Start a web to build concepts and vocabulary related to this week's lesson and the unit theme.

- Draw the Inquiry Concept Web.

- Read the sentence with the word *damage* again. Ask students to pronounce *damage* and discuss its meaning.

- Place *damage* in an oval attached to *Crimes or problems.* Discuss how *damage* from a crime or accident is a problem to investigate and solve. Read the sentences in which *case* and *court* appear. Have students pronounce the words, place them on the Web, and provide reasons.

- Brainstorm additional words and categories for the Web. Keep the Web on display and add words throughout the week.

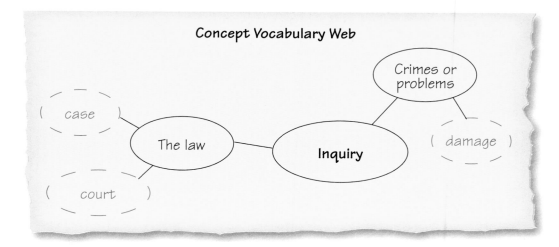

*Concept Vocabulary Web*

# Something Fishy

*by Robert Kausal*

Long ago, in the ancient city of Antigua, Guatemala, there lived a poor traveler by the name of Juan Rios. He arrived in the great city like many travelers before him, hungry and tired but filled with hope. With but a few coins in his pocket, he headed over to the market to enjoy nothing more than a bowl of beans and a few tortillas.

As Juan sat on a crate, eating his beans, he smelled the most delicious aroma of fried fish coming from the fish seller's stall. Juan leaned back, closed his eyes, and traveled back to his boyhood village and the memory of fishing with his father.

He remembered how he and his father would fill their canoe with fat fish that flopped around inside the boat. Later, his mother would spend the afternoon frying the fish—enough to fill the bellies of all of his brothers and sisters.

Suddenly, someone kicking at his leg pulled Juan from his daydream. He opened his eyes to see the fish seller, standing over him, his hands on his hips, his brows arched in anger. For several moments he stared at Juan before he said, "You owe me one silver coin."

"Excuse me?" Juan said trying to make sense of this request.

"You owe me one silver coin!" he shouted.

Juan was at a loss for words. Had he done something wrong? "Excuse me sir," Juan said, "but I am only eating a bowl of beans, which I paid for with my own money."

"Yes, I can see that," replied the fish seller, "but you have been sampling the smells of my fish as you sat here, have you not?"

"Well, yes," Juan stammered, "but—"

"But nothing! You owe me a silver coin for the fish you have been smelling."

The two men argued for some time before it was decided by some observers that they should take their case to don Miguel, a wise and trusted judge who settled disputes at the market.

Don Miguel had a court set up at the back of the market. Over the years, don Miguel had helped settle many disputes between buyers and sellers at the market. Everything from damage to goods or prices that were too high, no problem escaped his wise council.

The two men went before don Miguel, and each took a turn arguing his side of the story. Don Miguel listened patiently, his lips pursed as he twisted one end of his mustache with his fingers.

Finally, don Miguel said to Juan, "Sir, you did indeed enjoy the smells of this man's fish, did you not?"

*(Continued on TR1.)*

---

## Activate Prior Knowledge

Before students listen to the Read Aloud, explain that Guatemala is a country in Central America. Discuss how markets in many Latin American countries are different from markets in the United States.

## Set Purpose

Read aloud the title and ask students to predict what the story will be about.

Have students listen to identify parts of the story's plot, discovering what happens when a poor traveler is charged money for smelling fish.

## Creative Response

Have students imagine the thoughts that might be running through each character's mind at the end of the day's events. Have them choose one character and write a short monologue describing the character's thoughts. Students can present their monologues to the class. ***Drama***

**ELL**

**Access Content** Before reading, share this summary: A hungry traveler smells cooking fish coming from the fish seller's stall. The fish seller demands that the traveler pay him one sliver coin for smelling the fish. A clever judge finds a way to settle the case so each man gets what he deserves.

**Homework** Send home this week's Family Times newsletter.

SKILLS ↔ STRATEGIES IN CONTEXT

# Plot
# Prior Knowledge

## OBJECTIVES

- Identify elements of plot.
- Use prior knowledge to understand plot.

| Skills Trace | |
|---|---|
| **Literary Elements: Plot** | |
| Introduce/Teach | TE: 4.4 440–441, 488–489; 4.6 686–687 |
| Practice | TE: 171, 449, 455, 459, 497, 693, 699, 703 PB: 173, 177, 178, 193, 197, 198, 273, 277, 278 |
| Reteach/Review | TE: 4.2 171; 4.4 401, 465b, 507b, DI·56, 4.5 621; 4.6 711b PB: 66, 156, 246 |
| Test | Selection Test: 69–72, 77–80, 109–112; Benchmark Test: Unit 4 |

## INTRODUCE

Remind students of a recently read story and ask them to identify elements of its plot. *(Students should recognize the story's problem or conflict, how it builds, and how it is solved.)*

Have students read the information on p. 488. Explain the following:

- The *problem* is the central conflict in a story.
- The *rising action* includes events in which the problem gets worse as characters try various ways to solve it.
- The *climax* is the "high point" of the story where the conflict is directly confronted.
- The *resolution* is when the problem is solved.
- You can often use your own knowledge and experiences to understand plot elements.

Use Skill Transparency 20 to teach plot and prior knowledge.

---

**Comprehension**

| |
|---|
| **Skill** Plot |
| **Strategy** Prior Knowledge |

## Plot

- A plot, or underlying story structure, is found only in fiction.
- A plot begins when a character has a problem or conflict.
- The problem builds up during the rising action, is met directly at the climax, and comes to an end, as the action winds down, during the resolution.

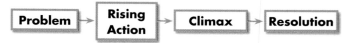

Problem → Rising Action → Climax → Resolution

 **Strategy: Prior Knowledge**

Good readers use their prior knowledge as they read. They ask themselves, "What do I already know about what is happening in this story?" You can use things you already know to help you understand the events in the rising action and the climax.

### Write to Read

1. Read "Oh, NO!" Make a graphic organizer like the one above to outline the parts of the story's plot.

2. Use your graphic organizer to write a summary of the plot.

488

---

**Strategic Intervention**

**Plot** Students having difficulty understanding plot may need practice identifying the key elements of problem and solution. Refer back to other stories in this book, and help students determine each story's problem and solution. Talk about familiar movies and determine their problems and solutions. Help students understand that all good stories, whether read or viewed, have a plot.

**ELL**

**Access Content**

**Beginning/Intermediate** For a Picture It! lesson on plot, see the ELL Teaching Guide, pp. 134–135.

**Advanced** Before reading "Oh, NO!" have volunteers explain the idiom "to catch up" (p. 489, paragraph 7).

Catherine was very excited when she learned that both she and her friend Shelley had gotten parts in the class play. She had always wanted to try acting. Mr. Kiley, the director, explained that it was important for everyone to attend each rehearsal. •⎯⎯⎯

On the fourth day of rehearsals, Catherine felt feverish. That night her fever became worse, and the next morning she had to remain in bed. •⎯⎯⎯

The doctor told Catherine that she would probably miss a week of school. "Oh, *no!* I can't miss that much!" she cried. "I'll be replaced in the class play."

That evening Catherine heard the telephone ring. Several minutes later her mother came into her bedroom.

"That was Mr. Kiley, your director, on the telephone," she told Catherine.

"He called to tell me I've been replaced, no doubt," Catherine moaned, suddenly feeling worse. •⎯⎯⎯

"No," said her mother. "He asked if Shelley could visit you after each rehearsal to keep you informed about the play. Then you'll be able to catch up when you get back next week."

"Oh, *yes!*" Catherine screamed excitedly and jumped out of bed. •⎯⎯⎯

"Hey!" laughed her mother. "Do you want your fever to *ever* go down?"

**1** **Skill** What does Catherine want to do? Could something prevent that from happening? This is the problem.

**2** **Strategy** Use your knowledge of being very sick. How did you feel? Did you miss school? What will happen to Catherine?

**3** **Skill** You might conclude that this is where the problem will be met directly. What do you predict will happen?

**4** **Strategy** How have you felt when you expected bad news and received good news? Can you understand Catherine's reaction?

489

Available as **Skill Transparency** 20

BEFORE READING

## TEACH

**1** **SKILL** Use the first paragraph to identify plot elements.

 Think Aloud **MODEL** I know that Catherine is very excited about being in this play. I also know the director says it's important for them to come to every rehearsal. I think something could happen that will prevent Catherine from coming to a rehearsal. That could be the story's problem.

**2** **STRATEGY** Discuss how prior knowledge can help students understand the plot.

Think Aloud **MODEL** When I have a fever, I feel terrible. My head hurts, and all I want to do is sleep. Based on my experiences of being sick, I think Catherine is going to miss school and miss her play practice.

## PRACTICE AND ASSESS

**3** **SKILL** Answers will vary, but some students may predict that Mr. Kiley has kicked Catherine out of the play.

**4** **STRATEGY** Answers will vary, but students should talk about their own feelings when they have received unexpected good news. Most will say they understand Catherine's reaction.

**WRITE** Have students complete steps 1 and 2 of the Write to Read activity. You might consider using this as a whole-class activity.

| **Monitor Progress** |
| :---: |
| 🔄 **Plot** |

| **If...** students are unable to complete **Write to Read** on p. 488, | **then...** use Practice Book p. 193 to provide additional practice. |
| --- | --- |

---

### Literary Elements • Plot

- A **plot**, or underlying story structure, is found only in fiction.
- A plot begins when a character has a problem or **conflict**. The problem builds up during the **rising action**, is met directly at the **climax**, and comes to an end, with the action winding down, during the **resolution**.

**Directions** Read the following passage. Then complete the diagram below.

Cory was trying out for a dance group that performed at city festivals. After waiting for four hours, it was finally her chance to dance. She had practiced so much, she did not think about individual steps. As Cory moved to the music, she focused on the rhythm and her feet knew what to do. When she'd finished, she knew she had danced her best. Cory had to wait again to find out if she had made it. Finally, a dance coach found her. "Welcome to Junior Jazz," the coach said. "Hooray!" shouted Cory.

| Problem ↓ | 1. Cory was trying out for a dance group. |
| --- | --- |
| **Rising Action** ↓ | Cory waited for her turn. |
| **Rising Action** ↓ | 2. Cory danced. |
| **Climax** ↓ | 3. Cory made it into the dance group. |
| **Resolution** | 4. Cory cheered. |

5. What do you know about tryouts that helps you to understand the plot events?
   Possible answer: Tryouts are competitive.

**School + Home** **Home Activity** Your child read a short passage and identified its plot structure. Read a story with your child, and work with him or her to identify the problem, rising action, climax, and resolution of the plot.

▲ **Practice Book** p. 193

*Encyclopedia Brown and the Case of the Slippery Salamander*   **489**

## Tech Files ONLINE

Students can search the Internet to find out more about real-life mysteries. Have them use a student-friendly search engine and the keywords *mystery stories*.

**Build Background** Use ELL Poster 20 to build background and vocabulary for the lesson concept of inquiry.

▲ **ELL Poster** 20

# Build Background

## ACTIVATE PRIOR KNOWLEDGE

**CREATE A WEB** about mystery stories.

- Display a concept web with *Mystery Stories* in the center circle.
- Invite students to talk about mystery stories they have read or mystery movies or TV shows they have seen. Prompt them to identify famous mysteries, as well as common elements of mystery stories, such as a crime, a detective, clues, and suspects.
- Record students' ideas in the outer circles of the web. Add circles to the web as needed.
- Tell students that *Encyclopedia Brown and the Case of the Slippery Salamander* is a mystery story. Have them look for additional ideas to add to the web as they read.

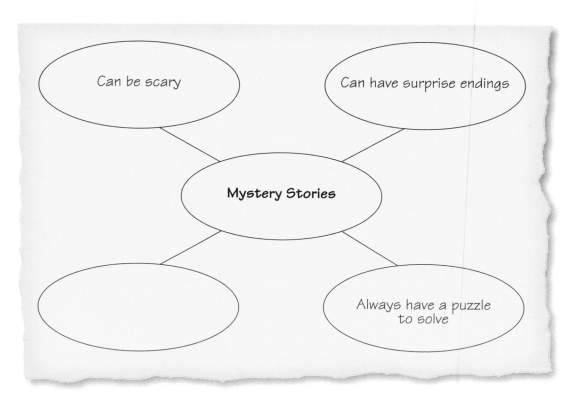

▲ **Graphic Organizer** 15

**BACKGROUND BUILDING AUDIO** This week's audio focuses on a police detective and crime solving. After students listen, discuss what they learned and how this career relates to the concept of mysteries.

**Background Building Audio**

# Introduce Vocabulary

## WORD CLUES

Ask questions about the lesson vocabulary words, challenging students to provide examples, synonyms, antonyms, and categories.

Display the lesson vocabulary words. Have students share what they know about the words. Ask questions like the ones below. ***Activate Prior Knowledge***

- What are some examples of *reference* books? *(dictionary, atlas)*

- How are all *amphibians* alike? *(They are cold-blooded and have backbones; they can breathe on land and in water for parts of their lives; they have moist, smooth skin.)*

- What do all *crimes* have in common? *(They are all against the law.)*

- What animal could you find in an *exhibit* of *reptiles*? *(snakes, lizards, turtles, alligators, or crocodiles)*

- How do you feel when you are the opposite of *stumped*? *(sure, knowing)*

- Is a *salamander* an *amphibian* or a *reptile*? *(amphibian)*

Have students identify the lesson vocabulary word with the digraph *ph*. (Amphibian) Point out *ph* is often a signal that a word comes from ancient Greek. Explain the prefix *amphi-* means "on both sides," and the root *bio* means "life." Have students tell how both meanings are expressed in the word *amphibian*. *(An amphibian lives both in water and on land.)* ***Word Origins***

Use the Multisyllabic Word Routine on p. DI·1 to help students read multisyllabic words.

Students can write their own questions about lesson vocabulary words at the end of the week and discuss them in small groups.

---

### Lesson Vocabulary

#### WORDS TO KNOW

**T amphibians** cold-blooded animals with backbones and moist, scale-less skins. Their young usually have gills and live in water until they develop lungs for living on land.

**T crime** activity of criminals; violation of law

**T exhibit** act of displaying; public showing

**T lizards** reptiles with long bodies and tails, movable eyelids, and usually four legs. Some lizards have no legs and look much like snakes.

**T reference** used for information or help

**T reptiles** cold-blooded animals with backbones and lungs, usually covered with horny plates or scales.

**T salamanders** animals shaped like lizards, but related to frogs and toads. Salamanders have moist, smooth skin and live in water or in damp places.

**T stumped** puzzled

#### MORE WORDS TO KNOW

**confided** told as a secret

**frustration** a feeling of anger and helplessness

**specimen** one of a group taken to show what the others are like;

**T** = Tested Word

---

### Vocabulary

**Directions** Choose the word from the box that best matches each definition. Write the word on the line.

amphibians    **1.** cold-blooded animals with backbones and moist skins

stumped    **2.** confused because something is hard to understand or solve

reference    **3.** a source used for information

lizards    **4.** reptiles with long bodies and tails and movable eyelids

salamanders    **5.** animals shaped like lizards but related to frogs and toads

**Check the Words You Know**
__amphibians
__crime
__exhibit
__lizards
__reference
__reptiles
__salamanders
__stumped

**Directions** Choose the word from the box that best completes each sentence. Write the word on the line.

David raced over to the new **6.** exhibit at the zoo. Nothing was there! He was baffled and **7.** stumped. Had there been a **8.** crime in which the animals were stolen? Had they escaped? He checked the sign as a **9.** reference about the animals that should be in the new exhibit. Suddenly he noticed where all of the rattlesnakes and other **10.** reptiles were hiding! The large sign had hidden them from view.

**Write a Description**
On a separate sheet of paper, write a description of an imaginary animal. Use as many vocabulary words as you can.

Descriptions should use words from the vocabulary list and include specific sensory details about an imaginary animal.

**Home Activity** Your child identified and used vocabulary words from *Encyclopedia Brown and the Case of the Slippery Salamander.* Read an encyclopedia article with your child. Have your child point out unfamiliar words. Work together to try to define each word by using the synonyms or antonyms around it.

▲ **Practice Book** p. 194

# Vocabulary Strategy

**OBJECTIVE**

Use context clues to determine word meaning.

## INTRODUCE

Discuss the strategy for synonyms and antonyms as context clues by using the steps on p. 490.

## TEACH

- Have students read "It Is Not All in the Family," paying attention to how vocabulary is used.

- Model using context clues to determine the meaning of *exhibit.*

**MODEL** In paragraph 3, I read that I can see live animals up close at a zoo *exhibit,* so I think that an exhibit is a place where the animals are shown. I read on and find a synonym, *display,* that supports my idea. Animals in an *exhibit* are part of a public display so visitors can see them.

---

## Words to Know

lizards

salamanders

reptiles

amphibians

stumped

reference

exhibit

crime

**Remember**

Try the strategy. Then, if you need more help, use your glossary or a dictionary.

# Vocabulary Strategy
## for Synonyms and Antonyms

**Context Clues** When you read, you may come across a word you don't know. Sometimes the author will use a synonym or an antonym as a clue to the word's meaning. Synonyms are words that mean almost the same thing. Antonyms are words with opposite meanings.

1. Reread the sentence with the unknown word. Look for a synonym or an antonym of the word. If you find one, try it in the sentence. Does the synonym make sense in the sentence? Does the antonym give the sentence an opposite meaning?

2. If there is not a synonym or an antonym in the same sentence as the unknown word, check the sentences around it. You may find a synonym or an antonym there. If you do, try it in the sentence.

As you read "It Is Not All in the Family," look for synonyms and antonyms to help you understand the meanings of vocabulary words.

490

---

## DAY 2   Grouping Options

**Reading**

**Whole Group** Discuss the Question of the Day. Then use pp. 490–493.

**Small Group** Differentiated Instruction
**Read** *Encyclopedia Brown.* See pp. 488f–488g for the small group lesson plan.

**Whole Group** Use p. 507a.

**Language Arts**
Use pp. 507e–507k.

---

**Strategic Intervention**

**Context Clues** Have partners reread paragraph 2 of "It Is Not All in the Family." Ask them to decide whether *slimy* skin feels wet or dry and to explain how the context helped them decide.

**Access Content** Use ELL Poster 20 to preteach vocabulary. Choose from the following to meet language proficiency levels.

**Beginning** Point out clues on p. 491, paragraph 3, that help define *reference* ("encyclopedia") and *exhibit* ("display").

**Intermediate** Before reading "It Is Not All in the Family," have students use the title and vocabulary words to predict the content.

**Advanced** Teach the lesson on pp. 490–491. Have pairs ask and answer their own vocabulary questions using the list on p. 490b.

Resources for home-language words may include parents, bilingual staff members, bilingual dictionaries, or online translation sources.

# IT IS NOT ALL IN THE FAMILY

Are you interested in the world of snakes, frogs, turtles, lizards, toads, and salamanders? You probably think of all of these animals as one big creepy family. In fact, they are not. Snakes, turtles, and lizards are all reptiles. Frogs, toads, and salamanders are all amphibians. Look at pictures of these animals. Can you tell how they are different? If you are stumped, read on.

Amphibians have skin that must be kept wet. If you touch the skin, it feels slimy. This is because amphibians live near water. They lay their eggs in water because the eggs have no shell. Reptiles, on the other hand, have dry skin that is covered with scales. Their eggs have a tough covering. These eggs can be laid on land.

If you are still baffled or confused about these animals, read about them in a reference book, such as an encyclopedia. The next time you are at a zoo, look them up. A zoo exhibit has live animals that you can see up close. The display gives facts about the animals. And remember, it is not a crime to ask questions! Zoo workers like to share what they know.

## Words to Write

Be a reporter. Write a news story about a group of young people who are helping the environment. Use as many Words to Know as you can.

491

## PRACTICE AND ASSESS

- Have students determine the meanings of the remaining words and explain the context clues they used.

- Explain that an article about how two things are different will often include words that point out contrasts, such as *however* and *on the other hand.* Have students find the phrase *on the other hand* (p. 491, paragraph 2) and use antonyms to compare and contrast the eggs or skin of amphibians and reptiles.

- If you introduced the oral questions activity (p. 490b), have students create additional questions using vocabulary words and other words related to reptiles, amphibians, and zoo exhibits.

- Have students complete Practice Book p. 195.

**WRITE** News stories should include several vocabulary words as well as other words about helping the environment.

### Monitor Progress

#### Context Clues

| If... students need more practice with the lesson vocabulary, | then... use Tested Vocabulary Cards. |
| --- | --- |

### Vocabulary • Context Clues

- **Synonyms** are words with the same or almost the same meaning.
- **Antonyms** are words with opposite meanings.
- When you read, you may come across a word you don't know. Look for synonyms or antonyms as clues to the unknown word's meaning.

**Directions** Read the following passage. Then answer the questions below.

Tamika's science fair exhibit, or display, featuring rattlesnakes was amazing. She presented a rattlesnake's skin and explained that unlike amphibians, reptiles have scales. Tamika also included pictures of the rattlesnake's diet, which included rabbits, rats, and squirrels.

Her best friend, Ty, was stumped and confused. He asked, "How can a snake eat animals that are larger than itself?" Tamika had been baffled by this herself, but now she was enlightened. She showed Ty her encyclopedia. Together, they looked at pictures of the snake's jaws expanding.

Possible answers given for 2, 5.

1. What does *exhibit* mean? What synonym helps you determine its meaning?
   display; the words "or display"

2. Explain why *reptile* and *amphibian* are not antonyms.
   Words can have different meanings without being opposites.

3. What does *baffled* mean? What synonym helps you determine its meaning?
   confused; the word "confused"

4. What does *enlightened* mean? What antonym helps you determine its meaning?
   understanding; the word "baffled"

5. Write a sentence using a word from the passage and its synonym or antonym.
   larger; The rat was larger than the mouse, but it was smaller than the cat.

**Home Activity** Your child identified vocabulary words using synonyms and antonyms in context. With your child, read an article about an animal and ask your child to identify unfamiliar words. Encourage your child to figure out the meanings using context clues such as synonyms and antonyms.

▲ **Practice Book** p. 195

*Encyclopedia Brown and the Case of the Slippery Salamander* **491**

# Prereading Strategies

## GENRE STUDY

### Realistic Fiction

*Encyclopedia Brown and the Case of the Slippery Salamander* is realistic fiction. Remind students that realistic fiction tells about people and events that aren't real, but could be. We use what we already know about people and the world to understand realistic stories.

## PREVIEW AND PREDICT

Have students preview the story title and illustrations. Discuss who they think the boy is and what he might be thinking about. Encourage students to use lesson vocabulary words as they talk about their predictions.

**Ask Questions** Have students ask questions about the main character and the mystery he may try to solve. They can answer their questions in the Strategy Response Log activity on p. 497.

## ENCYCLOPEDIA
### written by DONALD J. SOBOL

**Genre**

**Realistic fiction** tells about events that could really happen. As you read, think about how the events in this story are similar to events in real life.

492

**ELL**

**Access Content** In some other languages, adjectives come after nouns. This is not a story about a brown encyclopedia. Explain that Encyclopedia Brown is the unusual nickname of the main character.

Consider having students read the selection summary in English or in students' home languages. See the Multilingual Summaries in the ELL Teaching Guide, pp. 138–140.

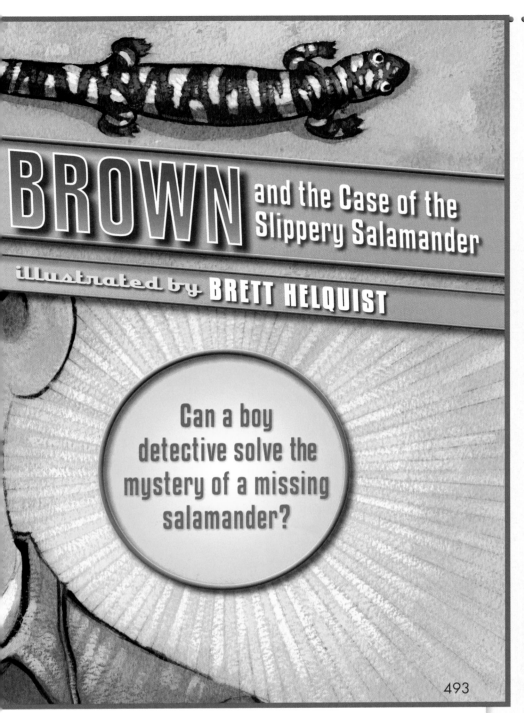

# BROWN and the Case of the Slippery Salamander

illustrated by **BRETT HELQUIST**

Can a boy detective solve the mystery of a missing salamander?

493

## SET PURPOSE

Read the first five paragraphs of the story aloud to students. Ask them what they'd like to find out about the mystery and Encyclopedia Brown as they read the rest of this story.

Remind students to think about the plot of this story as they read.

## STRATEGY RECALL

Students have now used these before-reading strategies:

- preview the selection to be aware of its genre, features, and possible content;
- activate prior knowledge about that content and what to expect of that genre;
- make predictions;
- set a purpose for reading.

Remind students to be aware of and flexibly use the during-reading strategies they have learned:

- link prior knowledge to new information;
- summarize text they have read so far;
- ask clarifying questions;
- answer questions they or others pose;
- check their predictions and either refine them or make new predictions;
- recognize the text structure the author is using, and use that knowledge to make predictions and increase comprehension;
- visualize what the author is describing;
- monitor their comprehension and use fix-up strategies.

After reading, students will use these strategies:

- summarize or retell the text;
- answer questions they or others pose;
- reflect to make new information become part of their prior knowledge.

Audio CD **AudioText**

# Guiding Comprehension

 **Vocabulary • Context Clues**

**What does *resided* mean on p. 494, paragraph 4? What clues can help you figure out what it means?**

Meaning: lived, dwelled, stayed; Clues: in a red brick house; 13 River Avenue; lived

| **Monitor Progress** | |
|---|---|
| ** Context Clues** | |
| **If...** students have difficulty using context clues to define *resided*, | **then...** use the vocabulary strategy instruction on p. 495. |

**2** **Facts and Details • Literal**

**Why hasn't the Brown family told everyone Encyclopedia is an amazing crime-solver?**

They don't want to boast, and they don't think anyone would believe them anyway.

**3** **Draw Conclusions • Critical**

**How does the chief feel about the crime he can't solve? How can you tell?**

Possible response: He is bothered by it. He rubs his forehead and doesn't eat his dinner.

**Tech Files ONLINE**

Students can search the Internet to learn more about reptiles and amphibians. Have them use a student-friendly search engine and the keywords *reptile* and *amphibian*.

---

To a visitor, Idaville looked like an ordinary seaside town.

It had churches, two car washes, and three movie theaters. It had bike paths, sparkling white beaches, a synagogue, and plenty of good fishing spots.

But there was something out of the ordinary about Idaville: For more than a year, no child or grown-up had gotten away with breaking a law.

People wanted to know: How did Idaville do it?

**1** The secret resided in a red brick house at 13 Rover Avenue. That was where Idaville's police chief lived with his wife and son.

Chief Brown was a smart, kind, and brave man. But he wasn't the one who kept crooks from getting away with their crimes. No, the brains behind it all was his ten-year-old son, Encyclopedia.

Encyclopedia's real name was Leroy. But only his parents and teachers called him that. Everyone else called him "Encyclopedia" because his brain was filled with more facts than a reference book.

Sometimes the Brown family was tempted to tell the world about Encyclopedia's amazing talent as a crime-solver. But so far they hadn't leaked a word. For one thing, the Browns didn't like to boast. For another, who would believe that Idaville's top

**2** detective was a fifth-grader?

13 Rover Avenue, Idaville

**ELL**

**Access Context** Pages 494–495 contain terms and phrases common to mysteries, such as *police chief, crooks, detective, breaking the law, getting away with,* and *cracked the case.* Discuss their meanings and connection to crime solving. Suggest students make a list of crime-solving words to help them understand mysteries.

One Monday night Chief Brown sat at the dinner table, staring at his plate of spaghetti. So far he hadn't slurped up a single strand. Encyclopedia and his mother knew the reason.

The chief wasn't eating because he had come up against a crime that he couldn't solve.

Encyclopedia waited for his dad to tell him about the case. Whenever Chief Brown was stumped, Encyclopedia cracked the case for him, usually by asking just one question.

At last Chief Brown looked up. "There was a theft at the aquarium today," he said, rubbing his forehead.

Last summer an aquarium had opened near the beach. The most popular attractions were the giant shark tanks, the dolphin shows, and the Den of Darkness.

The Den of Darkness was a huge indoor exhibit of reptiles and amphibians. Encyclopedia especially liked visiting the frogs and salamanders in the amphibian section.

495

## Salamanders

The salamander is an amphibian with soft, moist skin and a long body. Most salamanders are small, just a few inches long. However, there is a species in Japan that can grow to be five feet long. They have long tails for swimming and long, sticky tongues for catching insects. Often mistaken for lizards, salamanders actually are more closely related to frogs. Most go through the same process of metamorphosis as frogs, losing gills and developing lungs as they grow. Salamanders, which can be found in all but the coldest parts of the world, are most common in Asia, Europe, and North America.

## VOCABULARY STRATEGY

# Context Clues

## TEACH

- Remind students to use context clues to figure out the meanings of unfamiliar words. Sometimes the clues are synonyms or antonyms in nearby sentences.
- Explain that synonyms are words with almost the same meaning, and antonyms are words with opposite meanings.
- Model how to use a synonym to determine the meaning of *resided* on p. 494, paragraph 4.

**Think Aloud** **MODEL** When I read "the secret *resided* …" I'm not sure what *resided* means, so I'll keep reading to look for clues. I see that I'm given an address where the secret *resided*. Then the next sentence says that address is where the police chief lived. I think *resided* means about the same as *lived*. When I use *lived* in the sentence, it makes sense: "*The secret* lived *in a brick house at 13 Rover Avenue.*" Now I'll keep reading to find out who or what the secret is.

## PRACTICE AND ASSESS

Have students identify context clues they could use to determine the meaning of *aquarium* (p. 495, paragraph 4) and define the word. *(Clues: shark tanks, dolphin shows; Meaning: a building used to show collections of water animals)*

# Guiding Comprehension

 **4**  **Plot • Inferential**

**What is the main problem in this story?**

A salamander has been stolen from the aquarium, and Chief Brown doesn't know who has taken it.

---

### Monitor Progress

####  Plot

| **If...** students have difficulty identifying the story's problem, | **then...** use the skill and strategy instruction on p. 497. |
|---|---|

---

**5** **Summarize • Inferential**

**What has Chief Brown already done to try to solve the problem?**

Possible response: He's talked to the director of the aquarium. He's questioned the three people who were working at the aquarium when the salamander was stolen.

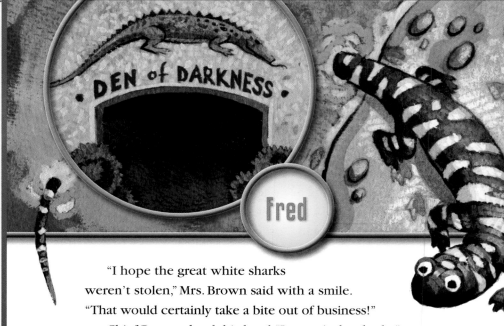

DEN of DARKNESS

Fred

"I hope the great white sharks weren't stolen," Mrs. Brown said with a smile. "That would certainly take a bite out of business!"

Chief Brown shook his head. "It wasn't the sharks."

Encyclopedia put down his fork and listened carefully as his father explained that Fred, a tiger salamander, had been stolen.

"Fred was shipped to the aquarium only two days ago," Chief Brown said. "He was being kept apart from the other animals until the officials were sure he was healthy. If he got a clean bill of health, he was to go on display next month."

"Do you have any clues, dear?" Mrs. Brown asked.

The chief frowned. "Not many. All we know is that the salamander disappeared this morning, sometime between ten-thirty **4** and eleven forty-five."

"Why would someone steal a salamander?" Mrs. Brown wondered.

"Fred is the aquarium's only tiger salamander," her husband explained. "From what the director of the aquarium told me, someone could sell him for a lot of money."

"Really?" Mrs. Brown's eyes widened. "Do you think a visitor might have stolen him?"

496

 **ELL**

**Build Background** When a doctor gives a *clean bill of health* (p. 496, paragraph 4), he or she asserts a person or animal is healthy. The term originated a long time ago when ships had to show a certificate (a bill of health) stating that none of the crew had a contagious disease.

"It's very unlikely," Chief Brown replied. "Employees and volunteers are the only ones who have access to the back room in the Den of Darkness where Fred was being kept."

Chief Brown told Encyclopedia and Mrs. Brown that three people had been working at the exhibit that morning: Mrs. King, who volunteered at the aquarium every Monday; Sam Maine, the man in charge of cleaning and maintaining the exhibits; and Dr. O'Donnell, an expert on reptiles and amphibians.

"Did you question the three of them?" Mrs. Brown asked.

The chief nodded. "Dr. O'Donnell spent the morning examining a new crocodile from Australia. Sam Maine told me he was busy cleaning out exhibits and feeding some of the lizards. Several people saw him working," Chief Brown added, "so it looks like he's telling the truth."

"What about Mrs. King?" his wife prodded.

497

## Develop Vocabulary

### PRACTICE LESSON VOCABULARY

Students orally respond *yes* or *no* to questions and provide a reason for each answer. Possible reasons are given.

**1. Does a person who is *stumped* know the answer?** *(No; a person who is stumped is unable to solve a problem.)*

**2. Is an atlas a type of *reference* book?** *(Yes; it contains maps and other helpful information.)*

**3. Are lizards *reptiles*?** *(Yes; lizards are cold-blooded animals with a backbone, lungs, and scales.)*

### BUILD CONCEPT VOCABULARY

Review previous concept words with students. Ask if students have come across any words today in their reading or elsewhere that they would like to add to the Inquiry Concept Web.

SKILLS ⬌ STRATEGIES IN CONTEXT

# Plot

## TEACH

- The plot of most stories has these parts: *problem, rising action, climax,* and *resolution.* Discuss the meaning of each term.
- Use p. 496 to model determining a story's problem.

**Think Aloud** **MODEL** I know that a strong plot usually begins with a problem. We know that in this story, a salamander has been stolen. Since Mr. Brown is the chief of police, it is his job to catch thieves, but he doesn't know who took the animal. That's the story's problem.

## PRACTICE AND ASSESS

Remind students that after a problem is identified in a story, the rising action begins. Have students identify the rising action on p. 497. (*The chief tries to solve the case by questioning workers at the aquarium and discussing what he learns with his family.*)

### Strategy Response Log

**Answer Questions** Have students look at the questions they wrote before reading the story. (See p. 492.) Tell students that if they can answer their questions, write the answers in the log, and then write a new question about the rest of the story.

## EXTEND SKILLS

### Word Play

Word play emphasizes the differences in word meanings for humorous effects. Point out the example on p. 496: "That would certainly take a bite out of business!" Discuss how a shark can literally "take a bite out of" something and what Mrs. Brown means. Ask why the author might have used word play in the story.

*If you want to teach this selection in two sessions, stop here.*

*Encyclopedia Brown and the Case of the Slippery Salamander*   **497**

# Guiding Comprehension

*If you are teaching the story in two days, discuss predictions made so far and review the vocabulary.*

**6** Plot • Critical

*Text to Text* **How do events in this story remind you of other realistic fiction stories you have read?**

Responses will vary, but students should compare the problem, rising action, or climax of this story to the plots of other realistic stories.

**7** Compare and Contrast • Inferential

**By the end of p. 499, how are Encyclopedia's and Chief Brown's feelings about the case the same and different?**

Same: Both care about solving the case. Different: Chief Brown is frustrated and baffled, but Encyclopedia is excited and satisfied because he thinks he's solved it.

---

### Monitor Progress

**REVIEW** **Compare and Contrast**

| If... students are unable to compare and contrast the characters' feelings, | then... use the skill and strategy instruction on p. 499. |
|---|---|

---

## DAY 3 Grouping Options

**Reading**
**Whole Group** Discuss the Question of the Day.

**Small Group** Differentiated Instruction
Read *Encyclopedia Brown.* See pp. 488f–488g for the small group lesson plan.

**Whole Group** Discuss the Reader Response questions on p. 501. Then use p. 507a.

**Language Arts**
Use pp. 507e–507k.

---

Chief Brown frowned. "Actually, Sam Maine seems very suspicious of Mrs. King," he confided. "And after talking with her I can see why. Mrs. King is fascinated with salamanders."

"Fascinated with salamanders?" Mrs. Brown echoed.

The chief nodded again. "She told me she has dozens of them at home as pets, and that Fred is the first tiger salamander she's ever seen." He shook his head. "Mrs. King does seem odd—she thinks salamanders are sacred creatures with magical powers."

Encyclopedia spoke up. "In ancient times, people used salamanders for medicine. They also believed that salamanders could eat fire and live in flames."

"Maybe Fred wasn't stolen for money," Mrs. Brown said thoughtfully. "Maybe Mrs. King took Fred just because she thinks he's a special specimen!"

"That's exactly what I've been thinking," Chief Brown admitted. "But there's no proof that Mrs. King had the opportunity to steal Fred. She was with a group of school children from ten-thirty to eleven-fifteen. After that she went over to the cafeteria for a coffee break. One of the cashiers said he saw her there."

498

**E L L**

**Access Content** Explain the term *opportunity* (p. 498, last paragraph) means "chance" or "possibility" in this context. Ask students to explain why it may not have possible for Mrs. King to steal the salamander.

Chief Brown sighed with frustration. "I hate to admit it, but this case has me baffled!" **6**

Encyclopedia closed his eyes. His parents watched him hopefully. They knew that when Encyclopedia closed his eyes, it meant he was doing his deepest thinking.

A moment later Encyclopedia was ready. He opened his eyes and asked his one question:

"Has Sam Maine been working at the aquarium long, Dad?"

"Actually, he was hired only two weeks ago," Chief Brown answered. "But he has a lot of experience. Sam told me he's been taking care of salamanders and other lizards for more than nineteen years."

That was all Encyclopedia needed to hear.

"Oh no, he hasn't!" Encyclopedia declared with a satisfied smile. "If he's a lizard expert, then I'm the Queen of England! Sam Maine is lying, and I can prove it!"

How does Encyclopedia know? **7**

499

## Develop Vocabulary

### PRACTICE LESSON VOCABULARY

Have students complete each sentence as a group. Possible responses are given.

1. An *amphibian* is an animal that lives *(in water when it's young and on land when it's older)*.

2. Unlike mammals and birds, lizards are *(cold-blooded animals)*.

3. *Salamanders* are related to *(frogs and toads)*.

4. An art *exhibit* might contain *(paintings, sculptures, or other art)*.

### BUILD CONCEPT VOCABULARY

Review previous concept words. Ask students if they have come across any words today in their reading or elsewhere that they would like to add to the Inquiry and Investigation Concept Web, such as *expert* and *odd*.

SKILLS ↔ STRATEGIES IN CONTEXT

# Compare and Contrast REVIEW

## TEACH

Remind students that to *compare and contrast* means to tell how two things are alike and different. Use p. 499 to model comparing and contrasting the characters' feelings about the case.

**Think Aloud** **MODEL** Both Encyclopedia and Chief Brown care about solving the case. They spend time talking about it, trying to figure it out. It says at the top of p. 499 that the Chief *sighed with frustration.* He can't solve the case, and it's bothering him. But at the bottom of p. 499, I see Encyclopedia has a *satisfied smile* and he says he can prove something about one of the suspects. Unlike his father, Encyclopedia feels good about the case because he thinks he's solved it.

## PRACTICE AND ASSESS

- Have students compare Mrs. King's and ancient people's beliefs about salamanders. (*Mrs. King believes they have magical powers. So did some ancient people, who thought they could eat fire and live in flames.*)

- To assess, use Practice Book p. 196.

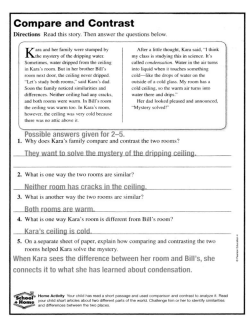

**Compare and Contrast**

**Directions** Read this story. Then answer the questions below.

> Kara and her family were stumped by the mystery of the dripping water. Sometimes, water dripped from the ceiling in Kara's room. But in her brother Bill's room next door, the ceiling never dripped. "Let's study both rooms," said Kara's dad. Soon the family noticed similarities and differences. Neither ceiling had any cracks, and both rooms were warm. In Bill's room the ceiling was warm too. In Kara's room, however, the ceiling was very cold because there was no attic above it.
>
> After a little thought, Kara said, "I think my class is studying this in science. It's called *condensation*. Water in the air turns into liquid when it touches something cold—like the drops of water on the outside of a cold glass. My room has a cold ceiling, so the warm air turns into water there and drips."
>
> Her dad looked pleased and announced, "Mystery solved!"

Possible answers given for 2–5.

1. Why does Kara's family compare and contrast the two rooms?

They want to solve the mystery of the dripping ceiling.

2. What is one way the two rooms are similar?

Neither room has cracks in the ceiling.

3. What is another way the two rooms are similar?

Both rooms are warm.

4. What is one way Kara's room is different from Bill's room?

Kara's ceiling is cold.

5. On a separate sheet of paper, explain how comparing and contrasting the two rooms helped Kara solve the mystery.

When Kara sees the difference between her room and Bill's, she connects it to what she has learned about condensation.

**School + Home** **Home Activity** Your child has read a short passage and used comparison and contrast to analyze it. Read your child short articles about two different parts of the world. Challenge him or her to identify similarities and differences between the two places.

▲ **Practice Book** p. 196

*Encyclopedia Brown and the Case of the Slippery Salamander* **499**

STRATEGY SELF-CHECK

# Prior Knowledge

Discuss how prior knowledge can help solve this mystery. (*Possible response: A reader who knows about salamanders may know Mr. Maine is lying about being an expert. People who lie in mysteries are often guilty of a crime.*)

Have students use a plot structure diagram and identify the problem, rising action, climax, and resolution of this story.

## SELF-CHECK

Students can ask themselves the following questions to assess understanding of the story.

- Can I identify the problem, rising action, climax, and resolution in this story?
- Did I think about what I already know to help me understand story events?

### Monitor Progress

#### 🔄 Plot and Prior Knowledge

| If... students have difficulty using prior knowledge to identify and understand the plot, | then... use the Reteach lesson on p. 507b. |
|---|---|

---

**Literary Elements • Plot**

- A **plot,** or underlying story structure, is found only in fiction.
- A plot begins when a character has a problem or **conflict.** The problem builds up during the **rising action,** is met directly at the **climax,** and comes to an end, with the action winding down, during the **resolution.**

**Directions** Read the following passage. Then answer the questions below.

The Bahamas is home to exotic wildlife. Many species of lizards and other reptiles live there. One summer, three men arrived at the islands. They said they were studying animals at a college in Europe. Local residents became suspicious when they noticed one of the men. He looked like someone who had stolen animals from the island many years earlier. Could it be the same person? After some debate, the residents contacted the police.

The three men were stopped at the airport, and their luggage was inspected. Five hundred live lizards were hidden in their luggage! The men had planned to take the lizards to Germany and sell them. Instead, the men were arrested, and the lizards were returned home alive.

Possible answers given.
1. In this story, what is the problem?
Local residents think three men might be stealing animals.

2. What is one event in the rising action?
Local residents report the three men to the police.

3. What event is the climax of the plot?
Police find 500 lizards in the three men's luggage.

4. What is the resolution?
The men are arrested, and the lizards are set free.

5. What did you already know about the Bahamas that helped you understand this passage?
People like visiting the Bahamas because of the warm weather there.

**School + Home** Home Activity Your child read a short passage and identified its plot structure. Read a story with your child. Work together to identify the problem, rising action, climax, and resolution of the plot.

▲ **Practice Book** p. 197

---

# SOLUTION to the Case of the Slippery Salamander

Encyclopedia knew that Sam Maine was lying because he told Chief Brown he'd been taking care of "salamanders and other lizards for more than nineteen years." Anyone who'd been taking care of salamanders for that long would know that salamanders are not lizards. They are classified as amphibians. Lizards are classified as reptiles.

Sam Maine admitted stealing the valuable new tiger salamander that morning. After he returned Fred to the aquarium, he was fired from his job as caretaker.

500

**Extend Language** Remind students to break unfamiliar words into smaller parts. *Caretaker* (paragraph 2) can be broken into *care + taker:* someone who "takes care" of a place.

# Reader Response

**Open for Discussion** Does Encyclopedia Brown remind you of anyone you know? Does he remind you of someone you would like to know? Explain your thoughts.

1. Idaville isn't real, but the author includes details to make it seem like a real town. Find at least three details that make Idaville seem real. **Think Like an Author**

2. A plot has a conflict, but the conflict isn't always between two characters. What is the conflict in this story? How is the conflict resolved? **Plot**

3. Think about what you know about how crimes are solved. What does Chief Brown do that is like what most detectives would do? What does he do that's different? **Prior Knowledge**

4. As a detective on the case, what notes might Encyclopedia Brown have jotted in his notebook? Write some of them, using words from the Words to Know list and the story. **Vocabulary**

**Look Back and Write** Whom do you think Chief Brown suspects of stealing the salamander before Encyclopedia solves the crime? Use details from the story to support your answer.

Meet author **Donald J. Sobol on page 771 and** illustrator **Brett Helquist on page 781.**

501

---

**Scoring Rubric** | **Look Back and Write**

**Top-Score Response** A top-score response uses information from the story to determine that Chief Brown initially suspects Mrs. King of stealing the salamander.

**Example of a Top-Score Response** It seems Chief Brown initially suspects Mrs. King. He knows that only three people had access to the salamander, and the other two seem to have solid alibis. Also, Mrs. King is known to have a strange fascination with salamanders. She has many salamanders at home as pets.

**For additional rubrics, see p. WA10.**

---

# Reader Response

**Open for Discussion** **Personal Response**

**Think Aloud** **MODEL** I don't know anyone like Encyclopedia Brown, but I'd like to. It would be great to have a friend who could remember everything he read.

**Comprehension Check** **Critical Response**

1. Idaville had churches, car washes, and bike paths, just like a real town. ***Author's Purpose***

2. The conflict is that someone stole a salamander from the aquarium. Chief Brown doesn't know who did it. The conflict is solved when Encyclopedia figures out Sam Maine did it.  ***Plot***

3. Possible response: Chief Brown asks the people who work at the aquarium questions. Unlike real detectives, he asks his son, who solves the case. ***Prior Knowledge***

4. Responses should include details of the case and vocabulary words. ***Vocabulary***

**TEST PRACTICE** **Look Back and Write** For test practice, assign a 10–15 minute time limit. For assessment, see the Scoring Rubric below.

## Retell

Have students retell *Encyclopedia Brown and the Case of the Slippery Salamander.* Use the Retelling Rubric on p. 502.

| **Monitor Progress** |
|---|
| **Check Retelling** Rubric 4 3 2 1 |

| If... students have difficulty retelling the story, | then... use the Retelling cards and the Scoring Rubric for Retelling on p. 502 to assist fluent retelling. |
|---|---|

SUCCESS PREDICTOR

**Check Retelling** Let students listen to other retellings before attempting their own. For more ideas on assessing students' retellings, see the ELL and Transition Handbook.

# Write Now

**Look at the Prompt** Each sentence in the prompt has a purpose.

- Sentence 1 presents a topic.
- Sentence 2 suggests students think about the topic.
- Sentence 3 tells what to write—a plot summary.

## Strategies to Develop Organization/ Paragraphs

Have students

- make sure one paragraph leads to the next and has transition words.
- write a concluding sentence that presents closure.

The boy learns an important lesson—love is more valuable than money.

For additional suggestions and rubric, see pp. 507g–507h.

## Strategy Response Log

**Summarize** When students finish reading the selection, provide this prompt: Imagine that a friend has asked you what the case of the slippery salamander is about and how it is solved. In four or five sentences, explain the case.

# Write Now

## Plot Summary

**Prompt**

The plot of *Encyclopedia Brown* keeps readers interested until the very end. Think about the plot of a favorite book or movie.

Now write a plot summary explaining what happened in that book or movie to a friend.

**Writing Trait**

Each **paragraph** a plot summary sh focus on one impo event in the plot.

**Student Model**

Each paragraph summarizes one section of the story—beginning, middle, and end.

Writer uses present verb tense.

> At the beginning of The King in the Kitchen, a guard leads a peasant to the dungeon. The peasant has just asked the King for the Princess's hand in marriage. However, the King wants the Princess to marry the wealthy Duke because the kingdom needs money. The King is also unhappy because his soup tastes awful.
>
> The King claims he can make a better soup blindfolded. Then he starts to cook. No one, including the King, knows what he has made. The King decides to have a contest. Whoever can gue what he has made will get to marry the Princess.
>
> The Duke guesses first. His answer—pudding— is wrong. After tasting the concoction, he can

502

## Scoring Rubric — Narrative Retelling

| Rubric 4 3 2 1 | 4 | 3 | 2 | 1 |
|---|---|---|---|---|
| **Connections** | Makes connections and generalizes beyond the text | Makes connections to other events, stories, or experiences | Makes a limited connection to another event, story, or experience | Makes no connection to another event, story, or experience |
| **Author's Purpose** | Elaborates on author's purpose | Tells author's purpose with some clarity | Makes some connection to author's purpose | Makes no connection to author's purpose |
| **Characters** | Describes the main character(s) and any character development | Identifies the main character(s) and gives some information about them | Inaccurately identifies some characters or gives little information about them | Inaccurately identifies the characters or gives no information about them |
| **Setting** | Describes the time and location | Identifies the time and location | Omits details of time or location | Is unable to identify time or location |
| **Plot** | Describes the problem, goal, events, and ending using rich detail | Tells the problem, goal, events, and ending with some errors that do not affect meaning | Tells parts of the problem, goal, events, and ending with gaps that affect meaning | Retelling has no sense of story |

## Retelling Plan

☑ **Week 1** Assess Strategic Intervention students.

☑ **Week 2** Assess Advanced students.

☑ **Week 3** Assess Strategic Intervention students.

☑ **Week 4** Assess On-Level students.

☑ **This week assess any students you have not yet checked during this unit.**

> Use the Retelling Chart on p. TR16 to record retelling.

**Selection Test** To assess with *Encyclopedia Brown and the Case of the Slippery Salamander,* use Selection Tests, pp. 77–80.

**Fresh Reads for Differentiated Test Practice** For weekly leveled practice, use pp. 115–120.

SU
PRED

no longer speak. The peasant is the only other contestant. The clever peasant takes a whiff of the King's mixture and uses a dab of it to fix his shoe. He declares that the King has made the best glue ever. He predicts that the King will make a fortune from his new product. The peasant marries the Princess, and the King starts a good business.

**Use the model to help you write your own plot summary.**

## Hints for Writing Good Paragraphs

- Write an opening sentence that engages readers and lets them know your topic or main idea. Your opener might be a topic sentence, a question, or an interesting fact.
- Use transition words and phrases such as *now, before, then, also, unlike, for example,* and *as a result* to connect ideas, sentences, and paragraphs.
- Make sure each sentence in the paragraph supports the topic or main idea.
- In a summary paragraph, give only the highlights of the plot.

503

## Writer's Checklist

☑ **Focus** Do sentences stick to the plot of the book or movie?

☑ **Organization** Is there a logical progression of ideas?

☑ **Support** Do details give readers information about plot?

☑ **Conventions** Are paragraphs indented?

# Science in Reading

## PREVIEW/USE TEXT FEATURES

Ask students to preview "Young Detectives," taking note of how this article looks different from other articles they have read.

After they preview, ask:

- **How does the headline grab the reader's attention?** *(It causes the reader to wonder how middle school students could be detectives.)*

- **What information do you expect the direct quotations in this article to give you?** *(The quotations will probably tell what the kids at Potterville Middle School think.)*

### Link to Science

Provide inkpads and paper so students can make their own fingerprints. Let them work in small groups to compare their results.

### DAY 4 Grouping Options

**Reading**
**Whole Group** Discuss the Question of the Day.

**Small Group** Differentiated Instruction
**Read** "Young Detectives of Potterville Middle School." See pp. 488f–488g for the small group lesson plan.

**Whole Group** Use p. 507a.

**Language Arts**
Use pp. 507e–507k.

---

## Science in Reading

### Newspaper Article

**Genre**
- Newspaper articles provide information about current events and topics of human interest.
- They are often short and to-the-point. They tell *who, what, when, where, why*. Human-interest stories are generally longer and more descriptive.

**Text Features**
- A catchy title, or headline, grabs the reader's attention.
- The first paragraph sums up the article and sets up for what comes next.
- The use of direct quotations makes the article personal and interesting.

**Link to Science**
Make a set of your fingerprints. Then compare and contrast your fingerprints with those of a classmate.

Crime scene investigation: Students use tools such as microscope to evaluate evidence at the scene of a "cr

504

---

| Content-Area Vocabulary | Science |
|---|---|
| analysis | an examination made carefully and in detail |
| blood type | any one of the groups into which human blood may be divided |
| data | facts from which conclusions can be drawn |
| microscope | device with a lens or lenses for making small things look larger |

**Activate Prior Knowledge** Ask students to describe how a detective solves a crime. Introduce *fingerprinting* and *blood samples* into the discussion.

# ily Journal

— Monday

# Young Detectives
## of Potterville Middle School

by Bonnie Kepplinger

Sixth-graders in a Michigan middle school solve crimes during one class period each day. Their classroom has become a crime lab. Their tools are microscopes, rubber gloves, goggles, and fingerprinting brushes and powder. These students work together to evaluate evidence at a "crime" scene. Hair and fiber analysis can answer questions that identify criminals. Does this hair belong to a dog, a cat, or a human? What kinds of fibers were found on the victim's clothes? What do clues tell us about anyone else present at the scene of the crime?

**Prior Knowledge** | Think about what you know about what detectives do.

505

## NEWSPAPER ARTICLE

Use the sidebar on p. 504 to guide discussion.

- Explain a newspaper article is designed to provide current information about real people and events.

- Tell students newspapers have different kinds of articles. "Young Detectives" is a human-interest story. This kind of article shows how an event or situation affects real people.

- Read the first paragraph of the article and discuss whether students would enjoy this kind of class.

Audio CD  AudioText

**Prior Knowledge**

To help generate ideas, have students think of TV shows, movies, or books they have read.

## Experiments

TIME FOR Science

Scientists use a system known as the Scientific Method to learn about the world. First, the scientist observes an event or situation. Next, the scientist formulates a possible explanation for the observation called a *hypothesis*. Then, predictions are made based on this hypothesis. The predictions are tested through experiments. If the predictions do not prove true, the scientist will suggest different hypotheses and different experiments. If the predictions prove true over time, the scientist may conclude the hypothesis is true. A hypothesis proved true over time is called a *theory*.

TEST PRACTICE ✓

## Strategies for Nonfiction

**USE DIRECT QUOTATIONS** Remind students newspaper articles often include direct quotations. Explain we can sometimes use direct quotations to answer test questions. Provide the following strategy.

### Use the Strategy

1. Read the test question to find out what you need to know.
2. Scan the article, looking for direct quotations related to the test question.
3. If you find a quote or quotes that seem to relate to the test question, read the information carefully to see if you can find an answer to the test question.

**GUIDED PRACTICE** Have students discuss how they would use the strategy to answer the following question.

How do students in Ms. Dykstra's forensics class feel about the class? Provide two details from the article to support your answer.

**INDEPENDENT PRACTICE** After students answer the following test question, discuss the process they used to find information.

What does Jeff Hudak, a crime scene investigator, think about these forensics classes in school? Use details from the article to support your answer.

---

A young detective analyzes "blood" samples.

"We rush to this class," said one student. "No one's ever really tardy because we like to come."

"I don't want to leave this class," added another student. "We get to solve crimes. It's fun because we get to find out by ourselves instead of having someone else tell us or show us."

Several high schools in mid-Michigan offer forensic science classes. (*Forensic* refers to science that can be used in legal courts.) However, Potterville Middle School is believed to be the first in the area to bring such classes to younger students. These classes teach students how to think, question, and solve problems. Young Potterville detectives enjoy improving their science skills through investigation.

During the nine weeks of classes, students have several projects. One week they were given a burglary scene with four possible suspects. Their job was to analyze fake blood samples. Then they matched one suspect's blood type with the sample found at the crime scene.

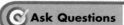 **Ask Questions** What questions do you have that the author answers?

506

 **ELL**

**Independent Practice** For the Independent Practice test question, direct student attention to the last paragraph of the article. Identify Jeff Hudak as an investigator, or person who tries to solve crimes. Read Hudak's quotes aloud. Help students decide whether he seems to think the class is good or bad for students.

## The Daily Journal

Teachers say that this is a way to get students interested in and excited about science. "We have never seen kids this excited about science as we have this year," said sixth-grade teacher Maureen Dykstra. "They have become close observers and careful recorders of data." Like all good detectives, students learn how to collect and weigh information. They even draw pictures of the crime scene. Students also have a place to stage the crimes. This is a portable unit outside the school that used to be a music room.

Guest speakers visit the class to talk about careers. Visitors have included a forensic scientist, a police officer, and a detective. Jeff Hudak is a crime investigator for the local police department. He knows that working with

young students encourages them to think about future jobs. "It lets them know what they have to do to get involved in crime scene investigation," he said. "It's never too early to get them interested."

### Reading Across Texts

Do you think Encyclopedia Brown should sign up for a forensics class at Potterville Middle School?

**Writing Across Texts** Explain why you answered the question about Encyclopedia Brown as you did.

507

## CONNECT TEXT TO TEXT

### Reading Across Texts

Have students create a list of activities students do in forensics class. Then have them create a list to describe Encyclopedia Brown's personality and interests. Students can compare the two lists to decide whether Encyclopedia should sign up for the class.

**Writing Across Texts** Write a letter to Encyclopedia to convince him to enroll, or not enroll, in the class. Include reasons from your list and examples from the article.

**Ask Questions**

Possible responses: What do students do in forensics classes? What other schools have classes like this? What experts come and talk to the students?

## Fluency Assessment Plan

☑ **Week 1** Assess Advanced students.

☑ **Week 2** Assess Strategic Intervention students.

☑ **Week 3** Assess On-Level students.

☑ **Week 4** Assess Strategic Intervention students.

☑ **This week assess any students you have not yet checked during this unit.**

Set individual goals for students to enable them to reach the year-end goal.
- Current Goal: 110–120 WCPM
- Year-End Goal: 130 WCPM

Provide opportunities for English language learners to read aloud to younger children. This allows them to practice their oral reading and improve their fluency.

To develop fluent readers, use Fluency Coach.

### DAY 5 — Grouping Options

**Reading**

**Whole Group**
Revisit the Question of the Week.

**Small Group**
**Differentiated Instruction**
**Reread** this week's Leveled Readers. See pp. 488f–488g for the small group lesson plan.

**Whole Group**
Use p. 507b–507c.

**Language Arts**
Use pp. 507d–507l.

---

## CHARACTERIZATION/DIALOGUE
# Fluency

### DAY 1

**Model** Reread aloud "The Clever Magistrate" on p. 488m. Explain that you will read dialogue to express each character's personality and emotions and to make the dialogue sound the way real people speak. Model as you read.

### DAY 2

**Echo Reading** Read aloud p. 496, paragraphs 5–9, conveying Chief Brown's frustration about the unsolved case and Mrs. Brown's surprise at the salamander's value. Practice as a class by doing three echo readings.

### DAY 3

**Model** Read aloud p. 499, paragraphs 4–10. Have students notice how your voice reflects Encyclopedia's feelings of excitement and triumph when he solves the case. Practice as a class by doing three echo readings.

### DAY 4

**Partner Reading** Partners practice reading aloud p. 499, paragraphs 4–10, three times. They should read dialogue dramatically, showing Encyclopedia's personality and emotions and provide each other feedback.

### Monitor Progress | Check Fluency WCPM

As students reread, monitor their progress toward their individual fluency goals. Current Goal: 110–120 words correct per minute. End-of-Year Goal: 130 words correct per minute.

**If...** students cannot read fluently at a rate of 110–120 words correct per minute,
**then...** make sure students practice with text at their independent level. Provide additional fluency practice, pairing nonfluent readers with fluent readers.

**If...** students already read at 130 words correct per minute,
**then...** they do not need to reread three to four times.

SUCCESS PREDICTOR

### DAY 5

**Assessment**
**Individual Reading Rate** Use the Fluency Assessment Plan and do a one-minute timed reading of either selection from this week to assess students in week 5. Pay special attention to this week's skill, characterization/dialogue. Provide corrective feedback for each student.

## RETEACH

# Literary Elements/Plot

## TEACH

Review the definitions of *plot, problem, rising action, climax,* and *resolution* on p. 488. Students can complete Practice Book p. 198 on their own or as a class. Discuss the plot diagram on the Practice Book page. Point out that the information in the boxes is incomplete. Students will complete each sentence by summarizing part of the plot.

## ASSESS

Have students review the action in *Encyclopedia Brown and the Case of the Slippery Salamander* and identify the climax of the story. *(On p. 499, Encyclopedia declares that Sam Maine is lying and he can prove it.)*

For additional instruction of plot, see DI·56.

## EXTEND SKILLS

# Idioms

## TEACH

An idiom is a phrase or expression whose meaning cannot be understood from the ordinary meaning of the words that form it.

- Context clues will sometimes help you figure out the meaning of an idiom.
- Some idioms can be found in a dictionary by looking up a keyword contained in the idiom.

Have students read the last paragraph on p. 494. Ask the meaning of the sentence: "But so far they hadn't leaked a word." *(They hadn't spoken about it.)* Ask what clues in the paragraph could help them figure out the meaning. *(The Browns didn't like to boast, but they were tempted to tell the world.)*

## ASSESS

Have students write a paragraph in which they use three idioms. Students could work in small groups first to brainstorm idioms. If they have a difficult time thinking of idioms, suggest: *put up with, take charge, I'm all ears, change your mind, give someone a hand,* or *make up your mind.*

---

## OBJECTIVES

- Recognize plot structure.
- Use context clues to figure out the meaning of idioms.

### Skills Trace

#### Literary Elements: Plot

| | |
|---|---|
| Introduce/Teach | TE: 4.4 440–441, 488–489; 4.6 686–687 |
| Practice | TE: 171, 449, 455, 459, 497, 693, 699, 703 PB: 173, 177, 178, 193, 197, 198, 273, 277, 278 |
| Reteach/Review | **TE: 4.2 171; 4.4 401, 465b, 507b, DI•54, DI•56; 4.5 621; 4.6 711b, DI•54** |
| Test | Selection Test: 69–72, 77–80, 109–112; Benchmark Test: Unit 4 |

## ELL

**Access Content** Reteach the skill by reviewing the Picture It! lesson on plot in the ELL Teaching Guide, pp. 134–135.

---

**Literary Elements • Plot**

- A **plot,** or underlying story structure, is found only in fiction.
- A plot begins when a character has a problem or **conflict.** The problem builds up during the **rising action,** is met directly at the **climax,** and comes to an end, with the action winding down, during the **resolution.**

**Directions** Read the following passage. Then complete the diagram below.

Brett, Tyrelle, and Jon were racing imaginary cars. Their "cars" were really water bottles, and the "track," the slide in Tyrelle's backyard. After a few races, the boys were puzzled. Brett won every race. What was Brett's secret?
   When Ted came over, Tyrelle and Jon asked Ted if he could solve the mystery.

"I know!" Ted said. "Brett's bottle is empty. Tyrelle's and Jon's still have some water in them. The heavier bottles create more friction, which slows them down. Brett's bottle weighs less and creates less friction. That's why he wins." Brett admitted his secret was out.

| | |
|---|---|
| Problem ↓ | 1. The boys couldn't understand why Brett won every race. |
| Rising Action ↓ | Brett wouldn't tell his secret. |
| Rising Action ↓ | 2. The boys asked Ted to solve the mystery. |
| Climax ↓ | 3. Ted figured out why Brett won. |
| Resolution | 4. Brett admitted his secret. |

5. Explain how the problem in this story is solved.
   Possible answer: Ted explains that because Brett's bottle creates less friction, it goes faster.

**School + Home** Home Activity Your child read a short passage and identified its plot structure. With your child, read a story about someone who solves a problem. Ask your child to identify the problem, rising action, climax, and resolution in the story.

▲ **Practice Book** p. 198

# Vocabulary and Word Study

## VOCABULARY STRATEGY

### Context Clues

**SYNONYMS AND ANTONYMS** Review the meanings of *synonym* and *antonym*. Remind students that a synonym or an antonym may appear as a context clue near an unfamiliar word. Have students reread the last paragraph on p. 494 and look for a synonym for the word *leaked.* (*tell*) Then have pairs choose other story words, use a thesaurus to find a synonym and antonym for each word, and write sentences that include the story word and a synonym or antonym. Pairs can exchange sentences and identify the synonym or antonym and the word it helps define.

| Word | Synonym/Antonym | Sentence |
|---|---|---|
| stumped | puzzled/sure | I was *stumped*, and the chief looked just as *puzzled*. |
| | | |

## BUILD CONCEPT VOCABULARY
## Puzzles and Mysteries

**LOOKING BACK** Discuss the Big Idea question with students: *Is there an explanation for everything?* Then ask students how the concept vocabulary from each week of this unit relates to the unit theme of *Puzzles and Mysteries* and the Big Idea question. Ask students if they have any words or categories to add to this week's Concept Web. If time permits, create a Unit Concept Web

## Animal Classifications

Have students reread p. 500 and point out that lizards are classified as *reptiles* and salamanders are classified as *amphibians*. Discuss other animal groupings and examples for each group such as those listed below. Create a class chart and have students illustrate it.

**Reptiles:** lizards, snakes, alligators, crocodiles, turtles
**Amphibians:** salamanders, newts, frogs, toads
**Insects:** ants, bees, flies, butterflies, grasshoppers
**Arachnids:** spiders, scorpions, mites, ticks
**Mammals:** monkeys, cats, dogs, whales, dolphins
**Fishes:** sharks, rays, eels, perch, trout
**Birds:** ducks, geese, swans, owls, hawks, eagles, pigeons
**Crustaceans:** crabs, lobsters, shrimp

### Monitor Progress
#### Check Vocabulary

| **If...** students suggest words or categories that are not related to the concept, | **then...** review the words and categories on the Concept Web and discuss how they relate to the lesson concept. |
|---|---|

SUCCESS PREDICTOR

# Speaking and Viewing

## SPEAKING

## Newscast

**SET-UP** Have students investigate a problem and prepare an oral news report to tell about it. Discuss the role of investigative reporters. They find problems, explore their causes and effects, and suggest possible solutions to correct the problems. Students can work alone, in pairs, or as part of an investigative team.

**TOPICS** Suggest students focus on a problem at school. Help them brainstorm ideas, such as slow lines in the cafeteria, litter on school property, or insufficient technology resources.

**RESEARCH** Have students interview teachers, school staff, parents, or other students to gather information related to the problem. They could also conduct an Internet search to learn if other schools have experienced and successfully solved similar problems.

### Delivery Tips
- Identify the problem at the beginning of the news report.
- Provide specific examples of negative effects the problem causes.
- Conclude by suggesting one or two possible solutions.

## VIEWING

## Analyze Media

Have students form discussion groups to talk about an episode of a TV series or a movie they have watched recently. Have students think about the main problem of the episode or movie and how it was resolved. Groups can then work together to answer the following questions:

1. **What was the main problem?** *(Responses will vary.)*

2. **Was the problem solved right away or did other events happen first? Why do you think the episode or movie was organized this way?** *(Problems are usually solved near the end of a show or movie. Taking time to solve the problem and presenting complications usually increases tension and makes stories more interesting.)*

3. **How was the problem finally solved?** *(Responses will vary.)*

4. **Were you surprised by the solution? Why or why not?** *(For some genres like mysteries, endings may be intentionally surprising. Other genres may have more predictable resolutions.)*

**ELL**

**Support Vocabulary** Use the following to review and extend vocabulary and to explore lesson concepts further:
- ELL Poster 20, Days 3–5 instruction
- Vocabulary Activities and Word Cards in ELL Teaching Guide, pp. 136–137

**Assessment** For information on assessing students' speaking, listening, and viewing, see the ELL and Transition Handbook.

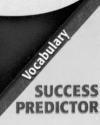

Vocabulary

**SUCCESS PREDICTOR**

# Grammar  Contractions and Negatives

## OBJECTIVES

- Define and identify contractions and negatives.
- Learn how to form contractions and negatives.
- Use contractions and negatives correctly in writing.
- Become familiar with contractions and negatives assessment on high-stakes tests.

### Monitor Progress

**Grammar**

| | |
|---|---|
| **If...** students have difficulty identifying contractions and negatives, | **then...** provide additional instruction and practice in The Grammar and Writing Book pp. 164–167. |

### DAILY FIX-IT

This week use Daily Fix-It Transparency 20.

 Spiral REVIEW

### ELL

**Grammar Support** See the Grammar Transition lessons in the ELL and Transition Handbook.

▲ **The Grammar and Writing Book**
For more instruction and practice, use pp. 164–167.

---

## DAY 1  Teach and Model

### DAILY FIX-IT

1. I was unware that salamanders and lizard's looked so similar. *(unaware; lizards)*

2. A salamander's skin is damp, a lizard's is'nt. *(damp. A; isn't)*

### READING-GRAMMAR CONNECTION

Write the following sentence from *Encyclopedia Brown* on the board:

> If <u>he's</u> a lizard expert, then <u>I'm</u> the Queen of England!

Point out that *he's* and *I'm* are **contractions.** Each contraction is made up of two words (*he is* and *I am*), with one letter replaced by an apostrophe.

Display Grammar Transparency 20. Read aloud the definitions and sample sentences. Work through the items.

#### Contractions and Negatives

A **contraction** is a shortened form of two words. An apostrophe takes the place of one or more letters. Some contractions are formed from a pronoun and a verb: *she is* = *she's.* Other contractions combine a verb and the word *not: would not* = *wouldn't.*

**Contractions with Pronouns and Verbs**

| I am | I'm | he is (has) | he's | she is (has) | she's |
|---|---|---|---|---|---|
| it is (has) | it's | you are | you're | we are | we're |
| they are | they're | I will | I'll | he will | he'll |
| she will | she'll | you will | you'll | we will | we'll |
| they will | they'll | I had (would) | I'd | he had (would) | he'd |
| she had (would) | she'd | you had (would) | you'd | I have | I've |
| you have | you've | we have | we've | they have | they've |

**Contractions with Verbs and *not***

| is not | isn't | are not | aren't | was not | wasn't |
|---|---|---|---|---|---|
| were not | weren't | has not | hasn't | have not | haven't |
| did not | didn't | does not | doesn't | will not | won't |
| would not | wouldn't | could not | couldn't | should not | shouldn't |
| cannot | can't | | | | |

**Directions** Write the contractions for the underlined words.

1. Chief Brown is <u>not</u> happy.  **isn't**
2. <u>He is</u> having difficulty solving a case.  **He's**
3. <u>It is</u> about a missing salamander.  **It's**

**Directions** Find two words in each sentence that can be written as a contraction. Write the contraction.

4. I have read another *Encyclopedia Brown* story.  **I've**
5. I could not guess what was going to happen.  **couldn't**
6. That boy did not have any difficulties.  **didn't**

Unit 4 Encyclopedia Brown  Grammar **20**

▲ **Grammar Transparency** 20

---

## DAY 2  Develop the Concept

### DAILY FIX-IT

3. Is it unfare to keep animals in captivity. *(unfair; captivity?)*

4. Some animal's dont seem to mind being in cages. *(animals don't)*

### GUIDED PRACTICE

Review the concept of contractions and negatives.

- A **contraction** is a shortened form of two words with an apostrophe taking the place of one or more letters.

- Contractions may be formed from a pronoun and a verb (*I + am = I'm*).

- Contractions may also be formed from a verb and the word *not* (*is + not = isn't*).

**HOMEWORK** Grammar and Writing Practice Book p. 77. Work through the first two items with the class.

#### Contractions and Negatives

A **contraction** is a shortened form of two words. An apostrophe takes the place of one or more letters. Some contractions are formed from a pronoun and a verb: *she is* = *she's.* Other contractions combine a verb and the word *not: would not* = *wouldn't.*

| **Contractions with Pronouns and Verbs** | | | | **Contractions with Verbs and *not*** | |
|---|---|---|---|---|---|
| I am | I'm | she will | she'll | is not | isn't |
| he is (has) | he's | you will | you'll | are not | aren't |
| she is (has) | she's | we will | we'll | was not | wasn't |
| it is (has) | it's | they will | they'll | were not | weren't |
| you are | you're | I had (would) | I'd | has not | hasn't |
| we are | we're | he had (would) | he'd | have not | haven't |
| they are | they're | she had (would) | she'd | did not | didn't |
| I have | I've | you had (would) | you'd | does not | doesn't |
| you have | you've | | | will not | won't |
| we have | we've | | | would not | wouldn't |
| they have | they've | | | could not | couldn't |
| I will | I'll | | | should not | shouldn't |
| he will | he'll | | | cannot | can't |

**Directions** Choose the correct contraction in ( ) to complete each sentence. Write the contraction.

1. (She'll, She's) read all the *Encyclopedia Brown* stories later.  **She'll**
2. (I'd, I'm) like to borrow a book from her.  **I'd**
3. I hear that (there, they're) all interesting.  **they're**
4. (Its, It's) hard to believe that anyone could be that smart!  **It's**
5. I (don't, hasn't) think I could be a detective.  **don't**

**Home Activity** Your child learned about contractions and negatives. Ask your child to show you how an apostrophe can make two words become one word. Encourage him or her to use contractions in oral sentences.

▲ **Grammar and Writing Practice Book** p. 77

---

# DAY 3 — Apply to Writing

## DAILY FIX-IT

5. Mouses seems perfectly happy as pets. *(Mice; seem)*

6. Im not so sure large animals, such as bears and mooses, enjoy zoos. *(I'm; moose)*

## CONTRACTIONS

Explain that using contractions makes writing sound like natural speech. Have students say these sentences: *I am glad he is here. I'm glad he's here.* Help students hear how the second sentence sounds more informal and natural than the first sentence.

• Have students review something they have written to see if they can use contractions to make their writing sound more like natural speech.

**HOMEWORK** Grammar and Writing Practice Book p. 78.

### Contractions and Negatives

**Directions** Complete the paragraph with contractions from the box.

isn't   won't   there's   We're   she'd   It's   he'd   he's

**1.** ___ trying to solve a mystery. **2.** Why ___ our cat behaving normally? **3.** ___ been staring out the window and yowling all evening. **4.** My mom said that ___ have to put the cat in the basement if it kept making that noise. **5.** My dad said ___ give it away. **6.** My brother told me that ___ a spaceship outside and that only the cat can see it! **7.** I think ___ making that up! **8.** At this rate, we ___ get much sleep.

1. __We're__   5. __he'd__
2. __isn't__   6. __there's__
3. __It's__   7. __he's__
4. __she'd__   8. __won't__

**Directions** Write a paragraph about something you hope to do in the next few days. Use at least three of the contractions in the box. Underline all the contractions you use.

I'm   she'll   we're   he's   isn't   can't   aren't   won't

Possible answer:

I'm trying to get some friends to come to my house. Jen says she isn't free on Friday, but she'll be able to come on Saturday. I've also asked Paula and Maria. They'll let me know later.

**Home Activity** Your child learned how to use contractions in writing. Ask your child to write an e-mail to a friend or family member, using contractions. Have your child show you the contractions he or she used.

▲ **Grammar and Writing Practice Book** p. 78

---

# DAY 4 — Test Preparation

## DAILY FIX-IT

7. When I visit a new city I always see if there's a aquarium. *(city,; an)*

8. I gone to one in florida last year. *(went; Florida)*

## STANDARDIZED TEST PREP

### Test Tip

Most contractions formed from a verb and the word *not* have an apostrophe in place of the *o* in *not* but no other letter changes: *isn't, aren't, don't, doesn't, wasn't, weren't, couldn't, shouldn't.* However, there are two exceptions: *will not = won't; cannot = can't.*

**HOMEWORK** Grammar and Writing Practice Book p. 79.

### Contractions and Negatives

**Directions** Mark the letter of the contraction that correctly completes each sentence.

1. ___ investigating a crime.
   A We're
   B We've
   C We'd
   D Were

2. It ___ be difficult to solve.
   A wont
   B won't
   C willn't
   D weren't

3. ___ got a kit for testing blood.
   A Shes
   B Shees
   C Shes'
   D She's

4. ___ fun being a policeman.
   A Its
   B Its'
   C It's
   D Itz

5. Criminals ___ have a chance against us.
   A don't
   B d'ont
   C dont
   D do'nt

6. ___ all be behind bars.
   A There'll
   B Theyll
   C They'll
   D Theyul

7. ___ going to be a detective.
   A I'd
   B Im
   C I'm
   D I'll

8. I ___ wait for my first case.
   A cann't
   B cant
   C cant'
   D can't

**Home Activity** Your child prepared for taking tests on contractions. Have your child look through advertisements in magazines or newspapers. Ask him or her to highlight the contractions and tell you what words they stand for.

▲ **Grammar and Writing Practice Book** p. 79

---

# DAY 5 — Cumulative Review

## DAILY FIX-IT

9. John loves snakes but hes' afraid of spiders. *(snakes, but he's)*

10. Lizard's look like dinosaurs, but their a lot smaller. *(Lizards; they're)*

## ADDITIONAL PRACTICE

Assign pp. 164–167 in The Grammar and Writing Book.

**EXTRA PRACTICE** Grammar and Writing Practice Book p. 141.

**TEST PREPARATION** Grammar and Writing Practice Book pp. 155–156.

## ASSESSMENT

**CUMULATIVE REVIEW** Grammar and Writing Practice Book p. 80.

### Contractions and Negatives

**Directions** Choose the correct contraction in ( ) to complete each sentence. Write the contraction.

1. There (isn't, doesn't) an aquarium in our town. __isn't__
2. (I'll, I've) been to the aquarium in Boston. __I've__
3. (It's, Its) right on the waterfront. __It's__
4. (They've, They're) got a huge tank full of sharks and rays. __They've__
5. I looked for a dolphin, but I (don't, didn't) see one. __didn't__
6. Next time we visit, (we're, we'd) going on a whale watch. __we're__

**Directions** Find two words in each sentence that can be written as a contraction. Write the sentence using the contraction.

7. I am reading a book about amphibians.
   I'm reading a book about amphibians.
8. It is very interesting.
   It's very interesting.
9. Amphibians are not reptiles.
   Amphibians aren't reptiles.
10. They do not have dry skin.
   They don't have dry skin.
11. They should not live far from water.
   They shouldn't live far from water.
12. Maybe you would like to borrow the book.
   Maybe you'd like to borrow the book.

**Home Activity** Your child reviewed contractions and negatives. Ask your child to say "stop" every time he or she hears you use a contraction in conversation. Have your child identify the words that make up each contraction.

▲ **Grammar and Writing Practice Book** p. 80

*Encyclopedia Brown and the Case of the Slippery Salamander*   **507f**

# Writing for Tests  Plot Summary

## OBJECTIVES

● Write a plot summary for a test.
● Identify key words in a prompt.
● Focus on organization/paragraphs.
● Use a rubric.

**Genre** Plot Summary
**Writer's Craft** Eliminate Wordiness
**Writing Trait** Organization/Paragraphs

**Organization/Paragraphs** Explain that transition words make order clear in writing. Write *first, next, then, after, before, also,* and *but* on index cards, one to a card, and model their meaning and use. Help language learners use these transition words in their writing.

## Writing Traits

**IDEAS/FOCUS** The plot is clearly described. The summary succeeds in its purpose of informing the reader.

**ORGANIZATION/PARAGRAPHS** The summary closely follows the plot. There is a paragraph for each important section.

**VOICE** The writer tells the story with enthusiasm and clearly intends to interest the reader.

**WORD CHOICE** Lively language (*brainy*) matches the enthusiastic voice.

**SENTENCES** An exclamatory sentence lightens the style. Sentences vary in length, as in natural speech.

**CONVENTIONS** The summary is free of technical errors.

### READING-WRITING CONNECTION

• When you write a response for tests, remember that clear organization will strengthen your answer.

• Think about how the story *Encyclopedia Brown* is organized to tell the story in a logical order.

**MODEL ORGANIZATION/PARAGRAPHS**
Discuss Writing Transparency 20A. Then discuss the model and the writing trait of organization/paragraphs.

 I see that this plot summary is organized into paragraphs. The very first sentence gives us the main idea of the beginning of the story. "Chief of Police Brown has a problem." The paragraph goes on to describe the events of the story in order. The last sentence sums up the ending. "As usual Encyclopedia Brown has the answer." The plot summary clearly tells me what happened when in the story.

### WRITER'S CRAFT
**Eliminate Wordiness**

Display Writing Transparency 20B. Read the directions and work together to practice eliminating wordiness.

 **ELIMINATE WORDINESS**
Tomorrow we will be writing a plot summary of a favorite story. A summary is shorter than the actual story. It is important to be brief, not wordy. Usually, people want a summary because they do not have time to read the whole story. I will practice communicating ideas with only a few words.

**GUIDED WRITING** Challenge students to write directions for getting from one part of town (or school) to another. Work with students to create the briefest, most accurate set of directions.

---

### Writing for Tests

**Prompt** Write a brief plot summary of a book or movie that you have enjoyed. Tell a friend what happens in the book or movie. Include the important details in the summary. Leave out unnecessary information.

#### Encyclopedia Brown

Introduction briefly describes the problem.
> Chief of Police Brown has a problem. He needs to know who has stolen the valuable tiger salamander from the Idaville Aquarium. Chief Brown turns to his brainy son Leroy—known as Encyclopedia—for help. One of the suspects is Sam Maine. Sam has only recently been hired, but he claims to have been "taking care of salamanders and

Summary quotes directly from story to give an important clue.
> other lizards for more than nineteen years."

Solution includes only necessary information.
> This statement makes Encyclopedia suspicious. If Sam really knew his salamanders, he wouldn't have said they were lizards. Salamanders are not lizards! If Sam can lie about a former job, he can lie about the crime.

As usual, Encyclopedia has the answer.

Unit 4 Encyclopedia Brown          **Writing Model 20A**

▲ **Writing Transparency** 20A

---

### Eliminate Wordiness

Contractions are one way to **eliminate wordiness.** Also, you can drop awkward phrases or replace them with a word or two (*sadly* for *with great sadness; red* for *red in color; if* for *in the event that; because* for *due to the fact that, the reason was because,* or *on account of*).

| | |
|---|---|
| Wordy | The reason he was puzzled was because he could not solve the case. |
| Improved | He was puzzled because he couldn't solve the case. |
| Wordy | Encyclopedia Brown solved the case with great cleverness. |
| Improved | Encyclopedia Brown cleverly solved the case. |
| Wordy | Call Encyclopedia Brown in the event that you need help. |
| Improved | Call Encyclopedia Brown if you need help. |

**Directions** Improve the sentences by making the underlined phrases less wordy. Rewrite each sentence.

1. Ed looked up at the sky, which was gray in color.
   Ed looked up at the gray sky.

2. He thought it might snow on account of the fact that it was so cold.
   He thought it might snow because it was so cold.

3. In the event that the weather is bad, his party might be canceled.
   If the weather is bad, his party might be canceled.

4. Suddenly, the clouds blew away, and the sun shone down in a warm way.
   Suddenly, the clouds blew away, and the sun shone down warmly.

5. Ed grinned with a lot of cheerfulness and ran home.
   Ed grinned cheerfully and ran home.

**Directions** Write an e-mail of three or four sentences to a friend, explaining why he or she should read an *Encyclopedia Brown* story. Avoid wordiness.

Possible answer: You should read *Encyclopedia Brown* stories because they are exciting. The hero is very smart, and you can learn things from him. For example, I learned that salamanders aren't lizards!

Unit 4 Encyclopedia Brown          **Writer's Craft 20B**

▲ **Writing Transparency** 20B

# DAY 3 Prewrite and Draft

## READ THE WRITING PROMPT

*The plot of* Encyclopedia Brown *includes a problem, rising action, a climax, and resolution.*

*Think about the plot of a book or movie.*

*Now write a plot summary explaining what happened in that book or movie.*

### Writing Test Tips

1. **Read the prompt carefully.**
   - Find key words.
   - Consider your purpose and audience.
2. **Develop a plan.** Think about what you want to say before writing. Fill out a graphic organizer, such as a story sequence chart showing beginning, middle, and end or a T-chart for a comparison/contrast essay.
3. **Support your ideas.** Use facts, examples, and details to strengthen your response. Avoid making general statements that are unsupported.
4. **Use a variety of sentence structures.** Include complex and compound sentences, sentences with varied beginnings, and sentences of different lengths and types.
5. **Choose clear, precise words.** Use words that create pictures and help readers understand what you mean.
6. **Check your writing.** If this is a timed test, neatly add, delete, or change words and make corrections in spelling, punctuation, or grammar instead of recopying. Make sure your handwriting is legible. Reread your work before handing it in.

# DAY 4 Draft and Revise

## EDITING/REVISING CHECKLIST

☑ **Focus** Do sentences stick to the topic of the story being summarized?

☑ **Organization** Is summary developed in a logical, sequential order with transition words?

☑ **Support** Do specific words make the summary informative? Is the voice objective?

☑ **Conventions** Have I indented correctly to make my organization clear? Did I use apostrophes with contractions? Have I used correct punctuation and capitalization to make the summary easy to follow?

**ASSESSMENT Use the scoring rubric to evaluate students' work.**

# DAY 5 Connect to Unit Writing

| Story | |
|-------|---|
| Week 1 | Story About a Discovery 415g–415h |
| Week 2 | Travel Brochure 439g–439h |
| Week 3 | Business Letter 465g–465h |
| Week 4 | Feature Story 487g–487h |
| Week 5 | Plot Summary 507g–507h |

## PREVIEW THE UNIT PROMPT

*Write a story about something that happens on a real or an imaginary trip. Try to include suspense or humor and dialogue.*

### APPLY

- A story has a beginning, middle, and end and focuses on one incident or event.
- Writers of good stories avoid using unnecessary words.

## Writing Trait Rubric

| | 4 | 3 | 2 | 1 |
|---|---|---|---|---|
| **Organization/ Paragraphs** | Organization clear; main idea for each paragraph | Organization generally clear; some confusion | Organization unclear | No organization; paragraphs nonexistent |
| | Plot summary easy to follow | Plot summary generally easy to follow | Plot summary difficult to follow | Plot summary impossible to follow |

# Spelling & Phonics Prefixes *un-*, *dis-*, and *in-*

## OBJECTIVE

● Spell words with the prefixes *un-*, *dis-*, and *in-*.

### Generalization

**Connect to Phonics** When adding prefixes *un-*, *dis-*, and *in-*, make no change in the base word: *discount, uncertain, incomplete*. Adding these prefixes does not, therefore, change the sound of the base word.

### Spelling Words

| | |
|---|---|
| 1. distrust | 11. unopened |
| 2. uncertain | 12. disrespect |
| 3. incomplete | 13. unimportant |
| 4. unlikely* | 14. unlisted |
| 5. unfair | 15. disrepair |
| 6. discontinue | 16. inability |
| 7. unaware | 17. disapprove |
| 8. disorder | 18. unsolved |
| 9. discount | 19. disobey |
| 10. indirect | 20. unsuspecting |

### Challenge Words

| | |
|---|---|
| 21. disintegrate | 24. unappetizing |
| 22. disillusioned | 25. intolerant |
| 23. unconscious | |

*Word from the selection

**Spelling/Phonics Support** See the ELL and Transition Handbook for spelling support.

---

## DAY 1 Pretest and Sort

### PRETEST

Use the Dictation Sentences from Day 5 to administer the pretest. Read the word, read the sentence, and then read the word again. Guide students in self-correcting their pretests and correcting any misspellings.

#### Monitor Progress

**Spelling**

| | |
|---|---|
| **If...** students misspell more than 5 pretest words, | **then...** use words 1–10 for Strategic Intervention. |
| **If...** students misspell 1–5 pretest words, | **then...** use words 1–20 for On-Level practice. |
| **If...** students correctly spell all pretest words, | **then...** use words 1–25 for Advanced Learners. |

**HOMEWORK** Spelling Practice Book, p. 77.

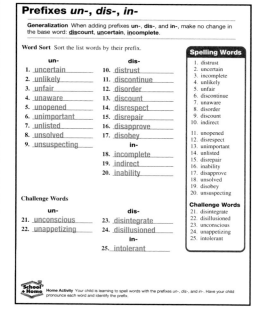

▲ **Spelling Practice Book** p. 77

---

## DAY 2 Think and Practice

### TEACH

When adding prefixes *un-*, *dis-*, and *in-*, make no change in the base word. Write the words *uncertain, distrust*, and *incomplete* on the board. Point out that the spelling of the base words does not change when the prefix is added. Guide students in applying this rule to other spelling words.

uncertain   distrust
incomplete

**USE A DICTIONARY** Ask students to look up a spelling word in a dictionary and find other words with the same prefix.

**HOMEWORK** Spelling Practice Book, p. 78.

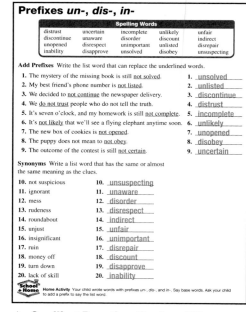

▲ **Spelling Practice Book** p. 78

---

# DAY 3 Connect to Writing

## WRITE AN INVITATIION

Ask students to write an invitation to some fictional event using at least four of the spelling words. The event might be a birthday party, a dinner, or any social gathering.

### Frequently Misspelled Words

*until*    *into*

These words may seem easy to spell, but they are frequently misspelled by fourth-graders. Alert students to these frequently misspelled words.

**HOMEWORK** Spelling Practice Book, p. 79.

**Prefixes *un-*, *dis-*, *in-***

**Proofread a Letter** Circle seven misspelled words in the letter. Write the words correctly. Add the missing punctuation mark.

Dear Mayor␣

It seems that you are ⟨unaware⟩ of the state of the city playground. The workers seem to have ⟨discontined⟩ their work, even though the project is still ⟨incomplete⟩ There is ⟨inorder⟩ everywhere. It appears that you think the needs of children are ⟨immportant⟩ We think it is best that you keep this unsafe place to play ⟨disopened⟩ ⟨untill⟩ everything is fixed.

Yours truly,
The Fourth Grade Class

| Spelling Words |
|---|
| distrust |
| uncertain |
| incomplete |
| unlikely |
| unfair |
| discontinue |
| unaware |
| disorder |
| discount |
| indirect |
| unopened |
| disrespect |
| unimportant |
| unlisted |
| disrepair |
| inability |
| disapprove |
| unsolved |
| disobey |
| unsuspecting |

1. unaware   2. discontinued   3. incomplete
4. disorder   5. unimportant   6. unopened
7. until

**Missing Words** Circle the letter of the word that is spelled correctly. Write it.

8. I love finding bargains at the ___ store.
   A. discont   (B) discount   C. miscount
9. I am ___ of the exact directions to the museum.
   A. uncertan   B. incertain   (C) uncertain
10. In the ___ event of a flood, go up the hill.
    A. unlikly   B. unlikely   C. inlikely
11. Why does your dog always ___ your commands?
    (A) disobey   B. disbayo   C. diobey
12. I have an ___ to keep a knapsack neat and in order.
    A. unability   (B) inability   C. inability

| Frequently Misspelled Words |
|---|
| until |
| into |

8. discount
9. uncertain
10. unlikely
11. disobey
12. inability

**School + Home** **Home Activity** Your child identified misspelled words with prefixes *un-*, *dis-*, and *in-*. Say a prefix and have your child name list words that begin with the prefix.

▲ **Spelling Practice Book** p. 79

# DAY 4 Review

## REVIEW PREFIXES *un-*, *dis-*, *in-*

Have each student create an activity in which the goal is to match a prefix with a base word. They can exchange their activities with a partner to review the spelling words.

### Spelling Strategy
**Problem Parts**

Although other prefixes and suffixes sometimes require changes in the spelling of the base word, *un-*, *dis-*, and *in-* do not.

Urge students to remember this rule when spelling words with prefixes.

**HOMEWORK** Spelling Practice Book, p. 80.

**Prefixes *un-*, *dis-*, *in-***

| Spelling Words | | | |
|---|---|---|---|
| distrust | uncertain | incomplete | unlikely | unfair |
| discontinue | unaware | disorder | discount | indirect |
| unopened | disrespect | unimportant | unlisted | disrepair |
| inability | disapprove | unsolved | disobey | unsuspecting |

**Match** Add a prefix to complete each list word. Write the complete word.

1. ___obey
2. ___listed
3. ___direct
4. ___opened
5. ___trust
6. ___ability
7. ___fair
8. ___repair
9. ___complete
10. ___order

1. disobey
2. unlisted
3. indirect
4. unopened
5. distrust
6. inability
7. unfair
8. disrepair
9. incomplete
10. disorder

**Cryptogram** Complete the words and the grid. The clue letters will help you.

| A | B | C | D | E | F | G | H | I | J | K | L | M | N | O | P | Q | R | S | T | U | V | W | X | Y | Z |
|---|---|---|---|---|---|---|---|---|---|---|---|---|---|---|---|---|---|---|---|---|---|---|---|---|---|
| 12 | 19 | 9 | 7 | 13 | 18 | 11 | 24 | 25 | 6 | 4 | 22 | 14 | 26 | 8 | 16 | 3 | 1 | 23 | 21 | 10 | 20 | 17 | 5 | 15 | 2 |

11. incomplete
12. unimportant
13. unlikely
14. inability
15. unaware
16. disapprove
17. indirect
18. unsolved
19. disrespect
20. unsuspecting

**School + Home** **Home Activity** Your child read, spelled, and wrote words with prefixes *un-*, *dis-*, and *in-*. Look through other printed materials to find more words with these prefixes.

▲ **Spelling Practice Book** p. 80

# DAY 5 Posttest

## DICTATION SENTENCES

1. We distrust someone who is not honest.
2. I am uncertain about the answer.
3. The road work is still incomplete.
4. It is unlikely that it will rain today.
5. The contest was unfair.
6. The store will discontinue that item.
7. Mia was unaware of our plans.
8. My room is in disorder.
9. I got a discount on my ticket.
10. A shy person may be indirect.
11. The gift was unopened.
12. I did not treat you with disrespect.
13. That task is unimportant.
14. Her phone number is unlisted.
15. The car was in a state of disrepair.
16. His inability to swim kept him away from the pool.
17. My mom would disapprove of that game.
18. The puzzle remains unsolved.
19. I would never disobey my parents.
20. She was an unsuspecting victim of my prank.

## CHALLENGE

21. The waves will disintegrate the sand castle.
22. I became disillusioned when I realized the truth.
23. I was completely unconscious of my surroundings.
24. That leftover food looks very unappetizing.
25. That person is intolerant of others.

*Encyclopedia Brown and the Case of the Slippery Salamander*    **507j**

## OBJECTIVES

- Formulate an inquiry question that is connected to this week's lesson focus.
- Effectively and efficiently find, evaluate, and communicate information related to an inquiry question using electronic sources.

| New Literacies | |
| --- | --- |
| Day 1 | **Identify Questions** |
| Day 2 | **Navigate/Search** |
| Day 3 | **Analyze** |
| Day 4 | **Synthesize** |
| Day 5 | **Communicate** |

## NEW LITERACIES

# Internet Inquiry Activity

## EXPLORE SUCCESSFUL PROBLEM SOLVING

Use the following 5-day plan to help students conduct this week's Internet inquiry activity on problem solving. Remind students to follow classroom rules for using the Internet.

### DAY 1

**Identify Questions** Discuss the lesson focus question: *How can attention to detail help solve a problem?* Help students brainstorm ideas for inquiry questions related to problem solving. For example, students might want to learn about how police detectives or FBI agents conduct investigations, how doctors invent vaccines to prevent diseases, or how geniuses such as Einstein worked. Have students work individually, in pairs, or in small groups to write an inquiry question about problem solving.

### DAY 2

**Navigate/Search** Discuss the importance of choosing specific keywords to find helpful Web sites related to inquiry questions. For example, if students want to know how Jonas Salk invented a vaccine to prevent people from getting polio, the keyword *polio* is too broad and will produce too many results. Students can narrow their search using a string of specific keywords such as *Jonas Salk polio vaccine.* Suggest students keep track of keywords that do or don't work well, and help them draw conclusions about effective uses of keywords. By the end of the day, students should have identified a few helpful sites to explore further.

### DAY 3

**Analyze** Have students explore the Web sites identified on Day 2. As they analyze these sites for relevant information, remind them to use note cards or graphic organizers to record their findings and sources.

### DAY 4

**Synthesize** Have students synthesize information gathered on Day 3. Be sure they understand that they will need to integrate information from several sources as they try to answer their inquiry questions.

### DAY 5

**Communicate** Have students share their inquiry results. They can play the role of the problem solver, telling what problem they solved and how they solved it.

# RESEARCH/STUDY SKILLS
# Card Catalog/Database

## TEACH

Ask students how they would find books about salamanders in the library. Explain that a **card catalog** and **library database** provide information to help readers find library books. If possible, visit the school library to show examples of both types of reference tools. Explain these terms:

- A **card catalog** has drawers with cards on each book in the library.
- The cards are organized alphabetically. You can search for a book by **author, title,** or **subject.**
- The **call number** is an identification number that shows where each book is stored on the library shelves.
- A **library database** is the online version of the card catalog.

Have students use a card catalog or library database to answer questions such as these:

1. **Find three books on salamanders. List the title, author, and call number of each book.** *(Responses will vary.)*
2. **Look up the title for one of the books on salamanders. What information is given besides the book's title?** *(Both a card catalog and library database will likely provide the author, illustrator (if any), call number, description, subject, and number of pages. The database may also give the book's status.)*

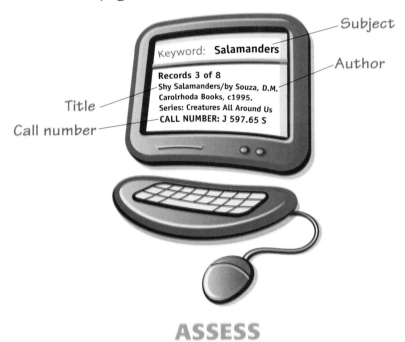

## ASSESS

As students work, check that they can search for books by subject, author, and title and identify a call number. You may wish to have students use a call number to actually find the book in the library.

For more practice or to assess students, use Practice Book pp. 199–200.

### OBJECTIVES

- Review terms associated with a card catalog and library database.
- Use a card catalog and library database to find information.

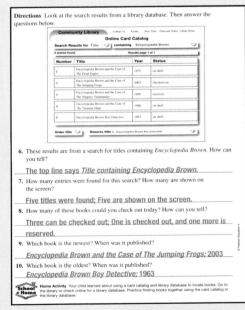

▲ **Practice Book** p. 199

▲ **Practice Book** p. 200

# Assessment Checkpoints *for the Week*

## Selection Assessment

**Use pp. 77–80 of** Selection Tests **to check:**

 **Selection Understanding**

 **Comprehension Skill** *Plot*

 **Selection Vocabulary**

| | |
|---|---|
| amphibians | reference |
| crime | reptiles |
| exhibit | salamanders |
| lizards | stumped |

ASSESSMENT

Scott Foresman
**Selection Tests**
Teacher's Manual

- Assess comprehension of weekly selections
- Assess understanding of weekly comprehension skills
- Assess knowledge of selection vocabulary

Reading STREET Grade 4

## Leveled Assessment

On-Level
Strategic Intervention
Advanced

**Use pp. 115–120 of** Fresh Reads for Differentiated Test Practice **to check:**

 **Comprehension Skill** *Plot*

 **REVIEW Comprehension Skill**
*Compare and Contrast*

 **Fluency** *Words Correct Per Minute*

ASSESSMENT  Teacher's Manual

Scott Foresman
**Fresh Reads**
**for Differentiated Test Practice**

Leveled passages—strategic intervention, on-level, and advanced—for

- Fluency checks
- Practice and application of weekly comprehension skills
- Answer key for all practice pages

Reading STREET Grade 4

## Managing Assessment

**Use** Assessment Handbook **for:**

 **Observation Checklists**

 **Record-Keeping Forms**

 **Portfolio Assessment**

ASSESSMENT

Scott Foresman
**Assessment Handbook**

- Suggestions for preparing students for high-stake tests
- Ideas for classroom-based assessment
- Forms in English and Spanish for students to record interests and progress
- Forms in English and Spanish for teachers to record observations of students' reading and writing abilities and progress
- Assessment and Regrouping charts reproduced from *Reading Street* Teacher's Editions

Reading STREET Grades 3–6

# Unit 4
# Concept Wrap-Up

**CONCEPT QUESTION**

### Is there an explanation for everything?

Students are ready to express their understanding of the unit concept question through discussion and wrap-up activities and to take the Unit 4 Benchmark Test.

## Unit Poetry

Use the poetry on pp. 508–511 to help students appreciate poetry and further explore their understanding of the unit theme, Puzzles and Mysteries. It is suggested that you

- **read the poems aloud**
- **discuss and interpret the poems with students**
- **have students read the poems for fluency practice**
- **have students write interpretive responses**

## Unit Wrap-Up

Use the Unit Wrap-Up on pp. 512–513 to discuss the unit theme, Puzzles and Mysteries, and to have students show their understanding of the theme through cross-curricular activities.

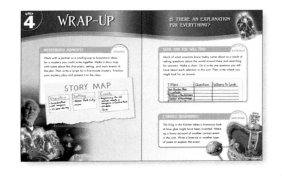

## Unit Project

On p. 391, you assigned students a unit-long inquiry project, a short speech describing a mystery of nature and the scientific explanation or theories for it. Students have investigated, analyzed, and synthesized information during the course of the unit as they prepared their speech. Schedule time for students to give their speeches. The project rubric can be found at the right.

### Unit Inquiry Project Rubric

| 4 | 3 | 2 | 1 |
|---|---|---|---|
| • Research is accurate and very detailed. Sources are reliable and relevant to inquiry question. <br> • Speech on a mystery of nature is informative, well organized, and clearly presented. | • Research is generally accurate and detailed. Most sources are reliable and relevant. <br> • Speech is generally informative and clearly presented, but includes minor inconsistencies in organization. | • Research includes inaccuracies, irrelevant information, or little detail. Some sources are unreliable. <br> • Speech is somewhat informative and organized, but parts are unclear. | • Research is not accurate, detailed, or relevant. Most sources are unreliable. <br> • Speech is incomplete, unclear, or confusing. It shows little or no organization. |

# Unit 4
# Reading Poetry

## OBJECTIVES

- Listen and respond to poems.
- Identify how meaning is conveyed through word choice.
- Read poetry fluently.
- Connect ideas and themes across texts.

## Model Fluent Reading

Read "Who Knows?" aloud. Remind students that people raise the pitch of their voices slightly at the end of questions. Have students notice how you raise your voice at the end of each question.

## Discuss the Poem

**1 Compare and Contrast • Inferential**
**What do the questions the speaker asks have in common?**

Possible responses: They are all about nature. They are all thought-provoking and difficult to answer.

**2 Author's Craft • Critical**
**If no one knows the answers to the speaker's questions, why might he or she ask them?**

Possible response: The speaker might ask such questions to encourage readers to think about the unknown.

## EXTEND SKILLS

### Repetition

Explain that repetition is the use of some aspect of language—sounds, words, thoughts, or sentences—over again, sometimes many times. Discuss how repetition of key words and structures unifies a poem and emphasizes its main idea.

**UNIT 4 Poetry**

## Who Knows?

### by Fatou Ndiaye Sow

Who knows
How many stars
Are in the roof of the sky?
How many fishes
In the deep seas?
How many people
In the whole wide world?
Who knows
Where, every evening
The sun flees to?
**1** Where the moon lights up?
Where dawn starts,
Where the endless horizon ends,
**2** Who knows?... Who knows?

508

## Practice Fluent Reading

Have partners take turns reading "Who Knows?" aloud. Tell students to pay attention to the way the pitch of their voices goes up when they come to a question mark. Then have students listen to the AudioText of the poem and compare and contrast their readings with the CD recording.

**Audio CD** Audio Text

## Poetry

**by Eleanor Farjeon**

What is Poetry? Who knows?
Not a rose, but the scent of the rose;
Not the sky, but the light in the sky;
Not the fly, but the gleam of the fly;
Not the sea, but the sound of the sea; ❶
Not myself, but what makes me
See, hear, and feel something that prose
Cannot: and what it is, who knows? ❷

509

## Model Fluent Reading

Tell students they can use their voices to stress important words in a poem. Read "Poetry" aloud, stressing the words in each line that tell what poetry is: *scent, light, gleam,* and so on.

## Discuss the Poem

**❶ Imagery • Inferential**

**What images does the poet use to define poetry? To which senses does she appeal?**

Possible responses: The poet says poetry is *the scent of the rose* (smell), *the light in the sky* and *gleam of the fly* (sight), and *the sound of the sea* (hearing).

**❷ Compare and Contrast • Literal**

**According to the poet, in what main way does poetry differ from prose?**

Possible response: Poetry helps you see, hear, and feel things in a way that prose cannot.

## WRITING POETRY

Have partners write their own "mystery" poems. Students might want to ponder questions about nature (why the sky is blue), about people (why babies cry), or about life in general (what happiness is). Suggest that students use repetition to emphasize their main idea.

# Unit 4
# Reading Poetry

## Model Fluent Reading

Read "The Seed" aloud. Ask students to listen for your tone of voice as you read. Which emotion are you communicating with your voice?

## Discuss the Poem

**1 Paraphrase • Inferential**

**In your own words, state the question the speaker is asking.**

Possible response: How does a tiny seed know what it is going to become?

**2 Draw Conclusions • Inferential**

**How do you think the speaker feels about the seed? Which words give you a clue about his or her feelings?**

Possible response: The speaker seems impressed by the seed's knowledge and power. He or she wonders how "a seed… so small…stores up all of the things it knows."

## The Seed
### by Aileen Fisher

How does it know,
 this little seed,
  if it is to grow
  to a flower or weed,
  if it is to be
  a vine or shoot,
  or grow to a tree
1  with a long deep root?
 A seed is so small,
 where do you suppose
 it stores up all
2  of the things it knows?

510

## Practice Fluent Reading

Have partners take turns reading "The Seed" aloud. Tell them to read the poem several times, using different tones of voice. Have them discuss which reading best conveys the poet's feelings.

**Audio CD** Audio Text

## Carolyn's Cat

by Constance Kling Levy

1 She's a house cat
pampered like a child,
cuddled and petted
and very well fed,
a stranger
to the wild
outside.
(She's the kind of cat
you'd invite to tea.)

Her life, it seems,
is peaceful and good
with only her house
for a neighborhood:
the plump pillows,
the soft chairs,
the smooth wood.

But I saw her one night
posed perfectly still,
like a china cat,
on the windowsill,
meeting, with moonlike
eyes,
the full moon's glow.

And I think
there are things
about Carolyn's cat
that even Carolyn
doesn't know. 2

511

## WRITING POETRY

Have students work in pairs to write a poem about an animal. What things, such as its looks or behavior, do they know about the animal? What things, such as its thoughts or feelings, might they never know?

## Model Fluent Reading

Read "Carolyn's Cat" aloud. Ask students to listen for the conversational tone as you read the poem. Point out that the speaker sounds as if he or she is revealing something in confidence to the reader.

## Discuss the Poem

**1** Simile • Inferential

**What comparison does the speaker make in the first two lines? What does this tell you about the cat?**

Possible response: The speaker says the cat is "pampered like a child." This tells you the cat is treated very well.

**2** Draw Conclusions • Critical

**What makes the cat appear mysterious to the speaker?**

Possible response: The speaker watches the cat staring at the Moon and realizes that what goes on in the cat's mind is unknown and mysterious.

## Connect Ideas and Themes

Remind students that this unit focuses on whether or not there is an explanation for everything. Have students discuss the topics each poet finds mysterious or puzzling. Ask students to list and discuss things that they wonder about.

# Wrap-Up

- Critically analyze unit theme.
- Connect content across selections.
- Combine content and skills in meaningful activities that build literacy.
- Respond to unit selections through a variety of modalities.

**PUZZLES AND MYSTERIES**

## Discuss the Big Idea

### Is there an explanation for everything?

Write the unit theme and Big Idea question on the board. Ask students to think about the selections they have read in the unit. Discuss how each selection and lesson concept can help them answer the Big Idea question from this unit.

Model this for students by choosing a selection and explaining how the selection and lesson concept address the Big Idea.

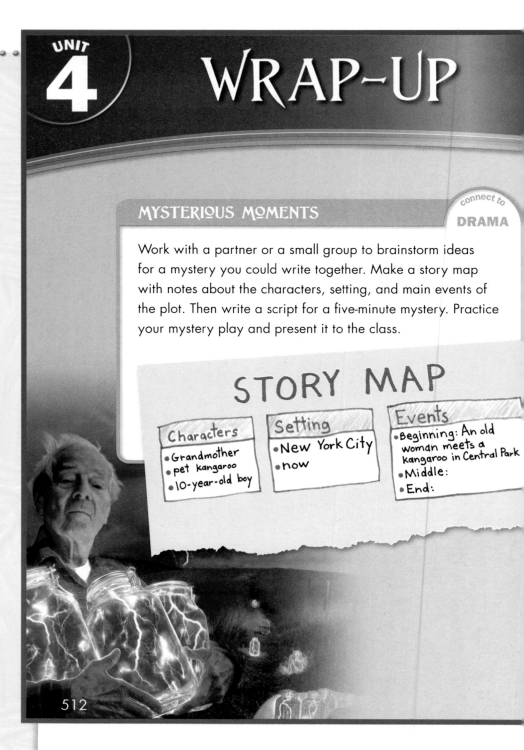

UNIT 4 WRAP-UP

MYSTERIOUS MOMENTS

connect to DRAMA

Work with a partner or a small group to brainstorm ideas for a mystery you could write together. Make a story map with notes about the characters, setting, and main events of the plot. Then write a script for a five-minute mystery. Practice your mystery play and present it to the class.

STORY MAP

Characters
- Grandmother
- pet kangaroo
- 10-year-old boy

Setting
- New York City
- now

Events
- Beginning: An old woman meets a kangaroo in Central Park
- Middle:
- End:

512

# IS THERE AN EXPLANATION FOR EVERYTHING?

## SEEK AND YOU WILL FIND

connect to
**SCIENCE**

Much of what scientists know today came about as a result of asking questions about the world around them and searching for answers. Make a chart. On it write one question you still have about each selection in this unit. Then write where you might look for an answer.

| Titles | Question | Where to Look |
|---|---|---|
| The Houdini Box | | |
| Encantado | | |
| The King in the Kitchen | | |
| Seeker of Knowledge | | |

## CURIOUS BEGINNINGS

connect to
**WRITING**

*The King in the Kitchen* takes a humorous look at how glue might have been invented. Make up a funny account of another curious event in this unit. Write a limerick or another type of poem to explain the event.

## Unit Inquiry Project Rubric

| 4 | 3 | 2 | 1 |
|---|---|---|---|
| • Research is accurate and very detailed. Sources are reliable and relevant to inquiry question.<br>• Speech on a mystery of nature is informative, well organized, and clearly presented. | • Research is generally accurate and detailed. Most sources are reliable and relevant.<br>• Speech is generally informative and clearly presented, but includes minor inconsistencies in organization. | • Research includes inaccuracies, irrelevant information, or little detail. Some sources are unreliable.<br>• Speech is somewhat informative and organized, but parts are unclear. | • Research is not accurate, detailed, or relevant. Most sources are unreliable.<br>• Speech is incomplete, unclear, or confusing. It shows little or no organization. |

# ACTIVITIES

## Mysterious Moments

**Write and Perform a Play** Discuss characteristics of mysteries and plays. Then have students follow the example of a story map in their books as they plan their plays. Tell students that when they write their scripts, they should focus on the characters' dialogue. They should also think about the characters' actions on stage and include stage directions. Students might plan ways to use simple props to enhance their performances.

## Seek and You Will Find

**Ask Questions** Have students skim the selections in the unit and think of a question they have about each one. Guide students to state their questions clearly and concisely on their charts. Point out that the best place to find answers to their questions may be in the selections themselves. Then have them consider print or online sources that would likely have information that answers their questions.

## Curious Beginnings

**Write a Funny Poem** Have students skim the selections for curious events about which they can write. You may wish to review the structure of limericks using the poems on p. 465.

# Glossary

## Page 784

### How to Use This Glossary

This glossary can help you understand and pronounce some of the words in this book. The entries in this glossary are in alphabetical order. There are guide words at the top of each page to show you the first and last words on the page. A pronunciation key is at the bottom of every other page. Remember, if you can't find the word you are looking for, ask for help or check a dictionary.

*The entry word is in dark type. It shows how the word is spelled and how the word is divided into syllables.*

*The pronunciation is in parentheses. It also shows which syllables are stressed.*

*Part-of-speech labels show the function or functions of an entry word and any listed form of that word.*

**an·ces·tor** (an′ses′tər), *NOUN.* person from whom you are descended, such as your great-grandparents: *Their ancestors had come to the United States in 1812.* ❑ *PLURAL* **an·ces·tors.**

*Sometimes, irregular and other special forms will be shown to help you use the word correctly.*

*The definition and example sentence show you what the word means and how it is used.*

784

## Page 785

### Aa

**a·board** (ə bôrd′), *ADVERB.* on board; in or on a ship, train, bus, airplane, etc.: *"All aboard!"* shouted the conductor, and everyone rushed for the train.

**a·bun·dance** (ə bun′dəns), *NOUN.* quantity that is a lot more than enough: *There is an abundance of apples this year.*

**af·ford** (ə fôrd′), *VERB.* to give as an effect or a result; provide; yield: *Reading a good book affords real pleasure.* ❑ *VERB* **af·ford·ed, af·ford·ing.**

**al·ti·tude** (al′tə tüd), *NOUN.* a high place: *At some altitudes, snow never melts.*

**a·maze** (ə māz′), *VERB.* to surprise greatly; strike with sudden wonder; astound: *He was amazed at how different the strand of hair looked under a microscope.* ❑ *VERB* **a·mazed, a·maz·ing.**

**am·phib·i·an** (am fib′ē ən), *NOUN.* any of many cold-blooded animals with backbones and moist, scaleless skins. Their young usually have gills and live in water until they develop lungs for living on land. Frogs, toads, newts, and salamanders are amphibians. ❑ *PLURAL* **am·phib·i·ans.**

**an·ces·tor** (an′ses′tər), *NOUN.* person from whom you are descended, such as your great-grandparents: *Their ancestors had come to the United States in 1812.* ❑ *PLURAL* **an·ces·tors.**

## Page 785 (continued)

**an·cient** (ān′shənt), *ADJECTIVE.* of times long past: *In Egypt, we saw the ruins of an ancient temple built 6000 years ago.* (Ancient comes from the Latin word *ante* meaning "before.")

**an·tic·i·pa·tion** (an tis′ə pā′shən), *NOUN.* act of anticipating; looking forward to; expectation: *In anticipation of a cold winter, they cut extra firewood.*

**ap·pear** (ə pir′), *VERB.* to be seen; come in sight: *One by one, the stars appear.* ❑ *VERB* **ap·peared, ap·pear·ing.**

**a·quar·i·um** (ə kwâr′ē əm), **1.** *NOUN.* tank or glass bowl in which fish or other water animals and water plants are kept in water. **2.** *NOUN.* building used for showing collections of live fish, water animals, and water plants.

**as·tro·naut** (as′trə nôt), *NOUN.* pilot or member of the crew of a spacecraft. ❑ *PLURAL* **as·tro·nauts.**

astronaut

**at·las** (at′ləs), *NOUN.* book of maps.

**a·vi·a·tion** (ā′vē ā′shən), *NOUN.* science or art of operating and navigating aircraft.

**a·vi·a·tor** (av′ē ā′tər), *NOUN.* person who flies an aircraft; pilot.

**a·void** (ə void′), *VERB.* to keep away from; keep out of the way of: *We avoided driving through large cities on our trip.* ❑ *VERB* **a·void·ed, a·void·ing.**

**awk·ward** (ȯk′wərd), *ADJECTIVE.* not easily managed: *This is an awkward corner to turn.*

### Bb

**back·board** (bak′bôrd′), *NOUN.* in basketball, the flat, elevated surface of glass, plastic, or wood, on which the basket is mounted. Bank shots are bounced off the backboard.

**bar·gain** (bär′gən), *NOUN.* agreement to trade or exchange; deal: *You can't back out on our bargain.*

| | | | |
|---|---|---|---|
| a in hat | ō in open | sh in she | |
| ā in age | ȯ in all | th in thin | |
| â in care | ô in order | ᵵH in then | |
| ä in far | oi in oil | zh in measure | |
| e in let | ou in out | ə = a in about | |
| ē in equal | u in cup | ə = e in taken | |
| ėr in term | ú in put | ə = i in pencil | |
| i in it | ü in rule | ə = o in lemon | |
| ī in ice | ch in child | ə = u in circus | |
| o in hot | ng in long | | |

785

## Page 786

**bawl** (bȯl), *VERB.* to shout or cry out in a noisy way: *a lost calf bawling for its mother.* ❑ *VERB* **bawled, bawl·ing.**

**be·wil·der** (bi wil′dər), *VERB.* to confuse completely; puzzle: *bewildered by the confusing instructions.* ❑ *VERB* **be·wil·dered, be·wil·der·ing.**

**bi·ol·o·gist** (bī ol′ə jist), *NOUN.* a scientist who studies living things, including their origins, structures, activities, and distribution.

**bluff¹** (bluf), *NOUN.* a high, steep slope or cliff.

bluff¹

**bluff²** (bluf), *VERB.* to fool or mislead, especially by pretending confidence: *She bluffed the robbers by convincing them that the police were on the way.*

**board·ing school** (bôr′ding skül), *NOUN.* school with buildings where the pupils live during the school term.

**bow¹** (bou), *VERB.* to bend the head or body in greeting, respect, worship, or obedience: *The people bowed before the queen.* ❑ *VERB* **bowed, bow·ing.**

**bow²** (bō), **1.** *NOUN.* weapon for shooting arrows. A bow usually consists of a strip of flexible wood bent by a string. **2.** *NOUN.* a looped knot: *The gift had a bow on top.*

**bow³** (bou), *NOUN.* the forward part of a ship, boat, or aircraft.

**bril·liant** (bril′yənt), *ADJECTIVE.* shining brightly; sparkling: *brilliant sunshine.*

**brisk** (brisk), *ADJECTIVE.* keen; sharp: *A brisk wind was blowing from the north.*

**bus·tle** (bus′əl), *VERB.* to be noisily busy and in a hurry: *The children were bustling to get ready for the party.* ❑ *VERB* **bus·tled, bus·tling.**

### Cc

**can·o·py** (kan′ə pē), *NOUN.* the uppermost layer of branches in forest trees.

**ca·pa·ble** (kā′pə bəl), *ADJECTIVE.* having fitness, power, or ability; able; efficient; competent: *He was such a capable student that everyone had great hopes for his future.*

**cap·sule** (kap′səl), *NOUN.* the enclosed front section of a rocket made to carry instruments, astronauts, etc., into space. In flight, the capsule can separate from the rest of the rocket and go into orbit or be directed back to Earth.

786

## Page 787

**car·go** (kär′gō), *NOUN.* load of goods carried by a ship, plane, or truck: *The freighter had docked to unload a cargo of wheat.*

**ce·les·tial** (sə les′chəl), *ADJECTIVE.* of the sky or outer space: *The sun, moon, planets, and stars are celestial bodies.*

**chant** (chant), *VERB.* to call over and over again: *The football fans chanted, "Go, team, go!"* ❑ *VERB* **chant·ed, chant·ing.**

**cho·rus** (kôr′əs), *NOUN.* anything spoken or sung all at the same time: *The children greeted the teacher with a chorus of "Good morning."*

**cock·pit** (kok′pit′), *NOUN.* the place where the pilot sits in an airplane.

**colo·nel** (kėr′nl), *NOUN.* a military rank below general.

**con·duct** (kon′dukt for noun; kən dukt′ for verb), **1.** *NOUN.* way of acting; behavior thought of as good or bad: *Her conduct was admirable.* **2.** *NOUN.* to direct; manage: *The teacher conducted our efforts.* ❑ *VERB* **con·duct·ed, con·duct·ing.**

conduct (def. 2)

**con·fide** (kən fīd′), *VERB.* to tell as a secret: *He confided his troubles to his brother.* ❑ *VERB* **con·fid·ed, con·fid·ing.**

**con·front** (kən frunt′), *VERB.* to face boldly; oppose: *Once she confronted her problems, she was able to solve them easily.* ❑ *VERB* **con·front·ed, con·front·ing.**

**con·scious** (kon′shəs), *ADJECTIVE.* aware of what you are doing; awake: *About five minutes after fainting, he became conscious again.*

**con·sist** (kən sist′), *VERB.* to be made up of; be formed: *A week consists of seven days.* ❑ *VERB* **con·sist·ed, con·sist·ing.**

**Con·sti·tu·tion** (kon′stə tü′shən), *NOUN.* the written set of fundamental principles by which the United States is governed.

**con·sult** (kən sult′), *VERB.* to seek information or advice from; refer to: *You can consult travelers, books, or maps for help in planning a trip abroad.* ❑ *VERB* **con·sult·ed, con·sult·ing.**

| | | | |
|---|---|---|---|
| a in hat | ō in open | sh in she | |
| ā in age | ȯ in all | th in thin | |
| â in care | ô in order | ᵵH in then | |
| ä in far | oi in oil | zh in measure | |
| e in let | ou in out | ə = a in about | |
| ē in equal | u in cup | ə = e in taken | |
| ėr in term | ú in put | ə = i in pencil | |
| i in it | ü in rule | ə = o in lemon | |
| ī in ice | ch in child | ə = u in circus | |
| o in hot | ng in long | | |

787

**con·ti·nent** (kon′tə nənt), NOUN. one of the seven great masses of land on the Earth. The continents are North America, South America, Europe, Africa, Asia, Australia, and Antarctica. (*Continent* comes from two Latin words, *com* meaning "in" or "together" and *tenere* meaning "to hold.")

**con·trap·tion** (kən trap′shən), NOUN. device or gadget.

**con·ver·gence** (kən vér′jəns), NOUN. act or process of meeting at a point. (*Convergence* comes from two Latin words, *com* meaning "in" or "together" and *vergere* meaning "incline.")

**cord** (kôrd), NOUN. measure of quantity for cut wood, equal to 128 cubic feet. A pile of wood 4 feet wide, 4 feet high, and 8 feet long is a cord.

**cow·ard** (kou′ərd), NOUN. person who lacks courage or is easily made afraid; person who runs from danger, trouble, etc.

**coy·o·te** (ki ō′tē or ki′ōt), NOUN. a small, wolflike mammal living in many parts of North America. It is noted for loud howling at night.

**cra·dle** (krā′dl), NOUN. a frame to support weight.

**crime** (krīm), NOUN. activity of criminals; violation of law: *Police forces combat crime.*

**crum·ble** (krum′bəl), VERB. to fall to pieces; decay: *The old wall was crumbling away at the edges.* ❑ VERB **crum·bled, crum·bling.**

**cur·i·os·i·ty** (kyür′ē os′ə tē), NOUN. an eager desire to know: *She satisfied her curiosity about animals by visiting the zoo every week.* (*Curiosity* comes from the Latin word *cure* meaning "care.")

## Dd

**dan·gle** (dang′gəl), VERB. to hang and swing loosely. ❑ VERB **dan·gled, dan·gling.**

dangle

**dap·pled** (dap′əld), ADJECTIVE. marked with spots; spotted.

**dar·ing** (dãr′ing), ADJECTIVE. bold; fearless; courageous: *Performing on a trapeze high above a crowd is a daring act.*

**de·ci·pher** (di sī′fər), **1.** VERB. to make out the meaning of something that is puzzling or not clear: *I can't decipher this poor handwriting.* **2.** VERB. to change something in cipher or code to ordinary language; decode. ❑ VERB **de·ci·phered, de·ci·pher·ing.**

**de·part** (di pärt′), VERB. to go away; leave: *Your flight departs at 6:15.* ❑ VERB **de·part·ed, de·part·ing.** (*Depart* comes from the Latin word *departire* meaning "to divide.")

**de·pot** (dē′ pō), NOUN. a railroad or bus station.

depot

**des·ti·na·tion** (des′tə nā′shən), NOUN. place to which someone or something is going or is being sent.

**de·struc·tion** (di struk′shən), NOUN. great damage; ruin: *The storm left destruction behind it.*

**dig·ni·fied** (dig′nə fīd), ADJECTIVE. having dignity; noble; stately: *The queen has a dignified manner.*

**dis·may** (dis mā′), NOUN. sudden, helpless fear of what is about to happen or what has happened: *I was filled with dismay when the basement began to flood.*

**dock** (dok), NOUN. platform built on the shore or out from the shore; wharf; pier. Ships load and unload beside a dock. ❑ PLURAL **docks.**

**dol·phin** (dol′fən), NOUN. any of the numerous sea mammals related to the whale, but smaller. Dolphins have beaklike snouts and remarkable intelligence. ❑ PLURAL **dol·phins.**

**dor·mi·to·ry** (dôr′mə tôr′ē), NOUN. a building with many rooms in which people sleep. Many colleges have dormitories for students whose homes are elsewhere.

**drab** (drab), ADJECTIVE. not attractive; dull; monotonous: *the drab houses of the smoky, dingy mining town.*

| a in hat | ō in open | sh in she |
| --- | --- | --- |
| ā in age | ô in all | th in thin |
| â in care | ô in order | ŦH in then |
| ä in far | oi in oil | zh in measure |
| e in let | ou in out | ə = a in about |
| ē in equal | u in cup | ə = e in taken |
| ėr in term | ů in put | ə = i in pencil |
| i in it | ü in rule | ə = o in lemon |
| ī in ice | ch in child | ə = u in circus |
| o in hot | ng in long | |

**draft** (draft), **1.** NOUN. current of air: *I caught cold by sitting in a draft.* **2.** NOUN. a rough copy: *She made two drafts of her book report before she handed in the final form.*

**drag** (drag), **1.** NOUN. the force acting on an object in motion, in a direction opposite to the object's motion. It is produced by friction. **2.** VERB. to pull or move along heavily or slowly; pull or draw along the ground: *We dragged the heavy crates out of the garage. I dragged along on my sprained ankle.* ❑ VERB **dragged, drag·ging.**

**drib·ble** (drib′əl), VERB. to move a ball along by bouncing it or giving it short kicks: *dribble a basketball or soccer ball.* ❑ VERB **drib·bled, drib·bling.**

**dude** (düd), **1.** NOUN. in the western parts of the United States and Canada, person raised in the city, especially an easterner who vacations on a ranch. **2.** NOUN. guy; fellow (slang). ❑ PLURAL **dudes.**

**duke** (dük), NOUN. nobleman of the highest title, ranking just below a prince.

**dun·geon** (dun′jən), NOUN. a dark underground room or cell to keep prisoners in.

**dunk** (dungk), VERB. to shoot a basketball by leaping, so that the hands are above the rim, and throwing the ball down through the netting. ❑ VERB **dunked, dunk·ing.**

**dwell** (dwel), VERB. to make your home; live: *He dwells in the city.* ❑ VERB **dwelled, dwell·ing.**

## Ee

**el·e·gant** (el′ə gənt), ADJECTIVE. having or showing good taste; gracefully and richly refined; beautifully luxurious: *The palace had elegant furnishings.*

**em·bar·rass·ment** (em bar′əs mənt), NOUN. shame; an uneasy feeling: *He blushed in embarrassment at such a silly mistake.*

**en·chant** (en chant′), VERB. to delight greatly; charm: *The music enchanted us all.* ❑ VERB **en·chant·ed, en·chant·ing.** ❑ ADJECTIVE **en·chant·ing.**

**en·coun·ter** (en koun′tər), NOUN. an unexpected meeting: *The explorers had a surprising encounter with a polar bear.*

encounter

**en·dur·ance** (en dúr′əns), NOUN. power to last and to withstand hard wear: *It takes great endurance to run a marathon.*

endurance

**en·grave** (en grāv′), VERB. to cut deeply in; carve in; carve in an artistic way: *The jeweler engraved my initials on the back of the watch.* ❑ VERB **en·graved, en·grav·ing.**

**es·cape** (e skāp′), VERB. to get out and away; get free: *The bird escaped from its cage.* ❑ VERB **es·caped, es·cap·ing.**

**es·cort** (e skôrt′), VERB. to go with another to give protection, show honor, provide companionship, etc. ❑ VERB **es·cort·ed, es·cort·ing.**

**etch** (ech), **1.** VERB. to engrave a drawing or design on a metal plate, glass, etc. **2.** VERB. to impress deeply: *Her face was etched in my memory.* ❑ VERB **etched, etch·ing.**

**ex·e·cute** (ek′sə kyüt′), VERB. to carry out; do: *He executed her instructions.* ❑ VERB **ex·e·cut·ed, ex·e·cut·ing.**

**ex·hale** (eks hāl′), VERB. to breathe out: *We exhale air from our lungs.* ❑ VERB **ex·haled, ex·hal·ing.**

**ex·hib·it** (eg zib′it), NOUN. display or public showing: *The village art exhibit drew 10,000 visitors.*

**ex·ile** (eg′zil or ek′sil), VERB. to be forced to leave your country or home, often by law as a punishment; banish: *Napoleon was exiled to Elba.* ❑ VERB **ex·iled, ex·il·ing.**

**ex·pect** (ek spekt′), VERB. to think something will probably happen: *They expected the hurricane to change directions.* ❑ VERB **ex·pect·ed, ex·pect·ing.**

**ex·po·sure** (ek spō′zhər), NOUN. condition of being without protection; condition of being uncovered.

| a in hat | ō in open | sh in she |
| --- | --- | --- |
| ā in age | ô in all | th in thin |
| â in care | ô in order | ŦH in then |
| ä in far | oi in oil | zh in measure |
| e in let | ou in out | ə = a in about |
| ē in equal | u in cup | ə = e in taken |
| ėr in term | ú in put | ə = i in pencil |
| i in it | ü in rule | ə = o in lemon |
| ī in ice | ch in child | ə = u in circus |
| o in hot | ng in long | |

# Glossary

## Ff

**fas·ci·nate** (fas′n āt), *VERB.* to interest greatly; attract very strongly; charm: *She was fascinated by the designs and colors in African art.* ❑ *VERB* **fas·ci·nat·ed, fas·ci·nat·ing.**

**fa·vor** (fā′vər), *NOUN.* act of kindness: *Will you do me a favor?*

**fee·bly** (fē′blē), *ADVERB.* weakly; without strength: *She walked feebly when she was first recovering from the flu.*

**flex** (fleks), *VERB.* to bend: *She flexed her stiff arm slowly.* ❑ *VERB* **flexed, flex·ing.**

**flex·i·ble** (flek′sə bəl), **1.** *ADJECTIVE.* easily bent; not stiff; bending without breaking: *Leather, rubber, and wire are flexible.* **2.** *ADJECTIVE.* able to change easily to fit different conditions: *My mother works from our home, and her hours are very flexible.*

**flexible** (def. 1)

**for·bid·ding** (fər bid′ing), *ADJECTIVE.* causing fear or dislike; looking dangerous or unpleasant: *The coast was rocky and forbidding.*

**fore·cast** (fôr′kast′), *NOUN.* statement of what is coming; prediction: *What is the weather forecast today?* ❑ *PLURAL* **fore·casts.**

**for·ma·tion** (fôr mā′shən), *NOUN.* series of layers or deposits of the same kind of rock or mineral. ❑ *PLURAL* **for·ma·tions.**

**foul** (foul), *VERB.* to make an unfair play against. ❑ *VERB* **fouled, foul·ing.**

**fra·grant** (frā′grənt), *ADJECTIVE.* having or giving off a pleasing odor; sweet-smelling: *fragrant roses.*

**friend·less** (frend′les), *ADJECTIVE.* to be without people who know and like you.

**frost** (frôst), **1.** *NOUN.* a freezing condition; temperature below the point at which water freezes: *Frost came early last winter.* **2.** *NOUN.* moisture frozen on or in a surface; feathery crystals of ice formed when water vapor in the air condenses at a temperature below freezing: *On cold fall mornings, there is frost on the grass.*

**frus·tra·tion** (fru strā′shən), *NOUN.* a feeling of anger and helplessness, caused by bad luck, failure, or defeat.

**fur·i·ous·ly** (fyur′ē əs lē), *ADVERB.* with unrestrained energy, speed, etc.

792

## Gg

**gash** (gash), *NOUN.* a long, deep cut or wound.

**gen·e·ra·tion** (jen′ə rā′shən), **1.** *NOUN.* all people born about the same time. Your parents and their siblings and cousins belong to one generation; you and your siblings and cousins belong to the next generation. **2.** *NOUN.* about thirty years, or the time from the birth of one generation to the birth of the next generation. There are three generations in a century. ❑ *PLURAL* **gen·e·ra·tions.**

**gen·ius** (jē′nyəs), *NOUN.* person having very great natural power of mind: *Shakespeare was a genius.*

**gla·cier** (glā′shər), *NOUN.* a great mass of ice moving very slowly down a mountain, along a valley, or over a land area. Glaciers are formed from snow on high ground wherever winter snowfall exceeds summer melting for many years.

**gleam** (glēm), *VERB.* to flash or beam with light: *The car's headlights gleamed through the rain.* ❑ *VERB* **gleamed, gleam·ing.**

**glid·er** (glī′dər), *NOUN.* aircraft without an engine. Rising air currents keep it up in the air.

**glider**

**glimpse** (glimps), **1.** *NOUN.* a short, quick view or look: *I caught a glimpse of the falls as our train went by.* **2.** *NOUN.* a short, faint appearance: *There was a glimpse of truth in what they said.* ❑ *PLURAL* **glimp·ses.**

**glint** (glint), *NOUN.* a gleam; flash: *The glint in her eye showed that she was angry.*

**glo·ri·ous** (glôr′ē əs), *ADJECTIVE.* magnificent; splendid: *a glorious day.* (*Glorious* comes from the Latin word *gloria* meaning "praise.")

**grand** (grand), *ADJECTIVE.* excellent; very good: *We had a grand time at the party last night.*

**gran·ite** (gran′it), *ADJECTIVE.* made from a very hard gray or pink rock that is formed when lava cools slowly underground: *a granite countertop.*

**griz·zly** (griz′lē), **1.** *ADJECTIVE.* grayish; gray. **2.** *NOUN.* grizzly bear; a large, gray or brownish gray bear of western North America.

| a in hat | o in open | sh in she |
| ā in age | ō in all | th in thin |
| â in care | ô in order | ᴛʜ in then |
| ä in far | oi in oil | zh in measure |
| e in let | ou in out | ə = a in about |
| ē in equal | u in cup | ə = e in taken |
| ėr in term | u in put | ə = i in pencil |
| i in it | ü in rule | ə = o in lemon |
| ī in ice | ch in child | ə = u in circus |
| o in hot | ng in long | |

793

## Hh

**hang·ar** (hang′ər), *NOUN.* building for storing aircraft. ❑ *PLURAL* **hang·ars.**

**hatch¹** (hach), **1.** *VERB.* to come out of an egg: *One of the chickens hatched today.* **2.** *VERB.* to keep an egg or eggs warm until the young come out: *The heat of the sun hatches turtles' eggs.*

**hatch²** (hach), *NOUN.* a trapdoor covering an opening in an aircraft's or ship's deck.

**heave** (hēv), **1.** *VERB.* to lift with force or effort: *The heavy cargo plane heaved off the runway.* **2.** *VERB.* to rise and fall alternately: *The waves heaved in the storm.* ❑ *VERB* **heaved, heav·ing.**

**her·mit** (hėr′mit), *NOUN.* person who goes away from others and lives alone.

**hi·er·o·glyph** (hī′ər ə glif), *NOUN.* picture, character, or symbol standing for a word, idea, or sound. The ancient Egyptians used hieroglyphics instead of an alphabet like ours. ❑ *PLURAL* **hi·er·o·glyphs.**

**home·land** (hōm′land′), *NOUN.* country that is your home; your native land.

**hoop** (húp or hüp), *NOUN.* ring; round, flat band: *a hoop for embroidery, a basketball hoop.*

**ho·ri·zon** (hə rī′zn), *NOUN.* line where the Earth and sky seem to meet; skyline. You cannot see beyond the horizon.

**howl·ing** (hou′ling), *ADJECTIVE.* very great: *a howling success.*

**hum·ble** (hum′bəl), *ADJECTIVE.* not proud; modest: *to be humble in spite of success.*

**hyp·no·tize** (hip′nə tīz), *VERB.* to put someone into a state resembling deep sleep, but more active, in which the person acts according to the suggestions of the person who brought about the condition. ❑ *VERB* **hyp·no·tized, hyp·no·tiz·ing.**

## Ii

**ice·berg** (īs′bėrg′), *NOUN.* a large mass of ice, detached from a glacier and floating in the sea. About 90 percent of its mass is below the surface of the water. ❑ *PLURAL* **ice·bergs.**

**iceberg**

794

**im·mense** (i mens′), *ADJECTIVE.* very large; huge; vast: *An ocean is an immense body of water.*

**im·pact** (im′pakt), *NOUN.* action of striking one thing against another; collision: *The impact of the heavy stone against the windowpane shattered the glass.*

**im·pres·sive** (im pres′iv), *ADJECTIVE.* able to have a strong effect on the mind or feelings; able to influence deeply.

**in·con·sol·a·ble** (in′kən sō′lə bəl), *ADJECTIVE.* not able to be comforted; brokenhearted: *The girl was inconsolable because her kitten was lost.*

**in·fe·ri·or** (in fir′ē ər), *ADJECTIVE.* not very good; below most others; low in quality: *an inferior grade of coffee.*

**in·jus·tice** (in jus′tis), *NOUN.* lack of justice, fairness, lawfulness: *We were angry at the injustice of the new rule.*

**in·land** (in′lənd), *ADVERB.* in or toward the interior: *He traveled inland from New York to Chicago.*

## Jj

**jer·sey** (jėr′zē), *NOUN.* shirt that is pulled over the head, made of soft, knitted cloth: *Members of the hockey team wear red jerseys.*

## Ll

**la·goon** (lə gün′), *NOUN.* pond or small lake, especially one connected with a larger body of water.

**land·lord** (land′lôrd′), *NOUN.* person who owns buildings or land that is rented to others.

**las·so** (la′sō), *VERB.* to catch with a long rope with a loop on one end. ❑ *VERB* **las·soed, las·so·ing.**

**lei·sure·ly** (lē′zhər lē), *ADVERB.* without hurry; taking plenty of time: *He walked leisurely across the bridge.*

**link** (lingk), *NOUN.* anything that joins or connects, as a loop of a chain does: *a link between his love of art and his career.*

**liz·ard** (liz′ərd), *NOUN.* any of many reptiles with long bodies and tails, movable eyelids, and usually four legs. Some lizards have no legs and look much like snakes. Iguanas, chameleons, and horned toads are lizards. ❑ *PLURAL* **liz·ards.**

| a in hat | o in open | sh in she |
| ā in age | ō in all | th in thin |
| â in care | ô in order | ᴛʜ in then |
| ä in far | oi in oil | zh in measure |
| e in let | ou in out | ə = a in about |
| ē in equal | u in cup | ə = e in taken |
| ėr in term | u in put | ə = i in pencil |
| i in it | ü in rule | ə = o in lemon |
| ī in ice | ch in child | ə = u in circus |
| o in hot | ng in long | |

795

## long•memorial

**long** (lòng), **1.** *ADJECTIVE.* measuring a great distance from end to end: *A year is a long time.* **2.** *VERB.* to wish very much; desire greatly: *long to see a good friend.* ❏ *VERB* **longed, long•ing.**

**loom** (lüm), *VERB.* to appear dimly or vaguely as a large, threatening shape: *A large iceberg loomed through the thick fog.* ❏ *VERB* **loomed, loom•ing.**

**lull** (lul), *VERB.* to soothe with sounds or caresses; cause to sleep: *The soft music lulled me to sleep.* ❏ *VERB* **lulled, lull•ing.**

**lum•ber•jack** (lum′bər jak′), *NOUN.* person whose work is cutting down trees and sending the logs to the sawmill; woodsman; logger.

**lu•nar** (lü′nər), *ADJECTIVE.* of, like, or about the moon: *a lunar landscape.*

**lurk** (lėrk), *VERB.* to move about in a secret and sly manner: *Several people were seen lurking near the house before it was robbed.* ❏ *VERB* **lurked, lurk•ing.**

### Mm

**ma•gi•cian** (mə jish′ən), *NOUN.* person who entertains by art or skill of creating illusions, especially a sleight of hand: *The magician pulled not one, but three rabbits out of his hat!*

**maj•es•ty** (maj′ə stē) *NOUN.* title used in speaking to or of a king, queen, emperor, empress, etc.: *Your Majesty, His Majesty, Her Majesty.*

**man•u•al** (man′yü əl), **1.** *ADJECTIVE.* done with the hands: *Digging a trench with a shovel is manual labor.* **2.** *NOUN.* a small book that helps its readers understand and use something; handbook: *A manual came with my pocket calculator.*

**mar•vel** (mär′vəl), *VERB.* to be filled with wonder; be astonished: *She marveled at the beautiful sunset.* ❏ *VERB* **mar•veled, mar•vel•ing.**

**mas•sive** (mas′iv), *ADJECTIVE.* big and heavy; bulky: *a massive boulder.*

**me•chan•i•cal** (mə kan′ə kəl), *ADJECTIVE.* like a machine; automatic; without expression: *The performance was very mechanical.*

**me•mo•ri•al** (mə môr′ē əl), *ADJECTIVE.* helping people to remember some person, thing, or event: *memorial services.*

**memorial**

## mesquite•mutual

**me•squite** (me skēt′), *ADJECTIVE.* any of several trees or bushes common in the southwestern United States and Mexico, which often grow in dense clumps or thickets. Mesquite pods furnish a valuable food for cattle. The wood is used in grilling food.

**mi•grate** (mī′grāt), *VERB.* to go from one region to another with the change in the seasons: *Most birds migrate to warmer countries in the winter.* ❏ *VERB* **mi•grat•ed, mi•grat•ing.**

**migrate**

**min•i•a•ture** (min′ē ə chùr or min′ə chər), *NOUN.* anything represented on a small scale: *In the museum, there is a miniature of the famous ship.* ❏ *PLURAL* **min•i•a•tures.**

**min•is•ter** (min′ə stər), *NOUN.* member of the clergy; spiritual guide; pastor.

**mir•a•cle** (mir′ə kəl), *NOUN.* a wonderful happening that is contrary to, or independent of, the known laws of nature: *His family considered his complete recovery from the accident to be a miracle.*

**mod•ule** (moj′ül), *NOUN.* a self-contained unit or system within a larger system, often designed for a particular function: *The lunar module circled the moon.*

**mon•u•ment** (mon′yə mənt), *NOUN.* something set up to honor a person or an event. A monument may be a building, pillar, arch, statue, tomb, or stone.

**monument**

**mu•tu•al** (myü′chü əl), *ADJECTIVE.* done, said, felt, etc., by each toward the other; both given and received: *They had mutual affection for each other.*

| a in hat | ò in open | sh in she |
|---|---|---|
| ā in age | ò in all | th in thin |
| â in care | ô in order | ŦH in then |
| ä in far | oi in oil | zh in measure |
| e in let | ou in out | ə = a in about |
| ē in equal | u in cup | ə = e in taken |
| ėr in term | ù in put | ə = i in pencil |
| i in it | ü in rule | ə = o in lemon |
| ī in ice | ch in child | ə = u in circus |
| o in hot | ng in long | |

## naturalist•payroll

### Nn

**nat•ur•al•ist** (nach′ər ə list), *NOUN.* person who makes a study of living things.

**nau•ti•cal** (nó′tə kəl), *ADJECTIVE.* of or about ships, sailors, or navigation.

**nav•i•ga•tion** (nav′ə gā′shən), *NOUN.* skill or process of finding a ship's or aircraft's position and course.

**no•ble** (nō′bəl), *ADJECTIVE.* high and great by birth, rank, or title; showing greatness of mind; good: *a noble person.*

**nour•ish•ing** (nėr′ish ing), **1.** *ADJECTIVE.* keeping well-fed and healthy; producing health and growth: *a nourishing diet.* **2.** *ADJECTIVE.* supporting, encouraging.

**nu•mer•ous** (nü′mər əs), *ADJECTIVE.* very many: *The child asked numerous questions.*

### Oo

**oath** (ōth), *NOUN.* a solemn promise: *The oath bound him to secrecy.*

**of•fend** (ə fend′), *VERB.* to hurt the feelings of someone; make angry; displease; pain: *My friend was offended by my laughter.* ❏ *VERB* **of•fend•ed, of•fend•ing.**

**out•spo•ken** (out′spō′kən), *ADJECTIVE.* not reserved; frank: *an outspoken person.*

### Pp

**pal•ette** (pal′it), **1.** *NOUN.* a thin board, usually oval or oblong, with a thumb hole at one end, used by painters to lay and mix colors on. **2.** *NOUN.* set of colors used by a painter. ❏ *PLURAL* **pal•ettes.**

**pan•to•mime** (pan′tə mīm), *VERB.* to express by gestures: *They pantomimed being hungry by pointing to their mouths and their stomachs.* ❏ *VERB* **pan•to•mimed, pan•to•mim•ing.**

**pantomime**

**par•lor** (pär′lər), **1.** *NOUN.* formerly, a room for receiving or entertaining guests; sitting room. **2.** *NOUN.* room or set of rooms used for various business purposes; shop: *a beauty parlor, an ice cream parlor.*

**pay•roll** (pā′rōl′), *NOUN.* list of persons to be paid and the amount that each one is to receive.

## peasant•prideful

**peas•ant** (pez′nt), *NOUN.* farmer of the working class in Europe, Asia, and Latin America.

**pe•cul•iar** (pi kyü′lyər), *ADJECTIVE.* strange; odd; unusual: *It was peculiar that the fish market had no fish last Friday.*

**plush** (plush), *ADJECTIVE.* luxurious; expensive; stylish: *a plush office.*

**pol•i•tics** (pol′ə tiks), *NOUN SINGULAR OR PLURAL.* the work of government; management of public business: *Our senior senator has been engaged in politics for many years.*

**pol•len** (pol′ən), *NOUN.* a fine, yellowish powder released from the anthers of flowers. Grains of pollen carried by insects, wind, etc., to the pistils of flowers fertilize the flowers.

**pol•li•nate** (pol′ə nāt), *VERB.* to carry pollen from anthers to pistils; bring pollen to. Flowers are pollinated by bees, bats, birds, wind, etc. ❏ *VERB* **pol•li•nat•ed, pol•li•nat•ing.**

**por•ridge** (pôr′ij), *NOUN.* food made of oatmeal or other grain boiled in water or milk until it thickens.

**pos•i•tive** (poz′ə tiv), *ADJECTIVE.* permitting no question; without doubt; sure: *We have positive evidence that the Earth moves around the sun.*

**po•ten•tial** (pə ten′shəl), *NOUN.* something possible: *a potential for danger.*

**prai•rie** (prâr′ē), **1.** *NOUN.* a large area of level or rolling land with grass but few or no trees, especially such an area making up much of central North America. **2.** *NOUN.* (regional) a wide, open space.

**pre•serve** (pri zėrv′), *VERB.* to keep from harm or change; keep safe; protect: *Good nutrition helps preserve your health.* ❏ *VERB* **pre•served, pre•serv•ing.**

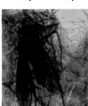

**preserve—** fly preserved in amber

**pride•ful** (prīd′fəl), *ADJECTIVE.* haughty; having too high an opinion of oneself.

| a in hat | ò in open | sh in she |
|---|---|---|
| ā in age | ò in all | th in thin |
| â in care | ô in order | ŦH in then |
| ä in far | oi in oil | zh in measure |
| e in let | ou in out | ə = a in about |
| ē in equal | u in cup | ə = e in taken |
| ėr in term | ù in put | ə = i in pencil |
| i in it | ü in rule | ə = o in lemon |
| ī in ice | ch in child | ə = u in circus |
| o in hot | ng in long | |

# Glossary

**pri·or·i·ty** (pri ôr'ə tē), *NOUN.* something given attention before anything else: *The young couple's first priority was to find a pleasant house.*

**pro·mote** (prə mōt'), *VERB.* to raise in rank, condition, or importance: *Pupils who pass the test will be promoted to the next higher grade.* ❑ *VERB* **pro·mot·ed, pro·mot·ing.**

**pul·pit** (pŭl'pit), *NOUN.* platform or raised structure in a church from which the minister preaches.

**pulse** (puls), **1.** *NOUN.* the regular beating of the arteries caused by the rush of blood into them after each contraction of the heart. By feeling a person's pulse in the artery of the wrist, you can count the number of times the heart beats each minute. **2.** *NOUN.* any regular, measured beat: *the pulse in music.* ❑ *PLURAL* **pul·ses.**

## Qq

**quaint** (kwānt), *ADJECTIVE.* strange or odd in an interesting, pleasing, or amusing way: *Many old photographs seem quaint to us today.*

**quar·an·tine** (kwôr'ən tēn' or kwär'ən tēn'), *NOUN.* detention, isolation, and other measures taken to prevent the spread of an infectious disease.

**quiv·er** (kwiv'ər), *VERB.* to shake; shiver; tremble: *The dog quivered with excitement.* ❑ *VERB* **quiv·ered, quiv·er·ing.**

## Rr

**re·call** (ri kól'), *VERB.* to call back to mind; remember: *I can recall stories told to me when I was a small child.* ❑ *VERB* **re·called, re·call·ing.**

**re·cruit·er** (ri krüt'ər), *NOUN.* a person who gets new members, who gets people to join or come: *The college recruiter attended our football game to watch our quarterback.*

**ref·er·ence** (ref'ər əns), *ADJECTIVE.* used for information or help: *The reference librarian can find the article that you need.*

**reign** (rān), **1.** *VERB.* to rule: *A king reigns over his kingdom.* **2.** *VERB.* to exist everywhere; prevail: *On a still night, silence reigns.* ❑ *VERB* **reigned, reign·ing.**

**re·mote** (ri mōt'), *ADJECTIVE.* out of the way; secluded.

**rep·tile** (rep'til), *NOUN.* any of many cold-blooded animals with backbones and lungs, usually covered with horny plates or scales. Snakes, lizards, turtles, alligators, and crocodiles are reptiles. Dinosaurs were reptiles. ❑ *PLURAL* **rep·tiles.**

**re·seat** (rē sēt'), *VERB.* to sit again. ❑ *VERB* **re·seat·ed, re·seat·ing.**

**re·sem·blance** (ri zem'bləns), *NOUN.* similar appearance; likeness: *Twins often show great resemblance.*

**res·er·va·tion** (rez'ər vā'shən), **1.** *NOUN.* arrangement to have a room, a seat, etc., held in advance for your use later on: *make a reservation for a room in a hotel.* **2.** *NOUN.* land set aside by the government for a special purpose: *an Indian reservation.*

**res·er·voir** (rez'ər vwär), *NOUN.* place where water is collected and stored for use: *This reservoir supplies the entire city.*

**re·sist·ance** (ri zis'təns), *NOUN.* thing or act that resists; opposing force; opposition: *Air resistance makes a feather fall more slowly than a pin.*

**re·spon·si·bil·i·ty** (ri spon'sə bil'ə tē), *NOUN.* the act or fact of taking care of someone or something; obligation: *We agreed to share responsibility for planning the party.*

**rift** (rift), *NOUN.* a split; break; crack: *The sun shone through a rift in the clouds.*

**rille** (ril), *NOUN.* a long, narrow valley on the surface of the moon.

**rim** (rim), *NOUN.* an edge, border, or margin on or around anything: *the rim of a wheel, the rim of a glass.*

**riv·er·bed** (riv'ər bed'), *NOUN.* channel in which a river flows or used to flow.

**round·up** (round'up'), *NOUN.* act of driving or bringing cattle together from long distances.

**rud·der** (rud'ər), *NOUN.* a flat piece of wood or metal hinged vertically to the rear end of an aircraft and used to steer it.

**rug·ged** (rug'id), *ADJECTIVE.* covered with rough edges; rough and uneven: *rugged ground.*

**rugged**

**ruin** (rü'ən), *NOUN.* often ruins, *PL.* what is left after a building, wall, etc., has fallen to pieces: *the ruins of an ancient city.* (*Ruin* comes from the Latin word *ruina* meaning "a collapse.")

| | | |
|---|---|---|
| a in hat | ō in open | sh in she |
| ā in age | ó in all | th in thin |
| â in care | ô in order | ᴛH in then |
| ä in far | oi in oil | zh in measure |
| e in let | ou in out | ə = a in about |
| ē in equal | u in cup | ə = e in taken |
| ėr in term | ú in put | ə = i in pencil |
| i in it | ü in rule | ə = o in lemon |
| ī in ice | ch in child | ə = u in circus |
| o in hot | ng in long | |

**rum·ble** (rum'bəl), *VERB.* to make a deep, heavy, continuous sound: *Thunder was rumbling in the distance.* ❑ *VERB* **rum·bled, rum·bling.**

**runt** (runt), *NOUN.* animal, person, or plant that is smaller than the usual size. If used about a person, *runt* is sometimes considered offensive.

## Ss

**sal·a·man·der** (sal'ə man'dər), *NOUN.* any of numerous animals shaped like lizards, but related to frogs and toads. Salamanders have moist, smooth skin and live in water or in damp places. ❑ *PLURAL* **sal·a·man·ders.**

**sas·sy** (sas'ē), *ADJECTIVE.* lively; spirited: *a sassy attitude.*

**scan** (skan), *VERB.* to glance at; look over hastily. ❑ *VERB* **scanned, scan·ning.**

**scent** (sent), *NOUN.* a smell: *The scent of roses filled the air.*

**schol·ar** (skol'ər), *NOUN.* a learned person; person having much knowledge: *The professor was a famous scholar.* ❑ *PLURAL* **schol·ars.** (*Scholar* comes from the Greek word *schol* meaning "discussion.")

**sculp·ture** (skulp'chər), **1.** *NOUN.* the art of making figures by carving, modeling, casting, etc. Sculpture includes the cutting of statues from blocks of marble, stone, or wood, casting in bronze, and modeling in clay or wax. **2.** *NOUN.* sculptured work; piece of such work. ❑ *PLURAL* **sculp·tures.**

**sculpture** (def. 2)

**sea·coast** (sē'kōst'), *NOUN.* land along the ocean or sea; seaboard: *the seacoast of Maine.*

**seek·er** (sēk'ər), *NOUN.* one who tries to find; one who searches: *That judge is a seeker of truth.*

**se·lect** (si lekt'), *VERB.* to pick out; choose: *Select the book you want.* ❑ *VERB* **se·lect·ed, se·lect·ing.**

**shat·ter** (shat'ər), *VERB.* to break into pieces suddenly: *A stone shattered the window.* ❑ *VERB* **shat·tered, shat·ter·ing.**

**shield** (shēld), *VERB.* to protect; defend: *They shielded me from unjust punishment.* ❑ *VERB* **shield·ed, shield·ing.**

**shim·mer** (shim'ər), *VERB.* to gleam or shine faintly: *Both the sea and the sand shimmered in the moonlight.* ❑ *VERB* **shim·mered, shim·mer·ing.** ❑ *ADJECTIVE* **shim·mer·ing.**

**shriek** (shrēk), *VERB.* to make a loud, sharp, shrill sound. People sometimes shriek because of terror, anger, pain, or amusement. ❑ *VERB* **shrieked, shriek·ing.**

**sil·hou·ette** (sil'ü et'), *NOUN.* a dark image outlined against a lighter background: *Silhouettes of skyscrapers could be seen against the moonlit sky.*

**silhouette**

**slith·er** (slim'ər), *VERB.* to go with a sliding motion: *The snake slithered into the weeds.* ❑ *VERB* **slith·ered, slith·er·ing.**

**slope** (slōp), *NOUN.* any line, surface, land, etc., that goes up or down at an angle: *If you roll a ball up a slope, it will roll down again.* ❑ *PLURAL* **slopes.**

**so·ci·e·ty** (sə sī'ə tē), **1.** *NOUN.* the people of any particular time or place: *twentieth-century society, American society.* **2.** *NOUN.* company; companionship: *I enjoy their society.*

**sol·emn·ly** (sol'əm lē), *ADVERB.* seriously; earnestly; with dignity.

**so·lo** (sō'lō), **1.** *ADJECTIVE.* without a partner, teacher, etc.; alone: *The flying student made her first solo flight.* **2.** *ADVERB.* on one's own, alone: *to fly solo.*

**spe·cies** (spē'shēz), *NOUN.* a set of related living things that all have certain characteristics. Spearmint is a species of mint.

**spec·i·men** (spes'ə mən), *NOUN.* one of a group or class taken to show what the others are like; sample: *He collects specimens of all kinds of rocks and minerals.*

**speech·less** (spēch'lis), *ADJECTIVE.* not able to talk: *He was speechless with wonder.*

| | | |
|---|---|---|
| a in hat | ō in open | sh in she |
| ā in age | ó in all | th in thin |
| â in care | ô in order | ᴛH in then |
| ä in far | oi in oil | zh in measure |
| e in let | ou in out | ə = a in about |
| ē in equal | u in cup | ə = e in taken |
| ėr in term | ú in put | ə = i in pencil |
| i in it | ü in rule | ə = o in lemon |
| ī in ice | ch in child | ə = u in circus |
| o in hot | ng in long | |

## spellbound•taunt

**spell·bound** (spel′bound′), *ADJECTIVE.* too interested to move; fascinated: *The children were spellbound by the circus performance.*

**sphere** (sfir), *NOUN.* ball or globe. The sun, moon, Earth, and stars are spheres.

**splen·dor** (splen′dər), *NOUN.* magnificent show; glory.

**spur** (spėr), *NOUN.* a metal point or pointed wheel, worn on a rider's boot heel for urging a horse on. □ *PLURAL* **spurs.**

**stag·ger** (stag′ər), *VERB.* to become unsteady; waver: *The troops staggered because of their exhaustion.* □ *VERB* **stag·gered, stag·ger·ing.**

**stall** (stòl), *VERB.* to stop or bring to a standstill, usually against your wish: *The engine stalled.* □ *VERB* **stalled, stall·ing.**

**steam·ship** (stēm′ship′), *NOUN.* ship moved by engines that work by the action of steam under pressure.

**stern¹** (stėrn), *ADJECTIVE.* harshly firm; hard; strict: *a stern parent.*

**stern²** (stėrn), *NOUN.* the rear part of a ship or boat.

**still** (stil), **1.** *ADJECTIVE.* staying in the same position or at rest; without motion; motionless: *to stand or lie still. The lake is still today.* **2.** *VERB.* to make or become calm or quiet: *The father stilled the crying baby.* □ *VERB* **stilled, stil·ling.**

**stump** (stump), *VERB.* to puzzle: *The riddle stumped me.* □ *VERB* **stumped, stump·ing.**

**sub·merge** (səb mėrj′), *VERB.* to put under water; cover with water: *A big wave momentarily submerged us.* □ *VERB* **sub·merged, sub·merg·ing.**

**sum·mon** (sum′ən), *VERB.* to stir to action; rouse: *We were summoning our courage before entering the deserted house.* □ *VERB* **sum·moned, sum·mon·ing.**

**sur·face** (sėr′fis), **1.** *NOUN.* the top of the ground or soil, or of a body of water or other liquid: *The stone sank beneath the surface of the water.* **2.** *NOUN.* the outward appearance: *He seems rough, but you will find him very kind below the surface.* **3.** *VERB.* to rise to the surface: *The submarine surfaced.*

**surge** (sėrj), *NOUN.* a swelling motion; sweep or rush, especially of waves: *Our boat was upset by a surge.*

**sus·pi·cious·ly** (sə spish′əs lē), *ADVERB.* without trust; doubtfully.

**swat** (swàt), *VERB.* to hit sharply or violently: *swat a fly.* □ *VERB* **swat·ted, swat·ting.**

## Tt

**taunt** (tònt), *VERB.* to jeer at; mock; reproach: *My classmates taunted me for being the teacher's pet.* □ *VERB* **taunt·ed, taunt·ing.**

## teem•towering

**teem** (tēm), *VERB.* to be full of; abound; swarm: *The swamp teemed with mosquitoes.* □ *VERB* **teemed, teem·ing.**

**tem·ple** (tem′pəl), *NOUN.* building used for the service or worship of God or gods. □ *PLURAL* **tem·ples.** (*Temple* comes from the Latin word *templum* meaning "temple.")

**ter·race** (ter′is), *VERB.* to form into flat, level land with steep sides; terraces are often made in hilly areas to create more space for farming. □ *VERB* **ter·raced, ter·rac·ing.** (*Terrace* comes from the Latin word *terra* meaning "earth, land.")

**terrace**

**ter·ror** (ter′ər), *NOUN.* great fear: *The dog has a terror of thunder.*

**thick·et** (thik′it), *NOUN.* bushes or small trees growing close together: *We crawled into the thicket and hid.* □ *PLURAL* **thick·ets.**

**tim·id** (tim′id), *ADJECTIVE.* easily frightened; shy: *The timid child was afraid of the dark.*

**tor·rent** (tòr′ənt), *NOUN.* a violent, rushing stream of water: *The mountain torrent dashed over the rock.* (*Torrent* comes from the Latin word *torrentum* meaning "boiling.")

**torrent**

**tow·er·ing** (tou′ər ing), **1.** *ADJECTIVE.* very high: *a towering mountain peak.* **2.** *ADJECTIVE.* very great: *Developing a polio vaccine was a towering achievement.*

| a in hat | o in open | sh in she |
|---|---|---|
| ā in age | ō in all | th in thin |
| â in care | ô in order | ᴛʜ in then |
| ä in far | oi in oil | zh in measure |
| e in let | ou in out | ə = a in about |
| ē in equal | u in cup | ə = e in taken |
| ėr in term | ů in put | ə = i in pencil |
| i in it | ü in rule | ə = o in lemon |
| ī in ice | ch in child | ə = u in circus |
| o in hot | ng in long | |

## translate•vanish

**trans·late** (tran slāt′ *or* tranz lāt′), *VERB.* to change from one language into another: *translate a book from French into English.* □ *VERB* **trans·lat·ed, trans·lat·ing.** (*Translate* comes from the Latin word *trans*, which means "across, through, or behind.")

**trans·mis·sion** (tran smish′ən *or* tranz mish′ən), *NOUN.* passage of electromagnetic waves from a transmitter to a receiver: *When transmission is good, even foreign radio stations can be heard.*

**treas·ur·y** (trezh′ər ē), *NOUN.* money owned; funds: *We voted to pay for the party out of the club treasury.*

**trench** (trench), *NOUN.* any ditch; deep furrow: *to dig a trench for a pipe.*

**tri·umph** (trī′umf), *NOUN.* victory; success: *The exploration of outer space is a great triumph of modern science.*

**trop·i·cal** (trop′ə kəl), *ADJECTIVE.* of or like the regions 23.45 degrees north and south of the equator where the sun can shine directly overhead: *tropical heat.*

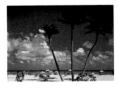

**tropical**

**trudge** (truj), *VERB.* to walk wearily or with effort. *We trudged up the hill.* □ *VERB* **trudged, trudg·ing.**

**twang** (twang), *VERB.* to make or cause to make a sharp, ringing sound: *The banjos twanged.* □ *VERB* **twanged, twang·ing.**

## Uu

**un·be·liev·a·ble** (un′bi lē′və bəl), *ADJECTIVE.* incredible; hard to think of as true or real: *an unbelievable lie.*

**un·cov·er** (un kuv′ər), *VERB.* to make known; reveal; expose: *The reporter uncovered a scandal.* □ *VERB* **un·cov·ered, un·cov·er·ing.**

**un·ex·plain·a·ble** (un ek splān′ə bəl), *ADJECTIVE.* not able to be explained; mysterious.

## Vv

**vain** (vān), *ADJECTIVE.* having too much pride in your looks, ability, etc.: *a good-looking but vain person.*

**van·ish** (van′ish), *VERB.* to disappear, especially suddenly: *The sun vanished behind a cloud.* □ *VERB* **van·ished, van·ish·ing.**

## vehicle•yearn

**ve·hi·cle** (vē′ə kəl), *NOUN.* device for carrying people or things, such as a car, bus, airplane, etc. Cars and trucks are motor vehicles. Rockets are space vehicles.

**ven·ture** (ven′chər), *VERB.* to dare to come or go: *We ventured out on the thin ice and almost fell through.* □ *VERB* **ven·tured, ven·tur·ing.**

## Ww

**wharf** (wôrf), *NOUN.* platform built on the shore or out from the shore, beside which ships can load and unload. □ *PLURAL* **wharves.**

**wil·der·ness** (wil′dər nis), *NOUN.* a wild, uncultivated region with few or no people living in it.

**wilderness**

**with·stand** (wiᴛʜ stand′), *VERB.* to stand against; hold out against; resist; endure: *These heavy shoes will withstand much hard wear.* □ *VERB* **with·stood, with·stand·ing.**

**won·drous** (wun′drəs), *ADJECTIVE.* wonderful; marvelous, remarkable.

**wreck·age** (rek′ij), *NOUN.* what is left behind after the destruction of a motor vehicle, ship, building, train, or aircraft: *The hurricane left behind much wreckage.*

## Yy

**yearn** (yėrn), *VERB.* to feel a longing or desire; desire earnestly: *I yearned for home.* □ *VERB* **yearned, yearn·ing.**

| a in hat | o in open | sh in she |
|---|---|---|
| ā in age | ō in all | th in thin |
| â in care | ô in order | ᴛʜ in then |
| ä in far | oi in oil | zh in measure |
| e in let | ou in out | ə = a in about |
| ē in equal | u in cup | ə = e in taken |
| ėr in term | ů in put | ə = i in pencil |
| i in it | ü in rule | ə = o in lemon |
| ī in ice | ch in child | ə = u in circus |
| o in hot | ng in long | |

# English/Spanish Selection Vocabulary List

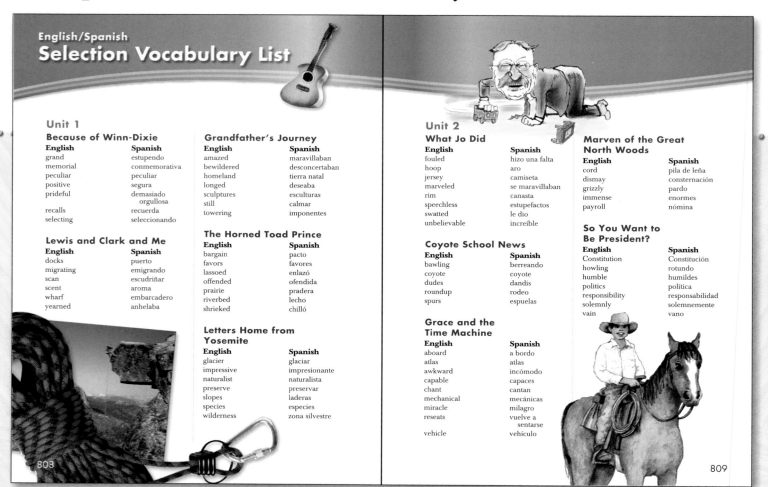

## English/Spanish Selection Vocabulary List

### Unit 1

**Because of Winn-Dixie**

| English | Spanish |
|---|---|
| grand | estupendo |
| memorial | conmemorativa |
| peculiar | peculiar |
| positive | segura |
| prideful | demasiado orgullosa |
| recalls | recuerda |
| selecting | seleccionando |

**Lewis and Clark and Me**

| English | Spanish |
|---|---|
| docks | puerto |
| migrating | emigrando |
| scan | escudriñar |
| scent | aroma |
| wharf | embarcadero |
| yearned | anhelaba |

**Grandfather's Journey**

| English | Spanish |
|---|---|
| amazed | maravillaban |
| bewildered | desconcertaban |
| homeland | tierra natal |
| longed | deseaba |
| sculptures | esculturas |
| still | calmar |
| towering | imponentes |

**The Horned Toad Prince**

| English | Spanish |
|---|---|
| bargain | pacto |
| favors | favores |
| lassoed | enlazó |
| offended | ofendida |
| prairie | pradera |
| riverbed | lecho |
| shrieked | chilló |

**Letters Home from Yosemite**

| English | Spanish |
|---|---|
| glacier | glaciar |
| impressive | impresionante |
| naturalist | naturalista |
| preserve | preservar |
| slopes | laderas |
| species | especies |
| wilderness | zona silvestre |

### Unit 2

**What Jo Did**

| English | Spanish |
|---|---|
| fouled | hizo una falta |
| hoop | aro |
| jersey | camiseta |
| marveled | se maravillaban |
| rim | canasta |
| speechless | estupefactos |
| swatted | le dio |
| unbelievable | increíble |

**Coyote School News**

| English | Spanish |
|---|---|
| bawling | berreando |
| coyote | coyote |
| dudes | dandis |
| roundup | rodeo |
| spurs | espuelas |

**Grace and the Time Machine**

| English | Spanish |
|---|---|
| aboard | a bordo |
| atlas | atlas |
| awkward | incómodo |
| capable | capaces |
| chant | cantan |
| mechanical | mecánicas |
| miracle | milagro |
| reseats | vuelve a sentarse |
| vehicle | vehículo |

**Marven of the Great North Woods**

| English | Spanish |
|---|---|
| cord | pila de leña |
| dismay | consternación |
| grizzly | pardo |
| immense | enormes |
| payroll | nómina |

**So You Want to Be President?**

| English | Spanish |
|---|---|
| Constitution | Constitución |
| howling | rotundo |
| humble | humildes |
| politics | política |
| responsibility | responsabilidad |
| solemnly | solemnemente |
| vain | vano |

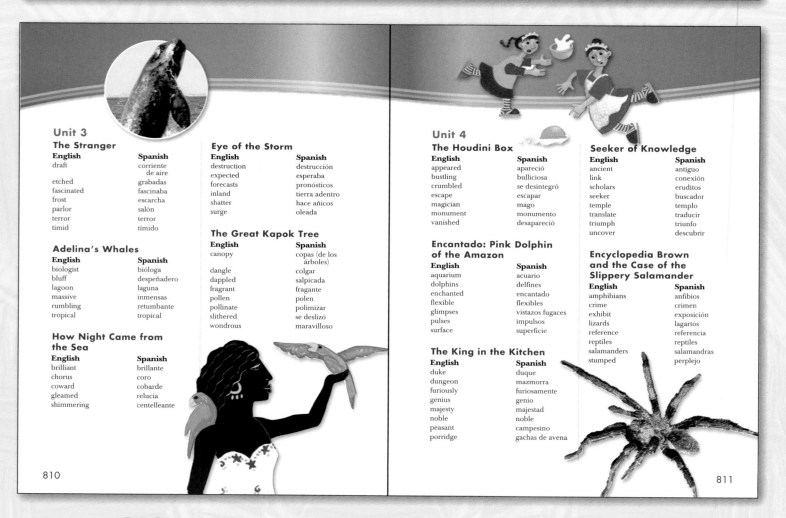

### Unit 3

**The Stranger**

| English | Spanish |
|---|---|
| draft | corriente de aire |
| etched | grabadas |
| fascinated | fascinaba |
| frost | escarcha |
| parlor | salón |
| terror | terror |
| timid | tímido |

**Adelina's Whales**

| English | Spanish |
|---|---|
| biologist | bióloga |
| bluff | despeñadero |
| lagoon | laguna |
| massive | inmensas |
| rumbling | retumbante |
| tropical | tropical |

**How Night Came from the Sea**

| English | Spanish |
|---|---|
| brilliant | brillante |
| chorus | coro |
| coward | cobarde |
| gleamed | relucía |
| shimmering | centelleante |

**Eye of the Storm**

| English | Spanish |
|---|---|
| destruction | destrucción |
| expected | esperaba |
| forecasts | pronósticos |
| inland | tierra adentro |
| shatter | hace añicos |
| surge | oleada |

**The Great Kapok Tree**

| English | Spanish |
|---|---|
| canopy | copas (de los árboles) |
| dangle | colgar |
| dappled | salpicada |
| fragrant | fragante |
| pollen | polen |
| pollinate | polimizar |
| slithered | se deslizó |
| wondrous | maravilloso |

### Unit 4

**The Houdini Box**

| English | Spanish |
|---|---|
| appeared | apareció |
| bustling | bulliciosa |
| crumbled | se desintegró |
| escape | escapar |
| magician | mago |
| monument | monumento |
| vanished | desapareció |

**Encantado: Pink Dolphin of the Amazon**

| English | Spanish |
|---|---|
| aquarium | acuario |
| dolphins | delfines |
| enchanted | encantado |
| flexible | flexibles |
| glimpses | vistazos fugaces |
| pulses | impulsos |
| surface | superficie |

**The King in the Kitchen**

| English | Spanish |
|---|---|
| duke | duque |
| dungeon | mazmorra |
| furiously | furiosamente |
| genius | genio |
| majesty | majestad |
| noble | noble |
| peasant | campesino |
| porridge | gachas de avena |

**Seeker of Knowledge**

| English | Spanish |
|---|---|
| ancient | antiguo |
| link | conexión |
| scholars | eruditos |
| seeker | buscador |
| temple | templo |
| translate | traducir |
| triumph | triunfo |
| uncover | descubrir |

**Encyclopedia Brown and the Case of the Slippery Salamander**

| English | Spanish |
|---|---|
| amphibians | anfibios |
| crime | crimen |
| exhibit | exposición |
| lizards | lagartos |
| reference | referencia |
| reptiles | reptiles |
| salamanders | salamandras |
| stumped | perplejo |

# English/Spanish Selection Vocabulary List

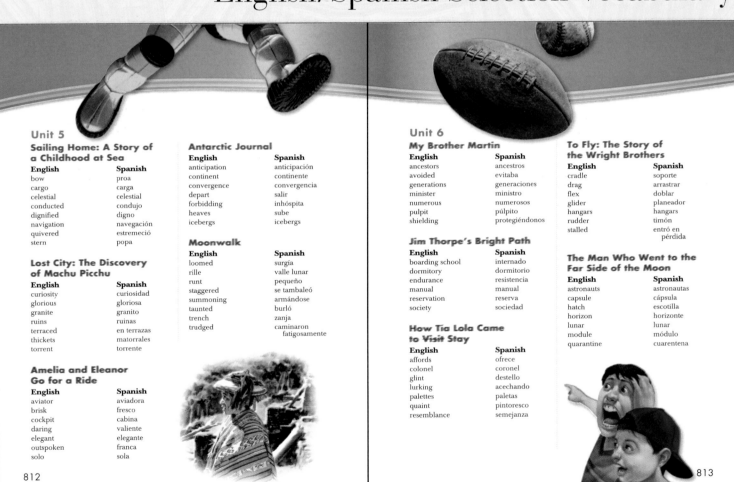

## Unit 5

### Sailing Home: A Story of a Childhood at Sea

| English | Spanish |
|---|---|
| bow | proa |
| cargo | carga |
| celestial | celestial |
| conducted | condujo |
| dignified | digno |
| navigation | navegación |
| quivered | estremeció |
| stern | popa |

### Lost City: The Discovery of Machu Picchu

| English | Spanish |
|---|---|
| curiosity | curiosidad |
| glorious | gloriosa |
| granite | granito |
| ruins | ruinas |
| terraced | en terrazas |
| thickets | matorrales |
| torrent | torrente |

### Amelia and Eleanor Go for a Ride

| English | Spanish |
|---|---|
| aviator | aviadora |
| brisk | fresco |
| cockpit | cabina |
| daring | valiente |
| elegant | elegante |
| outspoken | franca |
| solo | sola |

### Antarctic Journal

| English | Spanish |
|---|---|
| anticipation | anticipación |
| continent | continente |
| convergence | convergencia |
| depart | salir |
| forbidding | inhóspita |
| heaves | sube |
| icebergs | icebergs |

### Moonwalk

| English | Spanish |
|---|---|
| loomed | surgía |
| rille | valle lunar |
| runt | pequeño |
| staggered | se tambaleó |
| summoning | armándose |
| taunted | burló |
| trench | zanja |
| trudged | caminaron fatigosamente |

## Unit 6

### My Brother Martin

| English | Spanish |
|---|---|
| ancestors | ancestros |
| avoided | evitaba |
| generations | generaciones |
| minister | ministro |
| numerous | numerosos |
| pulpit | púlpito |
| shielding | protegiéndonos |

### Jim Thorpe's Bright Path

| English | Spanish |
|---|---|
| boarding school | internado |
| dormitory | dormitorio |
| endurance | resistencia |
| manual | manual |
| reservation | reserva |
| society | sociedad |

### How Tía Lola Came to Visit Stay

| English | Spanish |
|---|---|
| affords | ofrece |
| colonel | coronel |
| glint | destello |
| lurking | acechando |
| palettes | paletas |
| quaint | pintoresco |
| resemblance | semejanza |

### To Fly: The Story of the Wright Brothers

| English | Spanish |
|---|---|
| cradle | soporte |
| drag | arrastrar |
| flex | doblar |
| glider | planeador |
| hangars | hangars |
| rudder | timón |
| stalled | entró en pérdida |

### The Man Who Went to the Far Side of the Moon

| English | Spanish |
|---|---|
| astronauts | astronautas |
| capsule | cápsula |
| hatch | escotilla |
| horizon | horizonte |
| lunar | lunar |
| module | módulo |
| quarantine | cuarentena |

812

813

# Acknowledgments

## Acknowledgments

### Text

**22:** *Because of Winn-Dixie.* Copyright © 2000 by Kate DiCamillo; Cover Illustration Copyright © 2000 by Chris Sheban. Reprinted by permission of Candlewick Press, Inc., Cambridge, MA; **36:** "Fast Facts: Black Bears" by Kathy Kranking as appeared in *Ranger Rick*, August 1995. © Kathy Kranking. Reprinted with permission of the author; **44:** Text excerpt and selected illustrations from *Lewis and Clark and Me, A Dog's Tale* by Laurie Myers, illustrated by Michael Dooling. Text © 2002 by Laurie Myers, illustrations © 2002 by Michael Dooling. Reprinted by permission of Henry Holt and Company, LLC; **70:** From *Grandfather's Journey* by Allen Say. Copyright © 1993 by Allen Say. Reprinted by permission of Houghton Mifflin Company. All rights reserved; **92:** From *The Horned Toad Prince* by Jackie Mims Hopkins. Illustrated by Michael Austin. Text © 2000 by Jackie Mims Hopkins. Illustrations © 2000 by Michael Austin. Reprinted by permission of Peachtree Publishers; **108:** "Horned Lizards and Harvesting Ants," from *Journey into the Desert* by John Brown, copyright © 2002 by John Brown. Reprinted by permission of Oxford University Press, Inc.; **116:** From *Letters Home from Yosemite* by Lisa Halvorsen, Blackbirch Press. © 2000, Blackbirch Press. Reprinted by permission of The Gale Group; **130:** "This Land Is Your Land." Words and Music by Woody Guthrie. TRO - Copyright 1956 (Renewed), 1958 (Renewed), 1970 (Renewed), 1972 (Renewed), Ludlow Music, Inc., New York, NY. Used by permission; **134:** "We're All in the Telephone Book" from *The Collected Poems of Langston Hughes* by Langston Hughes, copyright © 1994 by The Estate of Langston Hughes. Used by permission of Alfred A. Knopf, a division of Random House, Inc.; **135:** "Speak Up" from *Good Luck Gold And Other Poems* by Janet S. Wong. Copyright © 1994 by Janet S. Wong. Reprinted with permission of Margaret K. McElderry Books, an imprint of Simon & Schuster Children's Publishing Division. All rights reserved; **136:** "City I Love" by Lee Bennett Hopkins. Copyright © 2002 by Lee Bennett Hopkins. First appeared in *Home to Me: Poems Across America*, published by Orchard Books. Reprinted by permission of Curtis Brown, Ltd.; **137:** "Midwest Town" by Ruth De Long Peterson, *The Saturday Evening Post*, Nov. 13, 1954. © 1954 (renewed). Used by permission of The Saturday Evening Post Society; **146:** "What Jo Did," from *Tall Tales: Six Amazing Basketball Dreams* by Charles R. Smith Jr., copyright © 2000 by Charles R. Smith Jr. Used by permission of Dutton Children's Books, A Division of Penguin Young Readers Group, A Member of The Penguin Group (USA) Inc., 345 Hudson Street, New York, NY 10014. All rights reserved; **158:** "Fast Break," from *Rimshots: Basketball Pix, Rolls and Rhythms* by Charles R. Smith Jr., copyright © 1999 by Charles R. Smith Jr. Used by permission of Dutton Children's Books, A Division of Penguin Young Readers Group, A Member of Penguin Group (USA) Inc., 345 Hudson Street, New York, NY 10014. All rights reserved; **160:** "Allow Me to Introduce Myself," from *Short Takes: Fast Break Basketball Poetry* by Charles R. Smith Jr., copyright © 2001 by Charles R. Smith Jr. Used by permission of Dutton Children's Books, A Division of Penguin Young Readers Group, A Member of Penguin Group (USA) Inc., 345 Hudson Street, New York, NY 10014. All rights reserved; **166:** Text and illustrations from *Coyote School News* by Joan Sandin. Copyright © 2003 by Joan Sandin. Reprinted by permission of Henry Holt and Company, LLC; **192:** "Grace and the Time Machine" adapted from *Starring Grace* by Mary Hoffman, Frances Lincoln Books, London. Copyright text © 2000 Mary Hoffman c/o Rogers, Coleridge & White Ltd., 20 Powis Mews, London W11 1JN. Reprinted by permission; **210:** "What's There to Do?" formerly titled "Help an Elderly Neighbor with Yard Work" and "Put on an Outdoor Arts-and-Crafts Show" from *101 Outdoor Adventures* by Samantha Beres, copyright © 2002 by Dutton Children's Books. Used by permission of Dutton Children's Books, A Division of Penguin Young Readers Group, A Member of Penguin Group (USA) Inc., 345 Hudson Street, New York, NY 10014. All rights reserved; **216:** From *Marven of the Great North Woods* by Kathryn Lasky Knight, illustrated by Kevin Hawkes. Text copyright © 1997 by Kathryn Lasky Knight. Illustrations copyright © 1997 by Kevin Hawkes. Reprinted by permission of Harcourt, Inc.; **239:** Adaptation of "Cook Shanty & Bunkhouse" from the Paul Bunyan Logging Camp Web site, paulbunyancamp.org. Reprinted by permission of the Paul Bunyan Logging Camp Museum, Eau Claire, WI; **244:** From *So You Want to Be President?* by Judith St. George, illustrations by David Small, copyright © 2000 by Judith St. George, text, copyright © 2000 by David Small, illustrations. Used by permission of Philomel Books, A Division of Penguin Young Readers Group, A Member of Penguin Group (USA) Inc., 345 Hudson Street, New York, NY 10014. All rights reserved; **260:** "His Hands", from *My Man Blue* by Nikki Grimes, copyright © 1999 by Nikki Grimes. Used by permission of Dial Books for Young Readers, A Division of Penguin Young Readers Group, A Member of Penguin Group (USA) Inc., 345 Hudson Street, New York, NY 10014. All rights reserved; **261:** "Homework" by Russell Hoban from *Egg Thoughts and Other Frances Songs*. Copyright © 1964 by Russell Hoban. Reprinted by permission of David Higham Associates Ltd.; **262:** "Lem Lonnigan's Leaf Machine" from *Here's What You Do When You Can't Find Your Shoe* by Andrea Perry. Text copyright © 2003 by Andrea Perry. Reprinted with the permission of Atheneum Books for Young Readers, an imprint of Simon & Schuster Children's Publishing Division; **272:** From *The Stranger* by Chris Van Allsburg. Copyright © 1986 by Chris Van Allsburg. Reprinted by permission of Houghton Mifflin Company. All rights reserved; **296:** From *Adelina's Whales* by Richard Sobol, copyright © 2003 by Richard Sobol. Used by permission of Dutton Children's Books, A Division of Penguin Young Readers Group, A Member of Penguin Group (USA) Inc., 345 Hudson Street, New York, NY 10014. All rights reserved; **318:** *How Night Came from the Sea* retold by Mary-Joan Gerson, illustrations by Carla Golembe. Text copyright © 1994 by Mary-Joan Gerson. Illustrations copyright © 1994 by Carla Golembe. Reprinted by permission of Goodman Associates Literary Agents as authorized agent for Mary-Joan Gerson and Carla Golembe; **334:** "The Ant and the Bear" from *Spirit of the Cedar People: More Stories and Paintings of Chief Lelooska* edited by Christine Normandin. A DK Ink Book, 1998. Reprinted by permission of the Estate of Don Lelooska Smith, Lelooska Foundation, www.lelooska.org; **342:** From *Eye of the Storm* by Stephen Kramer, photographs by Warren Faidley, copyright © 1997 by Stephen Kramer, text. Used by permission of G. P. Putnam's Sons, A Division of Penguin Young Readers Group, A Member of Penguin Group (USA) Inc., 345 Hudson Street, New York, NY 10014. All rights reserved; **364:** From *The Great Kapok Tree: A Tale of the Amazon Rain Forest*, copyright © 1990 by Lynne Cherry, reprinted by permission of Harcourt, Inc.; **380:** From *Living in a World of Green* by Tanya Lee Stone. Copyright © 2001 Blackbirch Press, Inc. Used by permission of Thomson Learning; **384:** "Autumn" by Charlotte Zolotow from *River Winding* by Charlotte Zolotow. Copyright © 1970 by Carlotte Zolotow. Reprinted by permission of Scott Treimel NY. All rights reserved; **386:** "Early Spring" from *Navajo: Visions and Voices Across the Mesa* by Shonto Begay. Copyright © 1995 by Shonto Begay. Reprinted by permission of Scholastic Inc.; **396:** From *The Houdini Box* by Brian Selznick. Copyright © 1991 by Brian Selznick. Reprinted and edited with the permission of Atheneum Books for Young Readers, Simon & Schuster Children's Publishing Division. All rights reserved; **412:** "So You Want to Be an Illusionist," from *Who Was Harry Houdini?* by Tui T. Sutherland, illustrated by John O'Brien, copyright © 2002 by Tui T. Sutherland, text. Used by permission of Grosset & Dunlap, A Division of Penguin Young Readers Group, A Member of Penguin Group (USA) Inc., 345 Hudson Street, New York, NY 10014. All rights reserved; **420:** Abridged from *Encantado: Pink Dolphin of the Amazon* by Sy Montgomery with photographs by Dianne Taylor-Snow. Text copyright © 2002 by Sy Montgomery. Photographs copyright © 2002 by Dianne Taylor-Snow. Reprinted by permission of Houghton Mifflin Company. All rights reserved; **444:** From "The King in the Kitchen" by Margaret E. Slattery in *30 Plays from Favorite Stories*, edited by Sylvia E. Kamerman. Copyright © 1964, 1997 by Plays/Sterling Partners, Inc. Reprinted by permission; **464:** "A Man for All Seasonings" from *The Spouse in the House* by Richard Armour, 1975, McGraw-Hill Book Company. Reprinted by permission of Geoffrey Armour; **465:** "A Confectioner" from *A Lollygag of Limericks* by Myra Cohn Livingston. Copyright © 1978 by Myra Cohn Livingston. Used by permission of Marian Reiner; **470:** From *Seeker of Knowledge: The Man Who Deciphered Egyptian Hieroglyphs* by James Rumford. Copyright © 2000 by James Rumford. Reprinted by permission of Houghton Mifflin Company. All rights reserved; **486:** "What is Picture Stories?" and "In the Desert" from www.instituteofthefuture.org. Used by permission of Rahul Bhargava, Institute of the Future; **492:** From *Encyclopedia Brown and the Case of the Slippery Salamander* by Donald J. Sobol and illustrated by Warren Chang, copyright © 1999 by Donald J. Sobol. Used by permission of Random House Children's Books, a division of Random House, Inc.; **508:** "Who Knows?" by Fatou Ndiaye Sow, translated by Véronique Tadjo from *Talking Drums:*



*A Selection of Poems from Africa South of the Sahara* edited and illustrated by Véronique Tadjo. © A & C Black Publishers, 2000. Reprinted by permission; **509:** "Poetry" from *Eleanor Farjeon's Poems for Children* by Eleanor Farjeon. Copyright 1938 by Eleanor Farjeon. Copyright renewed 1966 by Gervase Farjeon. Reprinted by permission of Harold Ober Associates Incorporated; **510:** "The Seed" from *Always Wondering* by Aileen Fisher. Copyright © 1991 by Aileen Fisher. Used by permission of Marian Reiner; **511:** "Carolyn's Cat" from *When Whales Exhale and Other Poems* by Constance Levy. Copyright © 1996 by Constance Levy (A Margaret K. McElderry Book). Reprinted by permission of Marian Reiner; **520:** *Sailing Home: A Story of a Childhood at Sea* by Gloria Rand, illustrated by Ted Rand. Text copyright © 2001 by Gloria Rand. Illustrations © 2001 by Ted Rand. Reprinted by arrangement with North-South Books Inc., New York. All rights reserved; **542:** From *Lost City: The Discovery of Machu Picchu* by Ted Lewin, copyright © 2003 by Ted Lewin. Used by permission of Philomel Books, A Division of Penguin Young Readers Group, A Member of Penguin Group (USA) Inc., 345 Hudson Street, New York, NY 10014. All rights reserved; **564:** From *Amelia and Eleanor Go for a Ride* by Pam Munoz Ryan, illustrated by Brian Selznick. Text copyright © 1999 by Pam Munoz Ryan, illustrations copyright © by Brian Selznick. Published by Scholastic Press/Scholastic Inc. Reprinted by permission; **586:** From *Antarctic Journal: Four Months at the Bottom of the World* by Jennifer Owings Dewey. Copyright © 2001 by Jennifer Owings Dewey. Used by permission of HarperCollins Publishers; **612:** "Moonwalk" by Ben Bova. Copyright © 2002 by Ben Bova. Reprinted with permission of Ben Bova and *Boys' Life*, November 2002, published by the Boy Scouts of America; **630:** "The Best Paths," from *Toasting Marshmallows: Camping Poems* by Kristine O'Connell George. Text copyright © 2001 by Kristine O'Connell George. Reprinted by permission of Clarion Books/Houghton Mifflin Company. All rights reserved; **631:** "Roller Coasters" by X. J. Kennedy. First appeared in *The Kite That Braved Old Orchard Beach*, published by Margaret K. McElderry Books. Copyright © 1991 by X. J. Kennedy. Reprinted by permission of Curtis Brown, Ltd.; **632:** "The Door" by Miroslav Holub from *Miroslav Holub: Selected Poems*, translated by Ian Milner and George Theiner. Copyright © 1967 by Miroslav Holub. Translation copyright © 1967 Penguin Books. Reproduced by permission of Penguin Books Ltd.; **642:** From *My Brother Martin* by Christine King Farris, illustrated by Chris Soentpiet. Text copyright © 2003 Christine King Farris. Illustrations copyright © 2003 Chris Soentpiet. Reprinted with the permission of Simon & Schuster Books for Young Readers, an imprint of Simon & Schuster Children's Publishing Division; **658:** "Haiku" by Cristina Beecham, *Skipping Stones*, Sept.-Oct. 2003. Reprinted with permission, Skipping Stones Magazine (www.SkippingStones.org); **659:** "When You Hope, Wish, and Trust" by Ek Ongkar K. Khalsa, *Skipping Stones*, Sept.-Oct. 2003. Reprinted with permission, Skipping Stones Magazine (www.SkippingStones.org); **659:** "My Life Is a Buried Treasure" by Dawn Withrow, *Ten-Second Rainshowers: Poems by Young People*, compiled by Sandford Lyne, Simon & Schuster Books for Young Readers, 1996; **664:** *Jim Thorpe's Bright Path* by Joseph Bruchac. Text copyright © 2004 by Joseph Bruchac, illustrations copyright © 2004 by S. D. Nelson. Permission arranged with Lee & Low Books Inc., New York, NY 10016; **690:** "Two Happy Months in Vermont" from *How Tia Lola Came to ~~Visit~~ Stay*. Copyright © 2001 by Julia Alvarez. Published by Dell Yearling and in hardcover by Alfred A. Knopf Children's Books, a division of Random House, New York. Reprinted by permission of Susan Bergholz Literary Services, New York. All Rights Reserved; **708:** From *Sadaharu Oh: A Zen Way of Baseball* by Sadaharu Oh and David Falkner, copyright © 1984 Sadaharu Oh and David Falkner. Used by permission of Times Books, a division of Random House, Inc.; **716:** Excerpts from *To Fly: The Story of the Wright Brothers* by Wendie C. Old. Text copyright © 2000 by Wendie C. Old. Abridged and reprinted by permission of Houghton Mifflin Company. All rights reserved; **737:** "Clement Ader's Eole" from First Flight Web site, http://firstflight.open.ac.uk. Used by permission of Dr. Peter Whalley; **742:** From *The Man Who Went to the Far Side of the Moon* by Bea Uusma Schyffert. Copyright © 1999 by Bea Uusma Schyffert. Reprinted with the permission of Chronicle Books LLC, San Francisco. www.chroniclebooks.com; **758:** "The Earth and the Moon" (originally titled "Earth", "The Moon" and "Exploring the Moon"), from *Scott Foresman Science*, Grade 4. Copyright © 2006 Pearson Education, Inc.; **762:** "Dream Dust" from *The Collected Poems of Langston Hughes* by Langston Hughes, copyright © 1994 by The Estate of Langston Hughes. Used by permission of Alfred A. Knopf, a division of Random House, Inc.; **762:** "Martin Luther King" from *No Way of Knowing: Dallas Poems* by Myra Cohn Livingston. Copyright © 1980 by Myra Cohn Livingston. Used by permission of Marian Reiner; **763:** "Martin Luther King Day" by X. J. Kennedy. First appeared in *The Kite That Braved Old Orchard Beach*, published by Margaret K. McElderry Books. Copyright © 1991 by X. J. Kennedy. Reprinted by permission of Curtis Brown, Ltd.; **764:** "Fall Football", from *Fearless Fernie: Hanging out with Fernie and Me* by Gary Soto, copyright © 2002 by Gary Soto, text. Used by permission of G. P. Putnam's Sons, A Division of Penguin Young Readers Group, A Member of Penguin Group (USA) Inc., 345 Hudson Street, New York, NY 10014. All rights reserved; **765:** "First Men on the Moon" by J. Patrick Lewis. © J. Patrick Lewis, 1998. Reprinted by permission of the author.

### Illustrations

**Cover**: Tim Jessell; **17, 22-33:** ©Kevin Hawkes; **21, 489:** Barry Gott; **37, 96, 259, 312, 515, 558, 612-622, 812:** Peter Bollinger; **48, 130-132:** Robert Crawford; **70:** Dave Stevenson; **89-91:** Laura Ovresat; **134-136:** Patrick Corrigan; **141, 192-208:** Matt Faulkner; **186:** Sachiko Yoshikawa; **189:** Shelly Hehenberger; **210:** Stephen Kroninger; **215:** Erika Le Barre; **260-262:** Lee White; **361:** Richard Downs; **391, 444, 462, 811:** Matthew Trueman; **391, 492-502:** Brett Helquist; **412-415:** Vitali Konstantinov; **441-443:** Christine Benjamin; **464:** Amy Vangsgard; **508-510, 609:** Joel Nakamura; **517:** Dan Andreasen; **630-632:** Franklin Hammond; **637, 664-680:** S.D. Nelson; **637, 690-706, 813:** Macky Pamintuan; **658:** Stephen Daigle; **662-663:** Gwen Connelly; **709-711:** SuLing Wang; **713:** Mark Neely; **756:** Bea Uusma Schyffert; **762-764:** Rafael Lopez.

### Photographs

Every effort has been made to secure permission and provide appropriate credit for photographic material. The publisher deeply regrets any omission and pledges to correct errors called to its attention in subsequent editions.

Unless otherwise acknowledged, all photographs are the property of Scott Foresman, a division of Pearson Education.

**Photo locators denoted as follows:** Top (T), Center (C), Bottom (B), Left (L), Right (R), Background (Bkgd).

**4:** ©Laurance B. Aiuppy/Getty Images; **6:** ©Paul King/Getty Images; **8:** ©Stewart Cohen/Getty Images; **10:** (TL, TR) ©ChiselVision/Corbis; **12:** ©Jerry Lofaro/Courtesy of Konica Minolta Business Solutions/American Artists Represents; **14:** ©Jerry Lofaro/Courtesy of Konica Minolta Business Solutions/American Artists Represents; **16:** ©Royalty-Free/Corbis; **17:** Corel; **20:** ©Stockbyte; **36:** ©Steve Kaufman/Corbis; **37:** (BL) ©Art Wolfe/Getty Images, (CR) ©Norbert Rosing/NGS Image Collection; **38:** (TR) ©George D. Lepp/Corbis, (BR) ©Art Wolfe/Photo Researchers, Inc., (Bkgd) ©Tim Davis/Photo Researchers, Inc.; **39:** (TCL) ©George F. Mobley/NGS Image Collection, (TR) ©Joe McDonald; **41:** (T) ©Royalty-Free/Corbis, (TR) Corbis; **42:** Getty Images; **43** ©Bettmann/Corbis; **46**: Getty Images; **48:** Getty Images; **53** Getty Images; **57:** Getty Images; **58:** Getty Images; **62:** ©brt Photo/Mira; **63:** ©Michael Haynes; **64:** (R) ©Michael Haynes, (TR) ©The Newark Museum/Art Resource, NY; **65:** Andreas Von Einsiedel/©DK Images; **67:** (BL) ©Arnold Genthe/Corbis, (TR) ©Bill Varie/Corbis; **69:** (TL) ©Joseph Sohm/Corbis, (TR) Corbis; **82:** ©Royalty-Free/Corbis; **84:** (TR) ©Dallas and John Heaton/Corbis, (BR) ©Roger Ressmeyer/Corbis; **87:** (TL) ©Dex Image, (TR) ©Orion Press/Getty Images, (CL) ©Roger Ressmeyer/Corbis, (CR) ©Ken Biggs/Getty Images; **113:** (B) ©Robert Y. Ono/Corbis, (BC) Getty Images; **114:** ©Royalty-Free/Corbis; **115:** (TL) ©Royalty-Free/Corbis, (TR) Corbis; **116:** (C) ©David Muench/Corbis, (TL, TR, CR) Getty Images; **117:** Getty Images; **118:** Getty Images; **119:** (CR) Getty Images, (BC) Corel, (T) ©Sam Clemens/Getty Images; **120:** (TC, BL) Corel; **121:**(TL) ©Sam Clemens/



Getty Images, (TR) Royalty-Free/Corbis, (BR) Corel; **122:** ©Harvey Lloyd/Getty Images; **123:** (CR) ©Royalty-Free/Corbis, (BR, T) Corel; **124:** (TL) ©Boyle & Boyle/Animals Animals/Earth Scenes, (CR) ©Don Mason/Corbis; **125:** (C, BL) Getty Images; **126:** ©Royalty-Free/ Corbis; **127:** (BR, TR) Getty Images, (TC) Corel, (CR) ©Phil Schermeister/Corbis; **128** ©Royalty-Free/Corbis; **138:** ©Laurance B. Aiuppy/Getty Images; **139:** Getty Images; **140:** ©Paul King/Getty Images; **143:** (TR, BC) Getty Images; **145** ©Royalty-Free/Corbis; **156:** (BR, BC) Getty Images; **163:** ©Yann Arthus-Bertrand/Corbis; **164:** Getty Images; **165:** ©Macduff Everton/Corbis; **190:** ©Jim Sugar/Corbis; **191:** ©W. A. Sharman/Corbis; **213:** ©ThinkStock/SuperStock; **232:** (BL, TR) Courtesy the Lasky Family; **236:** ©W. J. Lubken/Corbis; **237:** Corbis; **238:** (BL) ©E. F. Keller/Corbis, (BR) ©Bluford W. Muir/Corbis; **239:** ©Minnesota Historical Society/Corbis; **241:** ©William Manning/Corbis; **258:** Getty Images; **259:** (TL, CL) ©Royalty-Free/Corbis, (CR) ©Jeffrey Greenberg/Photo Researchers, Inc., (BC, BL) Getty Images, (TR) ©David Muench/Corbis; **264:** (BL) ©Paul King/Getty Images, (CR, CC) Getty Images; **266:** ©Stewart Westmoreland/ Corbis; **267:** (BCR) ©Warren Faidley/Weatherstock, (TC) ©Stewart Cohen/ Getty Images; **269** (T, BR) Getty Images; **271:** Getty Images; **288:** ©Royalty-Free/Corbis; **290:** ©ThinkStock/SuperStock; **291:** ©Chase Swift/Corbis; **293:** ©Tom Brakefield/Corbis; **294:** ©Alan Schein Photography/Corbis; **295:** Brand X Pictures; **310:** ©Natalie Fobes/Corbis; **311:** (CR) ©Flip Nicklin/Minden Pictures, (BL) ©Gunter Marx Photography/Corbis, (BC) Alaska Stock; **312:** (TR) ©Royalty-Free/Corbis, (CR) ©Natalie Fobes/Corbis; **313:** (TR) ©Joel W. Rogers/Corbis, (BL) ©Jeffrey L. Rotman/Corbis; **315:** Getty Images; **316:** Getty Images; **317:** (T) ©Carlos Dominguez/Corbis, (B) ©Carl & Ann Purcell/Corbis; **339:** Corbis; **340:** (BC) Getty Images, (BR) ©Space Frontiers/Getty Images; **341:** ©Walter Rawlings/Robert Harding World Imagery; **342:** ©Warren Faidley/Weatherstock; **343:** (TR, BR, BL) Getty Images; **344:** (TR, BL, BC, BR) ©Warren Faidley/Weatherstock, (B) Getty Images; **345:** (B, BR) ©Warren Faidley/Weatherstock, (BR) Getty Images; **346-348:** ©Warren Faidley/Weatherstock; **349:** (T) Warren Faidley/Weatherstock, (TL) Getty Images; **350:** (TC, TL, TCL, CL) ©Warren Faidley/Weatherstock; **351:** (B) ©Warren Faidley/Weatherstock, (CR) Getty Images; **352:** (TR) Getty Images, (T) ©Warren Faidley/Weatherstock; **353:** ©Warren Faidley/Weatherstock; **354:** ©Warren Faidley/Weatherstock; **356:** Corbis; **357:** (T) Getty Images, (CR) ©Ralph Wetmore/Getty Images; **358:** (T, BR, BC) Getty Images, (CR) ©David R. Frazier/The Image Works, Inc.; **359:** Getty Images; **362:** ©Schafer & Hill/Getty Images; **363:** (T) ©Peter Lilja/Getty Images, (BR) ©Chase Swift/Corbis; **380:** (TR) Brand X Pictures, (BC) Digital Vision; **381:** (TC) Corel, (BR) Frank Greenaway/ Courtesy of the Natural History Museum, London/©DK Images; **382:** ©Tom Brakefield/Corbis; **383:** Corel; **386:** ©Todd Gipstein/NGS Image Collection; **388:** ©Stewart Cohen/Getty Images; **389:** (CR) ©Comstock Inc., (CC) Getty Images; **390:** ©ChiselVision/Corbis; **393:** ©Bettmann/Corbis; **394:** Comstock Production Department/©Comstock Inc.; **395:** (TL) Dave King/©DK Images, (TR) ©Royalty-Free/Corbis, (BR) ©Myrleen Ferguson/PhotoEdit; **417:** (TR) Brand X Pictures, (CL) ©Royalty-Free/Corbis; **418:** ©Bob Krist/Corbis; **419:** (TR) ©Royalty-Free/Corbis, (BR) Getty Images; **420:** ©Todd Pusser/Nature Picture Library; **422:** ©Wolfgang Kaehler/Corbis; **423:** Getty Images; **424:** Getty Images; **428:** Brand X Pictures; **429:** ©Andre Baertschi; **430:** ©Royalty-Free/Corbis; **433:** Getty Images; **434:** (TL) ©Buddy Mays/Corbis, (B) ©Hong Kong Dolphinwatch, Ltd.; **436:** (BR) ©Darek Karp/Animals Animals/Earth Scenes, (TR) ©Dr. Morley Read/Photo Researchers, Inc.; **437:** (TR, BR) Getty Images, (CR) Andy Crawford/©DK Images; **438:** ©William Grenfell/Visuals Unlimited; **466:** ©Gianni Dagli Orti/Corbis; **468:** ©Royalty-Free/Corbis; **469:** ©Archivo Iconografico, S.A./Corbis; **472-482:** Getty Images; **484:** ©Royalty-Free/Corbis; **486:** (BL) ©Ralph A. Clevenger/Corbis, (BC, CC, BC, BL) Getty Images, (BL) ©Lisa Henderling/Images, Inc.; **487:** (TL, BL) ©Comstock, Inc., (TC, TCL, TCR, CR) Getty Images, (TR) ©Images/Corbis, (CL) ©Rubberball Productions, (BC) ©Royalty-Free/Corbis; **490:** Getty Images; **491:** Getty Images; **505:** ©Royalty-Free/Corbis; **506:** (TL) ©Becky Shink/Lansing State Journal, (BC) Getty Images; **507:** Getty Images; **512:** ©ChiselVision/Corbis; **513:** (BR) Brand X Pictures, (CR) Getty Images, (TR) ©ChiselVision/Corbis; **514:** (C, Bkgd) ©Royalty-Free/Corbis; **515:** ©Jennifer Owings Dewey; **519:** (TC) Getty Images, (BR) ©Royalty-Free/Corbis; **532:** (BC) San Francisco Maritime National Historical Park, (BR) Jefferson County Historical Society; **533:** (BL) Jefferson County Historical Society, (BC, BR) Ena Marie Sroat; **536:** ©Harry Benson; **537** ©Kevin Horan/Time Life Pictures/Getty Images; **539:** (TL) Corbis, (TR) ©Lowell Georgia/Corbis; **541:** (T) Getty Images, (B) ©Roger Ressmeyer/Corbis; **556:** ©Jim Erickson/Corbis; **558:** (CR) ©Roman Soumar/Corbis, (B) ©Dave Wilhelm/Corbis; **559:** (CL) ©Kevin Schafer/Corbis, (TR) ©Francesco Venturi/Corbis; **561:** Corbis; **562:** Corbis; **563:** (TC) ©National Aviation Museum/Corbis, (CC) Corbis; **575:** National Air and Space Museum/Smithsonian Institution; **578:** (B) Corbis, (TR) Library of Congress; **580:** (CL) Bridgeman Art Library, (TL) Library of Congress; **581:** (TL) Courtesy, Marin History Museum, (T) Digital Vision; **583:** ©Ralph A. Clevenger/Corbis; **584:** Getty Images; **585:** ©Joel W. Rogers/Corbis; **586:** Digital Vision; **590:** ©Jennifer Owings Dewey; **592:** (TR, CL, BC) National Science Foundation, (BR) ©Jennifer Owings Dewey; **594:** (BL, BC) ©Jennifer Owings Dewey; **595-602:** National Science Foundation; **604:** Corbis; **605:** ©Gabriella Miotto; **606:** (TL) ©Gabriella Minotto, (BR) AP/Wide World Photos; **607:** Corbis; **610:** ©1996/Original image courtesy of NASA/Corbis; **611:** (T) ©1996/Original image courtesy of NASA/Corbis, (TL) ©NASA/Roger Ressmeyer/Corbis, (TR, BR) Corbis; **626:** Getty Images; **627:** Getty Images; **628:** (B) ©1996/Original image courtesy of NASA/Corbis, (CL) Getty Images; **629:** (TL) Getty Images, (CR) NASA/Corbis; **634:** ©Jerry Lofaro/Courtesy of Konica Minolta Business Solutions/American Artists Represents; **635:** (BR) Corbis, (TR) ©Jerry Lofaro/Courtesy of Konica Minolta Business Solutions/American Artists Represents; **636:** ©Jerry Lofaro/Courtesy of Konica Minolta Business Solutions/American Artists Represents; **639:** ©Bettmann/Corbis; **640:** ©Comstock, Inc.; **641:** (BR, TR) ©Comstock Inc.; **661:** (T) Corbis, (TC) Getty Images; **678:** (CL, CR, BR) Cumberland County Historical Society/Carlisle, PA, (TL) Getty Images; **679:** (TL, BR, CC) Cumberland County Historical Society/Carlisle, PA, (BC) Getty Images; **682:** (T) ©Joseph Sohm/ChromoSohm, Inc/Corbis, (BC) ©Reuters/Corbis; **683:** ©Stephane Cardinale/Corbis; **684:** (TL) ©Robert W. Ginn/PhotoEdit, (TR) ©Kathleen Kliskey-Geraghty/Index Stock Imagery, (B, BL) ©Jonathan Nourok/PhotoEdit; **685:** (TR) ©The Times/AP/Wide World Photos, (TC) ©The Daily Oakland Press/AP/Wide World Photos; **687:** (TL) Getty Images, (TR) ©Royalty-Free/Corbis; **688:** ©W. Cody/Corbis; **689:** (TL) Getty Images, (TR) ©Bass Museum of Art/Corbis; **715:** (T, B) ©Royalty-Free/Corbis; **734:** (BR) Corbis, (TR) ©Underwood & Underwood/ Corbis; **735:** Getty Images; **736:** (BR, TCL) Corbis, (TL, TCR) ©Bettmann/Corbis, (TC) ©Underwood & Underwood/Corbis; **737:** The Granger Collection, NY; **739:** Getty Images; **741** (T, B, BR) Getty Images; **743-751:** NASA; **752:** NASA; **753:** NASA; **754:** ©Time Life Pictures/Getty Images; **755:** ©Time Life Pictures/Getty Images; **758:** Getty Images; **759:** Getty Images; **760:** Getty Images; **761:** Getty Images; **766:** (CL) ©Hulton-Deutsch Collection/Corbis, (BCL, CR, BCR) Corbis, (BL) ©Jerry Lofaro/Courtesy of Konica Minolta Business Solutions/American Artists Represents; **767:** Getty Images; **773:** ©Ted Lewin; **774:** ©Laurie Myers; **775:** ©Wendy Barry/ Houghton Mifflin Company; **785:** JSC/NASA; **786:** ©E. R. Degginger/Animals Animals/Earth Scenes; **787:** ©Oliver Benn/Getty Images; **788:** ©Stouffer Productions/Animals Animals/Earth Scenes; **791:** ©Robert Amft; **793:** ©Bernard Desestres/Vandystadt/Photo Researchers, Inc.; **794:** SuperStock; **797** (CL) ©Amy and Chuck Wiley/Wales/Index Stock Imagery, (CR) ©Rob Crandall/Stock Connection; **798:** Corbis; **799:** ©H. Taylor/OSF/Animals Animals/Earth Scenes; **801:** ©Robert Frerck/Odyssey/Chicago; **802:** SuperStock; **805:** ©Tim Brown/Index Stock Imagery; **806:** ©Steve Vidler/SuperStock; **807:** ©Michael Fogden/OSF/Animals Animals/Earth Scenes; **808:** (BR) Getty Images, (BL) ©Don Mason/Corbis; **813:** (TL, TC) Getty Images.

### Glossary

The contents of this glossary have been adapted from *Thorndike Barnhart Intermediate Dictionary*. Copyright © 1997, Pearson Education, Inc.

# Writing

# Assessment

# Student Tips for Making Top Scores in Writing Tests

**1** **Use transitions such as those below to relate ideas, sentences, or paragraphs.**

| | | | |
|---|---|---|---|
| in addition | nevertheless | finally | however |
| then | instead | therefore | as a result |
| for example | in particular | first | such as |

**2** **Write a good beginning. Make readers want to continue.**
- I shouldn't have opened that green box.
- Imagine being locked in a crate at the bottom of the sea.
- When I was four, I saw a purple dog.
- Have you ever heard of a talking tree?

**3** **Focus on the topic.**
If a word or detail is off-topic, get rid of it. If a sentence is unrelated or loosely related to the topic, drop it or connect it more closely.

**4** **Organize your ideas.**
Have a plan in mind before you start writing. Your plan can be a list, bulleted items, or a graphic organizer. Five minutes spent planning your work will make the actual writing go much faster and smoother.

**5** **Support your ideas.**
- Develop your ideas with fully elaborated examples and details.
- Make ideas clear to readers by choosing vivid words that create pictures. Avoid dull (*get, go, say*), vague (*thing, stuff, lots of*), or overused (*really, very*) words.
- Use a voice that is appropriate to your audience.

**6** **Make writing conventions as error-free as possible.**
Proofread your work line by line, sentence by sentence. Read for correct punctuation, then again for correct capitalization, and finally for correct spelling.

**7** **Write a conclusion that wraps things up but is more than a repeating of ideas or "The end."**
- After all, he was my brother, weird or not.
- The Internet has changed our lives for better and for worse.
- It's not the largest planet but the one I'd choose to live on.
- Now tell me you don't believe in a sixth sense.

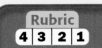

**Rubric**
4 | 3 | 2 | 1

**Focus/Ideas**

**Organization/ Paragraphs**

**Voice**

**Word Choice**

**Sentences**

**Conventions**

# Writing Traits

- **Focus/Ideas** refers to the main purpose for writing and the details that make the subject clear and interesting. It includes development of ideas through support and elaboration.

- **Organization/Paragraphs** refers to the overall structure of a piece of writing that guides readers. Within that structure, transitions show how ideas, sentences, and paragraphs are connected.

- **Voice** shows the writer's unique personality and establishes a connection between writer and reader. Voice, which contributes to style, should be suited to the audience and the purpose for writing.

- **Word Choice** is the use of precise, vivid words to communicate effectively and naturally. It helps create style through the use of specific nouns, lively verbs and adjectives, and accurate, well-placed modifiers.

- **Sentences** covers strong, well-built sentences that vary in length and type. Skillfully written sentences have pleasing rhythms and flow fluently.

- **Conventions** refers to mechanical correctness and includes grammar, usage, spelling, punctuation, capitalization, and paragraphing.

# Story

## OBJECTIVES

- Develop an understanding of a story.
- Include story elements such as characters, setting, and plot in a story.
- Write a good beginning for a story.
- Establish criteria for evaluating a story.

### Key Features
**Story**

**In a story, a writer narrates a series of related events involving specific characters in a specific setting.**

- Has a beginning, middle, and end
- Focuses on one incident or event
- Uses time-order words to show the sequence of events
- Has characters, plot, and a setting

### Connect to Weekly Writing

| Week 1 | Story About a Discovery 415g–415h |
| Week 2 | Travel Brochure 439g–439h |
| Week 3 | Business Letter 465g–465h |
| Week 4 | Feature Story 487g–487h |
| Week 5 | Plot Summary 507g–507h |

### Strategic Intervention

See Differentiated Instruction p. WA8.

### Advanced

See Differentiated Instruction p. WA9.

### ELL

See Differentiated Instruction p. WA9.

**Additional Resource for Writing**
Writing Rubrics and Anchor Papers, pp. 62–70.

**Writing Prompt:** *Puzzles and Mysteries*
Write a story about something that happens on a real or an imaginary trip. Try to include suspense or humor and dialogue.
Purpose: Entertain
Audience: Your Classmates

## READ LIKE A WRITER

Look back at *The King in the Kitchen*. Remind students how a play uses dialogue, the actual words a character says, to advance the plot. Point out that most effective **stories** use a combination of dialogue and description to keep the reader interested.

## EXAMINE THE MODEL AND RUBRIC

**GUIDED WRITING** Read the model aloud. Point out that the writer grabs the reader's attention in the first sentence by having a character shout an exclamation. Discuss how the model reflects traits of good writing.

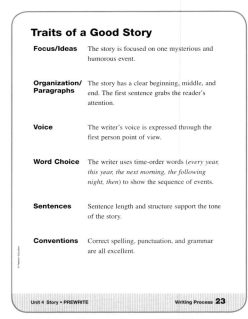

▲ **Writing Transparency** WP22     ▲ **Writing Transparency** WP23

## FINDING A TOPIC

- Have students discuss times when they experienced something puzzling or mysterious. Remind them that a real event can be in a fictional story.
- Ask students to think of people they know about, such as historical figures, celebrities, or family members. Point out that a writer may borrow characteristics from real people to create a believable character.
- Share classic stories. Have students answer the following questions about their favorites: Whose story is it? What is the problem? Tell them to consider these same questions when thinking about story ideas.

## NARROW A TOPIC

**A trip to Pluto**          I don't know much about this.

**A visit to a museum**      I saw a display that gives me a story idea.

**A plan to scare someone**  This wouldn't make a very good story.

## PREWRITING STRATEGY

**GUIDED WRITING** Display Writing Transparency WP24. Model how to complete a story chart.

**Think Aloud** **MODEL** This student has decided to write a story about a boy on a field trip to a museum. There is a clear order of events, a problem, and an imaginative solution. When details are added, I think this will be a very good story.

### PREWRITING ACTIVITIES

- Have students use Grammar and Writing Practice Book p. 172 to map out the characters, setting, events, and solution for their story.
- Students can brainstorm real and imagined trips as story ideas.

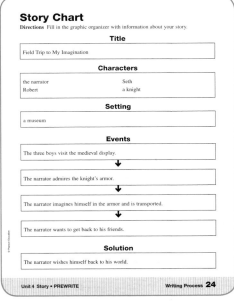

**Story Chart**
Directions Fill in the graphic organizer with information about your story.

**Title**
Field Trip to My Imagination

**Characters**
the narrator          Seth
Robert                a knight

**Setting**
a museum

**Events**
The three boys visit the medieval display.
↓
The narrator admires the knight's armor.
↓
The narrator imagines himself in the armor and is transported.
↓
The narrator wants to get back to his friends.

**Solution**
The narrator wishes himself back to his world.

Unit 4 Story • PREWRITE          Writing Process **24**

▲ **Writing Transparency** WP24

**Trips**

| Real | Imagined |
|------|----------|
| camping trip | trip to a star |
| day at the beach | flying a spaceship |
| field trip | time travel |

WRITING WORKSHOP 4                                    Story

Name

**Story Chart**
Directions Fill in the graphic organizer with information about your story.

**Title**

**Characters**
Answers should include details about students' stories.

**Setting**

**Events**

**Solution**

**172** Unit 4                    Grammar and Writing Practice Book

▲ **Grammar and Writing Practice Book** p. 172

## Writing Workshop

1 PREWRITE  2 DRAFT  3 REVISE  4 EDIT  5 PUBLISH

### Think Like a Writer

**Show an Emotion** A good storyteller provides vivid details, such as "a tear rolled down her cheek," instead of "she felt sad," to show a character's emotion. Descriptions of a character's actions can give the reader hints about how the character feels. The writer shows an emotion, rather than just telling the reader what the character is feeling. Show, not tell, is the rule for livelier writing.

### ELL

**Support Writing** If students include home-language words in their drafts, help them find replacement words in English. Resources can include

- conversations with you
- other home-language speakers
- bilingual dictionaries, if available
- online translation sources

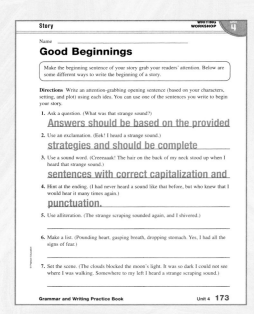

▲ **Grammar and Writing Practice Book** p. 173

## WRITING THE FIRST DRAFT

**GUIDED WRITING** Use Writing Transparency WP25 to practice writing good beginnings.

- Discuss why a good beginning is important to a story. Have students read the strategies for writing a good beginning.
- Read through the sentences and have students identify which strategy the writer used in each sentence.

**Think Aloud** **MODEL** Read these sentences and think about the strategies for writing a good beginning. How does each beginning sentence really grab the reader's attention? Let's identify the strategy used for each sentence. You might choose one of these strategies when writing your own stories.

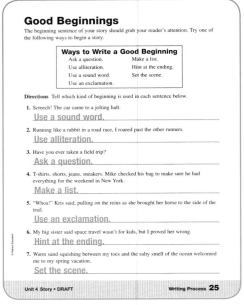

▲ **Writing Transparency** WP25

### WRITER'S CRAFT  Sensory Details

Here are some ways writers can involve the reader in the story.

- Consider what the character sees, smells, tastes, feels, and hears.
- Set the scene by beginning with a description of the place where events occur.
- Use details to enhance the mood of your story.

## DRAFTING STRATEGIES

- Have students review their story chart before they write.
- Students should use one strategy for writing a good beginning.
- Remind students to keep their audience and purpose in mind.
- Students should reread their story to see where they might add sensory details.
- Have students use Grammar and Writing Practice Book p. 173 to practice writing good beginnings.

## WRITER'S CRAFT Elaboration

**AVOID REPETITION** The repetition of nouns makes writing tedious to read. Explain that one way to elaborate is to use pronouns in place of nouns.

> **Repetitious**   Kevin said <u>Kevin</u> would ask <u>Kevin's</u> mother if <u>Kevin</u> could go to the concert.
>
> **Smoother**   Kevin said <u>he</u> would ask <u>his</u> mother if <u>he</u> could go to the concert.

Use Grammar and Writing Practice Book p. 174 to practice avoiding repetition by substituting pronouns.

## REVISING STRATEGIES

**GUIDED WRITING** Use Writing Transparency WP26 to model revising. Point out the Revising Marks, which students should use when they revise their work.

**Think Aloud** **MODEL** This is part of the story about a boy who is transported into a museum display by the power of his imagination. The sentence *I could imagine what it would feel like to be inside the armor* has been replaced with a sentence that provides sensory details. The boy imagines the cold feel of the metal and the weight of the sword. In the second paragraph, the writer has taken out the unnecessary word *still* and rewritten the sentence *They looked shocked.* The revised sentence shows exactly what the narrator sees: Robert with his mouth hanging open, and Seth holding his head in his hands. Using sensory details and showing, rather than telling, improve the writing.

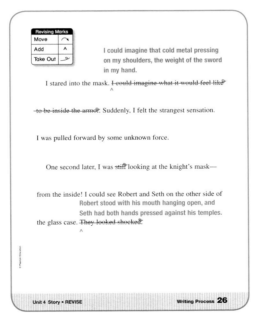

▲ **Writing Transparency** WP26

**PEER REVISION** Write the Revising Checklist on the board, or make copies to distribute. Students can use this checklist to revise their stories. Have partners read each other's first drafts. Remind them to be courteous and specific with suggestions.

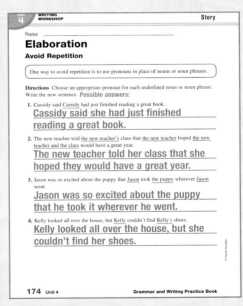

▲ **Grammar and Writing Practice Book** p. 174

# Writing Workshop

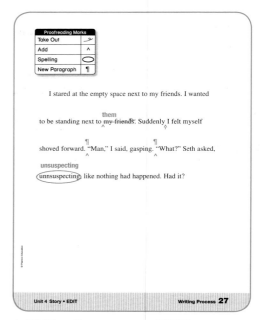

---

## Monitor Progress

### Differentiated Instruction

| **If...** students are using possessive pronouns incorrectly, | **then...** review the grammar lesson on pp. 487e–487f. |
|---|---|

## Editing Checklist

✔ Did I spell all contractions correctly?

✔ Did I use pronouns correctly?

✔ Did I check punctuation and capitalization for every sentence?

✔ Did I check words with the prefix *un-?*

---

## EDITING STRATEGY

**KEEP A DICTIONARY HANDY** Suggest that students use an editing strategy. They can check their spelling by looking up words they are unsure of in a dictionary.

**GUIDED WRITING** Use Writing Transparency WP27 to model the process of editing by keeping a dictionary handy. Indicate the Proofreading Marks, which students should use when they edit their work. Write the Editing Checklist on the board, or make copies to distribute. Students can use this checklist to edit their work.

 **MODEL** In the second sentence, the writer has replaced the words *my friends* with the pronoun *them.* The previous sentence ended with the antecedent, so the writer can refer back to that and eliminate wordiness. A comma has been added after the word *Suddenly.* A new paragraph must begin with each line of dialogue, so the paragraph symbol appears before the narrator's quote and again before Seth's response. In the last sentence, the writer has misspelled the word *unsuspecting.* He checks this in the dictionary. Yes, when *un-* is added to a base word, the spelling of the base does not change.

▲ **Writing Transparency** WP27

 **USING TECHNOLOGY** Students who have written or revised their stories on computers should keep these points in mind as they edit:

- Select a special font for your final draft to give your story a professional look. Choose script or a style that matches the mood of your story.

- If your program has a print preview or a page layout feature, you may wish to use it when you are finished typing your work. It will show you how the work will appear on your page before it is printed.

- When you have questions about how to do something on the computer, check with a friend or use the Help menu.

---

## ELL

**Support Writing** Invite students to read their drafts aloud to you. Observe whether they seem to note any spelling or grammatical errors by stumbling or self-correcting. Return to those errors and explain how to correct them. Use the appropriate Grammar Transition Lessons in the ELL Resource Handbook to explicitly teach the English conventions.

1 PREWRITE 2 DRAFT 3 REVISE 4 EDIT 5 PUBLISH

## SELF-EVALUATION

Prepare students to fill out a Self-Evaluation Guide. Display Writing Transparency WP28 to model the self-evaluation process.

**Think Aloud** **MODEL** I would give the story a 4.

**Focus/Ideas** Story focuses on one event.

**Organization/Paragraphs** The story has a clear beginning, middle, and end. The beginning sentence gets the reader's attention.

**Voice** The narrator's voice contributes to the mood of surprise and shock.

**Word Choice** The writer includes sensory details that show, rather than tell.

**Sentences** Sentences are varied. Fragments and exclamations create realistic dialogue.

**Conventions** Grammar, capitalization, and spelling are correct.

**EVALUATION** Assign Grammar and Writing Practice Book p. 175. Tell students that when they evaluate their own stories, assigning a score of 3, 2, or even 1 does not necessarily indicate a bad paper. The ability to identify areas for improvement in future writing is a valuable skill.

### Field Trip to My Imagination

Have you ever taken a field trip? Our last trip was to a museum. Robert, Seth, and I headed straight for the medieval display. We were almost as tall as the suits of armor! There were also swords, shields, and goblets. We stood with our noses pressed up against the glass, staring at a chain link suit.

I stared into the mask. I could imagine that cold metal pressing on my shoulders, the weight of the sword in my hand. Suddenly, I felt the strangest sensation. I was pulled forward by some unknown force.

One second later, I was looking at the knight's mask—from the inside! I could see Robert and Seth on the other side of the glass case. Robert stood with his mouth hanging open, and Seth had both hands pressed against his temples.

"I'm not looking for a fight," the knight on my left said.

"Whaaaa?" I jumped, turning to face him.

"You got a good imagination, kid. You transported yourself into the armor, but you didn't go far enough to actually make it to the battlefield."

"Battlefield? No! How do I get out of here?"

"Same way you got in," the knight said.

I stared at the empty space next to my friends. I wanted to be standing next to them. Suddenly, I felt myself shoved forward.

"Man!" I said, gasping.

"What?" Seth asked, unsuspecting, like nothing had happened. Had it?

Unit 4 Story • PUBLISH                    Writing Process **28**

▲ **Writing Transparency** WP28

## Ideas for Publishing

**Class Storybook** Bind the stories together in a class book. Have a student design a cover that reflects the theme of the unit.

**Stories on Stage** Choose a few stories and have students act them out for the class, incorporating emotions and dialogue.

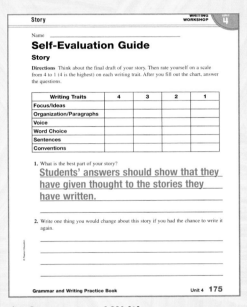

▲ **Grammar and Writing Practice Book** p. 175

## Scoring Rubric — Story

| Rubric 4 3 2 1 | 4 | 3 | 2 | 1 |
|---|---|---|---|---|
| **Focus/Ideas** | Story clearly focused on one event | Story generally focused on one event | Story lacks focus; event unclear | Story without focus; no event |
| **Organization/ Paragraphs** | Well organized, with clear beginning, middle, end | Organized with beginning, middle, end | Lacks clear beginning, middle, end | Lacks organization |
| **Voice** | Voice of character or narrator believable and engaging | Voice of character or narrator somewhat believable | Character or narrator lacking distinct voice | Voice of character or narrator not believable |
| **Word Choice** | Uses transitions to show sequence; includes sensory details | Uses some transitions to show sequence; some sensory details | Sequence of events unclear; no sensory details used | No attempt to show sequence or include sensory details |
| **Sentences** | Correct and varied sentences | Most sentences correct | Some sentences incorrect | Incorrect sentence structure |
| **Conventions** | Few, if any, errors | Several errors | Many errors in spelling, usage, and punctuation | Frequent errors that distract from story |

**For 6-, 5-, and 3-point Scoring Rubrics, see pp. WA11-WA14.**

# WRITING Workshop

## Story
# Differentiated Instruction

**WRITING PROMPT:** *Puzzles and Mysteries*

Write a story about something that happens on a real or an imaginary trip. Try to include suspense or humor and dialogue.

**Purpose:** Entertain

**Audience:** Your classmates

**ALTERNATIVE PROMPTS**

**MODIFY INSTRUCTION**

*Pick One*

## Strategic Intervention

### MODIFY THE PROMPT

Help emerging writers organize their ideas by transferring their story chart into three paragraphs. Write out the headings *Beginning, Middle,* and *End.* Encourage students to write a few sentences under each heading.

**PREWRITING SUPPORT**

- Invite a storyteller to your class to generate interest in storytelling and to demonstrate the power of storytelling.
- Ask students to identify elements of favorite stories that they might want to replicate in their stories.
- Interview students to get details about their characters, setting, and plot. Make suggestions about any elements they may be missing.

**OPTIONS**

- Give students the option of writing a group story under your supervision.

**CHECK PROGRESS** Segment the assignment into manageable pieces. Check work at intervals, such as graphic organizers and first drafts, to make sure writing is on track.

**ALTERNATIVE PROMPTS:** Narrative Writing

**Strategic Intervention** Think of a trip you take regularly, such as walking to school, shopping with a friend, or visiting a relative. Write your story about one event that happens during this trip.

**On-Level** Imagine a trip to a foreign country, a place you've never visited before. What interests you most about this country? Write a story in which you focus on one thing that you find mysterious about this place.

**Advanced** Think of a mystery you would like to solve. Send a cast of characters on a trip to solve the mystery. Include mood, dialogue, and sensory details in your tale. Remember to write a solution to the mystery too.

## MODIFY THE PROMPT

Expect advanced writers to write a story that includes a well-developed problem and a clear solution. They should incorporate sensory details that create a distinctive, identifiable mood. Their stories will most likely include a larger cast of characters and more dialogue.

### APPLY SKILLS

- As students revise their work, have them consider some ways to improve it.

    Consider a different beginning sentence, perhaps a question, a sound word, or an exclamation.

    Add sensory details to enhance the mood of the story.

    Look for places to add time-order words to clarify the sequence of events.

### OPTIONS

- Students can follow these steps to create their own class rubrics.

    **1.** Read examples of class stories and rank them 1–4, with 4 the highest.

    **2.** Discuss how they arrived at each rank.

    **3.** Isolate the six traits and make a rubric based on them.

**CHECK PROGRESS** Discuss the students' Self-Evaluation Guides. Work with students to monitor their growth and identify their strengths and weaknesses as writers.

## MODIFY THE PROMPT

Allow beginning speakers to dictate their stories to you or to a classmate to record. In the revising step, have students copy the story they have dictated.

### BUILD BACKGROUND

- Write the word *story* on the board. Ask students to think about the earliest stories. How were stories passed down before people had a written language? Ask for some examples of early stories and famous oral storytellers. *(Aesop, Homer)* Discuss the list of Key Features of a story that appears in the left column of p. W2.

### OPTIONS

- As students write their stories, guide them toward books, magazines, or Web sites that provide comprehension support through features such as the following:

    strong picture/text correspondence

    detailed photographs or illustrations

    text in the home-language

- For more suggestions on scaffolding the Writing Workshop, see the ELL and Transition Handbook.

**CHECK PROGRESS** You may need to explain certain traits and help students fill out their Self-Evaluation Guides. Downplay conventions and focus more on ideas. Recognize examples of vocabulary growth and efforts to use language in more complex ways.

## Scoring Rubric | Look Back and Write

**2 points** The response indicates that the student has a complete understanding of the reading concept embodied in the task. The response is accurate, complete, and fulfills all the requirements of the task. Necessary support and/or examples are included, and the information given is clearly text-based.

**1 point** The response indicates that the student has a partial understanding of the reading concept embodied in the task. The response includes information that is essentially correct and text-based, but the information is too general or too simplistic. Some of the support and/or examples may be incomplete or omitted.

**0 points** The response indicates that the student does not demonstrate an understanding of the reading concept embodied in the task. The student has either failed to respond or has provided a response that is inaccurate or has insufficient information.

## Scoring Rubric | Look Back and Write

**4 points** The response indicates that the student has a thorough understanding of the reading concept embodied in the task. The response is accurate, complete, and fulfills all the requirements of the task. Necessary support and/or examples are included, and the information is clearly text-based.

**3 points** The response indicates that the student has an understanding of the reading concept embodied in the task. The response is accurate and fulfills all the requirements of the task, but the required support and/or details are not complete or clearly text-based.

**2 points** The response indicates that the student has a partial understanding of the reading concept embodied in the task. The response that includes information is essentially correct and text-based, but the information is too general or too simplistic. Some of the support and/or examples and requirements of the task may be incomplete or omitted.

**1 point** The response indicates that the student has a very limited understanding of the reading concept embodied in the task. The response is incomplete, may exhibit many flaws, and may not address all requirements of the task.

**0 points** The response indicates that the student does not demonstrate an understanding of the reading concept embodied in the task. The student has either failed to respond or has provided a response that is inaccurate or has insufficient information.

## Scoring Rubric — Narrative Writing

**Rubric 4 3 2 1**

| | 6 | 5 | 4 | 3 | 2 | 1 |
|---|---|---|---|---|---|---|
| **Focus/Ideas** | Excellent, focused narrative; well elaborated with quality details | Good, focused narrative; elaborated with telling details | Narrative focused; adequate elaboration | Generally focused narrative; some supporting details | Sometimes unfocused narrative; needs more supporting details | Rambling narrative; lacks development and detail |
| **Organization/ Paragraphs** | Strong beginning, middle, and end; appropriate order words | Coherent beginning, middle, and end; some order words | Beginning, middle, and end easily identifiable | Recognizable beginning, middle, and end; some order words | Little direction from beginning to end; few order words | Lacks beginning, middle, end; incorrect or no order words |
| **Voice** | Writer closely involved; engaging personality | Reveals personality | Pleasant but not compelling voice | Sincere voice but not fully engaged | Little writer involvement, personality | Careless writing with no feeling |
| **Word Choice** | Vivid, precise words that bring story to life | Clear words to bring story to life | Some specific word pictures | Language adequate but lacks color | Generally limited or redundant language | Vague, dull, or misused words |
| **Sentences** | Excellent variety of sentences; natural rhythm | Varied lengths, styles; generally smooth | Correct sentences with some variations in style | Correctly constructed sentences; some variety | May have simple, awkward, or wordy sentences; little variety | Choppy; many incomplete or run-on sentences |
| **Conventions** | Excellent control; few or no errors | No serious errors to affect understanding | General mastery of conventions but some errors | Reasonable control; few distracting errors | Weak control; enough errors to affect understanding | Many errors that prevent understanding |

## Scoring Rubric — Narrative Writing

**Rubric 4 3 2 1**

| | 5 | 4 | 3 | 2 | 1 |
|---|---|---|---|---|---|
| **Focus/Ideas** | Excellent, focused narrative; well elaborated with quality details | Good, focused narrative; elaborated with telling details | Generally focused narrative; some supporting details | Sometimes unfocused narrative; needs more supporting details | Rambling narrative; lacks development and detail |
| **Organization/ Paragraphs** | Strong beginning, middle, and end; appropriate order words | Coherent beginning, middle, and end; some order words | Recognizable beginning, middle, and end; some order words | Little direction from beginning to end; few order words | Lacks beginning, middle, end; incorrect or no order words |
| **Voice** | Writer closely involved; engaging personality | Reveals personality | Sincere voice but not fully engaged | Little writer involvement, personality | Careless writing with no feeling |
| **Word Choice** | Vivid, precise words that bring story to life | Clear words to bring story to life | Language adequate but lacks color | Generally limited or redundant language | Vague, dull, or misused words |
| **Sentences** | Excellent variety of sentences; natural rhythm | Varied lengths, styles; generally smooth | Correctly constructed sentences; some variety | May have simple, awkward, or wordy sentences; little variety | Choppy; many incomplete or run-on sentences |
| **Conventions** | Excellent control; few or no errors | No serious errors to affect understanding | Reasonable control; few distracting errors | Weak control; enough errors to affect understanding | Many errors that prevent understanding |

## Scoring Rubric — Narrative Writing

**Rubric 4 3 2 1**

| | 3 | 2 | 1 |
|---|---|---|---|
| **Focus/Ideas** | Excellent, focused narrative; well elaborated with quality details | Generally focused narrative; some supporting details | Rambling narrative; lacks development and detail |
| **Organization/ Paragraphs** | Strong beginning, middle, and end; appropriate order words | Recognizable beginning, middle, and some order words | Lacks beginning, middle, end; incorrect or no order words |
| **Voice** | Writer closely involved; engaging personality | Sincere voice but not fully engaged | Careless writing with no feeling |
| **Word Choice** | Vivid, precise words that bring story to life | Language adequate but lacks color | Vague, dull, or misused words |
| **Sentences** | Excellent variety of sentences; natural rhythm | Correctly constructed sentences; some variety | Choppy; many incomplete or run-on sentences |
| **Conventions** | Excellent control; few or no errors | Reasonable control; few distracting errors | Many errors that prevent understanding |

## Scoring Rubric — Descriptive Writing

**Rubric 4 3 2 1**

| | 6 | 5 | 4 | 3 | 2 | 1 |
|---|---|---|---|---|---|---|
| **Focus/Ideas** | Excellent, focused description; well elaborated with quality details | Good, focused description; elaborated with telling details | Description focused; good elaboration | Generally focused description; some supporting details | Sometimes unfocused description; needs more supporting details | Rambling description; lacks development and detail |
| **Organization/ Paragraphs** | Compelling ideas enhanced by order, structure, and transitions | Appealing order, structure, and transitions | Structure identifiable and suitable; transitions used | Adequate order, structure, and some transitions to guide reader | Little direction from beginning to end; few transitions | Lacks direction and identifiable structure; no transitions |
| **Voice** | Writer closely involved; engaging personality | Reveals personality | Pleasant but not compelling voice | Sincere voice but not fully engaged | Little writer involvement, personality | Careless writing with no feeling |
| **Word Choice** | Vivid, precise words that create memorable pictures | Clear, interesting words to bring description to life | Some specific word pictures | Language adequate; appeals to senses | Generally limited or redundant language | Vague, dull, or misused words |
| **Sentences** | Excellent variety of sentences; natural rhythm | Varied lengths, styles; generally smooth | Correct sentences with variations in style | Correctly constructed sentences; some variety | May have simple, awkward, or wordy sentences; little variety | Choppy; many incomplete run-on sentences |
| **Conventions** | Excellent control; few or no errors | No serious errors to affect understanding | General mastery of conventions but some errors | Reasonable control; few distracting errors | Weak control; enough errors to affect understanding | Many errors that prevent understanding |

## Scoring Rubric — Descriptive Writing

**Rubric 4 3 2 1**

| | 5 | 4 | 3 | 2 | 1 |
|---|---|---|---|---|---|
| **Focus/Ideas** | Excellent, focused description; well elaborated with quality details | Good, focused description; elaborated with telling details | Generally focused description; some supporting details | Sometimes unfocused description; needs more supporting details | Rambling description; lacks development and detail |
| **Organization/ Paragraphs** | Compelling ideas enhanced by order, structure, and transitions | Appealing order, structure, and transitions | Adequate order, structure, and some transitions to guide reader | Little direction from beginning to end; few transitions | Lacks direction and identifiable structure; no transitions |
| **Voice** | Writer closely involved; engaging personality | Reveals personality | Sincere voice but not fully engaged | Little writer involvement, personality | Careless writing with no feeling |
| **Word Choice** | Vivid, precise words that create memorable pictures | Clear, interesting words to bring description to life | Language adequate; appeals to senses | Generally limited or redundant language | Vague, dull, or misused words |
| **Sentences** | Excellent variety of sentences; natural rhythm | Varied lengths, styles; generally smooth | Correctly constructed sentences; some variety | May have simple, awkward, or wordy sentences; little variety | Choppy; many incomplete or run-on sentences |
| **Conventions** | Excellent control; few or no errors | No serious errors to affect understanding | Reasonable control; few distracting errors | Weak control; enough errors to affect understanding | Many errors that prevent understanding |

## Scoring Rubric — Descriptive Writing

**Rubric 4 3 2 1**

| | 3 | 2 | 1 |
|---|---|---|---|
| **Focus/Ideas** | Excellent, focused description; well elaborated with quality details | Generally focused description; some supporting details | Rambling description; lacks development and detail |
| **Organization/ Paragraphs** | Compelling ideas enhanced by order, structure, and transitions | Adequate order, structure, and some transitions to guide reader | Lacks direction and identifiable structure; no transitions |
| **Voice** | Writer closely involved; engaging personality | Sincere voice but not fully engaged | Careless writing with no feeling |
| **Word Choice** | Vivid, precise words that create memorable pictures | Language adequate; appeals to senses | Vague, dull, or misused words |
| **Sentences** | Excellent variety of sentences; natural rhythm | Correctly constructed sentences; some variety | Choppy; many incomplete or run-on sentences |
| **Conventions** | Excellent control; few or no errors | Reasonable control; few distracting errors | Many errors that prevent understanding |

## Scoring Rubric — Persuasive Writing

Rubric 4 | 3 | 2 | 1

| | 6 | 5 | 4 | 3 | 2 | 1 |
|---|---|---|---|---|---|---|
| **Focus/Ideas** | Persuasive argument carefully built with quality details | Persuasive argument well supported with details | Persuasive argument focused; good elaboration | Persuasive argument with one or two convincing details | Persuasive piece sometimes unfocused; needs more support | Rambling persuasive argument; lacks development and detail |
| **Organization/ Paragraphs** | Information chosen and arranged for maximum effect | Evident progression of persuasive ideas | Progression and structure evident | Information arranged in a logical way with some lapses | Little structure or direction | No identifiable structure |
| **Voice** | Writer closely involved; persuasive but not overbearing | Maintains persuasive tone | Persuasive but not compelling voice | Sometimes uses persuasive voice | Little writer involvement, personality | Shows little conviction |
| **Word Choice** | Persuasive words carefully chosen for impact | Argument supported by persuasive language | Uses some persuasive words | Occasional persuasive language | Generally limited or redundant language | Vague, dull, or misused words; no persuasive words |
| **Sentences** | Excellent variety of sentences; natural rhythm | Varied lengths, styles; generally smooth | Correct sentences with variations in style | Carefully constructed sentences; some variety | Simple, awkward, or wordy sentences; little variety | Choppy; many incomplete or run-on sentences |
| **Conventions** | Excellent control; few or no errors | No serious errors to affect understanding | General mastery of conventions but some errors | Reasonable control; few distracting errors | Weak control; enough errors to affect understanding | Many errors that prevent understanding |

## Scoring Rubric — Persuasive Writing

Rubric 4 | 3 | 2 | 1

| | 5 | 4 | 3 | 2 | 1 |
|---|---|---|---|---|---|
| **Focus/Ideas** | Persuasive argument carefully built with quality details | Persuasive argument well supported with details | Persuasive argument with one or two convincing details | Persuasive piece sometimes unfocused; needs more support | Rambling persuasive argument; lacks development and detail |
| **Organization/ Paragraphs** | Information chosen and arranged for maximum effect | Evident progression of persuasive ideas | Information arranged in a logical way with some lapses | Little structure or direction | No identifiable structure |
| **Voice** | Writer closely involved; persuasive but not overbearing | Maintains persuasive tone | Sometimes uses persuasive voice | Little writer involvement, personality | Shows little conviction |
| **Word Choice** | Persuasive words carefully chosen for impact | Argument supported by persuasive language | Occasional persuasive language | Generally limited or redundant language | Vague, dull, or misused words; no persuasive words |
| **Sentences** | Excellent variety of sentences; natural rhythm | Varied lengths, styles; generally smooth | Carefully constructed sentences; some variety | Simple, awkward, or wordy sentences; little variety | Choppy; many incomplete or run-on sentences |
| **Conventions** | Excellent control; few or no errors | No serious errors to affect understanding | Reasonable control; few distracting errors | Weak control; enough errors to affect understanding | Many errors that prevent understanding |

## Scoring Rubric — Persuasive Writing

Rubric 4 | 3 | 2 | 1

| | 3 | 2 | 1 |
|---|---|---|---|
| **Focus/Ideas** | Persuasive argument carefully built with quality details | Persuasive argument with one or two convincing details | Rambling persuasive argument; lacks development and detail |
| **Organization/ Paragraphs** | Information chosen and arranged for maximum effect | Information arranged in a logical way with some lapses | No identifiable structure |
| **Voice** | Writer closely involved; persuasive but not overbearing | Sometimes uses persuasive voice | Shows little conviction |
| **Word Choice** | Persuasive words carefully chosen for impact | Occasional persuasive language | Vague, dull, or misused words; no persuasive words |
| **Sentences** | Excellent variety of sentences; natural rhythm | Carefully constructed sentences; some variety | Choppy; many incomplete or run-on sentences |
| **Conventions** | Excellent control; few or no errors | Reasonable control; few distracting errors | Many errors that prevent understanding |

## Scoring Rubric | Expository Writing

| Rubric 4 3 2 1 | 6 | 5 | 4 | 3 | 2 | 1 |
|---|---|---|---|---|---|---|
| **Focus/Ideas** | Insightful, focused exposition; well elaborated with quality details | Informed, focused exposition; elaborated with telling details | Exposition focused, good elaboration | Generally focused exposition; some supporting details | Sometimes unfocused exposition needs more supporting details | Rambling exposition; lack development and detail |
| **Organization/ Paragraphs** | Logical, consistent flow of ideas; good transitions | Logical sequencing of ideas; uses transitions | Ideas sequenced with some transitions | Sequenced ideas with some transitions | Little direction from beginning to end; few order words | Lacks structure and transitions |
| **Voice** | Writer closely involved; informative voice well suited to topic | Reveals personality; voice suited to topic | Pleasant but not compelling voice | Sincere voice suited to topic | Little writer involvement, personality | Careless writing with no feeling |
| **Word Choice** | Vivid, precise words to express ideas | Clear words to express ideas | Words correct and adequate | Language adequate but may lack precision | Generally limited or redundant language | Vague, dull, or misused words |
| **Sentences** | Strong topic sentence; fluent, varied structures | Good topic sentence; smooth sentence structure | Correct sentences that are sometimes fluent | Topic sentence correctly constructed; some sentence variety | Topic sentence unclear or missing; wordy, awkward sentences | No topic sentence; many incomplete or run-on sentences |
| **Conventions** | Excellent control; few or no errors | No serious errors to affect understanding | General mastery of conventions but some errors | Reasonable control; few distracting errors | Weak control; enough errors to affect understanding | Many errors that prevent understanding |

## Scoring Rubric | Expository Writing

| Rubric 4 3 2 1 | 5 | 4 | 3 | 2 | 1 |
|---|---|---|---|---|---|
| **Focus/Ideas** | Insightful, focused exposition; well elaborated with quality details | Informed, focused exposition; elaborated with telling details | Generally focused exposition; some supporting details | Sometimes unfocused exposition needs more supporting details | Rambling exposition; lacks development and detail |
| **Organization/ Paragraphs** | Logical, consistent flow of ideas; good transitions | Logical sequencing of ideas; uses transitions | Sequenced ideas with some transitions | Little direction from beginning to end; few order words | Lacks structure and transitions |
| **Voice** | Writer closely involved; informative voice well suited to topic | Reveals personality; voice suited to topic | Language adequate but may lack precision | Little writer involvement, personality | Careless writing with no feeling |
| **Word Choice** | Vivid, precise words to express ideas | Clear words to express ideas | Topic sentence correctly constructed; some sentence variety | Generally limited or redundant language | Vague, dull, or misused words |
| **Sentences** | Strong topic sentence; fluent, varied structures | Good topic sentence; smooth sentence structure | Sincere voice suited to topic | Topic sentence unclear or missing; wordy, awkward sentences | No topic sentence; many incomplete or run-on sentences |
| **Conventions** | Excellent control; few or no errors | No serious errors to affect understanding | Reasonable control; few distracting errors | Weak control; enough errors to affect understanding | Many errors that prevent understanding |

## Scoring Rubric | Expository Writing

| Rubric 4 3 2 1 | 3 | 2 | 1 |
|---|---|---|---|
| **Focus/Ideas** | Insightful, focused exposition; well elaborated with quality details | Generally focused exposition; some supporting details | Rambling exposition; lacks development and detail |
| **Organization/ Paragraphs** | Logical, consistent flow of ideas; good transitions | Sequenced ideas with some transitions | Lacks structure and transitions |
| **Voice** | Writer closely involved; informative voice well suited to topic | Sincere voice suited to topic | Careless writing with no feeling |
| **Word Choice** | Vivid, precise words to express ideas | Language adequate but may lack precision | Vague, dull, or misused words |
| **Sentences** | Strong topic sentence; fluent, varied structures | Topic sentence correctly constructed; some sentence variety | No topic sentence; many incomplete or run-on sentences |
| **Conventions** | Excellent control; few or no errors | Reasonable control; few distracting errors | Many errors that prevent understanding |

# Unit 4
# Monitoring Fluency

Ongoing assessment of student reading fluency is one of the most valuable measures we have of students' reading skills. One of the most effective ways to assess fluency is taking timed samples of students' oral reading and measuring the number of words correct per minute (WCPM).

## How to Measure Words Correct Per Minute—WCPM

### Choose a Text
Start by choosing a text for the student to read. The text should be:
- narrative
- unfamiliar
- on grade level

Make a copy of the text for yourself and have one for the student.

### Timed Reading of the Text
Tell the student: As you read this aloud, I want you to do your best reading and to read as quickly as you can. That doesn't mean it's a race. Just do your best, fast reading. When I say *begin*, start reading.

As the student reads, follow along in your copy. Mark words that are read incorrectly.

| Incorrect | Correct |
|---|---|
| • omissions | • self-corrections within 3 seconds |
| • substitutions | • repeated words |
| • mispronunciations | |
| • reversals | |

### After One Minute
At the end of one minute, draw a line after the last word that was read. Have the student finish reading but don't count any words beyond one minute. Arrive at the words correct per minute—wcpm—by counting the total number of words that the student read correctly in one minute.

## Fluency Goals
Grade 4 End-of-Year Goal = 130 WCPM

### Target goals by unit

| | |
|---|---|
| **Unit 1** 95 to 105 WCPM | **Unit 4** 110 to 120 WCPM |
| **Unit 2** 100 to 110 WCPM | **Unit 5** 115 to 125 WCPM |
| **Unit 3** 105 to 115 WCPM | **Unit 6** 120 to 130 WCPM |

## More Frequent Monitoring
You may want to monitor some students more frequently because they are falling far below grade-level benchmarks or they have a result that doesn't seem to align with their previous performance. Follow the same steps above, but choose 2 or 3 additional texts.

**Fluency Progress Chart** Copy the chart on the next page. Use it to record each student's progress across the year.

## Fluency Progress Chart, Grade 4

Name

| | 1 | 2 | 3 | 4 | 5 | 6 | 7 | 8 | 9 | 10 | 11 | 12 | 13 | 14 | 15 | 16 | 17 | 18 | 19 | 20 | 21 | 22 | 23 | 24 | 25 | 26 | 27 | 28 | 29 | 30 |
|---|---|---|---|---|---|---|---|---|---|---|---|---|---|---|---|---|---|---|---|---|---|---|---|---|---|---|---|---|---|---|
| 165 | | | | | | | | | | | | | | | | | | | | | | | | | | | | | | |
| 160 | | | | | | | | | | | | | | | | | | | | | | | | | | | | | | |
| 155 | | | | | | | | | | | | | | | | | | | | | | | | | | | | | | |
| 150 | | | | | | | | | | | | | | | | | | | | | | | | | | | | | | |
| 145 | | | | | | | | | | | | | | | | | | | | | | | | | | | | | | |
| 140 | | | | | | | | | | | | | | | | | | | | | | | | | | | | | | |
| 135 | | | | | | | | | | | | | | | | | | | | | | | | | | | | | | |
| 130 | | | | | | | | | | | | | | | | | | | | | | | | | | | | | | |
| 125 | | | | | | | | | | | | | | | | | | | | | | | | | | | | | | |
| 120 | | | | | | | | | | | | | | | | | | | | | | | | | | | | | | |
| 115 | | | | | | | | | | | | | | | | | | | | | | | | | | | | | | |
| 110 | | | | | | | | | | | | | | | | | | | | | | | | | | | | | | |
| 105 | | | | | | | | | | | | | | | | | | | | | | | | | | | | | | |
| 100 | | | | | | | | | | | | | | | | | | | | | | | | | | | | | | |
| 95 | | | | | | | | | | | | | | | | | | | | | | | | | | | | | | |
| 90 | | | | | | | | | | | | | | | | | | | | | | | | | | | | | | |
| 85 | | | | | | | | | | | | | | | | | | | | | | | | | | | | | | |
| 80 | | | | | | | | | | | | | | | | | | | | | | | | | | | | | | |
| 75 | | | | | | | | | | | | | | | | | | | | | | | | | | | | | | |
| 70 | | | | | | | | | | | | | | | | | | | | | | | | | | | | | | |

**Timed Reading**

# Assessment and Regrouping Chart

| Day 3 Retelling Assessment | | | Day 5 Fluency Assessment | | | Reteach | Teacher's Comments | Grouping |
|---|---|---|---|---|---|---|---|---|
| The assessed group is highlighted for each week. | Benchmark Score | Actual Score | The assessed group is highlighted for each week. | Benchmark wcpm | Actual Score | ✓ | | |
| **The Houdini Box** Compare/Contrast | | | | | | | | |
| Strategic | 1–2 | | Strategic | Less than 110 | | | | |
| On-Level | 3 | | On-Level | 110–120 | | | | |
| Advanced | 4 | | Advanced* | 110–120 | | | | |
| **Encantado** Compare/Contrast | | | | | | | | |
| Strategic | 1–2 | | Strategic | Less than 110 | | | | |
| On-Level | 3 | | On-Level | 110–120 | | | | |
| Advanced | 4 | | Advanced* | 110–120 | | | | |
| **King in the Kitchen** Character/Setting | | | | | | | | |
| Strategic | 1–2 | | Strategic | Less than 110 | | | | |
| On-Level | 3 | | On-Level | 110–120 | | | | |
| Advanced | 4 | | Advanced* | 110–120 | | | | |
| **Seeker of Knowledge** Graphic Sources | | | | | | | | |
| Strategic | 1–2 | | Strategic | Less than 110 | | | | |
| On-Level | 3 | | On-Level | 110–120 | | | | |
| Advanced | 4 | | Advanced* | 110–120 | | | | |
| **Encyclopedia Brown** Plot | | | | | | | | |
| Strategic | 1–2 | | Strategic | Less than 110 | | | | |
| On-Level | 3 | | On-Level | 110–120 | | | | |
| Advanced | 4 | | Advanced* | 110–120 | | | | |
| **Unit 4 Benchmark Test Score** | | | | | | | | |

- **RECORD SCORES** Use this chart to record scores for the Day 3 Retelling, Day 5 Fluency, and Unit Benchmark Test Assessments.

- **REGROUPING** Compare the student's actual score to the benchmark score for each group level and review the *Questions to Consider.* Students may move to a higher or lower group level, or they may remain in the same group.

- **RETEACH** If a student is unable to complete any part of the assessment process, use the weekly Reteach lessons for additional support. Record the lesson information in the space provided on the chart. After reteaching, you may want to reassess using the Unit Benchmark Test.

*Students in the advanced group should read above-grade-level materials.

# Unit 4
# Assess and Regroup

**FYI** In Grade 4 there are opportunities for regrouping every six weeks—at the end of Units 2, 3, 4, and 5. These options offer sensitivity to each student's progress although some teachers may prefer to regroup less frequently.

## Regroup for Unit 5

To make regrouping decisions at the end of Unit 4, consider students' end-of-unit scores for

- Unit 4 Retelling
- Fluency (WCPM)
- Unit 4 Benchmark Test

# Group Time

| On-Level | Strategic Intervention | Advanced |
|---|---|---|
| **To continue On-Level or to move into the On-Level group, students should** | **Students would benefit from Strategic Intervention if they** | **To move to the Advanced group, students should** |
| • score 3 or better on their cumulative unit rubric scores for Retelling | • score 2 or lower on their cumulative unit rubric scores for Retelling | • score 4 on their cumulative unit rubric scores for Retelling and demonstrate expansive vocabulary and ease of language in their retellings |
| • meet the current benchmark for fluency (110–120 WCPM), reading On-Level text such as Student Edition selections | • do not meet the current benchmark for fluency (110–120 WCPM) | • score 95% on the Unit 4 Benchmark Test |
| • score 80% or better on the Unit 4 Benchmark Tests | • score below 60% on the Unit 4 Benchmark Tests | • read above-grade-level material fluently (110–120 WCPM) |
| • be capable of working in the On-Level group based on teacher judgment | • are struggling to keep up with the On-Level group based on teacher judgment | • be capable of handling the problem solving and investigative work of the Advanced group based on teacher judgment |

## QUESTIONS TO CONSIDER

- What types of test questions did the student miss? Are they specific to a particular skill or strategy?
- Does the student have adequate background knowledge to understand the test passages or selections for retelling?

- Has the student's performance met expectations for daily lessons and assessments with little or no reteaching?
- Is the student performing more like students in another group?
- Does the student read for enjoyment, different purposes, and varied interests?

**Benchmark Fluency Scores**

Current Goal: **110–120** WCPM

End-of-Year Goal: **130** WCPM

# Leveled Readers

## Table of Contents

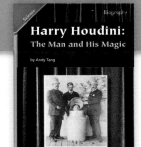

**Harry Houdini:**
The Man and His Magic
by Andy Tang

# Harry Houdini

**COMPARE AND CONTRAST**

**PREDICT**

**LESSON VOCABULARY** appeared, bustling, crumbled, escape, magician, monument, vanished

**SUMMARY** This short biography of Harry Houdini describes his rise from a poor immigrant Jewish family to the most famed magician of his age. Houdini's most famous magic tricks are described.

## INTRODUCE THE BOOK

**BUILD BACKGROUND** Before reading about Houdini, ask students to discuss their experiences seeing magic or card tricks at parties or on TV.

**PREVIEW/USE TEXT FEATURES** Explain that a biography is the nonfiction account of a person's life. As students page through the text, point out the photographs and invite students to predict what they will learn about the life of Houdini.

**ELL** Ask students to share in their home language for words associated with "magic." Ask students what magic or card tricks they may have seen performed in their home country.

**TEACH/REVIEW VOCABULARY** Write the vocabulary words on a large sheet of paper. Define each. Then ask each student to make up a sentence that uses two of these words in the same sentence.

## TARGET SKILL AND STRATEGY

**COMPARE AND CONTRAST** Explain to students that when we *compare* and *contrast* two objects, ideas, or pieces of text, we are looking for both similarities and differences. Ask students to compare and contrast cats and lions. Then encourage them, as they read, to use a graphic organizer to compare and contrast Houdini's handcuff escapes with his Upside-Down Water Torture Cell trick.

**PREDICT** Explain to students that to predict means to tell what you think might happen next in a story based on what has already happened. Ask students, as they read, to predict what will happen to Houdini after his Upside-Down Water Torture Cell escapade.

## READ THE BOOK

Use the following questions to support comprehension.

**PAGE 5** What were some of the sports Houdini played? *(swimming, boxing, and track)*

**PAGES 7 AND 14** Compare and contrast Houdini's Metamorphosis trick (p. 7) with his handcuff tricks (p. 14). *(Similarities: handcuffs used for both; differences: In Metamorphosis, Harry's brother also was involved. Also, Harry was both handcuffed and locked in a trunk. Also he escaped through a hatch.)*

**PAGE 8** What role did Houdini's wife play in his acts? *(Bess was Houdini's assistant for the rest of his career.)*

## TALK ABOUT THE BOOK

**READER RESPONSE**
1. Possible responses: Alike: Many require physical strength or endurance. Different: Some involve trap doors, while others use hidden lock picks or keys.
2. Possible response: Houdini saw a traveling magic show. He also read a book by a French magician.
3. Possible response: get out, break loose, get away, leave
4. Possible response: I learned that Bess put together a booklet in honor of her husband.

## RESPONSE OPTIONS

**WRITING** Instruct students to write a paragraph comparing and contrasting their Houdini and a modern illusionist like David Blaine or David Copperfield.

## CONTENT CONNECTIONS

**SOCIAL STUDIES** Ask students to form small groups and research more about Houdini's life. Suggest that they focus on the odds he was up against as an immigrant before the turn of the 20th century.

*Time for* SOCIAL STUDIES

# Compare and Contrast

- To **compare** is to tell how two or more things are alike or similar.
- To **contrast** is to tell how two or more things are different.

**Directions** Read the paragraphs. Then answer the questions below.

> For an act called the Metamorphosis, Harry Houdini was handcuffed inside a sack and locked in a trunk. Somehow he would free himself and switch places with his brother, who was standing beside the trunk. In 1898, Houdini developed his handcuff challenge. He said he would pay one hundred dollars to anyone who gave him handcuffs he could not escape from. He never had to pay. In 1913 he introduced his most famous stunt, the Upside-Down Water Torture Cell. In this act, Houdini was locked in a water-filled glass-and-steel cabinet while hanging upside down by his feet.
>
> Houdini explained some of his secrets. Many handcuffs could be opened with properly applied force. Sometimes he carried hidden lock picks or keys. In the Metamorphosis, the trunk had a hidden side panel that allowed Houdini to escape. Houdini also spent hours practicing holding his breath so he could stay submerged in the water trick.

**1.** Compare the Metamorphosis to the Water Torture Cell by finding one similarity.

_____

**2.** Contrast the Metamorphosis and the Water Torture Cell by finding one difference.

_____

**3.** Compare the Metamorphosis to the other handcuff tricks.

_____

**4.** Contrast the handcuff tricks with the Water Torture Cell by finding a difference.

_____

**5.** Find another difference between the Water Torture Cell and the handcuff tricks.

_____

**74**

Name _____

# Vocabulary

**Directions** Choose the word from the Word Box that best matches each definition. Write the word on the line.

> ### Check the Words You Know
>
> ___appeared    ___crumbled    ___magician    ___vanished
> ___bustling    ___escape    ___monument

1. The crowds at Houdini's shows were _____ with excitement.

2. Many people visit the _____ that was built to remember the president.

3. In some of Houdini's tricks, the magician or his partner _____ from view.

4. After Houdini vanished, he always _____ again.

5. The suspense of the crowd _____ as soon as Houdini reappeared.

6. It must have been exciting for the crowd when Houdini pretended to _____.

7. To be a good _____ takes months, sometimes years, of practice.

**Directions** For each word below, find the root word and write it on the line. Then use the root word or the vocabulary word in a sentence.

8. bustling _____

_____

9. crumbled _____

_____

10. vanished _____

_____

**75**

# Tricks to Doing Magic

- COMPARE AND CONTRAST
- PREDICT

**LESSON VOCABULARY** appeared, bustling, crumbled, escape, magician, monument, vanished

**SUMMARY** This book teaches students how to perform four simple magic tricks and explains how human vanishing acts work, as well. Students learn that a magician's demeanor is almost as important to carrying off the trick as the trick itself.

## INTRODUCE THE BOOK

**BUILD BACKGROUND** Ask students to share their experiences at magic shows or trying to do simple magic tricks. Ask students what they've noticed about the way magicians handle a crowd.

**PREVIEW/USE TEXT FEATURES** Ask students to examine the photos, drawings, section headings, and Glossary. Ask students what they expect to learn from this book.

**ELL** Encourage English language learners to share stories about "magic" in their native countries. Ask them to share vocabulary words connected to magic. These students may also enjoy showing coins from their native lands.

**TEACH/REVIEW VOCABULARY** Write the vocabulary words on the board and invite students to define the ones they know. Define the unfamiliar words. Play a synonym game. Ask students to come up with as many synonyms for each vocabulary word as they can.

## TARGET SKILL AND STRATEGY

**COMPARE AND CONTRAST** Remind students that when we *compare* and *contrast* two objects, ideas, or pieces of text, we are looking for similarities and differences. Encourage students, as they read, to compare and contrast the different magic tricks.

**PREDICT** Explain that to *predict* means to tell what you think might happen next in a text (or in a magic trick) based on what has already been explained or what has already happened. Ask students, as they read, to predict the outcome of each magic trick.

## READ THE BOOK

Use the following questions to support comprehension.

**PAGE 5** Why must your shirt be tucked in to do this trick? *(Otherwise, the coin will fall onto the floor).*

**PAGES 12–14** What can you predict about what the magician will do with the torn napkin? *(He or she will keep it tucked in the pocket).*

**PAGES 18 AND 19** What is the purpose of the post in the vanishing person trick? *(The mirrors are attached to it on an angle, creating the illusion that there is no place for a person to hide.)*

## TALK ABOUT THE BOOK

**READER RESPONSE**
1. Possible response: Because the audience is distracted, they don't see all the hand movements involved in many tricks. Also, because they expect the trick to work, they overlook some hand movements that are part of the trick.
2. Audiences may be shocked, surprised, or excited.
3. *Vanished* and *appeared* are antonyms. Also *front/back; left/right; show/hide*
4. Illustrations show how the trick is done and where hands should be at various points to pull off the trick.

## RESPONSE OPTIONS

**SPEAKING/PERFORMING** Have on hand props with which students can perform the magic tricks. Have them work in groups on different tricks. Then have the students practice performing the tricks in class.

## CONTENT CONNECTIONS

**SCIENCE** Invite students to research other kinds of optical illusions or magic tricks on the Internet or in the library. If time permits, have students make posters showing the optical illusions or magic tricks about which they've learned. Encourage them to use illustrations.

*TIME FOR Science*

# Compare and Contrast

- To **compare** is to describe how two ideas or concepts are similar or alike.
- To **contrast** is to describe how ideas or concepts are different.

**Directions** Read the paragraphs below. Then answer the questions.

When performing the *Disappearing Person* trick, the magician brings out a tall box. The magician talks and tells jokes or stories to the audience. In the center of the box, is a post that the audience cannot see. There are mirrors from the top to the bottom of the cabinet that swing from the sides to the center post. The magician's assistant steps inside and hides behind the mirrors. Presto! When the magician opens the box, the assistant is gone.

The *Guess Which Hand* trick is also an illusion. The magician keeps the audience's attention by talking and joking with them. First, he shows the audience a quarter. He also has a secret quarter in his belt. He shifts his hands to make it look like he's moving one quarter back and forth. In fact, each hand now has a quarter. When the audience picks which hand has the quarter, the magician shows the other hand. This way, the audience thinks they got it wrong.

1. Compare the magician's interaction with the audience in both tricks.

_____

2. Contrast the size of the props in these tricks.

_____

_____

3. How are these tricks similar?

_____

_____

4. Compare the set-up or preparation for these tricks.

_____

_____

5. Contrast the techniques the magician might use to practice these tricks.

_____

_____

**74**

# Vocabulary

**Directions** Choose the word from the Word Box that best matches each definition. Write the word on the line.

### Check the Words You Know

___appeared    ___crumbled    ___magician    ___vanished
___bustling    ___escape      ___monument

1. seemed to be, looked like        _____

2. disappeared suddenly             _____

3. made into small pieces           _____

4. to get free from                 _____

5. one who entertains with
   magic                            _____

6. noisily busy, excited            _____

7. something set up to honor
   a person or event                _____

**Directions** Choose the word (or words) from the Word Box that best completes each sentence. Write each word on the line.

8. The crowd outside the magic show was _____ with excitement.

9. First the assistant _____ from the box, but then she _____ again.

10. The magician was so famous that a _____ was put up to remember him after he died.

**75**

# Tricking the Eye

👁 **COMPARE AND CONTRAST**

👁 **PREDICT**

**LESSON VOCABULARY** accommodation, animate, cerebral cortex, computer-assisted animation, computer-generated animation, concave, frames, illusion, optical illusion, perception

**SUMMARY** This book explores several types of illusions and explains how the brain makes sense of tricks played on the human eye. The book discusses optical illusions, hand-drawn cartoons, and computer-drawn animations.

## INTRODUCE THE BOOK

**BUILD BACKGROUND** Ask students to share their experiences looking at optical illusions, and at computer-generated animations such as those in recent movies.

**PREVIEW/USE TEXT FEATURES** Ask students to examine the table of contents to clarify topics that will be covered in the text. Ask students to explain how they know the book is a work of nonfiction, just from the contents. Examine diagrams and illusions in the text. Talk about images that are particularly interesting.

**ELL** Pair English language learners with English speakers. Have them work together to research and further understand terms such as *computer-generated animation.*

**TEACH/PREVIEW VOCABULARY** Note for students that some concepts on the vocabulary list are so new (e.g., computer-generated animation) that they are not yet in mainstream dictionaries. Invite students to look up all of the vocabulary words, and to create sentences to share aloud.

## TARGET SKILL AND STRATEGY

👁 **COMPARE AND CONTRAST** Remind students that when we *compare* and *contrast* two objects, ideas, or pieces of text, we are looking for similarities and differences. Encourage students, as they read, to compare and contrast the optical illusions shown.

👁 **PREDICT** To *predict* means to tell what you think might happen next in a story or situation. Have students look at the illusions on page 19 before reading the text on page 18 and predict, for each illusion, what the author expects students to "see."

## READ THE BOOK

Use the following questions to support comprehension.

**PAGE 4** What is an optical illusion? *(an image in which the eye sees something different from what is actually portrayed)*

**PAGE 13** How does the cerebral cortex relate to vision? *(It receives signals from all senses and reinterprets visual cues to make sense of them.)*

**PAGES 6 AND 17** What is the difference between hand-drawn and computer-assisted animation? *(For hand-drawn animation, only one background was made, and fewer images of characters were used.)*

## TALK ABOUT THE BOOK

**READER RESPONSE**

1. Possible responses: Both create cartoons and animations. Computer-assisted animation is two-dimensional, while computer-generated animation is three-dimensional. Both bring still images and models to life.

2. Possible response: Their brains will perceive two different images in one picture.

3. Possible response: After the word, the text says "bent inward." The spoon photo also helped.

4. Labels show precise locations of body parts.

## RESPONSE OPTIONS

**WRITING** Have on hand books that include optical illusions. Instruct students to select one of the optical illusions on page 19 (or another illusion) and describe the drawing or diagram and explain how the illusion works.

## CONTENT CONNECTIONS

**SCIENCE** Invite students to prepare a poster on which they paste a favorite optical illusion and explain it.

# Compare and Contrast

- To **compare** is to describe how two ideas or concepts are similar or alike.
- To **contrast** is to describe how ideas or concepts are different.
- Clue words like **however, unlike, although,** and **on the other hand** suggest contrasts. Clue words like **also, similarly,** and **like** suggest similarities.

**Directions** Read the paragraphs below. Then answer the questions.

> In the early days, the many still pictures that make a cartoon had to be drawn by hand, and this took a lot of work. So animators came up with a few tricks to make their jobs easier. Instead of drawing a whole new picture for every frame, they decided to draw only the parts of the picture that needed to move. Usually this meant making one background drawing. The characters were drawn on clear plastic sheets and laid over the still background. The characters would change and look like they were moving, but only one background drawing was made. This method is called cel animation.
>
> Another old trick is called the slash-and-tear system. Here the moving characters are drawn on regular paper, but then they are cut out. This way the different images of the moving characters can be placed on top of the background drawing. Either way, what you think you see is the characters coming to life.

1. Compare the cel and slash-and-tear systems by finding two things that are similar.

   _____

2. Contrast the cel and slash-and-tear systems by finding a difference.

   _____

   _____

3. Contrast cel animation with making a cartoon without any tricks.

   _____

   _____

4. The book *Tricking the Eye* also discusses the use of clay models or puppets in animated films. Contrast this with cel animation.

   _____

   _____

© Pearson Education 4

**74**

# Vocabulary

**Directions** Choose the word from the Word Box that best matches each definition.
Write the word on the line.

---

### Check the Words You Know

___accommodation       ___concave

___animate       ___frames

___cerebral cortex       ___illusion

___computer-assisted animation       ___optical illusion

___computer-generated animation       ___perception

---

1. illusion having to do with sight or seeing _____

2. two-dimensional computer animation; a series of still computer images put together to create movement _____

3. to make lively _____

4. curved inward _____

5. the brain's understanding of something _____

6. the automatic adjustment of the lens of the eye to see objects at various distances
   _____

7. the process by which a computer uses models and formulas to make a still image move in lifelike ways, often in three dimensions _____

8. part of the brain that receives signals from the senses _____

9. individual still images that make up a cartoon _____

10. something that appears to be different from what it actually is
    _____

**75**

# Dolphins

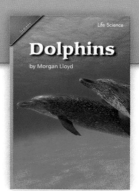

Life Science
**Dolphins**
by Morgan Lloyd

Unit 4 Week 2

  **COMPARE AND CONTRAST**

  **VISUALIZE**

**LESSON VOCABULARY** aquarium, dolphins, enchanted, flexible, glimpses, pulses, surface

**SUMMARY** This reader introduces various kinds of dolphins, characteristics of the species, growth patterns, and habitats. Mixed in with physical aspects, students can also read about the humanlike way dolphins whistle and click in their communications.

## INTRODUCE THE BOOK

**BUILD BACKGROUND** Ask students to describe what they know about dolphins and the environment today. Remind students that dolphins are mammals, as are humans.

**PREVIEW/USE TEXT FEATURES** Allow students to look through the reader. Draw students' attention to the labeled parts of the dolphin on pages 4–5. Have them suggest what the heads in the text tell about this book.

**TEACH/REVIEW VOCABULARY** Before reading, ask students to tell what they think each vocabulary word might have to do with dolphins. Have volunteers change a vocabulary word and find out how the word is used in the reader. After reading, have students point out what that word added to the reader.

## TARGETED SKILL AND STRATEGY

 **COMPARE AND CONTRAST** Remind students that to *compare* and *contrast* is to look for likenesses and differences. When several different kinds of dolphins are presented, readers are able to see both the similarities, or comparisons, as well as the differences, or contrasts. You may want to use a Venn diagram to compare and contrast just two kinds of dolphins, or use a cluster diagram to keep track of several kinds of dolphins.

 **VISUALIZE** Draw students' attention to "Bowriding" on page 7. Ask them to look at how the author described this action so that the reader could visualize how the dolphin glides through the water. Have the students describe in different ways how the dolphin uses less energy by taking this push from the boat.

## READ THE BOOK

Use the following questions to support comprehension.

**PAGE 5** Why do dolphins have a blowhole? *(This is how they take in air.)*

**PAGE 6** How will a baby dolphin recognize its mother? *(The mother whistles for several days after the baby is born.)*

**PAGE 8** In what ways is the Bottle-nosed Dolphin different from other dolphins? *(Answers will vary but may include that its beak is shaped like a bottle.)*

## TALK ABOUT THE BOOK

**READER RESPONSE**
1. Possible response: Dolphins breathe air and are mammals; dolphins are different colors and shapes. Every dolphin is unique.
2. Possible response: A blunt head with no beak helps me visualize the dolphin.
3. Possible response: Pulses are beats and are edible seeds from a pod.
4. Possible response: You can see the dorsal fin on top and pectoral fin on the bottom.

## RESPONSE OPTIONS

**WRITING** Suggest students make their own graphic organizer of different dolphins.

 **ELL** Lead a writing game to complete a sentence frame such as *I see a* _____. The more-proficient English speaker points to some element in a photograph in the reader and asks a less-proficient English speaker to write the word that completes the sentence frame.

## CONTENT CONNECTIONS

**SCIENCE** Discuss what dolphins can teach us about animal behavior.

TIME FOR Science

Name _____

# Compare and Contrast

- To **compare** is to tell how two or more things are alike and also how they are different.
- To **contrast** is to tell only how two or more things are different.

**Directions** Read the passage below. Then answer the questions.

All dolphins are mammals. Similar to other mammals, dolphins are warm-blooded. They live underwater but have lungs and breathe air. Dolphins all are born live and drink milk from their mothers.

There are many different kinds of dolphins. The bottle-nosed dolphin is found in coastal waters all over the world. Its name comes from the shape of its beak, which is usually a bit more than seven centimeters long. This type of dolphin varies from about two meters to nearly four meters long. These dolphins often travel in groups of 500 to 1000 members. Bottle-nosed dolphins usually have light gray upper bodies with pinkish gray bellies. By contrast, the hourglass dolphin's sharp black-and-white coloring makes it easy to recognize. It is only found in the cold waters surrounding Antarctica. At less than two meters long, it is somewhat smaller than other dolphins. Its black beak is so short that it might not be noticed. Hourglass dolphins travel in tiny groups of 2 to 40 dolphins.

1. Find two similarities among all dolphins.

_____

2. Contrast the coloring of bottle-nosed and hourglass dolphins.

_____

_____

3. Contrast the beaks of bottle-nosed and hourglass dolphins.

_____

_____

4. Compare or contrast where these two types of dolphin live.

_____

_____

78

© Pearson Education 4

Name _____

# Vocabulary

**Directions** Choose the word from the box that best matches each definition. Write the word on the line.

```
Check the Words You Know
___aquarium      ___glimpses
___dolphins      ___pulses
___enchanted     ___surface
___flexible
```

1. delightful, charming _____

2. short, quick viewings or looks _____

3. building used for showing collections of live fish, water animals and water plants

   _____

4. the top layer _____

5. regular, measured beats _____

6. sea mammals related to the whale, but smaller _____

7. easily bent, not stiff _____

**Directions** Choose the word from the box that best completes each sentence. Write the word on the line.

8. The _____ looked like they were skipping as they leapt from the water.

9. Some dolphins like to swim very near the _____ of the ocean.

10. The dolphin, with its sleek body and "smiling" face, is an

    _____ animal.

**79**

# Swimming with Dolphins

**COMPARE/CONTRAST**

**VISUALIZE**

**LESSON VOCABULARY** aquarium, dolphins, enchanted, flexible, glimpses, pulses, surface

**SUMMARY** By observing dolphins, scientists have been able to detail how they eat, sleep, breathe, and live in pods. Many of the dolphin behaviors, especially those involving caring for babies, have similarities with humans. For example, baby dolphins drink their mothers' milk and stay close to them for a full year.

## INTRODUCE THE BOOK

**BUILD BACKGROUND** Discuss what students know about dolphins. If they have seen dolphins at an aquarium or in the wild, have them talk about that experience.

**PREVIEW/USE TEXT FEATURES** Suggest that students notice the way the photographs are used in combination with diagrams. Draw attention to what they can learn from such combinations on pages 4–5, 6–7, and 10–11.

**TEACH/REVIEW VOCABULARY** To reinforce the contextual meaning of words like *glimpses,* read the opening paragraph on page 3 and show how *glimpses* into dolphin behavior have revealed a whole world to scientists. Continue in a similar fashion with the remaining vocabulary words.

**ELL** Students can compare the English terminology used in this book to describe the dolphin's behavior with translations of those words in their own language.

## TARGET SKILL AND STRATEGY

**COMPARE/CONTRAST** Remind students that to *compare* is to identify how two or more things are alike and to *contrast* is to identify how they are different. As students read through this book, have them look for similarities between humans and dolphins. Suggest they track similarities and differences using a graphic organizer.

**VISUALIZE** Remind students that to *visualize* is to create a picture in the mind. As students read, suggest that they visualize what it would be like to swim with the dolphins and learn their ways. Students may want to write about this later.

## READ THE BOOK

Use the following questions to support comprehension.

**PAGE 7** How does the way dolphins breathe compare with human breathing? *(Dolphins can hold their breath for ten minutes and are able to lower their heart rate to save oxygen.)*

**PAGE 9** Why do dolphins chase fish to the shoreline? *(They are able to catch more fish in areas where they can't escape easily.)*

**PAGE 11** Describe echolocation. *(Dolphin pulses create echoes that send sound back showing where its prey are.)*

## TALK ABOUT THE BOOK

**READER RESPONSE**

1. Possible response: *wild:* can be dangerous, hunt for food; *aquarium*: do tricks, swim with people; *both:* can hold breath for ten minutes

2. Possible response: Soft fin and tail flukes and the baby drinks from its mother

3. Possible response: *synonyms*: bendable, supple, elastic; *antonyms:* stiff, unbending, rigid

4. Indian, Pacific, and Atlantic Oceans

## RESPONSE OPTION

**WRITING** Suggest that students imagine what it would be like to swim with dolphins and write two paragraphs that describe that as vividly as possible.

## CONTENT CONNECTION

**SCIENCE** Students can learn more about the secrets of the ocean by researching on the Internet, at the library, and possibly even a trip to a zoo or an aquarium. Suggest that they learn more about how the family lives in a pod.

TIME FOR Science

# Compare and Contrast

- To **compare** is to tell how two or more things are alike and also how they are different.
- To **contrast** is to tell only how two or more things are different.

**Directions** Read the following passage. Then use the Venn diagram below to compare and contrast dolphins and yourself.

Dolphins can grow to be twelve feet long and weigh as much as one thousand pounds. They may look like fish, but they are mammals. They have to come up to the surface of the water to breathe. Dolphins are able to hold their breath for up to 10 minutes! Dolphins do not chew their food the way some mammals do. They have teeth, but they only use them to break up big pieces of food. They swallow little fish in one big gulp. Dolphins also can see both in and out of the water. While dolphins probably cannot smell their food, they can hear it coming.

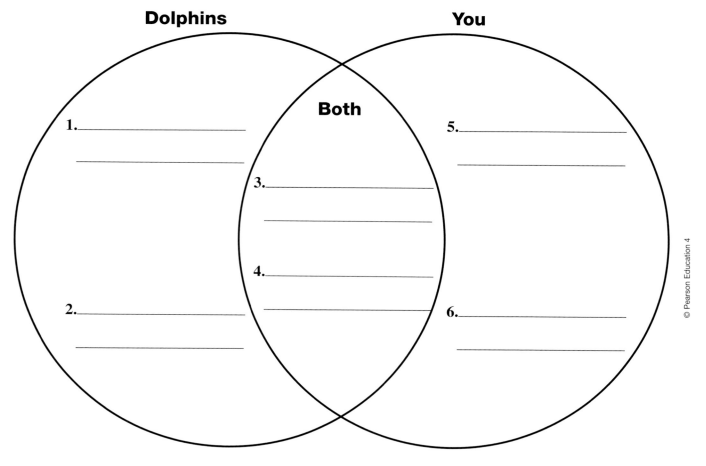

78

# Vocabulary

**Directions** Choose the word from the box that best matches each definition.
Write the word on the line.

> **Check the Words You Know**
>
> ___aquarium    ___glimpses
> ___dolphins    ___pulses
> ___enchanted   ___surface
> ___flexible

1. the top layer _____

2. delightful or charming _____

3. regular, measured beats _____

4. short, quick viewings or looks _____

5. sea mammals related to the whale, but smaller _____

6. easily bent, not stiff _____

7. building used for showing collections of live fish, water animals, and water plants

_____

**Directions** Write a short paragraph that uses three of your favorite words from the
above box.

**8-10.** _____

_____

_____

79

# Echolocation . . .

Echolocation:
Animals Making Sound Waves
by Laura Johnson

⦿ **COMPARE AND CONTRAST**

⦿ **VISUALIZE**

**LESSON VOCABULARY** anvil, cochlea, echolocation, hammer, larynx, lymph, melon, nose leaves, pinna, stirrup

**SUMMARY** Before reading about dolphins' and bats' abilities with echolocation, the author first presents a summary of the human ear and hearing. The way that both dolphins and bats use echolocation is detailed and clearly presented.

## INTRODUCE THE BOOK

**BUILD BACKGROUND** Before reading about bats and dolphins, introduce the idea of echolocation and ask what students know about this animal activity. Ask: How can mammals hear if they don't have ears?

**PREVIEW/USE TEXT FEATURES** Ask students to look at the heads to find the three parts to this reader. Also encourage them to look at the photos and read the captions. From the photos and the heads, ask what students can predict about echolocation.

**TEACH/PREVIEW VOCABULARY** Divide students into three groups for studying humans, dolphins, and bats. Suggest that each group look at the vocabulary words in their section of the book and, as they define them, make up example sentences that help the rest of the class better understand the words.

**ⒺⓁⓁ** Assist students with the term *echolocation,* as well as the names of the parts of the ear on pages 4–5. Suggest that the students make index cards with the English term on one side and the translations on the other.

## TARGETED SKILL AND STRATEGY

⦿ **COMPARE AND CONTRAST** Remind students that to *compare* and *contrast* is to identify how two or more things are alike and different. Have students chart comparisons and contrasts as they read. They can use a Venn diagram.

⦿ **VISUALIZE** Remind students that to *visualize* is to create a picture in the mind as they read. Encourage students to try the visualization exercise on page 21 and write about what they "see" based on the words they read.

## READ THE BOOK

Use the following questions to support comprehension.

**PAGE 3** How does vibration affect sound? *(This action can make sounds louder.)*

**PAGE 7** How does the melon function in echolocation? *(It directs the clicks that the dolphin sends out from its head.)*

**PAGE 14** How is the echolocation bats use similar to that of dolphins? *(Bats send out sound pulses that echo back from an object to eat.)*

## TALK ABOUT THE BOOK

**READER RESPONSE**
1. Answers will vary, but the organizer can show that dolphins produce sounds in nasal passages and some bats make them in their voice boxes.
2. Possible response: The pictures and the author's descriptions of each animal's parts that produce echolocation help the reader visualize.
3. Possible response: Because a hammer is used to pound nails, it clearly is not used the same way in the ear.
4. The captions provide additional topic information.

## RESPONSE OPTIONS

**WRITING** Some students may choose a section to focus on—either the dolphins or bats. Suggest that they write about echolocation from the animal's point of view.

## CONTENT CONNECTIONS

**SCIENCE** If possible, have on hand books and additional pictures illustrating echolocation. This subject is an excellent science experiment for readers of this age with an interest in "seeing through hearing."

TIME FOR Science

# Compare and Contrast

- To **compare** is to tell how two or more things are alike and also how they are different.
- To **contrast** is to tell only how two or more things are different.

**Directions** Read the following passage and answer the questions below.

Both bats and dolphins use echolocation, an ability to "see" using sound. Dolphins use their jaws, not their ears, to feel vibrations. Dolphins produce sounds called echolocation clicks. These clicks are short sound waves that bounce off objects in the water, then bounce back to the dolphin's jaw and then to the brain. Dolphins then create a mental picture of what is in the water around them. Echolocation clicks also can help a dolphin tell the direction an object is traveling, its speed, size and shape. Dolphins' tiny ear holes are only for hearing sounds above the surface of the water.

Bats produce their sound pulses differently than dolphins do. Dolphins produce sound in their nasal passages. Bats have a larynx or voice box that produces sound. Some bats send their sounds out of their mouths. Others snort the sound out of their noses. Bats' large ears can catch sound waves. When they catch sound waves, bats direct them to sound-sensitive cells inside their ears. These cells pass along signals to the brain.

**1.** What is one similarity between how bats and dolphins hear?

_____

**2.** Contrast how dolphins and bats produce sounds.

_____

_____

**3.** Contrast the way dolphins and bats receive echolocation sounds.

_____

_____

**4-5.** Compare and contrast dolphins' and bats' ears.

_____

_____

_____

**78**

© Pearson Education 4

# Vocabulary

**Directions** Choose the word from the box that best matches each definition. Write the word on the line.

> ### Check the Words You Know
>
> ___anvil       ___lymph
> ___cochlea    ___melon
> ___echolocation  ___nose leaves
> ___hammer    ___pinna
> ___larynx     ___stirrup

1. the skin-covered outer part of an ear _____

2. the outermost bone of three tiny bones in the middle ear _____

3. the fluid in the cochlea _____

4. a method of finding objects by using sound waves or vibrations

   _____

5. the flaps of skin on a bat's nose that direct sound forward

   _____

6. the fat-filled area in the front of a dolphin's head that focuses the echolocation clicks as they leave the dolphin's head _____

7. voice box _____

8. a spiral-shaped tube in the inner ear _____

9. the innermost of three tiny bones in the middle ear _____

10. the central bone of three tiny bones in the middle ear _____

**79**

# Inventing Oatmeal

**SUMMARY** A brother and sister are playing with their chemistry set and think they have invented oatmeal by mistake. They imagine what it would have been like to live in the Middle Ages, when porridge was on the menu.

## INTRODUCE THE BOOK

**BUILD BACKGROUND** Have volunteers talk about times when they thought they had made mistakes, only to have their errors turn into something positive. Point out that some inventions and scientific discoveries were found by accident.

**PREVIEW** Ask students to skim through the book looking at the illustrations. Have students describe the changes they see in the pictures beginning on page 9 and predict why the change occurs.

**TEACH/REVIEW VOCABULARY** Have students look up the words in the dictionary and write down the definitions and parts of speech. Have students use each word in a sentence.

**ELL** Have students write a group story. Have them choose one person to start the story by writing the first sentence. Then have students pass the story around the group, with each person writing a new sentence.

## TARGET SKILL AND STRATEGY

◉ **CHARACTER AND SETTING** Review with students that a *character* is a person that takes part in the events in a story. Remind students that the *setting* is the time and place in which events happen in the story. Have students identify the characters and setting in the story.

◉ **MONITOR AND FIX UP** Explain to students that when they monitor their reading, they are checking their understanding of what is happening in a story. Tell them that when they realize they do not completely understand something, they can use a fix-up strategy, like rereading, to review what they just read. Point out that using monitor and fix-up strategies can help them understand the characters and keep track of the setting in a story.

## READ THE BOOK

Use the following questions to support comprehension.

**PAGES 6–7** What can you tell about the characters Grace and Ben? *(Possible responses: Ben is messy and likes history; Grace likes science and teasing her brother.)*

**PAGE 9** What is the setting on this page? Are Grace and Ben really there? *(a castle in the Middle Ages; possible response: no, they're aren't really there, only imagining as Ben says)*

**PAGES 10–11** Monitor your understanding by answering this question: Who is the story about now, besides Grace and Ben? *(a well-dressed man, probably a duke, and a short, dirty man, probably a poor peasant)*

## TALK ABOUT THE BOOK

**READER RESPONSE**
1. dungeon (cold, empty), dining room (long, many candles), kitchen (full of people)
2. Possible response: students may mention they were confused when Ben and Grace found themselves in the castle. They may have reread.
3. Possible responses: some kind of jail; stone walls, no windows, dark, dirty, wet
4. Responses will vary but should include both the time and place for their time travel.

## RESPONSE OPTIONS

**WRITING** Let students use their responses to question 4 in Reader Response to write paragraphs in which they travel back in time. Their paragraphs should describe the people, places, and things they see.

## CONTENT CONNECTIONS

**SOCIAL STUDIES** Have students research how some important inventions were discovered, such as the light bulb or the telephone, and write brief reports describing the inventor's discovery process.

*Time for* **SOCIAL STUDIES**

# Character and Setting

- A **character** in a story is a person or animal that takes part in the events in a story.
- The **setting** is the time and place in which the events happen in a story.

**Directions** Complete the following table using evidence from the story *Inventing Oatmeal*. Remember, there is more than one setting and more than one important character in the story.

| Setting<br>The first part of the story takes place<br><br>_____<br><br>Evidence<br><br>_____<br>_____<br>_____ | Setting<br>The second part of the story takes place<br><br>_____<br><br>Evidence<br><br>_____<br>_____<br>_____ |
|---|---|
| Character<br>An important character in the story is<br><br>_____<br>Some of the traits of this character are<br><br>_____<br>_____<br>evidence<br><br>_____<br>_____<br>_____ | Character<br>An important character in the story is<br><br>_____<br>Some of the traits of this character are<br><br>_____<br>_____<br>evidence<br><br>_____<br>_____<br>_____ |

**82**

Name _____

# Vocabulary

**Directions** Read each of the following sentences about the Middle Ages. Circle the word from each pair that correctly completes the sentence.

___duke
___dungeon
___furiously
___genius
___majesty
___noble
___peasant
___porridge

1. A person who was poor and lived on land owned by rich people was a (noble/peasant).

2. A person who might have owned land and had nice clothes was a (duke/genius).

3. The criminal was thrown into the (porridge/dungeon) for stealing from the shopkeeper.

4. The king was angry that his laws had been broken, so he shouted (majesty/ furiously) at his guards.

5. Many people were poor farmers, so they ate a lot of (peasants/porridge).

6. A (genius/majesty) might be able to invent a time machine.

**Directions** Define the underlined word in each of the following sentences, and write your definition on the line.

7. In England, people might refer to the queen as "her majesty," or the <u>imperial</u> ruler.

_____

8. The ruler furiously stormed through the castle and <u>violently</u> destroyed every object in his path.

_____

9. The child hated porridge and threw his breakfast of <u>gruel</u> on the floor.

_____

10. Albert Einstein was a genius and was called an <u>intellect</u> of science.

_____

**83**

The Amazing,
Incredible . . .

The Amazing, **Incredible** Idea Kit
by Vana Douglas
illustrated by Burgundy Beam

**CHARACTER AND SETTING**

**MONITOR AND FIX UP**

**LESSON VOCABULARY** duke, dungeon, furiously, genius, majesty, noble, peasant, porridge

---

**SUMMARY** In this fictional story, twins, Paul and Beatrice, are trying to come up with an invention for their school science fair.

## INTRODUCE THE BOOK

**BUILD BACKGROUND** Ask students if they have ever had an idea for an invention. Have volunteers describe their inventions and how they came up with the ideas.

**PREVIEW** Read the first page of the selection with students. Discuss the main characters and what it is they are trying to do. Then have students skim through the rest of the book. Have them make predictions about the people pictured.

**TEACH/REVIEW VOCABULARY** To help students use context clues to understand unfamiliar words, write the word *duke* in a sentence on the board. Discuss how context clues can help them understand the meaning of *duke*. Assign the remaining vocabulary words to groups of students. Have each group use a dictionary to define the word and write the word in a sentence. Have groups exchange sentences, and tell each group to use the word in a sentence based on context clues.

**ELL** Have students write each vocabulary word on index cards and write two clues on the back of each card. Pair students and have partners give clues to each other to help guess the words.

## TARGET SKILL AND STRATEGY

**CHARACTER AND SETTING** Review with students that *characters* are the people in a story. Point out that authors sometimes give clues to a character's traits through the character's words and actions. Review with students that the setting is the time and place in which events happen. Have students identify the characters and setting as they read.

**MONITOR AND FIX UP** Explain to students that when they monitor their reading, they are checking their understanding of what is happening in a story. Tell them that

when they realize they do not understand something, they can use a strategy to fix up their comprehension. Point out that using monitor and fix-up strategies can help them understand the characters and setting in a book.

## READ THE BOOK

Use the following questions to support comprehension.

**PAGES 5–6** Describe the character traits of Granny Mae. *(She is wise, helpful, interesting, and thoughtful.)*

**PAGES 11–12** How did the setting change in the story? *(From Paul and Beatrice's house in the present to England in the past)*

**PAGES 14–16** What do we learn about Grandpa Nigel? *(He was an inventor and a genius.)*

## TALK ABOUT THE BOOK

**READER RESPONSE**
1. Responses will vary.
2. Responses will vary, but students should describe points in the story where they did not understand the content, and they should describe one of the fix-up strategies they used.
3. Responses will vary.
4. Responses will vary.

## RESPONSE OPTIONS

**WORD WORK** Have students use dictionaries to find the etymologies of the words *invent* and *genius*. Have students write one or two sentences comparing today's definitions of these words to their origins.

## CONTENT CONNECTIONS

**SOCIAL STUDIES** Have students research about an aspect of medieval daily life, such as knighthood, vassals and serfs, clothing, or food.

Time for
SOCIAL
STUDIES

# Character and Setting

- A **character** in a story is a person or animal that takes part in the events in a story.
- The **setting** is the time and place in which the events happen in a story.

**Directions** Complete the following chart about the main characters in *The Amazing, Incredible Idea Kit*. Make sure to give evidence from the story to support your ideas.

| Characters: Paul and Beatrice | | |
|---|---|---|
| Say/Think | Does | Others Say/Think |
| 1. _____ <br><br><br><br><br><br><br><br><br><br><br><br><br><br> | 2. _____ <br><br><br><br><br><br><br><br><br><br><br><br><br><br> | 3. _____ <br><br><br><br><br><br><br><br><br><br><br><br><br><br> |

**Directions** Describe the setting during the time when Granny Mae was a governess for James and Anastasia.

4-5. _____

_____

_____

82

# Vocabulary

**Directions** Unscramble each of the clue words. The clue words are the same as the vocabulary words in the box. Copy the letters in the numbered cells to other cells with the same number.

**Check the Words You Know**

___duke
___dungeon
___furiously
___genius
___majesty
___noble
___peasant
___porridge

**ROYLUSFIU**

☐☐☐☐☐☐☐☐☐
⠀2⠀9⠀⠀23⠀12

**DKUE**

☐☐☐☐
⠀⠀11

**MEJSATY**

☐☐☐☐☐☐☐
⠀7⠀16⠀18

**GUEDONN**

☐☐☐☐☐☐☐
⠀4⠀⠀14

**REIPORGD**

☐☐☐☐☐☐☐☐
19 13 20⠀5 10 22

**NELBO**

☐☐☐☐☐
8

**ESGINU**

☐☐☐☐☐☐
1⠀⠀21⠀17

**SAPAETN**

☐☐☐☐☐☐☐
6⠀⠀3⠀⠀15

☐☐☐☐☐☐☐⠀☐☐☐☐☐
1 2 3 4 5 6 7⠀8 9 10 11 12

[W]☐☐☐☐⠀☐☐☐☐☐☐☐
13 14 15 16⠀17 18 19 20 21 22 23

**83**

# Alexander Graham Bell . . .

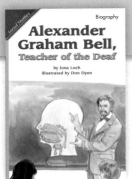

Biography
**Alexander Graham Bell, Teacher of the Deaf**
by Juna Loch
Illustrated by Don Dyen

**CHARACTER AND SETTING**

**MONITOR AND FIX UP**

**LESSON VOCABULARY** communicate, dedicated, frequency, harmonic, membrane, patent, vibrations, visible

**SUMMARY** This selection of historical fiction describes Alexander Graham Bell's search for tools to help the deaf, which led him to invent the telephone.

## INTRODUCE THE BOOK

**BUILD BACKGROUND** Have students brainstorm all the words and ideas that come to mind when they hear the name Alexander Graham Bell. If no one suggests the telephone, tell students that Bell is often credited with inventing the telephone.

**PREVIEW/USE TEXT FEATURES** Along with students, read through the table of contents. Based on the book and chapter titles, have students tell what type of work Bell pursued.

**TEACH/PREVIEW VOCABULARY** Demonstrate how to analyze an unfamiliar word using *communicate*. Show students how to break the word into syllables, or parts, and look at the parts to "solve" the word. Point out that students can also look for context clues in the story to help them define words. Then assign each vocabulary word to a group, and have groups tell the meanings of their words using word analysis and context clues.

## TARGET SKILL AND STRATEGY

**CHARACTER AND SETTING** Review with students that *characters* are the people or animals in a story. Point out that authors often give clues about a character's personality through the character's words, actions, or interactions with other characters. Then review with students that the *setting* is the time and place in which events happen in the story. Point out that sometimes settings affect a character's behavior.

**ELL** Have ELL students use Character Grid graphic organizers to take notes on the character traits of Alexander Graham Bell and the dog.

**MONITOR AND FIX UP** Explain to students that when they do not understand something, they can use a fix-up strategy for comprehension.

## READ THE BOOK

Use the following questions to support comprehension.

**PAGE 4** What makes the character of the narrator unusual? *(The narrator is a dog.)*

**PAGES 6–7** What is the setting of the story? How do you know? *(Boston, MA, a long time ago, because the narrator says so and the man on page 7 is wearing an old-fashioned suit)*

**PAGES 12–13** What fix-up strategies did you use to understand all the information on these pages? *(possible responses: reread, summarize)*

## TALK ABOUT THE BOOK

**READER RESPONSE**
1. Possible responses: Skye the dog; Bell works very hard; on page 8 the narrator describes Bell as dedicated to helping the deaf and working "like a dog."
2. Responses will vary, but students should describe a part of the story that was confusing and a fix-up strategy that helped them clarify information.
3. Possible responses: object, thing, model, tool; definitions and sentences will vary.
4. Responses will vary.

## RESPONSE OPTIONS

**VIEWING** Show students a film or video about the life of Alexander Graham Bell. Discuss the similarities and differences between the film and the selection. Then have students write brief paragraphs in which they tell whether they liked the film or the book better and why.

## CONTENT CONNECTIONS

**SCIENCE** Divide students into groups and assign each group one of Bell's inventions from the story. Have groups write reports about how the inventions work.

TIME FOR Science

# Character and Setting

- A **character** in a story is a person or animal that takes part in the events in a story.
- The **setting** is the time and place in which the events happen in a story.

**Directions** Answer the following questions using details from *Alexander Graham Bell, Teacher of the Deaf.*

1. Describe the character of the narrator. Tell the pages in the book where you find your evidence.

_____

_____

2. How do you learn about the narrator's character traits—through what the narrator says or thinks, what he does, or what others say or think about him?

_____

3. Describe Alexander Graham Bell. Tell the pages in the book where you find your evidence.

_____

_____

4. How does the reader learn about Alexander Graham Bell's character traits?

_____

5. How does the setting of the story influence what Alexander Graham Bell does in his life?

_____

_____

_____

**82**

# Vocabulary

**Directions** Use each of the following words in an original sentence about Alexander Graham Bell.

**1.** frequency

_____

**2.** harmonic

_____

**3.** vibrations

_____

**4.** communicate

_____

**5.** membrane

_____

**6.** visible

_____

**7.** dedicated

_____

**8.** patent

_____

© Pearson Education 4

🔘 **GRAPHIC SOURCES**

🔘 **ASK QUESTIONS**

**LESSON VOCABULARY** ancient, link, scholars, seeker, temple, translate, triumph, uncover

# The Rosetta Stone

**SUMMARY** This book tells the story of the Rosetta Stone—how it was discovered and how the discovery led to unlocking the secret of Egyptian hieroglyphs.

## INTRODUCE THE BOOK

**BUILD BACKGROUND** Ask students to share what they know about Ancient Egypt and Egyptian artifacts. Show students a page of text written in a language that most students in your class don't understand. Ask them how someone could figure out what it says.

**PREVIEW/USE TEXT FEATURES** Invite students to look through the book. Point out the map on page 3. Ask them how the photograph on that page relates to the map. Encourage students to look at the photos and pictures in the rest of the book and to read the headings.

**ELL** Point out the word "Mediterranean" on page 3. Tell students that the phrases in the parentheses tell them how to pronounce the word. Invite students to find other words and their pronunciations in the text. Have students work in pairs to create pronunciations for the vocabulary words.

**TEACH/REVIEW VOCABULARY** Have the students look up the vocabulary words in the dictionary, and write their Greek and/or Latin roots and the word's definition.

## TARGET SKILL AND STRATEGY

🔘 **GRAPHIC SOURCES** Remind students that *graphic sources* are charts, maps, photographs, drawings, and so on, that help strengthen their understanding of the text. Have students read the text on page 3 and then look at the map. Ask: How does the map help them understand what they read in the text?

🔘 **ASK QUESTIONS** Remind students that asking good questions about information can help them remember important ideas before, during, and after they read. Now that students have previewed the book, ask what are some of their questions about the text.

## READ THE BOOK

Use the following questions to support comprehension.

**PAGE 3** Look at the map. What features do you see? What country is shown? What town? *(Mediterranean Sea, Nile River; Egypt; Rosetta)*

**PAGE 7** What questions did you have about Egyptian hieroglyphics? Where did you find the answers? *(Possible response: What are hieroglyphs? How did they translate them? Answers found on pages 10, 13–15.)*

**PAGE 14** What helped Jean-Francois Champollion figure out hieroglyphics? *(Possible response: He liked learning, was good at languages, was interested in Egyptian culture, and spent a lot of time studying in Egypt.)*

## TALK ABOUT THE BOOK
**READER RESPONSE**
1. Responses should reflect the glyphs on the chart from page 10.
2. Possible response: What tools were needed to make hieroglyphics? I could get a book at the library or search the internet on Ancient Egypt.
3. The prefix *un–* means "not" or "the opposite of." Possible response: unfair, unsure, untie
4. Demotic script is the form of writing in the middle band of the Rosetta Stone.

## RESPONSE OPTION

**WRITING** Encourage students to create their own messages in code. Have them exchange their messages with other members of the class to decode.

## CONTENT CONNECTION

**SOCIAL STUDIES** Have students research more about the culture of Ancient Egypt. Have them present their findings to the rest of the class.

# Graphic Sources

- **Graphic sources** show information visually. They include visual aids such as maps, photographs and captions, time lines, and diagrams. You can use them to help you understand information in the text.

**Directions** Review *The Rosetta Stone* and write what happened in each year listed below.

**1.** 196 B.C.  _____

**2.** 30 B.C.  _____

**3.** 1799  _____

**4.** 1802  _____

**5–8.** On a separate sheet of paper, make a time line showing these important events.

# Vocabulary

**Directions** Use the definitions to solve the puzzle.

## Check the Words You Know

| | | | |
|---|---|---|---|
| ___uncover | ___ancient | ___triumph | ___link |
| ___translate | ___scholars | ___seeker | ___temple |

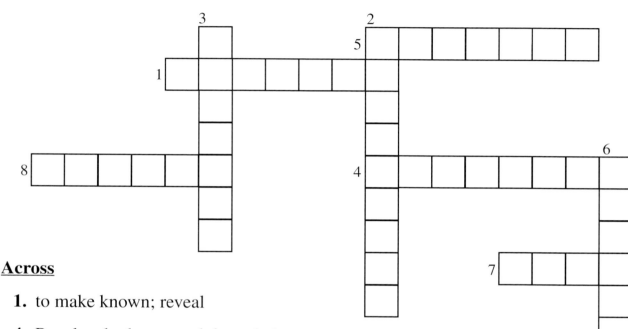

## Across

**1.** to make known; reveal

**4.** People who have much knowledge

**5.** Victory; success

**7.** Anything that joins or connects

**8.** A building used for worship

## Down

**2.** To change from one language into another

**3.** Of times long past

**6.** One who tries to find

87

# Cracking the German Code

**GRAPHIC SOURCES**

**ASK QUESTIONS**

**LESSON VOCABULARY** ancient, link, scholars, seeker, temple, translate, triumph, uncover

---

**SUMMARY** This book describes cracking of the German code during World War II. It focuses on the difficult task of the cryptologists who worked to crack that code.

## INTRODUCE THE BOOK

**BUILD BACKGROUND** Ask students what they know about World War II. What countries were involved in the War? Have students share their experiences creating or solving secret codes.

**PREVIEW/USE TEXT FEATURES** Have students look through the book at the headings, photos, and captions. Ask them how many different samples of code they see.

**ELL** Divide students into two groups and give each 16 index cards. Have the students write each vocabulary word on one card and either the translation into a home language or the word's definition on another card. Place all 10 cards facedown on a table. A student will turn up two cards, trying to match a word and its definition. When a match is made the group keeps those cards.

**TEACH/REVIEW VOCABULARY** Have students look up the vocabulary words in the dictionary. Have them write the word on one side of an index card and the Greek or Latin root (if there is one) and the word's definition on the other. Student pairs may work together to learn the words.

## TARGET SKILL AND STRATEGY

**GRAPHIC SOURCES** Remind students that *graphic sources* are maps, charts, photographs, drawings, and so on, that help strengthen their understanding of the text. Have students look at the photograph and caption on pages 4–5. Ask students what this photo tells them about what they will read on this page. Have students read the text. Discuss how the photo supports the text.

**ASK QUESTIONS** Ask students what questions they have about the text. Create a class chart to keep track of students' questions.

## READ THE BOOK

Use the following questions to support comprehension.

**PAGES 3–5** What questions did you have about World War II? What did you learn? *(Possible response: When did it begin? Who was involved? What did the German code have to do with it? Began in 1939. Allied powers were Great Britain, Russia, the United States, and their supporters; Axis powers included Germany, Italy, and Japan. Germans used secret code to send messages.)*

**PAGES 6–7** Why do you think there is a photo of an early cipher text? *(Possible response: It shows graphically that secret codes have been around for thousands of years.)*

**PAGE 12** Who solved the first piece of the Enigma puzzle? What did he do? *(Polish mathematician, Marian Rejewski. Built a working model of the Enigma)*

## TALK ABOUT THE BOOK

**READER RESPONSE**

1. EWMSOV

2. Possible response: How does the Enigma work? Works through a system of wheels and switching letter combinations. What did the code breakers do to crack the code? Spent years studying the Enigma

3. *Cryptography:* the process of recording, writing, or drawing, hidden messages or secret codes

4. Possible response: Winston Churchill paid a surprise visit to the code breakers at Bletchley Park in 1941.

## RESPONSE OPTION

**WRITING** Have students pretend they are code breakers working in secret at Bletchley Park. Have them write a short story about the experience.

## CONTENT CONNECTION

**SOCIAL STUDIES** Have students research the Navajo code talkers who helped the Allies in World War II. Encourage them to share their findings with the class.

*Time for* **SOCIAL STUDIES**

# Graphic Sources

- **Graphic sources** are maps, charts, photographs, drawings, and so on that help strengthen your understanding of the text.

**Directions**  Use the chart on pages 10–11 of *Cracking the German Code* to decode the message that is written in Morse code. Then write a message in Morse code.

```
 — . — —     — — —     . . —

 . —     . — .     .

 — . — .     . — .     . —     — . — .     — . —     . .     — .     — — .

 —     . . . .     .

 — —     — — —     . — .     . . .     .

 — . — .     — — —     — . .     .
```

**1.** What does it say?

_____

_____

_____

**2.** What did you notice about trying to solve this code?

_____

_____

_____

**3.** Write your own message in Morse code.

_____

_____

_____

_____

_____

**86**

# Vocabulary

**Directions** Use the root words and clues to solve the puzzle.

**Check the Words You Know**

| | | | |
|---|---|---|---|
| ___ancient | ___link | ___scholars | ___seeker |
| ___temple | ___translate | ___triumph | ___uncover |

## Across

**2.** *triumphare*

**3.** opposite of *cooperire*

**4.** *templum,* sanctuary

**5.** *schola,* school

**7.** strung together

## Down

**1.** *ante,* before

**2.** *translatus*

**6.** finder

87

# The Code Talkers

◎ **GRAPHIC SOURCES**

◎ **ASK QUESTIONS**

**LESSON VOCABULARY** ancient, ceremony, cryptography, decipher, fluently, recruit, reservation, scholars, tonal, translated

**SUMMARY** The secret of the Navajo Code Talkers is unveiled after years of silence. Graphic sources such as photographs, charts, and captions support the detailed text about Navajo culture and their contribution to World War II.

## INTRODUCE THE BOOK

**BUILD BACKGROUND** Ask a volunteer to look up the word *code* in a dictionary and read the definitions for the class. Ask students what of the word *code* means in the context of the title. Lead students to discuss why codes would be important during times of war.

**PREVIEW** Have students to share comments and questions that come to mind as they look at the heads, photographs, captions, charts, and Glossary. Invite volunteers to share their predictions as to what the book will be about.

**TEACH/PREVIEW VOCABULARY** Have students practice finding the meaning of unfamiliar words by looking at the surrounding words and sentences for context clues. Begin with the word *scholars* on page 4. Ask students to say the meaning of *scholars* in their own words, then explain which context clues helped them understand the word. Repeat this process for the remaining vocabulary words.

## TARGET SKILL AND STRATEGY

◎ **GRAPHIC SOURCES** Review with students how to use *graphic sources* to understand the text before, during, and after reading. Finish reading page 7. Say: During reading, we can look at graphic sources to help clarify the text. How do the photographs on page 7 help you understand the sacred ceremony of the *Blessing Way?* Read the caption on page 6. How does the caption help you interpret the photographs?

◎ **ASK QUESTIONS** Call attention to the photograph on page 17. Say: This photograph makes me wonder how many troops had Code Talkers? As you look at this photograph, what questions come to mind?

## READ THE BOOK

Use the following questions to support comprehension.

**PAGE 9** What questions come to mind as you read the second paragraph? *(Possible response: How are new codes invented?)*

**PAGE 15** How does the Code Talkers Dictionary clarify the text on page 14? *(Possible response: It helped me understand how they thought of Diné words to mean military terms.)*

**PAGE 20** Why do you think the Diné code is the only unbroken code? *(Possible response: Because the Diné language is very different from English and European languages)*

## TALK ABOUT THE BOOK

**READER RESPONSE**
1. Possible response: Hummingbird. They are fast.
2. Possible responses: Was it hard to keep your vow of secrecy? At a library or on the Internet
3. Possible responses: Photography, biography, geography
4. Possible response: *Traditional Ways*. Because an ancient ceremony is a tradition of the Diné people

## RESPONSE OPTIONS

**WRITING** Have students imagine that they are Code Talkers in battle. Prompt them to write a fictional letter to their family back home.

**ELL** Have students complete concept webs. Form small groups and assign each group a different topic for their web. Topics include the Diné people, World War II, and the Code Talkers Code.

## CONTENT CONNECTIONS

**SOCIAL STUDIES** Students can find out more about the role of codes in the battles of World War II by researching on the Internet or at the library.

*Time for* **SOCIAL STUDIES**

# Graphic Sources

- **Graphic sources** are maps, charts, photographs, drawings, and so on, that help strengthen your understanding of the text.

**Directions** Using the Code Talker's Dictionary on p. 15 of *The Code Talkers,* translate the Diné term in the proper English term for each of the following sentences:

1. The General ordered the CA-LO _____ to head out to sea.

2. The troops needed to cross the TOH-YIL-KAL _____, but the bridge was out.

3. Since the bridge was out, the Captain ordered the troops to use the CHAL _____ vehicle.

4. The Code Talkers did a great service to NE-HE-MAH _____ in the war.

5. The pilot of the GINI _____ was a true hero.

6. The DOLA-ALTH-WHOSH _____ cleared the rubble of the bombed-out house.

7. Fortunately the A-YE-SHI _____ missed the church as it fell.

8. The Army used the MAI-BE-HE-AHGAN _____ as a temporary headquarters.

9. The men stopped and drank from the little TOH-NIL-TSANH _____ .

10. The town was saved by the quick actions of the lone DA-HE-TIH-HI _____ .

**86**

Name _____

# Vocabulary

Fill in the blank with the word from the box that matches the definition.

**Check the Words You Know**

___ancient ___ceremony ___cryptography ___decipher ___fluently
___recruit ___reservation ___scholars ___tonal ___translated

1. _____ *adj.* of or relating to the high or low pitch of a sound.

2. _____ *v.* to sign up persons, especially for military service.

3. _____ *n.* a formal act or set of acts performed according to tradition for a special purpose.

4. _____ *adv.* smoothly, easily.

5. _____ *n.* land set aside by the government for a special use, especially for the use of a Native American nation.

6. _____ *n.* the art or process of creating or figuring out secret codes.

7. _____ *n.* people who have a great deal of knowledge.

8. _____ *v.* to make out the meaning of something that is puzzling.

9. _____ *v.* changed from one language to another.

10. _____ *adj.* very old or of times long past.

**Directions** Write a brief paragraph discussing the Code Talkers as described in *The Code Talkers,* using as many vocabulary words as possible.

_____

_____

_____

_____

**87**

© Pearson Education 4

The Code Talkers

**LR36** The Code Talkers • Week 4

Top Hat, The Detective
by Jason Lublinski
illustrated by Aleksey Ivanov

# Top Hat, The Detective

◉ **PLOT**

◉ **PRIOR KNOWLEDGE**

**LESSON VOCABULARY** amphibians, baffled, crime, exhibit, lizards, reference, reptiles, salamanders, stumped

**SUMMARY** In this mystery, Top Hat the detective uses his inquiry and problem-solving skills to find out what happened to his friend Sid's pet salamanders.

## INTRODUCE THE BOOK

**BUILD BACKGROUND** Invite volunteers to tell about times when they lost something important to them. Have students discuss how asking questions and looking at details helped them find the object.

**PREVIEW** Have students turn to page 5 in the book and skim the text and look at the picture. Discuss what the subject of this mystery seems to be. Then have students flip through the remaining pages of the book, stopping at page 15. Discuss what method Top Hat seems to use in searching for details about this mystery. *(questioning)*

**TEACH/REVIEW VOCABULARY** Write the vocabulary words on the board. Have students say each word, tell the part of speech, and give a possible definition.

**ELL** Talk with ELL students about the story and ask them to say the words in their native language.

## TARGET SKILL AND STRATEGY

◉ **PLOT** Remind students that the *plot* is an organized pattern of events in a story, and the *pattern* usually has a beginning, middle, and end. Point out that not all events in a story are important to the plot. Have students use a story map to write down the important events in *Top Hat, The Detective.*

◉ **PRIOR KNOWLEDGE** Explain to students that prior knowledge, either from personal experience or books, is what they already know about a topic. Point out that using their prior knowledge can help them understand the plot of a story. Since students know that the selection is a mystery, help them activate prior knowledge by discussing what they know about mysteries.

## READ THE BOOK

Use the following questions to support comprehension.

**PAGES 6–7** What information or event on these pages is important to the plot? What is not? *(Possible responses: all that was left of the fort was a puddle; the butterfly was beautiful.)*

**PAGE 12** In the third paragraph on this page, Top Hat talks about salamanders. Which statements in this paragraph are facts and which are opinions? Why? *(All of the statements are facts except the last one. This is Top Hat's opinion because it cannot be proved true or false.)*

**PAGES 16–17** Based on your prior knowledge of mysteries, did you expect that Top Hat would solve the puzzle? Why? *(Possible response: Yes, because in most mysteries, the detective solves the crime or puzzle.)*

## TALK ABOUT THE BOOK

**READER RESPONSE**
1. Possible responses: Second: Sid ran after a butterfly. Third: Sid found a large puddle when he came back.
2. Ice melts when the temperature is above 32° Fahrenheit, and since the ice fort was sitting in the hot sun, it would have melted.
3. Possible response: confused; not able to understand
4. Possible response: I would feel proud that I figured it out and happy that I could help my friend.

## RESPONSE OPTIONS

**SPEAKING** Divide students into groups, and have each group pick out a scene from the book that they think is important to the plot. Have each group act out its scene for the class and then explain why they thought the scene was important.

## CONTENT CONNECTIONS

**SCIENCE** Have students use encyclopedias, the Internet, or other books and resources to learn more about other amphibians. Tell students to prepare brief reports about their amphibians in which they include facts about their creatures and their own opinions about the animals.

*TIME FOR* **Science**

# Plot

- A story's **plot** is the important parts of a story.
- The parts include the **conflict**, the **rising action**, the **climax**, and the **resolution**.

**Directions**  Use the events in the story *Top Hat, The Detective*, to complete the plot map. Write page numbers to show where you found each event.

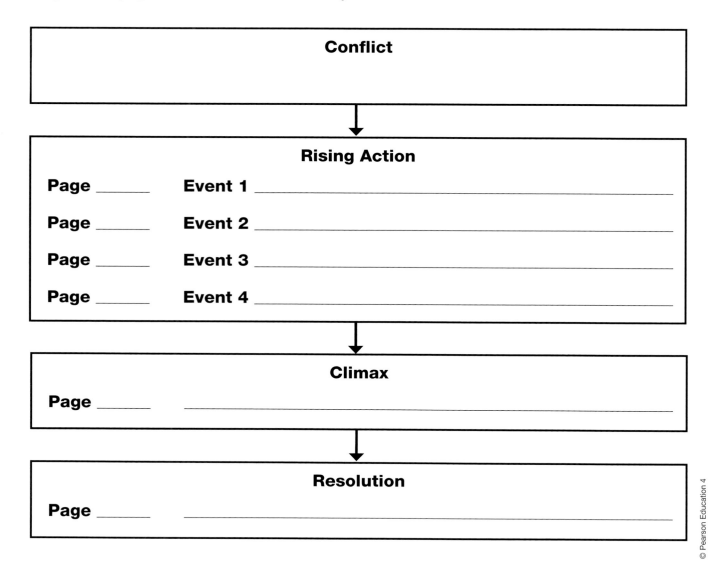

**Conflict**

**Rising Action**

Page _____  Event 1 _____

Page _____  Event 2 _____

Page _____  Event 3 _____

Page _____  Event 4 _____

**Climax**

Page _____  _____

**Resolution**

Page _____  _____

© Pearson Education 4

90

# Vocabulary

**Directions** Draw a line connecting each word in the left column with its definition in the right column.

1. **baffled**       display

2. **salamander**       confused

3. **lizard**       book of facts

4. **crime**       amphibian

5. **exhibit**       reptile

6. **reference**       unlawful act

**Directions** Read the words in each group below. Think about each word's meaning and part of speech. Circle the word in each group that does *not* belong in that group.

7. amphibians, salamanders, reptiles

8. lizards, reptiles, salamanders

9. baffled, amphibians, stumped

10. stumped, exhibit, reference

**91**

# The Case of the Missing Iguana

**PLOT**

**PRIOR KNOWLEDGE**

**LESSON VOCABULARY** amphibians, baffled, crime, exhibit, lizards, reference, reptiles, salamanders, stumped

**SUMMARY** In this mystery, a pet iguana is missing. Two young sleuths are on the case. By asking questions and paying attention to details the friends solve the puzzle.

## INTRODUCE THE BOOK

**BUILD BACKGROUND** Ask students if they have ever lost something important to them. Have them describe steps they took to find the lost object.

**PREVIEW/USE PICTURE CLUES** Read the book title aloud. Ask a student to suggest what type of story this is and how he/she knows this a mystery. Have the class skim through the pictures in the book. Ask: What are the characters doing?

**TEACH/REVIEW VOCABULARY** Assign vocabulary words to small groups of students. Groups look up words in a dictionary and come up with a synonym and an antonym. Have groups share their words.

## TARGET SKILL AND STRATEGY

**PLOT** Review the parts of a *plot*: conflict, rising action, climax, and resolution. Have students look for the conflict and climax. Have them write a sentence for each. *(conflict: Jacob, Shirley, and Pablo need to find Ziggy; climax: Shirley discovers the iguana on the bookshelf)*

**PRIOR KNOWLEDGE** Explain to students that *prior knowledge* is what they already know about a topic, either from personal experience or books. Point out that using their prior knowledge can help them understand the plot of a story. Discuss with students what they already know about mysteries and the subject of this mystery, iguanas.

## READ THE BOOK

Use the following questions to support comprehension.

**PAGE 4** How would you describe Shirley Hong? *(She is good at solving mysteries.)*

**PAGES 8–9** How does Shirley start to solve the mystery? *(She looks for clues and asks questions.)*

**PAGE 22** What clues does Shirley use to find Ziggy? *(The skylight in the attic is closed, so she thinks Ziggy must have gone downstairs. Then she looks for a high, warm place that Ziggy would like.)*

## TALK ABOUT THE BOOK

**READER RESPONSE**

1. His pet iguana is missing and he wants Shirley to help him find it.

2. Possible responses: K: they are a type of lizard, they have scaly skin, they like warm places; W: What do iguanas eat? How big do they get? Where do they live?; L: they are reptiles, they have dry skin, they absorb heat from their surroundings. More about iguanas may be found in the library or on the Internet.

3. To be completely absorbed in doing or thinking about something else

4. Possible responses: She is focused on the case; yes, I would laugh at Jacob's jokes.

**ELL** To help students understand the difference between amphibians and reptiles, have them create Venn diagrams to compare and contrast the words.

## RESPONSE OPTIONS

**WRITING** Draw a plot diagram on the board. Label the parts with the words "Conflict," "Rising Action," "Climax," and "Resolution." Ask students to copy the diagram and fill in the parts of the story under each heading.

## CONTENT CONNECTIONS

**SCIENCE** Have pairs of students research and prepare a report about a reptile. Put reports in a Reptile Encyclopedia.

**TIME FOR Science**

# Plot

- A story's **plot** is the important parts of a story.
- The parts include the **conflict**, the **rising action**, the **climax**, and the **resolution**.

**Directions** Use *The Case of the Missing Iguana* to help you answer each question. If the question is multiple choice, circle the letter of the correct answer.

1. *The Case of the Missing Iguana* is a mystery. What is often the conflict in a mystery story?

   **a.** The main character has to battle an enemy.

   **b.** There is a puzzle that has to be solved or explained.

   **c.** There is a disagreement between two characters.

   **d.** The main character has to overcome his or her fears.

2. What is the conflict in *The Case of the Missing Iguana*?

   _____

   _____

3. Jacob opened a closet to look for Ziggy and a moth flew out. Which element of the plot was this?

   _____

4. After Ziggy was found, Shirley explained how she used the clues to find the lost iguana. Which part of the plot was this?

   _____

5. Which of the following sentences from the story best describes the climax?

   **a.** "My pet iguana is missing," Pablo began.

   **b.** Pablo asked Shirley how she knew where to find Ziggy.

   **c.** There on the top shelf of a bookcase sat Ziggy.

   **d.** The three of us walked to Pablo's house.

**90**

© Pearson Education 4

# Vocabulary

**Directions** Choose the correct word from the box for each definition below.
Write the words on the lines.

| Check the Words You Know |
| --- |
| ___amphibians ___baffled ___crime ___exhibit ___lizard ___reference ___reptiles ___salamander ___stumped |

_____ **1.** amphibian

_____ **2.** lizards and iguanas

_____ **3.** stumped

_____ **4.** display

_____ **5.** offense

_____ **6.** fact book

_____ **7.** frogs, toads, and salamanders

_____ **8.** reptile

**Directions** For each category, list the words from the box that best fit the category.

| Animals | Mystery Words |
| --- | --- |
| 9._____ | 13._____ |
| 10._____ | 14._____ |
| 11._____ | 15._____ |
| 12._____ | |

91

# Professor Science . . .

Professor Science
AND THE SALAMANDER STUMPER
by Donna Latham
illustrated by Bill Petersen

🔍 **PLOT**

🔍 **PRIOR KNOWLEDGE**

**LESSON VOCABULARY** grotto, habitat, knowledgeable, observations, sedimentary, sketches, trowel

**SUMMARY** In this mystery, a boy named Doug uses his interest in science to find out why a new exhibit at the zoo has collapsed.

## INTRODUCE THE BOOK

**BUILD BACKGROUND** Discuss how science can answer everyday questions such as: Why does ice melt if left out in a warm room? *(Heat makes water molecules move, turning ice into water.)* Ask students for everyday questions that can be answered by science. *(Why do gas bubbles rise out of a newly opened soda bottle?)*

**PREVIEW/USE PICTURE CLUES** Have students skim through the pictures in the book. Ask: Which character seems to be "Professor Science?" *(the boy)* What do the people seem to be doing on pages 11–15? *(building something)*

**TEACH/PREVIEW VOCABULARY** Draw a chart like the one in question 3 of Reader Response. Divide the vocabulary words among the group. Have students complete the chart and share answers.

## TARGET SKILL AND STRATEGY

🔍 **PLOT** Review that the *plot* is what happens in a story and these events usually happen in chronological order. Remind students, however, that sometimes action is interrupted to discuss events in the past. This is called a *flashback*. Have students look for a flashback as they read.

🔍 **PRIOR KNOWLEDGE** Inform students that what they already know about a topic can help them understand a book as they read. Ask students what type of story this is and how they know this. Ask students what they might find in a mystery.

## READ THE BOOK

Use the following questions to support comprehension.

**PAGE 3** How would you describe Doug? *(He likes science and keeps his observations in a notebook.)*

**PAGES 11–13** Make a prediction: Why does the author include so much information about how the foundation is built? *(Possible response: It may be important in solving the mystery.)*

**PAGE 16** What parts of a mystery does the author include on this page? *(a puzzle—who broke the exhibit, clues— the fallen grotto and heat lamps, and a suspect—Todd)*

**ELL** Have students of different proficiency levels work together in pairs or groups to complete the vocabulary exercise. Remind students that *synonyms* are words that mean the same or nearly the same as another word.

## TALK ABOUT THE BOOK

**READER RESPONSE**
1. On page 7, Doug tells how he read to Sophie the night before; it shows that Doug and Sophie have a good relationship.
2. Possible response: Todd had a reason to harm the exhibit; he feared the salamander would be more popular than his dolphins.
3. Context clues: new habitat, rocky, cave, nooks, crannies, boulders, ledges; Definition: an imitation cave with natural features
4. Possible response: Doug solved the mystery of the salamander exhibit and could probably solve Todd's mystery.

## RESPONSE OPTIONS

**WRITING** Have each student write a two-page mystery including a puzzle, clues, a suspect, and a solution. Have students share their mysteries.

## CONTENT CONNECTIONS

**SCIENCE** Have pairs of students investigate an everyday science question, such as ones given in *Build Background.* Have each pair prepare a report and present it to the class.

TIME FOR Science

# Plot

- A story's **plot** is the important parts of a story.
- The parts include the **conflict**, the **rising action**, the **climax**, and the **resolution**.

**Directions** Answer the questions below about *Professor Science and the Salamander Stumper*. Use the story to help you find the answers.

1. In one sentence, describe a part of the story where there is rising action.

_____

_____

_____

2. What is the climax of the story?

_____

_____

_____

3. In one sentence, describe the conflict in the story.

_____

_____

_____

4. In one sentence, describe the resolution of the story.

_____

_____

_____

© Pearson Education 4

**90**

Name _____

# Vocabulary

**Directions** For each word below, write a word from the box that is its synonym.

1. drawings _____

2. well-informed _____

3. cave _____

4. home _____

**Directions** For each category, list the words from the box that best fit the category.

| Places | Plural Nouns |
|---|---|
| 5._____ | 7._____ |
| 6._____ | 8._____ |

| Adjectives | Tool |
|---|---|
| 9._____ | 11._____ |
| 10._____ | |

**12. Directions** How else might you group the words? Think of a new category. Write the name of the category and the words that belong in that group.

| Category: |
|---|
|  |
|  |
|  |

© Pearson Education 4

91

# Answer Key for Below-Level Reader Practice

## Harry Houdini: The Man and His Magic — LR1

### Compare and Contrast, LR2

Possible responses given. **1.** In both, Houdini was trapped inside a device. **2.** In the Metamorphosis, Houdini switched places with someone. **3.** In both, Houdini was stuck because he was locked up. **4.** the handcuff tricks did not involve water **5.** Houdini did not need to hold his breath.

### Vocabulary, LR3

**1.** bustling **2.** monument **3.** vanished **4.** appeared **5.** crumbled **6.** escape **7.** magician **8.** bustle, I went to the mall because I like the bustle of it. **9.** crumble, I watched the dirt clod crumble to pieces. **10.** vanish, I was so embarrassed I wanted to vanish.

## Dolphins — LR10

### Compare and Contrast, LR11

**1.** All are mammals that bear live young; all are warm-blooded **2.** Bottle-nosed dolphins have gray upper bodies with pinkish bellies. Hourglass dolphins have sharp black-and-white coloring **3.** Bottle-nosed dolphins' beaks about 7cm long; hourglass dolphins have shorter beaks **4.** Bottle-nosed dolphins are found in coastal waters, while hourglass dolphins are found in the cold waters off Antarctica.

### Vocabulary, LR12

**1.** enchanted **2.** glimpses **3.** aquarium **4.** surface **5.** pulses **6.** dolphins **7.** flexible **8.** dolphins **9.** surface **10.** enchanted

## Inventing Oatmeal — LR19

### Character and Setting, LR20

Possible responses given. **Setting:** in the present, in the garage of Grace and Ben. **Evidence:** pictures on pp. 3-8 show Grace and Ben in modern clothes. **Character:** Grace. that she likes science projects, being clean, she is interested in other times and places. **Evidence:** p. 3, she and Ben like to work on science projects; she wishes she could travel back to the Middle Ages. **Setting:** during the Middle Ages in an imaginary castle in England. p. 8, "'Picture us in a castle,'" he said. "we will be in England during the Middle Ages!'" **Character:** Ben. that he likes science projects, he has a good imagination. **Evidence:** p. 3, both like to work on science projects, he shows Grace how to imagine that they are in the Middle Ages.

## Vocabulary, LR21

**1.** peasant **2.** duke **3.** dungeon **4.** furiously **5.** porridge **6.** genius Possible responses given. **7.** royal, highest or most important **8.** angrily, in a mean and cruel way **9.** oatmeal, porridge **10.** a very smart person

## The Rosetta Stone: The Key that Unlocked the Secret of Hieroglyphics — LR28

### Graphic Sources, LR29

**1.** Rosetta Stone made **2.** Egypt becomes part of Roman Empire **3.** Rosetta Stone found **4.** Rosetta Stone displayed in The British Museum. **5–8.** Time lines should show the events in chronological order and the events should be spaced to reflect the time span between them.

### Vocabulary, LR30

**1.** uncover **2.** translate **3.** ancient **4.** scholars **5.** triumph **6.** seeker **7.** link **8.** temple

## Top Hat, the Detective — LR37

### Plot, LR38

Conflict: Sid's salamanders are missing. **Page 5, Event 1:** Top Hat and Sid talk to Penny Prundle. **Page 9, Event 2:** Top Hat and Sid talk to Ralph Moobly. **Page 11, Event 3:** Top Hat talks to Hugh and finds out that Hugh makes ice sculptures. **Page 14, Event 4:** Top Hat has one more question for Sid. **Page 16, Climax:** Top Hat returns with the salamanders in a box. **Pages 17–19, Resolution:** Top Hat explains how he solved the mystery.

### Vocabulary, LR39

**1.** confused **2.** amphibian **3.** reptile **4.** unlawful act **5.** display **6.** book of facts **7.** reptiles **8.** salamanders **9.** amphibians **10.** stumped

# Answer Key for On-Level Reader Practice

## Tricks to Doing Magic      LR4

 **Compare and Contrast, LR5**

Possible responses given. **1.** The magician talks to the audience to create excitement. **2.** the first trick uses a large box and another person; the second trick uses only two quarters **3.** they both involve disappearing props; both rely on the magician's clever talking **4.** for the *Disappearing Person*, the box must be built; for *Which Hand*, the magician needs to collect two quarters **5.** for the first, the magician creates dramatic presentation; for the second trick, the magician uses his hands to create illusion

**Vocabulary, LR6**

**1.** appeared **2.** vanished **3.** crumbled **4.** escape **5.** magician **6.** bustling. **7.** monument **8.** bustling **9.** vanished appeared **10.** monument

## Swimming with Dolphins      LR13

 **Compare and Contrast, LR14**

Possible responses given. DOLPHINS: **1.** can weigh 1,000 pounds **2.** can hold breath for 10 minutes BOTH: **3.** mammals **4.** have teeth YOU **5.** weigh 60 pounds **6.** don't swallow fish whole

**Vocabulary, LR15**

**1.** surface **2.** enchanted **3.** pulses **4.** glimpses **5.** dolphins. **6.** flexible. **7.** aquarium. **8–10.** Responses will vary.

## The Amazing Incredible Idea Kit      LR22

 **Character and Setting, LR23**

Possible responses given. **1.** Granny Mae is interesting and wise, p. 5; like to hear about Granny Mae's life, p. 9. **2.** help each other; created the idea kit, pp. 5, 22; listen to their parents, p. 20; work hard, p. 21. **3.** Granny Mae thinks Paul and Beatrice are smart and excellent students, p. 10; Mr. O'Hara thinks they made the best science fair exhibit, p. 23. **4–5.** The setting was England when Granny Mae was a college student. The house of the Goslings might have been in the country, because it had a garden for parties.

## Vocabulary, LR24

**1.** F U R I O U S L Y **2.** D U K E **3.** M A J E S T Y **4.** D U N G E O N **5.** P O R R I D G E **6.** N O B L E **7.** G E N I U S **8.** P E A S A N T **9.** G R A N D P A   N I G E L **10.** W R O T E   S T O R I E S

## Cracking the German Code      LR31

 **Graphic Sources, LR32**

**1.** *You are cracking the Morse code.* **2.** It can be difficult to tell the difference between letters. **3.** Responses will vary.

**Vocabulary, LR33**

**1.** uncover **2.** translate **3.** ancient **4.** scholars **5.** triumph **6.** seeker **7.** link **8.** temple

## The Case of the Missing Iguana      LR40

 **Plot, LR41**

**1.** b **2.** Ziggy is missing and needs to be found. **3.** rising action **4.** resolution **5.** c

**Vocabulary, LR42**

**1.** salamander **2.** reptile **3.** baffled **4.** exhibit **5.** crime. **6.** reference. **7.** amphibians. **8.** lizard **9.** amphibian **10.** lizard **11.** reptile **12.** salamander **13.** baffled **14.** crime **15.** stumped

# Answer Key for Advanced-Level Reader Practice

## Tricking the Eye      LR7

 **Compare and Contrast, LR8**

Possible responses given. **1.** both create animated characters; both use a basic background **2.** for the cel system, animators draw the characters on clear plastic; for the slash-and-tear, animators draw the characters on paper and cut them out **3.** in the first method, the animator draws every single frame from scratch; with cel animation, the animator only changes the characters **4.** puppets or clay models are three-dimensional; cel animation uses 2-D techniques

**Vocabulary, LR9**

**1.** optical illusion **2.** computer-assisted animation **3.** animate **4.** concave **5.** perception **6.** accommodation **7.** computer-generated animation **8.** cerebral cortex **9.** frames **10.** illusion

## Echolocation      LR16

 **Compare and Contrast, LR17**

**1.** They both use echolocation. **2.** Dolphins produce sound in their nasal passages; bats have a larynx. **3.** Bats receive sounds in their ears; dolphins receive sounds to their jaws. **4–5.** Bat ears are usually large; dolphins' ears are small. Bat ears are key to their use of echolocation; dolphin ears are useful only for hearing sounds above water.

**Vocabulary, LR18**

**1.** pinna **2.** hammer **3.** lymph **4.** echolocation **5.** nose leaves **6.** melon **7.** larynx **8.** cochlea **9.** stirrup **10.** anvil

## Alexander Graham Bell      LR25

 **Character and Setting, LR26**

Possible responses given. **1.** He is a talking dog who thinks he is handsome, and never lies, p.4. He also loves his master, Alexander Graham Bell, pp. 15, 18. **2.** Through what he thinks and what he does with his master. **3.** He was always interested in how things work, p. 4. He wanted to help deaf people talk and he worked hard, p. 10. **4.** Through what the narrator says and through what Bell does. **5.** The story is set before the telephone was invented. People far away from each other had to use a telegraph. Bell wanted to invent something to allow people to speak to each other from great distances.

## Vocabulary, LR27

Possible responses given. **1.** Bell thought that frequency was the key to creating a telephone. **2.** Bell and Watson worked together on the Harmonic Telegraph. **3.** Bell knew that different objects make different vibrations. **4.** Bell wanted to help the deaf communicate with others. **5.** Bell's telephone had a membrane that vibrated and made sound. **6.** The sound waves in Bell's telephone were not visible. **7.** Bell was dedicated to helping deaf people. **8.** Bell was the first to get a patent for the telephone.

## The Code Talkers      LR34

 **Graphic Sources, LR35**

**1.** destroyer **2.** river **3.** amphibious **4.** America **5.** dive bomber **6.** bulldozer **7.** bomb **8.** farm **9.** creek **10.** fighter plane

**Vocabulary, LR36**

**1.** tonal **2.** recruit **3.** ceremony **4.** fluently **5.** reservation **6.** cryptography **7.** scholars **8.** decipher **9.** translated **10.** ancient

## Professor Science      LR43

 **Plot, LR44**

Possible responses given. **1.** There is rising action when Doug watches the workers lay the foundation of the salamander grotto. **2.** The climax is when everyone discovers that the grotto has collapsed. **3.** The characters need to find out who or what caused the grotto to collapse. **4.** Doug figures out that the students building the grotto made the cement dry out, which caused the grotto to collapse.

**Vocabulary, LR45**

**1.** sketches **2.** knowledgeable **3.** grotto **4.** habitat **5.** grotto **6.** habitat **7.** sketches **8.** observations **9.** sedimentary **10.** knowledgeable **11.** trowel **12.** Possible responses given. Science Words: observations, sketches, sedimentary, habitat

# Differentiated Instruction

## Table of Contents

# Routine Cards

## Oral Rereading Routine

*Use this Routine when students read orally.*

**1 Read** Have students read the entire book orally.

**2 Reread** For optimal fluency, students should reread the text three or four times.

**3 Provide Feedback** Listen as students read and provide corrective feedback regarding their oral reading and their use of decoding strategies.

## Choral Reading Routine

*Use this Routine when students read chorally.*

**1 Select a Passage** Choose an appropriate passage from the selection.

**2 Divide into Groups** Assign each group a part to read.

**3 Model** Have students track the print as you read.

**4 Read Together** Have students read along with you.

**5 Independent Reading** Have the groups read aloud without you. Monitor progress and provide feedback. For optimal fluency, students should reread three to four times.

## Fluent Word Reading Routine

*Teach students to read words fluently using this Routine.*

**1 Connect** Write an example word. Isolate the sound-spelling or word structure element you will focus on and ask students to demonstrate their understanding.

**2 Model** When you come to a new word, look at all the letters in the word and think about its vowel sound. Say the sounds in the word to yourself and then read the word. Model reading the example words in this way. When you come to a new word, what are you going to do?

**3 Group Practice** Write other similar words. Let's read these words. Look at the letters, think about the vowel sounds, and say the sounds to yourself. When I point to the word, let's read it together. Allow 2-3 seconds previewing time for each word.

## Paired Reading Routine

*Use this Routine when students read in pairs.*

**1 Reader 1 Begins** Students read the entire book, switching readers at the end of each page.

**2 Reader 2 Begins** Have partners reread; now the other partner begins.

**3 Reread** For optimal fluency, students should reread three or four times.

**4 Provide Feedback** Listen as students read. Provide corrective feedback regarding their oral reading and their use of decoding strategies.

## Multisyllabic Word Routine

*Teach students this Routine to read long words with meaningful parts.*

**1 Teach** Tell students to look for meaningful parts and to think about the meaning of each part. They should use the parts to read the word and determine meaning.

**2 Model** Think aloud to analyze a long word for the base word, ending, prefix, and/or suffix and to identify the word and determine its meaning.

**3 Guide Practice** Provide examples of long words with endings (*-ing, -ed, -s*), prefixes (*un-, re-, dis-, mis-, non-*), and/or suffixes (*-ly, -ness, -less, -ful,* and so on). Help students analyze base words and parts.

**4 Provide Feedback** Encourage students to circle parts of the words to help identify parts and determine meaning.

---

## Multisyllabic Word Routine

*Teach students this Routine to chunk words with no recognizable parts.*

**1 Teach** Tell students to look for chunks in words with no meaningful parts. They should say each chunk slowly and then say the chunks fast to make a whole word.

**2 Model** Think aloud to demonstrate breaking a word into chunks, saying each chunk slowly, and then saying the chunks fast to make a word.

**3 Guide Practice** Provide examples of long words with no meaningful parts. Help students chunk the words.

**4 Provide Feedback** If necessary, reteach by modeling how to break words into chunks.

---

## Picture Walk Routine

*To build concepts and vocabulary, conduct a structured picture walk before reading.*

**1 Prepare** Preview the selection and list key concepts and vocabulary you wish to develop.

**2 Discuss** As students look at the pages, discuss illustrations, have students point to pictured items, and/or ask questions that target key concepts and vocabulary.

**3 Elaborate** Elaborate on students' responses to reinforce correct use of the vocabulary and to provide additional exposure to key concepts.

**4 Practice** For more practice with key concepts, have each student turn to a partner and do the picture walk using the key concept vocabulary.

---

## Concept Vocabulary

*Use this Routine to teach concept vocabulary.*

**1 Introduce the Word** Relate the word to the week's concept. Supply a student-friendly definition.

**2 Demonstrate** Provide several familiar examples to demonstrate meaning.

**3 Apply** Have students demonstrate understanding with a simple activity.

**4 Display the Word** Relate the word to the concept by displaying it on a concept web. Have students identify word parts and practice reading the word.

**5 Use the Word Often** Encourage students to use the word often in their writing and speaking. Ask questions that require students to use the word.

# Group Time

**DAY 1**

## Leveled Reader Database ONLINE

PearsonSuccessNet.com

### ① Build Background

**REINFORCE CONCEPTS** Display the Perception Concept Web. This week's concept is *perception*. Perception is what we see and think is happening. When our perception does not agree with what we know to be true or possible, we are faced with puzzles and mysteries. Discuss the meaning of each word on the web, using the definitions on p. 392l and the Concept Vocabulary Routine on p. DI·1.

**CONNECT TO READING** This week you will read about a magician who fooled people into believing that he could do impossible things, such as walk through a brick wall. How did the weavers in "The Emperor's New Clothes" fool the emperor into believing that their invisible cloth was real? *(They claimed that only foolish people and people who were unfit for their jobs could not see the cloth.)*

### ② Read Leveled Reader *Harry Houdini: The Man and His Magic*

**BEFORE READING** Using the Picture Walk Routine on p. DI·1, guide students through the text focusing on key concepts and vocabulary. Ask questions such as:

**p. 3** One of Harry Houdini's famous tricks was to make an elephant disappear. What do you know about how magicians do their tricks? *(They distract their audiences. They use special props.)*

**p. 5** As a young man, Harry Houdini was good at sports such as track. How do you think this might have helped him later as a magician? *(Sports made him strong and flexible.)*

**DURING READING** Read pp. 3–5 aloud, while students track the print. Do a choral reading of pp. 6–9. If students are capable, have them read and discuss the remainder of the book with a partner. Ask: How did Harry Houdini fool his audiences? What were some of the secrets to his tricks?

**AFTER READING** Encourage pairs of students to discuss Harry Houdini's tricks as they appeared to audiences and as he actually performed them. We read *Harry Houdini: The Man and His Magic* to learn how and why Harry Houdini became a magician. Knowing something about Harry Houdini's life will help us as we read *The Houdini Box*.

### Monitor Progress

**Selection Reading and Comprehension**

| | |
|---|---|
| **If…** students have difficulty reading the selection with a partner, | **then…** have them follow along as they listen to the Online Leveled Reader Audio. |
| **If…** students have trouble understanding Harry Houdini's tricks, | **then…** reread pp. 10–11 and discuss the photograph together. |

For alternate Leveled Reader lesson plans that teach ◎**Compare and Contrast,** ◎**Predict,** and **Lesson Vocabulary,** see pp. LR1–LR9.

## On-Level

### ① Build Background

**ROUTINE**

**DEVELOP VOCABULARY** Write the word *invisible* and ask students to define it in their own words. *(not visible, not able to be seen)* What are some things that are invisible? *(wind, thoughts, germs)* Repeat this activity with the word *illusion* and other words from the Leveled Reader *Tricks to Doing Magic.* Use the Concept Vocabulary Routine on p. DI·1 as needed.

### ② Read Leveled Reader *Tricks to Doing Magic*

**BEFORE READING** Have students create a three-column chart with the headings Trick, What People Think Happens, and What Really Happens. This book explains how to do several magic tricks. As you read about each trick, notice the difference between what people think happens and what really happens. Record this information in your chart.

**DURING READING** Have students follow along as you read pp. 3–11. Then let them complete the book on their own. Remind students to add information to their charts as they read.

**AFTER READING** Have students compare the information in their charts. Explain that knowing how to do magic tricks will help them as they read tomorrow's story, *The Houdini Box.*

## Advanced

### ① Read Leveled Reader *Tricking the Eye*

**ROUTINE**

**BEFORE READING** Recall the Read Aloud "The Emperor's New Clothes." How did the weavers trick the emperor and his people into seeing cloth that was not really there? *(They said that only foolish people and people who were unfit for their jobs could not see the cloth.)* Today you will read about other tricks people use to fool the eye.

**CRITICAL THINKING** Have students read the Leveled Reader independently. Encourage them to think critically. For example, ask:

- How has animation changed over time?
- Should people believe everything they see? Why or why not?

**AFTER READING** Have students find a synonym for *disappear* in the text on p. 7 and an antonym for *illusion* in the text on p. 21. Then have them write an analogy for each pair of words. For example, *disappear* is to *vanish* as *appear* is to *materialize; illusion* is to *reality* as *fake* is to *genuine.* Meet with students to discuss the selection and to share the analogies they wrote.

### ② Independent Extension Activity

**NOW TRY THIS** Assign "Now Try This" on pp. 22–23 of *Tricking the Eye* for students to work on throughout the week.

# The Houdini Box
# Group Time

AudioText
Audio CD

## Monitor Progress

### Word and Story Reading

| If... | then... |
|---|---|
| If... students have difficulty reading multisyllabic words in the selection, | then... have them look for and read meaningful parts in the words or have them chunk words with no recognizable parts. |
| If... students need practice reading words fluently, | then... use the Fluent Word Reading Routine on the DI tab. |
| If... students have difficulty reading along with the group, | then... have them follow along as they listen to the AudioText. |

## Strategic Intervention

ROUTINE

### 1 Word Study/Phonics

**LESSON VOCABULARY** Use p. 394b to review the meanings of *appeared, bustling, crumbled, escape, magician, monument,* and *vanished.* Have individuals practice reading the words from word cards.

**DECODING MULTISYLLABIC WORDS** Write *mysterious,* saying the word as you write it. Then model how to use meaningful parts to read longer words. First I look for familiar parts. I see the suffix *-ous.* I cover this suffix and read the base word: *mysteri.* That's not a real word; the base word must be *mystery.* I know that *y* sometimes changes to *i* when a suffix is added. Then I blend the base word and the suffix to read the whole word: *mystery ous, mysterious.* The suffix *-ous* means "having much; full of," so *mysterious* must mean "having much mystery" or "full of mystery."

Use the Multisyllabic Word Routine on p. DI·1 to help students read these other words from *The Houdini Box: wonderstruck, delighted, unexplainable, unsuccessful, congratulations, congratulated.* Be sure students understand the meanings of *wonderstruck* and *delighted.*

Use *Strategies for Word Analysis,* Lesson 21, with students who have difficulty mastering word analysis and need practice with decodable text.

### 2 Read *The Houdini Box,* pp. 396–403

**BEFORE READING** *Harry Houdini: The Man and His Magic* described how Harry Houdini became a famous magician. Think about what you know about Harry Houdini's life as you read *The Houdini Box.*

Using the Picture Walk Routine on p. DI·1, guide students through the text, asking questions such as those below. Read the question on p. 397. Together, set a purpose for reading.

**pp. 396–397** Who do you think the boy in this scene is? Who might the man be? What is strange or mysterious about this scene?

**p. 399** These illustrations show Victor trying to do two of Harry Houdini's tricks. Which tricks is he trying to do?

**DURING READING** Follow the Guiding Comprehension routine on pp. 398–403. Have students read along with you while tracking the print, or do a choral reading. Stop every two pages to ask what has happened so far. Prompt as necessary.

• Why does Victor want to be a magician?
• What happens in the train station on the way to Aunt Harriet's house?

**AFTER READING** What has happened so far? What do you predict will happen next? Reread passages with students as needed.

**DAY**
**2**

## Advanced

ROUTINE

### 1 Extend Vocabulary

🎯 **CONTEXT CLUES** Choose and read a sentence or passage containing a difficult word for which students can derive meaning from the context. For example, read the first paragraph on p. 7 of *Tricking the Eye* beginning with: *There are many other ways to animate. . . .* What does *animate* mean? *(to bring to life)* How did you figure out the word's meaning? *(I used context clues that tell about the models or puppets moving.)* What is an antonym for *animate*? *(still)* Discuss why context clues are helpful, and remind students to use the strategy as they read *The Houdini Box*.

### 2 Read *The Houdini Box*, pp. 396–403

**BEFORE READING** Today you will read a story about a boy who wants to become as great a magician as Harry Houdini, who thrilled audiences with his daring escapes and feats of magic. As you read, recall what you have learned about optical illusions and other tricks that fool the eye.

Have students write in their Strategy Response Logs predictions of what they expect to read about (p. 396).

**PROBLEM SOLVING** Have students read pp. 398–403 independently. Encourage them to problem solve. For example, ask:

• How might Victor succeed at one of the tricks he attempts?

**AFTER READING** Have partners discuss the story and share and confirm their Strategy Response Log predictions. Encourage them to predict whether or not Victor will learn Houdini's secrets and become a successful magician. Have individuals suggest a stage name for Victor and design a poster advertising his magic act.

**AudioText**

## The Houdini Box

# Group Time

Audio CD · AudioText

### 1 Reinforce Comprehension

**SKILL COMPARE AND CONTRAST** Have students tell what it means to compare and contrast *(to tell how two or more things are alike and different)* and name clue words that often signal comparisons and contrasts *(comparisons: like, as, same; contrasts: but, unlike, different).* If necessary, review the meaning and provide a model. To compare and contrast is to tell how two or more things are alike and different. Display two objects that have features in common, such as a coffee mug and a water bottle. Ask students to first tell how the objects are alike and then how they are different. Record their responses in a Venn diagram on the board.

Begin a Venn diagram with students to show how Victor and Harry Houdini are alike and different. *(alike: they're both interested in magic; different: Victor is a boy, Harry Houdini is a man; Victor is not successful at magic tricks, Harry Houdini is a successful magician)*

### 2 Read *The Houdini Box,* pp. 404–409

**BEFORE READING** Have students retell what has happened in the story so far. Ask: Do you think Victor will learn the secrets of Harry Houdini's tricks? Reread the last three paragraphs on p. 402 and all of p. 403. Model how to use details from the story and personal experience to make a prediction. Harry Houdini has invited Victor to his house. The invitation says "a thousand secrets await you," so Houdini must be planning to teach Victor his tricks. Victor is early for the meeting, though. Maybe Houdini isn't home. Also, the mood is a little uneasy. The door makes a heavy sigh when Mrs. Houdini opens it. And she is described as a sad woman who speaks softly. It feels like something is wrong. I predict that Victor won't get to meet Houdini. Remind students to make predictions as they finish reading *The Houdini Box.* **STRATEGY Predict**

**DURING READING** Follow the Guiding Comprehension routine on pp. 404–409. Have students read along with you while tracking print, or do a choral reading. Stop every two pages to ask students what has happened so far. Prompt as necessary.

- What does Mrs. Houdini do after Victor shows her the letter? Why?
- How do Victor and his son discover the grave of Harry Houdini? Why is this discovery important?

**AFTER READING** What makes someone, such as Harry Houdini, a great magician? Reread the story with students for comprehension as needed. Tell them that tomorrow they will read "So You Want to Be an Illusionist," an article that explains how Harry Houdini performed two of his famous tricks.

### Monitor Progress

#### Word and Story Reading

| **If...** students have difficulty reading multisyllabic words in the selection, | **then...** have them look for and read meaningful parts in the words or have them chunk words with no recognizable parts. |
| --- | --- |
| **If...** students have difficulty reading along with the group, | **then...** have them follow along as they listen to the AudioText. |

## Advanced

*ROUTINE*

### ① Extend Comprehension

🎯 **SKILL** **COMPARE AND CONTRAST** Have students compare and contrast the story's main characters (Harry Houdini, Victor, and Victor's mother) with people in their own lives. For example: *Victor reminds me of my little brother, Eric. When Eric first learned how to dive, he practiced over and over, just as Victor practiced his magic tricks over and over.*

🎯 **STRATEGY** **PREDICT** Have students scan the first half of the story to find the two mentions of Grandmother's trunk *(p. 399, fourth paragraph; p. 402, second paragraph).* Ask: What role does Grandmother's trunk seem to play in the story? Then have students predict whether or not Grandmother's trunk will appear in the second half of the story and, if so, in what context. Encourage students to provide logical support for their predictions.

### ② Read *The Houdini Box*, pp. 404–409

**BEFORE READING** Have students recall what has happened in the story so far. Remind them to compare and contrast characters and events and to predict how the plot will unfold as they read the rest of the story.

**CREATIVE THINKING** Have students read pp. 404–409 independently. Encourage them to think creatively. For example, ask:

• What is one detail you could change to alter the outcome of the story?

**AFTER READING** Have students complete the Strategy Response Log activity (p. 408). Then have them write a new ending for the story based on changing one detail.

**Audio CD**    **AudioText**

*The Houdini Box*

# Group Time

**ROUTINE**

**AudioText**

## **1** Practice Retelling

**REVIEW STORY ELEMENTS** Help students identify the main characters and the setting of *The Houdini Box*. Then guide them in using the Retelling Cards to list story events in sequence. Prompt students to include important details.

**RETELL** Using the Retelling Cards, have students work in pairs to retell *The Houdini Box*. Monitor retelling and prompt students as needed. For example, ask:

- What is the problem in this story?
- How is the problem solved?

## **2** Read "So You Want to Be an Illusionist"

**BEFORE READING** Read the genre information on p. 412. Write the words *expository* and *explain* on the board and help students make the connection that *expository* nonfiction *explains* something. Point out the diagram on p. 413. Tell students that diagrams are often part of this type of writing because they, too, help explain ideas. Ask: What do you think this article explains?

Read the rest of the panel on p. 412. Then have students scan the article to locate the title, headings, diagrams, and captions.

**DURING READING** Have students read along with you while tracking the print, or do a choral reading of the selection. As you read the description of each trick, pause to look at the accompanying diagram.

**AFTER READING** Have students share their reactions to the selection. Then guide them through the Reading Across Texts and Writing Across Texts activities, prompting if necessary.

- Which tricks did you read about in *The Houdini Box*?
- Which tricks did you read about in "So You Want to Be an Illusionist"?
- Which trick would you have liked to see Houdini perform?

### Monitor Progress

**Word and Story Reading**

| If... students have difficulty reading multisyllabic words in the selection, | then... have them look for and read meaningful parts in the words or have them chunk words with no recognizable parts. |
| --- | --- |
| If... students have difficulty reading along with the group, | then... have them follow along as they listen to the AudioText. |

## Advanced

### 1 Read "So You Want to Be an Illusionist"

**CRITICAL THINKING** Have students read pp. 412–415 independently. Encourage them to think critically. For example, ask:

- Which trick, the Vanishing Elephant Trick or the Brick Wall Trick, might be more likely to go wrong? Why do you think so?

- What are some of the risks of being a magician? What are some of the rewards?

**AFTER READING** Discuss Reading Across Texts. Have students complete Writing Across Texts independently.

### 2 Extend Genre Study

**RESEARCH** Have students use print or online resources to find other expository nonfiction that explains how magic tricks or illusions are performed. Have them take notes on a magic trick or illusion that they find especially interesting.

**WRITE** Have students use their notes to write a nonfiction article that explains the magic trick or illusion. Tell them to include a title, introduction, heading, and captioned diagram in their articles.

**AudioText**

*The Houdini Box*

# Group Time

DAY
**5**

ONLINE
PearsonSuccessNet.com

### ① Reread for Fluency

**MODEL** Read aloud pp. 3–5 of the Leveled Reader *Harry Houdini: The Man and His Magic,* using punctuation to guide your phrasing and voice modulation. Have students note where you pause and when your voice rises or falls. Then read pp. 6–7 in a monotone voice, disregarding punctuation. Have students tell you which model sounded better. Discuss how punctuation helps you group related words and know when to raise or lower your voice.

**PRACTICE** Have students reread passages from *Harry Houdini: The Man and His Magic* individually or with a partner. For optimal fluency, they should reread three or four times. As students read, monitor fluency and provide corrective feedback. Students in this group are assessed in Weeks 2 and 4.

### ② Retell Leveled Reader *Harry Houdini: The Man and His Magic*

Model how to use the photographs and captions to retell what the book was about. Then have students retell what they learned from the book, using the photographs and captions. Prompt them as needed.

- What do you see in this photograph? What does the caption say?
- How do the photograph and caption relate to Harry Houdini's life?

### Monitor Progress

#### Fluency

| **If...** students have difficulty reading fluently, | **then...** provide additional fluency practice by pairing nonfluent readers with fluent ones. |
|---|---|

For alternate Leveled Reader lesson plans that teach 🔄 **Compare and Contrast,** 🔄 **Predict,** and **Lesson Vocabulary,** see pp. LR1–LR9.

## On-Level

### 1 Reread for Fluency
**ROUTINE**

**MODEL** Read aloud p. 3 of the Leveled Reader *Tricks to Doing Magic,* using the punctuation to guide your phrasing and voice modulation. Have students note where you pause and when your voice rises or falls. Discuss how observing punctuation can make factual information easier to read and understand.

**PRACTICE** Have individuals or pairs reread passages from *Tricks to Doing Magic.* For optimal fluency, they should reread three or four times. As students read, monitor fluency and provide corrective feedback. Students in this group are assessed in Week 3.

### 2 Retell Leveled Reader *Tricks to Doing Magic*

Have students use the subheads and illustrations as a guide to summarize what they learned about each magic trick featured in the book. Prompt students as needed.

- What did you learn about being a magician from reading this book?
- Tell me how to do the quarter rubbing trick.

## Advanced

### 1 Reread for Fluency
**ROUTINE**

**PRACTICE** Have students reread passages from the Leveled Reader *Tricking the Eye* with a partner or individually. As students read, monitor fluency and provide corrective feedback. If students read fluently on the first reading, they do not need to reread three or four times. Assess the fluency of students in this group using p. 415a.

### 2 Revisit Leveled Reader *Tricking the Eye*

**RETELL** Have students retell what they learned from the Leveled Reader *Tricking the Eye.*

**NOW TRY THIS** Have students complete and present the projects they have been working on all week. You may wish to display the projects in the classroom for the whole class to see and enjoy.

# Group Time

**DAY 1**

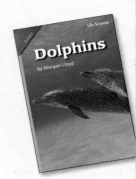

Dolphins
by Morgan Lloyd

Life Science

## Leveled Reader Database

### ONLINE

PearsonSuccessNet.com

---

### Strategic Intervention

**ROUTINE**

#### 1 Build Background

**REINFORCE CONCEPTS** Display the Animal Behavior Concept Web. This week's concept is *animal behavior*. Many animals exhibit very interesting, often mysterious behavior. Discuss the meaning of each word and phrase on the web, using the definitions on p. 416l and the Concept Vocabulary Routine on p. DI·1.

**CONNECT TO READING** This week you will read about some interesting animal behaviors and abilities. In "Sugar: Cross Country Traveler," what was so surprising about Sugar's journey? *(Sugar was able to find her owners after traveling 1,000 miles.)* What is it scientists wondered about? *(They wondered what signals from the Earth Sugar listened to.)*

#### 2 Read Leveled Reader *Dolphins*

**BEFORE READING** Using the Picture Walk Routine on p. DI·1, guide students through the text focusing on key concepts and vocabulary. Ask questions such as:

**pp. 4–5** This selection tells about dolphins. The diagram shows the unique body parts of a dolphin. Name these parts. How do you think dolphins use these body parts?

**pp. 8–13** Look at the different kinds of dolphins. Compare the dolphins on these pages. Tell how some are alike and some are different. (Answers should identify dolphin characteristics that are different and similar.)

**DURING READING** Read pp. 3–5 aloud, while students track the print. Do a choral reading of pp. 6–7. If students are capable, have them read and discuss the remainder of the book with a partner. Ask: What are some types of dolphins? In what ways do dolphins behave like fish and also like other mammals?

**AFTER READING** Encourage pairs of students to tell what they have learned so far about dolphin behavior. We read *Dolphins* to learn more about these friendly mammals. Understanding dolphin behavior will help us as we read *Encantado: Pink Dolphin of the Amazon.*

---

### Monitor Progress

#### Selection Reading and Comprehension

| If... students have difficulty reading the selection with a partner, | then... have them follow along as they listen to the Online Leveled Reader Audio. |
|---|---|
| If... students have trouble understanding the many types of dolphins, | then... reread pp. 8–13 and discuss the information together. |

---

For alternate Leveled Reader lesson plans that teach ↻**Compare and Contrast,** ↻**Visualize,** and **Lesson Vocabulary,** see pp. LR10–LR18.

## On-Level

### ❶ Build Background

**DEVELOP VOCABULARY** Write the word *agility* and ask students to define it in their own words. *(the ability to move quickly and easily)* Which would you expect to show more agility, a football player or a man with a broken leg? Repeat this activity with the word *pods* and other words from the Leveled Reader *Swimming with Dolphins.* Use the Concept Vocabulary Routine on p. DI·1 as needed.

### ❷ ᴿᵉᵃᵈ Leveled Reader
### *Swimming with Dolphins*

**BEFORE READING** Have students create Venn diagrams with the labels Dolphins, Land Mammals, and Both. This book tells how dolphins behave when seeking food and with other marine animals. As you read, look for ways dolphin behavior is similar to and different from the behavior of land mammals, such as wolves or humans. Record this information in your diagram.

**DURING READING** Have students follow along as you read pp. 3–9. Then let them complete the book on their own. Remind students to add facts to their Venn diagrams as they read.

**AFTER READING** Have students compare the facts on their diagrams. Point out that knowing how the many types of dolphins are alike and different will help them as they read tomorrow's selection *Encantado: Pink Dolphin of the Amazon.*

## Advanced

### ❶ ᴿᵉᵃᵈ Leveled Reader
### *Echolocation: Animals Making Sound Waves*

**BEFORE READING** Recall the Read Aloud "Sugar: Cross Country Traveler," a story about a disabled cat's long-distance journey to find her owners. Do you know of animals with unusual abilities? *(Some animals can detect earthquakes before they happen.)* Today we will read about the behaviors of the mysterious dolphins of the Amazon region.

**CREATIVE THINKING** Have students read the Leveled Reader independently. Encourage them to think creatively. For example, ask:

- How might a dolphin find food if it were a land-based mammal?
- What can we learn about ourselves from studying dolphin behavior?

**AFTER READING** Have students review the selection to find five or more unfamiliar words and determine their meanings by using context clues or by consulting a dictionary. Then ask them to write statements or questions about animal behavior that both include the words and express their meanings. Encourage students to meet as a group or with you to discuss the selections and the statements or questions they wrote.

### ❷ Independent Extension Activity

**NOW TRY THIS** Assign "Now Try This" on pp. 22–23 of *Echolocation* for students to work on throughout the week.

# Group Time

**Audio CD** AudioText

**DAY 2**

**ROUTINE**

## 1 Word Study/Phonics

**LESSON VOCABULARY** Use p. 418b to review the meanings of *aquarium, dolphins, enchanted, flexible, glimpses, pulses,* and *surface.* Have individuals practice reading the words from word cards.

**DECODING MULTISYLLABIC WORDS** Write *bowriding,* saying the word as you write it. Then model how to use meaningful parts to read longer words. First I look for meaningful parts of the word. If I see a part of the word I know, like *–ed* or *–ing,* I then look for a base word. I see *bow* at the beginning of the word, and *riding* at the end. I say the parts of the word: *bow rid ing.* Then I read the word: *bowriding.* A *bow* is the front part of a ship and *to ride* means to be carried along. So *bowriding* means "carried along by waves at the front of the ship."

Use the Multisyllabic Word Routine on p. DI·1 to help students read these words from *Encantado: Pink Dolphin of the Amazon: encounter, foreheads, abrupt,* and *waterway.* Be sure students understand the meanings of words such as *encounter* and *abrupt.*

Use *Strategies for Word Analysis,* Lesson 22, with students who have difficulty mastering word analysis and need practice with decodable text.

## 2 Read *Encantado: Pink Dolphin of the Amazon,* pp. 420–429

**BEFORE READING** *Dolphins* gave us interesting information about the many dolphins found around the world. Think about the behavior of these animals as you read *Encantado: Pink Dolphin of the Amazon.*

Using the Picture Walk Routine on p. DI·1, guide students through the text asking questions such as those listed below. Read the question on p. 421. Together, set a purpose for reading.

**pp. 422–423** Where do you think this village is?

**p. 425** This is a pink dolphin, or *encantado.* How might its behavior be different from that of other dolphins? *(It looks like it can twist around.)* Yes, the pink dolphin is more flexible than other dolphins.

**DURING READING** Follow the Guiding Comprehension routine on pp. 422–429. Have students read along with you while tracking the print or do a choral reading. Stop every two pages to ask what has happened so far. Prompt as necessary.

- How do the pink dolphins move through the dark water?
- Why are the pink dolphins so mysterious to outsiders?

**AFTER READING** What have you learned so far? What do you think you will read about tomorrow? Reread passages as needed.

### Monitor Progress

#### Word and Story Reading

| If... | then... |
|---|---|
| **If...** students have difficulty reading multisyllabic words in the selection, | **then...** have them look for and read meaningful parts in the words or have them chunk words with no recognizable parts. |
| **If...** students need practice reading words fluently, | **then...** use the Fluent Word Reading Routine on the DI tab. |
| **If...** students have difficulty reading along with the group, | **then...** have them follow along as they listen to the AudioText. |

## Advanced

ROUTINE

### 1 Extend Vocabulary

**CONTEXT CLUES** Choose and read a sentence or passage containing a difficult word, such as this passage from p. 4 of *Echolocation: When the sound waves make the eardrum vibrate, the vibrations make these bones move.* What does the word *vibrations* mean? *(Rapid movements to and fro.)* How did you determine the meaning? *(I used context clues sound waves and bones move.)* Discuss why context clues are helpful. Remind students to use the strategy as they read *Encantado: Pink Dolphin of the Amazon.*

### 2 Read *Encantado: Pink Dolphin of the Amazon,* pp. 420–429

**BEFORE READING** Today you will read a selection about the mysterious pink dolphin of the Amazon. As you read, think about how these dolphins are different from other dolphins you may know or have read about.

Have students write in their Strategy Response Logs what they know about the Amazon River (p. 420). Encourage them to think about new information and revise their ideas as they read.

**PROBLEM SOLVING** Have students read pp. 422–429 independently. Encourage them to think about how to solve the challenge of studying animals in remote areas. For example, ask:

• What is the best way to study an unknown animal?

**AFTER READING** Have partners discuss the selection and share their Strategy Response Log entries in a group or with you. Encourage them to think of other mysterious animals they would like to study. Ask students to create a plan of action to study animals deep in the Amazon region of South America. Have them write what they would do and what they might discover.

AudioText

# Encantado: Pink Dolphin of the Amazon
# Group Time

**DAY 3**

**Audio CD** AudioText

## Strategic Intervention

**ROUTINE**

### 1 Reinforce Comprehension

**SKILL COMPARE AND CONTRAST** Have students tell what it means to compare and contrast two or more items. Have them list clue words that often signal a comparison. *(like, as, but, instead, unlike)* If necessary, review comparing and contrasting and provide a model. To compare and contrast is to show how two or more things are alike and different. *The pink dolphin has a flexible body, but the bottle-nosed dolphin has a rigid body and cannot bend.* This shows how the two types of dolphins are different. This shows a contrast.

Ask students to compare and contrast the dolphins in other ways. For example, ask: What is one way the dolphins are alike? Use the clue word *both*. *(They are both mammals that need to surface for air.)* How are they different? Use the clue word *unlike*. *(The pink dolphin lives in the fresh water of the Amazon, unlike the bottle-nosed dolphin that lives in the ocean.)*

### 2 Read *Encantado: Pink Dolphin of the Amazon,* pp. 430–433

**BEFORE READING** Have students summarize what they have learned from the selection so far. Ask: What are some unusual characteristics of encantados? *(pink in color, live in fresh water, body shape is different from other dolphins)* Reread p. 426 and model how to visualize the journey in the canoe. As I read, I try to picture the canoe traveling on the river with trees on either side and low branches overhead. I see creatures, like spiders and eels, all around the canoe. Remind students to visualize as they read the rest of *Encantado: Pink Dolphin of the Amazon.* **STRATEGY Visualize**

**DURING READING** Follow the Guiding Comprehension routine on pp. 430–433. Have students read along with you while tracking the print or do a choral reading. Stop after each page to ask students what they have learned so far. Prompt as necessary.

- Why is it difficult to predict where a pink dolphin will surface?
- What happens to the dolphin's color as it exercises?

**AFTER READING** What have you learned about the behavior of the pink dolphin? What mysteries still remain? Reread with students for comprehension as needed. Tell them that tomorrow they will read "Mysterious Animals," a selection that tells about other strange animals found around the world.

## Monitor Progress

### Word and Selection Reading

| If... students have difficulty reading multisyllabic words in the selection, | then... have them look for and read meaningful parts in the words or have them chunk words with no recognizable parts. |
|---|---|
| If... students have difficulty reading along with the group, | then... have them follow along as they listen to the AudioText. |

## Advanced

### ① Extend Comprehension

**SKILL COMPARE AND CONTRAST** Have students compare and contrast a scientific expedition to the Amazon with an expedition to a park near home. Suggest students compare the vegetation and wildlife they might find in each locale.

**STRATEGY VISUALIZE** Have a volunteer read p. 426 while others close their eyes. Ask students which words or phrases help them visualize the canoe trip through the trees with low branches. Ask questions such as:

- What type of wildlife do you picture when you read this page?
- Would you like to live on the Amazon River? Why or why not?

### ② Read *Encantado: Pink Dolphin of the Amazon,* pp. 430–433

**BEFORE READING** Have students recall what they have learned about in the selection so far. Remind them to look for any comparisons and contrasts and to visualize as they read the remainder of the story.

**CREATIVE THINKING** Have students read pp. 430–433 independently. Encourage them to think creatively. For example, ask:

- How would you prepare for a canoe journey up the Amazon River?

**AFTER READING** Have students complete the Strategy Response Log activity on p. 432. Then have them research another animal found near the Amazon River and write a description of the animal. Tell students to include details about what a typical day might be like for the animal.

DAY 3

NCANTADO:

Audio CD  AudioText

# Group Time

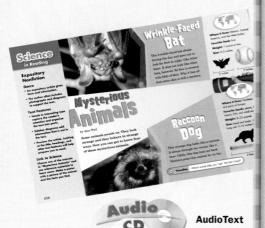

## 1 Practice Retelling

**REVIEW MAIN IDEAS** Help students identify the main ideas in *Encantado: Pink Dolphin of the Amazon.* List students' ideas and then ask questions to help them differentiate between essential and nonessential information.

**RETELL** Using the Retelling Cards, have students work in pairs to retell the important ideas. Show partners how to summarize in as few words as possible. Monitor retelling and prompt students as needed. For example, ask:

- What did you learn from reading this selection?
- Why do you think the author wrote this selection?

If students struggle, model a fluent retelling.

## 2 Read "Mysterious Animals"

**BEFORE READING** Read the genre information on p. 436. Have students recall other expository nonfiction books they have read and tell what the topics were.

Read the rest of the panel on p. 436. Have students tell about the text features they have seen in other nonfiction books, such as headings, diagrams, or captions. How did those text features help you as you read? Have students scan the pages of "Mysterious Animals" looking at the headings, sidebars, and the diagrams.

**DURING READING** Have students read along with you while tracking the print or do a choral reading of the selection. Stop to discuss text features such as maps and scales.

**AFTER READING** Have students share their reactions to the selection. Then guide them through the Reading Across Texts and Writing Across Texts activities, prompting if necessary.

- How are the pink dolphins mysterious? How are they different from the animals in "Mysterious Animals"?
- What characteristics do the pink dolphins and these animals share?

**Audio CD** AudioText

### Monitor Progress

**Word and Selection Reading**

| If... students have difficulty reading multisyllabic words in the selection, | then... have them look for and read meaningful parts in the words or have them chunk words with no recognizable parts. |
|---|---|
| If... students have difficulty reading along with the group, | then... have them follow along as they listen to the AudioText. |

ROUTINE

## Advanced

### 1 Read "Mysterious Animals"

**CRITICAL THINKING** Have students read pp. 436–439 independently. Encourage them to think critically. For example, ask:

- Why are these animals considered mysterious?
- How do the sidebars and their information help readers better understand these animals?

**AFTER READING** Discuss Reading Across Texts. Have students do the Writing Across Texts activity independently.

### 2 Extend Genre Study

**RESEARCH** Have students use online or print resources to find other expository nonfiction selections about mysterious animals or unusual animal behaviors. Have them make a list of titles, noting the animals each selection features.

**WRITE** Ask pairs of students to create posters with factual information of other mysterious animals from around the world. Have them include a brief "Did You Know?" feature for each animal.

**AudioText**

# Group Time

**ROUTINE**

**DAY 5**

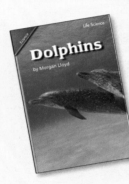

**ONLINE**

PearsonSuccessNet.com

### 1 Reread for Fluency

**MODEL** Read aloud pp. 3–5 of the Leveled Reader *Dolphins*, emphasizing the grouping of words to form phrases and sentences. Have students note how you group words together and pause after phrases to make your reading sound smooth. Then read pp. 6–7 word-by-word without pausing. Ask students to compare the two styles and tell which sounded better. Discuss how reading in phrases creates a more pleasing and natural rhythm.

**PRACTICE** Have students reread passages from *Dolphins* with a partner, with you, or individually. For optimal fluency, they should reread three or four times. As students read, monitor fluency and provide corrective feedback. Assess the fluency of students in this group using p. 439a.

### 2 Retell Leveled Reader *Dolphins*

Model retelling the selection using the subheads. Then ask students to retell the book, one section at a time. Prompt them as needed.

- What is this book mostly about?
- What did you learn about dolphins from reading this book?

## Monitor Progress

### Fluency

| **If...** students have difficulty reading fluently, | **then...** provide additional fluency practice by pairing nonfluent readers with fluent ones. |
|---|---|

For alternate Leveled Reader lesson plans that teach 🔄 **Compare and Contrast,** 👁 **Visualize,** and **Lesson Vocabulary,** see pp. LR10–LR18.

## On-Level

ROUTINE

### 1 Reread for Fluency

**MODEL** Read aloud pp. 4–5 of the Leveled Reader *Swimming with Dolphins,* emphasizing the grouping of words and phrasing. Have students note how you group words together and pause as you read. Discuss how pausing makes reading sound smooth and helps convey meaning.

**PRACTICE** Have students reread passages from *Swimming with Dolphins* with a partner or individually. For optimal fluency, they should reread three or four times. As students read, monitor fluency and provide corrective feedback. Students in this group are assessed in Week 3.

### 2 Retell Leveled Reader *Swimming with Dolphins*

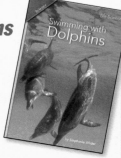

Have students use the photographs and captions as a guide to summarize the important facts they learned from the book. Prompt as needed.

- What is this book mainly about?
- What new information did you learn from reading this selection?
- What was the author trying to teach us?

## Advanced

ROUTINE

DAY 5

### 1 Reread for Fluency

**PRACTICE** Have students reread passages from the Leveled Reader *Echolocation: Animals Making Sound Waves* with a partner or individually. As students read, monitor fluency and provide corrective feedback. If students read fluently on the first reading, they do not need to reread three to four times. Students in this group were assessed in Week 1.

### 2 Revisit Leveled Reader *Echolocation: Animals Making Sound Waves*

**RETELL** Have students retell what they read about in the Leveled Reader *Echolocation*.

**NOW TRY THIS** Have students complete their projects from pp. 22–23 of the Leveled Reader *Echolocation*. You may wish to review their supplies and data and check whether they need any additional resources. Have them present their projects.

# Group Time

**Leveled Reader**
# Database
## ONLINE
PearsonSuccessNet.com

## Monitor Progress

### Selection Reading and Comprehension

| **If...** students have difficulty reading the selection with a partner, | **then...** have them follow along as they listen to the Online Leveled Reader Audio. |
|---|---|
| **If...** students have trouble understanding experiments that turned into successes, | **then...** reread pp. 3–4 and discuss how Ben and Grace's "invention" was different from that of the Kellogg brothers. |

---

## Strategic Intervention

**ROUTINE**

### 1 Build Background

**REINFORCE CONCEPTS** Display the Innovators Concept Web. This week's concept is *innovators*. Innovators are often people who solve puzzles or mysteries by changing the way things are done. Discuss the meaning of each word on the web, using the definitions on p. 440l and the Concept Vocabulary Routine on p. DI·1.

**CONNECT TO READING** This week you will read about ways people innovate with food. Some of these experiments are mistakes that turned into successes. Do you think what the Kellogg brothers did in "Corn Flake Kings" was a mistake that turned into a success? *(Yes, because the brothers took a mistake and turned it into a product that is still being produced and sold today.)*

### 2 Read Leveled Reader *Inventing Oatmeal*

**BEFORE READING** Using the Picture Walk Routine on p. DI·1, guide students through the text focusing on key concepts and vocabulary. Ask questions such as:

**p. 3** Ben and Grace have a gift from their aunt? What is it? *(a science kit)*

**p. 5** Using the book title and the picture on page 5, tell what you think they might do with the kit. *(invent something)*

**pp. 8–9** These pages show that Ben and Grace have moved from one time and place to another. Where have they gone? *(They have gone from home to a castle.)* Yes, they now seem to be in England during the Middle Ages. Could they have invented something that helped them do this? *(They used their imaginations.)*

**DURING READING** Read pp. 3–4 aloud while students track the print. Do a choral reading of pp. 5–8. If students are capable, have them read and discuss the remainder of the book with a partner. Ask: Where do Ben and Grace's imaginations take them? *(to England in the Middle Ages)* What do they find out about the oatmeal that Ben thought he had invented? *(It was invented in the Middle Ages and was called* porridge.*)*

**AFTER READING** Encourage pairs of students to discuss what they have learned about mistakes that led to successes. Knowing this will help you as you read *The King in the Kitchen.*

For alternate Leveled Reader lesson plans that teach **Character and Setting**, **Monitor and Fix Up**, and **Lesson Vocabulary,** see pp. LR19–LR27.

## On-Level

ROUTINE

### 1 Build Background

**DEVELOP VOCABULARY** Write the word *secret* on the board. Pantomime the act of telling a secret to one of the students. Ask: What do we do when someone tells us a secret? *(We keep it to ourselves; we don't tell anyone.)* Repeat this activity with the word *inventions* and other words from the Leveled Reader *The Amazing, Incredible Idea Kit.* Use the Concept Vocabulary Routine on p. DI·1 as needed.

### 2 Read Leveled Reader
**The Amazing, Incredible Idea Kit**

**BEFORE READING** Have students create T-charts with the labels Granny Mae and Grandpa Nigel. As you read, think of words that tell how these two characters from the book were innovators. Record the words on your T-charts.

**DURING READING** Have students follow along as you read pp. 3–9. Then let them complete the book on their own. Remind students to add words to their T-charts as they read.

**AFTER READING** Have students compare the words on their T-charts. Point out that they may find some of the words used to describe Granny Mae and Grandpa Nigel in tomorrow's story, *The King in the Kitchen.*

## Advanced

ROUTINE

### 1 Read Leveled Reader
**Alexander Graham Bell, Teacher of the Deaf**

**BEFORE READING** Recall the Read Aloud selection "The Corn Flake Kings." How were the Kellogg brothers innovative? *(They experimented with wheat and ended up inventing corn flakes.)* Today you will read about an inventor, Alexander Graham Bell, who has made our lives better because of his innovations.

**CRITICAL THINKING** Have students read the Leveled Reader independently. Encourage them to think critically. For example, ask:

• How did Bell's experiment with the piano as a child lead to his discovery of the Harmonic Telegraph?
• List Bell's innovations in what you think is the order of their importance to the world.

**AFTER READING** Have students find unfamiliar words in the selection and demonstrate how to break them into syllables in order to "solve" each word. Then have students write statements or questions that both include the words and convey their meanings. Encourage students to meet together or with you to discuss the selection and the statements or questions they wrote.

### 2 Independent Investigative Work

**CREATE A TIME LINE** Have students research the life and death of President Garfield and create a time line that includes events from Bell's life as well as those of the President. They will present their time lines at the end of the week.

# Group Time

**DAY 2**

**Audio CD** **AudioText**

## Monitor Progress

### Word and Story Reading

| | |
|---|---|
| **If...** students have difficulty reading multisyllabic words in the selection, | **then...** have them look for and read meaningful parts in the words or have them chunk words with no recognizable parts. |
| **If...** students need practice reading words fluently, | **then...** use the Fluent Word Reading Routine on the DI tab. |
| **If...** students have difficulty reading along with the group, | **then...** have them follow along as they listen to the AudioText. |

---

## Strategic Intervention

ROUTINE

### 1 Word Study/Phonics

**LESSON VOCABULARY** Use p. 442b to review the meanings of *duke, dungeon, furiously, genius, majesty, noble, peasant,* and *porridge.* Have individuals practice reading the words from word cards.

**DECODING MULTISYLLABIC WORDS** Write *potatoes,* saying the word as you write it. Then model how to chunk words that have no recognizable parts. When I see a word that doesn't have parts I recognize, I look at the syllables and say each syllable slowly, *po ta toes.* Then I say the syllables fast to make a word, *potatoes.*

Use the Multisyllabic Word Routine on p. DI·1 to help students read these other words from *The King in the Kitchen: marriage, vegetables, ingredients, teaspoon, imagination, relative, congratulations,* and *unexpected.* Be sure students understand the meanings of words such as *ingredients* and *relative.*

Use *Strategies for Word Analysis,* Lesson 23, with students who have difficulty mastering word analysis and need practice with decodable text.

### 2 Read *The King in the Kitchen,* pp. 444–451

**BEFORE READING** *Inventing Oatmeal* tells of two children who imagine they are inventors. In this story, a king tries to cook but becomes an inventor instead. Both stories have scenes that are set in a castle in the Middle Ages. Think about other similarities in characters and settings as you read.

Using the Picture Walk Routine on p. DI·1, guide students through the text asking questions such as those listed below. Read the question on p. 445. Together, set a purpose for reading.

**pp. 448–449** What can you tell from the picture about how the King is feeling? *(He's unhappy about something.)*

**pp. 450–451** What is the King doing on p. 450? *(He seems to be doing something blindfolded.)* What might happen if the king tries cooking while he is blindfolded?

**DURING READING** Follow the Guiding Comprehension routine on pp. 446–451. Have students read along with you while tracking the print or do a choral reading. Stop every two pages to ask what has happened so far. Prompt as necessary.

- Close your eyes and describe where this play takes place.
- Why did the King go to the kitchen?

**AFTER READING** What has happened so far? What do you think will happen next? Reread passages with students as needed.

## Advanced

### 1 Extend Vocabulary

**DICTIONARY/GLOSSARY** Read aloud the King's response to the Cook on p. 453: "Why, the hand of the Princess in marriage, of course." Say: The word *hand* has many definitions. I found seventeen in the dictionary I looked at. How would you decide which meaning fits in this sentence? Have students look up the word *hand* and choose the definition that fits the context. Remind students that they can use this strategy whenever they come across a word that has more than one meaning and whose meaning they are not sure of.

### 2 Read *The King in the Kitchen*, pp. 444–451

**BEFORE READING** You remember that in "The Corn Flake Kings," the Kellogg brothers wanted to make breakfast food. Today you will read a comedic play in which one of the main characters, a king, wants to make soup. As you read, think about whether the king's idea is a good one.

Have students write predictions they make in their Strategy Response Logs (p. 444). Remind students to add predictions as they read.

**CREATIVE THINKING** Have students read pp. 446–451 independently. Encourage them to think critically and creatively. For example, ask:

• Things are looking bleak for the peasant right now aren't they? What could happen that might change this outlook?

**AFTER READING** Have partners discuss the selection and share their Strategy Response Log entries. Encourage them to think of possible outcomes and write the one they want most to occur.

DAY 2

AudioText

# The King in the Kitchen

# Group Time

**Audio CD** AudioText

## Strategic Intervention

ROUTINE

### 1 Reinforce Comprehension

**SKILL CHARACTER AND SETTING** Have students tell what characters and setting mean to a story. (Characters are the people or animals who take parts in the events of a story, and the setting is the time and place of a story.) Have students name the characters and setting of *The King in the Kitchen*. Ask:

- If we were to put on a play about our class, who would the characters be?
- What would the most likely setting be?

### 2 Read *The King in the Kitchen*, pp. 452–461

**BEFORE READING** Have students retell what has happened in the play so far. Ask: What do you think the Princess will do next? Reread the last lines of dialogue on p. 451 beginning with: **PRINCESS:** Oh, here you are, Father. I've been looking everywhere for you. Remind students that rereading lines in a play often helps us get a sense of the action to come or helps us understand parts that may be unclear.

**STRATEGY Monitor and Fix Up**

**DURING READING** Follow the Guiding Comprehension routine on pp. 452–461. Have students read along with you while tracking print or do a choral reading. Stop every two pages to ask students what has happened so far. Prompt as necessary.

- What new idea did the King have when no one could figure out what to do with his invention?
- What made the King change his mind about the peasant?

**AFTER READING** How did the King's mistake, which turned into a successful invention, help the Princess and the peasant achieve their goal? Reread with students for comprehension as needed. Tell them that tomorrow they will continue reading about food and cooking, this time in poetry.

## Monitor Progress

### Word and Story Reading

| **If…** students have difficulty reading multisyllabic words in the selection, | **then…** have them look for and read meaningful parts in the words or have them chunk words with no recognizable parts. |
|---|---|
| **If…** students have difficulty reading along with the group, | **then…** have them follow along as they listen to the AudioText. |

## Advanced

**ROUTINE**

### 1 Extend Comprehension

**SKILL CHARACTER AND SETTING** Have students name a story they know that they think would make a good play. Have them assign parts to classmates and describe the setting.

**STRATEGY MONITOR AND FIX UP** Students can check their understanding of the story so far by telling why they think the King decided to hold a contest to identify what he has made in the kitchen.

### 2 Read *The King in the Kitchen,* pp. 452–461

**BEFORE READING** Have students recall what has happened in the selection so far. Remind them to identify the major characters and setting of the play and to reread if they need clarification.

**CRITICAL THINKING** Have students read pp. 452–461 independently. Encourage them to think critically. For example, ask:

• Who do you think is more creative—the King, who created the "invention," or the peasant who found a use for it? Tell why.

**AFTER READING** Have students complete the Strategy Response Log (p. 460). Then have them write a new ending for the play.

**AudioText**

# Group Time

**AudioText**

## Strategic Intervention

**ROUTINE**

### 1 Practice Retelling

**REVIEW STORY ELEMENTS** Help students identify the main characters and the setting of *The King in the Kitchen*. Then guide them in using the Retelling Cards to list story events in sequence. Prompt students to include important details.

**RETELL** Using the Retelling Cards, have students work in pairs to retell *The King in the Kitchen*. Monitor retelling and prompt students as needed. For example, ask:

- What are the two main problems in the story?
- How were these problems resolved?

If students struggle, model a fluent retelling.

### 2 Read Poetry

**BEFORE READING** Read the genre information on p. 464. Call attention to the three poems and ask what students think they may have in common. *(They're all about food.)* Talk about the meanings of the title words *seasonings* (something that gives a better flavor, such as salt) and *confectioner* (a person who makes or sells sweets).

**DURING READING** Have students read along with you while tracking the print of the poems. Discuss the importance of reading poetry line for line, letting one's voice pause at the end of lines with end punctuation. Call attention to the five-line pattern of the limericks to prepare students for writing their own.

**AFTER READING** Have students share their reactions to the poems. Then guide them through the Reading Across Texts and Writing Across Texts activities, prompting if necessary:

- What subject matter do the play and the poems have in common? *(food)*
- What words did you read in both *The King in the Kitchen* and the poems? *(salt, cooking, glue, sole, shoe, genius)*
- Which words might you use in the limericks you write?

---

### Monitor Progress

#### Word and Story Reading

| **If...** students have difficulty reading multisyllabic words in the selection, | **then...** have them look for and read meaningful parts in the words or have them chunk words with no recognizable parts. |
|---|---|
| **If...** students have difficulty reading along with the group, | **then...** have them follow along as they listen to the AudioText. |

## Advanced

**1** **Read** Poetry

**CRITICAL THINKING** Tell students that "A Man for All Seasonings" and "A Confectioner" are based upon problems and solutions. Have students tell the problem and solution in each poem.

**AFTER READING** Discuss Reading Across Texts. Have students do Writing Across Texts independently.

**2** **Extend Genre Study**

**RESEARCH** Have students use online or print resources to find other poems about food, people who grow it, cook it, or eat it. Have them list titles and topics of the poems.

**WRITE** Have students choose a "food" topic to write about in a poem. Encourage them to think of a problem and solution they might incorporate into their poems.

DAY
4

**Audio CD**　**AudioText**

# Group Time

**DAY 5**

## ONLINE
PearsonSuccessNet.com

### 1 Reread for Fluency

**MODEL** Read aloud pp. 3–4 of the Leveled Reader *Inventing Oatmeal*, highlighting important words by saying them with more emphasis. Have students note words that you say in a stronger voice or higher pitch. Then read pp. 6–7 without stressing any words. Have students tell you which model sounded better. Discuss how using emphasis when reading aloud makes listening more pleasurable.

**PRACTICE** Have students reread passages from *Inventing Oatmeal* with a partner or individually. For optimal fluency, they should read three or four times. As students read, monitor fluency and provide corrective feedback. Students in this group are assessed in Weeks 2 and 4.

### 2 Retell Leveled Reader *Inventing Oatmeal*

Model retelling the book by dividing it into parts: Ben and Grace before their trip to England; Ben and Grace in the castle in England; and Ben and Grace after their trip. Then ask students to retell the book, one part at a time. Prompt them as needed.

- What is the most important thing that happened in this part of the story?
- What was this book mostly about?

| Monitor Progress |
|---|
| **Fluency** |

| If... students have difficulty reading fluently, | then... provide additional fluency practice by pairing nonfluent readers with fluent ones. |
|---|---|

For alternate Leveled Reader lesson plans that teach
◉**Character and Setting,** ◉**Monitor and Fix Up,** and **Lesson Vocabulary,** see pp. LR19–LR27.

## On-Level

**ROUTINE**

**1** **ReRead for Fluency**

**MODEL** Read aloud p. 3 of the Leveled Reader *The Amazing, Incredible Idea Kit,* putting emphasis on certain important words. Give special treatment to the dialogue on the page. Discuss how stress and emphasis can make a reading or listening experience more interesting.

**PRACTICE** Have students reread passages from *The Amazing, Incredible Idea Kit* with a partner or individually. For optimal fluency, they should reread three or four times. As students read, monitor fluency and provide corrective feedback. Assess the fluency of students in this group using p. 465a.

**2** **Retell Leveled Reader**
**The Amazing, Incredible Idea Kit**

Have students use illustrations as a guide to summarize important events in the story. Prompt as needed.

*The Amazing, Incredible Idea Kit*
*by Vana Douglas*
*illustrated by Burgundy Beam*

- What is the problem in this story?
- How was the problem solved?
- Why do you think the author wrote this story?

## Advanced

**ROUTINE**

**1** **ReRead for Fluency**

**PRACTICE** Have students reread passages from the Leveled Reader *Alexander Graham Bell, Teacher of the Deaf* with a partner or individually. As students read, monitor fluency and provide corrective feedback. If students read fluently on the first reading, they do not need to reread three to four times. Students in this group were assessed in Week 1.

**2** **Revisit Leveled Reader**
**Alexander Graham Bell, Teacher of the Deaf**

**RETELL** Have students retell the Leveled Reader *Alexander Graham Bell, Teacher of the Deaf.*

*Alexander Graham Bell, Teacher of the Deaf*
*by Jena Loch*
*illustrated by Don Dyen*

**CREATE A TIME LINE** Students should complete and present the time lines they have been working on throughout the week. You may wish to review their sources and see whether they need any additional resources.

# Group Time

DAY **1**

ONLINE

PearsonSuccessNet.com

## Strategic Intervention

### 1 Build Background

**REINFORCE CONCEPTS** Display the Communication Concept Web. This week's concept is *Communication*. Communication is messages we share with one another. Communication is a good way to increase understanding. Discuss the meaning of each word on the web, using the definitions on p. 466l and the Concept Vocabulary Routine on p. DI·1.

**CONNECT TO READING** Communication is important, but communication can take place only when everyone understands the language you are speaking. This week you will read about an ancient language that everyone has forgotten. Think about "Silent Debate." Were the scholar and the boatman truly communicating with each other? Why or why not? *(No, because they weren't speaking the same language. They each meant something different by the symbols they were using.)*

### 2 Read Leveled Reader *The Rosetta Stone*

**BEFORE READING** Using the Picture Walk Routine on p. DI·1, guide students through the text focusing on key concepts and vocabulary. Ask questions such as:

**p. 6** This is the Rosetta Stone. What do you notice about the writing on the stone? *(There are three different kinds of writing.)* Yes, the stone has the same message written in three different scripts. This stone was a clue to figuring out the lost language of the ancient Egyptians.

**p. 10** What does the chart at the top of the page tell us? *(The symbols stand for sounds.)* The symbols are called *glyphs,* which is where we get the word *hieroglyphic.* If you know what sound a symbol stands for, you can translate from one language to another.

**DURING READING** Read pp. 3–5 aloud, while students track the print. Do a choral reading of pp. 7–9. If students are capable, have them read and discuss the remainder of the book with a partner. Ask: How do Egyptian hieroglyphics compare with the English alphabet? *(There are 700–800 symbols in Egyptian hieroglyphics compared with 26 letters in the English alphabet. Some symbols stand for objects or ideas as well as sounds.)*

**AFTER READING** Encourage pairs of students to discuss the problems of learning a "forgotten" language. Jean-François Champollion is given most credit for finding the key to unlocking the mystery of Egyptian hieroglyphics. Pronounce his name carefully and have students repeat after you. We will find out what that key was and how he found it when we read *Seeker of Knowledge.*

---

### Monitor Progress

#### Selection Reading and Comprehension

| If... students have difficulty reading the selection with a partner, | then... have them follow along as they listen to the Online Leveled Reader Audio. |
| --- | --- |
| If... students have trouble understanding why scholars had such difficulty reading hieroglyphics, | then... reread pp. 10–13 and discuss why a word-by-word translation was not possible. |

For alternate Leveled Reader lesson plans that teach
🔄 **Graphic Sources,** 🔄 **Asking Questions,** and
**Lesson Vocabulary,** see pp. LR28–LR36.

## On-Level

### 1 Build Background

**ROUTINE**

**DEVELOP VOCABULARY** Write the word *scholar* on the board and underline the letters *scho.* Ask students what other words they know that begin with these letters. *(school, scholarship, scholastic)* What meaning do all these words have in common? *("learning")* Have students use these words in sentences of their own. Repeat this activity with the word *transmit* and other words from the Leveled Reader *Cracking the German Code.* Use the Concept Vocabulary Routine on p. DI·1 as needed.

### 2 Read Leveled Reader
### *Cracking the German Code*

**BEFORE READING** Have students begin KWL charts, filling in what they know and what they want to know about codes. This book is about the code the Germans used during World War II. The German code, like most codes, was developed to communicate with certain people in a way that other people couldn't understand. As you read, look for facts about the German code, and record them in your KWL chart.

**DURING READING** Have students follow along as you read pp. 3–9. Then let them complete the book on their own. Remind students to record facts about the German code in their KWL charts as they read.

**AFTER READING** Have students compare their entries in the *W* and *L* columns of their charts. Point out that an understanding of codes and decoding processes will help them as they read tomorrow's biography, *Seeker of Knowledge.*

## Advanced

### 1 Read Leveled Reader
### *The Code Talkers*

**ROUTINE**

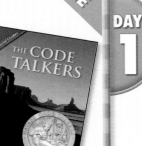

**BEFORE READING** Recall the Read Aloud "Silent Debate." Silent, or nonverbal, communication can be a powerful way to share ideas. Why did the scholar and the boatman *not* communicate with each other? *(Each thought the symbols they were using with each other meant something different.)* Today you will read about people who could talk in code because they agreed in advance what certain code words meant.

**CREATIVE THINKING** Have students read the Leveled Reader independently. Encourage them to think creatively. For example, ask:

- Why was the Diné language an effective one upon which to base a code?
- Look at the Code Talkers' Dictionary on p. 15. Choose three of the code words and tell why they are appropriate code words for the English terms given.

**AFTER READING** Have students find five or more unfamiliar words in the book and determine their meanings by using context clues or a dictionary. Have students rewrite the sentences, adding definitions or synonyms as appositives to the words they have chosen. Have students meet with you to discuss the selection and the sentences they wrote.

### 2 Independent Extension Activity

**NOW TRY THIS** Assign "Now Try This" on pp. 22–23 of *The Code Talkers* for students to work on throughout the week.

# Group Time

**AudioText**

**DAY 2**

## ① Word Study/Phonics

**LESSON VOCABULARY** Use p. 468b to review the meanings of *ancient, link, scholars, seeker, temple, translate, triumph,* and *uncover.* Have individuals practice reading the words from word cards.

**DECODING MULTISYLLABIC WORDS** Write *inscription,* saying the word as you write it. Then model how to chunk to pronounce longer words. I see a chunk at the beginning of the word: *in.* I see a part in the middle: *scrip.* I see a chunk at the end of the word: *tion.* I say each chunk slowly: *in scrip tion.* I say the chunks fast to make a whole word: *inscription.* Is it a real word? Yes, I know the word *inscription.*

Use the Multisyllabic Word Routine on p. DI·1 to help students read these other words from *Seeker of Knowledge: spellbound, trumpeting, defenseless, decipher,* and *conquered.* Be sure students understand the meanings of words such as *decipher* and *conquered.*

Use *Strategies for Word Analysis,* Lesson 24, with students who have difficulty mastering word analysis and need practice with decodable text.

## ② Read *Seeker of Knowledge,* pp. 470–477

**BEFORE READING** *The Rosetta Stone* describes the stone and its discovery, and it mentions Jean-François Champollion, who figured out the stone's secret. As you read *Seeker of Knowledge,* look for the key to understanding the stone's language and how Champollion found it.

Using the Picture Walk Routine on p. DI·1, guide students through the text asking questions such as those listed below. Read the question on p. 471. Together, set a purpose for reading.

**pp. 472–473** What do you see in the tan panels on these pages? *(Egyptian symbols and letters)* Why might they be important?

**p. 474** What are the men reading? *(hieroglyphics)* Yes, they are trying to learn about and decipher the Egyptian writing on the Rosetta Stone.

**DURING READING** Follow the Guiding Comprehension Routine on pp. 472–477. Have students read along with you while tracking the print or do a choral reading. Stop every two pages to ask what has happened so far. Prompt as necessary.

• What did Jean-François do to prepare himself for working on the puzzle of the Rosetta Stone?
• What happened to Jean-François after Napoleon was defeated at the Battle of Waterloo?

**AFTER READING** What has happened so far? What do you think will happen next? Reread passages with students as needed.

### Monitor Progress

**Word and Story Reading**

| | |
|---|---|
| **If...** students have difficulty reading multisyllabic words in the selection, | **then...** have them look for and read meaningful parts in the words or have them chunk words with no recognizable parts. |
| **If...** students need practice reading words fluently, | **then...** use the Fluent Word Reading Routine on the DI tab. |
| **If...** students have difficulty reading along with the group, | **then...** have them follow along as they listen to the AudioText. |

## Advanced

### 1 Extend Vocabulary

🔊 **WORD STRUCTURE** On p. 472, read the last sentence with *captured.* Explain that *capture* has the Latin root word *capere,* which means "take." Here are some more words with *capere* as a root: *capable, capacity, caption, captive.* Ask volunteers to find these words in a dictionary that gives etymologies, or word sources, and try to determine how the meaning of each word is related to "take." Ask these volunteers to report their findings to the class. Caution students that not every word that begins with *cap* has that same root.

### 2 Read *Seeker of Knowledge,* pp. 470–477

**BEFORE READING** Today you will read a biography of the man who was finally able to translate the Rosetta Stone and read Egyptian hieroglyphics. In many ways what he did was like breaking a code, in this case a code that scholars had been working on with little success for more than twenty years. As you read, think about how Jean-François Champollion might have done it. Have students create webs for their Strategic Response Logs (p. 470). Encourage them to add details as they read.

**PROBLEM SOLVING** Have students read pp. 472–477 independently. Encourage them to think critically and creatively. For example, ask:

- What sort of information do you think you would need to break a code?
- What quality of the Rosetta Stone convinced scholars that it could be the key to translating Egyptian hieroglyphics?

**AFTER READING** Have partners discuss the selection and share their Strategy Response Log webs. Have partners ask each other questions about this time in Jean-François's life, such as: *What was life like hiding in the woods? What experiences did Jean-François have?* Then have each pair of students collaborate in writing a journal entry as Jean-François.

AudioText

## Seeker of Knowledge
# Group Time

ROUTINE

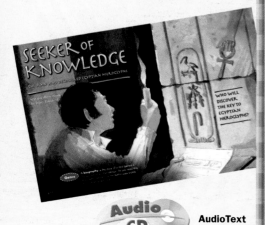

Audio CD  **AudioText**

### Monitor Progress

#### Word and Selection Reading

| | |
|---|---|
| **If...** students have difficulty reading multisyllabic words in the selection, | **then...** have them look for and read meaningful parts in the words or have them chunk words with no recognizable parts. |
| **If...** students have difficulty reading along with the group, | **then...** have them follow along as they listen to the AudioText. |

**DAY 3**

### 1 Reinforce Comprehension

**SKILL GRAPHIC SOURCES** Have students list a number of common graphic sources (*photograph, map, chart, diagram, icon, table, etc.*) and then point out the graphic sources that are in *Seeker of Knowledge (illustrations, sidebars with hieroglyphic examples).* Have students review the purpose of graphic sources. Why are graphic sources used in certain kinds of writing? *(to help readers understand the material better)* In what kinds of writing would you most expect to find graphic sources? *(nonfiction writing, writing with information that needs to be organized, writing about subjects to be visualized)*

Go through the pictures in the margins on pp. 472–473 as a group. Have students read and discuss the explanation under each drawing. Then ask them to look at the drawings included within the text. Reinforce that many of the drawings within the main text are shown and explained in the margins. Continue this activity on pp. 475–477.

### 2 Read *Seeker of Knowledge,* pp. 478–481

**BEFORE READING** Have students retell what happened in the selection so far. Ask: What did Napoleon promise to do for Jean-François after he had conquered the world? What happened instead? *(Napoleon promised to send Jean-François to Egypt. Instead, Napoleon was defeated and people who knew him were called traitors.)* Model asking questions: Remember, you can ask yourself questions as you read to make sure you understand the text. For example, I might ask: Why did Jean-François run away to hide in the woods? Remind students to ask themselves questions as they read the rest of *Seeker of Knowledge* **STRATEGY Ask Questions**

**DURING READING** Follow the Guiding Comprehension routine on pp. 478–481. Have students read along with you while tracking print or do a choral reading. Stop every two pages to ask students what has happened so far. Prompt as necessary.

• What was the link that Jean-François discovered between the pictures and Egyptian letters?
• How did he sound out the name of the pharaoh Thothmes? Point out that this process is rather like chunking to pronounce multisyllabic words.

**AFTER READING** How does this biography help explain how the Egyptians communicated with each other? Reread with students for comprehension as needed. Tell them that tomorrow they will read "Word Puzzles," a Web site about another kind of picture writing.

**Advanced**

## 1 Extend Comprehension

> **SKILL GRAPHIC SOURCES** Have students describe situations in their daily lives where pictures are used in combination with, or instead of words. What sort of information is generally communicated in those situations?

> **STRATEGY ASK QUESTIONS** Remind students that good readers ask themselves questions as they read to be sure they understand the text. Model:

- Here's a question I want to ask: What might Jean-François have discovered if Napoleon had sent him to Egypt?
- Here's another question: Why were some of the books written about hieroglyphic writing "unbelievable" or "ridiculous"?

Have students suggest questions they might ask.

## 2 Read *Seeker of Knowledge,* pp. 478–481

**BEFORE READING** Have students recall what happened in the selection so far. Remind them to look for and interpret graphic sources and ask themselves questions as they read the remainder of the biography.

**CREATIVE THINKING** Have students read pp. 478–481 independently. Encourage them to think creatively. For example, ask:

- If you were creating your own hieroglyphics, what pictures—like the crocodile meaning "trouble" or the wavy lines meaning "Nile River"—would you use to represent certain common words? List some words and draw pictures for them.

**AFTER READING** Have students complete the Strategy Response Log activity (p. 480). Then have them speculate as to why the ancient Egyptians used hieroglyphics instead of letters to communicate. (Hint: Many early written languages incorporated picture-symbols. The Phoenician alphabet was one of the first true alphabets in which one symbol represented one sound.) If you have time, suggest that students research the beginnings of our English alphabet.

DAY
3

Audio CD  **AudioText**

# Group Time

**DAY 4**

Audio CD    AudioText

## ① Practice Retelling

**REVIEW STORY ELEMENTS** Help students identify the main characters and the setting—including time—of *Seeker of Knowledge*. Then guide them in using the Retelling Cards to list biographical events in sequence. Prompt students to include important details.

**RETELL** Using the Retelling Cards, have students work in pairs to retell *Seeker of Knowledge*. Monitor retelling and prompt students as needed. For example, ask:

- Where and when does this biography take place?
- What was Jean-François Champollion determined to do? Did he succeed? How?

If students struggle, model a fluent retelling.

## ② Read "Word Puzzles"

**BEFORE READING** Read the title "Word Puzzles." Recall that the unit theme is Puzzles and Mysteries and comment that word puzzles are another kind of puzzle. Ask students what kind of word puzzles they know about. *(They may mention crosswords, riddles, etc.)* Now read the genre information on p. 484.

- A search engine can take us to Web sites where there is information about word puzzles. What kind of information about word puzzles would you expect to find? *(Possible answer: what word puzzles are and examples of different word puzzles)*
- What keywords might you try in order to find Web sites on word puzzles? *(Students might suggest keywords like* crossword *and* riddle. *Don't let them overlook the obvious keyword* word puzzle.*)*

Read the rest of the panel on p. 484. Then have students scan the pages to see what sort of material is on these Web sites.

**DURING READING** Have students read along with you while tracking the print or do a choral reading of the selection. Stop as necessary to discuss technical terms such as *engine, keyword, window, click,* or *link.*

**AFTER READING** Have students share their reactions to the selection. Then guide them through the Reading Across Texts and Writing Across Texts activities, prompting if necessary.

- How is it that pictures can help tell a story?
- What words about Jean-François Champollion can you represent with pictures.

### Monitor Progress

**Word and Selection Reading**

| **If...** students have difficulty reading multisyllabic words in the selection, | **then...** have them look for and read meaningful parts in the words or have them chunk words with no recognizable parts. |
|---|---|
| **If...** students have difficulty reading along with the group, | **then...** have them follow along as they listen to the AudioText. |

**Advanced**

**ROUTINE**

## 1 Read "Word Puzzles"

**CRITICAL THINKING** Have students read pp. 484–487 independently. Encourage them to think critically. For example, ask:

- How does the puzzle of a rebus story differ from the puzzle of Egyptian hieroglyphics before Jean-François Champollion?
- Do word puzzles serve a purpose, or are they merely a fun way to pass time?

**AFTER READING** Discuss Reading Across Texts. Have students do Writing Across Texts independently.

## 2 Extend Genre Study

**RESEARCH** If your school has search engines available for student use, have students compare two or more of them. Here are some prompts you can give them:

- Think of a topic you are interested in and list some keywords that you think will help you research that topic.
- Try the same keywords with each search engine. Do you get the same results?
- Is one search engine easier to use than another? In what way?
- After you have done your comparison, prepare a short oral report to give to the class.

**WRITE** Some people seem to be able to use a search engine and surf the Internet more easily than others. Suppose that your best friend has just gotten a computer and is not familiar with all its possibilities. Write a set of instructions for your friend to use a search engine to find information on a topic you know your friend is interested in. Be very thorough and very clear; remember, you are guiding your friend through every screen and every mouse click.

**AudioText**

# Group Time

**DAY 5**

## Leveled Reader Database
### ONLINE
**PearsonSuccessNet.com**

## Strategic Intervention

**ROUTINE**

### 1 Reread for Fluency

**MODEL** Read aloud pp. 7–9 of the Leveled Reader *The Rosetta Stone,* emphasizing the smooth flow of your interpretation. Have students note the grouping of your words and phrases for better understanding. Then read pp. 7–9 word-by-word, creating choppy phrases that do not help understanding. Have students tell you which model sounded better. Discuss how reading in phrases actually helps understanding.

Comment that, with some selections, it may be helpful to practice pronouncing certain words by themselves before reading a whole passage aloud. Have students suggest which words on these pages might give a reader difficulty in pronunciation. (For example: *Rosetta, inscribed, hieroglyphics, demotic, Egyptian, opponents, various, Persian*) Have the class read these words chorally.

**PRACTICE** Have students reread passages from *The Rosetta Stone* with a partner or individually. For optimal fluency, they should reread three or four times. As students read, monitor fluency and provide corrective feedback. Assess the fluency of students in this group using p. 487a.

### 2 Retell Leveled Reader *The Rosetta Stone*

Model how to skim the book, retelling as you skim. Then ask students to retell what they learned from the book, using the subheads as main topics in their retellings. Prompt them as needed.

- What is this section mostly about?
- Tell me about the major events in order.

## Monitor Progress

### Fluency

| **If...** students have difficulty reading fluently, | **then...** provide additional fluency practice by pairing nonfluent readers with fluent ones. |
|---|---|

For alternate Leveled Reader lesson plans that teach
⊙ **Graphic Sources,** ⊙ **Ask Questions,** and
**Lesson Vocabulary,** see pp. LR19–LR28.

## On-Level

ROUTINE

### 1 Reread for Fluency

**MODEL** Read aloud pp. 4–5 of the Leveled Reader *Cracking the German Code,* emphasizing the smooth flow of your interpretation. Have students note the grouping of your words and phrases for better understanding. Discuss how reading in phrases actually helps understanding by grouping and emphasizing ideas and relationships.

**PRACTICE** Have students reread passages from *Cracking the German Code* with a partner or individually. For optimal fluency, they should reread three or four times. As students read, monitor fluency and provide corrective feedback. Students in this group were assessed in Week 3.

### 2 Retell Leveled Reader *Cracking the German Code*

Have students use the subheads and illustrations as a guide to summarize the important facts they learned from each section of the book. Prompt as needed.

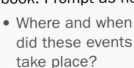

- Where and when did these events take place?
- Who are the heroes, and who are the villains?
- Tell me about the major events in order.

## Advanced

ROUTINE

### 1 Reread for Fluency

**PRACTICE** Have students reread passages from the Leveled Reader *The Code Talkers* with a partner or individually. As students read, monitor fluency and provide corrective feedback. If students read fluently on the first reading, they do not need to reread three to four times. Students in this group were assessed in Week 1.

### 2 Revisit Leveled Reader *The Code Talkers*

**RETELL** Have students retell what they learned from the Leveled Reader *The Code Talkers.*

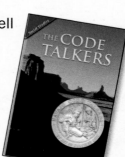

**NOW TRY THIS** Have students complete their projects. You may wish to review their keys to see whether they are set up correctly and are working for encoding and decoding messages. Did any partners accidentally come up with the same basic key? Discuss the chances of that happening. Finally, challenge students with step 5 on p. 23: trying to break the codes of other student teams without having their keys.

# Group Time

**DAY 1**

## ONLINE
PearsonSuccessNet.com

**ROUTINE**

### 1 Build Background

**REINFORCE CONCEPTS** Display the Inquiry Concept Web. This week's concept is *inquiry*. Inquiry is a search for information, knowledge, or truth. Discuss the meaning of each word on the web and how the words are related. Use the definitions on p. 488l and the Concept Vocabulary Routine on p. DI·1.

**CONNECT TO READING** This week you will read about a boy who solves a problem by inquiring into the details of a crime. Do you think Don Miguel in "Something Fishy" helped to solve Juan's problem by paying attention to details? If so, how? *(Yes, because Don Miguel noticed that if you can charge money for the smell of a cooking fish, you should be able to pay with the shadow of a coin.)*

### 2 Read Leveled Reader *Top Hat the Detective*

**BEFORE READING** Using the Picture Walk Routine on p. DI·1, guide students through the text focusing on key concepts and vocabulary. Ask questions such as:

**p. 4** This is Top Hat, the detective. What objects do you see that give you a clue that he is a detective? *(notepad, magnifying glass, camera, tape recorder)* Yes, these are all things that a detective would use in an investigation.

**p. 5** This picture shows Sid telling Top Hat about his missing salamanders. Like frogs, salamanders are amphibians. What do you know about amphibians?

**DURING READING** Read pp. 3–6 aloud, while students track the print. Do a choral reading of pp. 7–9. If students are able, have them read and discuss the remainder of the book with a partner. Ask: How does Top Hat conduct his investigation? What information is he looking for?

**AFTER READING** Encourage pairs of students to discuss the process of inquiry or what is involved in solving a mystery. We read *Top Hat, the Detective* to see how one detective tries to solve a mystery. Understanding the kinds of questions detectives ask about problems will help us as we read *Encyclopedia Brown and the Case of the Slippery Salamander*.

## Monitor Progress

### Story Reading and Comprehension

| If... students have difficulty reading the selection with a partner, | then... have them follow along as they listen to the Online Leveled Reader Audio. |
|---|---|
| If... students have trouble understanding why there was only a puddle left when the salamanders disappeared, | then... reread pp. 13–19 and go over plot details with them. |

For alternate Leveled Reader lesson plans that teach **Plot**, **Prior Knowledge**, and **Lesson Vocabulary**, see pp. LR37–LR45.

## On-Level

ROUTINE

DAY 1

### 1 Build Background

**DEVELOP VOCABULARY** Write the word *Investigation* and ask students to define it in their own words. *(to collect information about something, to study something)* When would you expect to investigate something? *(If I lost something and needed to find it, or to gather information for a school assignment)* Repeat this activity with the word *sleuth* and other words from the Leveled Reader *The Case of the Missing Iguana*. Use the Concept Vocabulary Routine on p. DI·1 as needed.

### 2 Read Leveled Reader
**The Case of the Missing Iguana**

**BEFORE READING** Have students create a time line and label it "Facts About the Case." This story is about the mysterious disappearance of a pet. As you read, you should note details that might be clues. You can use the time line to jot down facts about the case that could be important.

**DURING READING** Have students follow along as you read pp. 3–9. Then let them complete the book on their own. Remind students to add events to their time lines as they read.

**AFTER READING** Have students compare the events they entered in their time lines. Point out that paying close attention to the sequence of events in this investigation will help them as they read tomorrow's story *Encyclopedia Brown and the Slippery Salamander*.

## Advanced

ROUTINE

DAY 1

### 1 Read Leveled Reader
**Professor Science**

**BEFORE READING** Recall the Read Aloud story "Something Fishy." How did careful attention to the details of the case help the judge solve Juan's problem? *(He noticed that if the smell of cooking fish could be stolen, it could be paid for with the shadow of a coin.)* Today you will read how a boy's careful attention to detail helped him figure out what caused a disaster at a zoo.

**CRITICAL THINKING** Have students read the Leveled Reader independently. Encourage them to think critically. For example, ask:

- Why is "Professor Science" a good nickname for Doug?
- What qualities does Doug have that helped him solve the mystery?

**AFTER READING** Have students choose words from the story and make a list that describes the salamander's *habitat*. Then have them write sentences that demonstrate each word's meaning.

### 2 Independent Extension Activity

**SAVE THE SALAMANDER!** Have students read the article on p. 24 of *Professor Science*. Ask students how people could solve the problem of the possible extinction of the giant Japanese salamander. Have them research what people have already done to address the problem and any additional proposals for the future. Have students prepare posters to raise people's awareness of the problem. Students can work on their posters throughout the week.

# Group Time

**AudioText**

**DAY 2**

## 1 Word Study/Phonics

**LESSON VOCABULARY** Use p. 490b to review the meanings of *amphibians, crime, exhibit, lizards, reference, reptiles, salamanders,* and *stumped.* Have students practice reading from word cards.

**DECODING MULTISYLLABIC WORDS** Write *encyclopedia,* saying the word as you write it. Then model how to use chunking to read longer words. *I see a chunk at the beginning of the word: en. I see several more parts in the middle, cy clo pe. And I see two more parts at the end of the word, di and a. I say each chunk slowly: en cy clo pe di a. I say the chunks fast to make a whole word: encyclopedia. Is it a real word? Yes, I know the word encyclopedia.*

Use the Multisyllabic Word Routine on p. DI·1 to help students read these other words from *Encyclopedia Brown and the Case of the Slippery Salamander: synagogue, aquarium, business, exhibit, fascinated, specimen.* Be sure students understand the meanings of such words as *synagogue* and *fascinated.*

Use *Strategies for Word Analysis,* Lesson 25, with students who have difficulty mastering word analysis and need practice with decodable text.

## 2 Read *Encyclopedia Brown and the Case of the Slippery Salamander,* pp. 492–497

**BEFORE READING** *Top Hat, The Detective* showed how one detective investigated a case. Think about that investigation as you read *Encyclopedia Brown and the Case of the Slippery Salamander.*

Using the Picture Walk Routine on p. DI·1, guide students through the text asking questions such as those listed below. Read the question on page 493. Together, set a purpose for reading.

**pp. 494–495** Mr. Brown is the Police Chief of Idaville. What do you think this crime case will be about? *(an aquarium)*

**pp. 496–497** What do these illustrations tell you about the investigation? *(They probably show and name possible suspects.)*

**DURING READING** Follow the Guiding Comprehension routine on pp. 494–497. Have students read along with you while tracking the print or do a choral reading. Stop every two pages to ask what has happened so far. Prompt as necessary.

• What crime is Chief Brown investigating?
• What does he learn from questioning the suspects?

**AFTER READING** What has happened in the story so far? What do you think will happen next? Reread passages as needed.

### Monitor Progress

#### Word and Story Reading

| | |
|---|---|
| **If...** students have difficulty reading multisyllabic words in the selection, | **then...** have them look for and read meaningful parts in the words or have them chunk words with no recognizable parts. |
| **If...** students need practice reading words fluently, | **then...** use the Fluent Word Reading Routine on the DI tab. |
| **If...** students have difficulty reading along with the group, | **then...** have them follow along as they listen to the AudioText. |

## Advanced

ROUTINE

### 1 Extend Vocabulary

**⊙ CONTEXT CLUES** Choose and read a sentence or passage containing a difficult word, such as this sentence from p. 3 of *Professor Science:* "It is conveniently located just a few blocks away from my school."

What does the word *conveniently* mean? *(The word means "easy to use or easy to reach.")* How did you determine the word's meaning? *(I looked for nearby words and used the context clues just a few blocks away to help figure it out.)* Discuss why context clues can help determine word meanings. Remind students to look for context clues to help them determine the meanings of words as they read *Encyclopedia Brown and the Case of the Slippery Salamander.*

### 2 Read *Encyclopedia Brown and the Case of the Slippery Salamander,* pp. 492–497

**BEFORE READING** Today you will read a realistic fiction story about a boy detective who loves solving crimes. As you read, compare this story with *Top Hat, The Detective.*

Have students write the questions they have about the main character in their Strategy Response Logs (p. 492). Encourage them to continue to record questions as they read.

**CREATIVE THINKING** Have students read pp. 494–497 independently. Encourage them to think critically and creatively. For example, ask:

- So far, we haven't heard a word from Encyclopedia. Why do you think that is? How can he be such an amazing crime-solver when he hasn't helped at all?

**AFTER READING** Have partners discuss the selection and share their Strategy Response Log entries. Encourage them to discuss the answers to their questions. Have students think about what it takes to be a detective. Have them write a brief character profile that describes Encyclopedia Brown.

DAY 2

Audio CD　AudioText

# Group Time

**DAY 3**

**Audio CD** AudioText

## Strategic Intervention

### 1 Reinforce Comprehension

**SKILL PLOT** Have students tell what they know about plot and list some elements of plot. If necessary, review the elements of plot and provide a model. The plot of a fiction story is the underlying structure. It starts with a character who has a problem. The problem builds to a climax but is eventually resolved as the story ends.

Ask students to identify the problem in *Encyclopedia Brown and the Case of the Slippery Salamander*. Model determining a story's problem: I know that a plot usually begins by introducing a problem. I know that a rare salamander is missing from a zoo exhibit and that Chief Brown doesn't know who took it. Since he is the Chief of Police, this is a problem.

### 2 Read *Encyclopedia Brown and the Case of the Slippery Salamander*, pp. 498–500

**BEFORE READING** Have students retell what happened in the story so far. Ask: What kinds of information do detectives usually try to find out about a crime? Reread the first three paragraphs on p. 498 and model how to use prior knowledge. I know that a detective usually wants to know where suspects were at the time of the crime. I expect Chief Brown to be very interested in where the aquarium employees were on the day of the theft. Remind students to use what they already know about collecting facts as they read the rest of *Encyclopedia Brown and the Case of the Slippery Salamander*.

**STRATEGY Prior Knowledge**

**DURING READING** Follow the Guiding Comprehension routine on pp. 498–500. Have students read along with you while tracking the print or do a choral reading. Stop every two pages to ask what has happened so far. Prompt as necessary.

- Where was Mrs. King when the salamander was stolen?
- What does Mrs. Brown think about the case?

**AFTER READING** How does this selection help you understand the process of solving mysteries? Reread with students for comprehension as needed. Tell them that tomorrow they will read "Young Detectives of Potterville Middle School," which tells how some sixth graders solve crimes in real life.

---

### Monitor Progress

#### Word and Story Reading

| **If...** students have difficulty reading multisyllabic words in the selection, | **then...** have them look for and read meaningful parts in the words or have them chunk words with no recognizable parts. |
|---|---|
| **If...** students have difficulty reading along with the group, | **then...** have them follow along as they listen to the AudioText. |

## Advanced

### 1 Read *Extend Comprehension*

🎯 **SKILL PLOT** Have students list the plot elements from the story so far—the characters and the problem. Ask: Has the story reached a climax? Have students describe what they think happened and how it will be resolved. Have them use details from the story's plot to make their case.

🎯 **STRATEGY PRIOR KNOWLEDGE** Ask students what they know about real detectives. Have them use what they know to compile a list of steps a detective might take when he or she can't figure out who committed a crime. How might other members of Chief Brown's department help him solve the crime?

### 2 Read *Encyclopedia Brown and the Case of the Slippery Salamander,* pp. 498–500

**BEFORE READING** Have students recall what has happened in the selection so far. Remind students to summarize plot elements and to use their prior knowledge as they read the rest of the story.

**CREATIVE THINKING** Have students read pp. 498–500 independently. Encourage them to think creatively. For example, say: Imagine you are Mrs. King and you are in Chief Brown's office. Explain your interest in Fred the salamander. Use details from the story.

**AFTER READING** Have students complete the Strategy Response Log Activity (p. 502). Then have students write a paragraph that adds to the plot of the story. From Sam Maine's point of view, explain what you were going to do with Fred the salamander after you stole him.

 **AudioText**

# Group Time

Science in Reading

Newspaper Article

**The Dng State Journal**

Young Detective of Potterville Middle Sch

Audio CD    AudioText

## Strategic Intervention

ROUTINE

### 1 Practice Retelling

**REVIEW STORY ELEMENTS** Help students identify the main characters and setting of *Encyclopedia Brown and the Case of the Slippery Salamander*. Then guide them in using the Retelling Cards to list story events in sequence. Prompt students to include important details.

**RETELL** Using the Retelling Cards, have students work in pairs to retell *Encyclopedia Brown and the Case of the Slippery Salamander*. Monitor retelling and prompt students as needed. For example, ask:

- What was the problem in the story?
- How was the problem solved?

If students struggle, model a fluent retelling.

### 2 Read "Young Detectives of Potterville Middle School"

**BEFORE READING** Read the genre information on page 504. Newspaper articles convey information about the world and about what people have done or are doing. Newspaper articles most often are about current events. This article is about a middle school class learning about crime-solving techniques.

Read the rest of the panel on p. 504, and discuss the text features with students. Then have students scan the article and note the headline, introductory paragraph, and placement of direct quotations.

**DURING READING** Have students read along with you while tracking the print or do a choral reading of the selection. Stop to clarify and discuss the meaning of the word *forensic* with students (*science that can be used in a court of law*).

**AFTER READING** Have students share their reactions to the selection. Then guide them through the Reading Across Texts and Writing Across Texts activities, prompting if necessary.

- What did Encyclopedia Brown do that makes you think he might enjoy the class at Potterville Middle School?
- How is what Encyclopedia Brown did like what the middle school students do in their class? How are these things different?

## Monitor Progress

### Word and Story Reading

| **If...** students have difficulty reading multisyllabic words in the selection, | **then...** have them look for and read meaningful parts in the words or have them chunk words with no recognizable parts. |
|---|---|
| **If...** students have difficulty reading along with the group, | **then...** have them follow along as they listen to the AudioText. |

ROUTINE

DAY 4

## Advanced

### 1 Read "Young Detectives of Potterville Middle School"

**CREATIVE THINKING** Ask students to read pp. 504–507 independently. Encourage them to think creatively. For example, ask:

- Would you like to be a detective? Think of both positive and negative aspects of the occupation of detective.
- Write a list of your reasons both for and against being a detective.

**AFTER READING** Discuss Reading Across Texts. Have students do Writing Across Texts independently.

### 2 Extend Genre Study

**RESEARCH** Have students list the titles of stories from the front section of today's local newspaper. Have them note the elements of each story that make it appealing to a journalist. Why did the writers choose these stories to write about?

**WRITE** Have students write an outline for a newspaper article. Have them write a headline for the story and several subheads.

AudioText

# Encyclopedia Brown and the Case of the Slippery Salamander

# Group Time

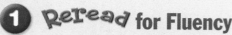

**DAY 5**

**Leveled Reader Database ONLINE**

PearsonSuccessNet.com

**Strategic Intervention**

ROUTINE

## 1 Reread for Fluency

**MODEL** Read aloud pp. 4–5 of the Leveled Reader *Top Hat, the Detective,* emphasizing dialogue and expressing characters' emotions. Have students note your efforts to make the dialogue sound the way people actually speak. Then read pp. 6–7 quickly and in a monotone. Have students tell which model sounded better. Discuss how reading with emotion and trying to express characters' personalities creates a more interesting reading.

**PRACTICE** Have students reread passages from *Top Hat, the Detective* with a partner or individually. For optimal fluency, they should reread three or four times. As students read, monitor fluency and provide corrective feedback. Assess any students you have not yet checked during this unit.

## 2 Retell Leveled Reader *Top Hat, the Detective*

Model how to use illustrations to help recall the events as you retell the story. Then ask students to retell the book, using the illustrations. Prompt them as needed.

• What is Top Hat like?
• Tell me what this story is about in just a few sentences.

### Monitor Progress

**Fluency**

| **If...** students have difficulty reading fluently, | **then...** provide additional fluency practice by pairing nonfluent readers with fluent ones. |

For alternate Leveled Reader lesson plans that teach 🔍**Plot**, 🔍**Prior Knowledge**, and **Lesson Vocabulary**, see pp. LR37–LR45.

## On-Level

**ROUTINE**

### 1 Reread for Fluency

**MODEL** Read aloud pp. 12–13 of the Leveled Reader *The Case of the Missing Iguana,* conveying Shirley's confidence that Juan had something to do with Ziggy's disappearance, Juan's guilty feelings, and Pablo's puzzlement. Have students notice how your voice reflects the characters' emotional states.

**PRACTICE** Have students reread passages from *The Case of the Missing Iguana* with a partner or individually. For optimal fluency they should reread three or four times. As students read, monitor fluency and provide corrective feedback. Assess any students you have not yet checked during this unit.

### 2 Read Retell Leveled Reader *The Case of the Missing Iguana*

Have students use illustrations as a guide to retell the story. Prompt as needed.

- What is the problem in this story?
- How was the problem solved?
- Has anything like this ever happened to you?

## Advanced

**ROUTINE**

### 1 Reread for Fluency

**PRACTICE** Have students reread passages from the Leveled Reader *Professor Science* with a partner or individually. As students read, monitor fluency and provide corrective feedback. If students read fluently on the first reading, they do not need to reread three to four times. Assess any students you have not yet checked during this unit.

### 2 Revisit Leveled Reader *Professor Science*

**RETELL** Have students retell the Leveled Reader *Professor Science and the Salamander Stumper.*

**SAVE THE SALAMANDER!** Have students present the posters they created during the week about efforts to save the giant salamander.

# Compare and Contrast

Noticing, understanding, and making comparisons and contrasts can clarify for students what they read. Use this routine to teach comparing and contrasting.

**1 DEFINE THE TERMS**

Explain that when you compare and contrast, you tell how two things are alike and different.

**2 GIVE AN EXAMPLE**

Provide a simple example, such as comparing a dog and a chameleon.

- Alike: Both are animals; both have four legs and a tail; both can be pets.

- Different: One is a mammal, the other is a reptile; one has fur, the other does not.

**3 DISCUSS CLUE WORDS**

Students should look for clue words that signal comparisons and contrasts as they read. List some examples on the board:

**Compare and Contrast**

| | |
|---|---|
| like | unlike |
| on the other hand | alike |
| similarly | however |

**4 USE A VENN DIAGRAM**

Students can use a Venn diagram to record comparisons and contrasts.

**5 PROVIDE PRACTICE**

- Ask students to compare and contrast two characters in a story or two characters in different stories.

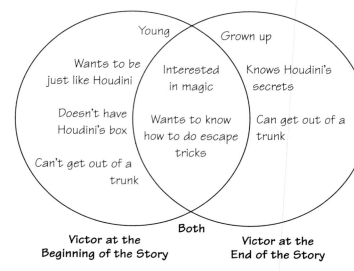

▲ **Graphic Organizer** 18

---

## Research on Compare and Contrast

"*Comparisons are one means of making concepts clear to the reader, and some writers use comparisons simply and effectively.*"

Rebecca J. Lukens,
*A Critical Handbook of Children's Literature*

Lukens, Rebecca J. *A Critical Handbook of Children's Literature.* Pearson Education, 2003, p. 286.

# Compare and Contrast

Noticing, understanding, and making comparisons and contrasts can clarify for students what they read. Use this routine to teach comparing and contrasting.

### 1 DEFINE THE TERMS

Explain that when you compare and contrast, you tell how two things are alike and different.

### 2 GIVE AN EXAMPLE

Provide a simple example, such as comparing a dog and a chameleon.

- Alike: Both are animals; both have four legs and a tail; both can be pets.

- Different: One is a mammal, the other is a reptile; one has fur, the other does not.

### 3 DISCUSS CLUE WORDS

Students should look for clue words that signal comparisons and contrasts as they read. List some examples on the board:

**Compare and Contrast**

| | |
|---|---|
| like | unlike |
| on the other hand | alike |
| similarly | however |

### 4 USE A VENN DIAGRAM

Students can use a Venn diagram to record comparisons and contrasts.

### 5 PROVIDE PRACTICE

- Ask students to compare and contrast information in a nonfiction article.

▲ **Graphic Organizer** 18

## Research on Compare and Contrast

"Comparisons are one means of making concepts clear to the reader, and some writers use comparisons simply and effectively."

Rebecca J. Lukens,
*A Critical Handbook of Children's Literature*

Lukens, Rebecca J. *A Critical Handbook of Children's Literature.* Pearson Education, 2003, p. 286.

# Character

Understanding characters helps readers comprehend a story and make good predictions about what will happen next. Use this routine to help students understand characters.

**①  REVIEW CHARACTER TRAITS**

Remind students that readers learn about characters by thinking about what they do, say, think, and how they interact with other characters. Readers infer character traits by thinking about these clues and their own experiences.

**②  TEACH CHARACTER DEVELOPMENT**

Explain that events in a story often cause a character to change in a significant way, such as in attitudes or beliefs. Students should read to see if this happens to the main character.

**③  MODEL INFERRING TRAITS**

Provide an example from a story you have read. Model inferring character traits from the character's words and actions. Point out how and why the character changes. Compare characters with each other and with real people.

**④  APPLY TO A SELECTION**

Read with students a story in which there are well-developed characters. Have students draw conclusons about character traits from clues in the story and their own experiences.

**⑤  USE A GRAPHIC ORGANIZER**

Have students record clues about a character in a web. They can record details about what the character said and did and how characters interacted.

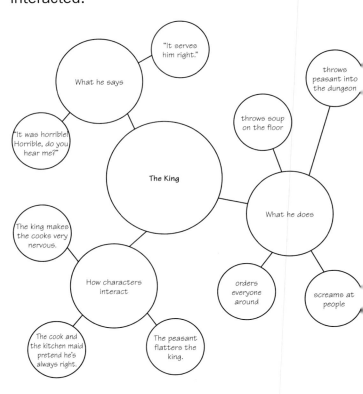

▲ **Graphic Organizer** 16

## Research on Character

"In life and in books, children can sense differences in human beings and are capable of recognizing and responding to well-developed characters. Even in the simplest stories it is possible to find characters that verify truths about human nature."

Rebecca J. Lukens,
*A Critical Handbook of Children's Literature*

Lukens, Rebecca J. *A Critical Handbook of Children's Literature.* Pearson Education, 2003, p. 94.

# Graphic Sources

Graphic sources can be a valuable aid to readers in previewing and comprehending text. When students interpret and create graphics as they read, they often strengthen their understanding of the text. Use this routine to teach graphic sources.

## 1 DISCUSS GRAPHIC SOURCES

Explain that a graphic is a way of showing information visually. Graphics can include pictures, charts, graphs, maps, diagrams, schedules, and so on. Graphics often show information from the text in a visual way. They can organize many facts or ideas.

## 2 USE GRAPHICS TO PREVIEW

Remind students to look for graphics when they preview. Graphics are often a good way to discover what the story or article is about.

## 3 COMPARE GRAPHICS TO TEXT

Have students compare the text with graphics in a selection and discuss the author's purpose for including graphics. Captions, charts, diagrams, and maps may present information that is nowhere else in the article, or they may help the reader better understand text information.

## 4 CREATE GRAPHICS

Give students opportunities to create their own pictures, charts, and other graphics to help them organize and understand text information.

## 5 USE A GRAPHIC ORGANIZER

Have students create a chart from information in a selection. Depending on the content, they may use a two-, three-, four-, or five-column chart.

| Pictograph | Related Word | How They Are Related |
|---|---|---|
| Ibis bird | Discover | The bird looks like it's looking for something. A discovery is something you find. |
| Crocodile | Trouble | A hungry crocodile could be trouble! |
| Waves | Nile | The Nile river has waves. |

▲ **Graphic Organizer** 26

## Research on Graphic Sources

"Teaching students to organize the ideas that they are reading about in a systematic, visual graph benefits the ability of the students to remember what they read and may transfer, in general, to better comprehension and achievement in Social Studies and Science content areas."

National Reading Panel,
*Teaching Children to Read*

National Reading Panel. *Teaching Children to Read: Reports of the Subgroups.* National Institute of Child Health & Human Development, National Institutes of Health, 2000, p. 4-45.

# Plot

When students have a clear understanding of the typical plot structure of stories, they can tell which events are most important and why they happen. Use this routine to support students' understanding of plot.

## 1 REVIEW PLOT

Review plot as the beginning, middle, and end of a story. Help them chart the beginning, middle, and end of familiar stories.

## 2 TEACH NEW TERMS

Introduce the following terms: *problem, rising action, climax,* and *resolution.* Tell students that these words describe a common plot structure.

## 3 IDENTIFY THE PROBLEM

Have students look for a problem or goal in a story you have read. Explain that they might see a conflict

- between two characters.

- between a character and nature, such as a character trying to survive in the desert.

- within a character, as when a character needs to make a decision.

Show students how to record the problem on a plot structure map.

## 4 RECORD PLOT STRUCTURE

Have students identify and record the major events in the story, the climax (when the problem is directly confronted), and the resolution (when the problem is resolved).

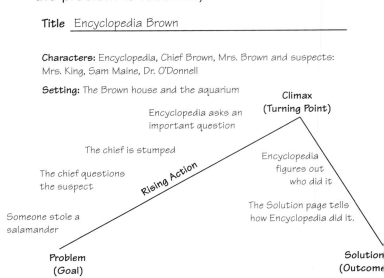

Title  Encyclopedia Brown

**Characters:** Encyclopedia, Chief Brown, Mrs. Brown and suspects: Mrs. King, Sam Maine, Dr. O'Donnell

**Setting:** The Brown house and the aquarium

Encyclopedia asks an important question

The chief is stumped

The chief questions the suspect

*Rising Action*

Someone stole a salamander

**Problem (Goal)**

**Climax (Turning Point)**

Encyclopedia figures out who did it

The Solution page tells how Encyclopedia did it.

**Solution (Outcome**

▲ **Graphic Organizer** 13

## Research on Plot

"By studying plot, children can learn to identify patterns that appear over and over again in the books they read. With older students, plot maps can be drawn to focus on key events in particular chapters or to discover the shapes of whole books."

Linda DeGroff and Lee Galda,
*"Responding to Literature: Activities for Exploring Books"*

DeGroff, Linda, and Lee Galda. "Responding to Literature: Activities for Exploring Books." In *Invitation to Read: More Children's Literature in the Reading Program,* edited by Bernice E. Cullinan, International Reading Association, 1992.

**Providing students with reading materials they can and want to read is an important step toward developing fluent readers. A running record allows you to determine each student's instructional and independent reading level. Information on how to take a running record is provided on pp. DI•59–DI•60.**

## Instructional Reading Level

Only approximately 1 in 10 words will be difficult when reading a selection from the Student Edition for students who are at grade level. (A typical fourth-grader reads approximately 115–130 words correct per minute.)

- Students reading at grade level should read regularly from the Student Edition and On-Level Leveled Readers, with teacher support as suggested in the Teacher's Editions.
- Students reading below grade level can read the Strategic Intervention Leveled Readers. Instructional plans can be found in the Teacher's Edition and the Leveled Reader Teaching Guide.
- Students who are reading above grade level can read the Advanced Leveled Readers. Instructional plans can be found in the Teacher's Edition and the Leveled Reader Teaching Guide.

## Independent Reading Level

Students should read regularly in independent-level texts in which no more than approximately 1 in 20 words is difficult for the reader. Other factors that make a book easy to read include the student's interest in the topic, the amount of text on a page, how well illustrations support meaning, and the complexity and familiarity of the concepts. Suggested books for self-selected reading are provided for each lesson on p. TR14 in this Teacher's Edition.

Guide students in learning how to self-select books at their independent reading level. As you talk about a book with students, discuss the challenging concepts in it, list new words students find in sampling the book, and ask students about their familiarity with the topic. A blackline master to help students evaluate books for independent reading is provided on p. DI•58.

## Self-Selected/Independent Reading

While oral reading allows you to assess students' reading level and fluency, independent reading is of crucial importance to students' futures as readers and learners. Students need to develop their ability to read independently for increasing amounts of time.

- Schedule a regular time for sustained independent reading in your classroom. During the year, gradually increase the amount of time devoted to independent reading.
- Encourage students to track the amount of time they read independently and the number of pages they read in a given amount of time. Tracking will help motivate them to gradually increase their duration and speed. Blackline masters for tracking independent reading are provided on p. DI•58 and p. TR15.

## Choosing a Book for Independent Reading

When choosing a book, story, or article for independent reading, consider these questions:

_____ 1. Do I know something about this topic?

_____ 2. Am I interested in this topic?

_____ 3. Do I like reading this kind of book (fiction, fantasy, biography, or whatever)?

_____ 4. Have I read other things by this author? Do I like this author?

If you say "yes" to at least one of the questions above, continue:

_____ 5. In reading the first page, was only about 1 of every 20 words hard?

If you say "yes," continue:

_____ 6. Does the number of words on a page look about right to me?

If you say "yes," the book or article is probably at the right level for you.

## Silent Reading

Record the date, the title of the book or article you read, the amount of time you spent reading, and the number of pages you read during that time.

| Date | Title | Minutes | Pages |
|------|-------|---------|-------|
|  |  |  |  |
|  |  |  |  |
|  |  |  |  |
|  |  |  |  |
|  |  |  |  |
|  |  |  |  |
|  |  |  |  |
|  |  |  |  |
|  |  |  |  |
|  |  |  |  |
|  |  |  |  |
|  |  |  |  |
|  |  |  |  |
|  |  |  |  |
|  |  |  |  |
|  |  |  |  |
|  |  |  |  |
|  |  |  |  |
|  |  |  |  |
|  |  |  |  |

## Taking a Running Record

A running record is an assessment of a student's oral reading accuracy and oral reading fluency. Reading accuracy is based on the number of words read correctly. Reading fluency is based on the reading rate (the number of words correct per minute) and the degree to which a student reads with a "natural flow."

### How to Measure Reading Accuracy

1. Choose a grade-level text of about 80 to 120 words that is unfamiliar to the student.
2. Make a copy of the text for yourself. Make a copy for the student or have the student read aloud from a book.
3. Give the student the text and have the student read aloud. (You may wish to record the student's reading for later evaluation.)
4. On your copy of the text, mark any miscues or errors the student makes while reading. See the running record sample on page DI·60, which shows how to identify and mark miscues.
5. Count the total number of words in the text and the total number of errors made by the student. Note: If a student makes the same error more than once, such as mispronouncing the same word multiple times, count it as one error. Self-corrections do not count as actual errors. Use the following formula to calculate the percentage score, or accuracy rate:

$$\frac{\text{Total Number of Words} - \text{Total Number of Errors}}{\text{Total Number of Words}} \times 100 = \text{percentage score}$$

### Interpreting the Results

- A student who reads **95–100%** of the words correctly is reading at an **independent level** and may need more challenging text.
- A student who reads **90–94%** of the words correctly is reading at an **instructional level** and will likely benefit from guided instruction.
- A student who reads **89%** or fewer of the words correctly is reading at a **frustrational level** and may benefit most from targeted instruction with lower-level texts and intervention.

### How to Measure Reading Rate (WCPM)

1. Follow Steps 1–3 above.
2. Note the exact times when the student begins and finishes reading.
3. Use the following formula to calculate the number of words correct per minute (WCPM):

$$\frac{\text{Total Number of Words Read Correctly}}{\text{Total Number of Seconds}} \times 60 = \text{words correct per minute}$$

### Interpreting the Results

An appropriate reading rate for a fourth-grader is 115–130 (WCPM).

## Running Record Sample

**Running Record Sample**

All the maple trees that grow in the
northeastern United States and parts of
Canada have shaken off their slumber.
During the next few months, they put all ^of^
their energy into growing. Maple trees
can live for hundreds of years. During
their first hundred years of existence,
they grow about *one* a foot each year.

The maple tree's roots anchor the
tree to the ground. They burrow /bore/ deep in
the soil and push out in every direction.
The huge network of roots (has) spread
like an enormous ^H^ open hand with dozens
and dozens of outstretched fingers in
the ground. The deep roots help keep
the tree from toppling over during strong
winds. The roots also gather (SC) nutrients the
tree needs to make sap.

—From *The Maple Tree*
On-Level Reader 4.3.1

**Symbols**

**Accurate Reading**
The student reads a word correctly.

**Insertion**
The student inserts words or parts of words that are not in the text.

**Substitution**
The student substitutes words or parts of words for the words in the text.

**Mispronunciation/Misreading**
The student pronounces or reads a word incorrectly.

**Omission**
The student omits words or word parts.

**Hesitation**
The student hesitates over a word, and the teacher provides the word. Wait several seconds before telling the student what the word is.

**Self-Correction**
The student reads a word incorrectly but then corrects the error. Do not count self-corrections as actual errors. However, noting self-corrections will help you identify words the student finds difficult.

**Running Record Results**
Total Number of Words: **122**
Number of Errors: **5**

Reading Time: **61 seconds**

▶ **Reading Accuracy**

$$\frac{122 - 5}{122} \times 100 = 95.9 = 96\%$$

Accuracy Percentage Score: **96%**

▶ **Reading Rate—WCPM**

$$\frac{117}{61} \times 60 = 115.08 = 115 \text{ words correct per minute}$$

Reading Rate: **115 WCPM**

# Teacher Resources

## Table of Contents

## Something Fishy    from p. 488m

"Well, yes," Juan said, "I did don Miguel, but..." The fish seller smiled with delight at this reply as he predicted justice leaning in his favor.

Don Miguel then turned to the fish seller and asked, "How much does one of your best fish cost?"

"One silver coin," the fish seller quickly replied.

The market judge looked sternly at Juan and said, "This is how you shall repay the fish seller. Please follow me outside." The fish seller and Juan followed don Miguel outside, Juan with downcast eyes, and the fish seller with a look of righteous pride.

The judge then said to Juan, "Do you have a silver coin?"

"Why, yes, don Miguel, but it is all that I have to my name."

The judge looked kindly on Juan and said, "Would you be so kind to hold your coin up in the air for all of us to see?" Juan reached into his pocket and pulled out the last of his money. Don Miguel then cleared his throat and said, "If the price of a fish is a silver coin, then the price for a smell of a fish is just a shadow of a silver coin." The judge then turned to the fish seller and said, "Please take the shadow that the coin casts."

And that is how Juan Rios found hope and justice in the great city of Antigua.

## Unit 1

| | Vocabulary Words | | Spelling Words | | | |
|---|---|---|---|---|---|---|
| **Because of Winn-Dixie** | grand | prideful | **Short vowels VCCV** | | | |
| | memorial | recalls | admire | soccer | intend | happen |
| | peculiar | selecting | magnet | engine | fabric | cannon |
| | positive | | contest | sudden | flatten | |
| | | | method | finger | rascal | |
| | | | custom | accident | gutter | |
| | | | rally | mitten | mammal | |
| **Lewis and Clark and Me** | docks | | **Long a and i** | | | |
| | migrating | | sigh | spray | tight | sleigh |
| | scan | | right | braid | raisin | freight |
| | scent | | weigh | bait | trait | |
| | wharf | | eight | grain | highway | |
| | yearned | | detail | slight | frighten | |
| | | | height | thigh | dismay | |
| **Grandfather's Journey** | amazed | | **Long e and o** | | | |
| | bewildered | | sweet | throat | croak | seaweed |
| | homeland | | each | float | shallow | hollow |
| | longed | | three | foam | eagle | |
| | sculptures | | least | flown | indeed | |
| | still | | freedom | greet | rainbow | |
| | towering | | below | season | grown | |
| **The Horned Toad Prince** | bargain | | **Long e** | | | |
| | favor | | prairie | movie | collie | trolley |
| | lassoed | | calorie | country | breezy | misty |
| | offended | | honey | empty | jury | |
| | prairie | | valley | city | balcony | |
| | riverbed | | money | rookie | steady | |
| | shrieked | | finally | hockey | alley | |
| **Letters Home from Yosemite** | glacier | | **Long u** | | | |
| | impressive | | usual | scooter | pupil | |
| | naturalist | | huge | juice | groove | |
| | preserve | | flute | cruise | confuse | |
| | slopes | | mood | truth | humor | |
| | species | | smooth | bruise | duty | |
| | wilderness | | threw | cruel | curfew | |
| | | | afternoon | excuse | | |

| Unit 2 | Vocabulary Words | Spelling Words | | | |
|---|---|---|---|---|---|
| **What Jo Did** | fouled<br>hoop<br>jersey<br>marveled<br>rim<br>speechless<br>swatted<br>unbelievable | **Adding -s and -es** | | | |
| | | monkeys<br>friends<br>plays<br>supplies<br>taxes<br>holidays | months<br>companies<br>costumes<br>sandwiches<br>hobbies<br>daisies | delays<br>scratches<br>counties<br>teammates<br>memories<br>bunches | batteries<br>donkeys |
| **Coyote School News** | bawling<br>coyote<br>dudes<br>roundup<br>spurs | **Irregular Plurals** | | | |
| | | videos<br>teeth<br>potatoes<br>themselves<br>lives<br>leaves | cliffs<br>roofs<br>halves<br>moose<br>radios<br>sheep | cuffs<br>beliefs<br>patios<br>banjos<br>tornadoes<br>tomatoes | hoofs<br>loaves |
| **Grace and the Time Machine** | aboard<br>atlas<br>awkward<br>capable<br>chant<br>mechanical<br>miracle | reseats<br>vehicle | **Words with ar, or** | | |
| | | morning<br>forest<br>garbage<br>form<br>alarm<br>corner | story<br>argue<br>backyard<br>start<br>partner<br>storm | Florida<br>apartment<br>sport<br>force<br>forward<br>sharp | garden<br>Arkansas |
| **Marven of the Great North Woods** | cord<br>dismay<br>grizzly<br>immense<br>payroll | **Digraphs ng, nk, ph, wh** | | | |
| | | Thanksgiving<br>among<br>think<br>blank<br>graph<br>young | wheel<br>nephew<br>belong<br>whiskers<br>whisper<br>elephant | white<br>shrink<br>wharf<br>trunk<br>strong<br>blink | chunk<br>skunk |
| **So You Want To Be President?** | Constitution<br>howling<br>humble<br>politics<br>responsibility<br>solemnly<br>vain | **Words with our, ur, ear, ir** | | | |
| | | return<br>courage<br>surface<br>purpose<br>first<br>turkey | heard<br>early<br>turtle<br>birthday<br>journal<br>courtesy | nourish<br>purse<br>furniture<br>search<br>curtain<br>burrow | hamburger<br>survey |

## Unit 3

| | Vocabulary Words | | Spelling Words |
|---|---|---|---|

### The Stranger

**Vocabulary Words**

| | |
|---|---|
| draft | parlor |
| etched | terror |
| fascinated | timid |
| frost | |

**Spelling Words**

#### Adding -ed and -ing

| | | | |
|---|---|---|---|
| watched | stopped | noticed | hurried |
| watching | stopping | noticing | hurrying |
| danced | dried | robbed | |
| dancing | drying | robbing | |
| studied | happened | slipped | |
| studying | happening | slipping | |

### Adelina's Whales

**Vocabulary Words**

| | |
|---|---|
| biologist | massive |
| bluff | rumbling |
| lagoon | tropical |

**Spelling Words**

#### Homophones

| | | | |
|---|---|---|---|
| piece | by | aloud | there |
| peace | bye | allowed | their |
| break | beat | past | |
| brake | beet | passed | |
| threw | thrown | weight | |
| through | throne | wait | |

### How Night Came from the Sea: A Story from Brazil

**Vocabulary Words**

| |
|---|
| brilliant |
| chorus |
| coward |
| gleamed |
| shimmering |

**Spelling Words**

#### Vowel sound in shout

| | | | |
|---|---|---|---|
| however | towel | browse | eyebrow |
| mountain | ounce | announce | boundary |
| mound | coward | hound | |
| scout | outdoors | trout | |
| shout | flowerpot | drowsy | |
| couch | scowl | grouch | |

### Eye of the Storm

**Vocabulary Words**

| |
|---|
| destruction |
| expected |
| forecasts |
| inland |
| shatter |
| surge |

**Spelling Words**

#### Compound words

| | | | |
|---|---|---|---|
| watermelon | upstairs | touchdown | loud-speaker |
| homemade | thunder-storm | campfire | laptop |
| understand | | skateboard | flashlight |
| sometimes | shortcut | anyway | |
| shoelace | doorbell | fireworks | |
| highway | jellyfish | haircut | |

### The Great Kapok Tree

**Vocabulary Words**

| |
|---|
| canopy |
| dangle |
| dappled |
| fragrant |
| pollen |
| pollinate |
| slithered |
| wondrous |

**Spelling Words**

#### Possessives

| | | |
|---|---|---|
| its | mens | teacher's |
| ours | girl's | teachers' |
| mine | girls' | aunt's |
| yours | hers | aunts' |
| family's | theirs | boy's |
| families' | brother's | boys' |
| man's | brothers' | |

## Unit 4

| Unit 4 | Vocabulary Words | Spelling Words |
|--------|------------------|----------------|

**The Houdini Box**

Vocabulary Words:
appeared
bustling
crumbled
escape
magician
monument
vanished

**Contractions**

| | | | |
|---|---|---|---|
| don't | doesn't | where's | when's |
| won't | I've | hadn't | haven't |
| wouldn't | here's | aren't | |
| there's | wasn't | they're | |
| we're | shouldn't | it's | |
| you're | couldn't | we've | |

**Encantado: Pink Dolphin of the Amazon**

Vocabulary Words:
aquarium
dolphins
enchanted
flexible
glimpses
pulses
surface

**Final -le, -al, -en**

| | | | |
|---|---|---|---|
| chicken | natural | paddle | tangle |
| eleven | needle | animal | frighten |
| given | single | spiral | |
| jungle | citizen | marble | |
| national | threaten | oval | |
| several | diagonal | mumble | |

**The King in the Kitchen**

Vocabulary Words:
duke
dungeon
furiously
genius
majesty
noble
peasant
porridge

**Words with final -er, -ar**

| | | | |
|---|---|---|---|
| brother | similar | filter | theater |
| together | regular | hangar | deliver |
| dinner | summer | never | |
| popular | clever | shelter | |
| center | supper | cellar | |
| calendar | pitcher | caterpillar | |

**Seeker of Knowledge**

Vocabulary Words:
ancient
link
scholars
seeker
temple
translate
triumph
uncover

**Consonants /j/, /ks/, and /k/**

| | | | |
|---|---|---|---|
| village | knowledge | Texas | quilt |
| except | question | fudge | expert |
| explain | equal | excellent | |
| quick | queen | exercise | |
| charge | excited | quart | |
| bridge | expect | liquid | |

**Encyclopedia Brown and the Case of the Slippery Salamander**

Vocabulary Words:
amphibians
crime
exhibit
lizards
reference
reptiles
salamanders
stumped

**Prefixes un-, dis-, in-**

| | | |
|---|---|---|
| distrust | disorder | disrepair |
| uncertain | discount | inability |
| incomplete | indirect | disapprove |
| unlikely | unopened | unsolved |
| unfair | disrespect | disobey |
| discontinue | unimportant | unsuspecting |
| unaware | unlisted | |

## Unit 5

| | Vocabulary Words | Spelling Words |
|---|---|---|

### Sailing Home: A Story of a Childhood at Sea

**Vocabulary Words**

bow, cargo, celestial, conducted, dignified, navigation, quivered, stern

**Spelling Words**

**Multisyllabic words**

| | | | |
|---|---|---|---|
| reaction | refreshment | unhappily | question-able |
| prerecorded | unbreakable | watchfully | displace-ment |
| incorrectly | declaration | gleefully | midship-man |
| incredibly | retirement | sportsman-ship | |
| disobedient | misdialed | repayment | |
| disagreeable | undefined | | |

### Lost City: The Discovery of Machu Picchu

**Vocabulary Words**

curiosity, glorious, granite, ruins, terraced, thickets, torrent

**Spelling Words**

**Syllable patterns V/CV and VC/V**

| | | | |
|---|---|---|---|
| basic | olive | beware | tribute |
| vacant | tiger | emotion | lizard |
| secret | spinach | cabin | |
| honor | second | tripod | |
| local | donate | dragon | |
| novel | locust | habit | |

### Amelia and Eleanor Go for a Ride

**Vocabulary Words**

aviator, brisk, cockpit, daring, elegant, outspoken, solo

**Spelling Words**

**Greek word parts**

| | | | |
|---|---|---|---|
| telephone | barometer | telegraph | periscope |
| biography | microscope | perimeter | mega-phone |
| telescope | headphones | paragraph | |
| photograph | microphone | phonics | |
| microwave | autograph | symphony | |
| diameter | microchip | saxophone | |

### Antarctic Journal: Four Months at the Bottom of the World

**Vocabulary Words**

anticipation, continent, convergence, depart, forbidding, heaves, icebergs

**Spelling Words**

**Words with Latin roots**

| | | | |
|---|---|---|---|
| dictionary | locate | erupt | disrupt |
| abrupt | portable | passport | dislocate |
| predict | transport | export | |
| import | bankrupt | contradict | |
| locally | dictate | rupture | |
| verdict | location | interrupt | |

### Moonwalk

**Vocabulary Words**

loomed, rille, runt, staggered, summoning, taunted, trench, trudged

**Spelling Words**

**Related words**

| | | |
|---|---|---|
| please | production | meter |
| pleasant | heal | metric |
| breath | health | compose |
| breathe | triple | composition |
| image | triplet | crumb |
| imagine | relate | crumble |
| product | relative | |

## Unit 6 | Vocabulary Words | Spelling Words

**My Brother Martin**

Vocabulary Words:
- ancestors
- avoided
- generations
- minister
- numerous
- pulpit
- shielding

### Schwa

| | | | |
|---|---|---|---|
| stomach | remember | fortune | cement |
| memory | forget | giant | yesterday |
| Canada | suppose | architect | |
| element | iron | normal | |
| mystery | gravel | notify | |
| science | difficult | privilege | |

**Jim Thorpe's Bright Path**

Vocabulary Words:
- boarding school
- dormitory
- endurance
- manual
- reservation
- society

### Prefixes *mis-, non-, re-*

| | | | |
|---|---|---|---|
| misplace | mishandle | nonfiction | nonstick |
| nonsense | nonstop | rebound | misquote |
| reread | recover | mistreat | |
| repack | reseal | readjust | |
| misfortune | misbehavior | misprint | |
| remove | reunion | nonprofit | |

**How Tía Lola Came to Visit Stay**

Vocabulary Words:
- affords
- colonel
- glint
- lurking
- palettes
- quaint
- resemblance

### Suffixes *-less, -ment, -ness*

| | | | |
|---|---|---|---|
| countless | statement | tireless | needless |
| payment | breathless | amazement | painless |
| goodness | restless | amusement | |
| fairness | enjoyment | greatness | |
| hopeless | pavement | punishment | |
| treatment | flawless | timeless | |

**To Fly: The Story of the Wright Brothers**

Vocabulary Words:
- cradle
- drag
- flex
- glider
- hangars
- rudder
- stalled

### Suffixes *-ful, -ly, -ion*

| | | | |
|---|---|---|---|
| careful | recently | yearly | correction |
| tasteful | extremely | successful | eagerly |
| lonely | certainly | playful | |
| powerful | wisely | thoughtful | |
| suggestion | harmful | actually | |
| peaceful | monthly | pollution | |

**The Man Who Went to the Far Side of the Moon: The Story of Apollo 11 Astronaut Michael Collins**

Vocabulary Words:
- astronauts
- capsule
- hatch
- horizon
- lunar
- module
- quarantine

### Words with silent consonants

| | | |
|---|---|---|
| island | half | rhyme |
| column | calf | climber |
| knee | whistle | limb |
| often | autumn | plumbing |
| known | knuckles | ghost |
| castle | numb | clothes |
| thumb | Illinois | |

## Grade 3 Vocabulary

**Use this list of third grade tested vocabulary words for review and leveled activities.**

**A**
admire
airport
amount
antlers
anxiously
arranged
attention
attic
average

**B**
bakery
barrels
batch
bay
beauty
beneath
blade
blizzards
blooming
board
boils
boom
bottom
bows
braided
budding
bulbs
bundles
buried
burro
bursts
business

**C**
cardboard
carpenter
carpetmaker
celebrate
cellar
channel
cheated
check
chilly

chimney
chipped
chores
clearing
clever
clutched
coins
collection
college
complained
continued
cotton
crops
crown
crystal
cuddles
curious
current
custom
customer

**D**
dangerously
delicious
depth
described
deserts
dew
dimes
disappeared
discovery
dough
downtown
doze
drifting
drowned

**E**
earned
earthquakes
echoed
encourages
enormous
errands
excitedly

**F**
factory
famous
farewell
feast
festival
fetched
fierce
fined
fireflies
fireworks
flights
flippers
flutter
foolish
force
foreign
frozen

**G**
gardener
giggle
glaring
glassblower
goal
graceful
gully

**H**
handkerchief
hatch
homesick
humor

**I**
imagined
ingredients
interest

**J**
journey
joyful

**K**
knead
knowledge

**L**
labeled
languages
laundry
lazy
liberty
local
looping

**M**
marketplace
medals
melody
memories
mending
mention
merchant
million
mixture
models
motioned

**N**
narrator
narrow
native
nickels
notepad

**O**
outrun
overhead
overnight

**P**
paces
pale
partners
patch
peak

pecks
perches
pick
pitcher
plenty
poked
popular
preen
public
puffs

**Q**
quarters

**R**
raindrops
realize
recipe
recognizing
reeds
reply
rhythm
rich
ruined

**S**
sadness
scattered
scoop
scrambled
settled
shiny
shivered
shocked
showers
skillet
slammed
snug
snuggles
social
spare
spell
spoil
sprouting
stamps

steady
steep
stirred
stoops
strain
straying
strokes
struggled
supplies
support
surrounded
swooping
symbol
symphony

**T**
tablet
thousand
thread
tides
torch
treasure
trembles
tune
twist

**U**
unaware
unforgettable
unveiled
unwrapped

**V**
valley
value
volcanoes

**W**
waterfalls
wealth
wobbled
worth

# Grade 5 Vocabulary

Use this list of fifth grade tested vocabulary words for leveled activities.

## A

abdomen
accomplishments
achieved
acquainted
admiringly
adorn
advice
advised
agreement
algae
appreciate
architect
armor
artificial
assignment
astonished

## B

background
barber
bass
behavior
benefactor
bleached
bluish
blunders
branded
bronze

## C

cable
cannon
carcasses
cartwheels
caterpillar
cavities
choir
circumstances
civilization
clarinet
cleanse
cocoon
combination
complex

concealed
confidence
conservation
constructed
contribute
cramped
critical
criticizing
cruised

## D

daintily
debris
decay
demonstrates
depressed
devastation
diplomat
disrespect
distribution
drenching
driftwood

## E

economic
eerie
elbow
emerge
enables
encases
enthusiastic
environment
envy
episode
era
erected
essential
expanded
explosion
explosions
extinct

## F

fashioned
fastball

fate
fearless
fidgety
fleeing
focus
forgetful
foundations

## G

gait
glimmer
gnawed
gratitude
gravity
guaranteed
gymnastics

## H

hammocks
handicapped
headland
hesitation
hideous
hustled
hydrogen

## I

immigrants
independence
inspired
interior
intersection
investigation
issue

## J

jammed

## K

kelp

## L

lair
lamented

landscape
lifeless
limelight
lingers
lullaby
luxury

## M

magnified
midst
migrant
miniature
mocking
mold
monitors
mucus

## N

newcomer
nighttime

## O

occasion
ooze
outfield
overrun

## P

parasites
peddler
permit
philosopher
pitch
plunged
pondered
precious
prehistoric
procedures
procession
profile
proportion

## R

ravine
realm

reassembled
recommend
refugees
released
eligious
representatives
reputation
resourceful
rival
robotic
role
rustling

## S

sacred
scarce
scoundrel
scrawled
scrawny
sea urchins
secondhand
sediment
serpent
severe
shellfish
sinew
sketched
skidded
slavery
somber
somersault
sonar
specialize
specific
spectacles
spoonful
starvation
steed
sterile
sternly
strategy
strict
subject
superiors
suspicions

## T

teenager
therapist
thieving
throbbing
tidied
traditions
tundra
tweezers

## U

unique
unscrewed

## V

vacant
veins
visa

## W

weakness
wheelchair
wincing
windup
withered
workshop
worshipped
worthless

# Legibility

When handwriting is legible, letters, words, and numbers can be read easily. Handwriting that is not legible can cause problems for the reader and make communication difficult. Legibility can be improved if students are able to identify what is causing legibility problems in their handwriting. Focus instruction on the following five elements of legible handwriting.

### Size

Letters need to be a consistent size. Students should focus on three things related to size: letters that reach to the top line, letters that reach halfway between the top and bottom line, and letters that extend below the bottom line. Writing letters the correct size can improve legibility. Often the letters that sit halfway between the top and bottom line cause the most problems. When students are writing on notebook paper, there is no middle line to help them size letters such as *m, a, i*, and *r* correctly. If students are having trouble, have them draw middle lines on their notebook paper.

### Shape

Some of the most common handwriting problems are caused by forming letters incorrectly. These are the most common types of handwriting problems:

- Round letters such as *a, o*, and *g* are not closed.
- Looped letters such as *l, e*, and *b* have no loops.
- Letters such as *i, t*, and *d* have loops that shouldn't be there.

Have students examine one another's writing to indicate which words are hard to read, and then discuss which letters aren't formed correctly. They can then practice those particular letters.

### Spacing

Letters within words should be evenly spaced. Too much or too little space can make writing difficult to read. A consistent amount of space should also be used between words in a sentence and between sentences. Suggest that students use the tip of their pencil to check the spacing between words and the width of their pencil to check the spacing between sentences.

### Slant

Correct writing slant can be to the right or to the left, or there may be no slant at all. Slant becomes a legibility problem when letters are slanted in different directions. Suggest that students use a ruler to draw lines to determine if their slant is consistent.

### Smoothness

Written letters should be produced with a line weight that is not too dark and not too light. The line should be smooth without any shaky or jagged edges. If students' writing is too dark, they are pressing too hard. If the writing is too light, they are not pressing hard enough. Usually shaky or jagged lines occur if students are unsure of how to form letters or if they are trying to draw letters rather than using a flowing motion.

# D'Nealian™ Cursive Alphabet

a b c d e f g
h i j k l m n
o p q r s t u
v w x y z

A B C D E F G
H I J K L M N
O P Q R S T U
V W X Y Z . , ' ?

1 2 3 4 5 6
7 8 9 10

# D'Nealian™ Alphabet

a b c d e f g h i
j k l m n o p q r s t
u v w x y z

A B C D E F G
H I J K L M N O
P Q R S T U V
W X Y Z . , ' ?

1 2 3 4 5 6
7 8 9 10

# Manuscript Alphabet

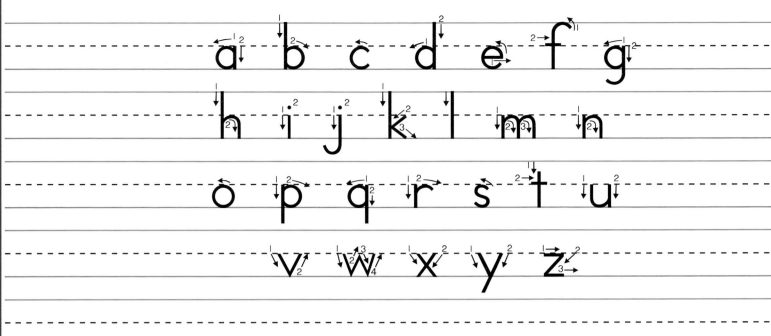

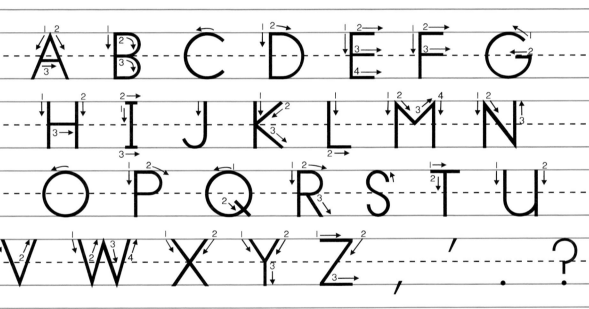

## Unit 4 *Puzzles and Mysteries*

| | Below-Level | On-Level | Advanced |
|---|---|---|---|

### The Houdini Box

**To Read Aloud!**
**Abiyoyo Returns**
by Pete Seeger (Simon and Schuster Books for Young Readers, 2001) When a giant is banished from town by a magician, the town realizes how much they need him to help save the town from flooding.

**Harry Houdini: Escape Artist**
by Patricia Lakin (Aladdin Paperbacks, 2002) This book gives an entertaining overview of the childhood of the most famous magician ever to live: Harry Houdini.

**Atariba and Niguayona**
by Harriet Rohmer and Jesus Guerrero Rea (Children's Press, 1988) When a macaw tells Niguayona that he can save his sick friend by finding a special fruit, he starts out on a magical journey.

**Wizards: An Amazing Journey Through the Last Great Age of Magic**
by Candace Savage (Greystone Books, 2004) This book explores the 17th century, when magic was part of everyday life.

### Encantado: Pink Dolphin of the Amazon

**To Read Aloud!**
**Mouse Views: What the Class Pet Saw**
by Bruce McMillan (Holiday House, 1993) See what a typical classroom looks like...from a mouse's point of view!

**Animal Fact/Animal Fable**
by Seymour Simon (Crown, 1987) Fun and humorous illustrations help kids discover the truth behind some of the animal kingdom's greatest myths.

**Alice and the Boa Constrictor**
by Laurie Adams and Allison Coudert (Houghton Mifflin, 1983) Alice buys a snake, Sir Lancelot, after her science teacher explains that boa constrictors make good pets.

**Puffins**
by Susan E. Quinlan (Carolrhoda, 1999) This book discusses the characteristics, habitat, and life cycle of the world's three different kinds of puffins.

### The King in the Kitchen

**To Read Aloud!**
**When Riddles Come Rumbling: Poems to Ponder**
by Rebecca Kai Dotlich (Boyd's Mill Press, 2001) The poems in this book describe everyday objects but with a twist: readers have to guess what each poem is describing.

**One Riddle, One Answer**
by Lauren Thompson (Scholastic, 2001) A princess composes a riddle in order to find a smart man who can solve it and thereby become her husband.

**The Malachite Palace**
by Alma Flor Ada (Atheneum, 1998) A princess, who lives in a palace with her family, is told she is not allowed to play with the children outside of the palace gates.

**True Lies**
by George Shannon (Greenwillow Books, 1997) A collection of eighteen folk tales in which readers must explain how the main characters both lie and tell the truth at the same time.

### Seeker of Knowledge

**To Read Aloud!**
**Voices of Ancient Egypt**
by Kay Winters (National Geographic Society, 2003) This book of poems about ancient Egypt is told through the voices of various people who lived and worked during that time.

**There's a Monster in the Alphabet**
by James Rumford (Houghton Mifflin, 2002) The story of Cadmus, a Phoenician hero who brought the alphabet to Greece.

**Out of Darkness: A Story of Louis Braille**
by Russell Freedman (Clarion, 1997) A profile of Louis Braille, a blind man, whose experiments made it possible for the blind to read.

**The Mystery of the Hieroglyphs**
by Carol Donoughue (Oxford University Press, 1999) As readers learn about the Rosetta Stone and the scientists who deciphered it, they must do their own deciphering and reading of hieroglyphics.

### Encyclopedia Brown and the Case of the Slippery Salamander

**To Read Aloud!**
**Bunnicula: A Rabbit Tale of Mystery**
by Deborah Howe (Aladdin Paperbacks, 1996) When a family finds a small bunny in the theater after seeing Dracula, their dog Harold and cat Chester are instantly suspicious and decide that the bunny must be a vegetarian vampire.

**The Case of the Dirty Clue**
by George Edward Stanley (Aladdin Paperbacks, 2003) When Misty's new bike is run over by a car, she and her friends use their brainpower (and a little help from their teacher) to solve the crime.

**Encyclopedia Brown: Boy Detective**
by Donald Sobol (Bantam, 1985) Ten-year-old "Encyclopedia" Brown solves ten mysteries in this interesting book, while challenging the reader to figure out how he solved each one.

**Inspector Forsooth's Whodunits**
by Derrick Niederman (Sterling Publishing, 1998) This book includes twelve mysteries with tons of clues to ponder before making a decision. A question and answer guide at the back helps lead the reader down the right path.

# Unit 4 Reading Log

Name _____

| Dates Read | Title and Author | What is it about? | How would you rate it? | Explain your rating. |
|---|---|---|---|---|
| From _____ to _____ | | | Great<br>5  4  3  2  1<br>Awful | |
| From _____ to _____ | | | Great<br>5  4  3  2  1<br>Awful | |
| From _____ to _____ | | | Great<br>5  4  3  2  1<br>Awful | |
| From _____ to _____ | | | Great<br>5  4  3  2  1<br>Awful | |
| From _____ to _____ | | | Great<br>5  4  3  2  1<br>Awful | |

© Pearson Education

# Unit 4 Narrative Retelling Chart

**Selection Title** _____    **Name** _____    **Date** _____

| Retelling Criteria/Teacher Prompt | Teacher-Aided Response | Student-Generated Response | Rubric Score (Circle one.) |
|---|---|---|---|
| **Connections** Has anything like this happened to you? How does this story remind you of other stories? | | | 4   3   2   1 |
| **Author's Purpose** Why do you think the author wrote this story? What was the author trying to tell us? | | | 4   3   2   1 |
| **Characters** Describe _____ (character's name) at the beginning and end of the story. | | | 4   3   2   1 |
| **Setting** Where and when did the story happen? | | | 4   3   2   1 |
| **Plot** Tell me what the story was about in a few sentences. | | | 4   3   2   1 |

**Summative Retelling Score**   4   3   2   1

**Comments** _____

_____

_____

# Unit 4 Expository Retelling Chart

**Selection Title** _____

**Name** _____

**Date** _____

| Retelling Criteria/Teacher Prompt | Teacher-Aided Response | Student-Generated Response | Rubric Score (Circle one.) | | | |
|---|---|---|---|---|---|---|
| **Connections**<br>Did this selection make you think about something else you have read?<br><br>What did you learn about as you read this selection? | | | 4 | 3 | 2 | 1 |
| **Author's Purpose**<br>Why do you think the author wrote this selection? | | | 4 | 3 | 2 | 1 |
| **Topic**<br>What was the selection mostly about? | | | 4 | 3 | 2 | 1 |
| **Important Ideas**<br>What is important for me to know about _____ (topic)? | | | 4 | 3 | 2 | 1 |
| **Conclusions**<br>What did you learn from reading this selection? | | | 4 | 3 | 2 | 1 |

**Summative Retelling Score**  4  3  2  1

**Comments** _____

_____

_____

# Reading

| Concepts of Print and Print Awareness | Pre-K | K | 1 | 2 | 3 | 4 | 5 |
|---|---|---|---|---|---|---|---|
| Develop awareness that print represents spoken language and conveys and preserves meaning | • | • | • | | | | |
| Recognize familiar books by their covers; hold book right side up | • | • | | | | | |
| Identify parts of a book and their functions (front cover, title page/title, back cover, page numbers) | • | • | • | | | | |
| Understand the concepts of letter, word, sentence, paragraph, and story | • | • | • | | | | |
| Track print (front to back of book, top to bottom of page, left to right on line, sweep back left for next line) | • | • | • | | | | |
| Match spoken to printed words | • | • | • | | | | |
| Know capital and lowercase letter names and match them | • | • T | • | | | | |
| Know the order of the alphabet | • | • | • | | | | |
| Recognize first name in print | • | • | • | | | | |
| Recognize the uses of capitalization and punctuation | | • | • | | | | |
| Value print as a means of gaining information | • | • | • | | | | |

| Phonological and Phonemic Awareness | Pre-K | K | 1 | 2 | 3 | 4 | 5 |
|---|---|---|---|---|---|---|---|
| **Phonological Awareness** | | | | | | | |
| Recognize and produce rhyming words | • | • | • | | | | |
| Track and count each word in a spoken sentence and each syllable in a spoken word | • | • | • | | | | |
| Segment and blend syllables in spoken words | | | • | | | | |
| Segment and blend onset and rime in one-syllable words | | • | • | | | | |
| Recognize and produce words beginning with the same sound | • | • | • | | | | |
| Identify beginning, middle, and/or ending sounds that are the same or different | • | • | • | | | | |
| Understand that spoken words are made of sequences of sounds | • | • | • | | | | |
| **Phonemic Awareness** | | | | | | | |
| Identify the position of sounds in words | | • | • | | | | |
| Identify and isolate initial, final, and medial sounds in spoken words | • | • | • | | | | |
| Blend sounds orally to make words or syllables | | • | • | | | | |
| Segment a word or syllable into sounds; count phonemes in spoken words or syllables | | • | • | | | | |
| Manipulate sounds in words (add, delete, and/or substitute phonemes) | • | • | • | | | | |

| Phonics and Decoding | Pre-K | K | 1 | 2 | 3 | 4 | 5 |
|---|---|---|---|---|---|---|---|
| **Phonics** | | | | | | | |
| Understand and apply the **alphabetic principle** that spoken words are composed of sounds that are represented by letters | • | • | • | | | | |
| Know letter-sound relationships | | • T | • T | • T | | | |
| Blend sounds of letters to decode | | • | • T | • T | • T | | |
| Consonants, consonant blends, and consonant digraphs | | • | • T | • T | • T | | |
| Short, long, and r-controlled vowels; vowel digraphs; diphthongs; common vowel patterns | | | • T | • T | • T | | |
| Phonograms/word families | | • | • | • | • | | |
| **Word Structure** | | | | | | | |
| Decode words with common word parts | | • | • T | • T | • T | • | • |
| Base words and inflected endings | | | • T | • T | • | • | • |
| Contractions and compound words | | | • T | • T | • T | • | • |
| Suffixes and prefixes | | | • T | • T | • T | • | • |
| Greek and Latin roots | | | | | | • | • |
| Blend syllables to decode words | | | • T | • T | • T | • | • |
| **Decoding Strategies** | | | | | | | |
| Blending strategy: Apply knowledge of letter-sound relationships to decode unfamiliar words | | • | • | • | • | | |
| Apply knowledge of word structure to decode unfamiliar words | | • | • | • | • | • | • |
| Use context and syntax along with letter-sound relationships and word structure to decode | | • | • | • | • | • | • |
| Self-correct | | | • | • | • | • | • |

| Fluency | Pre-K | K | 1 | 2 | 3 | 4 | 5 |
|---|---|---|---|---|---|---|---|
| Read aloud fluently with accuracy, comprehension, appropriate pace/rate; with expression/intonation (prosody); with attention to punctuation and appropriate phrasing | | | • T | • T | • T | • T | • T |
| Practice fluency in a variety of ways, including choral reading, partner/paired reading, Readers' Theater, repeated oral reading, and tape-assisted reading | | • | • | • | • | • | • |

• instructional opportunity          **T** tested in standardized test

| | Pre-K | K | 1 | 2 | 3 | 4 | 5 | 6 |
|---|---|---|---|---|---|---|---|---|
| toward appropriate fluency goals by the end of each grade | | | •T | •T | •T | •T | •T | •T |
| regularly in independent-level material | | | • | • | • | • | • | • |
| silently for increasing periods of time | | | • | • | • | • | • | • |

## cabulary (Oral and Written)

| | Pre-K | K | 1 | 2 | 3 | 4 | 5 | 6 |
|---|---|---|---|---|---|---|---|---|
| **rd Recognition** | | | | | | | | |
| gnize regular and irregular high-frequency words | • | • | •T | •T | | | | |
| gnize and understand selection vocabulary | | • | • | •T | • | • | • | • |
| erstand content-area vocabulary and specialized, technical, or topical words | | | • | • | • | • | • | • |
| **rd Learning Strategies** | | | | | | | | |
| lop vocabulary through direct instruction, concrete experiences, reading, listening to text read aloud | • | • | • | • | • | • | • | • |
| knowledge of word structure to figure out meanings of words | | | • | •T | •T | •T | •T | •T |
| context clues for meanings of unfamiliar words, multiple-meaning words, homonyms, homographs | | | • | •T | •T | •T | •T | •T |
| grade-appropriate reference sources to learn word meanings | • | • | • | • | •T | •T | •T | •T |
| picture clues to help determine word meanings | • | • | • | • | • | | | |
| new words in a variety of contexts | • | • | • | • | • | • | • | • |
| nine word usage and effectiveness | | • | • | • | • | • | • | • |
| te and use graphic organizers to group, study, and retain vocabulary | | | • | • | • | • | • | • |
| **end Concepts and Word Knowledge** | | | | | | | | |
| emic language | • | • | • | • | • | • | • | • |
| sify and categorize | • | • | • | • | • | • | • | • |
| nyms and synonyms | | | • | •T | •T | •T | •T | •T |
| ographs, homonyms, and homophones | | | | • | •T | •T | •T | •T |
| ple-meaning words | | | • | • | •T | •T | •T | •T |
| ted words and derivations | | | | | • | • | • | • |
| ogies | | | | | • | | • | |
| notation/denotation | | | | | | • | • | • |
| ative language and idioms | | | • | • | • | • | • | • |
| criptive words (location, size, color, shape, number, ideas, feelings) | • | • | • | • | • | • | | • |
| utility words (shapes, colors, question words, position/directional words, and so on) | • | • | • | • | | | | |
| and order words | • | • | • | • | • | • | • | • |
| sition words | | | | | | • | • | • |
| origins: Etymologies/word histories; words from other languages, regions, or cultures | | | | | • | • | • | • |
| tened forms: abbreviations, acronyms, clipped words | | | • | • | • | • | •T | |

## xt Comprehension

| | Pre-K | K | 1 | 2 | 3 | 4 | 5 | 6 |
|---|---|---|---|---|---|---|---|---|
| **nprehension Strategies** | | | | | | | | |
| ew the text and formulate questions | • | • | • | • | • | • | • | • |
| and monitor purpose for reading and listening | • | • | • | • | • | • | • | • |
| ate and use prior knowledge | • | • | • | • | • | • | • | • |
| e predictions | • | • | • | • | • | • | • | • |
| itor comprehension and use fix-up strategies to resolve difficulties in meaning: adjust reading rate, ad and read on, seek help from reference sources and/or other people, skim and scan, summarize, text features | | | • | • | • | • | • | • |
| te and use graphic and semantic organizers | | • | • | • | • | • | • | • |
| ver questions (text explicit, text implicit, scriptal), including *who, what, when, where, why, what if, how* | • | • | • | • | • | • | • | • |
| ok back in text for answers | | | • | • | • | • | • | • |
| swer test-like questions | | | • | • | • | • | • | • |
| erate clarifying questions, including *who, what, where, when, how, why,* and *what if* | • | • | • | • | • | • | • | • |
| ognize text structure: story and informational (cause/effect, chronological, compare/contrast, ription, problem/solution, proposition/support) | • | • | • | • | • | • | • | • |
| marize text | | • | • | • | • | • | • | • |
| call and retell stories | • | • | • | • | • | • | • | • |
| entify and retell important/main ideas (nonfiction) | • | • | • | • | • | • | • | • |
| entify and retell new information | | | | • | • | • | • | • |
| alize; use mental imagery | | • | • | • | • | • | • | • |
| strategies flexibly and in combination | | | • | • | • | • | • | • |

## Comprehension Skills

| | Pre-K | K | 1 | 2 | 3 | 4 | 5 |
|---|---|---|---|---|---|---|---|
| Author's purpose | | | • T | • T | • T | • T | • T |
| Author's viewpoint/bias/perspective | | | | | • | • | • |
| Categorize and classify | • | • | • | • | | | |
| Cause and effect | | • | • T | • T | • T | • T | • T |
| Compare and contrast | • | • | • T | • T | • T | • T | • T |
| Details and facts | | • | • | • | • | • | • |
| Draw conclusions | | • | • T | • T | • T | • T | • T |
| Fact and opinion | | | | • T | • T | • T | • T |
| Follow directions/steps in a process | • | • | • | • | • | • | • |
| Generalize | | | | | • T | • T | • T |
| Graphic sources | | • | • | • | • | • T | • T |
| Main idea and supporting details | | • T | • T | • T | • T | • T | • T |
| Paraphrase | | | • | • | • | • | • |
| Persuasive devices and propaganda | | | • | • | • | • | • |
| Realism/fantasy | • | • | • T | • T | • T | • | • |
| Sequence of events | • | • T | • T | • T | • T | • T | • T |

## Higher Order Thinking Skills

| | Pre-K | K | 1 | 2 | 3 | 4 | 5 |
|---|---|---|---|---|---|---|---|
| Analyze | | | | • | • | • | • |
| Describe and connect the essential ideas, arguments, and perspectives of a text | | | • | • | • | • | • |
| Draw inferences, conclusions, or generalizations, support them with textual evidence and prior knowledge | • | | • | • | • | • | • |
| Evaluate and critique ideas and text | | | • | • | • | • | • |
| Hypothesize | | | | | | • | • |
| Make judgments about ideas and text | | | • | • | • | • | • |
| Organize and synthesize ideas and information | | | • | | | • | • |

| Literary Analysis, Response, & Appreciation | Pre-K | K | 1 | 2 | 3 | 4 | 5 |
|---|---|---|---|---|---|---|---|
| **Genre and Its Characteristics** | | | | | | | |
| Recognize characteristics of a variety of genre | • | • | • | • | • | • | • |
| Distinguish fiction from nonfiction | • | • | • | • | • | • | • |
| Identify characteristics of literary texts, including drama, fantasy, traditional tales | | • | • | • | • | • | • |
| Identify characteristics of nonfiction texts, including biography, interviews, newspaper articles | | • | • | • | • | • | • |
| Identify characteristics of poetry and song, including nursery rhymes, limericks, blank verse | • | • | • | • | • | • | • |
| **Literary Elements and Story Structure** | | | | | | | |
| **Character** | • | • T | • T | • T | • T | • T | • T |
| Recognize and describe traits, actions, feelings, and motives of characters | | • | • | • | • | • | • |
| Analyze characters' relationships, changes, and points of view | | • | • | • | • | • | • |
| Analyze characters' conflicts | | | | • | | • | • |
| **Plot and plot structure** | • | • T | • T | • T | • T | • T | • T |
| Beginning, middle, end | • | • | • | • | • | | |
| Goal and outcome or problem and solution/resolution | | • | • | • | • | • | • |
| Rising action, climax, and falling action/denouement; setbacks | | | | | | • | • |
| **Setting** | • | • T | • T | • T | • T | • T | • |
| Relate setting to problem/solution | | | | | | • | • |
| Explain ways setting contributes to mood | | | | | | • | • |
| **Theme** | | • | • T | • T | • | • | • |
| **Use Literary Elements and Story Structure** | • | • | • | • | • | • | • |
| Analyze and evaluate author's use of setting, plot, character | | | | • | • | • | • |
| Identify similarities and differences of characters, events, and settings within or across selections/cultures | • | • | • | • | • | • | • |
| **Literary Devices** | | | | | | | |
| Allusion | | | | | | | |
| Dialect | | | | | | • | • |
| Dialogue and narration | • | • | • | • | • | • | • |
| Exaggeration/hyperbole | | | | | • | • | • |
| Figurative language: idiom, jargon, metaphor, simile, slang | | | • | • | • | • | • |

• instructional opportunity     **T** tested in standardized test

| | Pre-K | K | 1 | 2 | 3 | 4 | 5 | 6 |
|---|---|---|---|---|---|---|---|---|
| ...back | | | | | | • | • | • |
| ...hadowing | | | | | | | • | • |
| ...l and informal language | | | | • | • | • | • | • |
| ...r | | | | | • | • | • | • |
| ...ery and sensory words | | | • | • | • | • | • | • |
| | | | | | • | • | • | • |
| ...nification | | | | • | • | • | • | • |
| ...of view (first person, third person, omniscient) | | | | | • | • | • | • |
| ...and word play | | | | • | • | • | • | • |
| ...d devices and poetic elements | • | • | • | • | • | • | • | • |
| ...eration, assonance, onomatopoeia | • | • | • | • | • | • | • | • |
| ...me, rhythm, repetition, and cadence | • | • | • | • | • | • | • | • |
| ...d choice | | | | • | • | • | • | • |
| ...olism | | | | • | • | • | • | • |
| | | | | | | | • | • |

### ...or's and Illustrator's Craft

| | Pre-K | K | 1 | 2 | 3 | 4 | 5 | 6 |
|---|---|---|---|---|---|---|---|---|
| ...guish the roles of author and illustrator | • | • | • | • | | | | |
| ...gnize/analyze author's and illustrator's craft or style | | | • | • | • | • | • | • |

### ...rary Response

| | Pre-K | K | 1 | 2 | 3 | 4 | 5 | 6 |
|---|---|---|---|---|---|---|---|---|
| ...lect, talk, and write about books | • | • | • | • | • | • | • | • |
| ...ct on reading and respond (through talk, movement, art, and so on) | • | • | • | • | • | • | • | • |
| ...and answer questions about text | • | • | • | • | • | • | • | • |
| ...e about what is read | • | • | • | • | • | • | • | • |
| ...evidence from the text to support opinions, interpretations, or conclusions | | | • | • | • | • | • | • |
| ...port ideas through reference to other texts and personal knowledge | | | • | • | • | • | • | • |
| ...ate materials on related topic, theme, or idea | | | • | • | • | • | • | • |
| ...erate alternative endings to plots and identify the reason for, and the impact of, the alternatives | • | • | • | • | • | • | • | • |
| ...esize and extend the literary experience through creative responses | • | • | • | • | • | • | • | • |
| ...connections: text to self, text to text, text to world | • | • | • | • | • | • | • | • |
| ...ate and critique the quality of the literary experience | | | • | • | • | • | • | • |
| ...observations, react, speculate in response to text | | | • | • | • | • | • | • |

### ...rary Appreciation/Motivation

| | Pre-K | K | 1 | 2 | 3 | 4 | 5 | 6 |
|---|---|---|---|---|---|---|---|---|
| ...an interest in books and reading; engage voluntarily in social interaction about books | • | • | • | • | • | • | • | • |
| ...se text by drawing on personal interests, relying on knowledge of authors and genres, estimating text ...lty, and using recommendations of others | • | • | • | • | • | • | • | • |
| ...a variety of grade-level appropriate narrative and expository texts | | • | • | • | • | • | • | • |
| ...from a wide variety of genres for a variety of purposes | • | • | • | • | • | • | • | • |
| ...independently | | • | • | • | • | • | • | • |
| ...lish familiarity with a topic | | • | • | • | • | • | • | • |

### ...ural Awareness

| | Pre-K | K | 1 | 2 | 3 | 4 | 5 | 6 |
|---|---|---|---|---|---|---|---|---|
| ...op attitudes and abilities to interact with diverse groups and cultures | • | • | • | • | • | • | • | • |
| ...ect experiences and ideas with those from a variety of languages, cultures, customs, perspectives | • | • | • | • | • | • | • | • |
| ...stand how attitudes and values in a culture or during a period in time affect the writing from that ...e or time period | | | | | | • | • | • |
| ...are language and oral traditions (family stories) that reflect customs, regions, and cultures | | • | • | • | • | • | • | • |
| ...gnize themes that cross cultures and bind them together in their common humanness | | | | | | • | • | • |

## ...guage Arts

| ...ting | Pre-K | K | 1 | 2 | 3 | 4 | 5 | 6 |
|---|---|---|---|---|---|---|---|---|

### ...cepts of Print for Writing

| | Pre-K | K | 1 | 2 | 3 | 4 | 5 | 6 |
|---|---|---|---|---|---|---|---|---|
| ...op gross and fine motor skills and hand/eye coordination | • | • | • | | | | | |
| ...own name and other important words | • | • | • | | | | | |
| ...using pictures, some letters, and transitional spelling to convey meaning | • | • | • | | | | | |
| ...te messages or stories for others to write | • | • | • | | | | | |

| | Pre-K | K | 1 | 2 | 3 | 4 | 5 |
|---|---|---|---|---|---|---|---|
| Create own written texts for others to read; write left to right on a line and top to bottom on a page | • | • | • | | | | |
| Participate in shared and interactive writing | • | • | • | | | | |

## Traits of Writing

### Focus/Ideas

| | Pre-K | K | 1 | 2 | 3 | 4 | 5 |
|---|---|---|---|---|---|---|---|
| Maintain focus and sharpen ideas | | • | • | • | • | • | • |
| Use sensory details and concrete examples; elaborate | | • | • | • | • | • | • |
| Delete extraneous information | | | • | • | • | • | • |
| Rearrange words and sentences to improve meaning and focus | | | | • | • | • | • |
| Use strategies, such as tone, style, consistent point of view, to achieve a sense of completeness | | | | | | • | • |

### Organization/Paragraphs

| | Pre-K | K | 1 | 2 | 3 | 4 | 5 |
|---|---|---|---|---|---|---|---|
| Use graphic organizers to group ideas | | • | • | • | • | • | • |
| Write coherent paragraphs that develop a central idea | | | • | • | • | • | • |
| Use transitions to connect sentences and paragraphs | | | • | • | • | • | • |
| Select an organizational structure based on purpose, audience, length | | | | | | • | • |
| Organize ideas in a logical progression, such as chronological order or by order of importance | | • | • | • | • | • | • |
| Write introductory, supporting, and concluding paragraphs | | | | • | • | • | • |
| Write a multi-paragraph paper | | | | • | • | • | • |

### Voice

| | Pre-K | K | 1 | 2 | 3 | 4 | 5 |
|---|---|---|---|---|---|---|---|
| Develop personal, identifiable voice and an individual tone/style | | • | • | • | • | • | • |
| Maintain consistent voice and point of view | | | | | | • | • |
| Use voice appropriate to audience, message, and purpose | | | | | | • | • |

### Word Choice

| | Pre-K | K | 1 | 2 | 3 | 4 | 5 |
|---|---|---|---|---|---|---|---|
| Use clear, precise, appropriate language | | • | • | • | • | • | • |
| Use figurative language and vivid words | | | | • | • | • | • |
| Select effective vocabulary using word walls, dictionary, or thesaurus | | • | • | • | • | • | • |

### Sentences

| | Pre-K | K | 1 | 2 | 3 | 4 | 5 |
|---|---|---|---|---|---|---|---|
| Combine, elaborate, and vary sentences | | • | • | • | • | • | • |
| Write topic sentence, supporting sentences with facts and details, and concluding sentence | | | • | • | • | • | • |
| Use correct word order | | | • | • | • | • | • |
| Use parallel structure in a sentence | | | | | | | • |

### Conventions

| | Pre-K | K | 1 | 2 | 3 | 4 | 5 |
|---|---|---|---|---|---|---|---|
| Use correct spelling and grammar; capitalize and punctuate correctly | | • | • | • | • | • | • |
| Correct sentence fragments and run-ons | | | | | • | • | • |
| Use correct paragraph indention | | | • | • | • | • | • |

## The Writing Process

| | Pre-K | K | 1 | 2 | 3 | 4 | 5 |
|---|---|---|---|---|---|---|---|
| **Prewrite** using various strategies | • | • | • | • | • | • | • |
| **Develop first drafts** of single- and multiple-paragraph compositions | | • | • | • | • | • | • |
| **Revise** drafts for varied purposes, including to clarify and to achieve purpose, sense of audience, precise word choice, vivid images, and elaboration | | • | • | • | • | • | • |
| **Edit and proofread** for correct spelling, grammar, usage, and mechanics | | • | • | • | • | • | • |
| **Publish** own work | • | • | • | • | • | • | • |

## Types of Writing

| | Pre-K | K | 1 | 2 | 3 | 4 | 5 |
|---|---|---|---|---|---|---|---|
| Narrative writing (such as personal narratives, stories, biographies, autobiographies) | • | • | • T | • T | • T | • T | • T |
| Expository writing (such as essays, directions, explanations, news stories, research reports, summaries) | | • | • T | • T | • T | • T | • T |
| Descriptive writing (such as labels, captions, lists, plays, poems, response logs, songs) | • | • | • T | • T | • T | • T | • T |
| Persuasive writing (such as ads, editorials, essays, letters to the editor, opinions, posters) | | • | • T | • T | • T | • T | • T |

## Writing Habits and Practices

| | Pre-K | K | 1 | 2 | 3 | 4 | 5 |
|---|---|---|---|---|---|---|---|
| Write on a daily basis | • | • | • | • | • | • | • |
| Use writing as a tool for learning and self-discovery | | | | • | • | • | • |
| Write independently for extended periods of time | | | • | • | • | • | • |

## ENGLISH LANGUAGE CONVENTIONS in WRITING and SPEAKING

| | Pre-K | K | 1 | 2 | 3 | 4 | 5 |
|---|---|---|---|---|---|---|---|
| **Grammar and Usage in Speaking and Writing** | | | | | | | |
| Sentences | | | | | | | |
|   Types (declarative, interrogative, exclamatory, imperative) | • | • | • T | • T | • T | • T | • T |
|   Structure (simple, compound, complex, compound-complex) | • | • | | • | • | • T | • T |

• instructional opportunity      **T** tested in standardized test

| | Pre-K | K | 1 | 2 | 3 | 4 | 5 | 6 |
|---|---|---|---|---|---|---|---|---|
| ...ts (subjects/predicates: complete, simple, compound; phrases; clauses) | | | | • T | • | • T | • T | • T |
| ...gments and run-on sentences | | • | • | • | • | • | • | • |
| ...mbine sentences, elaborate | | | • | • | • | • | • | • |
| ...of speech: nouns, verbs and verb tenses, adjectives, adverbs, pronouns and antecedents, ...nctions, prepositions, interjections | | • | • T | • T | • T | • T | • T | • T |
| ...e | | | | | | | | |
| ...ject-verb agreement | | • | • T | • | • | • T | • T | • T |
| ...noun agreement/referents | | | • T | • | • | • T | • T | • T |
| ...placed modifiers | | | | | | • | • T | • T |
| ...used words | | | | | • | • | • | • T |
| ...atives; avoid double negatives | | | | | • | • | • | • |

## ...hanics in Writing

| | Pre-K | K | 1 | 2 | 3 | 4 | 5 | 6 |
|---|---|---|---|---|---|---|---|---|
| ...alization (first word in sentence, proper nouns and adjectives, pronoun *I*, titles, and so on) | • | • | • T | • T | • T | • T | • T | • T |
| ...uation (apostrophe, comma, period, question mark, exclamation mark, quotation marks, and so on) | | • | • T | • T | • T | • T | • T | • T |

## ...lling

| | Pre-K | K | 1 | 2 | 3 | 4 | 5 | 6 |
|---|---|---|---|---|---|---|---|---|
| ...independently by using pre-phonetic knowledge, knowledge of letter names, sound-letter knowledge | • | • | • | • | • | • | • | • |
| ...ound-letter knowledge to spell | • | • | • | • | • | • | • | • |
| ...sonants: single, double, blends, digraphs, silent letters, and unusual consonant spellings | | • | • | • | • | • | • | • |
| ...vels: short, long, *r*-controlled, digraphs, diphthongs, less common vowel patterns, schwa | | • | • | • | • | • | • | • |
| ...nowledge of word structure to spell | | | • | • | • | • | • | • |
| ...e words and affixes (inflections, prefixes, suffixes), possessives, contractions and compound words | | | • | • | • | • | • | • |
| ...ek and Latin roots, syllable patterns, multisyllabic words | | | • | • | • | • | • | • |
| ...high-frequency, irregular words | | • | • | • | • | • | • | • |
| ...frequently misspelled words correctly, including homophones or homonyms | | | • | • | • | • | • | • |
| ...neaning relationships to spell | | | | | • | • | • | • |

## ...dwriting

| | Pre-K | K | 1 | 2 | 3 | 4 | 5 | 6 |
|---|---|---|---|---|---|---|---|---|
| ...ncreasing control of penmanship, including pencil grip, paper position, posture, stroke | • | • | • | • | | | | |
| ...legibly, with control over letter size and form; letter slant; and letter, word, and sentence spacing | | • | • | • | • | • | • | • |
| ...lowercase and capital letters | • | • | • | • | | | | |
| ...nuscript | • | • | • | • | • | • | • | • |
| ...sive | | | | • | • | • | • | • |
| ...numerals | • | • | • | | | | | |

## ...tening and Speaking

| | Pre-K | K | 1 | 2 | 3 | 4 | 5 | 6 |
|---|---|---|---|---|---|---|---|---|

### ...ening Skills and Strategies

| | Pre-K | K | 1 | 2 | 3 | 4 | 5 | 6 |
|---|---|---|---|---|---|---|---|---|
| ...n to a variety of presentations attentively and politely | • | • | • | • | • | • | • | • |
| ...nonitor comprehension while listening, using a variety of skills and strategies | • | • | • | • | • | • | • | • |
| ...n for a purpose | | | | | | | | |
| ...enjoyment and appreciation | • | • | • | • | • | • | • | • |
| ...expand vocabulary and concepts | • | • | • | • | • | • | • | • |
| ...obtain information and ideas | • | • | • | • | • | • | • | • |
| ...follow oral directions | • | • | • | • | • | • | • | • |
| ...answer questions and solve problems | • | • | • | • | • | • | • | • |
| ...participate in group discussions | • | • | • | • | • | • | • | • |
| ...dentify and analyze the musical elements of literary language | • | • | • | • | • | • | • | • |
| ...gain knowledge of one's own culture, the culture of others, and the common elements of cultures | • | • | • | • | • | • | • | • |
| ...gnize formal and informal language | | | • | • | • | • | • | • |
| ...n critically to distinguish fact from opinion and to analyze and evaluate ideas, information, experiences | | • | | • | • | • | • | • |
| ...ate a speaker's delivery | | | | • | • | • | • | • |
| ...ret a speaker's purpose, perspective, persuasive techniques, verbal and nonverbal messages, and ...f rhetorical devices | | | | | • | • | • | • |

### ...aking Skills and Strategies

| | Pre-K | K | 1 | 2 | 3 | 4 | 5 | 6 |
|---|---|---|---|---|---|---|---|---|
| ...k clearly, accurately, and fluently, using appropriate delivery for a variety of audiences, and purposes | • | • | • | • | • | • | • | • |
| ...oroper intonation, volume, pitch, modulation, and phrasing | | • | • | • | • | • | • | • |
| ...k with a command of standard English conventions | • | • | • | • | • | • | • | • |
| ...appropriate language for formal and informal settings | • | • | • | • | • | • | • | • |

| | Pre-K | K | 1 | 2 | 3 | 4 | 5 |
|---|---|---|---|---|---|---|---|
| Speak for a purpose | | | | | | | |
|   To ask and answer questions | • | • | • | • | • | • | • |
|   To give directions and instructions | • | • | • | • | T | • | • |
|   To retell, paraphrase, or explain information | | • | • | • | • | • | • |
|   To communicate needs and share ideas and experiences | • | • | • | • | • | • | • |
|   To participate in conversations and discussions | • | • | • | • | • | • | • |
|   To express an opinion | • | • | • | • | • | • | • |
|   To deliver dramatic recitations, interpretations, or performances | • | • | • | • | • | • | • |
|   To deliver presentations or oral reports (narrative, descriptive, persuasive, and informational) | • | • | • | • | • | • | • |
| Stay on topic | • | • | • | • | • | • | |
| Use appropriate verbal and nonverbal elements (such as facial expression, gestures, eye contact, posture) | • | • | • | • | • | • | • |
| Identify and/or demonstrate methods to manage or overcome communication anxiety | | | | | | • | • |

## Viewing/Media

| Viewing/Media | Pre-K | K | 1 | 2 | 3 | 4 | 5 |
|---|---|---|---|---|---|---|---|
| Interact with and respond to a variety of print and non-print media for a range of purposes | • | • | • | • | • | • | • |
| Compare and contrast print, visual, and electronic media | | | | | • | • | • |
| Analyze and evaluate media | | | • | • | • | • | • |
| Recognize purpose, bias, propaganda, and persuasive techniques in media messages | | | • | • | • | • | • |

# Research and Study Skills

| Understand and Use Graphic Sources | Pre-K | K | 1 | 2 | 3 | 4 | 5 |
|---|---|---|---|---|---|---|---|
| Advertisement | | | • | • | • | • | • |
| Chart/table | • | • | • | • | • | • | • |
| Diagram/scale drawing | | | • | • | • | • | • |
| Graph (bar, circle, line, picture) | | • | • | • | • | • | • |
| Illustration, photograph, caption, label | • | • | • | • | • | • | • |
| Map/globe | • | • | • | • | • | • | • |
| Order form/application | | | | | | • | • |
| Poster/announcement | • | • | • | • | • | • | • |
| Schedule | | | | | | • | • |
| Sign | • | • | • | • | | • | |
| Time line | | | • | • | • | • | • |

| Understand and Use Reference Sources | Pre-K | K | 1 | 2 | 3 | 4 | 5 |
|---|---|---|---|---|---|---|---|
| Know and use parts of a book to locate information | • | • | • | • | • | • | • |
| Use alphabetical order | | | • | • | • | • | |
| Understand purpose, structure, and organization of reference sources (print, electronic, media, Internet) | • | • | • | • | • | • | • |
|   Almanac | | | | | | • | • |
|   Atlas | | • | | • | • | • | • |
|   Card catalog/library database | | | | • | • | • | • |
|   Dictionary/glossary | | • | • | • | • T | • T | • T |
|   Encyclopedia | | | | • | • | • | • |
|   Magazine/periodical | | | | • | • | • | • |
|   Newspaper and newsletter | | | | • | • | • | • |
|   *Readers' Guide to Periodical Literature* | | | | | | • | • |
|   Technology (computer and non-computer electronic media) | | • | • | • | • | • | • |
|   Thesaurus | | | | • | • | • | • |

| Study Skills and Strategies | Pre-K | K | 1 | 2 | 3 | 4 | 5 |
|---|---|---|---|---|---|---|---|
| Adjust reading rate | | | • | • | • | • | • |
| Clarify directions | • | • | • | • | • | • | • |
| Outline | | | | • | • | • | • |
| Skim and scan | | | • | • | • | • | • |
| SQP3R | | | | | | • | • |
| Summarize | | • | • | • | • | • | • |
| Take notes, paraphrase, and synthesize | | | • | • | • | • | • |
| Use graphic and semantic organizers to organize information | | • | • | • | • | • | • |

• instructional opportunity      **T** tested in standardized test

| Test-Taking Skills and Strategies | Pre-K | K | 1 | 2 | 3 | 4 | 5 | 6 |
|---|---|---|---|---|---|---|---|---|
| ...rstand the question, the vocabulary of tests, and key words | | | • | • | • | • | • | • |
| ...er the question; use information from the text (stated or inferred) | | • | • | • | • | • | • | • |
| ... across texts | | | • | • | • | • | • | • |
| ...plete the sentence | | | • | • | • | • | • | • |

| Technology/New Literacies | Pre-K | K | 1 | 2 | 3 | 4 | 5 | 6 |
|---|---|---|---|---|---|---|---|---|
| **...-Computer Electronic Media** | | | | | | | | |
| ...o tapes/CDs, video tapes/DVDs | • | • | • | • | • | • | • | |
| ... television, and radio | | • | • | • | • | • | • | • |
| **...mputer Programs and Services: Basic Operations and Concepts** | | | | | | | | |
| ...accurate computer terminology | • | • | • | • | • | • | • | • |
| ...te, name, locate, open, save, delete, and organize files | | • | • | • | • | • | • | • |
| ...mput and output devices (such as mouse, keyboard, monitor, printer, touch screen) | • | • | • | • | • | • | • | • |
| ...basic keyboarding skills | | • | • | • | • | • | • | • |
| **...onsible Use of Technology Systems and Software** | | | | | | | | |
| ... cooperatively and collaboratively with others; follow acceptable use policies | • | • | • | • | • | • | • | • |
| ...gnize hazards of Internet searches | | • | • | • | • | • | • | • |
| ...ect intellectual property | | | | | • | • | • | • |
| **...rmation and Communication Technologies: Information Acquisition** | | | | | | | | |
| ...electronic web (non-linear) navigation, online resources, databases, keyword searches | | | • | • | • | • | • | • |
| ...visual and non-textual features of online resources | • | • | • | • | • | • | • | • |
| ...net inquiry | | | • | • | • | • | • | • |
| ...ntify questions | | | • | • | • | • | • | • |
| ...ate, select, and collect information | | | • | • | • | • | • | • |
| ...alyze information | | | • | • | • | • | • | • |
| ...valuate electronic information sources for accuracy, relevance, bias | | | | • | • | • | • | • |
| ...Understand bias/subjectivity of electronic content (about this site, author search, date created) | | | | | | • | • | • |
| ...nthesize information | | | | | | • | • | • |
| ...mmunicate findings | | | | • | • | • | • | • |
| ...fix-up strategies (such as clicking *Back, Forward,* or *Undo;* redoing a search; trimming the URL) | | | • | • | • | • | • | • |
| **...munication** | | | | | | | | |
| ...borate, publish, present, and interact with others | | • | • | • | • | • | • | • |
| ...online resources (e-mail, bulletin boards, newsgroups) | | | • | • | • | • | • | • |
| ...a variety of multimedia formats | | | • | • | • | • | • | • |
| **...lem Solving** | | | | | | | | |
| ...ct the appropriate software for the task | • | • | • | • | • | • | • | • |
| ...technology resources for solving problems and making informed decisions | | | • | • | • | • | • | • |
| ...rmine when technology is useful | | | | • | • | • | • | • |

| ... Research Process | Pre-K | K | 1 | 2 | 3 | 4 | 5 | 6 |
|---|---|---|---|---|---|---|---|---|
| ...se and narrow the topic; frame and revise questions for inquiry | | • | • | • | • | • | • | • |
| ...se and evaluate appropriate reference sources | | | | • | • | • | • | • |
| ...te and collect information | • | • | • | • | • | • | • | • |
| ... notes/record findings | | | | • | • | • | • | • |
| ...bine and compare information | | | | • | • | • | • | • |
| ...uate, interpret, and draw conclusions about key information | | • | • | • | • | • | • | • |
| ...marize information | | • | • | • | • | • | • | • |
| ...e an outline | | | | • | • | • | • | • |
| ...nize content systematically | | • | • | • | • | • | • | • |
| ...municate information | | • | • | • | • | • | • | • |
| ...ite and present a report | | | | • | • | • | • | • |
| ...nclude citations | | | | | | • | • | • |
| ...Respect intellectual property/plagiarism | | | | | | • | • | • |
| ...lect and organize visual aids | | • | • | • | • | • | • | • |

# A

**Abbreviations,** 4.6 685e–685f.

**Accountability.** *See* **Adequate yearly progress.**

**Achieving English proficiency.** *See* **ELL (English Language Learners) suggestions.**

**Activate prior knowledge.** *See* **Prereading strategies.**

**Adequate yearly progress (AYP),** 4.1 16g–16h, 4.2 140g–140h, 4.3 266g–266h, 4.4 390g–390h, 4.5 514g–514h, 4.6 636g–636h

**Adjectives,** 4.4 537e–537f
  **articles,** 4.5 537e–537f
  **comparative and superlative,** 4.5 559e–559f
  **proper,** 4.4 537e

**Advanced learners**
  **critical thinking,** 4.6 654
  **group time,** 4.1 18f–18g, 40f–40g, 66f–66g, 88f–88g, 112f–112g, DI·3, DI·5, DI·7, DI·9, DI·11, DI·13, DI·15, DI·17, DI·19, DI·21, DI·23, DI·25, DI·27, DI·29, DI·31, DI·33, DI·35, DI·37, DI·39, DI·41, DI·43, DI·45, DI·47, DI·49, DI·51, 4.2 142f–142g, 162f–162g, 188f–188g, 212f–212g, 240f–240g, DI·3, DI·5, DI·7, DI·9, DI·11, DI·13, DI·15, DI·17, DI·19, DI·21, DI·23, DI·25, DI·27, DI·29, DI·31, DI·33, DI·35, DI·37, DI·39, DI·41, DI·43, DI·45, DI·47, DI·49, DI·51, 4.3 268f–268g, 292f–292g, 314f–314g, 338f–338g, 360f–360g, DI·3, DI·5, DI·7, DI·9, DI·11, DI·13, DI·15, DI·17, DI·19, DI·21, DI·23, DI·25, DI·27, DI·29, DI·31, DI·33, DI·35, DI·37, DI·39, DI·41, DI·43, DI·45, DI·47, DI·49, DI·51, 4.4 392f–392g, 416f–416g, 440f–440g, 466f–466g, 488f–488g, DI·3, DI·5, DI·7, DI·9, DI·11, DI·13, DI·15, DI·17, DI·19, DI·21, DI·23, DI·25, DI·27, DI·29, DI·31, DI·33, DI·35, DI·37, DI·39, DI·41, DI·43, DI·45, DI·47, DI·49, DI·51, 4.5 516f–516g, 538f–538g, 560f–560g, 582f–582g, 608f–608g, DI·3, DI·5, DI·7, DI·9, DI·11, DI·13, DI·15, DI·17, DI·19, DI·21, DI·23, DI·25, DI·27, DI·29, DI·31, DI·33, DI·35, DI·37, DI·39, DI·41, DI·43, DI·45, DI·47, DI·49, DI·51, 4.6 638f–638g, 660f–660g, 686f–686g, 712f–712g, 738f–738g, DI·3, DI·5, DI·7, DI·9, DI·11, DI·13, DI·15, DI·17, DI·19, DI·21, DI·23, DI·25, DI·27, DI·29, DI·31, DI·33, DI·35, DI·37, DI·39, DI·41, DI·43, DI·45, DI·47, DI·49, DI·51. *See also* **Grouping students for instruction.**
  **leveled readers,** 4.1 LR7–LR9, LR16–LR18, LR25–LR27, LR34–LR36, LR43–LR45, 4.2 LR7–LR9, LR16–LR18, LR25–LR27, LR34–LR36, LR43–LR45, 4.3 LR7–LR9, LR16–LR18, LR25–LR27, LR34–LR36, LR43–LR45, 4.4 LR7–LR9, LR16–LR18, LR25–LR27, LR34–LR36, LR43–LR45, 4.5 LR7–LR9, LR16–LR18, LR25–LR27, LR34–LR36, LR43–LR45, 4.6 LR7–LR9, LR16–LR18, LR25–LR27, LR34–LR36, LR43–LR45
  **resources,** 4.1 18i, 40i, 66i, 88i, 112i, 4.2 142i, 162i, 188i, 212i, 240i, 4.3 268i, 292i, 314i, 338i, 360i, 4.4 392i, 416i, 440i, 466i, 488i, 4.5 516i, 538i, 560i, 582i, 608i, 4.6 638i, 660i, 686i, 712i, 738i
  **writing,** 4.1 WA9, 4.2 WA9, 4.3 WA9, 4.4 WA9, 4.5 WA9, 4.6 WA9

**Adverbs,** 4.5 581e–581f
  **comparative and superlative,** 4.4 607e–607f

**Advertisement.** *See* **Graphic sources.**

**Affective domain.** *See* **Habits and attitudes, Literary response and appreciation.**

**Affixes.** *See* **Spelling,** word structure; **Word structure,** prefixes, suffixes.

**Alliteration.** *See* **Sound devices and poetic elements.**

**Almanac.** *See* **Reference sources.**

**Alphabetical order,** 4.2 253, 4.4 453, 4.6 662b. *See also* **Vocabulary strategies.**

**Analogies.** *See* **Vocabulary strategies.**

**Analyzing.** *See* **Reading across texts.** In addition, analytical thinking questions are raised throughout Guiding Comprehension and Reader Response.

**Answering questions.** *See* **Questions, answering.**

**Antonyms,** 4.2 242b, 4.4 394–395, 405, 415c, 490–491, 495, 507c. *See also* **Vocabulary strategies.**

**Application.** *See* **Graphic sources.**

**Appropriate word meaning,** 4.1 20b, 68–69, 79, 87c, 4.2 231, 4.3 270–271, 277, 291c, 316b, 4.4 418–419, 427, 439c, 457, 4.6 640b, 662–663, 669, 673, 685c, 714b

**Art activities.** *See* **Cross-curricular activities.**

**Art, interpreting.** *See* **Literary craft,** illustrator's craft/style.

**Asking questions.** *See* **Questions, asking.**

**Assessment**
  **classroom-based.** "If/then" assessment occurs throughout lessons and Guiding Comprehension.
  **fluency,** 4.1 39a, 65a, 87a, 111a, 133a, WA15–WA16, DI·57, DI·58, 4.2 161a, 187a, 211a, 239a, 259a, WA15–WA16, DI·57, DI·58, 4.3 291a, 313a, 337a, 359a, 383a, WA15–WA16, DI·57, DI·58, 4.4 415a, 439a, 465a, 487a, 507a, WA15–WA16, DI·57, DI·58, 4.5 537a, 559a, 581a, 607a, 629a, WA15–WA16, DI·57, DI·58, 4.6 659a, 685a, 711a, 737a, 761a, WA15–WA16, DI·57, DI·58
  **formal,** 4.1 35, 61, 83, 107, 129, 134a, WA7, WA10–WA14, 4.2 157, 185, 209, 235, 257, 260a, WA7, WA10–WA14, 4.3 287, 309, 333, 355, 379, 384a, WA7, WA10–WA14, 4.4 411, 435, 463, 483, 503, 508a, WA7, WA10–WA14, 4.5 535, 555, 577, 603, 625, 630a, WA7, WA10–WA14, 4.6 657, 681, 707, 733, 757, 762a, WA7, WA10–WA11
  **scoring guide (rubric),** 4.1 34, 35, 60, 61, 82, 83, 106, 107, 128, 129, 134a, WA7, WA10–WA14, 4.2 156, 157, 184, 185, 208, 209, 233, 234, 256, 257, 260a, WA7, WA10–WA14, 4.3 286, 287, 308, 309, 332, 333, 354, 355, 378, 379, 384a, WA7, WA10–WA14, 4.4 410, 411, 434, 435, 462, 463, 482, 483, 501, 502, 508a, WA7, WA10–WA14, 4.5 534, 535, 554, 555, 576, 577, 602, 603, 624, 625, 630a, WA7, WA10–WA14, 4.6 655, 656, 680, 681, 706, 707, 732, 733, 756, 757, 762a, WA7, WA10–WA14
  **self-assessment,** 4.1 WA7, 4.2 WA7, 4.3 WA7, 4.4 WA7, 4.5 WA7, 4.6 WA7
  **spelling,** 4.1 39j, 65j, 87j, 111j, 133j, 4.2 161j, 187j, 211j, 239j, 259j, 4.3 291j, 313j, 337j, 359j, 383j, 4.4 415j, 439j, 465j, 487j, 507j, 4.5 537j, 559j, 581j, 607j, 629j, 4.6 659j, 685j, 711j, 737j, 761j
  **test-taking strategies,** 4.1 34, 38, 60, 64, 82, 106, 110, 128, 133g–133h, 138, 4.2 156, 160, 184, 187, 208, 211, 233, 256, 259, 259g–259h, 4.3 286, 290, 308, 312, 332, 336, 354, 378, 382, 383g–383h, 4.4 410, 414, 434, 438, 462, 482, 501, 506, 507g–507h, 4.5 534, 551, 554, 558, 576, 602, 606, 624, 628, 4.6 655, 659, 680, 684, 706, 710, 732, 756, 760

**writing,** 4.1 WA7, WA10–WA14, 4.2 WA7, WA10–WA14, 4.3 WA7, WA10–WA14, 4.4 WA7, WA10–WA14, 4.5 WA7, WA10–WA14, 4.6 WA7, WA10–WA11

**Atlas.** *See* **Reference sources.**

**Attitudes, personal.** *See* **Habits and attitudes.**

**Authors (of reading selections)**
  **Alvarez, Julia,** 4.1 139d, 4.6 690–705
  **Armour, Richard,** 4.4 464
  **Beecham, Cristina,** 4.6 658
  **Begay, Shonto,** 4.3 386–387
  **Beres, Samantha,** 4.2 210–211
  **Bova, Ben,** 4.1 139l, 4.5 612–623
  **Brown, John,** 4.1 108–111
  **Bruchac, Joseph,** 4.1 139j, 4.6 664–679
  **Cherry, Lynne,** 4.1 139l, 4.3 364–377
  **Chief Lelooska,** 4.3 334–337
  **Daniel, Claire,** 4.5 604–607
  **Dewey, Jennifer Owings,** 4.1 139f, 4.5 586–601
  **Díaz, Katacha,** 4.5 556–559
  **DiCamillo, Kate,** 4.1 22–33
  **Falkner, David,** 4.6 708–711
  **Farjeon, Eleanor,** 4.4 509
  **Farris, Christine King,** 4.1 139j, 4.6 642–654
  **Fisher, Aileen,** 4.4 510
  **Gavin, Susan,** 4.2 258–259
  **George, Kristine O'Connell,** 4.5 630
  **Gerson, Mary-Joan,** 4.3 318–331
  **Grimes, Nikki,** 4.2 260
  **Guthrie, Woody,** 4.1 130–133
  **Halvorsen, Lisa,** 4.1 116–127
  **Hoban, Russell,** 4.2 261
  **Hoffman, Mary,** 4.1 139d, 4.2 192–207
  **Holub, Miroslav,** 4.5 632–633
  **Hopkins, Jackie Mims,** 4.1 92–105
  **Hopkins, Lee Bennett,** 4.1 136
  **Hughes, Langston,** 4.1 134, 4.6 762
  **Kennedy, X. J.,** 4.5 631, 4.6 763
  **Kepplinger, Bonnie,** 4.4 504–507
  **Khalsa, Ek Ongkar K.,** 4.6 659
  **Klobuchar, Lisa,** 4.2 186–187
  **Kramer, Stephen,** 4.1 139f, 4.3 342–353
  **Kranking, Kathy,** 4.1 36–39
  **Lasky, Kathryn,** 4.1 139j, 4.2 216–232
  **Levy, Constance Kling,** 4.4 511
  **Lewin, Ted,** 4.1 139f, 4.5 542–553
  **Lewis, J. Patrick,** 4.6 765
  **Livingston, Myra Cohn,** 4.4 465, 4.6 762
  **Massie, Elizabeth,** 4.1 62–65
  **Montgomery, Sy,** 4.4 420–433
  **Myers, Laurie,** 4.1 44–59
  **Nayer, Judy,** 4.5 626–629
  **Oh, Sadaharu,** 4.6 708–711
  **Old, Wendie C.,** 4.6 716–731
  **Perez, Marlene,** 4.6 682–685
  **Perry, Andrea,** 4.2 262–263
  **Peterson, Ruth De Long,** 4.1 137
  **Rand, Gloria,** 4.5 520–533
  **Rumford, James,** 4.4 470–481
  **Ryan, Pam Muñoz,** 4.5 564–575
  **Sandin, Joan,** 4.1 139h, 4.2 166–183
  **St. George, Judith,** 4.2 244–255
  **Say, Allen,** 4.1 70–81, 139h
  **Schyffert, Bea Uusma,** 4.6 742–755
  **Selznick, Brian,** 4.4 396–409
  **Singer, Marilyn,** 4.3 385
  **Slattery, Margaret E.,** 4.4 444–461
  **Smith Jr, Charles R.,** 4.2 146–155, 158–159, 160–161
  **Sobol, Donald J.,** 4.1 139d, 4.4 492–500
  **Sobol, Richard,** 4.3 296–307
  **Soto, Gary,** 4.6 764
  **Sow, Fatou Ndiaye,** 4.4 508
  **Stone, Tanya Lee,** 4.3 380–383

**D**

**E**

**Textbook-reading techniques,** 4.3 337l

**Text features,** 4.1 36, 62, 84, 108, 111l, 4.2 186, 210, 211l, 236, 258, 4.3 288, 310, 334, 356, 380, 4.4 412, 415l, 436, 464, 484, 504, 4.5 536, 537l, 556, 578, 604, 626, 4.6 682, 708, 734, 758

**Text structure (method of presenting information),** 4.1 66l–66m, 111, 4.5 582–583, 593, 595, 601, DI·36, DI·37, 4.6 660, 661, 671, 675, 679, 685, 709, DI·16, DI·17

**Theme (as a story element),** 4.5 582l–582m, 621, 4.6 686l–686m, 686–687, 699, 703, 711b, DI·54

**Themes for teaching and learning,** 4.1 16–17, 17a, 18a, 40a, 66a, 88a, 112a, 138–139, 4.2 140–141, 141a, 142a, 162a, 188a, 212a, 240a, 264–265, 4.3 266–267, 267a, 268a, 292a, 314a, 338a, 360a, 388–389, 4.4 390–391, 391a, 392a, 416a, 440a, 466a, 488a, 512–513, 4.5 514–515, 515a, 516a, 538a, 560a, 582a, 608a, 634–635, 4.6 636–637, 637a, 638a, 660a, 686a, 712a, 738a, 766–767, DI·26, DI·27

**Thesaurus.** *See* **Reference sources.**

**Think-aloud statements.** Think-alouds and teacher modeling are demonstrated throughout weekly lessons as a basic teaching strategy.

**Thinking strategies.** *See* **Critical thinking.**

**Time line.** *See* **Graphic sources.**

**Time sequence.** *See* **Sequence.**

**Tone.** *See* **Fluency, reading; Literacy devices.**

**Topic, recognizing.** *See* **Main idea.**

**Trade books**
as reference source, 4.1 133l, 4.3 337l
trade book library, 4.1 18i, 40i, 66i, 88i, 112i, 4.2 142i, 162i, 188i, 212i, 240i, 4.3 268i, 292i, 314i, 338i, 360i, 4.4 392i, 416i, 440i, 466i, 488i, 4.5 516i, 538i, 560i, 582i, 608i, 4.6 638i, 660i, 686i, 712i, 738i

**Types of literature.** *See* **Genres.**

# U

**Unfamiliar word meaning,** 4.1 114b, 4.2 164–165, 173, 177, 187c, 214–215, 239c, 242–243, 253, 259c, 316–317, 325, 337c, 4.4 442–443, 453, 465c, 468b, 4.5 562–563, 573, 581c, 4.6 688–689, 701, 711c, 714–715, 721, 729, 737c

**Unit inquiry projects.** *See* **Projects.**

**Usage.** *See* **Adjectives, Adverbs, Conjunctions, Contractions, Nouns, Prepositions and prepositional phrases, Pronouns, Sentences, Subject/verb agreement, Verbs.**

# V

**Venn diagram.** *See* **Graphic and semantic organizers,** types.

**Verbs**
action, 4.3 291e–291f
helping, 4.3 313e–313f
irregular, 4.3 383e–383f
linking, 4.3 291e–291f
main, 4.3 313e–313f
tense, 4.3 359e–359f
voice, 4.3 299

**Viewing**
**kinds of media**
art, 4.1 65d, 4.6 685d, 711d
illustration, 4.1 65d, 4.6 685d, 711d
movies/video, 4.2 161d, 211d, 4.4 415d, 465d, 507d
multimedia, 4.5 607d
photography, 4.1 62, 111d, 133d, 4.3 359d, 380, 4.5 536, 556, 559d, 626, 4.6 711d, 761d
**print media**
illustration, 4.1 65d, 4.6 685d, 711d
speech, 4.2 259d
**responding to media**
analyzing, 4.1 65d, 4.2 161d, 211d, 4.4 439d, 465d
oral, 4.1 65d, 111d, 133d, 4.2 161d, 211d, 259d, 4.3 352d, 4.4 415d, 465d, 507d, 4.5 559d, 607d, 4.6 685d, 711d, 761d
written, 4.1 111d, 4.2 259d, 4.3 359d, 4.4 465d, 4.5 559d, 607d, 4.6 685d, 761d
**uses of media**
analysis, 4.1 65d, 111d, 133d, 4.3 359d, 4.6 685d, 711d
enjoyment, 4.2 161d, 4.3 415d, 4.4 465d, 507d
persuasion, 4.2 259d
research, 4.5 559d, 607d, 4.6 761d

**Visualizing,** 4.3 314–315, 327, 329, 331, 4.4 416–417, 429, 431, 433, 437, 4.5 516l–516m, 538–539, 549, 553, 559, DI·16, DI·17

**Vocabulary development**
classifying words, 4.1 42b, 4.2 144b, 242b, 4.3 270b, 294b, 4.5 518b, 562b, 610b, 4.6 662b
concept vocabulary, 4.1 39c, 65c, 87c, 111c, 133c, 4.2 161c, 187c, 211c, 239c, 259c, 4.3 291c, 313c, 337c, 359c, 383c, 4.4 415c, 439c, 465c, 487c, 507c, 4.5 537c, 559c, 581c, 607c, 629c, 4.6 659c, 685c, 711c, 737c, 761c
connotation and denotation, 4.4 442b
content-area vocabulary, 4.1 36, 62, 108, 130, 4.2 186, 210, 258, 4.3 288, 310, 340b, 354, 380, 4.4 412, 436, 464, 504, 4.5 536, 540b, 556, 584b, 604, 626, 4.6 682, 708, 758
etymologies for meaning, 4.2 164b, 4.4 418b, 468, 479, 487c, 490b, 4.5 540–541, 547, 559, 559c, 562b, 584–585, 597, 599, 607c
graphic organizers for grouping, studying, and retaining, 4.1 20b, 42b, 90b, 4.2 144b, 190b, 214b, 242b, 4.3 294b, 340b, 362b, 4.4 394b, 418b, 442b, 468b, 4.5 518b, 562b, 584b, 4.6 662b, 714b
introducing selection vocabulary, 4.1 20b, 42b, 68b, 90b, 114b, 4.2 144b, 164b, 190b, 214b, 242b, 4.3 270b, 294b, 316b, 340b, 362b, 4.4 394b, 418b, 442b, 468b, 490b, 4.5 518b, 540b, 562b, 584b, 610b, 4.6 640b, 662b, 688b, 714b, 740b
listening for vocabulary development, 4.1 18l–18m, 40l–40m, 66l–66m, 88l–88m, 112l–112m, 4.2 142l–142m, 162l–162m, 188l–188m, 212l–212m, 240l–240m, 4.3 268l–268m, 292l–292m, 314l–314m, 338l–338m, 360l–360m, 4.4 392l–392m, 416l–416m, 440l–440m, 466l–466m, 488l–488m, 4.5 516l–516m, 538l–538m, 560l–560m, 582l–582m, 608l–608m, 4.6 638l–638m, 660l–660m, 686l–686m, 712l–712m, 738l–738m
practice lesson vocabulary, 4.1 27, 33, 53, 59, 77, 81, 99, 105, 123, 127, 4.2 151, 155, 175, 183, 201, 207, 223, 231, 251, 255, 4.3 279, 285, 303, 307, 327, 331, 349, 353, 371, 377, 4.4 403, 409, 429, 433, 451, 461, 477, 481, 497, 499, 4.5 527, 533, 549, 553, 571, 575, 593, 601, 619, 623, 4.6 649, 653, 671, 679, 697, 705, 725, 731, 751, 755

**reading for vocabulary development,** 4.1 20b, 42b, 68b, 90b, 114b, 4.2 144b, 164b, 190b, 214b, 242b, 4.3 270b, 294b, 316b, 340b, 362b, 4.4 394b, 418b, 442b, 468b, 490b, 4.5 518b, 540b, 562b, 584b, 610b, 4.6 640b, 662b, 688b, 714b, 740b
**related words in meaning (derivatives),** 4.1 87c, 4.2 190b, 4.6 740b
**speaking for vocabulary development,** 4.1 18l, 40l, 66l, 88l, 112l, 4.2 142l, 162l, 188l, 212l, 240l, 4.3 268l, 292l, 314l, 338l, 360l, 4.4 392l, 416l, 440l, 466l, 488l, 4.5 516l, 538l, 560l, 582l, 608l, 4.6 638l, 660l, 686l, 712l, 738l
**specialized/technical words,** 4.2 144b
**writing vocabulary,** 4.1 39g–39h, 65g, 87g, 111g, 133g, WA7, 4.2 161g–161h, 187g, 211g, 239g, 259g, WA7, 4.3 291g, 313g, 337g–337h, 359g, 383g, WA7, 4.4 415g, 439g, 465g, 487g, 507g, WA7, 4.5 537g, 559g–559h, 581g, 607g, 629g–629h, WA7, 4.6 659g, 685g, 711g, 737g, 761g, WA7

*See also* **Vocabulary strategies.**

**Vocabulary strategies**
alphabetical order, 4.6 662b
analogies, 4.3 270b
antonyms, 4.2 242b, 4.4 394–395, 405, 415c, 490–491, 495, 507c
base words, 4.5 518b
compound words, 4.1 68b, 4.2 214b, 4.6 662b
connotation, 4.4 442b
context clues, 4.1 20b, 90–91, 101, 111c, 4.3 270–271, 277, 291c, 294–295, 305, 313c, 316–317, 325, 337c, 4.4 394–395, 405, 415c, 418–419, 427, 439c, 490–491, 495, 507c, 4.5 518–519, 525, 537c, 562–563, 573, 581c, 610–611, 617, 629c, 4.6 662b, 688–689, 701, 711c, 714–715, 721, 729, 737c, 740–741, 749, 761c
dictionary/glossary, 4.1 68–69, 79, 87c, 4.2 164–165, 173, 177, 187c, 214–215, 221, 231, 239c, 242–243, 253, 259c, 4.4 442–443, 453, 457, 465c, 4.6 662–663, 669, 673, 685c
endings, 4.1 42–43, 51, 55, 65c, 68b, 4.3 270b, 340–341, 349, 359c, 362b, 4.4 394b, 4.6 640–641, 647, 659c
Greek and Latin roots, 4.4 418b, 468, 479, 487c, 4.5 540–541, 547, 559, 559c, 562b, 584–585, 597, 599, 607c
homographs, 4.5 518–519, 525, 537c
homonyms, 4.3 294–295, 305, 313c, 4.5 518–519, 525, 537c, 4.6 740–741, 749, 761c
homophones, 4.1 42b, 4.6 688b
multiple-meaning words, 4.1 20b, 68–69, 79, 87c, 4.2 231, 4.3 270–271, 277, 291c, 316b, 4.4 418–419, 427, 439c, 457, 4.6 640b, 662–663, 669, 673, 685c, 714b
noun phrases, 4.3 294b
nouns and verbs, 4.3 362b
picture clues, 4.1 90b
prefixes, 4.2 144–145, 151, 161c, 190–191, 199, 211c
related words, 4.2 190b, 4.6 740b
specialized vocabulary, 4.2 144b
suffixes, 4.1 20–21, 29, 39c, 114–115, 121, 133c, 4.2 144b, 144–145, 151, 161c, 4.3 362–363, 375, 383c, 4.4 394b, 4.6 640b
synonyms, 4.1 90–91, 101c, 111c, 4.4 394–395, 405, 415c, 490–491, 495, 507c, 4.5 562b, 610b, 610–611, 617, 629c
unfamiliar words, 4.1 114b, 4.2 164–165, 173, 177, 187c, 214–215, 239c, 242–243, 253, 259c, 316–317, 325, 337c, 4.4 442–443, 453, 465c, 468b, 4.5 562–563, 573, 581c, 4.6 688–689, 701, 711c, 714–715, 721, 729, 737c
word origins, 4.2 164b, 4.4 490b

# ACKNOWLEDGMENTS

## Teacher's Edition

### Text

**KWL Strategy:** The KWL Interactive Reading Strategy was developed and is used by permission of Donna Ogle, National-Louis University, Evanston, Illinois, co-author of *Reading Today and Tomorrow*, Holt, Rinehart & Winston Publishers, 1988. (See also *The Reading Teacher*, February 1986, pp. 564–570.)

Page 392m: "The Emperor's New Clothes," from *Scott Foresman Reading*. Copyright © 2002 Pearson Education.

Page 416m: "Cross Country Traveler" (originally titled "Sugar: Cross Country Traveler") adapted from *Animals Who Have Won Our Hearts* by Jean Craighead George. Text copyright © 1994 by Jean Craighead George. Used by permission of HarperCollins Publishers.

Page 440m: From "Corn Flake Kings: The Kellogg Brothers" from *Everyday Inventions* by Meredith Hooper. Published by Angus and Robertson, 1972.
Reprinted by permission of David Higham Associates.

Page 466m: "Silent Debate," *Asian Tales and Tellers* by Cathy Spagnoli. Copyright © 1998 by Cathy Spagnoli. Published by August House Publishers, Inc., and reprinted by permission of Marian Reiner.

### Artists

Tim Jessell: cover, page i

### Photographs

Every effort has been made to secure permission and provide appropriate credit for photographic material. The publisher deeply regrets any omission and pledges to correct errors called to its attention in subsequent editions.

Unless otherwise acknowledged, all photographs are the property of Scott Foresman, a division of Pearson Education.

Photo locators denoted as follows: Top (T), Center (C), Bottom (B), Left (L), Right (R), Background (Bkgd)

Page 18j: Mapquest

Page 66k: Digital Wisdom, Inc.

Page 87l: ©Royalty-Free/Corbis

Page 133l: ©Royalty-Free/Corbis

Page 162m: Hemera Technologies

Page 188k: Digital Wisdom, Inc.

Page 268j: Digital Wisdom, Inc.

Page 268m: Getty Images

Page 338m: Getty Images

Page 516m: Digital Vision

Page 608m: Ultimate Symbol, Inc.

Page 685l: Getty Images

Page 712m: Getty Images